Wierzbnik train station, 1939. Courtesy of the Wierzbniker Society of Toronto.

Wierzbnik-Starachowitz; a memorial book (Wierzbnik, Poland)

Translation of
Sefer Wierzbnik-Starachowice

Wierzbnik-Starachowitz; a memorial book

Original Yizkor Book Edited by: Mark Schutzman
Wierzbnik-Starachowitz Societies in Israel and the Diaspora,
Published in Tel Aviv, 1973

Published by JewishGen

**An Affiliate of the Museum of Jewish Heritage—A Living Memorial to the Holocaust
New York**

Memorial Book of Wierzbnik-Starachowitz
(Wierzbnik-Starachowitce, Poland)
Translation of: *Sefer Wierzbnik-Starachowice:*

Copyright © 2020 by JewishGen, Inc.
All rights reserved.
First Printing: September 2020, Elul 5780

Editor of the original Yizkor Book: Mark Schutzman
Translation Project Coordinator: Stan Zuckerman
Layout: Jonathan Wind
Cover Design: Nina Schwartz, Impulse Graphics
Name Indexing: Bena Shklyanoy

This book may not be reproduced, in whole or in part, including illustrations in any form (beyond that copying permitted by Sections 107 and 108 of the U.S. Copyright Law and except by reviewers for public press), without written permission from the publisher.

Published by JewishGen, Inc.
An Affiliate of the Museum of Jewish Heritage
A Living Memorial to the Holocaust
36 Battery Place, New York, NY 10280

JewishGen, Inc. is not responsible for inaccuracies or omissions in the original work and makes no representations regarding the accuracy of this translation. Digital images of the original book's contents can be seen online at the New York Public Library website.

The mission of the JewishGen organization is to produce a translation of the original work, and we cannot verify the accuracy of statements or alter facts cited.

Printed in the United States of America by Lightning Source, Inc.

Library of Congress Control Number (LCCN): 2020935350

ISBN: 978-1-939561-62-6 (hard cover: 676 pages, alk. paper)

Cover Credits:

Front Cover:

Front cover, top left: *Sura Malach with her grandfather, Chaskel Grynszpan, 1929.* Courtesy of Carolynne Veffer. Taken shortly before Veffer's mother, aged 9, emigrated to Toronto with her parents, Gershon and Esther Malach, and siblings, Rachmiel, Moshe, Shmuel and Fajga.

Front cover, right: *Dov and Idel Shlesinger (nee Zilberman) with sons Meir, Abraham and Alexander, Wierzbnik, 1937.* Abe Zukerman collection. Ontario Jewish Archives, Blankenstein Family Heritage Centre, accession 2017-9-1.

Front cover, bottom: *Two Jewish soldiers in Polish army uniform, Wierzbnik,1920s.* Abe Zukerman collection. Ontario Jewish Archives, Blankenstein Family Heritage Centre, accession 2017-9-1. Photo lightly corrected for mottling.

Back Cover:

Back cover, top: *Kleinberg family, May 1930.* Photo courtesy of Nina Flom. Syma (Zelda) and Herschel Kleinberg with children Raisa, Fredi, Yitzhak (back center), Howard (front) and Anchel. Almost dead when Bergen-Belsen was liberated in 1945, Howard was nursed by a fellow Wierzbniker, Nechama Baum, who had also been in the camp. Each emigrated to Toronto separately; they re-met, and married in 1950.

Back cover, bottom: *Gravestone, Starachowice Jewish cemetery.* ©2014 by Janet Isenberg, courtesy of the photographer. The text reads: In the year 5664/Here lies the important and modest woman, careful in following the commandments, Ms.*/RACHEL, daughter of our teacher, the rabbi, Rabbi/Yitzchak. She passed away the 19th day in the month of Kislev (December 8, 1903). May her soul be bound up in the bond of life.
*The abbreviation before Rachel's name can be read as either Mrs. or Miss. Since her marital status is unclear from the stone (no husband is mentioned), it is translated here with the modern term Ms.

JewishGen and the Yizkor Books in Print Project

This book has been published by the **Yizkor Books in Print Project**, as part of the **Yizkor Book Project** of JewishGen, Inc.

JewishGen, Inc. is a non-profit organization founded in 1987 as a resource for Jewish genealogy. Its website [www.jewishgen.org] serves as an international clearinghouse and resource center to assist individuals who are researching the history of their Jewish families and the places where they lived. JewishGen provides databases, facilitates discussion groups, and coordinates projects relating to Jewish genealogy and the history of the Jewish people. In 2003, JewishGen became an affiliate of the **Museum of Jewish Heritage—A Living Memorial to the Holocaust** in New York.

The **JewishGen Yizkor Book Project** was organized to make more widely known the existence of Yizkor (Memorial) Books written by survivors and former residents of various Jewish communities throughout the world. Later, volunteers connected to the different destroyed communities began cooperating to have these books translated from the original language—usually Hebrew or Yiddish—into English, thus enabling a wider audience to have access to the valuable information contained within them. As each chapter of these books was translated, it was posted on the JewishGen website and made available to the general public.

The **Yizkor Books in Print Project** began in 2011 as an initiative to print and publish Yizkor Books that had been fully translated, so that hard copies would be available for purchase by the descendants of these communities and also by scholars, universities, synagogues, libraries, and museums.

These Yizkor books have been produced almost entirely through the volunteer effort of researchers from around the world, assisted by donations from private individuals. The books are printed and sold at near cost, so as to make them as affordable as possible. Our goal is to make this important genre of Jewish literature and history available in English in book form, so that people can have the personal histories of their ancestral towns on their bookshelves for themselves and for their children and grandchildren.

A list of all published translated Yizkor Books in the project with prices and ordering information can be found at:
http://www.jewishgen.org/Yizkor/ybip.html

Lance Ackerfeld, Yizkor Book Project Manager
Joel Alpert, Yizkor-Book-in-Print Project Coordinator

This book is presented by the
Yizkor-Books-In-Print Project
Project Coordinator: Joel Alpert

Part of the Yizkor Books Project of JewishGen. Inc.
Project Manager: Lance Ackerfeld

These books have been produced solely through efforts of volunteers from around the world. The books are printed using the Print-on-Demand technology and sold at near cost, to make them as affordable as possible.

Our goal is to make this intimate history of the destroyed Jewish shtetls of Eastern Europe available in book form in English, so that people can experience the near-personal histories of their ancestral town on their bookshelves and those of their children and grandchildren.

All donations to the Yizkor Books Project, which translated the books, are sincerely appreciated.

Please send donations to:

Yizkor Book Project
JewishGen, Inc.
36 Battery Place
New York, NY, 10280

JewishGen, Inc. is an affiliate of the
Museum of Jewish Heritage
A Living Memorial to the Holocaust

Acknowledgment

The Wierzbniker Society, the publisher of this book, is located in Toronto Canada and was originally formed in the 1930s. At the current time, the Society has 185 members. The Society's goals include conducting not-for-profit activities pertaining to the World War II Jewish Holocaust. Our Society and its name are based on a town in Poland, Wierzbnik, which merged with the Town of Starachowice in 1939 and is now known as Starachowice. Some of the Society's current members lived in Wierzbnik Poland before and during the Holocaust and many others are descendants of Jews who lived in this town.

In 1973, the Wierzbniker Society published its original Memorial book with articles on life in Wierzbnik before and during the Holocaust written by Society members or their relatives, documenting the various aspects of Jewish life in Wierzbnik. This was published for future generations to read, appreciate and remember. The contents were mostly written in Hebrew, with some articles in Yiddish and a few in English.

Since the original book, many current members have expressed an interest in the book and indicated that they, their children and grand-children would like to get a copy of the articles written in English. In 2007, the Executive of the Society undertook the project of arranging the translation of the articles from the original book into English for the benefit of the membership and their families, future generations and other interested parties. To ensure that this project was economical, the articles have been re-published on compact discs and will be made available to all Society members. It is our belief that this book will become an important and significant addition to our members' libraries and we encourage all members to give copies to their family members. Members who would like a paper book version may take the compact disc to a printing store for such purpose.

The Society thanks the following persons who assisted in this publication of the English version of the Memorial book: Ran Snir of Israel for translating the Hebrew articles into English, Judy Grossman of Israel for translating the Yiddish articles, Lisa Zukerman for retyping the original English articles and re-organizing articles, Stanley Zukerman for coordinating this project, the Society Executive for their ideas and encouragement and especially the authors of the original articles, many of whom are no longer alive, without whom this project and book would not be possible.

Stanley Zukerman
Samuel Lepek
Mel Stein

May 8, 2008

Notes to the Reader:

We apologize ahead of time for the poor quality of images in the book. Often these images had been scanned from the original Yizkor books which were of poor quality to begin with, being copies of old photographs. Each transfer results in loss of quality. We have done the best we could, given the original material and the resources and technology at hand. Even though images often appear of higher quality on computer screens, that does not transfer to high quality images in print. Not all images are included due to technical difficulties. A reader can view the all the original scans on the web sites listed below.

Within the text the reader will note "{34}" standing ahead of a paragraph. This indicates that the material translated below was on page 34 of the original book. However, when a paragraph was split between two pages in the original book, the marker is placed in this book after the end of the paragraph for ease of reading.

Also please note that all references within the text of the book to page numbers, refer to the page numbers of the original Yizkor Book.

The original book can be seen online at the New York Public Library site:

https://digitalcollections.nypl.org/search/index?utf8=%E2%9C%93&keywords=wierzbnik

or at the Yiddish Book Center web site:

https://www.yiddishbookcenter.org/search?search_api_views_fulltext=wierzbnik&Submit+search=&restrict=

In order to obtain a list of all Shoah victims from Wierzbnik, the reader should access the Yad Vashem web site listed below; one can also search for specific family names using family name option. These lists are continually updated by Yad Vashem, so it is worthwhile to periodically search these lists.

There is much valuable information available on this web site, including the Pages of Testimony, etc.
http://yvng.yadvashem.org

A list of this book and all books available in the Yizkor-Book-In-Print Project along with prices is available at:
http://www.jewishgen.org/Yizkor/ybip.html

Geopolitical Information:

Wierzbnik, Poland

The town is located at 51°03' N, 21°05' E, 25 miles S of Radom, 24 miles NE of Kielce, 11 miles SW of Iłża. Since 1952, Wierzbnik is part of Starachowice

Period	Town	District	Province	Country
Before WWI (c. 1900):	Wierzbnik	Iłża	Radom	Russian Empire
Between the wars (c. 1930):	Wierzbnik	Iłża	Kielce	Poland
After WWII (c. 1950):	Wierzbnik			Poland
Today (c. 2000):	Wierzbnik			Poland

Alternate names for the town: Wierzbnik [Pol], Vierzhbinik [Yid], Vyerzhbnik [Rus], Wierzbnik-Starachowice [Pol, 1939-1952], Starachowice, Starakhovits, Strachovitza, Verzhbnik, Wierzbnik Starachow, Verzhbnik Starakhov, Vyerzbnik, Vyerzhbanik

Nearby Jewish Communities:

- Wąchock 3 miles WNW
- Bodzentyn 9 miles SW
- Skarżysko-Kamienna 9 miles WNW
- Iłża 11 miles NE
- Suchedniów 11 miles W
- Kunów 11 miles SE
- Waśniów 12 miles SSE
- Nowa Słupia 13 miles S
- Wierzbica 14 miles N
- Jastrząb 15 miles NNW
- Krajno 15 miles SW
- Ostrowiec Świętokrzyski 16 miles ESE
- Szydłowiec 16 miles NW
- Sienno 17 miles E
- Denków 17 miles ESE
- Łagów 18 miles S
- Skaryszew 20 miles NNE
- Daleszyce 20 miles SW
- Ćmielów 22 miles ESE
- Opatów 23 miles SE
- Kazanów 23 miles NE
- Kielce 24 miles SW
- Iwaniska 24 miles SSE
- Wolanów 24 miles NNW
- Ciepielów 25 miles NE
- Raków 25 miles S
- Radom 25 miles N
- Lipsko 26 miles ENE
- Skrzynno 27 miles NW
- Bogoria 28 miles SSE
- Tarłów 28 miles E
- Ożarów 28 miles ESE
- Pierzchnica 28 miles SSW
- Przysucha 30 miles NW
- Przytyk 30 miles NNW
- Solec 30 miles E
- Zwoleń 30 miles NE

Jewish Population: 975 (in 1897), 2,159 (in 1921)

Wierzbnik located in Poland

Hebrew Title Page of Original Hebrew/Yiddish Book

ס פ ר
וירזבניק - סטרכוביץ

מפעל הועד הציבורי
של יוצאי וירזבניק־סטרכוביץ בארץ ובתפוצות

אלול תשל״ג   תל־אביב   אוגוסט 1973

Translation of the Title Page of the Original Hebrew Book

Wierzbnik – Starachowitz

Book

**Enterprise of the Public Committee
of the Former Residents of
Wierzbnik - Starachowitz in Israel and the Diaspora**

Elul 5733   Tel-Aviv   August 1973

הועד למען "ספר הזכרון" וירזבניק והסביבה
קאמיטעט פארן "יזכור בוך" ווערזבניק און אומגעגנט

ישראל	קנדה
שמחה מינצברג	לוי ברוטבקר
משה קורבל (סלי)	חנה זילברשטין
צבי פיינבוים	אברהם צוקרמן
רומק זינגר	הרשל טננבוים
אברהם שיינר	גרשון רוזנוולד
ישעיהו דרקטלר (זקן)	
מלכה ויסבלום	אמריקה
ראובן ליס (שועלי)	צבי מורנשטרן
פנחס הוכמיץ	יעקב כץ
	לייביש הרבלום
	אמיל ניימן
	יצחק גוטרמן

ועענזועלא

יוסף קלייגר

עקוואדאר

מרדכי מסלוביץ

ברזיל

יעקב מנלה

גרמניה

דוד כהן

ה מ ע ר כ ת

שמחה מינצברג, משה סלי, צבי פיינבאום, ירחמיאל (רומק) זינגר

העורך : מ. שוצמן

דפוס "מופת", י. רייכמן, תל-אביב, רח' עידהקורא 6 טל. 32968. בהוצאת "מנורה"

Translation of previous page

Committee for the Wierzbnik and Surrounding Area "Yizkor Book"

Israel
Simcha Minzberg
Moshe Sali-Kerbel
Zvi Faigenbaum
Jerahmiel Romek Singer
Abraham Shiner
Yeshayahu Dekel (Dreksler)
Malka Weisblum
Reuven Shuali (Lis)
Pinchas Hochmitz

Canada
Levi Brotbeker
Hanna Zilberstein
Abe Zukerman
Hershel Tenenbaum
Gershon Rosenwald

United States
Yaakov Katz
Leibish Herblum
Emil Naiman
Yitzchak Guterman
Tzvi Morgenstern

Venezuela
Yosef Kleiner

Ecuador
Mordechai Maslowicz

Brazil
Yaakov Manela

Germany
David Cohen

Editorial Board:
Simcha Minzberg, Moshe Sali-Kerbel, Zvi Faigenbaum, Jerahmiel Romek Singer

Editor: M. Schutzman

Table of Contents

Preface and Acknowledgement	1
Forward For Eternal Memory	4
Eternal Memory	8
On the Book Publication	13
Forward – Moshe Sali (Kerbel)	15
Introduction – Moshe Sali (Kerbel)	20
In Times of Peace – Simcha Mincberg	24
Wierzbnik – Before the Flood – Simcha Minzberg	30
Jews in the Ghettoes of Poland (poem) – Malka Weisbloom	35
The Jewish People Lives! – Yaakov Katz	38
Wierzbnik: the Town, its Location and Growth – Excerpt from a Geographic Dictionary	40
A Precious Pearl Shattered – Moshe Sali (Kerbel)	41
Chronicles of the Town and its Jews – Jerachmiel Singer	43
My Shtetl Wierzbnik – Moshe Sali (Kerbel)	58

Religious and Traditional Life

Rabbis of the Community – Zvi Fajgenbaum	64
The Synagogues in Wierzbnik – Zvi Fajgenbaum	69
Heders and Melameds – Zvi Fajgenbaum	76
The Tale of a Torah Scroll – Reuven Lichtenstein	80
Traditional Folklore – Sara Postawski-Steinhardt	83

Social and Public Life

The Youth Movements in Wierzbnik – Yitzhak Kerbel	87
The Young Pioneer Movement in Wierzbnik – Moshe Sali (Kerbel)	88
The Gordonia Movement and the National Labor Committee for Palestine Youth League – Reuven Lis Shuali	91
The Zionist Youth Movement – Rivka Greenberg (Mincberg) and Rachel Laor (Dreksler)	93
Wierzbnik, a Proud Example of Zionism - Moshe Sali (Kerbel)	96
It Was our Whole World – Yaakov Katz	100
Beit-Yaakov School for Girls – Zehava Zitelna	102
The Batya Organization – Chava Fajgenbaum (Shraga)	104
The Establishment of Beit-Yaakov in our Town – Yaakov Korenwaser	105
The Maccabi Society – Reuven Lis Shuali	105
Maccabi's Youths – Pinchas Hochmitz	108
The Gviazda Sports Society – Shmuel Nudelman	110
The Beitar Movement – Yaakov Snir	111
The Revisionist Movement in Wierzbnik – Gershon Rosenwald	113

Jerusalem of Old and Jerusalem the Golden – Yaakov Katz	114

Memories

Memories – Reuven Shuali (Lis)	118
On Market Days – M. Ben-Yehuda	122
On Holidays We Gave Out Honey and Fish – Benyamin Weisbloom	123
A Bundle of Memories – Uri Shtramer	124
Fifty Years Ago – Yossef Kornwasser	126
The Blood Libel Miracle – Yaakov Korenwaser	128
The Tributaries of the Wisla – Moshe (Michael) Samet	128
We Baked Matzahs for Passover – Levi Brodbeker	130
The Hebrew Midwives – Zvi Faigenbaum	131
The Drama Society – Moshe (Michael) Samet	131
Kupat Cholim – V. H.	133
From Wierzbnik to Israel through the Paviak Prison – Moshe Sali (Kerbel)	134
A Compilation of Memories from Wierzbnik – Yoseph Citrinbaum	138
The Carousel – Yitzhak Kerbel	140
Memories of my Home – Moshe Sali – Kerbel	141

Characters

Town Dignitaries (Characters) – Zvi Faigenbaum	146
Pola Laks, the Noble Woman – Jerachmiel Singer	150
Reb Shmuel Kleiner's House – M. Sali-Kerbel	151
The Admor of Chmielów – Sara Postawski-Steinhardt	156
Memories from my Home – Moshe Sali (Kerbel)	159
Memories of our Home – Mania Rosenkrantz – Bagno (Minka)	161
And His Time Never Came – Sarah Miriam Ribak	167

During the Holocaust

The Holocaust of the Jews of Europe – G. H.	171
Dark Days of Horror and Ruin (The Tragedy of Wierzbnik) – Jerahmiel Singer	172
Ilza, the Beginning of the Scourge – Zvi Faigenbaum	183
In the "Camps for the Correction of Man" – Pinchas Nudelman	187
The Day of Holocaust and the Extermination of our Town – Leibish Herblum	189
The Synagogue is Burning – Zvi Faigenbaum	190
A Source of Life Gone Dry – Moshe Sali (Kerbel)	195
Waiting in Line for Bread – Sara Postawski-Steinhardt	196
The First Murder – Sara Postawski-Steinhardt	198

Testimonies

Wierzbnik, Auschwitz, Bergen-Belsen – Malka Cohen (Leopold)	201
On this Day They Shall Mourn – Sarah Brodbeker	203
In the Jaws of Destiny – Menachem Mincberg	205

Diaspora – M. Magen	209
On the Road to Treblinka – Menachem Efrati	211
My Journeys Through the Valley of the Shadow of Death – Rivka Greenberg (Mincberg)	214
On the Edge of the Abyss – Hanna Tenzer	220
To the Wilderness of the Taiga – Rachel Laor (Dreksler)	226
Going to Palestine – Chava Faigenbaum (Shraga)	229
In the Claws of Death's Minions – Avraham (Moshe) Minkowski	231
In Desperation – Pinchas Hochmitz	234
The Death March from Auschwitz – Ida Rosenberg (Bialik)	235
A Mountain of Corpses in Korenwasser's Yard – Gershon Rosenwald	236
We Ate Grass and Coal – Natan-Neta Gelbart	237
Only Graves Remain – Moshe Weintraub	239
Where No Birds Fly – Abe Zukerman	241
Father, I am Going to the Crematorium – Pinchas Helstein	243
From Wierzbnik to Mauthausen – Zvi Unger (Heshek)	244
A Gruesome Reality – Yaffa Barkai – Rosenwald	249
Sorrowful Reunions Tragic Encounters – Esther Zukerman-Zilberman	249
Wierzbnik's Lament - Anonymous	254
Memorial Candle – M. K.	257
Bar Mitzvah in the Forest – Malka Weisbloom	258
We were Ten Brothers – Pinchas Hochmitz	258
The Deception: "Work Sets You Free" – Malka Weisbloom	264
Echoes from the Valley of Tears – Yoseph Honigsberg	265
Aiding Children in the Holocaust – Sara Postawski-Steinhardt	271
The Little Orphaned Shoes – Esther Zukerman-Zilberman	273
Like Dark Clouds – Mindl Rosenwald-Farbman	275
The Beginning of the Downfall – Simcha Minzberg	276
Days of Misery and Ruin – Simcha Mincberg	284
Mengele's "Promise" – Zvi Unger (Heshek)	291
Polish Cooperation in the Extermination of Jews – Beniek Zukerman	292

Resistance and Rebellion

Led Like Lambs to the Slaughter – Zvi Faigenbaum	301
Hell's Dungeon – Chava Faigenbaum (Shraga)	309
The Policeman Shot and Missed – Abraham Shiner	312
A Hole in the Floor of the Railway Car – Pinchas Hochmitz	316
We Jumped from the Railway Car of Death – Zvi Faigenbaum	317
Aba Kumetz Dared to Swear – Jerachmiel Singer	320

Active Resistance

In the Woods of Wierzbnik (With the Partisans) – David Sali	322
Fighting the Nazi Conqueror – Yaacov Snir	331
In the Ranks of the Polish Army – Moshe (Michael) Samet	339

He Died on the Way to Freedom – Hania Kuper (Reichzeig)	343
Shmuel Dov Faigenbaum Fell in the Line of Duty – Zvi Faigenbaum	344
Hela Sacrificed Her Life – Tzipora Snir (Faiga Lustman)	346
Guta Blass-Weintraub Snatched the Gun – Jerachmiel Singer	347
In the Shade of the Thick Forest – Gershon Rosenwald	348
Memorial (poem) – Reuven Shuali (Lis)	352
We Wished to Die as Heroes (poem) – Malka Weisbloom	352
Flames Rose from the Steam – Avraham Shiner	353
Knives by the Crematoriums – Rivka Greenberg (Mincberg)	354
Saved by Finkelstein's Sacrifice – Malka Weisbloom	356
The Heroism of Esther Manela – Malka Weisbloom	356
A Gap in the Fence – Avraham Shiner	357
Deep in the Forest – Gershon Rosenwald	359
Hunted and Murdered by Polish Partisans – Avraham Shiner	364

After the War

After my Liberation – Simcha Mincberg	370
Yizkor… – Moshe Sali (Kerbel)	373
Murders – after Liberation – Perele Brodbeker-Unger	374
The Nazis' Followers – Chava Fajgenbaum (Shraga)	375
The Encounter in Munich – Yitzhak Kerbel	376
It Began on an Autumn Day – Dvora Rubinstein-Erlichsohn	377
I Ran Away and Returned Home – Yitzhak Edison-Erlichsohn	378
A Memorial Stone in Toronto Dedicated to the Wierzbniker Martyrs – Abe Zukerman	380
The Wierzbniker Society in Toronto – Abe Zukerman	381
Last Impressions of my Native City – Abe Zukerman	383
To the Cemetery in Wierzbnik – Sarah Postawski – Steinhart	389
The Town Elder Lied Deliberately – Yitzhak Kerbel	391
Hunted to Extinction – Moshe Neiman	393
From Slavery to Freedom – Zvi Magen (Hershel Pancer)	395
The Miraculous Journey of Mr. Hershel Wiser – M. S., Zvi Faigenbaum	398
To Mention – Through Allusion – Gershon Rosenwald	400

In Memory of the Missing Ones

Reb Mordechai Mendel Zilberstein, of Blessed Memory – Moshe Kerbel	403
Shmuel Morgenstern, of Blessed Memory – Yitzhak Kerbel	404
Mr. Noah Citrinbaum – His Daughter Esther	405
Hershel Froymán – Yaakov Katz	406
Israel Reisler, of Blessed Memory – Abe Zukerman	407
Shmuel Gelbard – David Plonsky	407
On the Grave of Yosef Citrinbaum – Moshe Sali (Kerbel)	408
Yoseph Citrinbaum (Harari) – His Sons, David and Amos	408
Mr. Moshe David Rothschild – Zvi Faigenbaum	410

I Cry for Them – Leibl Rabinowicz	411
In Memory of my Beloved Ones – Yehoshua Jerry Rolnizki	412
In Memory of our Family – Sternkranz Family	413
The House of Mr. Shmuel Kleiner – Moshe Sali (Kerbel)	414
At the Mass Grave of our Brethren – Moshe Sali-Kerbel	415
Conclusion – Yizkor Book Committee	417
Wierzbnik Necrology	419

English Section

In Memoriam (Introduction)	524
Sketches of a Town - Moshe Sali (Kerbel)	526
The Jewish People Lives! - Yaakov Katz	527
Twenty Years after the Loss of Jewry of the Cities of Wierzbnik and Drilz (Ilza) - Gershon Rosenwald	530
Remember, And Don't Forget - Yaakov Katz	531
Dark Days of Horror and Ruin (The Tragedy of Wierzbnik) - Jerachmiel Singer	534
In the Woods of Wierzbnik (With the Partisans) - David Sali	544
For the Next Generations - Reva Naiman Karstadt	551
German Trial Stirs Memory of Horror Camp - Wendy Tucker, Staff Reporter	553
The Sixteenth Day of Cheshvan - The Liquidation of our Town - Yaakov Katz	555
It Was a Great Shock - Necha Baranek	558
My Heart Began to Pound Loudly - Sam Stein	559
Jerusalem of Old and Jerusalem the Golden - Yaakov Katz	561
Lists	563
Photo Captions	625
Name Index	631

Starachowice

View of Starachowice (Wierzbnik), circa 1915. Public domain, Courtesy of Ośrodek Edukacyjno-Muzealny "Świętokrzyski Sztetl," Chmielnik, Poland, swietokrzyskisztetl.pl

Not in original Yizkor Book.

View of Starachowice (Wierzbnik), circa 1915. Public domain, Courtesy of Ośrodek Edukacyjno-Muzealny "Świętokrzyski Sztetl, Chmielnik, Poland, <u>swietokrzyskisztetl.pl</u>

Not in original Yizkor Book.

ספר
הזכרון

של קהילת

וירזבניק-
סטרכוביץ

[Page IX]

FORWARD
FOR ETERNAL MEMORY

There are very few of us remaining after the hellish fire which the Nazi vultures spread over the Jewish world. The sources of our being were depleted and yet, we must tell future generations what we suffered and what we lost. The embers of the past still glow in those who survived, but, from year to year, grows the fear of memories getting lost in the depth of our being.

However, we have inherited the last will of those who were murdered: we must remember what the Nazi Amalek did to us. We must, also, give the coming generations a reflection of what it was like, the sorrow and the orphaning, the unspeakable events. This is what our generation suffered.

We, the survivors of Wierzbnik, have the holy duty of preserving the memory of our sainted fellow citizens.

A general view of the Rynek (town square), in the direction of Kościólna Street

They lived there, to the bitter end, until they were cut down by the Nazi murderers and their collaborators.

The community of Wierzbnik-Strachovitz did not put on airs. It was not a pretentious group, but it was full of good Jews. They were plain, down-to-earth people and were devoted to God and to their fellow man.

When we recall the old times when the Jewish community existed, we see a multi-faceted Jewish life. In the mornings, dozens of Jews first went to the House of Learning and then to work in all parts of town. We see the mass of workers on one side and the intelligentsia on the other side. There were Rabbis and teachers and just ordinary people. Each one had his own way of living, his own memories and his own view of the world.

For many generations, when the Jews settled in Wierzbnik, our ancestors were imbued with deep and honest beliefs, good deeds and study of Torah, hard work, love of God and fellow man.

On Shabbat and Holidays, the streets of the town were filled with Jews rushing to synagogues and Houses of Learning. There, they prayed for good health, decent earnings and a happy life.

On other days of the week, one would hear in the streets the sounds of tools at work, the echo of life happening, the merchants selling, the carriers and the wagon drivers in the marketplace. In good times the marketplace was a center of Jewish life, but in the dark days of the Nazi occupation- the bloody station for transporting Jewish masses to their destruction.

In addition to the need for making a living, there was the excitement of intellectual and societal activity. Also, there was the beginning of national awakening of the Jewish youth. They were involved in the various streams of the Zionist movements. They dreamed of a life of enjoyment of man and nation and they prepared themselves to achieve the return to Zion and the rebuilding of the Land of Israel- homeland of the Jewish people.

Between dreaming and reality, there was a multi-colored and rich actuality, alert, lively activity in all phases of life.

****

The Jews of Wierzbnik were an important part of the population of the town- economy, industry, commerce and other aspects. They showed initiative, energy and knowledge and were highly involved in constructing factories and shops. They contributed greatly to the growth of the town.

Truth be told, the Wierzbnik Jews lived in a quiet, serene atmosphere. They conducted their affairs slowly and each person did his utmost. Suddenly, horrible winds began to blow. The sky was covered with black Vulcans. Satan entered and quickly destroyed the contented life. A stormy, bloody stream flooded the towns and villages of Europe. It was a terrible catastrophe that had not happened before in human history-not even in sad times of Jewish martyrdom.

The bright day was darkened with somber clouds and the Angel of Death entered the rows. He murdered without any pity.

How was the forest filled with people? How were the souls of Jews torn away from their bodies? How is it that our fathers, mothers, brothers, sisters and friends were hurt, tortured and eliminated? There were thousands, more than thousands, perhaps a million Jews who suffered through seven stages of hell. They were hit by the first bombs in Strachovitz. They were in the nightmare of the "counting" in the marketplace. They were, to the end, in the death camps and crematoriums of Auschwitz, Treblinka, Ravensbruck, and other murderous locations. The stories are told by the survivors, by a miracle, and were written, in blood and tears, in memorial books.

The tale of the struggle and the defiance of our fellow residents against the Nazi Satan is written in fiery letters. The Nazis had intended to annihilate the entire Jewish people. They fought, as best they could, not to give in to this terrible situation.

The majority of them did indeed pay with their lives, but they had not surrendered. They struggled hard and their heroic efforts will forever be etched in our memories.

The dark days were over and the world began to emerge from its nightmare. The nations began to repair, rebuild and construct anew whatever had been destroyed during the war and the occupation. There was a beginning of healing the wounds of war. Only one nation could not do it because its annihilation was almost total.

Only some survivors, remnants of the destruction, were able to breathe easily. They needed to stand on their own two feet because many others were too hurt and injured- physically and mentally. Among those remnants were some survivors from Wierzbnik. They were now scattered throughout the world.

Those active in the book committee in Israel. Standing from right: Malka Weisbloom, Pinchas Hochmitz, Reuven Lis-Shuali, Yeshaya Dekel-Dar Kesler, Chana Tantzer, Rivka Greenberg (Mincberg). Seated from right to left: Menachem Mintcberg, Moshe Sali, Simcha Mincberg, Yerachmiel Singer, Menachem Fajgenbaum, Tzvi Unger

Alas, on the banks of the Kamina river, there will no longer be Jewish life. The sounds of Yiddish or its melodies will not be heard. Everything is destroyed and nothing is left.

***

Despite the sad story of our existence, ignoring the terrible suffering, pogroms and persecutions, which our people had experienced for generations and despite the unbelievable catastrophe that annihilated a third of our members, we were fortunate to find the miracle of the Jewish state. However, our nation did not have peace. The initiative for this Yizkor Book, its editing and preparation, occurred here, in Israel. It is a time when our people are waging a bitter struggle for its existence, against our enemies who outnumber us many times. This is our lot, but just as in the dark days of the Nazis, we stand firm against the Arab neighboring countries who wish to find a solution for the "Jewish problem".

****

The difference between our status then and now is that our situation has changed. Then we were in foreign lands, but now we are in our own state and we wish to fight for our homeland. We are strong and steadfast because this is our land, our life and our being.

In order to describe clearly this change that has happened to the Jewish people, the ability to stand up to their enemies and fight for their being, it is necessary to tell the youth and the coming generations how it was before. It was different in exile.

It is important to tell how cheap Jewish life and Jewish blood were. This was when the Anti-Semitic murderers attacked the Jews. How we were kicked and stepped upon.

It is essential for the Jewish youth and the entire world to know how the people of Israel fight at the front. Their boldness and readiness to fight come not only from love of their homeland, but to show there will never again be a second Auschwitz.

For all the survivors and for all those who did not survive, to the thousands of Jews from Wierzbnik who were killed by the Nazi murderers, may these fiery letters in this Yizkor book, be a goblet filled with tears. These tears flow from crying hearts and bitter suffering of the survivors.

May these lines be a memorial on unknown graves standing on earth that is saturated with Jewish blood.

[Page XIII]

ETERNAL MEMORY

Eternal Candle

Very few of us were saved from the Nazi inferno that swept Europe. And so it is difficult for us to tell and describe to the world and the future generations all that we had and we lost.

The passing time is slowly gnawing the body and mind of those few who miraculously survived. Every year we feel more and more that a period will end soon, and with it a whole generation will disappear and all will be lost.

Winter in the town

Book committee in Toronto (Canada) Standing from the right: B. Zukerman, G. Rosenwald, A. Zukerman, Leibel Rabinowitz, Hershel Tennenbaum, Max Naiman. Seated from the right: Chana Naiman, Tova Wolfowitz, Esther Zukerman

But we have a holy commandment – to remember what the new Amalek did to us and to leave a legacy to the next generations of the sense of the historic ties to the bereavement and loss by our generation with all its horrendous events.

Therefore, we the remnants of the town of Wierzbnik came together with awe and compassion to memorialize our community and its martyrs, those that lived in it and were murdered by the Nazis and their helpers.

The community of Wierzbnik-Starachowice was not famous – its members were not shakers and movers and did not achieve fame in history. But this was a good and solid Jewish community. Humble and contentious, honest, hard-working people at peace with their creator and themselves.

As we look to those far away days when the Jewish Wierzbnik still existed we can see in our mind's eye the rich and vibrant community life. The Jewish population waking up to work and study – workers and those who are headed for the study halls; The well-educated and the simple people, rabbis and students and the multitudes – each of them with their worldview and their way of life.

*

In the many generations since the establishment of the Jewish community in Wierzbnik our forefathers worked hard to create a life of faith and prayer, balancing Torah and hard work, charity and honesty, God fearing and love of people. On Saturdays and during the holidays, the streets were overcrowded with people on their way to the synagogues. During the week the voices of hard work and the daily struggle for existence, the voices of the shopkeepers and merchants, porters and craftsmen, the wagon drivers all coming together in the Rynek (market) square - vibrant with life. And the same Rynek square, in the dark days of Nazi occupation became the place where multitudes of Jews were sent to their death by the murderers.

The book committee in the United States. Standing right to left: Motel Hilf, Yaakov Katz, Yerachmiel Naiman. Seated from the right: Leibish Herblum, Tzvi Morgenstern

At the same time the Zionist awakening of the Jewish youth played a major part as well. They threw themselves wholly and enthusiastically into the various national parties and organizations. They dreamed of salvation and prepared for the ultimate goal of return to Zion and building a home for the persecuted Jews. The everyday reality was colorful, active and lively. Wierzbnik-Starachowice Jews contributed to all aspects of the town's economic-growth – in commerce and industry. With the growth of the town, the Jews became involved in all facets of life, in all areas of creativity and craftsmanship still retaining their unique way of life. Wierzbnik was not especially rich, but people made a living and the mutual aid was evident everywhere.

Mountains of tears over unknown graves

Wierzbnik-Starachowice Jews lived for many generation their everyday lives: working, building their future and dreaming. But this peaceful existence ceased to exist with the horrendous and bloody hell – the likes of which was never known even in the history of the persecuted Jews. In place of the aspirations, wishes and good deeds destruction and catastrophe ensued. The few who miraculously survived eulogize on these pages with great pain in their hearts the incredible suffering, humiliation and torture imposed on our people. Since the first bombs fell on the munition factories in town our people suffered in an indescribable way – being pushed with great cruelty to the Rynek on their way to the death camps. There were some chapters of incredible heroism and opposition against the violent force of the Nazi machine – those daring souls and small groups who would not accept and would not surrender to the monstrosity. With great risk to themselves and without capabilities they opposed the enemy with all their might. Most of them paid with their lives for their bravery. But their brave actions and their sacrifice to save our oppressed nation will always live with us.

The dark days have finally passed and the world started to recover from the war: Nations started to rebuild their towns and villages and heal the wounds. Only one nation could not recover from the tragedy that befell us, especially in the hostile Anti-Semitic environment. And so, we picked-up our wandering staff again.

In spite of the bloody history and especially the holocaust that meant to wipe us off the face of the earth, the Jewish nation is alive! The remaining few decided to unite, to struggle and to rebuild our national home in our promised land. Although peace is still a dream for the future – we are no longer a powerless nation and a scapegoat for scheming enemies. We are a nation who fights bravely and with fortitude to protect and defend our homeland.

The inspiration, initiative and the preparation of this memorial book was in the state of Israel while our nation fights for its independence and physical existence against our many enemies.

How different is our situation today from the dark days of the holocaust. No more a dust scattered in a hostile environment, but a well-rooted nation in the soil of our homeland, strong in spirit and powerful, fighting bravely and with resourcefulness.

To illustrate more clearly the great difference in the Jewish nation and its ability to fight against its enemies and those who try to annihilate it, it is our duty to tell the world and the younger generation about the past. How the "enlightened" world was complicit during the holocaust. How there was nobody to prevent these horrific events. How we must learn from the past, to never again be at the mercy of other nations. It is our sacred duty to keep describing how worthless were the lives of Jews in the diaspora, and how our foes were able to imagine the Jews as a lowly monster, an insect that can be easily squashed. It is important for our brave fighting youth to know and understand the history and suffering of our people in the darkest times and days. This will never happen again!

For eternal memory of the martyrs of Wierzbnik-Starachowice who were murdered by the blood thirsty Nazis and their helpers. This is a memorial to those who did not survive to see the establishment of the independent state of Israel with its open gates to the returning sons and daughters.

May these painful words that were written by the scattered remains be the tears on the unknown graves and solace and consolation for the sorrow, bereavement and grief that will never be forgotten.

On the Book Publication

Immense difficulties and obstacles were in front of us as we initiated and planned the publication of the memorial book of the holy community of Wierzbnik-Starachowice. In addition to monetary difficulties, we were also faced with the fact that we did not have any archival or official material about the history of our community. We often thought that the mission is more than we can bear. But thanks to the unending dedication of the doers we overcame the many difficulties and obstacles and we are blessed to see the completed book.

With that, we have to say that the book is not perfect. It is completely expected that there are areas in the book that are incomplete or not completely accurate. These are unavoidable taking into consideration all the limitations we encountered.

We were determined to make every effort to unearth every detail, every finding and every memory. The idea was to clearly and accurately describe everything that was, everything known and everything that people remembered and also to find the right balance of opinions about events and to let every voice be heard. In spite of all our efforts, we must see the limitations.

So few remained of the Wierzbnik-Starachowice community and they were the only source of information of the events. We have to stress again that there was no documentation whatsoever about the life in our town, so all the material in the book is based on the memories of the survivors. It is only natural that a person who lives in a certain area would be able to shed light only on his or her part of the world.

Editorial committee. Right to left: Moshe Sali-Kerberl, Simcha Mincberg, Yerachmiel Zinger, Tzvi Faigenbaum

It is possible that these circumstances caused some imbalance or lack of proportion when describing events. We did everything possible to minimize these.

This book is a collective product of the relentless dedication of many individuals who collected every shred of information to recreate truthfully the glorious past.

We want to thank all the members of our community in Israel and abroad who helped us in bringing this book to fruition. Their contributions and hard work are highly appreciated. May they all know that this was truly a work of love and a fulfillment of a holy duty.

May the memory of our town and community martyrs remain in our hearts and our souls. May we see the growth and prosperity of our homeland Israel. May our victories in the many battle fields be a consolation to all the tragedies that we saw in this generation and a source of hope and encouragement for the future.

The Book Committee

[Page xix]

Forward

Moshe Sali-Kerbel

We, the remnants of the Wierzbnik Jewish community, decided to publish a Yizkor book. We did it with enthusiasm and great respect. The book was to immortalize the multi-colored and lively Jewish life in our shtetl with its tragic end.

The Jewish community where we were brought up, we created and planned for our future, was destroyed by the bloody enemy. It no longer exists.

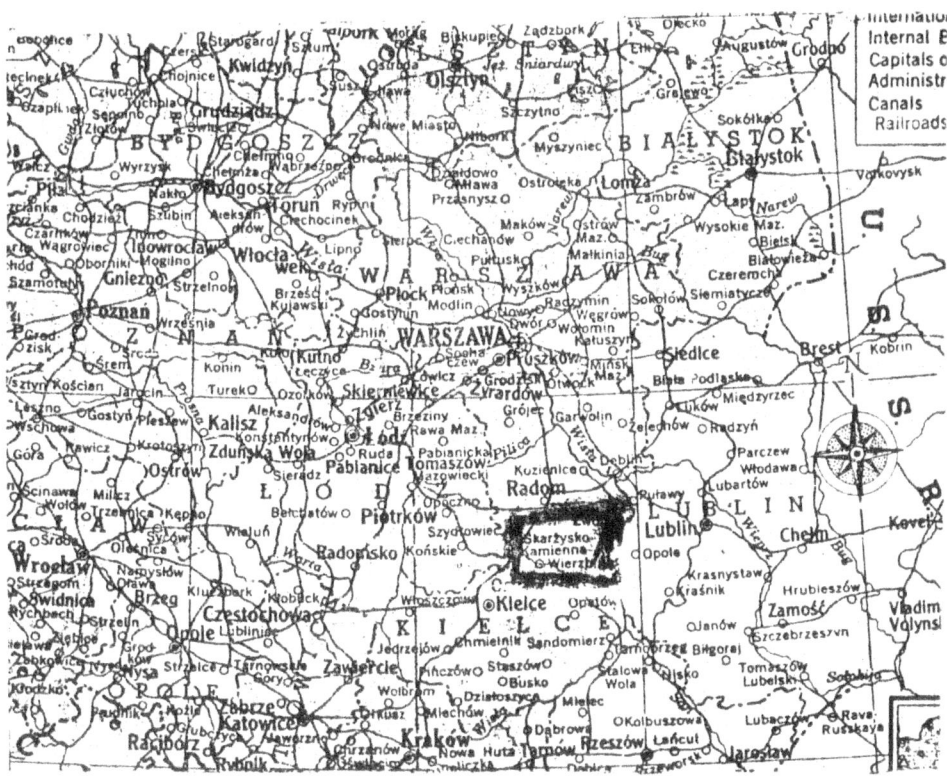

The idea of publishing a Yizkor book came out of the need to erect a monument which would immortalize and relate the story of the town. In this close-knit Jewish community which had its various political and cultural streams, there was a need to describe the struggle for equality and existence. There was suffering and happiness in the ordinary week days and the special Shabbat and Holidays. Later, there were the tragic days, months and years of annihilation of our own people by the blood-thirsty Nazi beasts and their helpers.

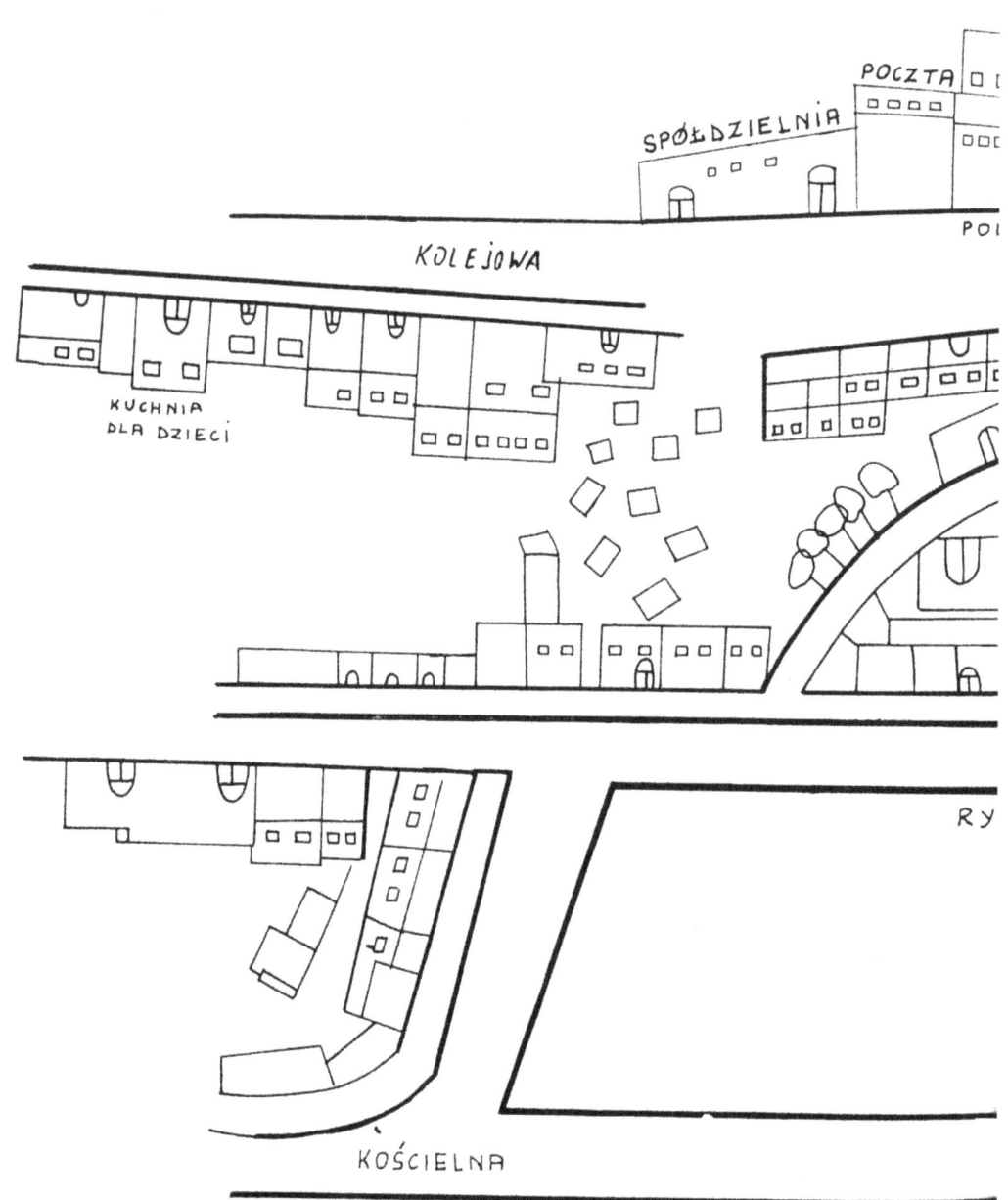

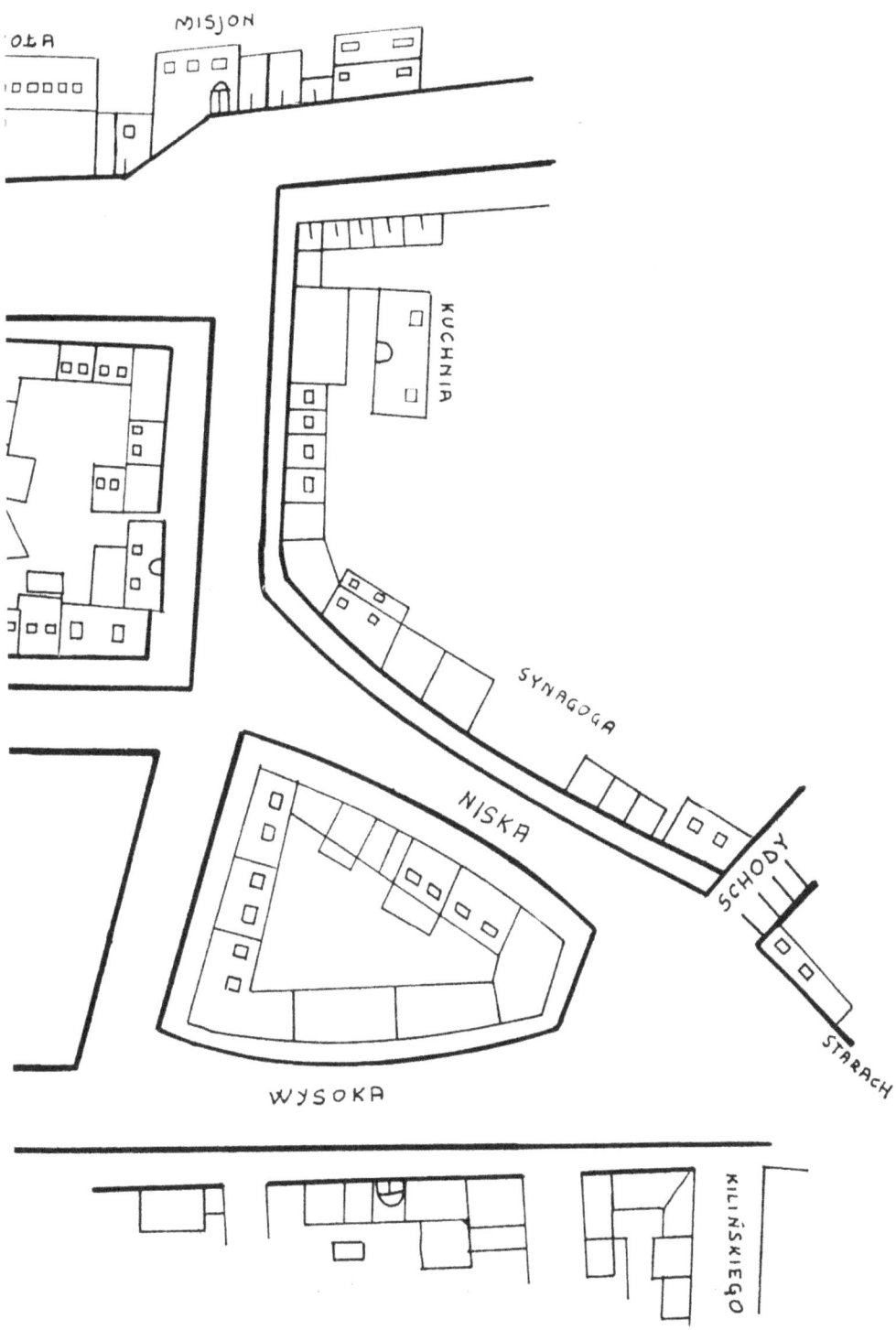

In the Yizkor Book we want to include memoirs and remembrances of our one-time home with its rich history. It is meant for us, and most importantly, for the future generations. It must reflect the true Jewish existence, from beginning to end.

Months and years passed since the first circulars were sent from Israel, to all former residents, to tell them about this holy project. Unfortunately, they did not have the proper reaction and the results were unsatisfactory. The disappointment and the despair were great at the passivity and indifference that did not allow for the realization of this important plan.

A new message

At one of the annual Holocaust memorial meetings, the writer of this article, volunteered to undertake the secretarial work involved. A new era dawned of regular, intensive work and the new activity culminated in a new, positive and dynamic trend. Again, circulars and letters were sent to all former residents in the country and outside of it. The importance of the historic meaning of this book was stressed - for those still living and for the future generations. Our martyrs must be immortalized.

In this manner there was correspondence between former residents in Israel, New York and Toronto. They were now involved in our enterprise. Yizkor book committees were established and there were special people who devoted themselves to this holy work.

This how, slowly, began the flow of material, articles and financial support. From day to day, interest in the Yizkor book grew. The warm and positive attitude of our former residents became the tribal force which strengthened us intensely in order to continue with this important book.

We made the effort to reflect, in the book, all aspects of the vibrant Jewish life and to demonstrate all its political, cultural, religious and national nuances and colors. The most important part of the book was dedicated to the tragic fate of our dearly beloved. This part was written completely by the survivors of the Nazi hell. They went through pain, suffering and bitter anger at the tragic events which were full of blood and tears.

There were many difficulties and strains during the preparation of the book. Not once did we think that we would have to resign from the entire project. The reasons were shortage of proper and able help, needed for such a complicated and difficult job.

In addition, it was not easy to obtain documents or material about the story of our town, its beginning and its existence. There were almost no sources for information about the establishment of the community - not in the library and not in the archives. We did not have proper financial assets, not enough workers to help and to continue the work. We awakened our people and called on them to fulfill their duty on both fronts. We asked for financial contributions and articles in order to immortalize their unforgettable families.

It is true that we made all efforts to eliminate errors and to assure that we honor our martyrs without any personal disagreements. It is probable that we were not successful in controlling everything.

There were many items that we did not include and so, many important details about events, special moments, immortalization of families, especially those which were completely annihilated are missing. However, my dearly beloved, when such an enormous project is planned, there are unavoidable omissions. We hope our expatriates will forgive us.

We did everything possible, under the circumstances, to transform ordinary people into writers. It was meant to include all descriptions as they were told by the survivors. The Yizkor book must be a book for all former residents who would be part of it. It would be done through the few remnants able to speak about historic moments.

This is our chance to thank all former residents who sent articles, memoirs and pictures. Thank you to everyone who did so willingly.

[Page 1]
Moshe Sali (Kerbel)

Introduction

With care and awe, we, the survivors of the town of Wierzbnik (Kielce county), approached the task of publishing a Yizkor book for our community, a book about life and demise.

This community, where we were raised and nurtured, was cut down by the bane and no longer exists.

At the memorial ceremony for the martyrs of our town, held in Tel Aviv. Sitting right to left: Tzvi Faigenbaum, Hershel Weiser, Moshe Sali, Simcha Mincberg, Y. Drexler-Dekel, Malka Weisbloom, and Avraham Sheiner.

{Signs at the top: right: The Yizkor book undertaking; left: Remember, and do not forget.}

{Sign at the bottom: May the people of Israel remember the martyrs of Starachowice-Wierzbnik who died in sanctification of the Divine Name. Their memory will never be forgotten from our midst.}

The notion of publishing a book commemorating the people of our town and its surrounding region was born from the need to leave behind an everlasting mark. This mark would take the form of a book that chronicles the town's history, its organizations and institutes, its everyday and holidays. It will also describe the Holocaust, the bravery and resolve of our fathers and mothers, our brothers and sisters, our relatives and friends who have all fallen prey to the bloodthirsty Nazi beasts. It will depict the human scenery of the vibrant community life, the activities and social struggles of its residents, as well as the special milieu during times of mourning.

The Bridge of the Kamienna River

In this commemorative book we seek to remind of the forgotten past and immortalize it, for our sake and the sake of future generations. We will tell not only about the torment suffered by our innocent loved ones, who valiantly bore the suffering and torture, but also about their rich lives, which were filled with a deep Jewish awareness of Bnei Torah. We will tell of activists and laborers, commoners and intellectuals; of the glory days of our community and its tragic fall.

Years have passed since the idea of immortalizing our town in a Yizkor book born. Those who brought up the idea were greatly disappointed by the apathy of our townsmen in Israel and the Diaspora. The few requests made years ago failed to touch our former townsmen and resulted in no activity toward the realization of the noble design hidden in their hearts.

The turnaround took place merely three years ago, when the author joined this sacred enterprise, allowing regular, intensive work towards the realization of the idea. We have sent out dozens of memos and prospects and hundreds of letters explaining the importance of the enterprise. We established close bonds with our landsleit in Israel and abroad, and managed to interest and even excite former townsmen in Toronto and New York, finding a few "fanatics" who joined the project wholeheartedly. We formed special committees and over the years have received considerable donations that would fund the project. This positive reaction encouraged and pushed us to continue work with increased vigor.

We tried to include the full scope of society in this book and to express every political notions found in the Jewish community of Wierzbnik. The book focuses mainly on the terrible Holocaust that doomed the Jews of the town. This part was written mostly by the survivors of our town, who expressed their outcry, their anguish, their pain and their terrible experiences.

We were faced with great difficulties while carrying out this mission and at times we felt that it was beyond us, because the financial support and the help offered in gathering the materials was insufficient.

At the memorial gathering dedicated to the publication of the book. Right to left: Tzvi Faigenbaum, Moshe Sali (speaking), Rabbi Eidelman, Simcha Mincberg, and Yerachmiel (Rumek) Singer)

It was also difficult to gather certified, accurate information about the history of the community, because we had limited sources to draw on, whether libraries or archives. Therefore we completed the enterprise with what limited means and few people we had at our disposal, knowing how inadequate we were for this enormous task.

Finally, we are able to say our work is done and the book pays homage to our townsmen. We know that this work is neither complete nor perfect. There are certainly deficiencies here and there as well as many missing details about eras, people and institutes. Nevertheless, we must accept this for a fact, as the members of the editorial board and those of the book committee, did anything in their power to find the material, encourage people to tell their tale and put in writing, for eternal memory, everything that could be gleaned from the memories of survivors in Israel and the Diaspora.

We wish to offer our thanks to all those who provided us with articles, lists and pictures, all those who helped, assisted, offered their support and encouraged, and special thanks to the members of the board, who worked tirelessly to create the book and publish it.

We also wish to thank all townsmen, wherever they may be, for the financial support they provided and which allowed us to publish this book. We wish to thank in particular the members of the book committee in Toronto and New York, who excelled at raising funds to finance this esteemed publication.

May our town and its martyrs become a part of our new life in the renewed State of Israel, which serves as some small consolation for our great tragedy and a source of hope and encouragement for all of our brothers and sisters.

[Page 4]
Simcha Minzberg

In Times of Peace

When I first came to Wierzbnik, before World War I, it was a peaceful, pastoral and growing town, and it I never guessed that my entire life would become entwined in the fate of this community and its Jews, from its beginning to its tragic downfall. But time has made that unforeseen future into a reality.

The first time I came to visit Wierzbnik I was accompanying my father, a lumber trader by profession who owned a lumber-mill in the town of Kunów. The purpose of this trip was a lumber deal with the famous firm "Heller". The owners of this firm have left their mark on the town's economy and did much for its growth. The owner of the factory, a German Jew named Noah Heller, was among the great lumber-traders of our time and procured many wooded areas near our town, which produced lumber that was processed in a special lumber-mill built for that purpose. This lumber-mill employed a full staff of workers and clerks, each an expert in his respective field and all of then naturally Jews, particularly nationalistic Jews.

Kolejowa Street in Wierzbnik

The manager was a great man, a Russian Jew called Mendel Rubin, a symbol of the nationalistic Jewish intellectuals among the Russian Jewry. He came from the town of Mir, birthplace of former Israeli president Mr. Zalman Shazar who mentions him, among other residents of his town, in his book "Morning Stars". Rubin has chosen a team of some 60 employees from among the townsfolk, among them some of the town's elite such as Avraham Mordechai Rotbart, Heinich Kazimierski, Moshe Bernstein, Nachumovski, Gendler, Aichler, Tenzer and others.

This factory was practically a different realm. It provided income for major parts of town; gave the town's development a financial and industrial push and also spread Zionism among the Jews.

The firm owned by the Brothers Lichtenstein encouraged and spread these values and promoted the community, establishing a plywood factory in the forest-surrounded town, among the first pioneers to promote this industry in Poland. The enterprise was initiated by the brothers' father, Mr. Meir Zanvil, who built a great lumber-mill on the road to Starachowice. As the surrounding neighborhood grew, the main street came to be called Starachowicka Street.

The lumber factory of the Lichtensztajn family

The plywood factory was owned by the four Lichtenstein brothers: Moshe Pinchas, Yoseph Reuven, Avraham and Daniel. Each brother was a remarkable person in his own right, and each had unique character, innovativeness, a spiritual, cultured attitude which brought them from the big city of Lodz and their fundamental Jewish lifestyle that won the respect of townsfolk. To this we add the fact that many of the local Jews found employment in their factory, and their contributions to various charities were generous.

We should therefore note a few aspects about the lives of the four brothers, whose positive contribution was both evident and significant:

Daniel was the key founder of the factory. He and his wife, Helcha, were highly educated people who took part in the turbulent events of 1905, a time of rebellion against the Tsarist regime and of political storms that swept the country. This involvement has forced them to leave the country around the turn of the century, leaving the factory in the hands of the other brothers. As Jewish nationalist revolutionaries, they naturally chose Israel as the place to realize their national ambitions. In Israel they were among the founders of Petah Tiqwa. During World War I they were deported, among all other Russian citizens, by the Turkish government that ruled Israel at the time, never to return from this exile.

Moshe Pinchas was a learned Jew, whose countenance and manners revealed his nobility. He took an active part in the social life of the community and was among the founders and managers of the Talmud Torah School. His pleasant voice could be heard at the synagogue located by the Talmud Torah, attracting worshipers and increasing attendance.

Daniel Lichtensztajn   *Halchia*   *Moshe Pinchas Lichtensztajn*

He was also a member of the Shtibl of the Gur Hasidim and as a long-time follower of the Rabbi of Gur, visited them frequently. He willingly and faithfully supported each institute and synagogue. While he lived at the center of town (at Laskovski's house), his residence was a gathering place for scholars, attracting many of the town's public activists and elite. As his future son-in-law, I had the chance to attend a Purim party at his house in 1913. This party, which was attended by important townsfolk, left a great impression on me despite being used to such events at my father's house.

Yoseph Reuven was a unique man, gifted with many talents, both an experienced lumber-trader and a scholar with a rare memory. His intellect and his kindness drew all the scholars, young and old, to him. He related to and kept in touch with the Rogachev Gaon[1]. In the years before his passing, he lost his sight and therefore memorized various religious writings by heart.

Avraham was an expert lumber-trader and represented the factory, while still being publicly active in both Wierzbnik and Lodz, the city he lived in until he immigrated to Israel.

Clearly, the Lichtenstein family added an important layer to the fruitful activity of social and public life in town, and their influence was considered positive indeed. It is not surprising that Hershel Lichtenstein, son of Moshe Pinchas, was among the young Zionist activists in town even before a branch of The Zionist Organization[2] was founded there.

As a matter of fact, even before marrying a girl from Wierzbnik, I was socially active in my town of Ostrowiec, which was already related to Wierzbnik. You may recall that the rabbi of that community was Rabbi Yaakov Aharon Regensberg, and among his followers and supporters were both workers from the Heller factory and the Lichtenstein brothers. My brother-in-law, Gershon, who later immigrated to Israel, was also one of his devout followers.

After the bloody clashes in Lemberg in 1918, the Jews of Ostrowiec were called to gather at the Beit Midrash[3] to mourn the victims. I have arranged for Rabbi Yaakov Aharon of Wierzbnik to say the eulogy during that touching event. As a social activist familiar with the rabbi and his skills, I worked to secure the permission of public activists, the Gabai[4] and particularly that of the Ostrowiec Gaon. This proved to be a fine choice, as the rabbi's eulogy was touching and left a lasting impression on those attending.

I had many opportunities to make contacts with the many families related to my fatherin-law. Thus I made friends with the family of Menashe's son Fishel (Fishel Najman), his son-in-law, the butcher Israel Szarfharc, the Gutermans, Dreksler, Tenenbaum, Kornwaser, Brodbeker, Herblum, Frimerman, Singer, Kleiner and others.

Yosef Reuven Lichtensztajn   *Avraham Lichtensztajn*

The atmosphere in Wierzbnik was Zionist even before my arrival, and so when I moved there, backed by a considerable record of social and public life, I became acquainted with members of the Zionist movement – Yoseph Dreksler, Moshe Birenzweig, Moshe Feldman, Leibale Tenenbaum, Avraham Zylberberg, Yitzhak Laks, Yoseph Tenzer, Itche Singer, Yoseph Unger and others, including of course my brother-in-law Hershel Lichtenstein. We made plans and focused our attention on expanding and increasing Zionist activism. And indeed we managed to widen the existing frameworks and introduce Zionism and Zionist contents to additional classes and members of town. These welcome enterprises and cooperation have helped in the founding of the Tarbut Hebrew School, a cornerstone for spreading the Hebrew language and imparting Jewish nationalistic values, particularly among the young.

As the son of a devout, traditional Jewish family, I tried to prevent Zionist activism from conflicting with tradition, instead characterizing and reflecting all the different trends of Zionism. We established a Zionist "Minyan" within the Zionist organization, which won the appreciation of both critics and sympathizers. This Minyan was particularly useful during the holidays, offering chances to collect donations to the Jewish National Fund, the Keren Hayesod Foundation Fund and others. During the ten days before Yom Kippur I was granted the honor of leading prayer, a role in which another of our members, Mordechai Lipstein, excelled as well. Our prayers were accompanied by the Zionist choir led by Yoseph Unger. And so the Zionist activity branched, becoming a guide and symbol for all nearby towns.

As the chairman of this vibrant organization during most of its prosperous period, before its tragic demise, I was always on top of events and did my best to act, motivate[5] and create Zionist cells and youth movements, guided and supported by the entire Zionist structure.

But my interests were not limited to the political field only. We were also aware of the financial aspects of most social classes, and managed to accomplish an impressive feat, establishing a Jewish bank in town with myself as its manager. This bank has eventually earned the trust of craftsmen who needed loans and they no longer had to depend on the good will of gentiles.

As an activist in both the public and financial fields I had extensive contacts among the different classes of the Jewish public as well as constant contact with representatives of the polish public and the authorities.

The "Tartak" (sawmill)

When the Jewish residents were allowed to take part in the elections for City Hall, they have chosen several men of means as representatives: Yoseph Dreksler, Shmuel Isser, Peretz Troper, Shimshon Frimerman, Yitzhak Singer, Chaim Brodbeker and myself. I also had the honor of being chosen as chairman and coordinator of the Jewish group. We participated in city council meetings and were charged with protecting the rights of the Jewish population, preventing or dulling the edge of the Polish edicts and suggestions that would limit and constrain the Jewish population in various manners.

I was thrice chosen as a member of the city council and once as a member of city council management. During this time I gained access to all the local authorities and could intervene and influence things in times of need. Along with the representatives of the Polish public I made public appearances on special occasions and these appearances have clearly earned us the respect of the gentiles. I'd like to take this opportunity to pay my respects to my partner in these activities,

Yoseph Dreksler, a great man and a conscientious Jew who was dedicated to the cause. I also fondly remember my friend Avraham Zylberberg, who despite being an orthodox Jew devoted his heart and his soul to the Zionist cause, dedicating to it much of his time and energy.

Before the formal organization of the community, public activity related to both religious and general public affairs was handled by the chosen leader of the community, Shmuel Isser. An organized committee was elected later, once again led by Shmuel Isser, and I was chosen as one of its members. Over time, the representatives changed and the community was led by Mr. Gelbtuch, an important activist from Wąchock. He was succeeded as community leader by Avraham Mordechai Rotbart, who did much to strengthen the boundaries of the community and revive it.

During the last two years before the outbreak of World War II, the community was led by the noble and educated Shmuel Pochachevski, who put much work and effort into turning the synagogue into a proper house of prayer, a pleasant place worthy of communion with our maker, a task he accomplished during his cadence.

Woefully, this holy place was stormed by soldiers as soon as the war broke out, and burned to the ground. This was the first sign of the dark days ahead, a sign that the unique chain of sacred Jewish values and the development of independent Jewish public activity were shrinking each day, becoming almost impossible. As aforesaid, I have witnessed the growth of activity in town and intertwined my fate with it, and so I also bore witness to the doom, the enslavement, the obstruction of any spark of Jewish initiative or independence, the desecration of a person's dignity and the image of God.

1. Highest rabbinical authority
2. Histadrut
3. Religious seminary
4. Manager of the synagogue's affairs
5. Religious quorum of ten men necessary for prayer

[Page 10]

Simcha Minzberg

Wierzbnik – Before the Flood

Before WWI, when I came to Wierzbnik, a small *shtel* with a pastoral appearance, for the first time, I could never have imagined that my entire future would be intertwined with that *shtetl* and its community, its Jews, its thriving and development – until its tragic demise. What could not have been thought of at that time became converted into reality.

I came at that time in the company of my father, a major lumber merchant and the owner of a sawmill in the nearby town of Kunow. The purpose of my father's trip was a lumber transaction in the well-known firm "Heller".

The Heller firm had placed its stamp on the *shtetl's* development. The owner of that firm, a German Jew called Noah-Nachi Heller, one of the most distinguished lumber merchants at that time, had then bought large lumber tracts in the Wierzbnik area, to exploit them for the sawmill he had built, and which employed a large staff, with clerks and specialists, almost all of higher ranks in different fields, and especially Jews with national pride.

The director-in-chief of the concern was a Russian Jew called Mendel Rubin, a personality, who symbolized a type of Russian Jew, a nationalistic intelligent class.

He originated from the town of Stoibtz (Stolbtsy), the birthplace of our distinguished President of Israel, Mr. Zalman Shazar, who mentions him among the characters in his book "*Kochvei Boker*".

Director Rubin had a staff of about 60 people under him, clerks and laborers, among whom were important personalities, such as Avraham-Mordechai Rotbard, Henech Kazimierski, Moshe Bernstein, Nachumawski, Gendler, Eichler, Yosef Tencer, and others. The concern was like a kingdom in itself, which provided an income for a large proportion of the *shtetl*, thereby also bringing about the economic development of the *shtetl*, and it also had a spiritual influence on the community, because the majority of them were consciously nationalist-Zionist Jews.

The Lichtenstein Brothers company also contributed to the economic and spiritual progress of the community. As pioneers in the veneer industry, the Lichtenstein brothers built up one of the first veneer factories in Poland. The one who started the investments in Wierzbnik was the father of the Lichtenstein brothers, Meir Zeinwel, of blessed memory, who built a large sawmill on the road that leads to Starachowice, which with building and development received the name 'Starachowice Street'.

The owners of the veneer factory were four brothers: Moshe-Pinchas, Yosef-Reuven, Avraham and Daniel. Each of the brothers was a personality in his own right. Coming from the big city of Łódź and leading a big-city lifestyle, they naturally aroused a feeling of respect in the Jews of the town. This feeling only increased because they employed the largest proportion of Jews, and generously donated a large amount for the charitable activities of the community.

I should mention a few aspects of the characteristics and life of the four brothers, whose contribution to the community was so positive and outstanding.

1. Daniel, the main founder of the factory, its dynamo, and his wife Helcze, both highly intelligent people, in the stormy years after 1905, at the time of the Polish revolt against the Russian Tsar, also took part in political activity. That is why after the failure of the rebellion they had to leave Poland and leave the factory in the hands of the three remaining brothers. Having to leave Poland, as their new country they chose our old country – Israel. Here in Israel Daniel and his wife were among the founders of Petach-Tikva. During World War I the Turkish regime deported all Russian citizens from the country, among them Daniel and his wife, who never returned from the deportation.

2. Moshe-Pinchas, a learned man, whose physiognomy and behavior expressed his natural nobility. In addition he also took apart in the communal life of the *shtetl*. He was one of the founders of the Talmud Torah [religious school] and was one of the directors of this important institution. His talent as a cantor also contributed to the synagogue in the Talmud Torah. His sweet voice, along with the beautiful version, used to attract many people to pray in the *minyan*. He was obviously also a contributor to the support of important public institutions. It is needless to add that Moshe-Pinchas did all this voluntarily. He also held a notable place in the prayer house of the Gur Hassidim[iii], as a Gur Hassid for generations, and there his prayers were a spiritual joy to the worshippers. Living in the center of town (in Laskawski's house), his house served as a committee room, where the distinguished men of the town used to gather. I personally had the opportunity to attend a meeting in 1913, at Purim. I was invited then for Purim, as a new bridegroom. The Purim evening in which the most important property owners took part made a deep impression on me, even though our house was a meeting place for sages.

3. Yosef-Reuven, was a very characteristic type, a great scholar. On the one hand he was a professional in the lumber industry, and on the other hand a scholar with a phenomenal memory. With his intellectual qualities, which were interwoven with friendliness to people, he was also a drawing card for all kinds of learning and intelligence, young and old. He also corresponded by mail with the Gaon of Rogaczewo, who was, by the way, also a relative of his. In his older years, when he lost his sight, he studied *Mishna* with interpretations by heart.

4. Avraham Lichtenstein, who was a specialist in the lumber industry, also didn't limit himself to commerce, but was also active in the community, not only in Wierzbnik, but also in Łódź, where he dealt with the factory's external business. He moved there and from there immigrated to Israel.

The Lichtenstein family was generally Zionist in outlook, and contributed a great deal to the progress of the Zionist activity in the *shtetl*. Hershel Lichtenstein, Moshe-Pinchas' son, was a Zionist activist even before the founding of the Zionist organization and its institutions in the town.

But even before my marriage, as a "prelude" to my social activity in Wierzbnik, I had already taken the first step in that direction in Ostrowiec, namely that at that time the rabbi of the community in Wierbznik was Rabbi Yaakov-Aharon Regensberg, one of whose main adherents and supporters was, together with the clerical staff of the Heller factory and the Lichtenstein brothers, my brother-in-law Gershon, who later immigrated to Israel, and who was also his devoted disciple.

After the pogrom in Lvov in 1918, a mass eulogy also took place in the synagogue in Ostrowiec, in memory of the victims of the pogrom. They invited the rabbi of Wierzbnik, Rabbi Yaakov-Aharon, to deliver the eulogy. This had to be approved by the Gaon of Ostrowiec, of blessed memory. As I was already then a public activist, and on the other hand, well acquainted with the Wierzbnik rabbi, I received the permission for the eulogy in the synagogue, which was packed with thousands of people, and the sermon by the Wierzbnik rabbi really did leave an extraordinary impression. With the passing of time, it was seen that I was in touch with many distinguished families, who had business with my father-in-law. Among others, I was friends with Fishl Neiman's family, with his son-inlaw – Israel Scharfhartz, the ritual slaughterer, the Guttermans, the Drekslers, Kornwassers, Tennenbaums, Brodbekers, Herblums, Frimmermans, Singers, Kleiners and others.

If the Zionist work will not be done, there will be religious encouragement in opposition

Even before I came to Wierzbnik, extensive Zionist propaganda activity had already developed, and among the first row of activists that I got to know in my Zionist work were my brother-in-law, Hershel Lichtenstein, Yosef Dreksler and also Moshe Feldman, Lebele Tennenbaum, Avremele Zilberberg, Yitzhak Laks, Yosef Tencer, Itcze Singer and others.

When I came to Wierzbnik I had already undergone an internship of community work in Ostrowiec, and so I immediately approached the above-mentioned Zionist activists, to develop, deepen and expand the Zionist work.

Thanks to our joint initiative, we established the base for the Tarbut School, which over time became the foundation, the center for the extension, deepening and instilling of Zionist thought in the broader sectors of the Jewish people in the town.

Stemming from an extremely religious, traditional family, I made great efforts to ensure that the Zionist work would not be done contrary to religious outlooks, but would be able to characterize and permit the expression of all the elements and varied streams of Zionism. We created a Zionist '*minyan*', which was very warmly attended by the members of the Zionist organization and also by various sympathizers. The holidays had a special character, and were marked by collections for the Jewish National Fund, Keren Hayesod and other monetary activities.

On the High Holidays I was especially honored with a seat in the front of the synagogue, as a public persona. My friend Mordechai Lipstein, who also excelled in this area, had his prayers accompanied by the choir led by Yosef Unger. This is how the Zionist work grew and spread, which served as an example for the entire province and neighboring area. As the chairman of the Zionist organization throughout all the years, until the tragic downfall, I always kept my hand on the pulse and attempted to fix and strengthen the work, founding Zionist youth cells, which would draw their nourishment from the Zionist stem.

Traditional and national spirit – were the foundation of life

But we were not only motivated by political problems, we also dedicated our interest to the economic side of the Jewish masses in the town.

A special event was the establishment of a Jewish bank under my direction, which immediately gained the trust of the Jewish merchants and tradesmen, who no longer needed to approach the Gentile bank for loans. Being in the framework of Zionist work and also active publicly and economically, I came into contact with broader sectors of the Jewish masses and I achieved close contact with the representatives of the Christian population.

Over time there were elections for the city council in which the Jewish population also took part, and a Jewish circle was formed in the city council, in which I took part together with the following property owners: Yosef Dreksler, Shmuel-Isser, Peretz Traper, Shimshon Frimmerman, Yitzhak Singer, Haim Brodbeker, and I was elected to be the chairman of the Jewish circle.

Taking part in the city council, the Jewish representatives had a permanent duty to defend the interests of the Jewish residents against the anti-Semitic decrees and pursuits to reduce Jewish rights, to economically limit them.

I was elected for three terms as a member of the city council, and during one term I was selected to be a member of the municipality.

Thanks to my constant public work, I had access to all government offices and was able to intervene when necessary.

My public excursions to various arenas and celebrations for the Polish public became known, and they brought much honor to the Jewish population.

At this opportunity I would like to emphasize that one of the most distinguished figures in the Zionist social work was my close friend Yosef Dreksler, who was very active and stood out for his devotion and temperament in all areas. The same applies to my friend Avremele Zilberberg, who was a nationalistic Jew, religiously observant and achieved a lot for Zionist-cultural purposes.

Before the rise of the community, communal activity was led by Shmuel-Isser. Over time, the representatives that led the community changed. For a certain time the person at the top was the important businessman Gelbtuch from Vanchikovtsy, and afterwards the position was filled by the talented, distinguished public activist, Avraham Mordechai Rotbard, who achieved a great deal for the welfare needs of the Jewish community. The last two years before the outbreak of the war, the work of the Jewish community was led by the active, energetic Shmuel Puchaczewski, who contributed a great deal of energy and effort to beautify every place, so that it would be pleasant to pray and study there – and he succeeded in achieving his goal.

But unfortunately, to our great regret, with the outbreak of the war the first place to be destroyed was the synagogue, which was burnt to ashes. This was the first portent that grim days were coming, and that the chain of the specifically Jewish cultural values and social activities was being limited and cut off. Just as my life was closely tied to the development of the town, so I was a witness to its destruction.

1. Followers of the Hassidic rabbi of Gur [Góra Kalwaria]

[Page15]

Jews in the Ghettoes of Poland (poem)

A German storms into your home,
Like a wind, a gale
He shoots the wife and kills
Oh little child, who will save him
In the cupboard he hides, stay in the cupboard
And please cry not
From the town square the cries of the tortured sound
Hearts turn heavy as stones
Children are crying loudly
Mother we are doomed, this is the end.
They also sent my father away
And I was left all alone
Homeless, a vagabond
Alone as a stone in the field.
The heart aches so much
Jews are marching there in a row
Brothers, sisters, mother and father
To the common grave
Why is it, why oh why
Surely you know –
Tell me why.

Malka Klara Weisbloom

Wierzbnik residents during the winter, before the disaster struck

Bnot Yaakov

{Written in the top photo: Wierzbnik, girls of Bnot Yaakov, 5693 Av (summer 1933)}

[Page 17]
Yaakov Katz

The Jewish People Lives!

With awe and reverence, ardently and with a heart quivering with a holy fear, I wish to join in expressing something of the purpose and meaning behind the publication of a memorial book for the Jewish community of Wierzbnik-Strachowitz.

This was a grand community with a long heritage and deep Jewish roots. In her, we first wove the fabric of our lives and futures, and in her foundation of tradition were laid in our souls forever. In Wierzbnik-Strachowitz's synagogues and study halls we imbibed the living Torah. To her came the blood thirsty Nazi beasts and she went up in smoke. The town is gone and only scattered remnants have escaped.

There has emerged therefore, a felt need to establish a lasting memorial to Wierzbnik-Strachowitz. A living monument in the form of a memorial book was conceived. Its pages were to tell of the life and death of this bustling community in whose shade we had been secure, of the war and of the struggles to save her. It would once again advance the contention that, "The Holy One of Israel will not fail."

For each and everyone of us, it is thus a sacred duty to aid and support to the fullest possible extent those engaged in this holy work, as it is written (Exod. 17, 14), "Write this for a memorial in the book." We must be for them "...aiding and supporting brethren."

In this memorial book we must recall from the depths of the past tortures and torments those dear innocents who bore their suffering with exalted courage. But we must also, so far as the human pen is able, record and eternalize the rich tapestry of tradition: steeped lives, of God; fearing and learned men, men of action and labourers, simple persons and seekers of enlightenment. In brief, we must chart the community's life course from its shining dawn tills its sunset. We must memorialize all for the sake of those who were not privileged to witness the enemy's downfall and the consolations of Zion and Jerusalem. We must memorialize for the sake of our dear ones who went up in flames, sanctifying the Holy Name.

Led to slaughter, they breathed their last pure breath on the altar of their will to remain Jews. Sons of a chosen nation, "stiff-necked" people, they chose to guard the spark of Judaism, despite all. We must memorialize too for our own sakes; we, "splinters saved from the fire" a last remnant which has emerged from bondage and been vouch saved a glimpse of redemption. We must memorialize also for the sake of future generations.

Wierzbnik-Strachowitz was a thriving and flowering branch of the splendid, deeply rooted tree of Polish Jewry and an ornamented link in its chain, a fruitful and productive shoot of Jewish stock. But when the axe of the German hangman was aimed at that beautiful tree, even the gentle and wonderful branch of Wierzbnik-Strachowitz was cut in its prime.

Twenty-eight years have passed since the Nazi terror directed its poison darts at Israel, employing weapons and tactics of destruction hitherto undreamed of by mankind. We were (Jeremiah 9,21), " As dung upon the open field and as the handful after the harvestman which none gathereth..."

Even in the long, blood-drenched history of Jewish martyrdom there is no likeness or parallel to those deeds of destruction.

We, the survivors and mourners, will never forget our loss. Our agony must be unceasing for those who, innocent and pure, fell victims at the hands of the scum of the earth. Let us hope that the conscience of an enlightened world will finally awaken, clearly realize the situation and learn the necessary lessons from this unparalleled Holocaust. Even now, we must be on guard against those who call for a new genocide and who deceitfully schemed to uproot us from the land of our Fathers, our eternal homeland since Abraham.

We are thus commanded on the basis of every consideration to kindle an eternal flame of memorial for our fathers, families, and relatives. May it burn before us forever, sanctifying their name in public mind and all the holy of Israel.

For us it is a privilege and a holy obligation to eternalize the history and events of the village, her social and spiritual life, organizations, public institutions and personalities. Only thus can we understand the proud and brave stand of our fathers and mothers, brothers and sisters, blood relatives and dear friends who were brought to the slaughter with lips trembling at the thought of vengeance.

Their last words were of, "The G-d of Israel who is a G-d of Vengeance" of, "The people of Israel which lives and endures." The downfall of Hitler and his cohorts must certainly not be of any less importance or significance to us than that of Amalek, Haman, Pharoah, or any of Israel's enemies throughout the generations. We were commanded to remember Amalek to celebrate Purim with joy and the reading of the Scroll of Esther. We celebrate Passover and tell stories of the Exodus till morning. Doubly so, should it be out holy obligation and that of all Israel to externalize in flaming letters and in public what the monstrous figure of Hitler bode for us. Unquestionably, enormous difficulties will arise in the practical implementation of such a weighty task. Those pioneers who have unselfishly shouldered the burden of this sacred duty will certainly meet many financial and social problems. Most difficult perhaps, will be the patient "ant's work", of collecting the mass of material, connecting its diverse threads and of finally reworking it for publication.

More than once doubts have arisen whether the strength of these pioneers, Jews and non-Jews alike, would suffice to overcome all the difficulties inherent in this invaluable task.

For those working on this particular volume, the scattering of the descendants of Wierzbnik-Strachowitz throughout the wide world, and their differing relations and attitudes towards the nation's spiritual treasures, weighs as a heavy problem. There is also a lack of substantial and reliable information about the history and events of Jewish Wierzbnik-Strachowitz.

Despite all difficulties, however, our great faith in the "Rock of Israel" together with our belief that (Jeremiah 51,5), "Israel is not widowed" have renewed in us the hope that our combined efforts will suffice, "to roll off the stone from the lip of the well." We will succeed. To me it seems as if our requests and prayers have already been answered. After long, fatiguing efforts, we are now finally entering the advanced stages of the projects realization. G-d willing, the book will soon appear in a format which will do honor to those from the town and its surroundings.

We realize that the work cannot be altogether faultless or complete, certain details regarding personages or historical periods may be missing. We may, however, accept such deficiencies, secure in the knowledge that the editors and all those involved in the project have done everything possible to obtain source materials, to encourage participation and to bring to light memoirs and information about events and feelings in the life of the villagers.

Let me take this opportunity to give my blessing and encouragement to all those engaged in this holy task and to all who have given it material and spiritual aid. Special mention must be made of the small group of organizers of the project who have not spared pain or effort to ensure the book's speedy publication. Similarly, we must thank all those who have actively participated in this lofty cause, whether by volunteering information or contributing financially. May they all be blessed!

May the memory of those who are not with us serve the State of Israel and all the House of Israel. May their merit help protect us from those in every generation who hate us and would seek to destroy us.

May the memory of our town and her holy martyrs be bound up with the eternal life of the renewed State of Israel in which we conceive some small consolation for our great loss. May the State be a source of hope and encouragement to all our brothers and sisters everywhere, thus strengthening the weakened ties among Jews. May her influence serve to forge a new link in the splendid, continuing chain of Jewish learning and values in the tradition of the prophets.

Let us say Amen – may such be thy Heavenly Will!

"Again will I build thee and thou shalt be built, O virgin of Israel."

[Page 19]

Wierzbnik: the Town, its Location and Growth – Excerpt from a Geographic Dictionary

Wierzbnik is an urban settlement, formerly a township, in the Iłża County. It is considered both the local and regional authority.

It is located on the Łysogürski plains, on the left bank of the Kamienna River, flowing some four kilometers from town, into a large lake (near Michałüw).

The settlement is located in a valley formed by the joining of several rivers, collecting water from broad forested regions. The most important among those rivers is the Łubianka, branching from the eastern bank of the Kamienna. On the opposite bank lies Starachowice.

Wierzbnik is located about 4 miles east of Wąchock and 20 miles south of Iłża. There is a stone Catholic Christian church in town, an elementary school, a town courthouse, a municipal office, a railroad station which is part of the Dombrowiec line connecting Będzin and Ostrowiec, about 17 wiorst[1] from Będzin and 15 wiorst from Kunów.

A market day takes place every Friday, and a fair takes place once a year.

The Œwiętokrzyski monastery ruled over the large forested areas by the shores of the Kamienna, bordering on the estates of the Cysters of Wąchock, and the two cooperated in efficiently exploiting this wilderness.

This may be the reason that prince Radoshevski, royal secretary and cardinal of Kiev, secured a concession from Polish king Sigismund the 3rd and decided to found the settlement of Wierzbnik in 1624, locating it 6 miles from Wąchock and opposite to Starachowice. The king gave the place his sanction according to Magdeburg Law, authorizing the weekly market days and three fairs a year. The Cysters protested, claiming that the land the town was built on was under the municipal authority of Wąchock and the controversy over this matter continued unabated for nearly a century.

Prince Opatówski built a stone church in Wierzbnik and gave the town various concessions. 167 tax payers were accounted for in 1674 while the legal issues with the Cysters were still under debate in the court of Radom. Both parties eventually agreed to delimit the area. According to a census, 9,887 souls lived in the Iłża County that year, among them 651 Jews. This county included the settlements Brody, Dziurów, the Hercules mines, Jabłonna, Kochów, Krzyżowa Wola, Michałüw, Ruda, Stikov, Svirta, Wenecja, Rajdowa, Książ, Starachowice and Wierzbnik.

(From a Geographic Dictionary, vol. 13, Warsaw, 1893)

1. Approximately 1 kilometer

[Page 20]
Moshe Sali (Kerbel)

A Precious Pearl Shattered

The community of Wierzbnik exists no more. Bloodthirsty murderers cut this bough from the great tree that was the Polish Jewry, eradicating it. Its memory shall live on in the hearts of the hundreds of survivors scattered in Israel and the Diaspora.

It was one Jewish settlement among the many that took root and became a part of their surroundings. Before its downfall it has reached a peak of national and public life, of enlightenment and experience, everything that was good and glorious about this enterprise – independent Jewish life in exile. The sleepy, seemingly peaceful town of Wierzbnik was like a living, conscious cell in the larger organism called the Polish Jewry, reflecting the struggles of the lives of Jews in Poland before the Holocaust.

The great stream composed of all the national social and political movements of the Polish Jewry flowed in every direction in Wierzbnik. It is true that the hundreds of children and youths considered the traditional home, the Heder[1] and the Melamed[2] to be their main sources of education. However under the influence of the youth organizations and the local Zionist movement, the desire for active Zionism spread and Israel was on the minds of all.

Everything was seen in a new light during those turbulent times. The Jewish youths learned that the routine existence offered no escape from the hardships of exile, because it failed to answer demands of time, the longing and the yearning for redemption hidden in their hearts. The youths therefore reached the conclusion that they have lost their way in life and strove for a change, a way out. While the Zionist movement served as the source for the Zionist spirit and the Hebrew language, HeHalutz and the other youth ovements served as the anvil on which the realization of Zionism was forged.

With great effort they shaped moral values that became general consensus. We transformed from the ones who received and were inspired into the ones who gave and offered inspiration – and the Jewish community underwent a process that changed its cultural values, as many started to weave their lives into the movement with great enthusiasm and faith.

One by one I imagine the people and characters of the town, like a colorful mosaic; public and individuals, with their lives, their ways, their manners and their actions during everyday and holidays. This wondrous gallery of characters and institutes, which grew from the colorful background of various classes: the commoners, the craftsmen, the grocers and traders, the rich, the professionals, religious scholars and ordinary Jews, this was the life of the vibrant town yearning for human and national salvation, one of the many holy communities that were destroyed. Like precious pearls shattered and torn away from the necklace that adorned the Jewish people.

The light was extinguished, the fire of enthusiasm quenched, the fountainhead of Jewish vigor, initiative and ingenuity dried up.

1. Religious elementary school
2. Religious teacher

[Page 21]

Jerachmiel Singer

Chronicles of the Town and its Jews

A small settlement called Wierzbnik was founded at the center of Poland, on the bank of the Kamienna River, a tributary of the Wisła River,, growing as time went by into a vibrant town. I remember that the residents of the place used to tell that the town received its name from the abundance of willow trees ("Wierzba" in Polish) in the area. Whether this claim is true I cannot prove, because in my time the surrounding area was full of conifers, and willows were not numbered among them…

The town lay in a valley, surrounded by hills. To one side were the ridges of Wenecja, and on the other, the hills of Starachowice. Two roads and railroads stretched out from the town, one being via Wąchock, leading to the industrial city of Skarżysko, and the other being via Kunów, stretching to the town of Ostrowiec. A third road led to the city of Iłża.

During the reign of pre-revolutionary Russia, until World War I, the town was part of Radom County, while following 1918 it became part of Kielce County, in the region of Iłża. Although the region bore the name of another town, the existence of railroad tracks placed it in Wierzbnik.

The lumber factory of the Lichtensztajn family

As aforementioned, the town was surrounded by forests and the land around it was rich in high quality iron deposits, although ones that were misused. There were also deep deposits of fireproof clay located midway between Wierzbnik and Wąchock, around Proszowice. All of the above contributed to the development of industry in town and around it. First and foremost was the metal industry. At first, the raw iron was smelted where it was dug using primitive methods that prevented mass utilization. However during the second half of the 19th century, a smelting furnace was built in the neighboring town of Starachowice. This would be a good opportunity to mention a rarely known fact: the initial establishment of the metal industry based on these iron deposits was carried out by the Rotvand family, one of the most respected Jewish families in Poland, which built the large metal factory called "Starachowice Factories". This family played an important role in building the Polish economy. Along with the Volberg family they also opened the high technical college in Warsaw. The factories I mentioned earlier were expanded during the Russian regime and the steel-mill known as Stalownia, where the steel was manufactured using the Martin approach was another legacy of that era.

The wartime acquisition policy of Poland changed between 1920-1922 and the government decided, among other things, to establish a military industry in Starachowice. As a result of this decision, all of the existing factories that manufactured war supplies became government property. Among them the government also inherited the factories that were owned by the Rotvand family (51%), but over the years the name was forgotten, despite the fact that its owner was among the founders and builders of the factory. Furthermore, although these factories were expanded and developed to employ as many as 20,000 workers, they failed to employ even a single

Jew. Only during the German occupation were the Jews forced to work there allowed to peek inside this behemoth, which was out of bounds for them in the past.

It should also be noted that this factory was formally owned by an organized body called in Polish "The Central Industrial Organization", which also controlled the factories in Nisko, Ostrowiec, Skarżysko, Radom, Blizin and Pionki.

There was also a factory called Rogalin in our town, which manufactured bricks and ceramics.

The lumber industry

The lumber industry, in which Jews took a prominent part, deserves some attention. Since my family was connected to this field, I will allow myself to dwell on it in detail.

My grandfather, Yidl Mysliborski, built a factory that produced turpentine, which was necessary for manufacture of chemicals. The production of turpentine was carried out by burning the tar of the conifers that filled the forests surrounding town.

I remember a legend I was told by my grandfather, about the Russian Tsar and his wife who spent their vacation in their palace in Spała. One day, while they were riding in the countryside, the queen caught a whiff of smoke and inquired about its source. When she was told that it came from the burning of tar, she stated that it might harm the birds of the forest... and as you know, the queen's will is near-absolute and her subordinates were immediately ordered to move the factory to Martzola, on the road to Iłża. After World War I, it was moved again to Starachowice, near the home of the Isenberg family.

However during the 1905 revolution, the factory was a dangerous place to live by, since it was located in the forest, inviting common bandit attacks and visits from the Russian Tsar's Ochrana. My grandfather therefore decided to move to Wierzbnik. Chaim Zajfman, who lived on Starachowicka Street, advised him to buy land nearby and my grandfather accepted his advice and built the famous courtyard "Mysliborski Hoif" which in time became practically a town of its own.

A typical Jewish house in Wierzbnik.
Mordechai Sztarkman (Michlower) next to his house

The first houses and public structures

Here is another detail worth mentioning. When my grandfather purchased his land, Starachowice road was already lined with the houses of the following families: Kalman Winograd (Goldzhak), the parents of Mendel Binstock, Pesach Isenberg, and near Lower Starachowice, the house of the Mora family. As far as I know, the family of Yaakov Mawer (who currently lives in the United States) was one of the oldest in town and the home of Yeshayahu Guterman was one of the first houses built. Its architecture was unique, in particular the entrance and the cellar which were reminiscent of castle labyrinths. The owner was not a local, but his wife Zelda, a daughter of the Mawer family, was a native of Wierzbnik. As the town grew, this house became a central location and was even nicknamed "Rot-hoiz". As many as 20-25 Jewish families lived there at the time. Nevertheless, it fell victim to urbanization plans and was torn down just before the outbreak of World War II. The ancient house on Niska Street, which belonged to Yaakov (Yankel) Kornwaser, suffered a similar fate. Kornwaser was one of the most respected families in town, along with Brodbeker, Dreksler, Herblum, Tenenbaum, Mawer, Winograd, Binstock and other families. Those families were among the first to settle in town, and originally made their by living baking bread for the miners and factory workers in the area.

I remember the synagogue on Niska Street, which underwent considerable renovation during my time. Some claim that it was built toward the turn of the previous century. As for the Mikveh, it was burned to the ground during World War I and was rebuilt with the assistance of the Joint and other philanthropic organizations.

I must note, however, that the majority of the Jewish population in town came from the nearby settlements and villages, moving there on their own or through marriage. This is indicated by the people named after their place of origin, such as Yaakov (Yankel) Razfiner, Avraham Lubianiker, Bzhezher Leibish Prendechiner, Shmeril Mlyneker and others. It is unclear if the large butcher families of Herblum and Rubinstein were direct descendants of Wierzbnik, while people like the Rotmanovich family (the parents of Avraham-Buba) and Hanna the baker, the wife of Shmuel Isser, were most likely among the "original" residents of the town.

The economic foundation of the Jews of Wierzbnik

The lumber industry was an important source of employment for the Jews of Wierzbnik. The surrounding forests provided lumber for house-building and industrial purposes, as well as support beams for the mines. Merchants from the Russian and German occupation zones came to Wierzbnik, to purchase this lumber, and the lumber trade gradually expanded, even earning a special nickname – "brakazh". The lumber sold had to be loaded girded into freight cars, and many Jewish porters and craftsmen were hired for this purpose.

Uncaptioned: Inscription on photo reads: Wierzbnik, 1/1 1934. To the Frajdman family on the occasion of their aliya to the Land of Israel

After a time, the four sons of the famous merchant Meir Zanvil Lichtenstein – Yoseph Reuven, Moshe Pinchas, Daniel and Avraham Lichtenstein – opened a plywood factory. The factory was built by the road to Iłża, near the lake in which the lumber was immersed so that the layers used for the plywood and furniture industries could be peeled off it.

A lumber drying branch was also established near the factory, and those structures changed the architectonic looks of the entire area, giving the formerly rural scenery clear urban characteristics. The factory employed many workers and craftsmen, including clerks brought from the big cities – Warsaw and Lodz – making it an important, vibrant public institute. It seem to have been the first factory of its kind, manufacturing parts for the furniture industry and spreading its reputation beyond the town, doing business with important merchants all over the country.

Another part of the lumber business was the lumber-mill by Starachowicka Street, also managed by the Lichtenstein brothers. And as we talk of this family, which played a major part in building and developing the town, we must mention that the first Jews to immigrate from Wierzbnik to Israel came from that family.

While on the subject of the Lichtenstein family, Daniel's wife, Mrs. Helcha Lichtenstein, was an exceptionally active member of the socialist party. Rumors told that she used to "ambush" workers by the factories after work and give them speeches while standing on a barrel...

Her speeches were passionate and called for the workers to rise against the regime. However the Russian Tsar's Ochrana quickly discovered her actions and began persecuting her. In light of this development and since the family was involved with the Hovevei Zion movement (Lovers of Zion, an immigration movement), they all decided to immigrate to Israel.

When they came to Israel, most of them settled in Petah-Tiqwa and the ones who followed them settled there as well.

Like the Lichtenstein brothers, who were important to the economic foundations of the Wierzbnik Jewry, the Heller family too was a prominent part of the Jewish public. The family originally came from Russia, and the factory they have opened grew over the years into a giant that branched well into Russia, Poland and South America. The founder of this great concern was Hershel Heller, son-in-law of the famous Jewish millionaire Wissotzky. The factory was later renamed "Hortzi", after the aforementioned founder. This firm was also active in the east of Poland, in Karsi, in Mikaszewice, near Łuniniec, in Solec and around Bydgoszcz.

When Poland gained its independence, the owners of the concern built a lumber-mill in the area, by the Kamienna River, and years later they added a modern plywood factory. The foundation of these factories following World War I was important for the establishment of the Jewish community. It provided employment, offered material aid to the lower social classes and supported social, cultural and political organizations and institutions.

In order to fulfill the needs of the manufacturing processes, the factories attracted people who emigrated from Russia to Poland after the revolution. These people were members of Hovevei Zion, intellectuals mainly, whose habits and social-cultural traditions greatly encouraged the awakening Zionism.

Brit Hachayil (Covenant of the Soldiers) in Wierzbnik in 1938: Godel Kadiszowicz, Shlomo Drajnodel, Noach Frajd, Gershon Rozenwald, Mordechai Maslowicz, Leo Zulcer, Avraham Nisker

Bnot Agudat Yisrael (Agudat Israel Girls). Standing right to left: Weizer, Cohen, Sheindel Herblum, Tova Cohen, Dina Rabinowicz, Rivka Przyticka, Komec, Dvora Tenenbaum. Seated from the right: Rabinowicz, Malka Kornwaser, in the center, the teacher Lea Wajntraub.

During 1921-22, youth groups organized and took up physical labor at the factories in order to prepare for immigration to Israel. Some of their work involved the driving of carts to the factory, which they did while singing in Hebrew as they worked. The living spirit of this group was Hochblit, brother of Moshe Bernstein's wife Abigail. Yaakov Goldgrub recruited a Hebrew teacher named Zheloni from the town of Kielce, who taught the boys the Hebrew language, Hebrew songs and military foot drills.

Among the participants of these groups were Avraham and Shmuel Unger, Uri Helstein, Moshe Birenzweig, the sons of Shmeril and Efraim Pratzovnik, both Manela brothers, Ovadia Goldberg, Shlomo Goldberg and the sole member who actually made it to Israel, a man named Bar.

The field next to the railway station.

The Heller Factories

Having temporarily worked at the Heller family's factories, where many Jews found employment, I remember well the excellent working conditions and work relations. One of the prominent employees was the factory manager, Mr. Rubin, a talented man and a visionary who was the subject of legends; Gincberg, the Rosenstein brothers, Getzko, Moshe Bernstein, Benyamin Helstein, Berl-Yidl Rosenberg, Yitzhak Mendel Kerbel, Avraham Goldstein, and during the last years, before the outbreak of the war, Yaakov Shiner.

As aforesaid, the firm employed many Jews and was an important part of the Jewish economy in Wierzbnik.

Before the holidays, the company provided the Jewish community with monetary donations and leftover lumber, to be distributed among the poor.

After the passing of the factory owner, his family immortalized him by building a brick fence around the cemetery in his memory.

During World War I

It is a fact that the constant motions of the fighting armies during World War I brought the front line closer to Wierzbnik. Eventually, the Russian authorities ordered the place evacuated and forced the residents to migrate to the town of Iłża.

This order came out of the blue for the Jewish residents and most, if not all, were unprepared for such a radical and sudden move.

Elementary school class in Wierzbnik with the teacher

The slowness of their preparations clearly showed their reluctance and the Russians used drastic measures to rush the eviction, driving people out while screaming and shouting, "Come on, come on!"

The people were understandably agitated and fear and terror were in the atmosphere. People had to leave in a hurry and could only take with them the bare necessities and the clothes on their back. It was a sad, depressing sight, this entire crowd of refugees fleeing for their lives with their belongings and babies in their arms, headed for the nearest town, Iłża. They naively assumed that when they arrive in town, they can rest a while and perhaps even find food, but the Russians allowed them no rest and they were forced to march on, to the city of Radom, exhausted and worn-out as they were. When they reached Radom they joined with other refugees and were forced to stay there two months, suffering from destitution and misery, although many found residence among the local Jewish families. Our family lived in the house of a famous wealthy lady named Malka Korman.

Fortunately, the front line shifted once again and we could return to our homes in Wierzbnik. The days rolled by, and the effects of the historic events taking place in this world were evident everywhere, including our town. New frameworks and patterns started emerging here and there, in traditional areas of life and especially social life. The Jews in town assimilated all those processes and played an active role in them.

The leader of our community at the time was Heinich Kazimierski, son-in-law of Eli Kalmanzon, who was known as the informal patron of the Jews of Wierzbnik. He was a well-educated, intelligent man, wise and kind hearted. These fine traits earned him respect and access to the authorities, allowing him do much for his community.

Following the war, several Jewish families received official permits to trade in food products such as sugar, salt, oil and so on. This was a necessary arrangement since the needs of the hour dictated a rationing of such commodities.

Zionist activity

This period also foreshadowed the awakening of the Jewish youths, who sought a purpose in life and wanted to shape their future path. Many turned to the work circles and a few found enthusiasm in the Zionist idea. Among the first residents of town to realize this dream and immigrate to Israel were Ovadia Goldberg, today a resident of Benyamina, and Shlomo Goldgrub.

There were other residents who did not see Poland as their future, although their conclusions carried them in other directions, and they immigrated to Brazil, the United States and Canada. To Brazil went Anchel Grossman, the brothers Manela from Krutka Street, the son of Pinchas Manela, the sons of Shmeril and Efraim Pratzovnik, and the sons of Itzik Mendel Kerbel. To the United States and Canada left the sons of the tanner Hershel Kleinberg, Urish and Yoseph and his daughters – Sheindl and Mania. Another phenomenon, unique to this period and noteworthy, is the seminary students, who spent years studying nothing but the Torah and now abandoned the seminary, changed their manners and dress and joined the secular movements.

Among those Yeshiva students were: Leibale Tenenbaum, Moshe Birenzweig, Moshe Feldman, Yaakov Kaiser-Tenenbaum, the son of Pinchas Manela and others.

It was about that period that Mr. Simcha Mincberg, son-in-law of Moshe Pinchas Lichtenstein, began his public activity. He was already famous for public activism in his own hometown, but when he moved to our town he worked extensively with a group of people who labored in the factories owned by the Lichtenstein brothers and the Heller family.

They had two different goals: one was increasing and expanding the Zionist concept, establishing organizational movements, teaching the youth Zionist activism, teaching the Hebrew language, and so on. Their other goal was ensuring the existence and peace of the Jewish public, and expressed itself mainly by waging battle against the authorities and municipal administration, protecting the rights of every Jewish citizen and resident. Among the activists who gathered around Simcha Mincberg were: Yoseph Dreksler, Hershel Lichtenstein, Yoseph Tenzer, Moshe Feldman, Moshe Birenzweig, Yoseph Unger, Leibale Tenenbaum, Yeheskel Morgenstern, Meir Baumstein, Yitzhak Rosenberg, the Rosenwald brothers, Yeshayahu Yona Szarfharc, Avraham Frimerman, Berish Guterman, my father and others.

Other activists in this field were Shimshon Frimerman, Shmuel Isser and Shmuel Cohen.

One of the typical phenomena of those times was the special places of worship that served as a kind of substitute for those activists who left the seminary, the various "Shtiblach" that adopted the ideals of national renaissance. Searching for spiritual "bonds", they organized groups for public prayer sessions, and held these sessions at private residences. One such place, where people prayed for years, was Zajfman's Hotel. Avraham Zylberberg, Mordechai Lipstein and my father read the Torah regularly, while Simcha Mincberg was the Baal Kore[1]. Prayers such as El Adon were sung by a choir, led by the sweet voices of the Unger brothers. Incidentally, two of the brothers, Becalel and Shmuel, eventually became cantors.

Prayers were also sung at the end of Yom Kippur, with the musical accompaniment of Motele Isenman and Moshe Lustig, filling the atmosphere with a sense of warmth and elation.

Tashlich processions were organized by the Zionist Organization for the New Year, during which the youth marched in both directions, singing marches in Hebrew. As time went by, the movement acquired its own gathering places. The first among them was the home of the Taubman family, and later the house of the Drajnudel family and the house of Yeheskel Szternkrantz. The movement also increased and expanded its activity from one year to the next. Among the results of this activity was the Tarbut School. For a time, just after its inception, the Zionist movement in Wierzbnik acted as a single, organized body, but the events and divisions that took place in the world led to similar developments in our town. When the Beitar movement was established, some activists joined the new organization, which wielded considerable power, while the more religiously-orthodox Zionists organized a separate group, led by Shmuel Tenenbaum. At first, they gathered on the ground floor of the Talmud-Torah and later they moved to Ilzhezka Street and even opened their own school. Some of the movements famous throughout Poland – the Bund and HaShomer HaTzair – were missing from our town, but we had a group called "The Evening Class Alliance", which turned out to be tightly linked to Poalei Zion the Left, founded by Yaakov Zerubavel. This group was led by Shimon (Shimale), an educated man with a staunch proletarian mindset, and Chaim Binstock, Yaakov Vigdorovich and Marmel Furman. This group was the axis around which the proletariat youth gathered. They fought for better conditions at their workplaces, organized night classes for impoverished workers to provide them with a proper education and even founded a library and a sports club, sponsoring a sports team called "Gviazda". Their first activities were public lectures given at the home of Avraham Zylberman and eventually they became a decidedly leftist movement. When Zerubavel returned to the Zionist Organization, they too changed their approach to the Organization and showed willingness to cooperate with it instead, but the war that broke out in 1939 destroyed all their nice plans and lofty ambitions.

Bnot Zion (Daughters of Zion)

A women's organization called "Bnot Zion" was also established. Its members gathered in the attic of Pesach Isenberg's house. Among the activists in this organization were: Pola Laks, my aunt Gucia Tenzer, Macia Lichtenstein-Mincberg, Esther Guterman, Frania Unger, Mania Zylber. Among the clerks were Hilia Rosenstein, Bernstein, Gincberg, Shmuel Heller's wife and others.

The women of the organization collected donations for Zionist goals, and also acted in the field of culture, organizing festive events, plays and so on. One such unique event was etched into my memory, though I no longer recall the actual name of the play. It was staged in the firefighters' lot on Koleyova Street, which was later turned into an elementary school. I recall that my aunt, Mrs. Tenzer, played the role of Rebecca and Pola and Isaac Laks participated in it as well. They have borrowed the costumes from Rabbi Yaakov Regensberg's wife. It was the first play I have ever seen and it left me with a sensation of marvelous fantasy…

Another event I recall from those days was a play called "Achashverosh", performed just before Purim at the municipal movie theatre "Pshigoda". Among the actors were Hochblit, playing the role of Vaizata, and the photographer Ostrian from Radom playing the role of Achashverosh. I also recall a skit performed at the firefighters' lot in which Hershel Lichtenstein played a drunk and sang the famous song "A Jew goes to the bar".

The women's example and success has inspired the start of a musical band, comprised mostly of violinists accompanied by a few wind instruments. They organized public performances in our town and sometimes played in nearby towns as well. An excellent violinist called Moshe Lustig (who later immigrated to the United States) lived in our town at the time. Another man, called Isenman, was a first class clarinet player, and the fame he won eventually earned him a first chair in the city orchestra of Lodz. Among the other participants of the Wierzbnik town band I remember were the talented klezmer[2] Yoseph Plaitze, Gershon Lichtenstein, Moshe Birenzweig, Sheine Goldstein, Max Heinich and Yitzhak Vaigenshperg. They were all youths filled with the need of doing and versatile artistic activity, resulting in a glorious cultural enterprise.

The political direction

The activists of the Zionist movement subscribed to a variety of different viewpoints. The majority were followers of "Al-Hamishmar", led by Yitzhak Grinbaum and Moshe Kleinbaum (Sne).

I would like to take this chance to note that Yitzhak Grinbaum tried organizing the middle class (we used to joke that "Mitelshtand – Shtand una mitel") to immigrate to Israel and settle Wadi Havari, today's Emek Hefer. Many were excited about the idea, but only two actually emigrated: Dov Frydman, who currently resides in Kfar Yanai, and Shaul Weisbloom, a resident of Kfar Vitkin.

Among the more organized members of the public were the craftsmen, who even had their own club, on Visoka Street, at the home of Ovadia Goldberg's parents. The leaders of this group were Yaakov Kopf, Yeheskel Szternkrantz, Avraham Rubinstein and Ephraim Lustiger. Their main duties were securing proper permits from the authorities that would allow the craftsmen to work unhindered; arranging the payment of taxes; and so on. They paid no heed to political issues, although during elections to the community board or magistrate they supported the candidacy of Shmuel Isser.

Rabbinical disputes

Wierzbnik had a long lasting reputation of rabbinical disputes that broke out from time to time. Before World War I it was the descendants of rabbi from Lipsk who claimed their "right" to the role of Wierzbnik's Rabbi and they had the support of the large Guterman family. There were other times, however, when the Russian authorities nominated a rabbi, among them the famous rabbi Jechiel Kestenberg from Radom. Nevertheless, during 1920-23 the office of town rabbi belonged to Rabbi Yaakov Regensberg, the son of the Rabbi of Zambrów. Yaakov's son-in-law was a rich Jew, a landowner from the vicinity of Wąchock. Rabbi Regensberg was said to be a well mannered man and popular despite the fact that many objected to his appointment for office. He died at a very young age.

His successor as town rabbi was a man from Bodzentyń, who had the support of Shmuel Isser's group, but a few years later he immigrated to Canada, bequeathing his position to his son-in-law, Rabinowicz, who was the last rabbi of the Wierzbnik community before the bane came upon it. Rabbi Rabinowicz perished in Treblinka and left behind three daughters who currently reside in Canada (see also the detailed article "Rabbis of the community by Zvi Fajgenbaum).

Portraits

A Jew named Azriel Najman lived in town during the last years before World War I, and his role was maintaining relations between the Jewish population and the gentile authorities. He had a colorful, interesting persona, and was the subject of many stories and tales. Despite his old age, Azriel would drag himself from office to office and from clerk to clerk in order to settle certain issues that the Jews in town placed in his care. His second role was delivering back messages and letters from the authorities, and even postcards sent to the people of Wierzbnik by their relatives and acquaintances. He would distribute these postcards at the synagogue between Minhah[3] and Maariv[4]. Since he sometimes spent the whole day idling, he entertained himself by reading the contents of the postcards, and so when he arrived at the synagogue he already knew the contents by heart... It is said that he used to play all manner of "pranks" on people. A girl who asked him about a postcard she was expecting was told that "They offered you a match, a wise scholar, but I know you already have a man, so I tore up the postcard on the way here..." Another man was told "they offered you a metal deal, but what would you do with metal? You're a lumber trader... I figured it was a mistake and threw the postcard in the trash."

Municipal life

As the years went by, social frameworks were formed, patterns of public life were set, institutes were established, and the Jewish community began integrating itself into the public life of the town and from time to time chose its own representatives for the municipal authority, men who represented the special interests of their senders before the authorities. Every cadence of the local authority also included a Jewish member, who was part of the municipal authority's management.

Among those members of the local authority or senior bureaucracy I recall Yoseph Dreksler, Simcha Mincberg, Yitzhak Singer, Shmuel Isser, Shimshon Frimerman and, during a period of transition, Moshe Bernstein. I will also name the heads of the local authority I remember serving in our town during the different periods: Guralchik, Sokul, and Miernik. This may be a good opportunity to mention that Sokul was by far the most agreeable mayor; he was a fisherman who voluntarily left office at the beginning of the Nazi occupation. When the Nazis set the synagogue on fire at the end of Yom Kippur 1939, he innocently assumed that the fire broke out by accident, and called for the local residents to help put it out and save the sacred building.

The unification of Wierzbnik and Starachowice caused a decline in the influence of the Jews over the local authority.

Community board

It is hard to piece together the different compositions of that institute, which constantly guided the public affairs of the Jewish community. I remember several members of the community board: Yona Bzhichiner, who served for many years in the role of community board secretary (Gmina) and later "bequeathed" this position to his son-in-law, the teacher Mordechai Lis.

I also recall Shmuel Isser, who served as head of the community board and was succeeded by Avraham Mordechai Rotbart, followed by Shmuel Pochachevski. I also recall the short tenures of Willie Gelbtuch and the lawyer Shtramer, both residents of Wąchock, as heads of the Gmina.

In order to explain the unusual circumstances under which this came to pass, I must note that during the early 1930s, the two towns of Wierzbnik and Wąchock were considered one municipal authority, and the residents of the two towns therefore chose their delegates for the local authority together.

Aside from its usual activities, the community board served as management for the Talmud Torah School, which was funded by the American Joint. This funding also provided the pupils with a bun and a glass of milk every morning.

It should be mentioned that financial activities carried out by the community board, such as tax collection and payments, failed to match its budget needs. Those paid by the Gmina often had their pay delayed and faced other difficulties.

Nevertheless, the members of this institution changed in 1937, replaced by shrewd, resourceful men, who instituted extensive changes under the leadership of Shmuel Pochachevski, Yoseph Tenzer, Simcha Mincberg, Moshe Birenzweig and Gustav Drobner. One of their first acts was the restoration of the crumbling synagogue, but more important was the fact that their activity sent a general surge of awakening in the communal life of the town.

Shmuel Pochachevski, who served as head of the new board, owned a lumber-mill and a share in Eli Kalmanzon's gristmill. He had extensive plans for founding and building Jewish institutes, but the outbreak of World War II put a stop to all his ambitious plans.

Torah teachings

There were no actual Yeshivas[5] in Wierzbnik. I already mentioned the Talmud Torah School, but there were also many Heders and people studied the Torah in seminaries and even at private houses. Following are the names of teachers who spent their time and effort teaching the Torah and general knowledge to the children of Israel: Sani Green, Yeshayahu, Zelig, Jermiahu, Mailech and Shlomo. But from among all those who taught the children of Israel the language of the past, a place of honor on the eastern wall is reserved for the great teacher Mordechai Lis.

As the years rolled by we witnessed the founding of the "Tarbut" and "Hamizrachi" schools, as well as the Bnot-Yaakov School for girls.

Elementary schooling was mandatory in Poland after World War I, but only Jewish girls were allowed to attend it at first; it was years before Jewish boys were allowed to attend as well. Wierzbnik had no high schools for many years, but the Jewish parents spared no expense to offer their children secondary education, sending them to high schools in other towns.

Following are examples of those devotion and deep care showed by Jewish parents, who sent their children far away to acquire knowledge.

Salka and Yoseph Kleiner studied at the Jewish high school in Kielce, along with Eshcha Bernstein. My sister, Pola, graduated from high school in Lodz and my sister Gucia and I graduated from the Jewish high school called Shoharei Da'at in Radom. Hilel Frimerman also studied at that school. During the last years before the outbreak of World War II, Wierzbnik had dozens of high school graduates, who studied in Radom, Piotrków and Starachowice.

Relations with the Christian population

As a result of the town's unique nature and its many industrial factories, the majority of the Christian population was part of the proletariat and shared the perspective and political approaches of the socialist party, which had a considerable impact on its tolerance of the Jewish population. The occupational profile had another effect: the town was a center for marketing the produce of the factories and craft shops, and dozens of villagers flowed into it to sell their agricultural produce and purchase the industrial products.

Under these circumstances, the financial conditions of town residents in general, and Jews in particular, were relatively good, which had an impact on neighborly relations.

This was also the reason why the famous financial crisis of 1929 largely spared the town and hardly affected it.

Another phenomenon that should be mentioned in this context is "the turbid wave" that swept Poland following Polish Prime Minister Składkowski's infamous instigation to put financial pressure. This wave hardly had any effect on Wierzbnik, despite the efforts of outsider anti-Semites to organize boycotts, strikes, and so on. These attempts failed entirely, due to the disinterest of the Polish residents of Wierzbnik, who maintained their loyal relations with the Jewish population.

There were also some incidents typical of the relations between Jews and Poles in Wierzbnik, like the rumor which spread among the gentiles about the coming of "The Jewish God", as the doctor was known. During those dark days, many Poles have changed their skins, cooperating and serving Satan. Worse, when the war ended and the Nazis were defeated, a handful of Jewish survivors returned to their homes, only to fall prey to a traitorous attack. Eleven Jews were murdered – men, women and children. The rest escaped while they could.

The criminal behavior of these Polish murderers following the terrible Holocaust, spilling the blood of innocents during times of peace, will be remembered in eternal disgrace and the victims who fell to villains will forever be commemorated.

1. The man who prepares the Torah for reading
2. Jewish folk musician
3. Afternoon prayer
4. Evening prayer
5. Rabbinical colleges, sing. Yeshiva

[Page 32]
Moshe Sali (Kerbel)

My Shtetl Wierzbnik

With a frightened shiver and a deep reverent fear I approach, to put on paper just something of my memories of my *shtetl* Wierzbnik from my earliest childhood years, which have been engraved and preserved in my memory to this day.

I was sixteen years old when I left the *shtetl*. As a pioneer I left for the *hachshara* in a kibbutz, in order to realize my life's ideal. At the age of nineteen I was already an immigrant in the Land of Israel, and was in fact the first one of my townspeople who dared to contend with all difficulties, to break down walls and gates and become an immigrant in the Land of Israel. At that time, most Zionists just fulfilled their duty through polite Zionist activity, by collecting money for the national funds, and obtaining a certificate [an immigration permit from the British Mandate] was as hard as parting the Red Sea.

It was a great privilege for me and those like me, who had the honor of struggling, fighting and taking part in the preparations for laying the cornerstones on which the free and independent Jewish state was erected. It is an obligation to frankly relate about the life of the Jews in our *shtetl* Wierzbnik, which was noisy, filled with the lust for life, and the Jewish masses that placed Zion at the head of all their joys, with adherence and longing and with the prayer "may our eyes behold your return to Zion", and with widespread Zionist activity. Sabbath and holiday Jews, whose hearts were filled with love for the Jewish people and for Zionism. From the day of their birth, people who were immersed in the wells of Jewishness, and who also spun the thread of redemption in the dark bunkers, in the death camps and in the terrible years of the oppression, anti-Jewish measures and death.

Our *shtetl* wasn't blessed with many sources of income. Most of the Jews were engaged in commerce: lumber, food shops, manufactured goods, shoes, faience, fancy goods, and some were also craftsmen and laborers. The shops and the craftsmen mainly served the large Christian population of the *shtetl* and the surrounding villages. Who doesn't remember the market (*rynek*), which was entirely Jewish, and the Gentiles used to gather every Thursday for market days. The thousands of Polish workers who worked in the government iron-casting factories in Starachowice were the principal customers of the Jewish shops in the *shtetl*. It really was a poor *shtetl*, and its inhabitants lived a life that was far from luxurious. However, everyone earned a living, some more and some less, and there was almost no one who hungered for a piece of bread.

That Jewish community had lived a lively independent Jewish life for decades, and perhaps centuries. It grew and developed, created and formed frameworks and life models of a cultural, social life full of content. All streams of Judaism received their expression in that variegated mosaic. On the one side – the strict observance and enthusiasm of G-d-fearing Hassidim, an interconnected network of '*shtiblech*' [small, one-room prayer rooms], Hassidim who were tied and bound heart and soul with the "courts" of the famous rabbis from the Polish cities (Góra Kalwaria, Aleksandria, Mszczonów, Radzyń, etc.). On the other side – deep feelings of nationalistic revival, and an impetuous longing for redemption, which grew out of the stubborn-courageous Jewry of that time, whose roots were deep and widespread.

The dear Jewry, which drew its vision from the stories of redemption, from the Book of Books and from the Bible, from the limitless faith that "the Lord of Israel will not lie", from the stories of the Biluim [pioneers to Israel], which was nourished by the period of the Hovevei-Zion [pioneers in Israel] and the generation of the *Haskala* [Enlightenment], and from the Zionist emancipation, which was carried over the waves in that generation. It was able to give Zionist thought a special, individual structure, and to convert it to common property, in a mighty, extensive folk movement.

I can still very well remember the splendid parades, the serious propaganda and the activities, oral and written, the great acts to instill Zionist thought in every square and corner, in everyone's hearts and minds – to achieve a homeland in Zion for our oppressed and tortured people, which was to be our own home. The *Lag Baomer* academies, the exhibitions, the fairs for the Jewish National Fund, the processions – all filled our hearts with light and joy, lightened our yokes, and their waves carried the majority of the Jews in the *shtetl* with them, and the very best of the learning and working youth.

The cultural and social life of the Zionist circles in the *shtetl* was exceptionally lively. Each organization and each sector strengthened and extended the mighty tree of Zionism. These were the Zionists of Al-Hamishmar, Et Livnot, Mizrachi, Hapoel-Hamizrachi, or Young Mizrachi, revisionists, youth organizations, pioneers, religious groups, Poalei Zion, *hachshara* kibbutzim, schools - Tarbut schools and evening schools for Hebrew – the lectures, recital evenings, libraries, discussion groups, etc. etc.

Simultaneously and parallel to all this, religious Jews also carried out extensive socially organized activities in their way, and spread out a network of Agudat Yisrael, Young Agudat Yisrael and their Beis-Yaakov schools. But the very crown of Jewish national action in the *shtetl* was the Zionist activity, which represented the foundation of the social action in the place. They didn't underrate the smallest thing, they did every work and service: collecting penny after penny and occupying themselves with this and that. Everything for the great aspiration in life – to prepare the conditions and infuse the hearts with loyalty and devotion, and with permanent fostering for many long years, together with the realization-Zionism of the pioneering youth movements – with many young people in our *shtetl* having prepared themselves for Zion, to which their eyes were directed day and night, as they dreamt of the State of Israel. Unfortunately, they were not able to be with us, because their pure, innocent lives were cut off by the bloodthirsty Nazi beasts.

Actually, life in the *shtetl* was monotonous and gray, but there was a hope in everyone's heart that days of great and important acts still awaited him/her, that the day would come when the hope of thousands of years would be fulfilled in the free Jewish country of our dreams.

The Zionist movement and its youth movements in all streams succeeded in bringing a shine to the gray life in a variegated way, and inflate it with a spirit of hope, interest and activity. Now, when we glance back, we see with what a rich content, with what a heavenly simplicity and joy of life the social life in our *stetl* was filled. In every institution and organization there were always the "fanatics", who expended their time, their energy and their soul on activity, in order to strengthen and expand the work on behalf of Zion even more.

As I stated, Jewish society in our *shtetl*, if it was not fanatically religious, nevertheless had a religious-traditional hue, imbued with all the signs of a true Jewish house, with its symbols and special holidays, which were filled with Jewish content. Also the *heders* [schools for young boys] and the Talmud Torahs [religious schools] spread the spirit of the deeply-rooted Jewish tradition.

I won't pretend and say that an ideal state of peace and tranquility always prevailed in our *shtetl*. The main part of life, as usual, was concentrated around the Jewish community and its breadwinners, around the synagogue and its beadles, and more than once there were arguments and conflicts between one group and another about the ways of the system of power in the community , about the representation of the community to the organs of power, about the control of public property. However, these negative events were also the results of an active social life, which gave flavor and meaning to life in the *shtetl*. Although the worries over earning a living and providing for the family occupied everyone, they still found the time to take an active part in the good and the bad, and believing in G-d's laws they accepted everything with love, not doubting the will of the Lord.

This small Jewish settlement, which, as stated, didn't have much in the way of writers, artists, intellectuals, journalists, and was also not blessed with exceptionally talented businessman, was nevertheless a settlement that truly breathed a well-organized social Jewish life, with large, extensive Jewish institutions.

Generally speaking, our *shtetl* was outstanding in its variety and vibrancy. It was a deep-rooted Jewry, with all its different strata: laborers, merchants and store-keepers, educated people and "simple folks", who lived a modest life and who struggled hard for their economic existence.

All this was destroyed and torn up by the roots. In fire and water, with killing and suffocation, and with every imaginable horror, our dear, unforgettable fathers and mothers, brothers and sisters, were brought to their deaths. Even when they were brought to the death camps and to the gas chambers, they remained firm in their faith, in Judaism.

I remember that the Jewish community in its period of grandeur was surrounded with the rays of light of a communal life, with culture, progress, a fighting spirit and longing for redemption; with an incessant struggle for life and existence – a life of honesty, that was based on foundations of happiness and righteousness.

Now, I would like to relate about all this, in order to inscribe the memories for an eternal monument of our dear martyrs with a human pen. Like an eternal flame, which should cast its light on all of those that look into these pages, which were written by relatives, children and grandchildren of the pure martyrs, whose memory will never be torn out of our hearts.

In conclusion, as someone who grew up in "Hechalutz" [a pioneering Zionist youth movement], thanks to which I found the way to make *aliya* [immigrate] to Israel in those years – an *aliya* that encountered colossal difficulties and problems and all the mitzvoth, I will dedicate a few lines to the activities in this youth movement, which placed the development of Zionism in the spirit of a working people at the head of its pursuits.

The economically better off Jews and their sons and daughters regarded the children of the worker and laborer Jews, who seemed inferior in their eyes, with scorn and derision. This, understandably, was the result of generations of upbringing. And then Hechalutz appeared in our *shtetl* like a rousing wind, and with a mighty effort broke down the barriers that had existed for years between the different classes of young people in the *shtetl*, and as though with a magic wand, a cardinal change took place in the attitude and approach, so that at gatherings and circles we began to see young people from the working, merchant and property owner classes, rich and poor – all, all together.

The majority of the young people were attracted to innovation and a change in existence, which was directed at one goal: to prepare oneself to join the members of a labor Israel.

In the evenings the clubhouse was filled with the loud sounds of young people, boys and girls who studied, formed and wove the face of their future, without barriers and ancestral prestige. There were complaints and problems, but we overcame them all. We were the first ones to go out to *hachshara*, far from home. We worked at very hard work in the sawmills, the forests, chopping wood – in order to adapt ourselves and become accustomed to all kinds of hard work, and to the most difficult conditions. The letters that were received at home from those who had the privilege of going for self-realization, were filled with wonder at the extremely interesting and daring life together (boys and girls), something that was not accepted at that time , because of the condemnation that held sway then in the life of the Jewish *shtetl*.

Who doesn't remember the tempestuous *hora* dances that filled the hearts with joy and happiness, and which used to sweep along the observers, young and old. Thanks to that pioneering youth and to the other Zionist youth organizations, the Jewish youth were rescued from purposelessness and their life became filled with a deep movement content. The youth learned and knew that the Land of Israel needed workers with a profession, and every evening there were study groups for various subjects, such as Hebrew, Yiddish, general history, agriculture, Yiddish and Zionist literature. There were also activities for the national funds and there were stormy debates on the topics that were then on the agenda.

More than once there were evenings and parties in the club, which certainly disturbed the neighbors' rest. However, they always forgave us and didn't complain, knowing that this was the spark that gave flavor and meaning to the life of their sons and daughters. Our hands were filled with work and activities, as it was said that the young people should promote as much knowledge as possible of the Hebrew language. We learned together about Dr. Herzl, H. Brenner, and A. D. Gordon, and a flame was lit in our hearts. We educated the youth to go outside the walls of the house and the ghetto, to the broad fields, mountains and valleys, to hike, to live communally, to breath air from meadows, lakes and forests.

All these things made us strong and determined our character. Sometimes this really wasn't an easy war and the youth had an inner argument with themselves, but in the end we overcame everything and we came out stronger and determined, knowing that we had a single clear way for us.

The members of Hechalutz and of the other youth organizations lived a lively, sparkling and cultural life, a communal life, which was permeated with the striving to convert dependence and idleness – to a good, independent life of self-realization.

And this variegated life was torn apart. A storm came and tore up the widespread and deeply-rooted tree of Zionism, and it tore it out with its roots and trunk, with its branches and leaves.

That is why these pages should be like a consolation and a source of life and knowledge, on which those for whom the memory of the martyrs is dearer than all else will draw.

Religious and Traditional Life

[Page38]
Zvi Fajgenbaum

Rabbis of the Community

The township of Wierzbnik, renamed Starachowice near the end of its days, was a young community no more than 100 years old at the time of its tragic demise, its downfall unimaginable for those who saw it last during its days of glory, as one of the most advanced and established communities in Poland.

As a young community with no historical record, Wierzbnik kept no official record of its rabbis, enterprises and events as was customary in older Jewish communities. We are therefore called to perform the holy work of drawing the information from the recesses of memory, recalling what we learned from our ancestors in days gone by.

Following is the record of the rabbinates and rabbis who served the community of Wierzbnik, delivered in chronological order:

The first rabbi of our community was known affectionately and admiringly as "The Old Rabbi". This nickname set him aside from his son David, the young rabbi, who later served as rabbi for the Lipsk community. We can imagine how loved he was by his community given that his surname, Rotfeld, was practically forgotten, and he was known in public by his nickname.

Stories told about him describe him as a devout man and a scholar, like all outstanding rabbis of his generation. In his role as a spiritual father, he helped his flock and led it justly and peacefully.

I know this due to of my family ties with him. As a little boy, I listened to conversations between my mother and her sisters, my aunts, who would gather at the home of their mother, my grandmother, the pious Rivka Zisl, to talk about their own grandmother, "Grandma Libale" and her brother "The Old Rabbi".

He also had a big family in town: his sister, my great grandma Libale, after whom the granddaughters were named, was also the mother of Shlomo Krozman. Therefore, the Krozman family and that of my grandfather, David Yehoshua Brodbeker, who was married to my grandmother, Rivka Zisl, as well as the families of Yaakov and Rachel Birenzweig and Leibl Furman, were all descended from her. So was the great Najman family: Fishel and his brother Zvi (who passed away in Toronto), their sister Zotl, who married Chaim Mordechai, the brothers Benyamin Fishel and Isaac Najman and their offspring. All of them were members of this family.

Next in the golden chain of incumbents was Rabbi David Rotfeld, the Rabbi of Lipsk, a nickname bestowed on him due to his previous, lengthy rabbinical office.

Following the passing of The Old Rabbi, his friends and relatives insisted that his son David, who was worthy of that role, would take his father's place as community rabbi. They were opposed by the Tenenbaum family and its followers, who demanded that the position of town rabbi would be given to Menachem Mendel Tenenbaum, a learned man who was unable to present his candidacy in other, bigger towns due to natural causes. The dispute eventually reached rabbinical arbitration. A court of religious scholars was convened but the scales were eventually tipped by a third alternative, and Rabbi Morgenstern was appointed town rabbi, while Rabbi Menachem

Mendel Tenenbaum was appointed judge and rabbi David moved to Lipsk, where he served as rabbi for the rest of his days.

One of Rabbi David's sons – Rabbi Elimelech Rotfeld, son-in-law of the rabbi of the Radom community, Rabbi Jechiel Kestenberg, served as a rabbi of the community of Poddębice. Aside from being a scholar, he also made an excellent orator, and was well versed in both manners and public relations. He was also considered the "foreign minister" of Alexander's court, due to his superior personality. Father and son perished in the Holocaust along with their families and the other members of their communities.

Rabbi Yaakov Arie Morgenstern, who was called among the people of Wierzbnik "Dar Wyszkower Rov" (the Rabbi of Wyszków), was an impressive man, a great and wise scholar, grandson of the Rabbi of Kock, son of the Admor Rabbi Zvi of Łomży and sonin- law to the Admor Rabbi Menachem of Amshinov. The last helped him win the position of Wierzbnik's community rabbi, since our town hosted a Shtibl of the Amshinov Hasidim, whose members were among the town's wealthy elite.

Our community, which was relatively small sixty years ago, was naturally not the last stop in the rabbinical path of such a dynamic, broad-minded person. His heart was set on a larger community, where he could nurture his skills and aspirations in the fields of rabbinic practice. He was soon invited to the important community of Wyszków, where his father served as the head religious arbitrator. Furthermore, when his father the Admor passed away, he too was given the title of Admor by the Łomży Hasidim, taking his father's place. With these two titles he led his flock in Otwock, the summer resort of Warsaw, capital of Poland, until the bane came upon them. He perished among the rest of Poland's martyred Jews.

He had many sons. The eldest among them, Rabbi Israel Yitzhak, served as rabbi of the Serock community. Rabbi Jerachmiel was son-in-law to Rabbi Mordechai, who served as rabbi of the nearby Skarżysko community and was in turn son-in-law to the famous industrialist, Mendel Feldman. Rabbi Dov-Berish, son-in-law of the Admor of Volumin; Rabbi Benyamin, son-in-law of the Admor of Sokołów. Rabbi David Shlomo served as rabbi of the Wyszków community, taking the place of his father. Rabbi Moshe became son-in-law to the Admor of Grochów. Yehuda Elimelech became son-in-law to the Admor Yoseph (Yosale). This entire noble family, innocent and pure, perished in the Holocaust, leaving behind only a single daughter, Ita Tova and her husband the Admor of Amshinov, Rabbi Meir'l, both of whom managed to escape the Polish Vale of Tears, and traveling through Japan to the United States. The Admor currently tends to the need of his parish, the Amshinov Hasidim, from his home in the Bait Vagan neighborhood in Jerusalem, where he also founded the "Shem Olam" Yeshiva, in honor of his late father, the Admor of Amshinov-Otwock, Rabbi Shimon. This Yeshiva is headed by the Admor's son-in-law, Rabbi Chaim Vilkovski.

Rabbi Jechiel Kestenberg was son of Rabbi Mendel Skarshiver, the Dayan[iii] of the Radom community. After the departure of the rabbi of Wyszków, Rabbi Kestenberg was appointed rabbi of the community, tempering youth with talent. His tenure in office was nevertheless brief. When the rabbi of Radom moved to the city of Lodz, the position of community rabbi in Radom was taken up by Rabbi Kestenberg, who became famous there. He served the town until the Holocaust, during which he died with his martyred parish, most of them in Treblinka.

Rabbi Menachem Mendel Tenenbaum served as a religious judge and arbitrator for the community. He was known as a formidable scholar even beyond our community, and many complex questions and financial disputes were sent to him from afar. He was admired by the public until he unexpectedly passed away in Iłża, a mere day before the German invasion of the town. It was there that he was also later buried, miraculously, at the last moment before the war broke out.

His offspring included a son, the Gaon Rabbi David, who served as a rabbi in the nearby town of Kunów. His personality and scholastic accomplishments made him worthy of a rabbinical position in a big city but he tragically died in his prime from typhus. Nevertheless, even while sitting on the rabbinical throne of tiny Kunów, his domain spread as far as the remarkable town of Ostrowiec, because the holy Admor and lord of the place, Rabbi Yeheskel, invited him into his home, to teach and pass judgment, a duty he persevered in until he passed away from his illness, in the prime of his life. He was buried in Wierzbnik and every resident of the community mourned him and paid him his last respects, in tears and sorrow.

His eldest daughter, Mrs. Kayla, had married in the United States to Rabbi Moshe Jechiel Halevi Epstein, the Admor of Ożarów. The Rabbi of Ożarów immigrated a few years ago to Israel and continues to lead his parish there according to the Torah and Hasidic traditions. He is a particularly prolific author, having written such books as Esh-Dat and Be'er-Moshe and so on. The rabbi also dedicates his time to public issues, in the highest sense of the term, and serves as the chairman of Moetzes Gedolei HaTorah.

His young daughter, Mrs. Mina, immigrated to Israel before World War II, as a member of a pioneer youth movement, where she married Mr. Moshe Bagno, who served in different public offices, including secretary of the National Religious Party in Bnei Brak, member of city council and later mayor. The two raised a remarkable, long lasting family.

The departure of the rabbi of Wyszków led to a dispute concerning the appointment of the next community rabbi. Two rabbis claimed precedence. Each had many supporters, since both were worthy of this important title. It is interesting to note that both their paths led them from Wąchock to Wierzbnik.

Rabbi Yoseph Eliezer Rabinowicz, who previously served as rabbi and Admor of Wąchock, came from the line of "The Holy Jew" from Przysucha. His father was Rabbi Pinchas of Końskie and his father-in-law was the famous Rabbi Shraga Yair from Białobrzeg. His heritage and his scholastic and righteous nature earned him many followers. His service as rabbi and Admor brought respect and glory to our entire community until the Shavuot holiday of 1915. Our town, which was surrounded by mountains, was trapped during World War I between the two fronts, the Russian and German armies. One Friday night, after three weeks of suffering, the town was infiltrated under the cover of darkness by Russian soldiers, who ordered the Jews to leave the place immediately. Eviction of the Jews from war zones was part of the Russian high command's strategy, because they were considered disloyal to the Tsar. The Jews, who had no means of transportation, were forced to leave the place "within the hour". We walked away, leaving all our property behind to be plundered.

We arrived as refugees in Radom on Shabbat. We stayed in Radom until the Ninth of Ab, the day the Germans entered the city. When the Jews returned to their town, they found that half of it was consumed by fire while the other half was plundered by their gentile neighbors. Everyone had to start all over again. Given the grim situation, the rabbi's followers in Radom asked him to stay with them, offering him a spacious apartment in 23rd Lubelska Street. It was only natural for the rabbi to accept their request and settle there permanently. From his new residence he also responded to every request for advice, until the bitter end of the entire Polish Jewry, including the metropolitan community of Radom.

Rabbi Yaakov Aharon Regensberg was the son of the famous rabbi from Lithuania, Gaon Rabbi Menachem Dov, presiding judge of the Zambrów community. His son-inlaw was the wealthy and well-respected Mr. Yankalevski, a businessman from Lithuania who resided in Wąchock. His son-in-law, the son of the rabbi of Zambrów, lived and studied the Torah with him. He was respected by those familiar with his positive, scholastic nature. Once a rabbinical position opened in our neighboring community, his followers suggested him as candidate – and he seemed to have the vote of majority, since the authorities have also given him their approval as rabbi of the Wierzbnik community. Nevertheless, since the opposition refused to surrender their position, the community had two rabbis for a time, each welcomed by his own followers. When the refugees returned from Radom, however, Rabbi Yaakov Aharon alone returned with them, and henceforth he remained as the sole rabbi of the community.

Eventually he was acknowledged by all, even his opposition, due to his integrity, good nature and broad education. Once accepted, he led the entire community through the turbulent days of World War I. I would like to take this opportunity to tell of an event from this period, which was etched into my memory: on the first (or second) day of Pesach, a regiment of Austrian soldiers came into town, 200 Jewish soldiers among them. These devout soldiers refused to eat leavened food and we had to make matzahs for them, despite the fact that the town residents had little enough for themselves. The rabbi, followed by the heads of the community, entered a regular flour storehouse (which was not prepared for Pesach) and on the rabbi's orders they took flour out of clean, dry bags, went to the matzah bakeries and helped bake matzahs for the visiting soldiers.

His tenure was nevertheless regrettably short. A plague of typhus broke out in Poland in those days, and it did not spare our town. Many perished, among them the beloved and admired Rabbi Yaakov Aharon Regensberg.

His widowed wife was left behind with four orphaned children, two boys and two girls. The youngest daughter married Gezl Katzenellenbogen of the Gur Hasidim, an honest, intelligent and well-respected man who came from a good family in Szydłowiec. But his son, David, who reached the United States, was the only survivor, as the rest were all led one bitter day to Treblinka and perished as martyrs.

Rabbi Shmuel Zvi Hirsch Zylberstein, the rabbi of Będzin. A fire broke out in the nearby town of Będzin near the end of World War I. The fire consumed nearly every Jewish house in town, according to custom, the Jews in nearby towns, Wierzbnik among them, held collections for their cause. This collection drive was initiated by the rabbi of the community, Rabbi Zylberstein, who visited different towns, including Wierzbnik.

Rabbi Zylberstein served his position proudly. He taught the Torah to advanced students and knew how to represent the community with dignity. One of his enterprises was the building of a new Jewish bathhouse in place of the old crumbling one, without imposing any financial burden on the community itself. Various aid organizations from the United States sent expeditions in an effort to restore some of the damages the war has caused to the East European Jewry. Their main activities were in the fields of nutrition, health and sanitation. Rabbi Zylberstein immediately found a field of action that suited his nature. His enterprise succeeded: he gathered food for the needy, made plans for a bathhouse and a Mikveh for purification and secured the funding necessary for its construction.

However our community was too small for Rabbi Zylberstein's broad horizons and after a few years he went on a visit to America. The temporary visit became a permanent stay when he became rabbi of the Toronto community in Canada and it was not long before his family joined him. He nevertheless saved our community the need to look for a new rabbi, as he left his son-in-law behind to take his place.

It should be added that Rabbi Zylberstein was also a prolific author and composed a whole series of religious books. I would like to share with you a short, relevant anecdote: after immigrating to Israel, I have visited the Meron, near the gravesite of Rabbi Shimon Bar-Yochai. While touring the synagogue there, one of the books on the bench captured my attention. Looking at the cover, all aflutter, I confirmed that it was indeed "Zivchei Shmuel" by Rabbi Avraham Shmuel Zvi Hirsch Zylberstein, a rabbi from Toronto who previously served as rabbi in the communities of Będzin and... Wierzbnik! The commemoration inside the book was dedicated to his wife and his offspring, first among them his daughter, Mrs. Guta and her husband...

Rabbi Ben-Zion Rabinowicz, the last presiding judge of the Wierzbnik community, which was his first step in the rabbinical field. Three reasons led to his election: he was the son of Rabbi Yoseph Eliezer, a former rabbi of the town; he had the support of the Końskie- Białobrzeg-Wąchock Hasidim, as a descendent of "The Holy Jew"; and last but most important, he was the son-in-law of Rabbi Zylberstein, who left him as a temporary substitute while visiting America. Much like that visit, his status became permanent. The elections held later formalized his position as community rabbi. He led his community, supported by the virtues of his ancestors and his wife was his right hand, offering both her experience with her father's court and her own considerable intelligence.

Rabbi Rabinowicz served as rabbi of the community until its tragic annihilation, dying in the Holocaust with his beloved community. On November 6th, 1941, that bitter, fatal day when the enemy attacked our sacred community, razed it to the ground and marched its Jews – men, women and children, led by the rabbi – to the gas chambers of Treblinka, where they all died as martyrs. May their blood cover the land forever.

The rabbi and his wife were fortunate that three of their daughters – Ratzale, Dina and Chasha – survived. Their great-grandfather, who lived in Canada, immediately arranged for the three to move to America, where they wed, built homes and continue to weave the golden thread of the house of Israel.

Rabbi Moshe Goldberg sought to serve in Wierzbnik by right of possession, as a family member of the rabbi of Lipsk called "the rabbi from Warsaw", who lived in our town until the Jews were exiled by the Russian army to Radom. I cannot describe him properly, nor do I know his name; as a child I saw him as a dignified man who offered his petitioners advice and prayer. Rabbi Goldberg was very noble and kind to all. He was among those who stayed in the camps. He suffered much but lived to be among those who survived the camps. Upon his liberation he settled in France, where he served as rabbi at the Fleishman synagogue in the Plazil in Paris.

He visited Israel nearly ten years ago, staying at the Mea Shearim Hotel in Jerusalem. During his stay at the hotel, the Jordanian artillery opened fire on that neighborhood and a shell's shrapnel hit his head. He was taken to a hospital where he lay for a week before passing away. He was buried at Har Menuhot in Jerusalem.

This article was written from memory, unaided, and its purpose – to make a record of the rabbis of our town, even if we could not do them and their many actions justice, for which we hope they would forgive us. May their souls rest in peace.

1. Religious judge

[Page 42]
Zvi Feigenbaum

The Synagogues in Wierzbnik

Historical accuracy requires that we mention first that a "synagogue", in its common form, has not been built in our town yet.

It is common knowledge that old, established communities had two kinds of places to worship in: a Beit Kneset was dedicated solely for praying and studying the Torah. A Beit Midrash, on the other hand, was used for studying the Torah, praying and other activities such as overseeing public affairs and so on. As such, it contained certain things a man might require while studying the Torah such as smokes, drinks to quench his thirst and food to eat.

Wierzbnik, as a relatively young community still establishing itself, did not build a community synagogue. It is also possible that the leaders of the community, who were mostly members of the Hasidic movement and who considered a Shtibl or a Kloyz to be a social-educational ideal, did not consider the building of a synagogue their first priority. It was for these reasons that the synagogue remained nothing more than a plan, the shape of things never to come.

As a matter of fact, there was one central house of worship which was open for all, and that was the Beit Midrash.

The following memories are dedicated to this Beit Midrash, to the other places of worship in town, and to all those who came there to pray and study the Torah, in hope that my humble writings will do them justice.

The great Beit Midrash, built on the spacious public lot in Niska Street, was the second one to be built during the short history of the community. It was preceded by "the old Beit Midrash" which was smaller in size.

Nearly 100 years ago, when the Jewish community was starting to establish itself in this colony (the town's status during those days), the first act of the founders was to buy a lot at the center of town and build a Beit Midrash on it, to serve as a house of worship for the entire community. It was a wooden structure whose size would fit the size of the community at that time and in the foreseeable future.

As the community grew, the Beit Midrash became too small to contain the increasing numbers of worshippers, and the leaders of the community, led by the community's rabbi, decided to tear down the old Beit Midrash and build a larger stone Beit Midrash, one that stood until Yom Kippur 1939, when the Nazi enemy set fire to it.

When this temple was first built, it was the only place in town for a person to worship in or study the Torah. Even after the foundation of Hasidic houses of worship for our people, the great Beit Midrash was considered the only place of study, a custom that lasted until after World War I. Nevertheless, it was around this time that diligent Yeshiva students came to town and made their home at the Hasidic Shtibl, claiming that "Humility benefits the study of Torah." So long as the Beit Midrash stood, the sounds of Torah echoed from within its walls from dawn to the late hours of the night. Yeshiva students supported by their fathers-in-law studied there, as did youths and learned men of means, and regular lessons for commoners were held there as well.

Among the scholars who offered advanced lessons to Torah seeking youths, we should mention Rabbi Yitzhak Meir Konigsberg, the kosher butcher (and my father-in-law), who had many students and passed away on the second day of the Succoth Holiday of 1930, as well as my uncle, Rabbi Yoseph Brodbeker, who was a kosher butcher for the Stopnica community until its bitter end. He was a dedicated scholar, with many positive attributes and people sought to learn Torah from him.

The aforementioned were only additions to the large public of worshipers who showed up evening, morning and noon to pray and say psalms and Maamadot with awe and reverence.

Those who came to pray were considered equal in status – the rich and the poor, merchants, craftsmen and workers. All came to visit the temple in the morning, before work, and in the evening, after their Talmud studies.

The Beit Midrash was a center of community life in the full sense of the word. These innocent Jews knew the value and import of studying the Torah, and as soon as they finished praying they left, leaving the place free for the various students.

The women's gallery

It is only natural that the sermons given by rabbis on special occasions – such as Shabbat Gadol and Shabbat Tshuva – or on specific occasions, were given at the Beit Midrash. Wandering orators, who visited our town from time to time, also spoke within its confines. One should mention that when the listeners liked an oratory, the butcher Shmuel Rubinstein, who was a large man, took his place by the door, collecting "donations" for the orator. The sum would then be double and triple the usual amount, because none wanted to risk invoking "uncle" Shmuel's ire by giving him mere pittance.

The men took up nearly half the space in the Beit Midrash, while the other half consisted of a women's gallery, a place for the innocent, humble women. On Shabbat mornings, the women who were not saddled with young children would arrive there. On Shabbat Mevarchin, the women's gallery was nearly full. The numbers were even greater during the holidays. On Rosh Hashanah and Yom Kippur, the building was too small to hold the many ladies praying.

I recall that when I was 4 years old, I felt the need to go to my mother – that is, to venture into the women's gallery. I barely managed to reach her, and it took a great effort for me to escape, because the place was so very crowded.

The women's gallery served an additional purpose beyond its main function as a place of worship: teachers who taught young children and who lived far from the homes of those children would bring their students there for lessons. This hall also served as an emergency shelter. Refugees, poor folk and survivors of fires, floods and any other disaster would head first to the women's gallery. The Beit Midrash was not only spacious but also served multiple purposes.

In the new age following the end of World War I, the Beit Midrash gained an additional aspect of public activity. It began hosting public gatherings, typically organized by political parties, during which people spoke before a large crowd about other public events. During these days, the Yeshiva students started joining the Hasidic Shtiblach, as described in the next article.

Hasidic Shtiblach

The Hasidic house of Amshinov was the first to be established. Several important men of wealth among the previous generation followed the Admors of Amshinov: Moshe Tenenbaum, Shlomo Krozman, Yitzhak, Yaakov and Shlomo Brodbeker, who were sons of the famous Rabbi Hirsch, Fishel Dreksler, Mordechai David Kornwaser, Simcha Buchbinder and Rabbi Yitzhak Meir, all of them were among the Amshinov Hasidim. Other members of this Hasidic group were the brothers Yaakov, Reuven and Yeheskel Herblum. The eldest brother Yaakov, who was sonless, dedicated part of his house to be a Hasidic residence, increasing the reputation of this Shtibl, which hosted the finest of the Hasidim in Wierzbnik during that era.

Those of the second generation, the sons and sons-in-law of the aforementioned, followed the teachings of the Amshinov Hasidim, which can be described as "good for heaven and pleasant to people". I will like to mention the religious arbitrator Rabbi Menachem Tenenbaum, Jechiel Pszytycki and his brother-in-law Mendel Brodbeker; the brothers Noah and Neta Kornwaser; Gershon Herblum and his brother Leibish Herblum, who survived the Holocaust. Among the members of the third generation was also a group of Hasidic Yeshiva students, and prominent among them were Tanchum Lighteizen, Simcha Taiblum and Shmuel Avraham Eisenshtat, the lone survivor who moved to America.

The "strategic location" of the Shtibl, that is, a closed courtyard, allowed its members to continue their prayers and religious studies there until the last minute possible. Even under the Nazi occupation, during the days of the ghetto and quarantine, this place offered a place for prayer, Torah and companionship – until the last, bitter and fatal day, November 9th, 1941.

The Hasidic house of Gur, which of late was considered the most important one, gained its prominence not by right of seniority. Unlike the Amshinov Hasidim, who were residents of the town since days gone by, the Gur Hasidim were newcomers. They arrived from various places; some on business, such as Rabbi Chanoch Biderman and Moshe Pinchas Lichtenstein, and some chosen as husbands for the daughters of wealthy men, such as Yeshayahu Guterman, Heinich Kojfman, Zelig Stern and Moshe David Rothschild. The Shtibl grew and expanded, until it achieved self-residence. But the main virtue of the Gur Hasidic group was its human content. Most members were religious scholars who believed in Torah and knowledge. The sons of Hasidim from other groups joined them as well, such as Chaim Herblum of the Amshinov Hasidic group.

The writer of these lines was also among those who joined the Gur Hasidim.

At the end of World War I, this group enjoyed an influx of new members. Among the merchants who joined it were Shmuel Cohen, Israel Yitzhak Spitzer, Avraham Brodbeker, Gezl Katzenellenbogen, Shimon Urbach and others. This was in addition to several locals, such as Israel Yaakov and Yoseph, the sons of Yeshayahu Guterman, and others.

The next wave, the third and last one, was also the greatest. Leading this wave was Yeshiva student Rabbi Yitzhak Goldknopf, who arrived from Warsaw to wed the daughter of Moshe David Rothschild. Rabbi Yitzhak was a scholar well versed in religious matters, a man of character, both intelligent and versed in matters of this world. He attracted many young men as his followers, teaching them Torah and etiquette. He was accompanied by other Yeshiva students such as the scholar Pinchas Vigdorovich, Teibil Lichtiger, Moshe Yitzhak Rosenbloom (son-in-law of Zvi Shtayrat), Shmuel Zoberman (son-in-law of Rabbi Yitzhak Meir), Berl Hercig and others. Three of his students who survived the Holocaust were Zissman Citrinbaum, Jechiel Brodbeker (in Israel) and Jechiel Brodbeker (abroad).

Each of the aforementioned people is worthy of our respect. The lack of space, however, forces us to settle for saying "We mourn those lost and remember them".

The Hasidic group of Sokołów enjoyed seniority as well, due to the presence of two men who added their own fame to that of the community of Wierzbnik. One was the rabbi of Węgrów, Rabbi Shmuel Morgenstern, son of the Admor of Sokołów, who lived with his father-in-law, Moshe Tenenbaum. The other was Yoseph Dov Morgenstern, a descendent of the Admor of Kock, whose business brought him to reside in Wierzbnik. The two gathered learned Hasidim around them and established a Hasidic house in the Kock tradition. Regretfully, they each parted with the place under unfortunate circumstances. Yoseph Dov perished in a fire in 1905. When the Russian Tsar's authorities set the alcohol stores at the Monopol on fire, he jumped into the burning house of a relative to attempt a rescue. Caught in the inferno, he died before the very eyes of his wife Dvora and their 5 little children, still in his prime. The entire town joined his relatives in mourning this terrible fire. The rabbi of Węgrów's wife also died in her prime, forcing him to return to his father's house and leave town.

As aforesaid, their departure left a mark. One passed away and the other left alive, but due to his wife's passing. Both left and never came back. But their work was not in vain. The Hasidic house remained even after their departure. Among this group were Yoseph Lithuak (Brodbeker), Yoel Starachovitzer (Shenner) Yoel Kojfman, Natan Brodbeker, Avraham Moshe Weintraub, and others. Leibish Morgenstern, the son of Yoseph Dov Morgenstern, also returned from Ostrowiec to Wierzbnik. A learned man in his own right and the descendent of great men, he brought a spirit of rejuvenation into the group. His excellent sons also graced the Hasidic house of Sokołów, including the youngest brother, Zvi Morgenstern, who survived to live in the States. They gathered every Shabbat at the home of Avraham Moshe Weintraub to study the Torah and pray, until the enemy came and murdered them all.

The members of the Hasidic house of Wąchock were mostly craftsmen and workers. Their regular Minyan gathered on Shabbats and holidays at the house of the Rabbi Ben-Zion Rabinowicz, son of the Admor of Wąchock, who in lived in Wierzbnik in the past and spent his last days in the central city of Radom.

The followers of the Rabbi of Wąchock were not great scholars but were honest Jews. Mornings and evenings they came to the Beit Midrash to pray, and they worked faithfully and reaped the fruits of their labor. When faced with family issues or various other problems, they turned to the rabbi, who gave them his advice, his blessing and his guidance. Thus they live as honest folk.

Among the more prominent members of this group were:

Chaim Zajfman, a generous and hospitable man, who was also involved with public affairs in his youth. He served for a time as a faithful public servant and leader of the community. A sonless man, he raised orphaned girls and sought decent husbands for them. His wife was also kind and charitable. Together, they wrote a Torah book for the seminary. One of his "sons-in-law" was Moshe Shiner, who married an orphaned relative they have adopted. The brothers Avraham and Yaakov Shiner, who survived the Holocaust and live in Israel today, are considered their grandchildren.

Yoseph Avramovitz, the owner of a poultry butcher's shop, made his way every day from the end of Iłżacka Street to pray at the Beit Midrash. On Shabbats he spoke only in the holy tongue. His two sons, Yoseph Hirsch and Pinchas, immigrated before the war to Argentina, where they had families.

Avraham Rubinstein, a tailor, was also a community leader for a time. Like his predecessors he was honest, took part in all manner of charitable collections, paid respect to all and won their respect in return.

Mendel Radkowizer Kogut Sandlar, another commoner, served as leader in prayer at the Beit Midrash, reading the Torah during afternoon prayer on Shabbats and holidays.

Avraham Radkowizer Gotlib (his son-in-law) was a rustic Jew, whose solemn appearance, handsome, flowing beard and calm talk earned him respect. He was hospitable and kind to guests. These traits earned him the nickname "Father Avraham". His daughter and her husband Pinchas Helstein survived and made their home in Kiryat Motzkin.

Moshe Enisman was a tailor and a leader among reciters of Psalms. He was also a member of Hevra Kaddisha and sewed shrouds, free of charge, for community members who passed away.

Eliezer Rolnicki and Matil (Mordechai) Rosenwald both came from the nearby town of Słupia. Both were providers of kosher food, one of poultry and the other of dairy products. As a young child, even before World War I, the author of these memories had to sit and wait every Shabbat night (during wintertime) for an hour and a half until the Kiddush. My father stayed at the Beit Midrash after the rest of the public left to for supper. He spent this time teaching Midrash Rabbah to two honest Jews, who spent their weekdays hard at work but did not hurry home at the end of prayer to eat a hearty Shabbat feast, but first sat and enjoyed a course of Midrash.

Once the three finished their studies for the night, each went home to wish "Shabbat Shalom" to his family, bid "the angel who escorts a person from the synagogue home on Shabbat eve" with "Shalom Aleichem", to sanctify the wine and enjoy the pleasures of Shabbat with his family. These two who studied with my father, Moshe Baruch, were Eliezer Rolnicki and Matil Rosenwald. Matil's son, Mr. Gershon Rosenwald, survived the Holocaust and currently resides in Toronto in Canada, and working on publishing this Yizkor book.

Shmuel Isser, a leather trader, had a pleasant voice and was a good singer, serving as leader in prayer on Shabbats and holidays, especially at the Wąchock Shtibl located at the apartment of the Rabbi Ben-Zion Rabinowicz. They would also gather there for the third feast of the Shabbat, with the rabbi reciting from the Torah. As cantor, Shmuel Isser would sing during the three feasts. He was also a keen administrator, and knew how to organize people into a cohesive public force. This trait allowed him to win the position of community leader repeatedly, overcoming the rest of his talented rivals. This position allowed him to instate Rabbi Ben Zion Rabinowicz, grandson of the rabbi of Wąchock, Rabbi Yoseph Eliezer Rabinowicz, who was also the son-in-law of the previous rabbi, Shmuel Zvi Zylberstein (see the article about the rabbis of the community) as the new rabbi of the Wierzbnik community, and support him until the end.

The Hasidic house of Chmielów-Ożarów was open for prayer on Shabbat and holidays at the home of Jechiel Lerman. Prominent among this group were Hasidim and men of action: Gezl Neinudel, Zvi Steinhardt (butcher of the community), Yaakov Mandelzis and Zvi (Hershel) Froiman. The tale of this Hasidic house, its members and their actions, is told by Sarah Steinhardt Postawski, Zvi's daughter, who survived and lived to make a home in Bnei Brak, Israel.

In addition to the Beit Midrash and the kloyzn mentioned above, our town had other important houses of worship. Among them were the Talmud Torah School, the Bnot-Yaakov School for girls, the Hamizrachi School and the houses of worship of the General Zionists and the Revisionist Zionists. Since these organizations and their associated places of worship are mentioned elsewhere in this book, including praise for the people who led the organization and the management of the prayer houses, the reader should seek them in their proper place.

A few Hasidim who came from Hasidic lines not mentioned above also lived in our town. Some were true scholars, but there were not enough of them to form a special Minyan (of ten men). They retained their uniqueness, as loners, and they joined the existing Shtiblach for prayer and Torah studies. We commemorate Shmuel Kleiner, of the Radomsko Hasidim, Fishel Najman, Eli Wilenczyk and Yitzhak Meir Manela and also Leibish Kerbel, Michal Gotlib and Israel Szarfharc, who were Alexander Hasidim; and from among the Warka Hasidim – my honored father, Moshe Baruch Fajgenbaum and Yoseph Sztarkman, who was among the ten Hasidim who accompanied the Admor Rabbi Simcha Bonim from Warka on his way to board the ship in Odessa (Russia) that took him Israel, where he lived in Tverya.

Among the Warka Hasidim was also Zvi Wajzer, who immigrated to Israel before the Holocaust scourge and settled there permanently (see more about his personality in Characters). May the deceased rest in peace. May those who perished in the Holocaust be avenged by the Lord. May those who remain live long, and the memory of those gone never fade.

An old synagogoue destroyed in the Shoah

[Page 47]
Zvi Fajgenbaum

Heders and Melameds

"Man shall not live on bread alone". The Jews who lived in the community of Wierzbnik typically enjoyed a steady livelihood, however they did not earn their living doing easy work or working part-time on market days, but rather labored every day of the week.

Bread was not the only thing to sustain them, however. Their first calling was to pass Torah and knowledge to their sons. In those days, there was no elementary Jewish education and the Heder was charged with the duty of providing elementary education for the children of Israel, an important task undertaken by educated Jews who were appointed to teach the sons of Israel the Torah, and did not always receive proper appreciation.

The Mizrachi School in 1932. Standing from left to right: The teacher Lipsky, Moshe Szeiner, Yosel Jabner, Kornwasser, Shmuel Weisbloom, Shmuel Tenenbaum, Erlichman, Tennenbaum, Y. Szeiner, M. Neiman, Rotbard, Lipsztejn, Y. Kerbel, Fiszman, Kroizman, Ch. Tennenbaum, Z. Neiman, V. Kelman, Drajnwodel, Sh. Weisbloom

This profession was not enough, under the circumstances, to provide for the livelihood of its practitioners, and most of them lived in poverty. Nevertheless, they did their job dutifully, each according to his educational and pedagogic capabilities and his skill in explaining and teaching. These were the men who gave their all to nurture, grow and mold devout future generations of Jews. As teachers of Torah to the children of Israel they are worthy of commemoration by the survivors of the community and earned a separate chapter in this Yizkor book.

We will try to accomplish this mission in these lines, to the extent that memory allows, and our profuse apologies go to those we fail to mention or accord with the proper respect.

Young Agudat Israel Comitte: Right to left: Leibish the son of Reb Shlomo Morgensztern, Leibel Rabinowicz, Tzvi Mordensztern, Abba Komec, Mordechai Zeev Brodbaker

R' Zelig Stern

A scholarly, intelligent and clever Jew, one of the spokesmen for the Gur Hasidim and Agudath Israel. The class he taught was small, (8-12), comprised mostly of prized students whom he taught Talmud and interpretations. He came from the town of Szydłowiec, arriving in Wierzbnik as a groom for the daughter of one of the wealthy men in town, David Leib Dreksler. When he failed to prosper as a businessman, he turned to teaching because he was gifted with a pedagogic ability. All the students he taught made the Torah the center of their lives.

R' Jermiahu Steinhardt

Elder brother-in-law of the aforementioned Zelig, Jermiahu, who came from nearby Ostrowiec to be the son-in-law of David Leib Dreksler, was a scholar among the Gur Hasidim. He has always considered teaching to be his calling, since he had little experience with the world of trade. He also took in advanced students who already reached Talmud and its supplements. His home (apparently purchased with the dowry he received) was in Rot-Hoiz, across from the magistrate, and it was there he taught his classes. The place also served partly as a bakery for light pastries made by his wife Zelda and sold to earn a better living.

Leadership of the Young Agudat Israel movement. Right to left: Moshe Kornwasser, Zisman Cytrynbaum, Tzvi Morgensztern, Shmuel Weizer, Moshe Neiman, Shlomo Sztern

R' Yeshayahu Milrad (Iłżaher)

Yeshayahu was a Melamed of the old generation and among the most important members of the Amshinov Hasidim. He was noble, soft-spoken, handsome and well dressed. He taught Pentateuch, Rashi and the basics of Talmud. His students respected him, impressed by the respectful relations in his family. Yeshayahu Milrad also had a pleasant voice and used to lead prayer at the Amshinov Shtibl, his recitation rich with rhythm, intonation and emotion.

R' Shlomo Taichman Shenner

Arrived in Wierzbnik from the town of Sienno as son-in-law to Shmeril, the owner of the gristmill in the village of Młynek, who was a devout Jew schooled in Hasidic Torah. Shlomo taught with all his heart and the Heder at his home was a large one, espousing his own methods and strict discipline. He put much thought and effort into his teaching, making sure that his students will knew the weekly portion of the Bible, the Pentateuch, Rashi and basics of Talmud and passed their tests on Shabbat.

R' Yoel Kojfman

Another resident who came from the town of Sienno. He was a member of the Sokołów Hasidim and apparently moved to Starachowice based on their advice. A learned man and a Hasid, necessity forced him, like the other Melameds, to teach in his private apartment, but he did his work dutifully, and had many students.

He passed away unexpectedly before the war. May he rest in peace.

R' Shlomo Zalman Wieznik (Szydłower Melamed)

A Jew of character who made teaching his trade. He arrived in Wierzbnik from the town of Szydłowiec during the 1930s, organized and taught a class of nearly 20 students at his apartment on Visoka Street at a level of Pentateuch and some Talmud. Did his work dutifully and diligently, and beget many students.

Fathers and sons

Among the teachers were some for whom teaching was a generations old family practice. Two of these families will be mentioned here: Moshe Dan Guterman (of the Amshinov Hasidim), who was part Hasid and part loafer. He taught Hebrew and some Pentateuch to children at the Heder, but also served dutifully as a court attendant, particularly after the foundation of the Talmud Torah School.

He would sometimes perform wedding ceremonies, but being a devout and abstract thinker he would occasionally confuse things: instead of announcing that "The rabbi... is honored to arrange this wedding" he announced "honored to arrange godfathering" which amused the crowd, who knew it was an honest mistake.

His son, Simcha Guterman, was his opposite, a very claculated man, but also a learned member of the Amshinov Hasidim. After trying his hand at trade in vain, he returned to his father's profession and dedicated himself to teaching children.

R' Shmelke Grober and his son Elimelech

He was called "Shmelke Melamed" and he was one of the Końskie-Białobrzeg Hasidim. His Heder was at his apartment on Visoka Street, where he taught the alphabet to young children before World War I. During the years before the Holocaust, his students became important people and took up valued public positions. Most perished in the Holocaust, among them the son of Mailech Melamed, and only a handful survived. Elimelech considered himself as a natural born teacher of young children and fulfilled his task wholeheartedly. He knew how to endear himself to the children and taught them punctuation, letters and so on.

R' Shlomo (Szydłowiecr) Gdanski

Another man who considered teaching his calling. He was not a skilled negotiator, but could explain verses from the Pentateuch and Avoth to his young students. He taught at his Heder for a long time before World War I, until the end.

Among his students was Efraim Melamed (Rendil) who served as synagogue attendant in a special structure in the synagogue's yard. He taught young children the alphabet for years until he perished in the typhus plague during World War I (1917).

R' Shmelke Buchsbaum (Kunover)

His apartment was across from the synagogue. His Heder was remarkably tidy. He taught the Pentateuch, Rashi, Bible and Talmud using a special system. He was also, quietly and stylishly, a cantor at the synagogue.

R' Yosl Lithuak Brodbeker

One of the fathers of the large Brodbeker family. He studied at the Yeshivas of Lithuania, where he also married and started a family. Since his studies could not provide for his family he returned to the home of his ancestors as a scholar and a Hasid of Sokołów and started teaching children. The Heder was at the house he inherited, at the Rinek, where he taught advanced students until he died near the end of World War I.

The Yeshiva of Beit Yoseph

It should be noted that during the 1930s a Yeshiva opened in Wierzbnik, for two years. It was at the time that the leaders of the Beit Yoseph Novogrudok Yeshiva managed to leave Red Russia and decided to teach their lore in the State of Poland. They founded Yeshivas in several cities and towns. The people of the community supported this enterprise both with money and by hosting students, as customary in those days. However the Yeshiva did not last long because of the competition with the neighboring communities of Ostrowiec and Końskie. The Yeshivas in these towns drew more students, making it hard to meet standards and leading to the eventual dissolution of the Yeshiva despite the hospitality of the community.

[Page 51]
Reuven Lichtenstein

The Tale of a Torah Scroll

"Luck determines everything, even the fate of the Torah Scroll at the temple". I always believed that this saying is nothing more than an allegory, because what would luck have to do with a Torah scroll? But the events told here have convinced me that the saying is literally true.

In the late summer of 1938 I brought to Israel a Torah scroll from the town of Wierzbnik in Poland, a scroll currently housed at the great synagogue in my town while the community of Wierzbnik was razed completely and the synagogue from which I saved the Torah scroll was burned to the ground at the end of Yom Kippur 1940, along with all the books and holy writs it housed, according to Nazi custom in conquered lands.

This Torah scroll was donated to the synagogue in Wierzbnik by my parents over 40 years ago. Its "trees of life" are covered with silver foil etched with the names of my grandfather and grandmother. I knew nothing about it, since my parents came to Israel during the Second Aliya[iii] and passed away during the World War, when I was almost a boy. When I grew up I got back in touch with our large family in Poland, my uncles and aunts, and one of my uncles wrote to me about the Torah scroll kept at the Zionist synagogue in Wierzbnik and advised that I reclaim the book and have it sent to me. I wrote to the managers of the synagogue but to no avail. Using various excuses, they have reject my requests. I sought the support of the rabbinical office here in

Israel to strengthen my claim but to no avail. Negotiations with the managers continued for three years until in the summer of 1938, while visiting our family in Poland, I naturally visited the two uncles living in Wierzbnik, one of whom was encouraging me to reclaim the Torah scroll. Both were later shot by the Nazis at the center of town when they refused to leave with the death trains.

When I came to Wierzbnik, I embraced my uncle's recommendation, and immediately opened negotiations with the head manager, Simcha. He refuted my arguments claiming they had right of possession over the Torah scroll, which was in their possession for over 30 years. But after lengthy negotiation and discussions among the managers they seemed to agree to hand me the Torah scroll. Simcha told me the news and asked me to visit him on Friday at the bank office where he worked. From there he will go with me to the synagogue to hand me the Torah scroll. I accepted the news with mixed feelings, because I was not convinced of his intentions and felt that the promise was not given wholeheartedly, leaving me skeptic.

On Friday morning I came to the bank office. When I arrived, Simcha suggested that we sit and talk. I urged him to take me to the synagogue and he told me "Sit down, let us talk", but I refused. I was afraid that he was merely stalling again. "What more do we have to talk about?" I asked. The owner of the bank entered the room, an impressive Jew with bright eyes and a long beard. He welcomed me kindly and was glad to meet me, since he was another acquaintance of my late parents (we became fast friends). He was, naturally, aware of the dispute over the Torah scroll. I complained to him that Simcha said he would give me the Torah scroll today and now wants to start talking again. "When accepting the Torah", I said, "it is customary to do first and hear after. Therefore, I demand to receive the book before we talk." My demand hit the mark. The old man failed to hide his satisfaction when he heard me, because at first he thought that the youths in Israel strayed far from Torah and good manners. He immediately turned to Simcha with a commanding voice: "Mr. Simcha! This Jew is right. Please, go with him to the Beit Midrash and first give him the Torah scroll as he asks."

We arrived at the synagogue. Simcha asked me to wait a while at the entrance. He was in an awkward position: on the one hand he was my relative (married into our family) and wanted to do as I ask, unable to resist the pressures put on him by the family. But on the other hand, he had to consider the elder worshipers and the managers who were not inclined at all to return the Torah scroll and claimed that it was given at the time as a gift to the synagogue. Furthermore, this Torah scroll was famously well-written and was read often, which made parting with it hard after having it for 30 years. A few moments later and Simcha came back, satisfaction written on his face, and bid me enter.

It was during late morning hours. Two or three quorums of Jews wearing their tallits[2] sat by a long table at the "east", about to finish their "lesson". I immediately noticed that they were eyeing me askance, because I was there to take the scroll from them. Many of them must have known my parents and remembered them fondly, but they were now old and jealously guarding their property. This impatient, angry group made me feel sadness and pity. For some reason I saw them as a representation of Poland's Jewry, which by then faced a crisis of helplessness and hopelessness.

Finally I received the Torah scroll, wrapped in a shawl and ready to go. I was holding it in my arms, all aquiver. I wanted to lighten up the atmosphere. I said "Gentlemen, I would like to tell you three things: A) It is a great deed to bring a Torah scroll from the Diaspora to the holy land,

and an act of respect for the Torah; B) You knew my late father. He passed away at the end of the big war in Damascus and no one knows where he was buried. This book is meant for the synagogue in my town and will serve as a kind of headstone in his memory; C) As the Holy Ark preceded the people of Israel when they returned to Israel from Egypt, so will this Torah scroll be a holy ark for you, and may you and your sons come to Israel soon."

By the time I was finished I felt the listeners stirring. Their manner changed completely, as if a spark lit something within them. They kissed the book and many of them kissed me as well, wished me a safe journey and asked that I pray for them; some asked that I go to Jerusalem to pray for them before The Western Wall and some asked that I would pray before The Tomb of Rachel. At the time I did not know that Rachel will soon have to mourn her lost sons once more.

One other matter of coincidence and blind luck: a few years after the destruction of the Wierzbnik community and the burning of the synagogues, my family found a hidden cache and delivered to me a bundle of letters my parents sent abroad when they first moved to Israel. One of the letters, written by my mother in 1910 to her brother-in-law living abroad, included the following paragraph: "If you do come (to Israel) I would ask you a great favor. At the synagogue in Wierzbnik is my Torah scroll, that is, the one that belonged to my late father, and which I would ask you to bring with you. I will arrange everything in Jaffa so you would come to no trouble. I would be grateful for this. This is the most sacred keepsake I have left of my dear father" (he did not come then).

And so not only have I earned the chance to save a Torah scroll at the very last opportunity from the hands of the murderers, but also to grant my mother's request, which was made 28 years earlier without my knowledge.

According to the history of the Torah scroll and the many people mentioned in this story, it also serves as a kind of memorial candle burning always in memory of many dear souls who found rest on the wings of the Divine Presence.

1. Second great wave of immigration to Israel
2. Praying shawls

[Page 53]
Sara Postawski-Steinhardt

Traditional Folklore

It is not an easy task for a woman to remember and review the orthodox and Hasidic life and customs of our towns, because these subjects are mainly the domain of men. However when I was asked to relate in the Yizkor book of our community the nature of religious life in those days, I accepted this role with awe and reverence and I pray that I will be fit to carry out this sacred duty.

Houses of worship

I should start perhaps with the Beit Midrash, which had a pleasant exterior and a spectacular interior, a virtual glow hidden within its walls. It was a large building, which stood at the center of town, among the decidedly Jewish streets and residences. It served as a house of learning and prayer, and those who saw with their own eyes the Jews of the city rush to worship their maker in the morning, and glanced at the house of the Lord, could with great satisfaction admire the sanctity of "How beautiful are your tents, O Jacob, your dwelling places, O Israel!"[1] However it was also surrounded by the synagogues of the Hasidic courts, like pearls in the holy crown. These were the Shtiblach that could be found on almost every street and which hosted the majority of our Jewish brethren.

I distinctly recall the Minyan at the Bnot-Yaakov School on Iłzacka Street, or as it was called in Yiddish, "Drildjer Gas". Not far from it was the Shtibl of the Hasidic followers of the rabbi of Amshinov, located inside the courtyard of Leibish Herblum. Across from this Shtibl was another Shtibl, that of the Gur Hasidim. This synagogue, which was among the larger ones, sent to heaven songs that made hearts tremble. It was composed of two rooms and the Hasidic followers of the rabbi of Gur, respected Jewish scholars, prayed there. They were joined by learned Yeshiva students, who further peace in the world. A few of them I can remember and mention by name: Yeshayahu Guterman, his two sons and their children; Shmuel Cohen, Shmuel Zoberman, Yitzhak Goldknopf, my brother-in-law Moshe Rosenbloom, Dov (Berl) Hercig, and many others whose faces I still remember but whose names were swallowed by time.

Shtiblach

This subject was as many hued as a rainbow. Here we must mention the synagogue, which had a unique nature. For reasons of humility or perhaps to ward off the evil eye, it was only referred to by its acronyms.

Shtibl as well as another Shtibl, which was called "Vankhotsker", were located in Kilinska Street. One of them was at the house of Avraham Moshe Weintraub and the other at the home of the rabbi of Wierzbnik. Aside from the Shtiblach I mentioned, there were also synagogues in which people prayed only on Shabbats or holidays. A few of them resided in two story buildings, which generally distinguished them from the general architecture of the town.

The Chmielówer Synagogue

A synagogue I remember in particular is that of the Chmielów Hasidim, which shared a building with the community board, its women's gallery separated by a single wall from the rooms of the board. People prayed there only on Shabbats and holidays, and during the rest of the week it served as a school, which was taught using modern approaches. This school only accepted Yeshiva graduates and its two teachers graduated from the seminary of religious teachers in Warsaw.

Among the worshippers who attended this synagogue were: Gezl Drajnudel, Hershel Fruman, Yaakov (Yankel) Mandelzis, Shmuel Tenenbaum, Jechiel Lerman, Jechiel Hering, my brother Avraham, who earned a living as a butcher in nearby villages, my honorable father Hershel, Yaakov Zukerman, Reuven Rolnicki and his sons Yehoshua and Yaakov, who are in the United States, and Yaakov Katz.

At the end of every Shabbat these people would gather at our home for a Melava Malka feast and each would contribute something to this feast – one would bring a challah and another would bring ale, another would bring fruit and the fourth would bring beans and so on. They spent many long hours together, singing and reciting epigrams, legends and stories about rabbis and holy men all over the world. Among them was a youth, whose name I no longer remember, who knew how to play well using only an empty bottle, a feat none were able to copy.

This time wasn't meant for the adults alone but also for us, the children of the house, who got swept up in the excitement of the festive atmosphere. Since there was no school the following day (the schools were closed on Sundays, it being the Shabbat of Christians) I would stay up late and follow the course of the feast. I still remember the excitement of the participants, their eyes bright with joy, and how they would sometimes stare ponderously into the heavens, discussing matters that concerned the higher spheres. However more than anything I was impressed with their concentration when reciting the lore of scholars, the stories about miracles of saints, which they drank thirstily, tensions rising. And along with the Torah and the miracles came up the subject of the return to Zion and the yearning for Israel, especially after the immigration of the Citrinbaum family, followed by the Wajzer family. Many wanted to follow them but it was impossible since the gates of the country were closed.

The Torah procession

In 1935, Jechiel Lerman brought a Torah scroll to the Shtibl. During that time, my brother Avraham was enlisted in the Polish army and stationed in the city of Radom. We went to great trouble getting the chief of police to give him leave, so he could participate in the joy of the book's homecoming. Our petition was accepted, and there is no describing our joy when my brother came for leave exactly on the day meant for the Torah scroll procession. It was a wonder to astound any onlooker – a soldier dancing with the Torah scroll and sharing the mounting joy of the crowd.

A feast was served later at our house, and my mother and my sister Rivka offered the guests borscht with potatoes, intestine, and stuffed spleen, a feast worthy of a butcher's family. At the head of the laid table covered with pristine tablecloths, sat the rabbi of Chmielów, joined by many other people, and the festivities lasted until first light.

Another Torah scroll was brought later to the Shtibl by Gezl and his wife Sarah Neinudel (a childless couple) and another magnificent procession was held, with the participation of the rabbi. After my father passed away, the Chmielów Shtibl was moved into our house and a regular Minyan gathered in the room where my father used to pray and study, a custom that was continued until the outbreak of the war.

1. Numbers 24:5

Social and Public Life

[Page 57]
Yitzhak Kerbel

The Youth Movements in Wierzbnik

Our town had the same composition of youth movements as other towns in central Poland, from the radical leftist movements to Beitar, which was considered a rightist movement.

Despite its distance from large population centers, our town was teeming with Zionist activity, and the youths, who showed interest in every field of Jewish life, were aware of problems of the hour and willing to tackle them for the sake of the nation.

We also hosted certain training kibbutzim (collectives) who visited the town from time to time. Some of them worked at the large Tartak (lumber-mill), while others would wander around town carrying axes and saws, looking for work chopping wood for the harsh days of winter.

An aura of romance surrounded these kibbutzniks. Despite their financial struggles we youths saw them as "princes" and were jealous of them, because they were destined to travel to Israel soon.

This took place in ages past and much has been forgotten since, but I have no doubt that our youths were healthy in spirit, and I can recall no bullying or hooliganism. Each was part of a group, whether it was Beitar, HeHalutz, the Zionist Youth, the religious youth, the professional associations of tailors and carpenters, or movements such as "The Star" (Gviazda) or Maccabi, and so on. We should also mention the young members of Agudath Israel, among which I had the honor of studying Talmud. As a matter of fact, the education of youth in our town was divided as follows: from around the age of 4 we studied under Mailech the Melamed. Later, we studied under rabbi Yoel. Finally we studied under, Shlomo "Shenner", who was known as a devout but very bad-tempered Jew. That was the sum of the education received by of most youths in our town.

A minor educational revolution took place with the foundation of the first school, Tarbut, managed by the great educator Lupta, and that of the Hamizrachi School managed by the teachers Lipski of Opatów and Yaakov Tenenbaum, the son of the rabbi of Wierzbnik. This teacher was better known as "Yankel the Yellow" than by his surname, Tenenbaum.

The Polish school system naturally took part in general education, and throughout the years, until the Nazi holocaust, the Jewish students were treated with patience and objectiveness, regardless of the fact that most Jewish students excelled in all their subjects during those years. If memory serves, there were few high school graduates in our town because the town was far from large population centers and the parents feared sending their children far away, where they might pick up bad habits. Among the high school graduates we commemorate Sarah Kleiner and her brother Yoseph, who live today in Caracas in Venezuela. Sarah's husband, Dr. Wiesenfeld, serves as the leader of the Jewish community in Caracas and as the president of the Zionist organization there.

I may have forgotten some other high school graduates, but I would like to mention another of them here, Shmuel Gelbard, who fell during the War of Independence when the Syrians bombed Holon.

But although we were not rich with formal graduates, there were many of us with a general and Jewish education, even distinct scholars. The libraries of the tailors' organization and the

Zionist organization were always filled with those youths who had a thirst for knowledge, and on Shabbats it was a pleasure to see the endless trains of youths carrying books under their arms, headed toward the woods, or the lake, or the big rock up in the mountain by the riverside, where the groups sat and discussed important issues for many hours.

We also had ties to youth groups in nearby towns, such as Skarżysko, Opatów, Ostrowiec, Szydłowiec, and so on, and we would often pay visits to each other.

We remember the train of youths walking from the tavern of Berish Guterman on the corner of Starachowicka Street (Marszałkowska) to the floor-tile factory.

We would wander along this route in droves, sometimes stopping for a short while by the large picturesque courtyard of Mysliborski, or on the other side of the street, by Vigdorovich's barber shop, or by the Pshigoda movie theatre.

There are bundles of memories in my mind, but it is clear to me that I cannot bring them all forth. I have tried to draw a broad picture of the life of youths in our town, their dreams and their folklore which are now gone from us forever.

Let these recollections serve as a memory candle for all those youths who did not live to see days of freedom and the revival of the free State of Israel.

[Page 60]
Moshe Sali (Kerbel)

The Young Pioneer Movement in Wierzbnik

The bloody clashes that erupted in Israel in 1929 were echoed by an awakening among the youths in the Diaspora and a desire to establish branches of HeHalutz and training kibbutzim in every town in Poland, to train youths in physical labor and social customs and prepare them for immigration to Israel. This trend was just as evident in our town of Wierzbnik.

And so, the foundations for the Young Pioneer branch in Wierzbnik were laid.

Although there were only a few of us at first, it was not long before our numbers began to grow, as our fellow youths sought change and challenge in their lives, a change powered by the news that came from Israel. The youths were also attracted by the various classes taught by the movement, such as general and Jewish history and Hebrew, and by the party nights that were organized.

After a while, we learned about the existence of training kibbutzim in Grochów, Kłosów, Shcharia and other places. Although we did not clearly understand their nature, we knew that preaching was not enough and action was required as well. It was not enough to be an activist, to talk and preach immigration and realization. We needed to take other steps, to train ourselves physically and professionally for the day when we will be numbered among the immigrants in the long awaited homeland, which yearned for working hands.

The Young Hechalutz Committee. Standing from right to left: Hertzka Kleinman, Mottel Reizman, Mosheke Kerbel, Mendel Ribak. Sitting: Avraham Goldsztejn, Shmuel Meir Ribak, Hershel Herszman, Reuven Lis

Since most of our members never did any physical work, a few of us took up apprenticeship in such crafts as carpentry, construction, tinkering and so on. However it was quickly made clear to us that we will not get far in this manner and that we must start living in the tradition of the kibbutz life to prepare ourselves for this lifestyle. From this point onward, we had to find suitable places for organizing training kibbutzim. It was not easy because most parents objected, considering this lifestyle to be a reprehensible adventure.

Nevertheless, we have made our decision, one clear day. Three of the branch leaders, who were among its finest members – Meir Rolnicki, Mordechai Riseman and I – decided to break through this barrier and serve as an example for those we strove to teach.

We therefore left, with the blessing of the HeHalutz center in Warsaw, for the Borochov kibbutz in Suchedniów in order to familiarize ourselves with this lifestyle. Next, we turned to the town of Kielce where we intended to strike root and establish a kibbutz for youths filled with Zionist vision, who will train for immigration. Our plans were indeed realized, and we settled down there. This was not an easy assignment and we had to fight hard to overcome all manner of obstacles placed in our path, but we were determined to overcome this ordeal.

When we arrived in Kielce we immediately sought a meeting with the activists of the Zionist organizations and youth movements there, and explained our mission to them. They were impressed by our resolve and promised to help in any way possible, including finding us residence and work.

Nevertheless, I remember that when we first came before the esteemed merchant and industrialist Rutenberg, or the owners of the lumber-mill, the Golembiowski brothers, seeking work as common workers, they were largely amazed and though they were kind, they did not take us seriously. Although they too were dedicated Zionist activists, they tried to talk us out of this hard task. We were wellborn and barely out from under our mothers' skirts, they said, how can we compete with the strong gentiles who became accustomed to such hard work over generations?

Nevertheless, when they saw our determination and the reverence we felt toward this matter, they agreed to take us in on a trial basis.

We explained to them that we sought neither charity nor profits, and that all we wish is to train ourselves for physical work and sustain ourselves and our communal life, in a manner similar to the kibbutz in Israel. We were overjoyed when the local youths helped us find a small, dirty apartment, which we rented and cleaned thoroughly. We built minimal furniture from unsmoothed planks: sleep bunks (one atop the other), a dining table and a kitchen.

We were ten at first, including two brave girls, as we started to run our property and other affairs.

Our first day of work at the Golembiowski brothers' lumber-mill was a day of triumph for us, but also a disappointment. The foreman did not assign us to do hard labor with the other workers, but tasked us with lighter chores such as arranging planks, sawing lumber and so on. We were also offended by his coworkers, particularly the Christians, who laughed at our "delicate white hands". However this attitude has slowly faded and after a while, the management was convinced of our working prowess, our quick wit and our proper execution of every chore to the best of our ability, on par with the Christian workers who always worked there.

As time passed, the management started to assign us most of the hard jobs: carrying, loading and unloading, putting logs into the sawing machines and all manner of work. The kibbutz became famous in the area. However our ability to accept new members was limited because we lacked a proper residence for them. Eventually, when we moved to a bigger apartment, we accepted several dozens of new members who were sent to us from the HeHalutz center in Warsaw. We also broke into the business of loading and unloading at the train station and later at the nearby limestone quarries, and the more work we got, the more our numbers grew, until we were one of the greatest Polish collectives of pioneering youth.

And then it occurred to us that we shouldn't rest on our laurels but strive for new conquests, sow the seeds of training kibbutzim that would be branches of the mother kibbutz of Kielce.

Once again I was chosen, together with two other capable members. We toured the towns of congressional Poland, seeking the right environments that would serve as training centers. And indeed, after going back and forth through most towns of congressional Poland, we managed to strike root and lay the foundations for several training kibbutzim in Radom, Będzin, Dąbrowa Górnicza and so on.

I should take a moment to mention the excitement of our members as they went to work and back. Jews and gentiles alike were amazed to see the "Palestinazians" pass by, walking in a row and singing on the way to work and back, sometimes dressed only in tatters, but always full of vigor, joy and liveliness. Our living conditions and nutrition were not always satisfactory, but the camaraderie was never lacking and the singing and the dancing never stopped, day or night, in light of the goal that beckoned and set our bones on fire. We lovingly accepted all the hardships of striking root and training.

The fact that we were not alone but rather an inseparable part of a pioneering group gave us the courage to continue this work and lifestyle. The working conditions were naturally harsher during the winters, but we grew accustomed to that as well, through dedication and willpower. The female members, who increased in number, did not settle for housekeeping and sewing but worked hard alongside the men, at the lumber-mills or the limestone quarries. Order in the kibbutz was exemplary, and the daily schedule preplanned.

Work in the kibbutz was, as aforesaid, not only a means for material sustenance, but also a goal unto itself, meant to change a person. Its educational value lay in the fact that the person stopped being what he was before and started realizing his heart's desire. He carried out his own revolution, and did not pull back, did not go back home, despite the calls, the requests and the temptations offered by the parents.

Although some members dropped out here and there, the majority persevered and continued walking this path, which led to their heart's desire, immigration to Israel.

I would like to mention and commemorate two pioneers in particular, Meir Rolnicki and Mordechai Riseman, who were refined in the melting pot of training and traveled a hard, interesting path with me, but never realized their dreams and aspirations. The Devil's hand caught them and they were murdered in their prime, without reaching the homeland they have dreamed about for many years.

Let this therefore be a memory candle and a mark of their actions, honoring their memory.

[Page 64]
Reuven Lis Shuali

The Gordonia Movement and the National Labor Committee for Palestine Youth League

The extensive activities of the youths in Wierzbnik touched the social-public sphere, various fields of sports, the cultural, religious and national fields, and more.

The social movements that grew in the Jewish communities throughout Poland's hundreds of cities and towns found a place among the Jewish youths of Wierzbnik as well, in one form or another, and these youths were loyal to the organization processes, the activities and the desire to do that were typical of Jewish youths in every country.

We therefore find in Wierzbnik patterns and frameworks, movements and organizations, all of which were built and shaped over many years and nurtured with a dedicated and loving hand, diligently and with boundless loyalty.

Following are the various Zionist organizations: Poalei Zion Right and Poalei Zion Left, HeHalutz, Gordonia, Mizrachi Labor Federation. Akin to them but different in their political view were Agudath Israel on one hand and the leftist groups on the other, each loyal to their cause and belief, dedicating their time to the noble goal that was their hearts' desire.

All of them typically suffered from financial difficulties and were barely able to finance their extensive activity, which was never proportionate to their budget, but they made up for any shortages with dedication and sacrifice.

In addition to the social-public activity, there were also sports organizations – soccer, ping-pong and tennis – which attracted sports-loving youths and filled their hearts with pride for every achievement and every success.

Every group required material aid at some point and expected it from the body that was supposed to unit all echelons of the community, that is, the community board. This institute was, however, unable to fulfill all those wishes because of its own meager means and lack of authority, preventing it from sponsoring the entire public.

The League for Labor in Palestine

In 1933, the Gordonia group established a group called the League for Labor Palestine, which set out to impart to the Jewish youths among the members of Poalei Zion Right knowledge and ideological foundations concerning the return to Zion and the future of our people in Israel. The writer of these lines himself conducted a series of lessons and lectures for groups of organized youth regarding the history of the Jewish people, according to Graetz's books and Hebrew study. I also had friendly conversations with them and tried to use pioneer dancing and cultural nights at the clubs to inspire social values that would mentally prepare them for a future in Israel.

In my lectures before the Jewish youths of Wierzbnik, I often expressed support of the concepts espoused by the leaders of the movement – Zeev Jabotinsky and Yitzhak Grinbaum – concerning the evacuation of the Jews of Poland in light of the expected danger, which they predicted with their political foresight.

The approach which considered historical developments to be against us enjoyed some measure of support, but although some people, especially youths, wanted to draw the logical conclusion from the situation and immigrate to Israel, they were faced with an impenetrable barrier. It is common knowledge that immigration to Israel required certificates and that those certificates were given stingingly, only a few at a time. Living testimony of this plight were the dozens of men who came to our town for "training", anxiously waiting for the promised certificates, all their work in vain as they never got their wish.

Although the events described were not encouraging, the Jewish populace did not despair of returning to Zion and building a national home, as the idea was espoused in those days. Ideological life continued to flow through channels of interest and action.

I remember a lively symposium that took place during those days between the representatives of the religious youths, led by my father, Mordechai Lis, the chairman of the local community board, Shmuel Isser, and myself. I was demanding a change in the religious tone of the community, making it more nationalistic; dedication of greater efforts to broaden the national education, to impart knowledge and professional skills to the general public and to take care of the national and social affairs of the Jewish population. I presented before them the need to expand the education network of private schools, as well as cultural and sports enterprises, shifting emphasis from the opening of religious schools for children to the opening of kindergartens, and so on. I addressed this demand to the Zionist organization on other occasions as well, but to tell the truth, it was completely devoid of the need for a comprehensive political and social plan that will integrate the Jewish reality in the Diaspora with our future in Israel.

Our main desires, our resources and our attention were all directed at escaping the strait, leaving Poland in various ways – whether as tourists or capitalists or athletes traveling to the Maccabiyah or simply as immigrants. However despite our best intentions and no matter how hard we strove for this goal, only a few could achieve it and be counted among the blessed.

[Page 66]
Rivka Greenberg (Mincberg) and Rachel Laor (Dreksler)

The Zionist Youth Movement

Our childhood was wonderful. We were full of the excitement and joy of youth. The majority of youths in our town were swept into the stream of movement activity. Members of HeHalutz on one hand and members of Beitar on the other; Hamizrachi and Agudath Israel on one side of the camp and the socialists on the other side; and in the middle were other organizations and glorious movements: Akiva, the Zionist Youth and Labor Palestine. Everything. Men's sports organizations – Maccabi and Gviazda. Women organizations – WIZO[1], Bnot Yaakov and so on. There were hardly any margins left in the great torrent of inspired activism. Everything and everywhere was part of the boiling cauldron of gatherings and meetings. And parties and assemblies and singing and dancing until dawn!

Recreation coexisted with lively, passionate activism for the sake of the ideal, the cause. Who can forget the blue box carried by the boys and girls visiting the houses of Jews, collecting donations? Legends formed around such "operations", shrouded in an air of gravity and devotion to the cause, sometimes with an aura of romance and sometimes under strange circumstances and steeped in humor, nothing grand.

The center of activity

The youths of Wierzbnik carried out no great deeds, nor reached for the sky, and never made their way into parlors or fancy halls. Instead they set up a residence – a meeting place for scholars clearly signifying humility and modesty, but also much content. Everything centered around this building, from kindergarten through the Tarbut School, the Zionist Youth movement and the WIZO and HeHalutz organizations, and so on. All of them were entwined and combined, complementing each other. The public was small and children who finished their two years of kindergarten continued to a higher stage of schooling. It would be impossible to forget the kindergarten teacher, Hanka Glooschneider, a wonderful woman who made such efforts to impart the best of habits and values to her young charges. Activity inside the building was not limited to it, however. The surrounding atmosphere was also nurtured by the caring hands of people with a national conscience, who were not formally part of any organizational framework but nevertheless yearned greatly for Zion, seeking to impart this sentiment to the younger generation that will shoulder the burden of realization. Inspiration sometimes came from beyond the local public. This meeting place of the public movements was visited by messengers and lecturers from the big cities and even the capital, Warsaw.

Rachel tells us:

I remember an impressive visit of the great Zionist leader, Yitzhak Grinbaum, to our town. In preparation of his visit, I was charged with greeting him and presenting him with a bouquet of flowers. Naturally, I was excited about the visit of this important guest. When the day finally came and the noble guest arrived, everyone was excited. Thrilled, I approached to greet him when something unexpected suddenly happened, almost causing an incident. When I finished greeting him, Grinbaum held my hand and tried to kiss me on the cheek, but for me this was a highly unusual act and I pushed him away in apprehension ...

The audience swallowed its "surprise" and the Zionist leader merely smiled. Dozens of trying years later, after I immigrated to Israel, I met Y. Grinbaum by chance and reminded him of the event. He answered me, in his typical way: "If I failed then, I am more than willing to try again now. Perhaps I would be more successful this time?"

On another occasion we were visited by Dr. Leon Uris from Warsaw, who was the direct supervisor of all Tarbut schools in Poland.

Who was the first Jew?

Once, our school was visited by the regional supervisor, a man named Bernstein. I believe this was in 1932, during his patrol of his region. He was a small bald man, middle-aged and wearing a somber, solemn expression. The parents of students were invited to a gathering and during this event the supervisor asked questions and the students answered. I recall the question he asked me, and my answer which caused a stir. He asked me "Who was the first Jew?" and I, filled with self-esteem, answered "Moses, naturally!" but the disbelief on his face divided the class in two, one group supporting my answer while the other insisted that Avraham was the first Jew. The fact that so many dared disagree with me made me question myself as well, and I sought affirmation from my father, who was among those present. However to my great embarrassment, when I saw my father he was clasping his hands with disappointment.

My candy box

Cultural activities served an important role in the life of the Tarbut School and it enjoyed a broad range of enterprises and talents as well as a unique milieu, leaving an impression of more than just a pedagogic experience. For many it was a way of life that offered fulfillment and swept them into extensive activity, full of the talent and vigor so characteristic of youths.

Our performances, which were carried out solely in Hebrew, won particular acclaim throughout town. I remember a play from those days, called "Yaakov and Eisav", in which I had the honor of playing one of the central roles. I spent days and nights rehearsing my lines and expected a proper reward, in the form of applause. But in order to further entice the crowd, as was customary in those days, I asked my parents to throw a candy box to me.

This led to quite an incident, which became the talk of the town. The show went according to plan and the audience was excited, but when I reached the crowning moment of my role and expected the candy box to come flying, things went wrong. The candy box was given to a "neutral" person, to make things appear more "authentic", and that person was not gifted with particular theatrical sense. Instead of tossing the package when I was alone on the stage, he tossed it while I was with my friend, Hanka Laks, and next to her feet... she naturally stooped to pick up the candy box but I refused to accept the injustice taking place before me and screamed "It's mine!"

Hanka managed to reply "How do you know?" but the cat was already out of the bag...

Rivka tells us: Zionist upbringing

The field of education and particularly the school environment was filled with a valiant and firm connection to Israel. We sang folk songs, and identified heart and soul with the notion of returning to Zion. A great part in shaping these notions was played by the educators, among them our teacher Lupta of Łuniniec and the resourceful and energetic teacher Horowitz, who taught their students to love Israel and everything in it. The students, on the other hand, showed great interest in subjects and activities, songs and dances that brought them closer to Israel, and they continued practicing them outside school. It is important to note that these classes in Tarbut were our "second shift", as during the "first shift" of the day, morning to noon, we Jewish kids of Wierzbnik studied at the Polish school.

Graduates join Zionist Youth

The school was also the natural resource for the organized Zionist movements.

After graduation from the Tarbut School, the students would join a movement and throw themselves into extensive activity which included drills and exercises, joining the colonies (with their unique sense of a romantic adventure), cultural activity and among the older ages – independent training for immigration to Israel. Another field that occupied every class in some way was the activity surrounding the collection for the National Fund.

The methods of collecting donations for the National Fund formed into traditional patterns, such as walking rounds with the collection box, or emptying collection boxes at homes; collections in synagogues and public institutes, during holidays, gatherings, and so on.

The collection operations with the blue box became renowned and were often shrouded with youthful passion and entwined with many legends and adventures.

Holidays

The meaning of the words Moadim Lesimcha, Hagim U'zmanim L'sasson"[2], has never been more fully expressed than by the Zionist youth club, which was visited by all on such days and occasionally hosted special ceremonies. And the same applies for holy or traditional days as well.

1. Women's International Zionist Organization
2. "And you have given us holidays on which we rejoice, festivals and times for jubilation…"

[Page 69]
Moshe Sali (Kerbel)

Wierzbnik, a Proud Example of Zionism

It is with awe and reverence that I approach the task of writing down some memories from my youth in the town of Wierzbnik, memories I cherish to this day. In all honesty, I consider myself unworthy. I was only 16 years old when I left on behalf of HeHalutz for a training kibbutz and a life of realization, and I cannot dredge much from the depths of the past. At the age of 19 I immigrated to Israel and was, in fact, the first swallow among our landsleit, to dare and break through hardships and barriers and immigrate to Israel during the days when most Zionists served their duty through local activism, collecting donations for the Funds, and getting a certificate was as hard as splitting the Red Sea…

We were offered a great chance, I and the likes of me, to labor and struggle, to fight and take part in creating the foundations on which the sovereign, independent State of Israel was established. Nevertheless, it is my duty to emphasize that this great privilege was inspired by the Jewish life in our town Wierzbnik, a lively community that always considered Zion its first priority – some in yearning and some in prayer, hoping to return, some through extensive Zionist activity. They were people who considered Judaism and Zionism one and the same, good Jews who cherished their place of origin and continued to weave the thread of salvation everywhere, even in the valley of the shadow of death, the camps, during the years of oppression and damnation.

Our town was not blessed with many sources of livelihood. Most of the Jews were merchants selling lumber, groceries, cloth, shoes, house-wares, haberdashery and so on, and some were craftsmen who worked for a living. The stores and craftsmen typically served the large Christian population in town and the nearby villages.

It is impossible to forget the market (Rinek) which was entirely Jewish in nature and drew the gentiles to it every Thursday for market days, in addition to the large fairs on special days. The thousands of Polish workers that worked in Starachowice, in the steelmills of the government, were the main customers of the Jewish grocers and craftsmen. While life in town was far from luxurious, there was no shortage of livelihood. Some enjoyed plenty of it and some only sparingly, but few people were on the verge of starvation.

This Jewish settlement existed for tens and maybe even hundreds of years, teaming with life, growing and evolving, creating and shaping patterns and frameworks of meaningful social and cultural life, and all the various threads of Judaism found a place in this vibrant, unique tapestry of life. A wondrous mosaic of individuals and masses formed over the many years, with their different ideas, sensations and lifestyles. On the one hand was the devotion of the Hasidim and the orthodox men, a broad network of houses of learning (Shtiblach), who were tied heart and soul to the courts of the famous Admors of Poland's cities (Gur, Alexander, Amshinov, Radzyń, and so on). And on the other hand were feelings of national renaissance, a yearning for salvation that sprung from this precious Judaism and took root. This precious Judaism – which suckled its vision from the stories of salvation, from the holy book, the Bible, from unlimited faith in NILI[1], from the stories of Bilus, fed by Hibbath Zion and the enlightenment generation and by Zionist emancipation carried on the tides of that generation – managed to give a unique shape and flavor to the sublime Zionist ideal, to bring it to the masses and make it public domain, a great and popular movement.

I still remember the spectacular displays, the propaganda and the activism, both oral and in writing, the work carried out to spread the Zionist ideal everywhere, the return to Zion and the founding of a home for our persecuted people. The Lag Ba'Omer gatherings, the exhibitions and markets held for the National Fund, the processions – all those shed a great light on us, made us stand tall, and swept in their wake the majority of the Jewish population in town and most of its youths.

Particularly vibrant were the social and cultural lives of the Zionist groups: each organization and layer was a scion of Yishai, growing and branching out from the bough called "Zionism". These were the movements: Al-Hamishmar, Et-Livnot, Hamizrachi, Hapoel-Hamizrachi, Young Hamizrachi, revisionists, Poalei Zion and so on. We had training kibbutzim, Tarbut Schools and Hebrew night classes; gatherings, lectures, reading parties, libraries, friendly chats and so on.

At the same time, orthodox Judaism wove in its own path through the network of Agudath Israel, Agudath Israel Youths and the Bnot-Yaakov School for girls. But the crown jewel of Jewish activity in town was the Zionist movement in its various forms, which served as the spine of public activity in town.

They belittled nothing, took any job and gave any service, saved penny by penny, added deed to deed – all because of their great desire to realize this lofty ideal. We were brought this far by the training of bodies and hearts, carried out tirelessly for years, and the volunteers from the pioneering youth movements carrying out Zionism. Therefore it is a bitter fact that so many of our landsleit, who trained themselves wholeheartedly for Israel constantly looked forward to Zion, who did so much for it, did not live to be with us and were innocently cut down by bloodthirsty villains.

Life in town was seemingly monotonous, and yet every heart hoped for great events, for the day when the hopes of 2,000 years would be realized in the land of Israel.

The Zionist movement and its youth movements managed to put color, excitement and hope into the mundane life. Looking back, we can see how much substance, warmth and life could be found in the lifestyle of our townsmen – every institute and every organization had its own fanatics who spent their time and efforts working for Zion.

As aforesaid, the Jewish society in our town was, if not religiously devout, then mostly characterized by religious nature and tradition, giving a sense of the Jewish home and its symbols, the traditional Jewish family and its unique holidays, filled with many Jewish contents. The spirit of this milieu suffused the entire area and the Heders and Talmud Torah schools spread and taught in the spirit of traditional, fundamental Judaism.

I will further add that the Jews in town were always peaceful folk. Life typically centered on the Jewish community, its leaders and the synagogue and its managers. The various groups commonly disagreed and fought about the proper ways to govern the community, such as the ways it was represented before the authorities, control over public property, and so on. Such fight were, however, the result of an active social life that gave a purpose to the lives of the town's Jews, who despite the duty of providing for their families found the time to take part in the good and bad aspects of community life, and as Jews adhering to the precepts of their religion accepted everything with love, never doubting the will of God almighty.

This tiny Jewish settlement, which was blessed neither with an abundance of genius nor with groundbreaking leaders and trailblazers, was nevertheless a lively Jewish settlement, its individuals and public relentlessly and loyally active. This Jewry, which as aforementioned was comprised mostly of common workers and laborers, merchants and grocers who lived humble, moderate lives and struggled daily for their livelihood, was also aware of matters of the public and willing to join its cause.

It was all destroyed, in various ways, as the townspeople perished because of their faith and Judaism.

I recall that during its days of glory the Jewish community was steeped with a cultural, public life, seeking progress and yearning for redemption. The unrelenting struggle for life and subsistence, and the life of integrity and yearning for a just society, are both noble qualities of our community, which I wished to commemorate in this book, a monument for our martyrs, a candle that will shine for those who leaf through these pages, written by the relatives and family members of the pure martyrs who will never be forgotten.

The path of HeHalutz

As a former cadet of HeHalutz, an active Zionist youth movement that allowed my immigration to Israel during those days, when immigration was fraught with endless hardships, I would like to dedicate a few lines to this youth movement, which made its goal the realization of Zionism in the spirit of the working class. Jews of the higher classes looked in dismissal and shame at the sons of workers and laborers, who they considered for some reason to be inferior (naturally the result of ages of upbringing). HeHalutz came into our town like a breath of fresh air, and knocked down the barriers that existed between youth classes in town, and as if by magic the order of things was turned on its head, the approach reversed: you could see the sons of laborers, merchants and men of means, poor and rich, all together in gatherings and classes.

Most of the youths were drawn to this change, which had a single purpose: to undergo training and join the people of Labor Palestine.

During the nights the club was filled with young men and women who studied, shaped and spun their future, unfettered by heritage. We faced hardships and issues, but we conquered them all. First we left to train far from home; we labored in lumber-mills, in forests, doing any hard work (such as chopping down trees), adapting ourselves to all manners of work and harsh conditions. But despite these hardships, the letters we sent home were filled with excitement about our interesting life together (guys and girls cohabitating), a phenomenon made uncommon at the time by prejudice. It is impossible to forget the wild Hora dances that filled people with joy and drew the viewers, big and small, into the circle of dancers. Thanks to these realizing youths and the other Zionist youth organizations, the Jewish youths were saved from the void and their lives were filled with profound movement contents. The youths learned that Israel requires attentive workers, and classes in a variety of topics – Hebrew, Jewish and general history, geography, Jewish and Zionist literature – took place every night. There were activities for the National Fund and tumultuous arguments about the subjects at hand.

The balls and parties we often had at the club bothered the neighbors, but they were always forgiving and did not act against us, knowing that this was the spark giving life to their sons and daughters.

Our hands were full of work and action; we sought, as aforementioned, to impart knowledge of the Hebrew language to the youths, and we read and studied together about Herzl, Trumpeldor, the Tel-Hai incidents, Brenner and A.D. Gordon, all of whom set our hearts ablaze. We taught the youths to leave the house on trips, to spend time together in the open country, to hike across mountains, rivers and forests. These things built our strength and character. Although at times we had to wage harsh battles with ourselves, we eventually overcame everything and came out stronger. members of HeHalutz and other youth movements enjoyed a vibrant, cultural life, a social life that sustained our desire to make the dream into a reality.

This inspired life was cut off before its time.

Let these pages serve as a tear for the lives annihilated, as knowledge and a harsh lesson of all generations to come.

1. Nezah Israel Lo Yeshaker

Members of Young Hechalutz along with members of the Hamapil Kibbutz on hachshara in our town. Standing from right to left: Leibe Kroizman, Goldsztejn, Herman, Leibel Gruber, Yechiel Mor, Avraham Goldsztejn, Reuven Lis, Meir Rolnicki. Standing in the center: Yaakov Rolnicki. Edge of the left: Mottel Reizman. Sitting on the floor: rightmost edge: Avraham Manela

[Page 73]
Yaakov Katz

It Was our Whole World

Our great classicists did us a boon during the early 1920s, drawing many pictures of the Jewish life in the towns of Poland and Russia. Surely they never even imagined that these works of art would also serve as the swan song of the Jewish town. In the aftermath of the Holocaust of World War II 1939-1945, their authentic art became the tombstone of the Jewish town in the European Diaspora.

Throughout our exile, our historians knew how to immortalize heroes and heroic acts carried out in times of strife, since the exile of Babylon, through the wars of the Maccabim and to our days.

Today, over 30 years since the beginning of World War II, we still lack a national poet who will encompass the scope of the Holocaust and the terrors of the great ruination and the cruelest of wars the world has ever known.

Any historian who would wish to learn about the heroic deeds of anonymous men and women from the ruins of the towns and ghettos would find this burden beyond his abilities, since there were so many of them.

Many of the people who suffered hellish torture before breathing their last in the furnaces of the Nazis have left no trace of family and only a few were spared from every town, as the saying goes: two to a town and one to a family.

Remember and never forget

Therefore it is the sacred duty of the survivors to immortalize the names of the martyrs and the innocents so they will never be forgotten.

In the book of Exodus 17:14 it is said "Then the Lord said to Moses, 'Write this for a memorial in the book and recount it in the hearing of Joshua, that I will utterly blot out the remembrance of Amalek from under heaven'." It is seemingly possible to omit the word "this", but in Hebrew it marks the acronyms for "Remember (and) Never Forget".

In the book of Deuteronomy 25:17 we also find "Remember what Amalek did to you" "That you will blot out the remembrance of Amalek from under heaven. You shall not forget." The words "never forget" also mean never grow tired of remembering. Hence we learn that the duty to remember and the prohibition of forget is a supreme decree for each of us, "That you will tell your son and your son's son". We are the last generation enslaved and the first redeemed, ordered and bound to mark these memories for ourselves and for the next generations so they will be proud of their origins and so they will learn and know that many people were annihilated but The Jewish People Live and Nezah Israel Lo Yeshaker. These are not random sayings but a truth forged in the melting pot of history, proven and engraved in blood and fire by our guiltless martyrs who were burned to death.

The town of Wierzbnik-Starachowice may have been a small unimportant point on the greater map of Poland, but during the 1930s it was my whole world. A small town, surrounded by forests, fields, meadows, lakes and rivers. Although there were no asphalt roads or large houses, the wooden houses and the small antiquated buildings – that had no electricity, running water, or minimal sanitary infrastructure – were remarkably clean and a place where lively Jewish lives were lived. It is no wonder that our greatest authors, such as Shalom Aleichem, Mendele Mocher Sefarim, Y.L Perez and others, saw fit to immortalize the town Jews in realistic fashion. The commoners, who would wake up early and walk in the dark or by lamplight to the first Minyan at the Beit-Midrash, and from there on to their daily affairs, be it a store, a craft or a trade. Although the town enjoyed no glory or fame, there was never any shortage of scholars, students and philosophers of the Torah.

The Beit-Midrash was not only a place to study the Talmud but also a gathering place for every kind of public activity in town. It was a parliament house where public opinion concerning any local and public occasion was shaped. It was the place where the activists struggled to influence people using every tool at their disposal. It was where famous activists came to speak from time to time. And so the Jewish life ran its course peacefully for years.

Since Hitler's ascent to power in Germany, greater and greater shocks plagued the world and the Jewish world in particular. Anti-Semitism, which has always existed but was well hidden in the past, started rearing its head and showing some of its true colors. The feeling of financial insecurity grew and the Jewish youth started looking for a way and pondering its future.

And as if riding this gale came up the magic word, "Israel". In every Jewish town there was a surge of Jewish youth movements, both religious and secular, and in every city and town people made the return to Zion their hearts' desire. Clubs formed, offering an outlet for the energy built up among the youths. The parents did not accept this rebellious phenomenon easily, but many have accepted it in retrospect, believing that in time, the youths would carve their own path.

The youths have simply found their calling in life.

Wierzbnik

Wierzbnik was blessed with more than a few activists who spent their time and energy on this holy agenda, and gave their support and patronage to this blessed work. The movement served as an important, fundamental melting pot, teaching values, knowledge and learning, to the youths and broadening their horizons.

On the other hand were movements that adhered to the legacy of our people, the fountains of Torah, Talmud and judges, feeding with unending awe from the depths of religious interpretations, debate and legend, and becoming drunk with the biblical tales of Israel.

Wierzbnik-Starachowice is also a chapter filled with blood and tears, because the Polish enemies collaborated with the Nazi enslaver to decimate us.

We will not weep for its ruination, only for the loss of human dignity, for the life that was taken before its time and for the dear ones who lost their lives.

We will memorize and remember it to our last generation.

Remember what the Nazi Amalek did to you, may it be damned for eternity.

[Page 75]
Zehava Zitelna

Beit-Yaakov School for Girls

I arrived in Wierzbnik at the end of December 1932, to serve as the teacher in the Bnot-Yaakov School for girls. When I arrived, I found a typical Jewish-Polish town, whose Jewish residents were mainly merchants, but filled their lives with religion and tradition and observed their customs – the Shabbats, holidays and chastity – according to the laws of the Torah. I was invited to stay with the family of Moshe David Rothschild, who welcomed me in. We had to found the school from scratch. Since the others were all busy, I had to plan how we would set the first cornerstones for this school, which was an innovation in this town. I remember sitting idle for an entire week, which felt like a whole year to me. After a week of introspection, the town peers gathered and formed a committee for the Bnot-Yaakov School for girls. Among the founders were: Natan Kornwaser, Yoseph Brodbeker, and Fishel Hercig. At first I had seven girls of different ages and classes to start my educational work with. I rejoiced at the fact that new girls joined every day and gradually I succeeded in organizing three classes and planning a curriculum. On Shabbat eve, after lighting the candles, we welcomed the Shabbat together with prayer and the girls, dressed in clean Shabbat clothes and their faces bright, welcomed Shabbat the Queen. Everything was done with elegance; it was practically heaven.

In the next room, the men would prey in the tradition of the Gur Hasidim. This meant that there was a break between the Minhah and Kabalat Shabbat prayers. As a student of the seminary, I was used to reciting from the Song of Songs and therefore I asked the children to open their books at the Song of Songs. I read them the words of the wisest of all men and they listened. One Shabbat I could not attend and asked one of the gifted girls from the family of Faiga Wajzer to recite in my stead, to keep things in order. She did her job well, I would say. On my return to the school, I was told that most of the men from the nearby synagogue came to listen to the young girl flawlessly reciting the Song of Songs as if she understood the meaning of the words. That Friday night, many fathers started quizzing their sons, who were studying at the Heder, to see whether they can recite the Song of Songs with no mistakes, and the girls were naturally happy of their superiority over the boys, leading to a literary competition, reminiscent of "when authors vie, wisdom mounts".

A special chapter belongs to the activity of "Bnot Agudath Israel". These 16-20 years old girl would gather every night to study and perform. Every Shabbat eve, one of them had to give a lecture about the contents of the portion of the week. It was not an easy task, because most of them knew practically nothing about the Torah, but in order to make matters easier for them they were told in advance which portion they would have to lecture about, so they could prepare for the task ahead of time. And it was a glorious sight to see them prepare for this duty for months, while their parents, fathers and brothers alike helped them willingly with those preparations. It was a kind of scholastic, familial form of worship.

After the lectures were done we sang songs together late into the night and then walked each of the girls home.

The dead are dancing

A legend spread at the time among the girls. Some of them lived near the Christian cemetery and at first they avoided coming to the meetings on Shabbat eves. When I asked for the reason, they told me they were afraid of coming home late at night because that was when the dead danced at the cemetery and around it. I asked them to come and promised we would walk them home first and see the dancing dead together...

The girls indeed showed up and we kept our promise and escorted them home. Since the dead failed to dance before us, the girls showed up regularly from that day on and took part in Shabbat eves.

We also did social work. Every year I asked all the girls to collect spare warm clothes at home for needy children to use during the harsh Polish winter. Every girl also paid a monthly fee, and the money was spent on fixing torn shoes for needy children. On weeknights we gathered both to study and to do practical work. Some of the girls were tasked with collecting newspaper clips that would interest our group, a bit of recent news or a chapter from an interesting, suitable book. At the same time, the rest of the girls would darn socks and do other chores.

The purpose of this activity was, as aforesaid, to provide the needy with darned and worthy clothes. This work gave us great satisfaction because the girls felt the actual beneficial results of their work.

The girls found particular interest in distributing the Bnot-Yaakov magazine among people. I would order several magazines from the editorial office, based on the number of girls, and without qualms gave each of them a magazine for one zloty a month. It was an interesting, glorious time, and the girls yearned to read books and magazines in Yiddish to glean knowledge.

In 1935 I left and immigrated to Israel, and ever since I recall this time as one of the most beautiful periods in my life and my heart aches for this Jewish glory that fell victim to ravening Nazi beasts.

The class of the older girls of Beit Yaakov with the teaching staff. Right to left; Perl Herzog, Henia Wajntraub, Krolnik, Maslowicz, Pesia Wajnberg, Rivker Proman, Komec, Wajnberg. Sitting: Esther Sztern, Reizel Morgensztern, Ita Groszenkorn, (--), center – the teacher

Malka Leopold (Cohen), Malka Kornwasser, Rivka Cytryn, Bela Weizer, Markowicz, Golda and Esther Cytrynbaum

[Note added: Carolyn Veffer has identified her mother, Sura Malach, in back row, second from right, and circa 1929.]

[Page 79]
Chava Fajgenbaum (Shraga)

The Batya Organization

We are told of the activities of this organization by Mrs. Shraga, who was a member of the organization in her youth and today resides in Israel:

Next to the Bnot-Yaakov School for girls was kind of club for young girls, both those who were not attending school yet, and those of the lower classes, usually ages 6-9. It can be referred to as the social club of the students of Bnot-Yaakov, where they spent their time away from classes. The term "spending time" naturally carries a different meaning among the orthodox classes than it does among the secular classes, and during those days the distinction was even more obvious. It is therefore understandable that the teachers sought to teach these girls the important values in their lives from a very young age. First and foremost was memorizing and reciting the prayers. The young girls would often read Barchi Nafshi or sing other prayers together.

However the program also included social elements such as trips around town, nature hikes, or the telling of legends from the Talmud and interesting stories from the Bible.

The senior students of Bnot-Yaakov served as instructors of this club and they considered this social work the fulfillment of a higher calling, dedicating time and energy to carry it out as best as they could. They worked with dedication and received no reward. Although their positive image and activity lives on in my memory, I cannot mention their names, because the long, harsh passage of time has wiped them away. To this day I remember only the name of one of those instructors, Sarah Kumetz.

[Page 80]
Yaakov Korenwaser

The Establishment of "Beit-Yaakov" in our Town

Educating our young, both boys and girls, was a problem in those days, and matters escalated when the fine institute Talmud Torah School closed down. A temporary solution for the education of the boys was found in the form of private Heders, each taught by a rabbi. Other youths, who were not satisfied with this framework, traveled far to study. Our townsman Shmuel Wajzer went to distant Szydłowiec when he was merely 11 years old and was followed by Moshe Sally-Kerbel, who left for the Yeshiva of the rabbi of Sokołów, and by me, who studied in Ostrowiec with Rabbi Israel Meir.

Yet there was no solution for the fundamental issue of educating the girls. Although most of the girls were sent to the primary municipal school, they received no Jewish education there.

We were fortunate then, that the great educator Sarah Schneider laid the foundations for the Bnot-Yaakov teachers' seminar in Kraków.

One evening, the leaders of Agudath Israel Youths in our town, Hershel Morgenstern and Leibish Morgenstern, met with David, Zvi Wajzer and my father and decided to found a Bnot-Yaakov School and to contact the seminar in Kraków for a suitable teacher.

They have managed to sway my father, despite his many concerns and the daily affairs that kept him from public activity, and he used all his energy and influence to make this idea a reality, founding the Bnot-Yaakov School for girls.

[Page 81]
Reuven Lis Shuali

The "Maccabi" Society

I had the great privilege to witness the beginning of the Wierzbnik Maccabi Society, that source of attraction for the Jewish youths of our town, an outlet for their youthful vigor and energy. I joined the society in 1932 and was effectively one of the founding members.

My membership in Maccabi and my membership in the League of Labor Palestine, founded by the Gordonia Movement, seemingly contradicted each other. Special circumstances have nevertheless allowed for this fact, because in those days the Maccabi Society served as a challenge for the Jewish youths of Wierzbnik – including those of the working classes – who were not interested in public activity. The time was also right for the Jews to challenge the gentiles in the field of sports, and the Maccabi Society offered us the leverage necessary for that purpose.

Unidentified family seated at table, 1937. Abe Zukerman collection, Ontario Jewish Archives, Blankenstein Family Heritage Centre, accession 2017-9-1. Photo de-skewed, some editing for scratches. Not in the Original Yizkor Book.

Everything is hard at the beginning

We started out small, both because we lacked the means and because we were still inexperienced. First we collected money to buy uniforms for the soccer team, since this symbol effectively showed that the Society's has become an actual organization. In time we rented a room from the grandfather of the Shiner brothers, and it became a kind of sports and culture club.

The Jewish movement in Wierzbnik considered this club a meeting place and would gather there at night to spend their free time. As aforesaid, the club hosted not only sportive activities but also social ones. There was a ping-pong table there and many used it to play and practice, although we never reached competitive levels in this field.

As for the field of culture, members of the club would take active part in various public campaigns organized by the Zionist Organization, such as a "movie night" whose revenues were dedicated to the National Fund. The same applied to parties, balls and so on.

Among the other founding members of the Society I remember Avraham Goldstein, Chanan Rubinstein, Eli Erlichson, who was also the captain of the soccer team, and Akiva Binstock.

Soccer led the way

The crown jewel of this extensive activity was naturally the soccer team, which won the interest and adoration of the Jewish public in town – and discovered it was also worthy of it.

The team made admirable progress in the professional field and began arranging matches with Jewish teams from nearby towns. It has later reached the peak of its talent by competing with the local gentile team, "Tur".

A group of youth on bicycle at a sporting competition. The photo was taken before the competition

The Maccabee soccer team at one of their successful tournaments

I remember this game and the preparations for it, the general excitement among the Jews in town long before the actual match. On the day of the match itself, everyone has swarmed the field and watched in anticipation for the results of the game. The game ended with a loss for the Maccabi team, but I recall it was an honorable loss, which left us neither frustrated nor bitter.

In time, another soccer team called Gviazda was organized in our town, founded by the leftist circles of Poalei Zion (left), who intended for it to balance the sportive activity in political terms. From here on the relations between the two teams and their fans gradually heated up. Each team tried to outdo the other and there were occasional tensions over an attempt to "shift" players from one group to the other.

The Maccabiyah

In 1935 came up the issue of sending representatives for the Maccabiyah. The subject caused both internal and external arguments. First, we had to choose the candidates we will send, and then we had to struggle to keep our place, because the number of representatives was limited. A certain index based on the number of members in the society determined the number of candidates or delegations that could be sent. Our town, however, turned out short of the members and fans necessary for even a single mandate. Since our members only numbered 50 people, far below the index, we received a negative reply. As the secretary of the society, I was highly active in the attempts to send a delegate to the Maccabiyah but my efforts were likely doomed to fail has I not turned to another source for help. Along my activity in the Maccabi society I was also an activist for the League of Labor Palestine, and now I tried to fuse the two together to achieve the desired goal. I turned to Anchel Reis, one of the leaders of the League of Labor Palestine in Warsaw, and his many solicitations got me a position as an observer at the Maccabiyah on behalf of both institutes. Based on this decision, though not without difficulty, I immigrated to Israel. As policy and custom dictated during those days, I changed my status from observer to immigrant once I arrived at our future country.

[Page 85]
Pinchas Hochmitz

Maccabi's Youths

Since interest in various sports was not common in the days between the two wars, the relatively limited size of the Jewish population in Wierzbnik led to a void in this field, mostly for demographic reasons. The young generation, which was swept into sportive interest and shouldered the responsibility for organization and other issues, was whittled away as people aged and lost their affinity for sports before a new generation that would replace it has matured. As a result, there was a sense of organizational and public erosion which threatened to become complete disintegration. This process expressed itself in a lack of the fundamental conditions necessary for creating a common cause. While early in 1937 you could enter the Maccabi club in Piłsudskiego Street and still see people gathered to spend their time under the Hebrew slogans on the walls, by the end of the year the ranks started to grow thin. Fewer and fewer people came to the club, interest diminished, numbers decreased, monetary resources ran out and the club was finally closed down.

The Gviazda soccer team with its central activists

A natural resource

However there were some youths who served as natural resource, and they picked up the challenge of continuing this glorious tradition. Among them were Shlomo Weisbloom, Max Najman, the Shiner brothers, Yash, Arie Najman, Binstock, young Lipstein, the youths from Piłsudskiego Street and others who could not rebuild the club's permanent standing but still showed resourcefulness. Since our house was close to the mill and had a large courtyard nearby, they turned it into a gathering place for their sportive activities. They would also leave their uniforms there, and take them before meetings and matches.

As the time passed by, these youths became more and more talented and showed an ability to face other soccer teams, among them gentile teams, a challenge which was considered "daring" at the time.

I recall one match, which drew the interest of the entire public, in which the Maccabi Youths played a "warm up" game with the S.K.S (youth) soccer team before the match between the S.K.S Starachowice team and the famous soccer team Cracovia (one of the best in the Polish national league).

Interest in the game sparked long before the match and increased as the day drew closer. But the results of the game became a widespread sensation after the Jews beat the gentiles, and the tale echoed far away, well beyond anyone's expectations.

As usual, the happiness brought by victory was tempered by a small measure of bitterness that was already the lot of Jews when competing with gentiles. At the end of the game, the gentiles would beat up the Jews regardless of the result. When they lost, they spent their anger on the

Jews and if they won, they would drink and rampage, driven by success, and express their joy by beating up Jews.

As for myself, I was already seasoned in these matters and left the stadium before the end of the game, to save myself the physical battery.

[Page 86]
Shmuel Nudelman

The "Gviazda" Sports Society

As a youth, I have joined the sports team Gviazda, under somewhat curious circumstances. To tell you the truth, I always wanted to be on the Maccabi team. I was a fan of Beitar, and Maccabi was closer to those circles than Gviazda, which ran in more leftist circles of the labor movement. However when I applied for Maccabi, I was foiled by my young age and they refused to have me. Angry and miserable, I applied for the Gviazda team, which welcomed me with open arms. It was not long before I was playing in the starting lineup as an inside left and as it happens often on the soccer field, I somehow earned the nickname "Pile". Many members of the crowd got so used to that appellation that they forgot my real name and some of them call me that to this day.

Gviazda had a big hall where both the organizational activity of the soccer team and its social and public aspects were concentrated. People would come to play ping-pong, to practice for the drama club, or just to spend a nice evening with friends and acquaintances. The Gviazda soccer team was part of the regional league and therefore had matches against teams from other towns. However the most interesting matches were the ones played by Gviazda against its local opponent, Maccabi, events referred to as a "derby".

From the field to the hospital

The game was traditionally the center of interest for sports fans, and as matches drew closer, so did tensions flare. Nevertheless, both sides always played fairly and kept from taking their ambition to extremes. Matches against the gentiles, on the other hand, had the tendency of escalating into violence.

I remember a particularly sad event from those days, when our group played a gentile team known in the area as P.K.S, which was comprised of policemen. As fate would have it, the game went in our favor and the gentiles lost 3:0, ground their teeth and plotted to take revenge on us for our triumph.

Seeing that the game was coming to a close and they had no way of changing the outcome, they engaged in outright violence. Since I did particularly well during that game, having scored three times in a row, they targeted me. At some point, and for no reason because I did not even have the ball, one of their players, a large man, closed in on me and pushed hard enough to knock me down, then stepped on my foot and broke it. The entire Jewish public was outraged by the violence and showed solidarity and eagerness to help me, regardless of association with Maccabi or Gviazda.

I was immediately taken from the field on a stretcher and after receiving first aid I was sent to the hospital. I have stayed there for a long time and was visited every day by dozens of friends and acquaintances, as well as relatives and family members. But the clearest expression of my townsmen's sympathy was sending Vigdorovich to play his violin for me and break my tedium. Fraternity and solidarity were indeed exemplary.

Gviazda put on trial

One day, something unexpected happened to the society. The police came to the home of the society's chairman, Mr. Vigdorovich, and arrested him with none the wiser. They also arrested the society's coordinator, Shimshon Brobka (I was also worried of arrest because I served as the society's secretary for a time, but they never came for me). After their arrest they were transported to the county prison in Radom. These events happened out of the blue, taking our town completely by surprise. While people wondered about the cause for these arrests, the authorities charged the prisoners with responsibility for a communist resistance among the ranks of the society. Since the authorities could not capture the actual members of the resistance, who made their timely escape (Meir Pratzovnik escaped to Russia; Israel Kerbel left for France and the third member, whose name I no longer remember, vanished without a trace), they placed the society's leaders on trial in their stead. The trial itself took place in Radom and drew the attention of many Jews, who were anxious about the fate of the prisoners. Fortunately this mockery was stopped and the falsely accused were exonerated in the absence of evidence.

[Page 88]
Yaakov Snir

The Beitar Movement

Since my father was an activist in the revisionist movement for years and our house was filled with the ideals of this movement, it was only natural for me to join it eventually. And indeed, after a brief participation in youth movements like Akiva and Zionist Youth, I joined Beitar and became a rather active member of the movement.

Our club was located next to the home of a Jew named Goldstein, and we often met there during evenings to sing, hear lectures and study the Hebrew language, Palestinography and so on.

Since most of our members were youths, we felt that contact with nature was highly important, and therefore every once in a while we went on hikes to the nearby fields, where we carried out field training and drill exercises, in pre-military fashion. We would also visit Beitar clubs in other towns, sharing knowledge and experience and establishing social relations.

We would often have ideological debates with members of other parties about the proper way of realizing the Zionist ideal, in which we each emphasized our beliefs.

Jabotinsky's visit

The movement's activities were intensive, but the passage of time erased all but those central events that left a particular impression. I remember in particular the visit of our movement's leader, Zeev Jabotinsky, to the neighboring Ostrowiec. The event was preceded by many preparations and a general awakening among our members. Many planned to go to the convention, including myself.

During those days, transportation was still in its infancy and modern vehicles were expensive and beyond the reach of youths. Several of us have therefore banded together and acquired a cart which we drove to listen to Zeev Jabotinsky's lecture.

The road was hard and tiring, and we barely got there in time. Since we were tired, we could not concentrate on the speaker's words, despite his brilliant rhetorical talent.

He opened his speech in Hebrew but after a few sentences switched to Yiddish.

The hall where the lecture took place was filled wall to wall and the masses crowded outside, because thousands of people from nearby towns came and only a few could gain entrance. Spirits were high and the audience drank the words of the speaker thirstily, interrupting him from time to time with wild cheers.

Mourning Dov Gruner

One of the movement's sacred customs was holding mourning assemblies on the memorial days of the fathers of Zionism, such as the visionary Dr. B. Z. Herzl, Max Nordau and others. However a particular event that was etched into my memory was the mourning assembly dedicated to the memory of Dov Gruner, following his execution by the British authorities.

I remember the sadness and grief that surrounded us and the particular expression of a general sense of mourning.

A symbolic coffin was placed inside the club, covered with national flags carrying the Shield of David and flanked by Beitar activists serving as an honor guard. It was an event that left a strong impression on all movement members.

Leaving for an IZL course

In adherence to the principal of realization, the movement made a goal of imparting military skills to its cadets that would serve them in times of need.

Regular military training courses were conducted, teaching both familiarity with weapons and their practical use. These courses took place according to the rules of conspiracy, but were nevertheless known to the Polish authorities, who preferred to keep the fact secret.

In 1939 I was sent along with a few other Beitar members from Wierzbnik to the area of Kielce, where a special camp was set up for this purpose by the IZL. Several of the candidates from Wierzbnik were winnowed and only two were left: Peretz Nudelman and the author.

The course took place just before the outbreak of the war and ended two days ahead of schedule, when the war started.

On my return from this course I had a chance to bid goodbye to my father, who was drafted into the Polish army, and a while later I shared a similar fate with him and my brother Avraham, a story told elsewhere in this volume.

[Page 89]
Gershon Rosenwald

The Revisionist Movement in Wierzbnik

Our city distinguished itself with its special Zionist actions and activities. There was rich and varied cultural activity to spread and instill the Zionist spirit in the hearts of the youth who were searching for an ideal for their aspirations and feelings, to strengthen the base of their existence and to continue preserving the special values of the Jewish people.

At every meeting and initiative that was connected to Zion, the Revisionists gave the word and set the tone. The bold words of the honest Zionist activist were always said through us with great pathos and candor. That is why they were always effective and convincing, so that the strongest antagonists were carried along by the enthusiasm and supported our proposals. The impact of our political work could be felt not only in Jewish circles, but the Christian milieu also related to us with respect. That is why our public appearances and gatherings were attended in such large numbers.

As early as 1930, when the Zionist local was located in Haim Dreinudel's house, the future kernel of the Beitar branch was emerging within the Zionist organization, and we were represented by two members in the general Zionist committee. At that time the leaders of Beitar were the members Beniek Slezinger, Yeshaya-Yona Scharfharz and I, the writer of these words.

The Zionist organization in Wierzbnik showed extraordinary initiative and energy in collecting money for the Israel funds, and in creating new institutions. It was really a pleasure to see how the older prominent, distinguished Jews worked with the young people, even though there were always differences of opinion between them. The goal that united everyone was constantly before their eyes. Thanks to that the misunderstandings between the Zionist groups were always minor and transitory, and were never serious, because everyone understood the will of the youth, who were constantly full of enthusiasm and dedication for the work. Thus the younger members also knew how to appreciate the work of the older members in the Zionist groupings, and always listened to what they had to say and took their advice. And so together, shoulder to shoulder, the older and younger members worked together to collect money for the Jewish National Fund, in the "shekel actions", in culture, etc.

Over time the work of the Revisionists expanded and branched out. New activity cells were founded, such as a Beitar *kibbutz-hachshara* [training farm]; the "Brit Hehayal" was founded under the leadership of Shlomo Dreinudel, the Brit Yeshurun was founded, which developed extensive activity in the religious sectors, and the emergence of "Hazhar", which was headed by the deserving Zionist activist and learned man, Yaakov Kleiner. In this way the chain of productive Revisionist-Zionist branches, which grew Stronger from day to day and gained the sympathy of the wide masses of youth, was forged.

Thus the agricultural school in Bodzentyn was festively opened, in order to prepare the Revisionist youth for husbandry and agricultural work before their *aliya*. The opening was attended by delegates from the Kielce circle, such as Avraham Lichtenstein, David Mandelbaum, Menachem Chodorowski (afterwards Savidor) and the writer of these lines. It is also very necessary to recall the fact that thirty years previously, when Haim Arlozorov was shot in Israel on a Friday night and the press reported the news on Sunday, word spread that the Revisionists were involved in the murder. And I still remember that that same Sunday, the head of Beitar, Zeev

Jabotinsky, was supposed to appear in the largest hall in Ostrowiec, which was twenty-five kilometers away from our town. Thousands of people from the entire region had prepared to go hear the great fighter and leader. The air was filled with nervousness and tension. The entire Jewish population was incensed and in a bad state of mind. Finally evening arrived, the hall was packed full, and the atmosphere was strained. There was a smell of gunpowder, and people assumed that the evening would not pass peacefully. And then the tribune Jabotinsky began his speech, and right from the start a loud shout was heard, an exclamation of "down with the Revisionist murderers." The shouter was Zadok Tennenbaum from our town. There was immediately an uproar and commotion, and the large audience wanted to react strongly, but the head of Beitar shouted out in his thundering voice: "Everyone keep quiet and calm; I agree to the cry 'down with the murderers,' may the hand of the shooter be cut off." From the start Jabotinsky had demanded controlled behavior on the part of all the members of Beitar in the hall, so as not to allow the evening to be ruined. And in fact quiet again prevailed in the large hall and the speaker gave his speech without any disturbances.

Thus in my mind's eye I see Jabotinsky's last appearance shortly before the outbreak of war, in the Philharmonic Theater in Łódź, where he expounded the evacuation plan, described the sad future awaiting the Jews and called on them to leave Poland en masse. Rich and distinguished persons sat at the head table there, and Jabotinsky warned that the storm clouds were approaching and he shouted: "leave your fortunes behind, take only what is necessary with you, save yourselves and go to Israel. Jews, I love you, and that is why you should take my advice." But unfortunately, his words were like a prophecy.

And then the Hitler wave arrived, which darkened the entire bright horizon and cut off all the shoots of devotion and belief, the sources of hope and aspiration, and tore up everything, stem and roots, and brought destruction and annihilation on everything that breathed Jewish air.

Down with the Huns and the cannibals of the twentieth century!

The *Herrenvolk* that produced such wild beasts and scurrilous murderers should be stood against the wall of infamy!

[Page 91]
Yaakov Katz

From Jerusalem of Old to "Jerusalem the Golden"

For two thousand years, Jews all over the world never ceased hoping for a return to the land of Israel. They yearned to rebuild Jerusalem and transform her into the capital of the State of Israel for the people of Israel. As she was in times past when the Temple stood. Thrice yearly, all of Israel would pilgrimage to Jerusalem with songs and dancing laden with the choice fruits of the land and leading choice sheep and cattle.

Great was the preparation for the festival pilgrimage. From all corners of the land, kinsmen would depart together and the roads and paths bustled with pilgrims. The capital prepared to meet them. The Temple candelabrum lit up the surrounding hills, the priests came out to greet the visitors, and the Levites played and sang in their honour. Great was that joy!

To our great sorrow the Temple was destroyed and Jerusalem razed and gone were the joyful years. The nation was exiled. Only the Western Wall remained to recall Israel's past glory. But for two thousand years Israel continued to long for Jerusalem and did not cease to lament her destruction.

On the same date, the night of the 9th of Ab, both the First and Second Temple were destroyed. Thus, "She weepeth sore in the night." Doubly, did Jeremiah lament, once for the destruction of each Temple. "Mine eye, mine eye runneth down with water..." The verse's repetition of the word "eye" teaches us that the shedding of tears was ceaseless, without respite. On this night, year after long year, they sit upon the ground and keep silence, "the elders of the daughters of Zion"; they have cast dust upon their heads and they have girded themselves with sackcloth. They sat, stricken and motionless on the ground as though sunken into it. During the course of the year too, at Midnight Devotions and at prayer time, with tears streaming from their eyes, they turned towards Jerusalem, to that Western Wall known as the Wailing Wall, the Wall of Tears.

As long as the heavenly Gate of Tears was not shut, it was the wall, which drew Jewish prayers. Truly, lamentation was established for all generations, "And all of Israel shall bemoan the great conflagration which Lord kindled."

Moreover, one is required to rend one's garments in mourning upon the sight of the desolate Jerusalem. For Jerusalem our sages held, the customary single rent is insufficient.

Said Rabbi Helbe, as citing Ulla of Berai, who reported to Rabbi Eleazar: One who sees the cities of Judah in their [state of] ruin, recites the verse: "The holy cities are become a wilderness..." and rends his garments. [On seeing] Jerusalem in its [state of] ruin, one recites, "Our holy and our beautiful House, where our Fathers praised thee, is burned with fire and all our things are laid waste", and rends his garment. (Moed Katan, 26).

Similarly, in the 7th chapter of the tractate of Semachot, we read the following:

"These are the rents which may not be basted [when it was done]...for the ruined Temple...on seeing Jerusalem from Mount Scopus... One who sees Jerusalem from Mount Scopus must rend, when he enters [the city] he extends the rent, and if he goes up [again to Jerusalem], he must extend it further.

We may deduce then that for Jerusalem more than one rent is required.

Through all the ages of Jewish history, since the destruction, thousands of Jews journeyed from far off lands to weep over the ruined Jerusalem, to bow before the wall and to kiss it. Aged Jews came to die and be buried in their holy soil. Even those Jews, who never saw the land, felt the love of Jerusalem, which bound together Jews scattered in many different lands. All Jews from Jerusalem all felt a special brotherly closeness. In his poem, "Jerusalem", the poet A. HaMeiri expresses his longing and outpours his soul towards the city:

Peace to you, Jerusalem
From the summit of Mount Scopus
I'll fall on my face before you.
For a hundred generations I dreamt about you,
To be privileged to behold the light of your Countenance.

Finally, finally..."Your sin is ended, daughter of Zion. He will not exile you." The State of Israel was established! Hope became a reality and Jerusalem was restored to her former eminence. As the capital of our state, she contains the Parliament, the Presidential Residence, the Chief Rabbinate, and many other institutions. Torah and learning are wreathed about her every streets. For Jerusalem is no longer in strange hands, she is wholly ours by being deeply rooted in the collective soul of the Jewish people and firmly stamped in our consciousness. Torn in half, during the battle, she returned to us completely in the whirlwind of the Six Day War. In this miraculous and wonder filled whirlwind she appeared to us suddenly. On one hand, her return seemed strange and was dimly comprehended, but one the other it felt as natural as the rejoining of a lost object with its owner. Finally, finally the words of the poet, Saul Tschernichovsky, had become a reality:

> A wanderer through all the world you will be,
> But your homeland is one,
> Forget it not...until your grave.
> Even if the day of redemption may tarry...
> Don't despair, you prisoner of hope,
> Our sun will rise...
> My people too, again will blossom forth
> On the land a new breed will arise.
> Their iron chains will they remove,
> Eye to eye will they see the light.
> The soul yearnings of 2000 years have found their fulfillment:
> Rejoice you with Jerusalem, and be glad with her,
> All you that love her.

Happy are we, who have seen the fulfillment of the 2000 year old longing for the land of Zion and Jerusalem!

Memories

[Page 95]
Reuven Shuali (Lis)

Memories

My hometown Wierzbnik was a small town in the Kielce shire in Poland, surrounded by fields, mountains and forests.

Hardworking Jews lived there, alongside gentile workers manufacturing munitions and steel, who lived separately from the Jews. Most of the Jews were simple folk, craftsmen and traders. Wierzbnik was not filled with prominent scholars or rich folk, but it residents were a dignified people, putting their trust in themselves and in God. Generations lived and died here, generations followed them and they all followed Judaism to the letter, in prayer and daily practice, in thought and in action, by caring for the needs of the family and the individual and through their extensive activism for the public – each according to his own beliefs – until the bane killed them all.

The population

About 10,000 Jews lived here during my childhood. The town was surrounded by mountains, the main residence area of the Christians (several thousands) while the rest of them lived in Starachowice, by the heavy industry buildings. The town proper featured several gentile business places, along with the only Christian church visited every Sunday by hundreds of Christians with their families.

The peasantry

The peasants mostly labored manually in the fields, plowing and manually sowing seeds taken from a large backpack hanging from the right shoulder. Harvesting was carried out with a scythe, stacking with a rake, loading with a pitchfork and the grain was taken to the yards in large horse-driven carts. The grain was beat with sticks. The daughters of the peasants also worked in the fields, loading sheaves with pitchforks. They were fair maidens, their heads covered with colorful handkerchiefs, their braided locks poking through.

The market

At the center of the town was the market, located next to the plaza in which Jermiahu the scholar and Shlomo Kopf lived on opposite ends. The buildings were all made of wood and the market was surrounded by the shops of Jewish grocers: fabrics, haberdashery, hats, iron, housework, and so on. Hundreds of families made a living from those stores and it was a place of gathering for the peasants on market days, which were Thursdays. On these days, the neighboring villagers would come to town to sell their produce and buy what they needed and the town was filled with people and their produce. Rows of carts stacked with sacks of apples, pears and plums, potatoes, carrots and beets filled the market.

The synagogue and other places of worship

The large synagogue served as the central house of worship for the people – attended by butchers, craftsmen and carters, any Jewish person. It was the first and holiest house of worship in town. Although it served as a place of worship for the lower classes, it was also a central gathering place for the entire town. Great preachers and cantors, who expected a large audience, would come to pray there. It was also attended by the members of many Shtiblach, who would come here to listen to sermons on Shabbat afternoons, The commoners, who lived a hard life of labor, were the ones who listened most intently.

A group of Zionist movement. From right to left: Reuven Lis-Shuali, Moniek Cukerman, Shmuelik Gelbard, Avraham Goldsztein, Akiva Binsztok

Talmud Torah

The Jewish children in Wierzbnik were taught by a Melamed. They studied Hebrew and the Pentateuch and Rashi with Melameds until they were thirteen and ventured into the world to make their living. Only a few, who had their hearts set on studying the Torah, migrated to Yeshivas in other cities, while others who sought higher education traveled to high schools in other towns. As time went by, the Jewish children started learning the language of the land. It was not an easy custom to introduce, because the elders objected for a long time and considered it an act of conversion... however slowly the times changed and teachers appeared, among them my father Mordechai Lis, who would take home students "for a few hours". Several schools were founded later – the Tarbut school and the Bnot Yaakov academy for Girls – but they all followed new paths of Israeli culture, whether Zionism or Yiddishism.

The Talmud Torah has always served as the place of study for poor children and it was financed by contributions from men of means, who sent their children to private Melameds and Heders but also concerned themselves with the education of the barehanded masses.

Childish acts

The children of Israel had little time for merriment in Wierzbnik, because the Heder occupied most of their days and left little room for childhood, games and joy. They fought for every moment of happiness and what was not given freely they took for themselves whenever possible.

Jewish games

The major games played among the children of the Heder were: the nuts game on Pesach and Succoth, spinning tops on Hanukah and the "koilech", that is, cards marked with letters of the Hebrew alphabet. On Purim they played with Haman rattlers and with wooden swords, and on the Ninth of Ab they would throw pegs and thorns at the prayers.

Winter pictures

The children had several joys during winter. When snow blanketed the whole town and frost glimmered on the trees, when the awnings were decorated with shimmering icicles and the windows were covered with unique flowers, the Jewish children would leave their rooms at night by the light of oiled paper lanterns, walking and singing together, squirming in the snow, throwing snowballs and skating on the ice and snow. Those who could afford it bought themselves shiny steel ice-skates, and would skate over the ice, making faces and noises, all the way to the estuary by the forest.

They would build sleighs from old crates and slide across the snow with them. They would make scarecrows out of snow, huge ones; give them eyes and moustaches of coal, glue a large nose and tails when needed, and pour water over them so they would freeze and become a solid block of lasting ice.

Acts of charity

The people of Wierzbnik pursued several charity enterprises:

You could find a donation box of Rabbi Meir Ba'al-Hanes hanging in every house, and on Shabbat the ladies of the house would put their donations into them, weeping and moaning, naming our holy Fathers and Mothers. Envoys would come from a distance with a higher calling, from the holy land and the Yeshivas in the Diaspora, and the wealthy would walk with them from house to house and collect donations for the important cause. While carrying out their mission they make lively conversation about current affairs and the envoy offers news and tells of salvation. Tales of Hassidim and miracles are also told, and most importantly, are passed by word of mouth, finding their way to the broad public.

One must mention the custom of the Yom Kipur Eve bowl, respectfully placed at the center of the synagogue table. Every Jew would consider it his duty to place his traditional donation into it.

There was a unique atmosphere to those sublime, awe inspiring moments, when the holy day was coming, with all the preparations and excitement, and the way to the synagogue was paved with charity for the needy according to the donor's ability.

The National Fund

And first among the funds is the National Fund, because its scope and popularity outweighed those of all similar enterprises. The National Fund suffused the broad public and was a kind of ritual that people believed in and dedicated time and effort to. It would start in kindergarten and continue through school, the youth movements and clubs, at public places and in private homes. Boys and girls would go from house to house to empty the boxes or collect donations into their box; they would distribute stamps and sell pictures and do other things in order to increase the donations that were meant to redeem the lands of Israel. The youths worked diligently to raise the funds and their work bore fruit.

Emergency funds

Finally I should mention the traditional acts of collecting donations for unique traditional "enterprises" such as Hachnasat Kala[1], or aiding a person who needed immediate help. And above all were those donations that people do not mention and which are given in secret – both on the part of the donor and on the part of the receiver. All those made for a rich mosaic of public activities with which our town was blessed through the years, until the terrible times came and no mercy was given when it was needed by all.

1. Providing a bride with a dowry so she can be wed

[Page 98]
M. Ben-Yehuda

On Market Days

My beloved birthplace, Wierzbnik, had none of the particular beauty or uniqueness that marked other Jewish towns and communities in the Polish Diaspora. Nevertheless, it was loved by both residents and visitors for the forests, the rivers and the lakes that surrounded it, and the liveliness of hard work, craftsmanship, production, commerce, scholarship and learning. You were full of life and youthful vigor, Zionism and pioneering, and the yearning for Zion was felt by every Jew in town. A Jewish folk, humble, religious that also battled for its existence and human rights. A Jewry saturated with yearnings and dreams of things to come, fundamental, healthy and protective of its spiritual assets.

The shoemaker   On the road

There was nothing glorious about your streets and alleys and the residences exposed the financial standings of your citizens – but we loved you just the same. You were created by your residents, your builders. You symbolized their vigor and experience. Jews lived in you for generations, raising families, rearing sons and fighting for their survival no matter the circumstances.

My heart swells when I recall you, I love and admire your Jews because of their simplicity, humility and innocence and their quiet and pure way of life, their conduct which was characterized by a wonderful harmony of nobility and endless, limitless love of Israel.

It was a hospitable town. Those refugees that came to town during the Holocaust and at other times of need, escaping the war or the hatred of the regime, were welcomed as brothers and offered protection and support, easing their sorrows and nursing their wounds. No one ever said "there is no room".

Jews resided at the center of town, both at the central square that housed the marketplace and in the nearby streets. The majority of the Polish population resided in the distant suburbs.

The majority of villagers in the area were farmers who lived off the land, workers and laborers, and most of the shops and craftsmen in town were Jews (cattle merchants, carters, tailors, cobblers, upholsterers, hatters, smiths, carpenters and so on). The town was surrounded by several lumber-mills, mostly owned by Jews, which produced lumber and plywood. The local government factories, which produced iron, copper and munitions, hired thousands of Polish workers, the majority of them Christian.

I recall the market days in town, which were something of a holiday for the Jews because they served as a major source of income. These market days, which took place every fifth day of the week, were attended by residents of the town, its suburbs and villages, some coming on foot and some by vehicle., Whole convoys would head early in the morning towards the center square, called the Rinek. On the one side were the stalls and stands of tailors, cobblers, hatters, haberdashers and renters of orchards with their produce. Across from them were huts, carts and shelves filled with produce, vegetables, fruit, milk and dairy products. Wagons laden with chickens that could be heard from a distance and sacks full of potatoes, all spread throughout the market. The town square was full of visitors and buyers and profits abounded.

The main beneficiaries of this event were the stores and bars at the marketplace, which belonged mostly to Jews and were filled with visitors who bought plenty. At the far ends of the streets, where the smithies and craftsmen were located, profits rose and the sounds of bargaining could be heard in the distance. Everyone was buying kerosene or lumber, haberdashery or groceries, clothes or food and drink. The important thing was that this day provided the Jews with a living. Only when the evening grew later would the carts hurry back through the streets and the peasants rush back each to their home. The market square emptied of its thousands of visitors and the Jews in town thanked God for this plenty.

It is all gone now. The town square probably still exists, although changed over the years, but the sounds of Jewish commerce no longer echo there, because it was inherited by Polish murderers, mourned by the prophet who said "Have you murdered and also taken possession?" Nevertheless, one cannot uproot the memories of the youth we have spent in this town until the coming of the Holocaust that made life a hell without a savior.

[Page 99]
Benyamin Weisbloom

On Holidays We Gave Out Honey and Fish

A few memories from the town of Wierzbnik, where I spent my youth and the best years of my life.

We moved to the town of Wierzbnik from Opatów, leaving behind our social, ancestral and economical roots. At first I thought we would have a hard time settling in this new place, but I was quickly proven wrong. We found friends in Wierzbnik, amicable people who were always willing to help. My father was a retailer and dealt in gristmills all his life. After my grandfather passed away, my father (and grandmother) sold the gristmill we owned in the village of Nieksholank and with the help of his family bought a gristmill in Wierzbnik. Business was not bad. We would sell the flour to bakers in town and the nearby area. There was a small fish pond by the mill, some apiaries and some fruit trees, all of which provided us with sustenance and served as gifts for friends. My father xcelled at his hobby, beekeeping. I remember that on holidays, we would give our friends honey and fish. His mother, a descendent of the Steinhardt family, was an honest housewife and took care of our every need. At the end of every Shabbat, my father's friends would gather at our house: Borstein, Pratzovnik, Yosl Unger and others. My mother would make them food for Melava Malka and they would pass the time until midnight. My sister Rivka and her 3 years old son, Pinchas, came from Opatów to live with us after her husband, Yoseph Hochmitz, has passed away. My brother Shaul, my sister Haviva and I all managed to immigrate to Israel before the war. My sister Esther and Pinchas managed to survive the Holocaust and arrived in Israel after the war, while my two brothers, Leibish and Shlomo, my sister Rivka and my parents all died in the Holocaust.

There were many youth movements in Wierzbnik. I was part of HeHalutz Hatzair and later of "Hapoel-Hamizrachi". Our desire to immigrate to Israel was great. Our youths spent the best years of their lives with no purpose. I started looking for ways to immigrate to Israel. Finally, my father managed by sheer luck to secure a certificate, and I immigrated. My father planned to send my brothers first and then come himself. But cruel fate put an end to all of our hopes and aspirations, tearing us away from our loved ones who were lost during the Holocaust among the innocent and the pure.

[Page 100]
Uri Shtramer

A Bundle of Memories

I first became acquainted with Wierzbnik in 1937, when I opened an office there as a novice lawyer. During my professional road and life, I had an extensive chance to learn more about its foundations, basis and socioeconomic structure.

The town of Wierzbnik was connected to Starachowice and its financial existence relied mostly on munitions manufactured at the big factory in Starachowice, the coal mines in the area and some agriculture. The Jews, however, took no part in the economic foundations of the town. They did not work at the munitions factory because the owners were anti-Semites and refused to employ Jews. Prolonged historic disownment also kept them from taking part in coal mining or agriculture, leaving trade and mediation as the only venues still open to them. The financial lives of the Jews in Wierzbnik were therefore similar to the lives of Jews in other nearby towns, consisting of retail and some craftsmanship.

The Jews in Wierzbnik distanced themselves from the public life of the town in general, secluding themselves within the confines of their own public life, their institutes and enterprises and the national issues that occupied the Jewish public. First and foremost among those was the national revivification movement. Most of the youths and middle aged citizens were members of various Zionist parties and movements while the older folk had an affinity for Agudath Israel.

The youths were filled with national awareness and worked wholeheartedly to realize the Zionist concept. Most prominent in town were the Zionist movements of "Hamizrachi", the socialist, revisionist Zionists. When I came to Wierzbnik I joined the Herzl Association, a faction whose position closely mirrored my own views. My first steps as a novice lawyer in Wierzbnik were not easy, because the Polish society was full of anti-Semitic sentiment and any contact with the authorities met with hostility, hampering my activity. The infamous National-Democrat Party was the main political force in town and this fact was evident everywhere I turned. They conspired against a Jewish lawyer and piled obstacles and difficulties in my path. At times, they even posted "sentries" by my office, whose job was to turn away Poles who sought my services. I did my best to overcome their persecution because I wanted to settle down there, and slowly I succeeded, thanks to the loyal and dedicated assistance of our public leaders, particularly Simcha Mincberg, Shmuel Pochachevski, Yoseph Greenhaut and Yitzhak Singer, who spared neither time nor effort to stand by me and help me during my first days. The Singer and Greenhaut households practically became second homes for me, offering me any help I needed. Romek Singer and his sisters became my close friends, offering me social support.

In 1938 the governor of our county (Starosta) ordered to disperse the community board in Wierzbnik-Starachowice and put me in charge as supervisor. This administrative step was taken because the former board failed to attend the regular needs, collecting no taxes and leaving the treasury empty and us without the means of financing necessary expenses.

Advised by the heads of the Zionist movement in town and its key activists, I accepted the appointment and immediately assigned myself the following tasks:

a. To settle the financial difficulties of the community.

b. To restore the synagogues and renovate them.

c. To hold an election for the community board as soon as possible

With the generous help of Simcha Mincberg, who worked with me for several months, we managed to "clear the field" and divide the financial burden fairly among the public using a just taxation system intended to fund the regular needs of the community.

There was an ancient synagogue in Wierzbnik, built in an old and ornate fashion. This ancient synagogue inspired awe and a sense of sanctity in its visitors when they came to spend time with their God.

Time has nevertheless eroded the exterior of this sacred building, and it was vital to renovate and renew it.

Simcha Mincberg, Greenhaut, Shmuel Tenenbaum and I initiated a collection that would serve as a source of funding for the renovation enterprise. Realizing the importance of the task, the Jewish public complied generously and allowed us to act for the glorification of the ancient, historical synagogue.

Regrettably, World War II broke out soon after, and the Nazi soldiers came and defiled the synagogue, burning it down.

Following the renovation of the synagogue, I approached my next task, which was holding a new election. I admit that I was hoping for the Zionist movements to gain priority over the orthodox Aguda circles or those who have assimilated into the gentiles, turning their back on their people and their religion and wholeheartedly accepting the edicts of the "Starosta". And indeed, the national-minded public in Wierzbnik met my expectations, properly assessing the needs of the hour. Simcha Mincberg, Shmuel Tenenbaum and Yoseph Tenzer took action at my request and put much effort into guiding and convincing the public in the right direction. Our work paid off as all the Zionist factions joined together and presented a unified Zionist list for the community board elections. As a result, the first Zionist representative was chosen for as chairman of the community board – Pochachevski.

When World War II broke out, I bid goodbye to Wierzbnik, forced to flee the advance of the German soldiers, and I never returned. After the war I no longer had the courage to come back and witness with my own eyes the terrible reality, that this entire public that I loved, cared for and bonded with, was so tragically annihilated.

Thirty years have passed since I left Wierzbnik, but carved deep in my soul are the portraits of the vibrant youths of the town, the craftsmen, the intellectuals and the commoners, who prayed "may our eyes see your return to Zion" every day, who dreamed about a life in the land of their ancestors and who were regrettably denied the opportunity to live among us and build our old-turned-new homeland, the State of Israel.

A group of youths. Seated in uniform: Yosef Cytrynbaum. Standing from left to right: Fishel Hirszhorn the son of Reb Shlomo Slopia, Yoel Komec the son of Reb Moshe, Tzvi Herblum the son of Reb Gershon and Tzipora (his story is told in the chapter "Opposition and Rebelliousness" by Tzvi Faigenbaum)

[Page 102]
Yossef Kornwasser

Fifty Years Ago

It seems to me like a dream that began in 1920.

The surrounding area and the nature around the town of my birth, Wierzbnik, were very beautiful, but the earth burned beneath my feet and every day was one too many for me. I had already been walking around for a long time with the intention of going to the Land of Israel, but the thought of leaving my dearest and most beloved parents, sisters and brothers, as well as relatives and friends, prevented me from making a quick decision. Nevertheless, the day arrived when I decided to take the bold step and I traveled to Sosnowiec, which was close to the Polish-German border, because as I had been informed, there were opportunities there to cross the border illegally.

And in fact, when I reached there, I immediately approached the address of the smuggler, which I had been given while still in Wierzbnik.

After a great deal of effort and trepidation, I managed to find this smuggler and when I reached his house I was excited to encounter another three Jews from Wierzbnik there, who had come there for the same purpose. We were immediately overjoyed that a few of us 'hometown' people had encountered each other, and we even began to plan our common future. But our happiness didn't last long, because the smuggler informed us that he was regretfully unable to take us across, because a few days previously they had caught a couple of young Jews sneaking across and had arrested them. No one knew what would happen to them, but in the meantime the guarding had been greatly reinforced that week and it was extremely dangerous to risk it. Having no alternative, with deep pain and fury I returned to Wierzbnik.

Since then I could find no rest and the thought of making *aliya* [immigrating to Israel] constantly hammered at me, and didn't leave me alone.

Suddenly I discovered that in the capital, Warsaw, a Palestine Office had been founded, which dealt with the issues of sending pioneers to the Land of Israel. As soon as I knew about this, I didn't wait long, and immediately set out for Warsaw to try and fulfill my greatest dream. This time it seemed that the prospect for solving the problem was not bad and they required that I pay a deposit on the travel fare to the Land of Israel, and that gave me the hope that I would succeed. After a few months of very tense waiting, I finally received the permit to go to the Land of Israel legally. No one could equal my great joy and enthusiasm when I learned about it.

The day come, and the happy hour arrived when I left Wierzbnik for Warsaw and reported at the large station of the capital. There I had to wait for quite a while until I was able to leave for Austria. On the train I met other Jews, who had gathered to make the same journey as I. We got off the train in Vienna and reported at the Palestine Office. From there we were sent on to Trieste, and from there we were supposed to make our way to the Land of Israel on a ship. To our joy there was no border, but unfortunately, a disappointment awaited us there. We couldn't board the ship because news had been received that the Arabs were rioting in the Land of Israel, and we had to wait because it was very dangerous.

Four Friends in a Tent

However, it didn't take long, and on a beautiful bright day we boarded the freighter Campidoagla, and thirteen days later we reached the coast of our fatherland.

I encountered the realization of my dream with great emotion, and I took everything in good part. Unexpectedly, I right away encountered a friend from Wierzbnik, who had arrived before me. It was Zvi Enisman. I joined his group and immediately received a roof over my head. It was a tent, in which four of us slept. Just then there was no shortage of work, but food was very sparse. Nevertheless, our hearts were filled with joy. We had nothing and needed nothing. Everything was permeated with hope and the enjoyment of life, until the sad news reached us about the Nazi nightmare and the sad fate of our nearest and dearest, who perished together with the millions of Jews in Europe.

[Page 103]
Yaakov Korenwaser

The Blood Libel Miracle

Neta Crystal and his family, the parents of my grandmother Sarah who was the wife of Mordechai David Kornwaser, owned the Młynek farm by Brody and were known as a hospitable couple. Many received a place to stay and something to eat at their home, as well as a gift of supplies for the road.

On Passover eve, while the family and a few dozen guests were celebrating the Seder, the grandmother went to the cabinet to take out the Kitel that Hasidim and other elect people would wear during the Seder, but instead suffered a terrible shock. Inside the cabinet was the corpse of a young shegetz. A sudden activity outside the house made the people within fearful. The grandmother quickly told the grandfather, who ordered her to keep the matter secret and tell nothing to the rest of the family and their guests, to prevent a panic. Quickly and secretly, they hid the corpse elsewhere. But where and how can you hide it when the enemies of Israel might come knocking at the door at any moment?

Without delay they placed the corpse into the big pot that was used to cook pumpkin for the many guests and the grandfather and grandmother sat down again at the table. The grandfather ordered their guests not to open the door if someone knocks on it. They sanctified the wine and joyfully and loudly told of the miracle of the Exodus from Egypt.

Loud knocks came from the door while they were reading the Haggadah, but everyone continued reading and completely ignored the knocking. The knocking got louder and was followed by shouting and banging before the door was finally forced open. Policemen entered the house with their accomplices and started searching the place. They searched the entire house until they reached the cabinet where the "victim" of their libel was to be found. But the empty cabinet left them standing stunned and gaping, and so they had to leave in humiliation, their plot foiled, after apologizing for interrupting the Passover Seder.

[Page 104]
Moshe (Michael) Samet

The Tributaries of the Wisla

When I recall the *shtetl* of Wierzbnik, I am gripped by a deep sorrow and hatred deep in my heart, which has remained with me forever.

It is hard to understand how a person can speak as I have expressed myself about my *shtetl,* in which I was born and raised, where I spent my most beautiful and happy childhood years. But I believe that my acquaintances from the town who grew up with me will pardon me, because I am certain that the same feelings that I have, have remained for many years in the hearts of more than one of us.

Thirty-seven years ago, when I was a boy of twelve, a student in the fifth grade, something occurred: it was in a geography lesson, where in the seat behind me sat a Pole called Wojciechawski. It happened during the lesson of the relentlessly anti-Semitic teacher Kozbinski.

Suddenly the teacher called out my name and demanded that I answer a question: what is the name of the place from which the Wisła flows?

I stood up and answered that the Wisła flowed from Babia-Góra in the Tatra Mountains.

The next question was: what tributaries do we have, that flow into the Wisła? For this I began to calculate that we had the following rivers: Biała, Skawa, Raba, Bug, etc. Suddenly my neighbor who sat behind me and whose name was Wojciechawski interrupted me, shouting out the following to me in a loud voice: Hey ˉid [Jew], what right do you have to list the rivers that belong to us Poles with the words "we have"; you should say "they have".

I remember it as though the picture were now in front of my eyes. My blood boiled, I turned to him in a split second and punched him right in the face with all my might. When his nose began to bleed I understood that it would not end well for me. And yes, on the spot I received five lashes on my right hand from my teacher Kozbinski, and he sent me to the principal of the school, who naturally immediately sent me home with the warning that he would not let me return to the school.

I tried to convince him and wanted to tell what had happened and that I considered myself a citizen like other Polish children, but unfortunately and regretfully, I came up against the same anti-Semite, who didn't even want to listen to me.

I left his room with my book bag, which I carried in my left hand. Then I first noticed my swollen hand – red as blood, but I felt no pain. Nevertheless, I was seething and roaring inside, but deep in my heart I felt content and satisfied at having defended myself.I tried to justify myself. And thinking thus all the way, I opened the door of my house.

My mother, of blessed memory, stood frozen and white as chalk; my father, of blessed memory, opened his eyes wide in amazement at why I had suddenly come home during school hours. And looking at my worried parents, I began to regret the step that I had taken. Nevertheless I controlled myself and began to tell them the sorry truth, from the beginning to the end.

I looked, and my mother, of blessed memory, was crying silently inside and all the blood gathered in my father's face, and at that moment I thought that he would immediately attack me in all his anger, but that didn't happen. He quietly said the following words to himself: "This is the fate of our Jewish people, which is fragmented and dispersed throughout the world." Turning to me he added: "That is how your grandfather, of blessed memory, suffered, that is how I suffered and that is how you and your future children will suffer. We can do nothing to protect ourselves against this, because we are in the Diaspora."

At that time I thought that I understood that moment very well, although I was not yet an adult.

Later on, thanks to the fact that my father, of blessed memory, had many acquaintances in Polish circles and institutions, after great effort and running around he managed to get the school principal to allow me to attend the school.

This sad episode from my childhood engraved itself in my memory and aroused in me an enmity towards the Poles and the city of my birth, where I lived until the Nazi forces marched into the city. Shortly thereafter, having suffered the occupation of the murderous and barbarous Germans, I fled to the Soviet Union.

[Page 106]
Levi Brodbeker

We Baked Matzahs for Passover

I recall many events and important social activities when I think about specific memories of our *shtetl* Wierzbnik.

Because of the time that has passed, it is difficult for me to collect my thoughts and provide a survey of the history of the Jewish population, nevertheless, I consider it necessary to recall and emphasize two important good deeds from different periods that have a characteristic general significance and provide a special reflection of the expansive, blessed good-heartedness and the great sense of mutual assistance that were an integral part of many of the Jews of Wierzbnik.

A Permit to Bake for Passover

In 1917, during WWI, the rabbi of our community, was Rabbi Yaakov-Aharon Regensberg, of blessed memory, a son of the Dobrów rabbi, a great scholar and someone who knew how to take responsibility upon himself in certain situations, and also the proper decision.

I remember that it was the time of Passover when a train filled with Jewish soldiers from Austria suddenly arrived, and it was feared that because of the shortage of matzos the Jewish soldiers would be forced, Heaven forbid, to eat food not kosher for Passover. So he issued a permit to bake matzos during Passover. The Jewish population accepted this with great understanding and joy and set to work, so that the Jewish soldiers celebrated the holiday according to all the rules and regulations.

A Wagonload of Coal

In 1928 there was a very harsh winter in Poland and the cold was extreme, so that there was a threat of families freezing to death because they didn't have the means to obtain wood or coals to warm their homes. Consequently, a group of Jews from Mszczonów and others organized a campaign to bring a wagonload of coals and distribute it among the poor classes. The campaign for this charitable act was headed by Haim Broitbeker, Shlomo Broitbeker, Fishl Neiman (who was know as Fishl Manche's), my father, may he rest in peace, and others.

I have cited these two episodes to stress the fact and remind us all from where we stem and with what humanitarian values, virtues and way of life our parents raised us.

May their communal and individual acts serve us as an example and their way as a model for an honest and straightforward way of life. May it be the honorable perpetuation of their holy memory.

[Page 107]
Zvi Faigenbaum

The Hebrew Midwives

Matil Konigsberg, commonly known as "di alta shohatin", was a rare character, not only among the town's women but also outside the community.

An intelligent, skilled and experienced woman, she showed maternal affection for all. Many of the girls in town turned to her for advice, and she never turned them away.

Matil came to Wierzbnik from Ostrowiec, marrying Mordechai after the loss of his first wife. Her virtues and her dignified appearance quickly earned her the respect of the fine girls in town. In those days there was no maternity clinic in town, the newborn baby saw his home and residence as soon as it emerged into the world and the midwife was the one who reached out to comfort it when it finally decided that it deserved more spacious quarters and greater freedom.

Our community had two Hebrew midwives, one of them being the wife of Chaim Hersh and the other was "di alta shohatin". Both did their work dutifully, but di alta shohatin was more prominent due to her personality and her status as a kosher butcher's wife. Publicly recognized as a noble and enterprising woman, she came and went through the homes of such wealthy families as Lichtenstein, Mysliborski, Singer and so on, and the ladies of these privileged families did nothing without first consulting her when it came to matters of motherhood and raising children.

In addition to her role as midwife, Matil also provided assistance when a child broke or dislocated his limbs. Those who came to her pained and sad left feeling content and calm. She also knew how to ward off the evil eye with spells, and those who came to her upset left happy.

Even in her old age, when she was living with her son, Rabbi Yitzhak Meir, she remained a lively woman, assisting in the delivery of a triplet without the aid of a doctor at the age of 90.

Matil the midwife passed away of old age when she was 93, her reputation spotless and her town filled with the children that were delivered by her dedicated hands.

God bless her memory.

[Page 108]
Moshe (Michael) Samet

The Drama Society

The town's size and population were both too small to provide its citizens with their own theatre. This held true for the entire settlement, let alone for the Jewish community which numbered fewer than 3,000 souls. Nevertheless, the Jewish community never lacked for cultural activity and has not neglected dramaturgy either.

Fate, however, has decreed that my memories of this aforementioned activity, that is, the existence and activity of the drama society, would be tainted by a very dramatic and tragic event.

The Drama Club. Standing left to right: (--), Gucha Tencer, Miatek Wajgszperg. Seated from left to right: Rivka Lajbenszaft (nee Milman), Chana Sencer, Natsha Cirinska, Mondel Halsztejn, Fela Szarafharc, Yudik Ziskind, and Chaim-Yosef Milman

A brick to the head

I was drawn to the drama society since youth and started actively participating in it when I was older. The society was coached by a kind and pleasant man who put both his time and money into this public affair for no personal gain. He came early to rehearsals to prepare for the arrival of the cast, and he was the last to leave the club, noting down his impressions of the rehearsal.

One day, on his way back home from the society, while he was passing Piłsudskiego Street, he was hit in the head by a falling brick and fatally wounded. All efforts to save him have failed and the man passed away.

This despicable murder, which was maliciously plotted by anti-Semites, greatly enraged the Jewish community, while the authorities perfunctorily claimed that they cannot prosecute anyone because there was no proof that this act was a premeditated murder.

Wandering Stars

The clubhouse of the drama society was located in the backyard of the Unger Family (Pola Unger), where we met during the evenings, 15-20 guys and girls of various ages. We were highly enthusiastic about our work, and our efforts bore fruit. Every few months we put on a play at the firefighters' lot (next to the police building), which was always packed with people curious to see the "actors", whom they knew in real life, as well as the play itself.

Among the many shows we put up I remember "The Witch of Castile", by Shalom Ash, and particularly "Wandering Stars" by Shalom Aleichem, which was quite successful.

The club we rehearsed in also had a library and those who came early could spend time with a book or a newspaper, soaking up some culture. The outbreak of the war, which soured the atmosphere in town, has also naturally put an end to the society's activities.

Only memories remain.

[Page 109]
V. H.

Kupat Cholim

The institute that provides medical help for the needy must stem from such foreign institutes as the German KrankenKasse or the Polish Kasa Chorych, or else it would have been called "medical help society" or something of the sort.

But in terms of form, content and essence it should be noted that despite the great gap which existed between the Jewish and Christian populations, and all the ramifications and the affinity to various institutes, Kupat Cholim was among the few institutes which featured impeccable cooperation between these two communities.

In our town, Wierzbnik, this institute was even more unique because it resided in a house owned by a Jew, Pinchas Helstein, who owned a large store on the bottom floor while the top floor housed the Helstein family and the office of the Kasa Chorych.

The landlord, who currently resides with us in Israel, tells us that the Kasa Chorych was full of Jews every day of the year, although the majority of clients were Christians, workers at the weapons and munitions factories found mostly in Starachowice, the industrial part of town.

There were no Jewish doctors in the Wierzbnik Kasa Chorych, but the Polish doctors treated the Jewish population with all fairness, a fact worthy of note in light of the typical hostility of the Polish population towards the Jews of the town, a sentiment also common in other towns in the Polish kingdom.

We particularly recall a doctor named Borkovski, who can easily be numbered among the Righteous Gentiles. This doctor, a surgeon by profession, was kind, pleasant and helped people even at the risk of his social standing and more.

At the end of the war he saved a Jewish girl, the daughter of Shlomo Enisman, who was shot by Polish partisans – murderers from the A.K. gangs who pretended they were fighting the Germans but mostly murdered Jews. The girl suffered a supposedly "fatal" wound at the hands of the A.K. criminals, who left her for dead. Though she was still alive, she was mortally wounded and it was a miracle that she was saved by some villagers who found her. They brought her to doctor Borkovski, who took care of her dutifully. Although the A.K. has sent him threat letters, he ignored them until she was well once more.

[Page 110]
Moshe Sali (Kerbel)

From Wierzbnik to Israel through the Paviak Prison

The State of Israel was nothing more than a dream during those days, and the Law of legislated in the independent State of Israel, affording any Jew the right to immigrate to Israel and become a citizen, was something we never imagined even in our wildest dreams. Reality back then was much more "prosaic", grey, and hard, full of difficulties and obstacles. Earning an immigration certificate and immigrating to Israel were as difficult as parting the Red Sea. I have shared these concerns from the moment I aspired to immigrate to Israel, and had to go through much hardship and trouble before I could see the gate open before me.

Following the events of 1929, the desire to immigrate intensified and the youth movements and training kibbutzim bubbled and gushed with youths eager to join the warriors and builders in Israel. The British government, however, closed the gates to the country and would only offer a small number of certificates for immigration purposes, making an immigration certificate a great and invaluable prize.

It is no wonder that as an activist in a youth movement and the first swallow of our town I was told that I may immigrate by myself (without a fictitious wife, as was customary in those days) and I was a happy man when all I had left to do had to go to the Israeli Office in Warsaw, the capital of Poland, and settle the formalities concerning my future journey.

However a rueful experience stood like a demon between me and that goal, and even recalling it today sends a shiver down my spine.

It was a typical summer's day. The city was noisy, as always, a mass of people heading about on business, the street filled with the roar of engines and the neighs of horses harnessed to carriages (Piakers). The stores were filled with goods, the shop windows glittered, and I, according to the customs of the pioneers of that time, was striding in the streets of Warsaw wearing my Rubashka embroidered in our national colors, cerulean and white, headed for the Israeli Office. And although my thoughts were centered on this turning point in my life and the issues I will be facing, my natural curiosity drove me to observe the big city surrounding me, because such a visit was a rare privilege for me. Suddenly, as if arranged for the sake of the visitors and the curious, I walked into a leftist-communist protest march, organized by a group commonly referred to at the time as The Three Ls because they identified with leaders whose names started with the letter L: Liebknecht, Luxemburg and Lenin.

As the protest approached me, I stood on the sidewalk and watched the protesters. There was plenty to hear and see... the protesters made a lot of noise, cried out revolutionary slogans, and occasionally sang songs which were interrupted by shouts and loud announcements, all the while marching down the street carrying banners and flags, while sympathizers and curious bystanders stood on both sides of the street and watched – passerby such as myself.

Suddenly, the police have arrived and fell upon the protesters, trying to scatter them. Brawls broke out and the policemen used mixed methods, alternately beating people up and arresting them. The street became a human maelstrom and we were all mixed together, the people marching on the street and those who stood on the sidewalk becoming a single solution. The policemen grabbed anyone they could get their hands on, and in the process, caught me as well.

Taken into custody in the Defensiva

I was led with all due respect into the motor vehicle known as "Defensiva" and along with the others who shared my fate I was transported to a renowned prison in town to be interrogated.

When we reached the prison we learned that the "crop" indiscriminately harvested by the police was rich indeed. Hundreds of people stood crowded in the yard, and it took hours of waiting before our cases were even addressed. Finally, when our patience was beginning to wear thin, they started calling us in one by one for interrogation on the third floor of the building.

I went up the stairs feeling strange, like a stranger at a party. When I entered the room I was facing a large rectangular table, behind which the sat senior police officers, while spotlights were directed into my face, blinding me to the point of breakdown. The interrogation started with a question regarding my presence at the protest site. I told them that I was an innocent passerby and that I was brought there by mistake. To support my claims, I added that I was a member of the HeHalutz movement, intent on immigrating to Israel, and that I came to arrange my immigration – "and here are the documents supporting my claims," I said, removing the papers from my bag and placing them on the table.

Unfortunately my words fell on deaf ears. Not only did they refuse to listen to me, but the officers who stood around me with whips at the ready started whipping me, despite my protests.

They bombarded me with questions, all at once, confusing me. Each of them threatened me and demanded that I answer him, and if I answered one another took offense, giving them excuse to hit me again and again.

In the process they snatched my bag and started rummaging through my papers in excitement, occasionally making surprised but satisfied remarks such as "quite the bird we got here" or "that's a fat trout we caught ourselves".

Flustered by their cruel attitude, I was beginning to fear for my future.

Hanging upside down

When I saw how enthusiastic the policemen were with their false "discovery", and having already suffered through their violent actions, I began to imagine untold horrors about to befall me. I tried to no avail to overcome this depressing sensation, and tears welled in my eyes.

When they saw me cry, the policemen changed tactics. The stick was replaced by a carrot – as if they wanted to calm me down. However as soon as I recovered some of my wits, they resumed their former course of action and demanded again that I tell the truth, threatening me with even greater abuse.

My fears came to pass. Without another word, I was pulled into another room and strung upside-down.

Apparently I have not remained in this position for long, because 10 minutes later I passed out.

Nevertheless, my suffering was far from over and although I was near death, the policemen kept beating me even while I was hanging unconscious. Perhaps they thought to revive me in this manner, but when their savagery failed to achieve the desired result, they took me down and doused me with a bucket of water. This method also failed them, because I could not lie to them when they demanded that I tell them "the truth".

It would seem that other innocent people dragged there suffered the same fate I did, and so finally, the policemen decided to transfer me. We were told to go out to the yard, where a car was already waiting for us to climb into. However merely entering the car was too easy in the eyes of the inhuman policemen, and they shoved the prisoners and whipped us left and right, banging heads and wounding other body parts until the very last moment when the car started moving.

Where? They answered: to the infamous prison, Paviak.

There was no delay this time before we were placed in a dark cell that was already full of other prisoners. The cell was typically small – 2x2 meters – and the 12 prisoners in it made it unbearably crowded. It was impossible to even lean, let alone to sit. We were forced to stand.

At the top of the wall, near the ceiling, was a small hatch that let in a bit of sunshine that made it possible to see other people. Those were the "veteran" prisoners, most of them criminals, men of the underworld whose faces and expressions attested their "social standings".

Wearied by the events of the day I was too tired to stand and since I was unable to sit I tried to find something to lean against, but I could not reach the wall because the place was too crowded.

People suddenly started talking to me in Polish, and even in Yiddish. They asked me what brought me there, but when I told them what happened they disbelieved me. "Don't lie in here!" they thundered at me, hinting that there are rules to be honored "among thieves". But after repeating the facts again and again, I managed to convince them and they left me alone.

During our conversation we started to get used to the situation somehow, and I asked them why they were incarcerated. I received a detailed list of common crimes such as murder, manslaughter, rape and so on, as well as the appropriate sentence – 10, 15, 20 years and so on.

Helped by Urke Nachalnik

They were mostly interested to know if I had any money. I told them I didn't, even though I hid some guldens in my sandals for emergencies. Knowing that I came from "outside", they refused to leave me alone until I revealed my secret, saying that I only had enough for cigarettes. My honest plea failed to impress them. They took every coin I had and one of them beat me up on the spot. I started crying in despair and was approached by one of the Jewish prisoners, who whispered to me that I should lodge a complaint with the "cell leader". I did as he told me and reported to a middle-aged looking prisoner who was easily distinguished from the rest, since he was the only one who had a mattress... he was also addressed by everyone with the title "doctor". I didn't know whether this nickname was a result of vast scholarship or attendance of a university, but perhaps it had nothing to do with education in the first place. At any rate, I followed the example of others and turned to him with my story. He listened attentively without interrupting me and then called the prisoner who slapped me and judged him on the spot, carrying the sentence out himself by beating up the gentile and chastising him, saying "this is a friend of ours and may not be beat up".

As for the money that was taken, it became public property... but since I told them that I had some guldens for cigarettes they dedicated the money to the purchase of cigarettes, distributed by the cell leader among the prisoners.

This development taught me that at the very least my life was not completely forfeit and there was someone to protect me from the cruelty of the anti-Semite prisoners. I later found out that the man was the famous Urke Nachalnik.

Prison routine

I started settling into the prison routine. Looking around me, I began to see the typical characteristics of a prison. I saw the degeneration and the pressure people were in, I smelled the terrible stench from the indoors toilet in the cell, heard the secret language of the prisoners who tapped it on both sides of the wall and having no choice in the matter, settled into the social circle of prison life. And quite the literal circle it was, to be sure.

"Every person has his follies and every society its habits," as the saying goes, and that includes customs, traditions, games, and so on. The inmates in prison also have their own traditional customs and typical games. One such game that I was forced to partake in was called "the circle". Everyone forms a circle and one by one the prisoners have to walk along it, allowing other prisoners to kick them. You can imagine the state in which a person leaves such a game, particularly a novice like myself who didn't know how to protect himself and cover his vulnerable parts, but I had no choice. If I failed to partake in this game they would have hounded me every step of the way. I later found out that this game was an initiation that every new prisoner had to go through and it was set up especially for me...

As time went by, new prisoners were put in the circle occasionally while I, already one of the "veteran" residents, took an active part in the game (and not passively as before).

Set free by Yitzhak Grinbaum and Anchel Reis

While I was gone from my home and town, my acquaintances were searching for me in all manner of places because they knew where I went and for what purpose. Finally, they managed to locate me. In the process, they discovered that I was not the only one to disappear, and that others were swallowed by the city during the protest, captured and locked up like myself.

Representatives of my youth movement have therefore approached the leaders of our movement – Yitzhak Grinbaum and Anchel Reis – asking them to contact the authorities and arrange our release. It seems they had significant influence, because we were released within 48 hours from the moment they took action.

A jailor came into my cell early in the morning, calling my name. When I answered, I was told to come with him. The prisoners asked "Is he coming back?" and the jailor told them I was, otherwise they would have beaten me up according to their custom. Instead, he told them I was being taken for interrogation.

I followed him through long corridors and into a locker room where the clothes of the prisoners were kept, and received my clothes back. I checked my possessions and found that some things were missing, but I thought it was pointless to argue over. We went into a large hall where Yitzhak Grinbaum and Anchel Rice waited for us, and they took us to the Israeli Office where our papers were arranged on the spot. Two days later I immigrated to Israel.

[Page 113]
Yoseph Citrinbaum

A Compilation of Memories from Wierzbnik

When I was still a little boy, my family moved from the big city of Lodz to the quiet town of Wierzbnik. At first, I was enrolled into the Heder of Moshe Dan and later I studied under Zelikel, who was known at the time for his use of modern teaching methods, such as self-instruction. He made students study together, pairing an advanced student with a weak one and giving them the freedom to study all manner of sources and interpretations – MaHaRSha, Tzlach, Maharam and so on (difficult questions and arguments). He hardly interfered with our studies, merely overseeing the students. He would go from class to class, listening and observing, and tended to rub his hands in satisfaction when he was pleased with a correct answer.

Thursdays were our judgment days, as the testers quizzed us on what we studied during the week. Among them were learned scholars such as Mordechai Rotenberg's son-in-law, Welwl (who made us all quiver), Itche Meir the kosher butcher, Jechiel Pszytycki, Yankel Mandelzis, and Zvi Wajzer.

We were overjoyed when the renowned philanthropist Heller arranged for us to have classes on weekdays. The teacher Yitzhak Meir Melman came from Apta and for the first time we studied Hebrew and Polish. This teacher was a dignified Jew with a long flowing beard, well versed in his calling. On Hanukkah he organized a public test night at the great Beit Midrash, which was filled with people. He tested us one after the other: one student asked the question and another answered. The test started off easy, with the first grade students, and concluded with our class, the most advanced. At the end of the test we received prizes from Neta Kornwaser, the head of the board and the most dynamic activist.

Society and establishment

The town of Wierzbnik continued to develop, growing and expanding, following the growth and flourishing of the industry in Starachowice which affected the growth of the town as a whole.

Various institutes formed; the first and only Jewish bank in town was founded, under the management of Simcha Mincberg, providing great help to the merchants in town.

New houses were built, mostly in and around Starachowicka Street. A major part of Poland's iron industry (manufacturing the great Stalownia ovens from raw materials, as well as heavy weapons and the Prochownia gunpowder), its factories employed thousands of workers who worked two continuous shifts, naturally resulting in the quick growth of the town. The population grew as well, affecting the evolution of cultural and social life. The Tarbut School was founded, its classes taught by the excellent teacher Lupta, from Vilna. The political organizations filled with lively youths. Among the organization founded were the Jewish Organization, Mizrachi Youths, HeHalutz, the Aguda, Beit-Yaakov and later P.A.I, the craftsmen organization, and sports organizations such as Maccabi and Hapoel, which were active in various sports fields and even dared to challenge Polish sports organizations.

The Zionist Organization organized questions and answers nights, initiated by chairman Moshe Birenzweig, during which the members of various political associations – Zionist Youth, Bund, radical left – engaged in ideological and literate debates, while conducting themselves in a civil manner.

Wierzbnik was represented by all manner of Hasidic Shtiblach. The Jews also took part in the management of town affairs. They were members not only of the town council but also the town administration. Yoseph Dreksler and Simcha Mincberg were practically its permanent representatives, representing the Jews of Wierzbnik in a dignified and proud manner and protecting their special interests.

Dark days

However our town was not spared times of woe.

The event in question took place on Succoth eve. We were shocked to learn of the arrest of dignified activists of the merchants' organization: Neta Kornwaser, elderly Chaim Zajfman, Yaakov Kornwaser, Shmuel Isser and the community secretary Mordechai Lis. Despite our pleas to the town's authorities, they were marched through the streets to the train station in chains on the first day of Succoth and sent to the prison in Radom. This event turned out to be the result of a provocation by a county bureau clerk who framed them.

It took the town a long while to recover from this harsh blow.

Zionism and immigration

And thus the town grew and developed and so did its youths, who thirsted for knowledge. Some left for the big cities, to study in high schools or Yeshivas as well as to "train" for immigration to Israel. The youths, who saw no future for themselves in the Diaspora, waited many years for the chance to immigrate. Sadly, many of them never fulfilled their lives' dream. Some accepted the situation – perhaps temporarily – and settled for the time being in Wierzbnik, waiting for a chance to immigrate as well.

I would like to mention here one of the great fellows who lived in Wierzbnik, our good friend Yoel Kumetz. He joined our group along with my friends Fishel Hirschhorn and Hershel Herblum, nicknamed the eternal purple.

Yoel was a scholar, a genius quick of wit but also as humble as they come. Despite his youth, he was a man of Torah. His thirst for knowledge led him to spend days and nights reading, and he was lively, keen and energetic. His eyes burned with wisdom and a will to live. He mastered Hebrew and Polish quickly and had a rich vocabulary, drawing of course from the Bible and Talmud.

The letters he wrote to me while I was in the Polish army (some of which I still have) are a small remnant of his great spiritual wealth, which was yet to be fully developed and revealed. But he fell as quickly as he rose. He trained for potential immigration at the Sobaków kibbutz, but was killed in his prime and never lived to fulfill his heart's desire. It was at that time, during the early 1930s, that a few of the town's residents, among them my dear parents, rose, as if out of an inner urge, and fulfilled their dream of immigrating to Israel. They closed their businesses and immigrated, along with their families. Many were jealous of them for having the courage to make this bold move, but many misunderstood them and expressed their dismay.

Anti-Semitism and pogroms

The situation in Poland during those years was harsh in terms of both financial and personal security. A wave of rampant anti-Semite pogroms was raging around Poland at the time, led by the infamous lady doctor Pristor. The atmosphere turned ugly and pogroms took place in Przytyk, Przysucha and elsewhere, but the residents of Wierzbnik felt that "nothing could happen here". After all, our town was filled with modern workers. Unfortunately, the horrors of the Holocaust applied to Wierzbnik just the same and the community and its Jews were swallowed by oblivion. Wierzbnik, formerly a magnet for Jews in the area, near and far, was left empty of Jews. This town, which was saturated with a lush and fundamental Judaism, fell silent and vanished. Hardly any survived; a few members of each family.

I am reminded of a few righteous and honest people who walked among us: Chanoch Biderman, a wonderful Hasid who studied the Torah day and night, a humble and noble man; Yeshayahu Guterman, Moshe Tenenbaum, and the great scholar Rabbi Mendel Tenenbaum; Moshe Pinchas Lichtenstein, a generous and noble man who was among the town's dignitaries – all of them scholars, merchants, distinguished men of means.

The central town square (Rinek) was a vibrant commercial center, surrounded by Jewish stores and business places. And who can forget the great courtyard of Mysliborski, which was home to such town dignitaries as Itche Singer, Shmuel Kleiner and the Kornwaser, Dreksler, Brodbeker, Drajnudel, Rubinstein, Lis, Zukerman and Frimerman families, all of them among the pillars of our community.

I would also like to mention the Rabinowicz family, whose young son was the first victim shot in his store by an anti-Semite rioter.

Dear Jews of Wierzbnik, may the dirt be swept from your eyes. You, who were silenced without cause. May God avenge you. Your memories shall live on in our hearts.

[Page 115]
Yitzhak Kerbel

The Carousel

The arrival of the carousel, built in the courtyard by the old school, in front of the home of the Bernek family of tinsmiths, was a great event, practically a holiday for the entire town.

The carousel became the center of life and interest for children, youths and even adults. It was not one of the elaborate, electricity-powered carousels we have today, and required people to climb up a ladder and push it around and around. Ten children were required to move it, and for every five turns of the carousel they received a reward – a ride of their own on the carousel.

There was no shortage of candidates among the children and the only problem was escaping the Heder to do this "holy work". And here is our tale: A bunch of us were pupils of Shlomo Shenner, and we agreed one day to escape during recess, go push the carousel and then receive our free ride.

Unfortunately for us, our plot was discovered and our angry Melamed and his special cane paid a visit to the carousel.

As soon as we sat down, some on horse and some in cart, and the carousel started to move, our Melamed popped out of nowhere and whack! Raised his cane and smacked each kid passing him by on the carousel. And I dare you to try and jump off the carousel while it picks up speed with every turn.

Pork

This incident happened to me during my days in elementary school. During recess, I was approached by the shegetz Yozef Sobicinski, son of a butcher and pork seller, who stuffed a piece of pork into my mouth. As a Jewish boy from an orthodox household, it was only natural that I felt shame and humiliation, and in front of dozens of Jewish and Polish kids no less. I was not a very strong boy but I was driven by fury, and to this day I wonder where I got the strength to knock down such an ox of a shegetz and beat him bloody.

This event naturally came to the attention of our principal Toznik, who was a notorious anti-Semite, and often made disparaging remarks about the Jews.

We were called into his office to clear things up, but instead he directed a venomous question at me: "Are Jews beating up the Poles in Poland now?"

That was the extent of the discussion, and nothing I said helped. I was sentenced to a flogging, which I still felt for many days.

Nevertheless, in the aftermath of this event no shegetz dared raise his hand on a Jew at school, and clearly I became a hero to the Jewish students.

[Page 116]
Moshe Sali-Kerbel

Memories of my Home

The distance of time and the weight of the long years since I left my home have blurred and dimmed not a few of the experiences and events of my childhood and youthful years. Many of them have actually been forgotten. Nevertheless, I have firmly decided to do everything I can to gather together and exhaust every kernel of my past memories that can shed light on life in the home of my parents, from which I drew my desires and longing for the land of our fathers.

It was a home with deep roots and a rich tradition, a thoroughly Jewish home with an abundance of light, faith and warmth.

My father – was a scholarly and learned Jew, with a sharp mind, a refined pen and a well of knowledge. He was, in fact, an adjudicator and arbitrator, a "smoother out" of disputes between partners and competitors in matters of trade and commerce. Many people used to come to him for advice, begging for counsel. He was very popular and respected by everyone. His quick-wittedness and analytical ability paved his way to being at the head of the circles with which he came into contact. His appearance among Gentiles was that of a proud Jew with a straight back, whether it was on matters of taxes or business. He was an outspoken man of letters and the Book of Books never left his hand. He used to look into it at every opportunity. He especially loved "the holy language" and he made an effort to ensure that we would also be infected with this love for it. He was inundated with the best cultural and educational values, modest in day-today life, with admirable behavior and ways. The Bible and the Talmud, books by Hassidim and Maimonedes' *Guide for the Perplexed*, the *Kuzari* and the Hebrew newspaper *Hatzfira* and the monthly journal *Haolam* and the yellowed with age pages of *Hashiloah* – all found their place under one roof, and lay next to each other.

More than once, when he felt bad, expressions of his feelings would come tumbling out of his mouth, either poetry or humming Hebrew songs to himself. I drank from these springs like a thirsty man and absorbed the eternal values of the oppressed and beleaguered Jewish people.

I remember how on Sabbath afternoons students from the schools used to come to our house to let my father hear what they knew in the Bible or the Talmud, in order to receive a sign of approval from an expert and authority, from a literate and scholarly man, who was also knowledgeable in the ways of the world.

He suffered greatly when the dreadful period of destruction arrived, but he bore the torment with superhuman courage, and he always knew how to adapt himself to the conditions and limitations of the time. He aroused admiration with his animation and he struggled with his bitter fate. He bore his fate with stoic tranquility and with faith and complete awareness, with no illusions about what was decreed and what awaited him.

My Mother – She was the soul of the house and its heart. She was the epitome of warmth, feeling, love and modesty. An abundance of softness and gentleness shone from her entire being. She was humble and modest in all her ways. The family framework filled her entire life. Limitless devotion, an extraordinary love for her children, her house – those were her attributes. All heartaches, all sicknesses were reflected in her face. She was a real "Jewish mother", in the loftiest meaning of the word. Despite the distance between parents and children, she understood us and loved us dearly – and we, the children, paid her back in the same coin – with limitless love.

She was "a woman of valor", i.e. a capable woman, and her hands were always busy with work. She didn't know what it meant to rest, to be unoccupied or to take a break from work. From dawn until late at night she washed and cleaned, cooked, sewed and kept busy – she was an utterly dear mother and a wonderful housewife. It wasn't all that simple to raise children and to run a home expansively – and she did everything herself, worry about everything and everyone, big, and small. However, she never complained, even at the hardest times she knew how to hide her sorrow deep in her heart and suffer silently. The beautiful face of our dear and beloved mother, on Sabbaths and holidays, when everything shone from cleanliness and beauty, and everyone's heart was filled with joy – was like restoration for her deep motherly feelings and for her soul.

Although the roots of my parents' life were in the Diaspora, they loved the Land of Israel of the wonderful past, the Holy Land, the land of our fathers and mothers, the land of longing, of the *Maarot Hamachpela*[1], Rachel's Tomb and the Western Wall – just like it was told in the stories of the Bible.

The life of the Jews and of the family found their fullest expression on the Sabbath and on the Jewish holidays. How pleasant and uplifting these holidays in the bosom of the family were. How much beauty, warmth and joy the Sabbath brought every week. All the preparations and all the weekdays were like a corridor, to receive the Sabbath Queen. And the Sabbath was bathed in a halo of light and heavenly festivity that cannot be described in words – a sort of cult of holiness. There was a feeling of renewal, all the lamps were lit and the candles in the silver candlestick spread a streaming light throughout the whole house. Going to prayers and saying "Shalom Aleichem" and "Woman of Valor"[2] with a sweetly pleasant melody, and then the Kiddush and sitting around the beautifully set table, with the special Sabbath foods and the beautiful dishes made of real porcelain. We all felt like "royalty", like free men – free of all worries. And on the Sabbath morning – the celebration of the "*shalosh seudot*" [three meals – which it was obligatory to eat on the Sabbath], and the Sabbath songs and reading the holy books – and then came the *Havdala* ceremony [to separate the Sabbath from the rest of the week], which separated the sacred from the profane, and the "*Melaveh Malka*" meal [the last meal on the Sabbath, to accompany the Sabbath queen] together with the Hassidim of the Aleksandria rabbi. All this contained such a wonderful completeness and faith in Divine Providence, and in the mission of the Chosen People.

The Passover holiday was distinguished by extraordinary beauty. The preparations for this holiday went on for weeks, the house was truly turned inside out; the dishes were made kosher with boiling water, matzos were baked, and then the "search for leavened food" with the light of a candle [on the day before Passover], cleaning it up and selling it, and then came the main event: **the Seder evening**. The plate with *haroses* [mixture of fruit, nuts and wine, symbolically eaten at Passover] and bitter herbs and the bone, Elijah's cup, together reading the *Haggada* with the special melody, the Four Questions, asked by the youngest son, opening the door to let out the Lord's wrath, and the table that was prepared according to custom and was filled with delicious Passover dishes, with *kneidlech* [matzo balls] – and the wonderful story of the Exodus from Egypt was recited until late at night.

And the same was true for the other holidays – Lag Baomer – bows and arrows, Shavuot and dairy foods, Simchat Torah and dancing with the Torah scroll, every child with a flag and with great joy in their hearts, and stories about the heroism of the Maccabees; at Hanukah – latkes, games with the *dreidl* [top], Purim – wonderful masks, "*mishloach manot*" [exchanging goodies with the neighbors], *Hamantaschen* [triangular filled cookies], the noise of the rattles whenever Haman's name was mentioned, and the reading of the Book of Esther. At Succoth – engaging in the construction of the *sukkah*, dragging branches and decorations, ribbons and brightly-colored lanterns, purchasing a beautiful *etrog* [citron] and a kosher *lulav* [ceremonial frond composed of palm leaves, willow and myrtle]. The deep emotion and sacred preparations for Rosh Hashana and Yom Kippur [the Day of Judgment] are indescribable – selecting the "*kapparot*"[3] – a white rooster for the head of the family and white hens for the women. The trembling during the "ten days of repentance" [between Rosh Hashana and Yom Kippur] and traveling to the rabbi in Aleksandria or to the Ostrowec rabbi – all with deep, earnest faith, with great joy of life. Every holiday and

Sabbath were like a new occasion in themselves, which created extraordinary stimulation and excitement in us children.

Who can relate and describe the richness of the unforgettable experiences on the Jewish Sabbaths and holidays – the way they were celebrated with such glory and brilliance, with such deep content, with so much joy and youthful enthusiasm. The memories of the past, the acts of the present and the hopes of the future in the tradition of my home – filled our souls, and had an extraordinary, deep educational influence on us.

In my memory, and my sacred feelings I carry the memory of that life in my parents' house. Their ways are also instilled in me. At times of longing and yearning, the threads of my soul draw me to them, and with all my thoughts and feelings I become united with these dear beings, shedding a tear… Until that dreadful storm arrived, which ensured the annihilation of everything and shook up that magnificent tree, encountered its trunk and tore it up by the roots.

May their souls be inscribed in the Book of Life – may their memory forever shine in the Jewish people, which is renewing its life in its own eternal homeland.

If the priority of mankind against death is remembrance – then let us gather their images and let us bring them out in these memorial pages, let us give form to and perpetuate their special sound, which was silenced in such a tragic and cruel way from our symphony of life, through human beasts that boasted of being "people of a higher race", may their names be wiped out forever.

1. The cave in Hebron where Abraham and Sarah, Isaac and Rebecca and Jacob and Leah are buried.
2. A Woman of Valor, called Eshet Chayil in Hebrew, is a hymn which is customarily recited on Friday evenings, after returning from synagogue and singing "Shalom Aleichem" and before sitting down to the Shabbat evening meal. It is from the book of Proverbs (31).
3. In expiation of their sins, the sins were transferred to the chicken, which was then slaughtered. This is a survival of the scapegoat ceremony in the Temple in Jerusalem.

Characters

[Page 121]

Zvi Faigenbaum

Town Dignitaries (Characters)

Even an entire community of saints has certain prominent people whose attributes set them apart, whether they excel in Torah and lore, wealth and wisdom, heritage and virtue or leadership qualities and public work. They represent the public blessed by their presence, and the community looks up to them in times of trouble. And in times of joy and merriment, they are the great ones who represent our generation.

The community of Wierzbnik also had such great individuals of virtue, who were considered "the town's finest". With awe and a sense of deep respect I will try and commemorate those characters who were the "finest" of the Wierzbnik community before the Holocaust storm – some, but not all, because it is impossible to name them all. Those who deserve to be numbered among them and receive no mention here also deserve our respect and have my apologies.

Rabbi Chanoch Biderman

He was a distinguished man who studied the Torah and worked day and night. Even while entertaining guests, he was never seen without a book. Rabbi Hanoch also wrote a book on kabala, which he never got in print. He was an opinionated man and stood by his convictions even when it meant going against popular opinion. He never caved before others. Two events demonstrate this quality of his, insisting that he is right:

Individual opinion

During the days of World War I, most of the Jews in town (at the time under the rule of the Russian Tsar) considered German victory to be a salvation for Israel. They have prayed for such victory because they thought "it would be good for the Jews". Rabbi Chanoch was the only person to object to this reasoning, saying that the victory of the Russian Tsar would be better for the Jews than a victory for the enlightened Germans.

His opinion was considered controversial at the time, but we know now what good comes to the Jews from German victories and what aid and succor we can expect from the "forces of tomorrow" that vanquished the Tsar…

At the beginning of World War II, when all people in town except for a few youths left the place because of the bombings, Rabbi Chanoch and his wife Rivka were the only people who stayed behind. Everyone was astonished to see him intentionally put himself in the way of harm, but reality proved him right in retrospect. Nothing happened to the town, but those who followed "common sense" and escaped, like Jacob in his time, were subject to many perils and managed to return home (in part) only after many hardships…

A mark from King David

His livelihood came from a brewery he owned in Szydłowiec. His wife Rivkale Biderman, an intelligent woman graced with an air of nobility, assisted him. She managed the affairs of the brewery, allowing her husband to focus on matters of heaven. The two earned the respect of the entire community, including the gentiles. While they were fairly wealthy, they led a humble life, offering generous aid to the needy.

Rabbi Chanoch was also highborn. According to the tales of his ancestors, he was a direct descendant of King David. Like his father, Rabbi Moshe Biderman (of Szydłowiec), there was a kind of furrow circling his head, which legends told was formed on King David's head by the crown he wore, a mark he passed down to his descendants. Like his forefather, Rabbi Chanoch, he cherished this status and maintained its dignity.

Rabbi Yeshayahu Guterman

He was a descendant of Rabbi Yaakov Guterman, head of the Admor line of Radzyń. He was a dignified, soft-spoken man, radiating a sense of nobility that earned him the respect of all.

He was among the richest people in town even before World War I. Mrs. Zelda was known as a capable woman, who managed their wholesale tobacco shop.

In 1919-1920, during the Bolshevik army's invasion of Poland, when the Polish government announced a general draft to fend off the invaders, a Yeshiva student named Berish Blumenfeld was arrested for desertion and was to be court-martialed and possibly sentenced to death. Yoseph Tubman managed to convince (using bribe) the judge to set a high bail for his release until his trial. The plan was for him to entirely avoid the trial, which could only end in his death. Who would vouch for him? They turned to Yeshayahu Guterman, who never hesitated but went quickly to court, signing his wall house at the corner of Rinek-Iłżacka as bail for the return of the prisoner, knowing that he never intended to show up...

Yeshayahu returned to the home he just compromised, content in knowing that he risked his property to save a Hebrew soul.

His sons, Israel-Yaakov and Yoseph, were also like him. They were honest, virtuous and among the town's dignitaries.

Among his surviving descendants are: his son Berish and his wife Esther, who passed away in the United States but not before marrying their sons Yitzhak and Moshe who live today in the States.

His daughter – Chaya Gutsman, who also made a new home in this country, Libcha, his granddaughter (daughter of Yoseph) who married as well and lives in the great Jewish community in New York.

Rabbi Avraham Mordechai Rotbart

He was an intelligent scholar, who came to Wierzbnik from Wolin as a senior clerk of the Heller firm that controlled the woodcraft and lumber-mill trade in and around town. He was respected by the people, who acknowledged his understanding in matters of spirit and the needs of the public. Also served as head of the community.

He was among the founders of the Tarbut Torah and Beit Yaakov schools. This school for girls, which was appreciated by the entire population, was located in his wall house on Iłżacka Street.

Lastly, he served as manager for the Kopycki bank, the Jewish cooperative, along with Mr. Simcha Mincberg. This institute was also located at his home. In 1941 he fell ill, needed special medical help that was not available, and as a result suffered from toxemia and passed away.

Among his sons-in-law we met Rabbi Welwl and Yitzhak Shlomo, whose daughter Yehudit survived the Holocaust, married in Israel and lives in Tel-Aviv.

The brothers Rabbi Moshe Pinchas and Rabbi Yoseph-Reuven Lichtenstein

Both came from a house of "Torah and Greatness". The two came from Lodz and founded a plywood factory. Each had many positive traits. Yoseph Reuven was a great religious scholar, while Moshe Pinchas was a learned man in his own right, but excelled more in the field of management and trade. He was also a gifted singer. When he prayed in public on Shabbats and holidays he brought great spiritual joy to his fellow prayers. The two took part in every charity enterprise and contributed to every need of the community. Their house was a meeting place for scholars and their conduct august. Both were martyred by the bullets of the bane, on the bitter day when they could not find the strength to go to the Rinek where the Jews of our community were gathered, some to be sent to the furnaces of Treblinka and others sent for hard labor and torture in the camps, where only a few survived.

Among their surviving descendants who live in Israel are: Rabbi Simcha Mincberg, (son-in-law to Moshe Pinchas) with his son Menachem and his daughter Rivka, both of whom raised families.

The grandchildren of Reuven-Yoseph – Chava Kilman-Singer (wife of Jerachmiel Singer), her sister Renia Frimerman (in the United States) and her brother Zeev all raised families and live with them. Zeev's son, Yoseph, died as a hero protecting the people and country during The Six Day War.

Rabbi Shmuel Cohen

A scion of a noble family, he came to Wierzbnik from Warsaw after World War I, marrying Yocheved, daughter of Rabbi Mordechai David Kornwaser. He was an extraordinary person, a scholar who spoke many languages and knew much of the world, and an idealist who believed in people and trusted them. Assisted by his wife, Mrs. Yocheved, and his daughters Tova and Malka, he ran a wholesale store. He was an honest man, and respected by people. He was also chosen (for a single cadence) as member of the town council. Under the Nazi occupation he was appointed a member of the community board, which mainly handled matters of welfare, providing support for Jews in need.

His home was a meeting place for public activists, especially in the ghetto. People would gather in his apartment for morning and evening prayer and to say Kaddish (prayer for the dead), as well as to seek solutions and possible means of escape from the siege. During the time of Holocaust and ruin.

He lived through the hardships of the camps. He was dragged from camp to camp, labored hard and suffered famine. His desire to survive was never realized. Two weeks before his liberation he could suffer no more and died at the Flossenbürg concentration camp in Germany, joining his martyred family members who passed away before him in different times and under different circumstances: his wife and his youngest son in Treblinka, his son-in-law Yoseph shot before our very eyes during the march from the Rinek to Strzelnica and his infant grandchild also murdered before our very eyes at the ghetto in Szydłowiec.

Survived: his daughters Tova and Malka, and his son, David Cohen. All raised great families according to the tradition of their noble family.

Rabbi Jechiel Pszytycki

Although he was not a rich man but rather, suffered from poverty all his life, he earned himself a place at the eastern wall. This was due to his personal qualities: he was a Hasidic scholar who observed the commandments. He too was a public activist. For years he served as head of Hevra Kaddisha, skillfully managing its affairs, preserving the honor of the dead and the wellbeing of the living. He was gifted with a pleasant voice and a gentle manner. As a cantor, he excelled at leading prayer during holidays, the High Holidays and during the three pilgrim festivals.

His daughter Hanna, her husband Moshe Najman and their children, along with Jechiel and his wife Rachel, were all led with the rest of the town's martyrs to the furnaces of Treblinka, while their son Zvi died in similar fashion among the Jews of Szydłowiec. His daughter Rivka, on the other hand, who survived the furnaces of the Nazis, was murdered by Polish villains after the war, in the town of Gdynia, along with Ms. Miriam, daughter of Avraham Zylberberg.

R' Yoseph Dreksler

Yoseph Dreksler was an outstanding public activist, who had a large family in Wierzbnik. It is said that his family was related in some way to every other family in town.

As an employee of the local treasury he was coming and going among the senior clerks of the local authorities and he would often use his connections to help townsmen who required the aid of this office.

He acquired his extensive education on his own, and knew something about everything. Every evening he was visited by friends, his house serving as a meeting place for scholars. People would gather to read the "Haynt" or to talk about politics until the late hours of the night. He himself was a man of many positive attributes, remarkably patient and collected, even when others around him were distraught.

His daughter, Mrs. Rachel Laor (Dreksler) tells about him: "I remember a time when a woman came to talk with my father about her tax troubles. Her words made me believe that her claims are not quite justified, but my father refrained from bluntly pointing out her mistakes. The woman, however, reacted differently than one might expect. Ungratefully, she started swearing at my father and chastising him. I was amazed at the calm with which my father met her rudeness. He calmed her down and even promised to help. When she left, I asked him why he behaved in such an unusual manner, and he told me: "Don't judge your fellow men until you walked a mile in their shoes, the woman is in trouble and therefore we must show her plenty of tolerance and understanding."

Yoseph Dreksler was among the wealthy men in town, but his wealth never made him aloof, serving instead as a way of expressing his positive qualities, by offering people material aide in the form of anonymous donations, unknown to any but his close family. The virtues he was gifted with complemented each other; he was calm, reserved, and considered matters before making up his mind, but he also adhered to his own principles. Among his closest associates were Simcha Mincberg, Yoseph Unger, Moshe Birenzweig, Avraham Zylberberg and Yoseph Tenzer. They were a regular group and had much in common with each other, maintaining a years old friendship and acting in fact as the public leadership of the town Jews in the south.

When the war broke out, he left Wierzbnik with his family and traveled to Russia, where he worked in the virgin forests of the north around Arkhangelsk until his release following the agreement between Polish general Sikorski and the Russians, which affected the release of all former Polish citizens.

Honorable loser

Our elders knew the heroic secret of restraint, subduing urges and subjecting them to the laws of logic and reason, and their insight was conveyed with remarkable succinctness: Who is a hero? He who conquers his passions. It would seem that Yoseph Dreksler was gifted with this virtue, a man capable of conquering his passion even under circumstances that would make others furious.

His daughter Rachel recalls a typical event, when her father ordered large quantity of flour just before the prices dropped in a way that would incur him considerable losses. Since the goods were not delivered by the supplier yet, his partners advised him to break the deal. Advised isn't the right word for it; they begged, pleaded and pressured him, but he insisted on keeping his word. "When I say something," he told them, "I must keep my word, no matter what!" The partners refused to give up and continued pleading. At times, the discussion would heat to the point where they could hear across the line the sound of the receiver slamming down as it dropped from Yoseph Dreksler's shaking hands. He was a man of principles and hard to dissuade.

Dreksler was always a believer in the Zionist cause and did much to realize the return to Zion. Even during the harsh times he spent on the Russian taiga, faced with famine and a cold weather that dropped to -50??c, he had faith that he will reach Israel.

His dream came to pass. After his release from the camp in Siberia, he traveled with his family to Uzbekistan and from there, through Persia, to Israel.

Here he bore witness to the founding of the State of Israel. He passed away here in 1967.

[Page 125]
Jerachmiel Singer

Pola Laks, the Noble Woman

Pola Laks, of the Tenenbaum family, was born in Sandomierz and following her graduation from the Russian high school has dedicated her time to helpful public activity. Filled with a desire to help others, she worked both in the general-public field, and in a personal, direct way.

When the first refugees started pouring in from Germany during the years 1936-1937, she went to great pains to offer them the necessary help, and did even more during World War II, when the pogroms against our people were rapidly escalating.

She was a dedicated Zionist and one of the key movement activists in town, served as the head of the local WIZO organization and founded the local branch of "Young WIZO". Her virtues earned her the affection of the public in Wierzbnik and she was awarded with positions such as membership in the organizational board of the Tarbut school and sole representative of the Jewish community on the representative committee of the national high school in Starachowice.

Pola worked hard to raise the cultural level of the Jewish population in town, while taking constant care to improve the living conditions of the town's Jews. Her husband, Yitzhak Laks, a native of Sosnowych who later settled in Wierzbnik, served as her loyal partner in public activism and was as active as she was in the local movement.

Pola died during World War II, during the eviction on October 1941, while her husband died in Auschwitz in 1944.

Her blessed work and her noble character are inscribed in the hearts of our townsmen and her memory shall live forever.

[Page 126]
M. Sali-Kerbel

Reb Shmuel Kleiner's House

Reb Shmuel Kleiner's house was known and famed in the entire city as a welcoming and friendly house that was always open to all, and every person who suffered from pain, distress and a heavy heart, who needed either moral or material assistance, found it in that patriarchal house from the dear Jew who was imbued with sympathy for others, Reb Shmuel Kleiner and his family.

An extraordinary and special grace had been poured onto this house. An atmosphere of happiness and peace filled with sympathy reigned there. The refinement and the cultural, nationalistic and traditional methods of upbringing could be felt in every step, so that many Wierbznik families wondered at and viewed such a beautiful Jewish home with envy.

The head of the family, Reb Shmuel Kleiner, of blessed memory, as I stated, led a patriarchal Jewish home, which was permeated with and rooted in traditional Jewish national values. He himself was tall and was always modestly and neatly dressed, with great elegance and taste. He was a great philanthropist and also actively contributed to Mizrachi in collections for the Land of Israel, especially for Keren Hayesod. In a word, this was a house of "Torah and merchandise" [this rhymes in Yiddish and means of learning and material wealth]. It was a house in which old-time specifically Jewish books were mixed with new international books and writings, and produced a new forward moving generation whose gaze reached far horizons[1].

His gracious wife Sheindele, of blessed memory, was a true, typical "*Yiddishe mame*" [Jewish mother]. She managed the house with great modesty and devotion, worried about every little thing, and the house shone with light and cleanliness. She was a good-hearted woman, suffused with limitless love for Jews, and she was respected by everyone. Understandably, with such blessed parents the children received a proper upbringing, and they developed and grew and were a source of pride and pleasure for their parents. The entire house bubbled and shone with modernism, with cheerfulness, with life and a sense of accomplishment.

The oldest son Fishl, of blessed memory, was a young man with education gleaming from his face, a gentleman, a businessman and at the same time a great scholar, well versed in the "small print', as we say. He was known as a young man who incorporated in himself Jewish history, knowledge and current world culture, in a word "Torah and wisdom"[2].

The second son, Yaakov, of blessed memory[3], was a handsome young man with the face of a scholar, with an open mind and an open heart, aware and sharp, and talented in all areas, in affairs of commerce or problems of development, and in addition he was politically active in the echelons of the Zionist movement, and afterwards was one of the founders of the revisionist organization in the city.

In this way the family lived a harmonious, good life, and the house was simply an idyll, and the children had the greatest respect for their parents. With the passing of time Fishl and Yaakov successfully managed their lumber business together with their father.

Afterwards they married and each one separately began – with the help of the family – to build his own family nest. But they always had great respect for their parents, their warm home, and came to visit them frequently.

With the passing of time, the head of the family, Reb Shmuel Kleiner, passed away, and afterwards also his wife Sheindl. Then bitter fate cast its grim wrath on Fishl and his family and they all perished at the hands of the Nazi beasts. That was also the fate of the splendid young man Yaakov, in his best years. Yaakov's wife and his one and only daughter survived and now live in Israel.

Their daughter Sarale (Sala), who married the well-know attorney Leon Wiesenfeld from Tarnobrzeg, also survived the bloody time of the Hitler regime, and now lives in Caracas.

Their son Yossl, who on his young shoulders bore the entire period of torture in the concentration camps, married Roszke Kerbel of Wierbznik. They also presently live in Caracas, Venezuela. They both raised beautiful families, which can serve as an example for others as to what energy, perseverance, great effort, a strong character and a firm will can achieve.

These are two homes of Jewishness, philanthropy and good deeds, with a deep traditional-nationalistic drive to bring up their children in that direction.

Bina Grynszpan Family, circa 1920. In the second row on the left are Bina Grynszpan-Goldberg (Chaskel Grynszpan's daughter) and her husband Fiszel Goldberg, a bootmaker, with some of their children. Bina was born in Ilza and Fiszel in Sienno, but all their children in Wierzbnik. Courtesy of Carolynne Veffer.

Not in the original Yizkor Book

Esther Katz-Malach, with her five children, Wierzbnik, 1929. Veffer's mother, Sura Malach, is at far right. Courtesy of Carolynne Veffer. Not in the original Yizkor Book.

Sura Malach and her grandfather, Chaskel Grynszpan, in Wierzbnik or Ilza, 1928 or 1929. Malach emigrated to Toronto in 1929. Courtesy of Carolynne Veffer.

Not in the original Yizkor Book

The young remaining twigs of the large, many branched tree of the Kleiner house, which was cut down so tragically by the murderers, became stronger and more extensive, and took upon themselves the holy duty willed to them, of transplanting their life in the spirit that they had absorbed in the home of their parents.

These roots provided the strength and the will to pass on the cultural values and the good behavior and traits, the beautiful traditional mentality of their old home, to their children.

This is the great consolation for the family. May their holy and beloved souls remain forever in our heart and be eternally inscribed in our memory.

1. When looking at the gruesome dark days of the Nazi occupation, Reb Shmuel Kleiner was extremely distressed by the cruelty – and paid for it with his life, dying suddenly in 1940. His wife Sheindl perished at the hands of the Nazi murderers.
2. He perished during the German occupation together with his wife Goldele, his daughter Rivche and his son Berek
3. Yaakov was murdered in a terrible way by the Germans. Only his wife and their only daughter survived and presently live in Israel.

[Page 128]
Sara Postawski-Steinhardt

The Admor of Chmielów

The rabbi of Chmielów was practically a part of our town's spiritual landscape, because of the many followers he had there. His visits to Wierzbnik were always great public events.

The Admor of Chmielów accompanied by his Hassidim

The Admor of Chmielów was the son of the rabbi of Ożarów, the Admor Arie Leibish, who served before settling in Ożarów as a rabbi in the communities of Tarłów, Afla and Chmielnik. A renowned scholar, the rabbi was also known as a holy man of great and widespread influence.

The dynasty of the Ożarów Admors originates in Rabbi Leibish Epstein, who was one of the greatest students of the Seer of Lublin. The rabbi of Chmielów, who was the son of Rabbi Leibish, was therefore following the holy path outlined by his holy ancestors.

His radiant personality (he was a man of stature), scholarship and virtue constantly expanded the number of followers who wanted to study under him. It was only natural that he had Shtiblach (Hasidic chapters) in many communities. The capital city of Warsaw boasted a particularly sizeable community of Chmielów Hasidim.

In our town of Wierzbnik, his Hasidim were significant and outstanding, both in terms of quantity (five quorums) and in terms of individual quality. The members of this Hasidic group shared bonds of love, fraternity and dedication to each other. Their friendship was inspired by the rabbi himself, who was a peace lover in the full sense of the words, and concerned with the fate of all his fellow men.

My father, who in the past served as a kosher butcher for the Tarłów community, was appointed in 1934 to be a kosher butcher in Wierzbnik. We had no trouble acclimating into this new place and society, and required no transition period, as if we were born there. The warmth shown to us by the Chmielów Hasidim in that place contributed to that fact. My brothers, my sisters and I all found our place right away both in society and at school.

The rabbi's visits, an honor to our community, have greatly strengthened our congregation and raised moral. The rabbi was typically accompanied by elder Hasidim, especially his old manservant Meir Nisles who was in the past a son-in-law of our important townsman, Hershel Fruman, a Hasid of Chmielów himself.

The "receptions" by the railway station whenever the rabbi came to visit our town were very impressive, and those Shabbats were both beautiful and happy. His glory and grace were felt everywhere we turned.

The rabbi would regularly stay at the home of his follower Jechiel Lerman. During the week, the house was astir, bustling with people coming and going, looking for advice and blessing. And on Shabbat, Jechiel Lerman would rearrange the whole place, turning his store into a large hall that housed the many prayers and at its center, a table so long that it would reach from one end of the room to the other.

Members of every Hasidic circle would participate in the feasts (fast) on Shabbat eve and on Shabbat day, the elders sitting by the rabbi and around the table while the rest stood around in rows. Among the important people who enjoyed a prominent place at the table and who are still among us were rabbi Zvi Wajzer, who graced the event with his sweet tunes and his pleasant, strong voice, and Simcha Mincberg who was a relative of the rabbi, his cousin on his mother's side.

Martyrdom

My father in particular would be filled with joy during those days when the rabbi visited our community. The rabbi and my father have shared a bond of friendship since the rabbi's days in Tarłów, and maintained it even when the rabbi moved to Tarłów and my father to Wierzbnik. Wearing a "kitel", wrapped in a tallit and with a tefillin on his arm, the rabbi of Chmielów, the Admor Israel David Halevi, led the community of Chmielów to martyrdom in Treblinka, where they were annihilated with the multitude of Israel.

[Page 130]
Moshe Sali (Kerbel)

Memories from my Home

I am eager to write down an outline or some anecdotes that would describe my parents' house. Although the time that passed since I left home has blurred the experiences and events of my childhood and youth, and many of them were forgotten completely or faded and blurred, I have decided to try my best in collecting and gleaning from the depths of the past every last ounce of memory that may shed light on the fundamental life in my parents' house, from which I drew my yearning for our fatherland.

Our home had a long history and a rich tradition, a typical Jewish house, filled with faith and warmth.

Father was a scholar, intelligent and clever. This is the reason that he was chosen to serve as judge and arbiter, settling disputes among partners and rivals, in matters of trade and finance. Many sought his advice and all paid him respect. His intelligence and analytic capabilities paved his way to leadership in the circles he traveled. Among the gentiles he maintained the image of a proud, tall Jew, whether dealing with matters of tax or of trade and prakmatia. He loved books and rarely set down the Bible, reading in it whenever he had the time. Torah and Hasidim were the foundations of his life. He also loved the holy tongue and tried to teach us to love it. He combined the best of culture and education, a humble and kind man. The Bible and the six books[1], the Hasidic scripts and Guide to the Perplexed, The Kuzari and the Hatzfira weekly, Haolam magazine and the age-yellowed pages of "Hashaluch", all lived side by side on his shelf.

When depressed, he would often start singing or humming – "Take me under your wing" or "Di Blum". It was those fountains that quenched my thirst and from which I absorbed the eternal ideals of our afflicted and persecuted people.

I remember the young torah students that came to our house on Shabbat afternoons, to tell father what they learned and earn the approval of a knowledgeable authority, a scholar familiar with the ways of the world.

The coming of the Holocaust caused him a fair share of misery, but he carried his torment with heroic, superhuman courage and was always able to adapt to the conditions and time constraints, showing remarkable vitality and accepting his fate with calmness and faith, fully aware of it and struggling inwardly but entertaining no illusions about what was soon to come, thus ending the circle of his life.

Mother was the heart and soul of the house. She bathed us in love, warmth and care. Her very being radiated great gentleness. She was always humble and chaste. Our family was her entire life. Endless dedication and honest concern for her children and home, those were her virtues. Her face reflected her heartbreak and weariness. She was the Yiddish Mother in the full sense of the words. Despite the gap between parents and their children, she understood and loved us, and we loved her.

My mother was a capable woman and always had work to do. She never rested or took a break. From dawn to midnight she labored, the ideal mother and housewife. It was not simple to raise so many children and take care of the household by herself, cleaning, washing the floors, cooking, roasting, laundering and washing, and sewing and patching clothes, darning socks and making food, and handling every detail, big or small. She never complained, even during the hardest of times, able to hide the sorrow in her heart and suffer in silence. Mother's radiant face on Shabbats, when the place was glowing, shed their own light and joy on all members of the household and served as a draught for her soul and her deep maternal emotions.

Although my parents' lives were rooted in the Diaspora, they loved "The land of Israel" of the glorious past, the holy land, land of our ancestors, the yearned land of The Cave of Machpelah, our mother Rachel's Tomb and the Western Wall, according to the stories of legend and the Bible.

Both Judaism and closeness were best expressed during the Shabbats and holidays of Israel. How pleasant were my holidays with my family. How much beauty, warmth and joy the Shabbat brought with it. It was as though the massive activity during the six days of the week was but a corridor welcoming Shabbat the Queen, and it had an aura of indescribable light and festiveness, a kind of sacred ritual. There was a sense of renewal, as the entire house was lit by every lantern and by the silver candlesticks. We went to say our Shabbat prayers at the Shtibl and came back from prayer saying "Shalom Aleichem" and "A Woman of valor, who will find" in a pleasant, flowing singsong, sanctified the wine and sat around the table laid with all the best, the special Shabbat dishes in their polished bowls, making us feel as though we were free kings.

And the next day we would conduct the three feasts, sing, read the holy scripts, and later conduct the ceremony separating holy from secular, the Melava Malka, together with the Hasidim of the rabbi of Alexander. These acts all carried with them a sense of perfection and faith in Providence and the calling of "the chosen people".

Passover was particularly glorious. Preparations for the holiday took months; putting the house in order, whitewashing it, rinsing the dishes in scalding water to make them kosher, baking matzahs, looking for leavened food by candlelight, burning it and selling it, with the crowning event being the Seder. The unique bowl (including the Haroseth and Maror), Eliyahu's cup, telling the Haggadah together, the Four Questions asked by the youngest son, opening the door for "pour out your wrath", the table laid with a variety of tasty delicacies, chief among them the dumplings, and tales of the Exodus which lasted until late hours.

Reb Moshe Tennenbaum

The rest of the holidays were very much the same. On Lag Ba'Omer, a bow and arrow; on Shavuoth, papyrus bushes, vegetables and dairy products; on Simchat Torah, circling the synagogue, each child with his flag and much joy in his heart; on Hanukkah, fried pancakes, playing with a spinning top and wondrous tales about the heroics of the Hashmonaim-Maccabim; on Purim, costumes, Purim-gifts, Haman's ears, the noise of rattlers and reading the Book of Esther; on Sukkoth, the very participation in building the Sukkah, carrying the thatch and decorating the interior with ribbons and colorful lanterns, purchasing an elegant Etrog with a kosher Lulav and weaving a reed handle to hold the Arrabot and Hadasim.

The excitement and mental preparation for New Year and Yom Kippur are unimaginable. Choosing the Kaparot, a white rooster for the head of the family and chickens for the women, the shudder foretelling of the ten days of judgment and visiting the Rabbi of Alexander or the Rabbi of Ostrowiec, all offered a bit of innocence, faith and flavor to life. Thus every holiday and every Shabbat was a new, unique event that awakened us children to a unique way of life.

It is hard to fathom the depth of the experience that was the holidays of Israel celebrated in our home with grandeur and filled with content, joy and youthful mischief. The memories of the past, the deeds of the present and our wishes for the future mixed together in the best of our house's tradition, and had a deep, educative effect over us.

In my mind's eye I see the fabric of this life woven in my parents' house. Their essence is part of me, my heartstrings are drawn to them in times of yearning and longing, and the only thing on my mind is their precious, kind images, while the tears flow. Until the terrible storm came to devour everything, shook the family tree, wounded its trunk and uprooted it. May they rest in peace, their memory everlasting in the hearts of the people of Israel renewing its youth in its eternal homeland.

If man's advantage over oblivion is memory – let us keep their images in our memories and raise through these pages the unique tune that was so tragically and cruelly silenced, ripped from our lives by villains and predators who pretended to be members of a superior race, God damn them and their memory for ever more.

1. Of Talmud

[Page 132]
Mania Rosenkrantz – Bagno (Minka)

Memories of our Home

In order to reflect the Jewish life in our *shtetl* in all its forms, it is necessary to describe not only the collective general community, but we must also look more deeply at the individual; we mean at the basic cell of life – the character and life style of a Wierzbnik Jewish family.

And since such a thing requires being knowledgeable about the details and the fine points of family life, we will here present the memories of our own home.

Reb Mendel Tennenbaum

A special page is here devoted to the eldest son of Menachem-Mendel Tennenbaum, of blessed memory, who was a great scholar and a well-known Talmudist.

For over 50 years he was a teacher in the city, i.e., until the destruction of the community at the hands of the murderous Nazis he filled his position with honor. The man was never separated from the Torah. In a page of the Talmud he found his world, there he sought and also found the consolation to forget the great misfortune he had suffered.

The teacher Reb Mendel Tennenbaum was married to Sarah, of blessed memory – the daughter of the Æmielów rabbi. Unfortunately, she died young and left behind seven children – orphans. His oldest son David, of blessed memory, was the rabbi of Kunow, a great Torah prodigy and student of the Ostrowiec rabbi. He was inundated with Torah and knowledge, and in Kunow he was considered a real *tzaddik* [saintly person].

Religious and honest, he tortured his body for the sake of Heaven. He was his father's greatest pride and joy. Regretfully, he didn't live very long. He died after a serious and short illness. He was mourned by hundreds of people and his death produced a general state of sadness.

The second son, Yaakov (Yankel) Tennenbaum, of blessed memory, was noted for his sharp mind as a prodigy. He studied in the Sokołow yeshiva and afterwards in the Ostrowiec yeshiva. At a very young age he received a teacher's permit from the Ostrowiec rabbi himself.

Yankel Tennenbaum, of blessed memory, was not satisfied with only the education from the yeshivas, he was also drawn to general education, general literature, mathematics, etc. He obtained the general education, without the knowledge of his ultrareligious father. He studied alone, fought against all the difficulties. He was an autodidact and a prodigy in all aspects, and filled with education and knowledge.

In public life he was well known by the youth for taking part in sharp discussions about various world problems.

The third son, Zadok, of blessed memory, died in the army in the anti-Semitic ultranationalist Poland.

Reb Mendel Tennenbaum's eldest daughter, Kayla, of blessed memory, was married to the Osów rabbi, who later became the Chief Rabbi of New York, Rabbi Epstein. He was famous as a great Talmudist, as well as the author of many books, and also recently received the Rabbi Kook Institute in Israel award for his work on the Talmud.

The second daughter, Hanna, of blessed memory, was married to Yosef Orbach, of blessed memory, the well-known teacher of the Tarbut school in Kowal. He was distinguished in World War II for calling the Jews to resist and not to let themselves be slaughtered like sheep by the Germans. At the roll call at the time of the deportation, he was shot before the eyes of all the assembled Kowal Jews.

Of all his children, only his youngest daughter Minka survived, and she lives in Israel and is married to Moshe Bagno, a well-known activist in public affairs in this country [Israel]. For many years he had the honor of being the mayor of Bnei Brak. In recent years he has withdrawn from political and social work because of his bad state of health.

Reb Shmuel Tennenbaum

Shmuel Tennenbaum was very well known in the merchant circles of Wierzbnik. He ran a big business in the market from 1924. However, he was known in the city not only as a rich merchant, but also as one of the main founders of Mizrachi, and as such he was an adherent of the idea that proclaimed – "Torah and labor", "Torah and Zionism".

Shmuel Tennenbaum was a great public servant; he didn't just collect large sums of money for the Jewish National Fund, but he was also one of the major donors to Zionist causes. He even had a thank you letter from Menachem Ussishkin himself.

His greatest dream was to immigrate to the land of Israel. He even had certificates in 1939, but the outbreak of war interfered with the fulfillment of his deepest dreams.

Right at the beginning of the war, Shmuel was deported with blows falling on his head. The husband of his only daughter Roize fell in battle in the Polish army and left behind his pregnant wife. The business was demolished by the Nazi robbers and his wife was killed a short while later.

His daughter gave birth to the child in 1940, and afterwards she also died at the hands of the Nazis.

The little girl, his granddaughter, became an encumbrance for Shmuel Tennenbaum. The ground was burning under his feet, the times were coming when all Jewish children were sentenced to death and Shmuel Tennenbaum foresaw it with his realistic vision. At the last minute, with the help of a Polish woman he succeeded in placing the child in the forest near an orphanage run by priests.

The Christian woman entered the convent and stated that there was a child lying in the forest and crying. The priests took in the two-year old girl and asked her who her father was. The child had been born an orphan and actually never knew her father. She also didn't know her mother's name. She knew one thing – her name. In the register they listed the day that the child was found, the place where the child was found and her name.

Shmuel inscribed these details in blood in his memory and heart.

After this there was another disaster – the death of his son Moshe. The fact that he had given the little girl away gave him the strength to survive the most difficult times in the camps. He had to live at any cost – if not, what would be with the child, and he had to rescue her from the hands of the Catholics.

He survived the camps, and fate flung him to Rome. News reached there that the Polish anti-Semites were carrying out pogroms against the Jews and that specifically in Wierzbnik a few Jews had been murdered, who had barely come out of the hellish camps and had returned to Wierzbnik – to their former home. Disregarding this, Shmuel Tennenbaum returned to Poland to rescue the only child of his only beloved daughter. It wasn't that easy. With great effort and much money – he succeeded in getting the child out.

Today the girl has been in Israel for a long time. She married Dr. Mordechai Paz, who works in the Djeni Hospital in Jaffa – and is already herself the mother of two sweet children.

Unfortunately, Shmuel Tennenbaum did not live to enjoy this pleasure and satisfaction. He died in Rome in 1958, and left a will for his oldest son Haim, who lives in Brussels, requesting that he be brought to Israel and buried in the holy city of Jerusalem. His will was carried out.

Shmuel Tennenbaum's youngest son, Yerachmiel (Monia), lives in Rome, and manages his late father's well-known and only kosher hotel.

He follows the way of life of his late father, keeping a truly Jewish, religious home. His two sons study in yeshivas and are continuing their studies in Israel.

The Family of Reb Moshe Tennenbaum, of Blessed Memory

One of the oldest and most important families in Wierzbnik was the Tennenbaum family. The patriarch of the family, Reb Moshe Tennenbaum, the son of David Tennenbaum, was born in 1843. He was a great persona, well-known in the city as well as in other cities in the area – where he was called Moishel Wierzbniker [from Wierzbnik].

It is told that one time the Hassidim and scholars gathered together to travel to Wierzbnik, to the rich man, Reb Moishel, in order to receive donations for various causes – for yeshivas, for rabbis and ordinary donations for poor people. It was hard for them to pronounce the name Wierzbnik – so they began to think: why is it actually called Wierzbnik? Until they came to the conclusion that Wierzbnik is called Wierzbnik because Moishel Wierzbniker lives in Wierzbnik.

It sounds like a joke, but in fact, at that time – i.e. more than a hundred years ago, Wierzbnik was a small unknown *shtetl* and Jewish and Hassidic circles in Poland only knew it because Reb Moishel Tennenbaum lived there.

Now the question is, how did the man gain such popularity? It wasn't for nothing. Throughout his entire life (he lived to the age of 81 – passing away in 1924), he contributed to the public welfare. His life was never so dear for him as when it dealt with saving the life of other people.

In World War I he rescued many Jews from death – among them one of the Kornwasser family. More than that, he risked his life to go to Radom and get Jews who had been sentenced by the Russians out of prison. He ransomed them with his own money. His patriarchal appearance, with the full, long beard, invoked respect and opened the doors to all circles for him.

Reb Moishel Tannenbaum has special credit for the establishment of a Jewish community in Wierzbnik. He is the person who established the old synagogue in the city. He donated the land for the Jewish cemetery, as well as for other ritual purposes.

Reb Moishel Tannenbaum had a big business. He was the first Jew to form major business ties with the Christians.

He operated a tar works and had a large stone quarry, which took up an enormous amount of space. There he employed scores of Poles.

His hospitality at home was famous everywhere, and many rabbis lodged there. Whoever was looking for Torah, wisdom or simply a bit of warm food could receive all of them there.

When his wife Freidel, of blessed memory (born in Wierzbnik, nee Eidelman) complained that despite the servants she was always tired from entertaining so many people – Reb Moishel said:

hospitality is one of the greatest mitzvahs, and such arguments were enough for her to agree with her distinguished husband.

Numerous generations developed from Moishele Tennenbaum in Wierzbnik. His seven children married people from prestigious rabbinic families or families from the distinguished aristocratic Jewish world.

Reb Moishele Tennenbaum's children married into the family of the Æmielów rabbi, twice with members of the court of the Rabbi of Kock (Mendel Tauman and Morgenstern), into the family of the rabbi of Sokołów, Morgenstern, into the family of the rabbi of Kowal, Rabbi Szapiro, into the family of the rabbi of Solec, Rabbi R. Trofa, and also into the family of the rabbi of Kielce, Rabbi Rappoport.

All the children made their homes in Wierzbnik and brought a fresh spirit into the city. While still living, Reb Moishel Tennenbaum had over one hundred grandchildren and great-grandchildren.

During the time of the Nazi catastrophe many members of this family perished, but some of them were able to save themselves from the Nazi hell. Among them were highly educated people: doctors, engineers, university professors, etc.

Many of the Wierzbnik Jews in America read in the newspapers about "a new discovery", "a new electronic force!", "the sensational discovery by an Israeli doctor, Yehuda Perl" – and probably didn't know that he is a great-grandchild of Moishel Tennenbaum, a grandson of Rabbi Mendel Tauman from Wierzbnik, and the son of his daughter Tova. Also, when the American Jews from Wierzbnik hear about the great Dr. Morgenstern – they don't know that he is a grandson of Reb Moishel Tennenbaum and of the Węgrów rabbi, of blessed memory.

There are also more such important persons, such as Yitzhak, the son of Reb Moshe Bagno and Minka (the daughter of the teacher Mendel Tennenbaum, of blessed memory), etc.

Two of the late Rabbi Mendel Tauman's daughters presently live in Israel, and they are the granddaughters of Reb Moishel Tennenbaum and the rabbi of Kock.

- ·Tova – her husband, Eliezer Perl, has for many years been the secretary of the Bnei Brak municipality.
  Miriam, her husband Yehiel Rosenkrantz is the municipal engineer of Bnei Brak

- ·Four of the late Yosef Tennebaum's children also live in Israel: Rachel Meislicz, Golda, Yaakov Tennenbaum and Binyamin Tennenbaum, and also two daughters and a daughter-in-law of Reb Yaakov Tennenbaum, of blessed memory, who was married to the daughter of the rabbi of Kielce, Rabbi Rappoport, of blessed memory.

Peretz Trofa, of Blessed Memory

Every former resident of Wierzbnik who wants to recall what the *shtetl* used to look like, sees not only the streets, the market, the town hall, or for example the school – where he studied, or the synagogue where he prayed in his mind, but all of them in association with the people who were connected to this.

You can't just recall the school without immediately seeing Peretz Trofa's "cigarettes and writing materials" shop, which was across from the synagogue. There was really no person or child that didn't know the shop.

Peretz Trofa first opened his shop on Wisoko St. and then for many years on Nisko St., at the corner of Kaliewo, across the street from the synagogue.

He ran his store for almost fifty years from the time when he married Sarah- Beila, the daughter of Reb Moishel Tennenbaum, of blessed memory.

He was a very interesting person. He was a son of the rabbi of Solec, and spent his youth in yeshivas, excelling as a Talmudist. After his marriage, real life required that he be in the shop, while his spirit and soul demanded that he study Torah. He felt an internal struggle between the two. That is why he strove to have his wife and children run the shop. He made a "crafty merchant" out of his younger daughter Brachale at the age of 9-10.

When they were in the shop, or when there were customers in the shop, he cunningly moved himself away to the *Gemara*, which always lay open on his table in the room. He studied every day, except for Thursdays, because that was market day and the peasants from the neighboring villages filled the shop until late at night. The pleasure of studying Torah was quite difficult for him, because he didn't have suitable conditions for it.

"We were already living in Kielce, but I often came to visit my uncle Trofa, especially my cousin Brachale, who was not just my cousin but also my good friend. It was a cold winter day, around 6 AM. There was a frost outside, which could also be felt in the house; the windows were frozen and Brachale and I were sleeping in the kitchen, which also served as a dining room and at night as a children's room.

My uncle and aunt were sleeping in the other room. Suddenly I heard my uncle silently getting up, lighting the fire and sitting down quietly to study. But how can you study and not accompany it with a little melody? Then I again heard my aunt getting up and reproaching him: 'Why don't you let the girl sleep?' She was referring to me – the guest. 'Today is a (non-Jewish) holiday.'

I spoke up, saying that it didn't bother me, that it was a lullaby for me. However, my aunt took him into their bedroom and made him a place to study. It didn't take long, and there was a knock at the door. The owner of the house came in – a dark, wizened Gentile woman called Drozdowa. She was angry that people were 'shouting' on the day of their Lord's birth...

It appeared that my aunt's religious feelings were very hurt, and not paying any attention to the fact that the woman was standing in the room, she said to me in Yiddish:

'Nu, what do you have to say about this simpleton; she thinks that my Peretz is studying because her Lord was born today! Do you see with whom we share a wall?'

Brachale and I both hid under the comforter to hide our laughter. Mrs. Drozodowa left, my uncle changed his seat again – he was already upset – drank some hot tea and sank deep into the small print, but I am afraid that he no longer had any pleasure from the studying."

[Page 137]
Sarah Miriam Ribak

And His Time Never Came

My dear father Moshe Rybak died in his prime, while I was still a young girl. Although it has been a long time since he left us, I always remember his admirable figure, the way he moved and the light of his eyes.

The things I write here are in part my memories of my father and in part things I was told about him by members of his generation, relatives and friends who knew and admired him.

My father was known as a brave but sensitive man, one who would not hesitate to put himself at risk for the sake of others. He defended our people many a time against members of the hostile regime, who were only too happy to throw the book at any Jew who fell into their clutches. My father succeeded many times because of his impressive appearance, his dignity, his intelligence and his eloquence in the language of the gentiles (and speaking of languages, my father spoke not only Yiddish and Polish, which were common in our house, but also Hebrew, Russian and German, having learned them all on his own).

During the day my father was a trader, traveling near and far to sell and buy, and during the nights he studied, wrote and read. He studied the Torah and the writings of wise men of the old and new world, and wrote what his penetrating eyes have seen, about rare phenomena, about the wonders of existence and the great yearning for the unknown.

At night, my father would retire to his room, to his desk, and whenever I woke up at night or during the small hours I could still see a light coming from where he sat. He wrote on pristine sheets, his handwriting round and clean, every page numbered, locking the pages in the cupboard when he was done. In time, the writings have piled up and filled the cabinet but my father continued to learn and write until his last day. I would like to bring a few of the stories told about him by my dear uncle, Yoseph Dreksler, who passed away in Israel and is still with us in memory:

"I had the privilege of reading the writings of my brother-in-law, Avraham Moshe, and I found them to be a treasure trove of genius and wisdom, radiating from his pure, innocent soul.

I also read chapters from a diary of sorts, "My town Wierzbnik", and found descriptions, characters and anecdotes about the town that a person normally passes by without noticing. Only the eye and heart of the artist allow him to glean the interest in such things, those stirring or ridiculous aspects, and he, my brother-in-law, saw things and described them with love and compassion.

I told him – "You need to tell this to the world, let us publish your writings in a book!" But he hesitated, saying "It isn't time yet!"

And the time never came! My father was taken in his prime – and his writings? What became of them? They were no doubt lost during the long, painful journey my family has taken along with all our townsmen during the Holocaust.

During the Holocaust

[Page 141]

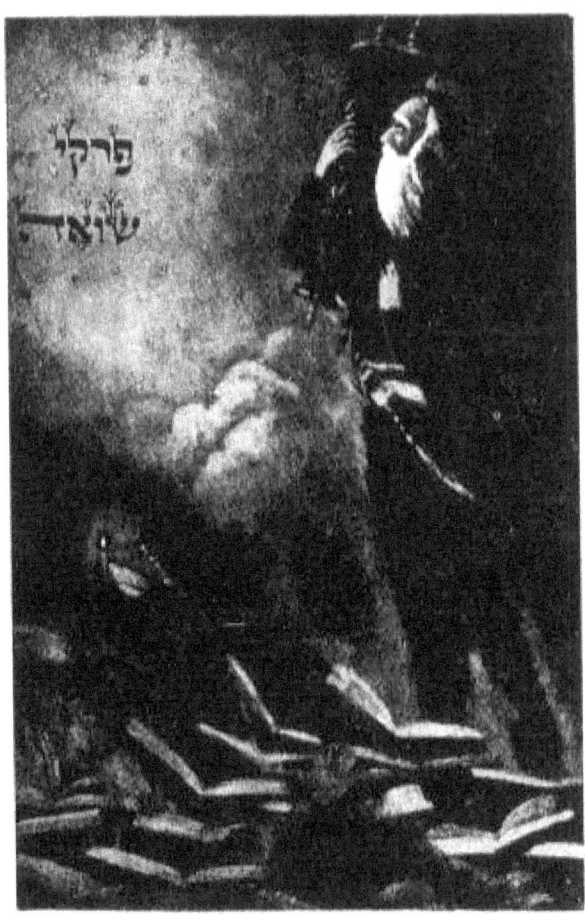

In every path and route, stands a destroyed community.

It is plowed over like silent grass

Standing mute, and asking a mute question

Why did you murder us, and for what reason?

Yitzchak Katznelson ("Woe Unto You")

[Page 143]
G. H.

The Holocaust of the Jews of Europe

Why?

The history of the Jewish people is drenched with suffering, tears and blood, starting with the Pharaoh of Egypt who enslaved and tortured the Jews, going as far as ordering their newborn sons thrown into the Nile. Another villain was Haman, who plotted to kill and annihilate them. The Spanish inquisition has burned thousands at the stake. The Ukraine pogromists, Chmielnicki and Petlura. And the Arabs, led by the mufti Hajj Amin al Husseini who carried out pogroms, robbing and murdering Jews.

Why?

But this entire bloody trail of suffering, persecution and murder could not amount, in scope or cruelty, to the vile precedent of the Nazi regime.

In the entire history of martyrdom, Jewish or gentile, there was never such genocide, planned and carried out in cold blood using advanced methods and calculated to the finest detail. Our generation was the first to see a such a mechanism attacking a peaceful, defenseless population – men, women, old, children, infants and babies – and destroying them in any manner of deaths: famine, shooting, hanging, killing, burning and suffocation, all carried out with terrible methodicalness while other countries kept silent and allowed the blood to flow. 8.25 million Jews lived in the European countries conquered by the Nazis before World War II. 6 million of them were murdered by the Nazis and their assistants during the Holocaust. The Jewish people, who numbered 18 million souls in 1939, number only 12.5 million souls today. The criminal precedent also lies in the fact that this unmatched mass-slaughter was not carried out of spontaneous urge or the plot of few, but rather by a criminal alliance, in which thousands and tens of thousands took part, whether in uniform or not, as well as organizations and units whose sole purpose was carrying out the criminal task.

[Page 144]
Jerahmiel Singer

Dark Days of Horror and Ruin
(The Destruction of Wierzbnik)

Dark clouds settled over Poland. Day by day, almost hour by hour one felt the oncoming war approaching and becoming inevitable. The skies turned black and threatening over the towns and villages where the Jewish population was concentrated. Every news item on the worsening situation, every runner with a mobilization order increased the uncertainty and fright among the masses.

The fact that there were ammunition and arms factories in town was sufficient to arouse people's thoughts of what was in store for the place once hostilities broke out. They thought, rightly as the events proved later, that the presence of those factories would invite the German bombers to unload their destructive charges on the densely populated area in the very near vicinity.

Fifth columnists knew how to exploit this fact in addition to their other subversive activities, only encouraged the rumours in order to create a panic amongst the people and create difficulties for the Polish army authorities.

Meanwhile the Poles themselves started to dismantle the arms factories with theintention of putting them up in some "safer" place (hear-say mentioned Kubel). This official step only increased the fear of what was ahead. Slowly, the shopkeepers emptied their stores and people prepared themselves to flee to the neighbouring towns and villages, which they thought to be safer. At about this time a Civil Defense was organized under the auspices of the authorities. Among the organizers were also Jews, Isaac Laks, Josef Unger, Yitzhak Singer, and others.

"We are all in the same boat"

I joined the Civil Defense when a neighbour, a cafeteria owner in our neighbourhood, presented himself as the man in charge of our block and appealed for volunteers among those who were free of army service or had not yet been called to the flag. He assigned me for duty on a certain stretch day and night because the blackout was already in force.

About a week before the war broke out the congregants of the Great Synagogue in Wierzbnik were indeed surprised when during the Friday night service no people appeared but the District Inspector of Police, in person. His sudden unprecedented appearance in "Shul" in those troubled days certainly was dramatic. He didn't waste any time and came straight to the point. As the responsible authority of the District including Civil Defense, he asked for volunteers to dig trenches in all parts of the town. To make the point, he stressed the fact that the Jews and Poles were now bound by the same bonds of destiny and in his own words, "We are all in the same boat." No one needed any convincing that indeed we were on the verge of war.

The next morning, in spite of the Shabbat, many volunteered to dig the trenches together with the Poles.

Special mention must be made here of Professor Godel Janisevitz, the leader of the Union for the light industry, who was the first to take an active part in this matter.

The inevitable came...On the first of September 1939, the first bomb fell on Wierzbnik next to the plywood factory of the Lichtenstein Brothers. This was followed in the afternoon by a second one, which fell near the house of Chaim Brodbekker, and although this was expected, it nonetheless shocked the people who became more wary as what was to come.

Next day, the atmosphere became somewhat lighter when the news came that England and France declared war on Germany.

Jews started to leave town, one after the other houses in the "Jewish" streets became empty. Only those who did not have the possibilities of hiring a cart to stack their belongings or those who had an active part in the Civil Defense stayed behind. The big yard of Maschliburski was nearly empty. In this block only my cousin, Josef Unger, my Father, my sister and myself were left.

When we heard that all the offices of the government and the local authority had been evacuated to the district capital and that the town mayor was advising everyone to leave, we too on second thoughts, decided to follow suit. On the 5th of September, we started out on foot, because no more vehicles of any description were available in town. It soon became apparent that more people shared our thoughts and decided on the last moment to leave town, amongst them, our family. Since they were setting out to Vashniew, we joined them.

German tanks crossed the village

I couldn't leave town without seeing two of my friends, Dr. Jacob Kramacz and Prof. Leon Korta, who were on duty this time of night at the public bathhouse and to warn them of the situation.

When I got there they were asleep. Without disturbing anyone I awakened them and in a whisper told them of my intention to leave town advising them to join me and after some hesitations and upon my insistence, they quietly and without anyone noticing came away with me.

Together, we made our way through the night uneventful. It was only at dawn, upon meeting the local police sergeant, Oupile, who told us that three German tanks had broken through the village down the road, that we became aware of any change.

These tidings greatly upset us. Instinctively we increased our pace until we started running... Thus we continued marching, taking a little rest here and there until at sunset we reached Vasniew. This was a typical Jewish village, which we found half deserted and in turmoil. We decided therefore to continue our flight.

By then we were quite exhausted and after a few hours sleep all of us, except Unger, took to the road again. This time we went in the direction of Ostrowic.

We felt the effort of the continuous marching and the walking became difficult, besides the strafing from the low flying German planes.

We reached Ostrowic in the early afternoon. The streets teemed with refugees, many from our town. Amongst them we met a close friend of the family, Mordechai Lipstein. Tired from our journey, we sat down to rest when suddenly the streets emptied as German troops were marching into the town.

The German Occupation

The Jews were horror struck, and feared of what was to come. Trouble started soon enough. The Germans immediately imposed a curfew from sunset till 6am. A few Jews on their way home from "Mincha – Mariv" prayers were killed by German patrols.

We stayed a few days with friends, Kleiman family. When we heard that the roads were clear, we decided to return to our town. We hired a horse and wagon and soon arrived back to Wierzbnik. The sight that met our eyes was shocking! There were few people around, all the stores had been broken into and looted. Our flat we found as we had left it so was our provision stock intact that we had prepared before the outbreak of the war.

The bakeries were ordered by the German authorities to open and the people, including Jews, were queuing up for bread. Soon the Poles started to point at the Jews, who were then forcefully removed by the German guards. Daily, Jews were being rounded up for all kinds of jobs: to clean German army vehicles, to clear public buildings of materials and furniture, loading, unloading, etc. This work was carried out with beatings and mistreatment.

The night after Yom Kippur, we smelt a strong smell of smoke. We climbed to the roof to see if we could detect anything, but in vain. Next day, however, an awful sight awaited us. The Synagogue in Nieska Street and the adjoining building of Talmud Torah had burned down completely with al the Torah scrolls, religious objects, the furniture as well as the community offices. (The burning of the Synagogue is described in a separate article by D.P.).

As it transpired later, the Germans had perpetrated this act, since this very same night many Synagogues went up in flames throughout Poland. The Germans had apparently intended to commit this arson on Yom Kippur night but were misled by the Jewish calendar. This event left a deep sorrow on the Jewish community in town.

Edicts

A series of proclamations, decrees and orders against the Jews followed one another. To cite only a few of them: the turning in of foreign currency, jewelry, gold, silver and other precious metals. Orders about restriction of movement: It was forbidden to go by train or any public vehicle without special permission, it was forbidden to raise prices as food rationing and new taxes were introduced and etc.

As life became more difficult, so the tension rose day by day. In many cases, Poles so called "Volksdeutsche" betrayed Jewish shopkeepers, whereupon the Germans put through ruthless searches. Not a day passed without a few Jewish families being ransacked. An enormous quantity of material was taken out of the cellars of Yaacov Guterman. The stores of Shmuel Cohen, Josef Drexler and others were completely emptied. The German authorities expropriated the sawing mills and timber yards of Mordechai Lipstein, Yitshak Rosenberg, Uri Helstein, Meir Steinbaum, Moshe Tentzer, Shmuel and Yaacov Kleiner, Weitzman, the father-in-law of Yaacov Zuckerman. The factory and sawmill of Shmuel Pochachewsky were confiscated, as was the plywood factory or Hortzi. Here I have to mention the tragic case of Shmuel Kleiner, who upon hearing the news that his timber yard had been expropriated had a heart failure and passed away on the spot.

The Sign of Dishonor

The current beatings and seizing of Jews paralyzed the life of the Jewish population altogether. And if the Jews still tried to get about in spite of the atmosphere, this became impossible with the latest and most humiliating of all decrees: the wearing of the yellow patch.

That decree caused great confusion amongst us, everyone felt as if he was being branded and a deep sense of shame overcame many. Not surprising therefore that the first days of the decree most of us did not leave our dwellings, but life continues and slowly people started to show their faces outside.

The Poles meeting us on the street grinned and smiled of satisfaction. In their satanic minds they were convinced that all the furor and enmity of the Germans would be directed only against the Jews, whilst they would enjoy special privileges. Whereas to the Germans, the yellow patch indicated a person who could be taken for forced labour without having to account to anyone.

Another order, which caused us great embarrassment and humiliation, ordered us to take off our hats before a Germans in uniform...

The local authority was taken over by German officials, and a "Volksdeutche" (a Pole who declared that he was of German origin) was named as its head.

At the same time the Germans set up a council through which they could govern the Jews, and demanded a special contribution for this purpose. This sum had to be handed over within 24 hours, and the people had to collect it within this time limit. With the setting up of the Jewish council, the random seizing of Jews in the streets ceased, but the council had to provide the necessary manpower in accordance with the German demands. Soon there were two groups: those who were always sent out to work on the one hand, whilst the other group comprised of those who paid ransom money.

The community was ordered to draw up a list of males between the ages of 14 and 65, which actually made up the available manpower for them to draw upon. The Germans made a point of it that all those who appeared on the lists underwent a so-called medical inspection. In fact it was a farce since the doctors did not receive any instructions on the subject. Jewish apostates too were forced to register and were included in the lists.

The Death of Engineer Hidokewitch

A Polish engineer named Hidokewitch, was murdered in the beginning of 1940 by partisans who suspected him of cooperating with the Germans in putting the ammunition factory into production again. Following this act, hundreds of Poles were arrested. The Germans were fully aware that Jews were not involved in this murder. Yet, they arrested a number of them. They were held a whole month in the central prison of Radom and were subjected to harsh treatment. Amongst them we count Dr. Leon Korta, Zwi Feigenbaum, Abraham Shmuel Eisenstadt, Beni Zuckerman and his Father, Josef Paflower and son, Meir and Moshe Brodbeker, Yaacov Guterman and others.

Since they did not succeed in finding the perpetrators, they released the Jews, but not before the community paid a decent sum as a special tax for their release.

Owing to transfer of population orders, which the Germans had enacted, Polish refugees of the Furmon region arrived in Wierzbnik. They found refuge in different places in town. In March a train-full of Jewish and Polish refugees arrived from Lodz. The Jewish community went all out to help them and saw to their needs as far as they could. Part of them traveled on to Warsaw, mostly those who had relations and friends there.

A short wile afterwards another train arrived with Jewish refugees from Plotzk, but now the community could not help much considering the previous influx and settling of refugees in town.

Refugees

The great number of refugees spelled out need and poverty, and it soon became necessary to put up a public kitchen, which provided them with regular meals. The community with the help of volunteers supported the kitchen. A great number of women were active, but special mention should be made of the few who excelled themselves in this task: Yehiel Schechman and his wife, Mrs. Avisa Milman-Herling, Mrs. Hochnitz, Yeshayahu Jona Sharfhertz, Haya Brank-Weisblum, Yeheskel Morgenstern and Moshe Feldman.

Most of the refugees belonged to intellectual circles and it was not easy for them to adapt themselves to the new conditions and to the fare of the public kitchen.

A special effort was made to provide additional nourishment to needy children. Every Friday bread was collected for them and at Shabbat they were guests at a communal meal with the family Steinbaum which was always accompanied with song.

Within this framework, my sister Gutzia Tentzer, organized a children performance "The Trial of the Good Mother". The following took part in this performance: Natasha Zirenska, Sara (Slusia) Scharfhertz, Rivka (Regi) Milman and her brother, Hanna Tentzer, Issy Siskind, Mietek Wiegensprech, Mondek Holtzman and Rachel Milman.

The children played their parts with great gusto and the event was no doubt a bright spot in their dark lives.

Quite a number of refugees were ill, stricken by an epidemic of typhoid, which spread amongst them. The community organized a hospital in one of the houses on Ilitzka Street, where conditions were not ideal due to overcrowding and other physical shortcomings.

The Ghetto

If my memory does not fail me, the ghetto was established, like in other parts of the "General Government" in mid-April 1940.

The district governor ordered the Jewish council to establish the ghetto and gave them 3 days time to arrange the evacuation of certain streets and to concentrate all the Jews within the quarter, which had been proclaimed as Jewish. The boundaries of the ghetto included as follows: the streets of Kilinskiego, Nieska, Wisoka, a small part of Rinach (ie. The pavement from the corner of Visoka until the corner of Nieska only, Krotka, Koliova, Jedushveskiego until the Jewish Cemetery, an alley leading from Koliova Street until the house of Miriam Drexler, Ilsetzka Street until the plywood factory of the Lichtenstein Brothers.

And yet there was something particular about the ghetto in Wierzbnik, which as we learned later was the only place where the ghetto was not completely closed up (where none could come or go). One was free to move to and from other quarters in town.

Credit for this exceptional feat is apparently due to the Community leaders who succeeded in influencing and convincing the Germans to demarcate the ghetto as described above.

This allowed the Poles to move freely in the ghetto, a fact that made life easier for us from the aspect of food supplies, as well as for communication with the outside world.

The refugees who had arrived earlier in Wierzbnik from Lodz and from Plotzk were ordered also to move into the ghetto. This meant overcrowding and with it a spreading of the typhoid epidemic.

Since the healing and the prevention measures called for the isolation of sick persons who were infected by this contagious disease, the overcrowding became still greater.

The Germans transferred part of the refugees from Plotzk to the neighbouring town of Bodzentin.

Mistreatment and Beatings

Life became almost unbearable as new decrees and orders followed one another. One of the decrees, which hit Jews most severely, was the restriction on trade. One had to procure a special license for each deal, and so high was the demanded payment that it was almost impossible to bear.

Many remained without making a living, with the setting up of the ghetto, and were forced to look elsewhere for their wellbeing.

Until May 1940, the Germans used the Jewish manpower for a variety of jobs: ie. Log cutting, cleaning of houses and offices, loading and unloading, street clearing, snow clearance, and etc. All this changed when one Saturday in May 1940, hundreds of men were taken from their homes to an iron ore mine at a distance of 12 kilometers from town. There they had to work hard labour. The Jews were not used to such hard physical tasks and this left them in a state of shock.

A few days afterwards saw the sudden appearance of S.S. troops belonging to the "Skull and Cross-Bones" Regiment. They entered the ghetto, broke open the doors of houses, meted out brutal beatings indiscriminately and forced everyone to the streets. From there they were driven in the direction of the metal factories, which were part of the Starachowice plant.

That same day I was in the office of the Jewish Council together with Moshe Feldman, Abraham Goldstein, the teacher Laps and twenty others. All of us had been called upon for secretarial work, when before we had time to settle down to work, the same S.S. men entered the building and started to beat everyone up with their rifle butts. We tried to flee to the other rooms in the building but none were available. They hit us mercilessly. I received a few blows to my head and ran home from there covered with blood. I had to stay for six weeks at home.

About the time of these bloody events, the Germans started to "employ" the Jews at the Starachowice factory. They were organized into working parties and worked in three shifts.

Until this period it was possible to avoid duties by paying ransom money, but now this became impossible and everyone, without exception, went out to work.

Food Rationing

With the entrance of the Germans in Wierzbnik they ordered the rationing of food, which was distributed in small quantities with food cards. When the factory was put into production again, the workers received supplementary rations of bread, marmalade, fish and a small quantity of sugar. The food rations were insufficient and the people turned to the black market that of course was very dangerous. Trading in the black market was punishable, even with the death penalty.

Hard Labour

In spite of the fact that the Jews worked in a factory, which had first priority, all the Jews were taken one summer afternoon and transported to the Lublin region to work in fortifications on the German-Russian border. Working conditions were beyond description, whilst their supervisors were brutal and whipped them.

Most of the men had families, who stayed behind without the minimal economic means of existence.

This happened on Thursday, Tisha Be' Av, with the women weeping in the streets bewailing their fate.

The council of Jews, after many efforts, succeeded in bringing about the release, after four weeks, of the married men. The bachelors were released after the fortifications were completed.

Hanging and Murders

During the summer of 1940 a German patrol was fired upon from a house at the end of the town, were upon all the inhabitants, Jews and Christians alike were arrested. The Germans soon came to the conclusion that the Jews were not guilty, and released them accordingly, whilst the Poles were held in prison. After a few days the Germans put up a scaffold in the middle of the Ring, and the whole non-Jewish population was forced to witness the execution of the arrested. Amongst the executed was an old woman of 67 years and babies.

Midst 1940, a well-known personality, Itzhak Rosenberg, was murdered by a Ukrainian policeman upon leaving his factory under the pretense that he had ignored this order to halt. This event caused great sorrow by all Jews in town, especially on the workers of the factory who had worked with him. He was a fervent Zionist and a staunch supporter of the national funds, to which he was the biggest donator.

The Collection of Furs

The beginning of 1941, the Jews were ordered to hand over all furs to the Germans. All had to bring in fur coats or any other article made of fur to the police station without receiving anything in return of course. Believing that the Jews had not handed in all furs, the Germans started house searches. A funny thing happened when a German policeman came to the house of Hershel Feigenbaum to look for concealed furs. Upon his question of "where is the fur?" everybody kept quiet except a little girl who thought he was asking about the cream of the milk, which in Yiddish has the same expression like fur, "Peltz". In all innocence she answered, "The cat has eaten it". The German chuckled and left the house without further ado.

Resistance Activities

In spite of the threats and depression exercised by the Germans in the ghetto, there were a few who had the courage to resist by all possible means, These activities were not without danger to their lives. Such was the group which members included (among others), Shmuel Cohen, Shlomo Lev, Buslig Melamed, Zvi Feigenbaum, Hershel Herblum, which somehow got hold of a radio set which they hid in one of the cellars. They used to gather regularly to listen to London radio, and afterwards spread the news "underground" from one to the other.

Every week they used to meet in the house of my wife's Grandfather, Josef Reuven Lichtenstein, a well versed and enlightened man, to discuss the political and military situation and to exchange ideas. They somehow got German newspapers and learned to read the truth between the lines, with the help of the radio in London.

What we feared happened when the Germans arrested Shlomele Ben Zelig Melamed and Itzhak Trupa, the son-in-law of Libish Binstock. Their friends were afraid under torture they would disclose all. But Shlomele assured Hershel Herblum, who was arrested by the Jewish police so as to get him in the prison to contact the arrested, that he would never give his friends away, even if it cost him his life.

From prison they were transferred to a concentration camp where Shlomo Lev died soon after his arrival. His wife received notification to that effect. Itzhak Trupa on the other hand, as told by his brother living now in Petah Tiqua, fell one day before the end of the war during a bombing raid.

The Witch Dance Around Work Permits

1942, was the worst and bitterest year fro the Polish Jewry. On Seder night, a relative of Simcha Mintzberg came to us, who had been in Lublin and had succeeded to escape from there during the expulsion of the Jews and had reached Wierzbnik. The girl by the name of Bianca told of the horrors, which had passed in Lublin, and of the expulsion of the whole Jewish population to an unknown direction. At the same time, news reached us of the concentration of all Jews from the surrounding villages of Warsaw, who were subject to expulsion as well. The Poles spread rumours that the Germans were transporting Jews in wagons to certain places in the Lublin region and returned with empty wagons from there. They also told us that German drivers replaced Polish engine drivers at a certain spot and that was as far as their knowledge went, but added that over the whole area hung a sickly smell of corpses.

It became also known that many of these Poles living in the area went down with jaundice.

Unfortunately, very few took these stories seriously and put them down, as pure fantasy since it did not dawn upon them that is was possible to destroy people, just like that, and without any reason.

The rumours persisted and became louder day-by-day, and fear overtook all for the future. The Germans were at the peak of their success at the front and the political situation worried the Jews still more. The Poles on the whole were hostile, and even those who were active against the Germans refused to take Jews into their ranks. When I addressed myself to an old acquaintance of mine, Jankowsky, on this subject, his answer was curt, "Impossible" without any explanation.

In the registry office I met a non-Jewish comrade with whom I had studied together at college in Konske, and he gave me, without any payment, identity papers with Aryan names for my two sisters, my wife Ida Birentzweig. The last two named in fact, hid themselves with the help of these identity papers with Polish families and thus saved themselves.

Beginning of the summer of 1942, the expulsions started in our vicinity: Ostrowice, Skarzysko, Radom, Kolzev and other places. Those who had succeeded to escape reached us and told of what was happening. With all these facts at hand, it became finally clear to the people that danger was approaching. At the same time it was rumoured that people who were engaged in essential work would be exempted from the expulsion order. This brought rise to a witch dance around the procurement of work permits, and all kinds of agents appeared overnight who led a brisk trade with these permits, which sold at exorbitant prices. The permits sold were fictitious and were especially wanted by elderly people. For them it represented a question of life or death and was therefore willing to pay these prices. There were those who acquired permits with their last savings, to be on the safe side, for a few priority factories like Starachowice, the electricity works "Zeorg" and the sawmill of Heler.

The town was full of refugees, and they too joined the market for work permits. This caused the prices to rise further still.

A month before the expulsion, a work camp was put up by the Germans in the Majowka district. The camp consisted of wooden huts and the non-local workers from Starachowice could live there. The Jewish workers willingly went to live there for two reasons. First of all they wanted to make sure that they had permanent employment in a high priority plant and secondly because it offered a certain security.

This plant was divided into two parts, upper and lower. Whilst the work camp in Majowka was intended for those working in the lower part, the other camp called Szczelnica served those working in the upper part.

In October 1942, Gestapo men and German gendarmes "visited" the houses of the "well off" and robbed and plundered all they could lay their hands on with a special eye on precious objects. Early one morning, I was still in bed, they came to our house too and without a word went straight to the cupboards and emptied them.

Seeing what was happening, the Jews tried to sell their belongings, at least what was left, to the local non-Jews. And that was not always easy; so many objects were passed to Polish neighbours for safekeeping.

As the days passed, the first signs appeared of the German's brutal intention of expulsion of the whole Jewish population from the town. Jews from other places like: Wychock, Szidlowiec, Suchedniow and other villages told of the dire fate of the Jews there when all men, women, and children were expulsed to an unknown place. Another fact which supported these forebodings, was the sudden demand of Germans, who had ordered shoes or suits with Jewish tradesmen, for their orders whether completed or not. This was most suspicious since no reasonable excuse was given.

These ominous signs brought dark shadows on every Jewish house. All the elderly feared and infirmed that they would be the first victims of the expulsion with all its consequences. The speculation begun with a logical reasoning that if and when the expulsion started, it would include all those who were within the ghetto whilst the workers who would be at work in the factories would not be affected. Tine was to prove their reasoning to be right. There were even those who tried to work two consecutive shifts at work, so as to spend as much time as possible in the factory and so to save themselves.

The Expulsion

The 27th of October 1942, this date will always be remembered with horror. Jewish police entered at dawn the courtyards of the houses in the ghetto and announced sorrowfully the German order that everyone without exception had to leave his home and concentrate in the Rynek. Everybody understood what it was all about and took with them small parcels of personal effects that had been kept at hand for some time now.

I was among the first who made their way with their families to the central square, Awaiting us were companies of S.S. troops, Germans gendarmes and for the first time we saw units of Lutishim (Latvians) who were the actual executors of the expulsion, They ordered us to line up five abreast. I stood facing Krotka Street.

The Separation of Families

After a short interval, the Latvians went through the lines and demanded that all money and precious objects be handed over to them. By force accompanied by insults they robbed what they could. An hour or so afterwards, they called on all who had work permits to step outside the lines and group up separately. This caused an immediate splitting up of families, since not all the members of one family had a permit. Heartrending were the scenes that took place.

People with work permits refused to part from their dear ones, relinquishing thereby voluntarily the opportunity to be exempt from the expulsion, but the Germans took them by force from their families into the other group.

Having completed the disposition of the groups, those with the work permits were ordered to march off in the direction of the Szczelnica camp at Starachowice under the guard of Ukrainians, who were called "Werkscutz". The distance from the Rynek until the camp was about 7 kilometers uphill, which we had to run with the guard at our heels beating, shooting into our ranks and murdering. Among the victims was the son-in-law of Shmuel Cohen, Josef. I remember this event very clearly because it happened right next to me and secondly because he was a close friend of mine.

Tired and exhausted we were pushed into a trench while Germans with machine guns at the ready towered over us at both sides, and again we were ordered to hand over money, precious objects and etc. At the same time they got a hold of Jacob Rubinstein to take him to the kitchen and asked him whether he had anything of worth in his possession. When he gave a negative answer, they searched him and found some money. The Germans wanted to execute him on the spot. Under the threat of death he begged for mercy and implored them for his life, with difficulty he did save himself. This incident was sufficient for all others to start to dig deep into their pockets and other hiding places and handed over all that was left to them.

Something unexpected happened when a young lad started to curse the Germans loudly. The commander, Althoff, murdered him on the spot. We were taken to the barracks in the camp, which was surrounded by a barbed wire fence and efficiently guarded.

The people who remained in Rynek were again divided into two groups, one group was taken for forced labour in the sawmill or in the electricity plant, whilst the rest were loaded into wagons and transported to Treblinka.

We learned later that 42 people, old and sick who could not or did not want to go to Rynek and remained in their homes, were murdered in cold blood. My wife's Grandfather, Reb Josef Reuven Lichtenstein and his wife Gitel were amongst them.

The Germans went through every house and murdered everyone indiscriminately they found; a young girl, the daughter of Pinchas Manela was among the victims.

Page 155]
Zvi Faigenbaum

Ilza, the Beginning of the Scourge

On the day the war broke out, September 1st 1939 (on Shabbat Eve) I was in the Polish city of Warsaw. I arrived there with my sister-in-law, Rivka Zoberman (today in Bnei-Brak), accompanying my brother-in-law Shmuel Zoberman, who was sent by the doctors for surgery at the stomatological institute in Warsaw. I stayed there from Friday evening to Sunday. My wife and children, unaware of my whereabouts, were concerned for me.

That night I already knew about the German bombardment that started on Friday. I was also told that the local residents were leaving town. Logic dictated that I look for cover in nonstrategic places until the threat was over, away from factories and railways which were the first targets for bombardment.

At first light I went outside to talk to neighbors and learn about the situation, but most of them have left the city. I went to the Beit Midrash to pray and met three people there (of which I remember only Akiva Shefla), who told me that everyone was leaving and they would be following them today as well. The people left in different direction but the majority left for Iłża.

I prayed. I never imagined that this was the last time I would pray in this synagogue.

When I finished my prayer I heard the buzz of airplanes followed immediately by strong explosions that covered the entire area with a cloud of dust, blotting out the sun. I ran home and noticed the impact crater of a bomb, whose fragments spread as far as my home. Curious, I picked up a fragment, something I have never seen before, but soon I realized that there was no time to wait and I immediately went to rent a vehicle (a wagon and horses) to take my family to Iłża.

After many hardships we arrived in Iłża during the night and found the place quiet and life going on as usual. Curiously, the situation actually led to some prosperity. People were renting rooms, selling goods and earning plenty of money. I too rented a room for my family and we started settling in...

We naively believed that this matter would not last more than a few weeks, and so I insisted on the right to extend the lease on the room for another two months beyond the month I paid for. We all felt we were acting according to common sense. Except for one person... the admirable and honorable Chanoch Biderman and his honorable wife Rivka. While some brave young men remained behind to watch their property, he was the only man of means who would not budge. He refused to listen to advice. He also never told other people what they should do. But he didn't want to go to Iłża.

Tuesday went by and Wednesday was normal until noon... we listened to the radio, intent on every piece of news. We also received news about events in our town from messengers, young men traveled back and forth between Wierzbnik and Iłża for this purpose.

On Wednesday noon... the radio fell silent! There was no more news. We imagined that the station in Warsaw was hit by a bomb. And here come the messengers... a tank division came as far as the entrance to Wierzbnik! The 42 antiaircraft cannons that surrounded the factories opened fire on them. Three were hit, leaving the damaged tanks behind...

We quickly learned that the radio station was unharmed, but the entire Polish defense was compromised. The future was already clear, but the tank battle also confirmed that our departure for Iłża was a smart move.

Thursday: news followed news. The Germans were advancing on all fronts, Kielce was also conquered as well as the nearby Słupia. Some of the people from Wierzbnik escaped to Słupia. Its innocent residents never imagined that the Germans would arrive so soon. The "experts" decided that it was a French armored force, coming to the aid of the Polish army. They were welcomed with cakes and flowers... a mistake that has saved them (and the refugees of Wierzbnik among them) from pogroms. Those details would have been amusing if they were not so tragic. We didn't know yet was the future held in store. What we already knew beyond doubt was that in a couple of days, we would also find ourselves in the maw of the vicious German beast, because it was unreasonable to assume that their advance would be halted at the gates of Iłża.

We prayed for one thing – an eventless transition. The fact that Iłża was a minor, negligible place, gave us hope that the place would change hands in a relatively uneventful manner, because we believed that the strategic or military value of the place was a key factor. The Polish high command, however, thought differently, and decided to stage the defense of the region in Iłża...

Buried on the front line

Among the refugees from Wierzbnik were the two rabbis of Wierzbnik, Rabbi Ben Zion Rabinowicz and Rabbi Menachem Tenenbaum. The latter, an old, frail man, was effected by the hardships and terrors and his condition degenerated. In the evening, a messenger came to inform me of his sudden death. I hurried to his apartment where I found Leibish Herblum (now in the States), his son-in-law (the husband of his daughter Rachel) Akiva Shefla and Shmuel Tenenbaum, who later passed away in Roma and was buried in Jerusalem. We immediately contacted the local Hevra Kaddisha and decided on a burial location and the time of the funeral, which would be held first thing in the morning.

The general situation was already tense and we barely gathered ten people for the funeral, among them four members of the Wierzbnik community: Akiva Shefla, another man whom I do not recall, Leibish Herblum and the author. The cemetery, which was customarily located outside of town, was on a hillside. On our way we stumbled across the front lines of the Polish army. The front line under the hill boasted soldiers armed with machineguns crouching in their ditches, horses standing and stretched telephone lines. Before we arrived at the open grave, I heard the observer make a phone call: "Hello, sergeant, the tanks are coming in on the left!" The Polish soldiers gave us no trouble, but I realized that we were directly between the two fronts and the oncoming clash. I said: "We must carry out our task as soon as possible, because there is no time to waste." The grave was still being dug and we tried to reach the necessary minimum. We lowered the deceased, placed the seal, covered everything with earth and asked forgiveness according to tradition. We then headed to town. I said again: "Gentlemen, we must get to town as quickly as possible, even if it means running, avoiding the main roads traveled by tanks and taking side paths instead."

My first act was gathering my family, wife and children. My second act was searching for a house with a concrete ceiling. The only such building I found was the bathhouse and that was where we headed, for the lack of other choice. Those who were inside the town had no idea what was about to happen. I told them that they must all find cover right away. The bathhouse filled with people, and the shooting began soon after. First light arms, then heavy arms. First machineguns, then light artillery, escalating more and more... the shells were falling among the houses! We heard more and more explosions. "This is no longer a joke," said some people. But suddenly the bathhouse was alight, burning all around us... we felt we must leave the building now or we never will. We burst out. Bullets whistled overhead. My daughter Faiga was grazed by a bullet. We jumped into the river passing through the town. We ran in the water until we found ourselves between houses. I noticed a stone house and we burst inside. The house was filled with people from Wierzbnik, the rabbi among them. We were welcomed with open arms. But the shooting continued. Suddenly I realized that my eldest daughter Chava wasn't with us. I could not get over my anxiety for her. After two hours we received word of her location. In another street. I took advantage of a short cessation in the shooting and ran to her. They day had come and gone. We are in the dark room of a Jew named Holtz, who was a soldier during the Japanese War. He was laughing at the explosions. Fires broke out in the neighboring houses. I stood in the doorway and after every explosion poked my head out to examine our situation. Polish soldiers were standing under the walls in the street next to us and firing. I went and talked to them in between the shots. And things continued in this manner until dawn. The Germans must have noticed the fire coming from our position and aimed their fire this way. We escaped, my daughter and I, and arrived together at the house I left to look for her. We were all together again, happy but afraid.

At 10 in the morning, the Polish army ceased fire. Quiet. But only for a short while. The buzz of aircraft deafened us. They flew in waves, unloading their bombs on the houses of Iłża and us inside them. A new wave unloaded its bombs on our street. The houses right next to us were shaking. The people gathered started crying Shma Israel! They were all upset, frightened and alert. The rabbi turns to me and asks, "Should we run out?" But before I can think of an answer comes the answer "from heaven"... a bomb hits the wall of the house and everyone rushed outside.

In the street, confusion. People are running in all directions. Another wave of airplanes fires into the crowd with machineguns. The fire is aimed right for us. We press against the walls and hide under them. A break. Vanishing. We run again, beyond the houses. Arrive in a small grove, lie on the ground among the trees. Around us the houses are burning and there are sounds of machinegun fire. Apparently we are close to the front line again. Late in the afternoon, after the bombardments, we had some casualties. Some are residents of Wierzbnik – Michael Gutholtz, the daughter of Noah Gutvil and her husband, the son of Shmuel Vakselman from Lipie.

Sunday morning, and we have yet to see a German soldier. They dare not enter the town yet. But things are quiet. Vehicles carrying the refugees of Wierzbnik, led by the brave, are starting to go back home. Yaakov Kornwaser rented a wagon. I joined him too. In the Marcule forest we met two men from the Hevra Kaddisha of Wierzbnik, Pinchas Manela and Kalman Lebman, who came to burry the Jewish soldiers that fell on the front lines, with the permission of the German authorities. Tanks were passing by the hundreds. No one addressed us. Only at the crossroads in Lubienia did we meet guards who ordered us down. They conducted a search, looking for weapons. They found me carrying the knife I used to butcher poultry. They took me aside, and everyone panicked, as did I. The guard asked me "What is this?" I managed to give an answer that seemed to satisfy him, and he released me. But I didn't realize it until the people in the wagon told me "Come back!"

When we reached home, we were surprised. Thank god, everything is still standing. There were no changes. Their tactics turned out to be beyond us. They were interested in leaving the factories whole and gaining control over them. They sought to use the bombardments to scare people and create a panic. To ensure that no one removed the machinery. They didn't touch the population either, in case the engineers and craftsmen necessary to run the factories were among it. That was the reason they left our town unharmed, after all of us save for Chanoch Biderman escaped from it. He turned out to be right, his intuition accurate.

By God's will we returned, but not all of us. Of those who left Iłża that afternoon, about 100 were arrested, beaten and led to the camp in Kielce. They were kept there for three days with no food or water. They underwent severe torture. Only on the fourth day were they allowed to return home as well.

We slowly became used to the new way of life, the German regime (whose first act was burning down the synagogue, a story told elsewhere), a time for saying "O that it were evening!" in the morning and "O that it were morning!" in the evening. And although the new hardships outweighed the old, we could never forget the beginning of the scourge, Iłża...

Dark clouds gathered over the Jewish town

[Page 158]
Pinchas Nudelman

In the "Camps for the Correction of Man"

About a month after the German occupation, the Germans have ordered all youths to "register". We assumed that registration would involve hard labor, and since I did not wish to labor for the Nazis, I decided to escape to the Russian side. I talked to friends – The Drajnudel brothers and Hershel Lipstein (alive today in Canada), and we took a train to Przemyœl. When we approached the border, we left the train and headed to the house of a smuggler, whose address we got in Wierzbnik. We found him according to the description we received and paid him to help us cross the border.

During the night he handed us over to the German guards he bribed, and they pretended to check us, looted a few choice items and allowed us to cross the border, accompanied by the mocking remark "Go ahead, off you go to paradise".

We crossed the river and continued through Russian territory until we arrived by train to the city of Lvov, where we found a pleasant surprise. We discovered a large group of townsmen from Wierzbnik, who also arrived there at different times and from different places. We debated whether we should go back to the German side or stay there, because the conditions were very harsh. The situation was very depressing and many have unfortunately returned to the Germans and perished later.

After a while, I was arrested along with other people who came from the German side, and imprisoned in Lvov for about nine months under unbearable conditions. 100 of us were crammed in a small cell and suffered from the lack of food and room. At the end of that period we were transferred to a prison in Cherson where the conditions were slightly improved, however shortly after our arrival we were given our verdict, which was in itself a farce. They hardly interrogated us, I heard no charges and there were no legal deliberations. There was neither defense nor prosecution. One day I was simply summoned to an office where they corroborated my personal details such as first name, surname, age and so on, and gave me papers to sign. When I asked what I was signing I was surprised to learn that I was put on trial in Moscow and the Troika sentenced me to 8 years at a labor camp. I innocently asked what would happen if I refused to sign the papers, since no trial was held for me, and the manager answered me, half mocking half dismissive, "If you don't sign, I'll sign". I laughed back and signed.

After that we were transported by train through Charkov to the northern area of Arkhangelsk, where the cold reached a temperature of -50c and below. The trip took 18 days, with the railroad cars closed and guarded by armed soldiers.

When we arrived we were led to the cabins and told that this was our new home. The prisoners were mostly Uzbeks, who were exiled there in droves back in 1936, practically whole villages of them. Many of them died of the cold there and the ones who survived have adapted somehow to the harsh conditions. They told us that their sentences were extended every so often and that they already accepted the fact that they will never leave this dark life of slavery. After a while we were divided into groups and sent to work in the forests every morning, accompanied by guards and dogs. We chopped down trees, laid railroad tracks, and also performed other tasks. Each of us was given a fairly big work quota and the food was distributed according to our productivity. Many perished because they could not stand the harsh conditions – the climate, the work, the cold, the diseases and the lack of nutrition. A disease called "Tsinga" was common there, brought on by the lack of vitamins and causing the gums to swell and teeth to fall out. I too wouldn't have been able to carry on if not for an older Polish prisoner I made friends with and who saved me: as partners, I gave him whatever tobacco we received because I did not smoke. Others would cherish it, while I gave him mine expecting nothing in return, a fact that made him like me very much. In time, he was discovered to be a surgeon and put in charge of the camp's hospital. In this role he was able to help me by keeping me at the hospital, giving me food and so on.

Word from Pratzovnik

After a long stay in that camp I was transported along with a group of other prisoners to a different camp, closer to the train station, because during my incarceration the Russians had signed an agreement with General Sikorski concerning the release of Polish citizens. In this camp I met one day with a Jew whose leg was amputated, and during our conversation I learned that he came from a town near Wierzbnik, Szydłowiec, and escaped with our townsman Meir Pratzovnik to Russia. The two of them have somehow ended up in the same labor camp. One day he suffered a bad accident; a tree he was cutting in the forest fell on his leg and the hospital staff was forced to amputate it. When I asked about Pratzovnik's whereabouts he replied that he believed the man dead, because he left him exhausted and in very bad shape.

After my release I arrived in the city of Samarkand and met the Dreksler family from our town. They told me that another man from Wierzbnik, Shlomo Lipstein, was in town, suffering from poor health and in need of help. Unfortunately I couldn't find him; I found another townsman called Hilel Frimerman, who also mentioned Lisptein and gave me 500 rubles to take to him, but I couldn't find the man I was looking for. A few days later I learned that Hilel Frimerman drowned while bathing in the local river. In the city of Karmina, where the Seventh Division was stationed, I met with our townswoman Malka Weisberg, who was at the time sick and feverish.

On board the last ship

The next day I was taken to the station and wanted to board the train going to Krasnovodsk, and then cross the Caspian Sea on my way to Israel. Luckily I met another acquaintance who put me in an officers' car, and the two of us got as far as the port city. Suddenly, I saw a ship being boarded by people while Russian policemen checked their certificates. These were the Poles who crossed the border according to the agreement with General Sikorski. I also wanted to board but I was pushed back by the Russians since I did not have the necessary papers. With me was another Jew and the two of us sought a way of boarding the ship. After much skulking we found the rope mooring the ship to the dock, climbed it and jumped into the boat. To our surprise I found the Dreksler family on board the same ship – and from that moment on, we traveled together.

After a relatively short trip we arrived in Persia, but since we had no papers we were arrested and taken to prison, where we met 30 other Jews. The local authorities wanted to return us to the Russians but we claimed that we were Polish citizens and fortunately, the Russians refused to take us back. In the meantime, a delegate from Israel came and promised to look after us. A few days later all the prisoners, and me among them, were drafted into the Polish army, where I also met our townsmen – Yoseph Birenzweig and Yehuda Rybak. The Poles brought us to Teheran and from there, through Iraq, we reached Israel.

[Page 160]
Leibish Herblum

The Day of Holocaust and the Extermination of our Town
October 27th, 1942 – 16th Cheshvan, 5703

It was a dark day for our town, Wierzbnik-Starachowice. At approximately 5 a.m. in the morning, we suddenly heard the SS beasts screaming and shouting: Jews out, out!

Anxious and miserable we left our homes, every Jew in town, and headed toward the marketplace, where the Nazi beasts were already waiting to line us up in rows of five. From time to time we heard the sounds of gunfire from the direction of Jewish houses, a bloody echo to the murder of those Jews who did not leave their houses "quickly enough".

My whole world was shattered

We were forced to stand like this until late noon, when they started screaming "fall in line!" and immediately thereafter we were forced to march forward on the road to doom. Downcast, our hearts bleeding, we marched toward the train station and during this march I was approached and pulled out of line by the oppressors, to serve in the cleanup unit (Raum Commando). I was shocked and didn't know what to do. I was wondering "What would come next?" "What should I do?" "Is this my last chance to bid my dead family and friends goodbye?"

I asked myself why I, Leibish Herblum, was chosen for this sacred task.

Apparently I was deemed worthy because of my 30 years of service to Hevra Kaddisha, a service that allowed me during this Holocaust to offer our martyrs a Jewish burial. And indeed, I only got one last look at the martyrs that were about to be shipped on their final journey, my wife, my children, my relatives and friends. My entire world was shattered and tears of blood fell from my eyes, soaking the road to death, while a silent prayer played in my mind: "God, avenge the spilled blood of servants, the blood of the innocent and the pure!"

The cleanup unit, which numbered about 20 men including myself, was ordered to march toward the Jewish cemetery in town. When we reached it we were struck dumb by the indescribable horrors we witnessed. Every few minutes came a new shipment of murdered town residents, practically a martyring. 48 corpses, among them 22 women and 26 men were found scattered across the terrain. We were ordered to burry the murdered victims and started digging two large graves, one for the women and one for the men. While we were working, a member of the cleanup unit, a young man from the town of Bodzentyń named Eliyahu Shapir, broke his leg and was squirming in agony. The murderers saw it and shot him on the spot. The bullet went through his mouth while he was thrashing and bleeding. Though he was still alive and fully conscious, the Germans ordered us to burry him as well. We wanted nothing more at that moment than for the earth to swallow us alive with the rest of the universe! How can you burry a living, breathing man? At the last moment, an order was somehow issued, to carry him to the cabin we stayed in, but his luck did not hold and the next day he was murdered, again.

With awe and respect I buried the following holy women: Dvora Morgenstern, Miriam Kojfman, Fraindl, the wife of Fishel Menashe. Among the 26 men murdered by the soldiers were Yoseph

Reuven Lichtenstein, Moshe Pinchas Lichtenstein, Henoch Kojfman, Fishel Dreksler, Moshe Kumetz, Moshe Krojzman and Shlomo Melamed. Three of them had tallits to cover the bodies with. I did above and beyond my ability to bind them respectfully, to honor them and our God. And so did our town fall before our eyes.

When I returned from the cemetery there were once again two SS soldiers waiting for me and I was told to follow them to the police station in town, where I found the bodies of two people who were shot earlier. They were the brothers Aharon and Noah Zylberberg, the sons of Avraham Zylberberg. When I left the police station I found another corpse, that of a child named Mordechai Kornwaser. Somehow I managed to get a cart, loaded the corpses on it and gave them a proper burial.

On Friday morning, the third day of that insane murder spree, I was once again led by an SS killer to a place where I was told to bury two young children. They belonged to Rosa, daughter of Shmuel Isser. My heart bleeding I used the rest of my strength to offer those young martyrs a proper burial. When I returned to the cabin, accompanied by the nightmares of this hell, I was called again by a Nazi killer to bury a young woman who was laid before the cabin, and immediately afterwards I was called to take another victim out from under a bed and bury him. The corpse was that of Moshe Naftalis.

I am incapable of describing in detail the horrors and murders we have witnessed as part of the cleanup squad I was with. I doubt any man can. May the lord avenge them and console us with redemption during our lifetime.

These are the horrifying facts that were delivered to me by one of our important survivors, the capable Mr. Leibish Herblum, who risked his life every moment and moment to carry out his sacred duty and provide a proper burial for the martyrs of our town. This dear Jew is worthy of special mention in this memorial book, for his courage and dedication during those days of despair and horror (Yaakov Katz)

[Page 162]
Zvi Faigenbaum

The Synagogue is Burning

"The town is burning", said the mourner of the Holocaust, describing the ruination of the European Jewry. The bane's first step in his destruction of Wierzbnik was burning down the house of our lord. The central synagogue of the community, a place which was sacred for every Jew in town, was set on fire at the end of Yom Kippur 1939. That is, during the year where the Jews have finally faltered before their persecutors, who defamed Israel's glory.

Compared with the situation elsewhere, it can be said that the Nazis did not treat the Jews of Wierzbnik harshly during the first days. In Lipsk, for example, the houses were set on fire while the Jews were still inside them, and those trying to escape were shot, among them a resident of Wierzbnik, 80 years old Efraim Zimerman. In Ostrowiec, a Yeshiva student named Berl Hercig was shot to death. In neighboring Kazanów, the Germans took 180 Jews and shot them to death, among them the brother of the honoured Zvi Wajzer. In the neighboring town of Wąchock, the Germans set the town houses on fire as soon as they arrived, while Wierzbnik enjoyed a relative calm.

G-d, gentiles have come into your property and defiled your holy sanctuary

The Polish mayor, Sokul, was assigned the continued management of the town affairs and the supply needs of the residents. The merchants were ordered to open their stores and sell merchandise to any client. The butchers received certificates that allowed them to venture to the villages, buy cattle, lead it to the slaughterhouse to be butchered and sell the meat in their shops. The kosher butchers also accompanied them and made sure the butchering was carried out properly and the Jewish community did not have to suffer a cleaning of teeth. Although some Jews, including myself, were abducted to carry out certain undignified tasks from time to time, we could still get by somehow and survive. There was only one exception: the synagogue was closed and gatherings were forbidden. However we did not see fit to provoke the sleeping dragon...

These events took place during the days of forgiveness, and the prayers were being said in privacy this time, each person in his home. On New Year's and even on Yom Kippur, the synagogue was empty of Jews. We have found an alternative by arranging for Minyans in private houses in different neighborhoods, where neighbors gathered to pray for the return of peace during our lifetime. For who could imagine that the annihilation of Europe's Jewry was already sealed, and we were sinking into oblivion?

Even two years later we could scarcely believe it was possible. What we felt was a need for heaven's mercies. The prayers were said quickly but wholeheartedly, the moans and the weeping accompanying them whispered in fear of eavesdroppers. Lookouts were placed for that purpose. Any hint of a German presence caused the house to empty immediately, the presence of prayers removed completely from the room. The occupation army instated blackout regulations. When we snuffed out the small candles we lit, we went to sleep feeling that this holy day is our private matter and the evil plans of outsiders have nothing to do with it.

Hear Oh Israel! Shema Yisrael!

On Yom Kippur morning the streets were quiet until the end of the Morning Prayer. At noon, however, while praying Musaf, we learned that they have not forgotten the Jewish date. The news of their appearance spread quickly and the Minyans emptied, but they managed to surprise a single Minyan in Iłżacka Street, at the home of Mordechai Rotbart. The supplicants were in the middle of the Musaf prayer when the Germans stormed the synagogue. The trembling, frightened Jews faced a group of loathsome pests with their arrogant commander. The order came: to work! And the Jews wrapped in tallits were led by an armed escort, silent as lambs with their heads bowed down. It was the reign of evil...

Late in the afternoon, they have finished unloading the coal from the cars on the railroad track. The work was carried out as ordered. Quickly and while still wearing the tallits. But the evil ones are still dissatisfied. They know it is a holy day for Jews and they want to oppress them completely. Now that the work is done, it is time for a few exercises, says the commander. His subordinates know his murderous intents. Exercise while wearing tallits! Drop, rise, drop, rise! Roll in the mud with your Tallits! On your back! Face up! Like so!

When they were done mocking us, they said "Now that you carried out the Perzenunstag properly, you can go home".

Word about this abuse spread quickly in every neighborhood. If they are capable of this, there is no end to their evil. And if that is the case, what will become of us? Concern started nagging even in the hearts of the most optimistic.

And then at midnight... we all woke up in a panic. Something terrible was taking place. A fire. A great fire nearby, which lit up the entire district, the yards and houses. This light, flickering from afar, came through the windows into my apartment...

A few minutes later, all of us – big and small – were dressed up. If the fire comes any closer, we will have to get away from it and perhaps save something. This concern gives way before a greater concern, since the gentile neighbor tells us: the synagogue is burning, it was set aflame...

Our world was shattered. The Devil outdid itself. There are 365 days in a year. In numerology, the number of the Devil is 364, because on one day of the year he is forbidden from prosecuting us, and that is on Yom Kippur. And now our sins have allowed him to claim this day as well. We thought that the holy day ended when we said the closing prayer, which was uttered from broken, gloomy hearts. But the prayer of Israel was rejected. The Devil reigns. He concluded the day by burning the holy place. Jews said the "separating prayer" and the prayer to "the maker of the orbs of fire" over a pair of lit candles, but the Devil felt the need for a great fire that would turn the glory of Israel into ashes...

But the need to do something overpowers me. The synagogue, with all its torah scrolls and book cases, is on fire. Those who see it are compelled to tear. Tearing instead of reading. But then I felt as if Yom Kippur was still upon us. I therefore went to my bookcase and took out the Book of Psalms, went back to the window and opened it in chapter 79, where the poet Asaf mourns the burning of the Temple. I started repeating his verses, which are compelling even in normal times. But now, under the light shed by the burning synagogue, I feel no distance between us, in neither time nor space, it seemed to me as though this temple is a part of the Temple in Jerusalem and the arsonists stand together with the soldiers of Titus and Nebuchadnezzar ... where are the priests who will climb to the roof with the keys of this synagogue and hold them up to the sky, to be joined with the keys of the Temple? And again, holding the book of psalms I feel as if my hand is holding the edge of Asaf's coat while he reads the words and I repeat after him "O God, the nations have invaded your inheritance; the have defiled your holy temple, we are objects of reproach to our neighbors, of scorn and derision to those around us... pour out your wrath on the nations that do not acknowledge you... why should the nations say 'where is their God?' May the groans of the prisoners come before you..."

Without realizing it I find sanctuary in the world of limitless thoughts, neither in place nor in time, and it comforts me. But I am immediately called back to the tragic reality: a German is in my yard. He approaches my apartment. I stood ready. I refused all suggestion to hide. He opens the door and turns directly to me. "Come!" I follow him. We leave the yard. Outside, the light and darkness blend together. Fire and smoke pour from the synagogue and the Talmud Torah. A group of soldiers and local firefighters are busy spraying water on nearby houses to contain the fire while another group of Germans is concerned mostly with ensuring that the synagogue burns down completely. I am also ordered to participate in the operation. I was placed by the well at the plaza between Niska, Visoka, Kilinska and Starachowicka Streets, ordered to turn the wheel drawing water from it. A few others are there with me, turning the wheels, drawing buckets of water and handing them to the firefighters, replaced by others and so on. I myself was in a daze, merely mumbling "pour out your wrath on the nations that do not acknowledge you..."

The fire was contained. Embers lay smoking on the floor of the synagogue. The soldier approaches me again and orders: "Home!"

Unintentionally I snatch another look at the burnt synagogue before marching back home. When I touched the lock to my house, I felt as if I was returned to a new reality that we could not imagine before.

What would happen next? What did the future hold in store for us? Were the stones and timber the final manifestation of the enemy's wrath, or was it just the beginning and a sign of things to come? It occurred to me that we say "Pour out your wrath" while the house is alight, on a night of redemption and freedom, while we should be saying it when the house is dark, on the night of the Ninth of Ab, a night of destruction and enslavement...

And the next day, when people wished each other "May you be inscribed in the book of life", the greeting came out tainted with concern. The lips of every person whisper "What is going on? What will happen later? What do you think?" Anxiety. News follows news. Germans appeared by the burned down synagogue, entered the home of a Jew living across from it, Shmuel Isser, and demanded of the neighbors to admit that the fire was caused by the Jews themselves, who lit candles on Yom Kippur eve at the synagogue according to their customs.

And before we could comprehend this appalling libel, we were surprised by a horrible rumor, a bad sign.

At 10 in the morning, two Gestapo officers came into the home of the community's rabbi, Rabbi Ben-Zion Rabinowicz, demanding a list of community elders in order to establish a "Judenrat". The rabbi mentioned a few people who are capable of representing the community even in times of danger, among them experienced public figures who, unawares of the danger, came forth. The order was clear: to establish a council of the Jewish "elders" (Judenrat). Following the Judenrat came the uniformed Jewish policemen (OrdnungsDinst). It was the beginning of a supposedly organized community under the reign of the Nazi conqueror.

It is only natural that this immediately became a matter for consideration, as the optimists (and me among them) wished to see it as a chance for shaping proper relations between the occupation force and the Jewish community. Perhaps things will work out after all, allowing us to weather the storm.

However the faint optimism was accompanied by the nagging and worries brought on by these terms which were both old and new: oppressors, elders, policemen...

In time, we learned the diabolical plan, calculated in fine detail, drawing on the persecution of every evil in this world: Pharaoh, Nebuchadnezzar and Titus, whom I imaged at the end of Yom Kippur, standing together with the arsonists by the burning synagogue.

[Page 165]
Moshe Sali (Kerbel)

A Source of Life Gone Dry

There was a Jewish community – Wierzbnik, but woe and alas – it no longer exists. The hands of the bloodthirsty murderers annihilated it and tore up the deeply-rooted and wide-branched tree of Polish Jewry. Their memory, inscribed in the hearts of the hundreds of survivors who are sown and spread throughout the world and in Israel, will live forever.

A Jewish settlement, one of many, one that was respected and enrooted in the area, which in the period before the destruction had reached the utmost heights of nationalsocial awareness, with all the light and shadowy aspects, with the positive and the negative that was embodied in that struggle for an independent Jewish life in the Diaspora and in an alien land. The Jewish *shtetl*, which seemed as though sleepy and sluggish – was actually a lively and very tangible cell in the body of Polish Jewry, and all the sectors of Jewish life in Poland before the destruction were reflected in it.

From the mighty stream of all the nationalistic, social and political movements of Polish Jewry, Wierzbnik contained branches of all the parties and movements. For the hundreds of Jewish children and young people the deep-rooted Jewish home was their foundation, and the *heder* [school for young children] and the *melamed* [teacher of young children] were the main source of their education and spiritual nurture. However, under the influence of the youth organizations and of the local Zionist movement, the aspiration for an active Zionism grew ever stronger, and the Land of Israel was the topic on everyone's lips. In those tempestuous times an inner awakening emerged, and everything was lit with a new light. The Jewish youth became convinced that they had no egress from material and moral pain. Concluding that they had lost their way in a complicated way of life, they began to actively strive for change, to abandon the regular daily way, because the continuation of the existing situation provided no solution for the requirements of the time and especially for the longings and desire for redemption that were concealed deep in their souls. And just as the Zionist movement served as the house for establishing the foundation of the Zionist spirit and the Hebrew language, so also Hechalutz and the other youth movements served as the anvil, on which pioneering labor Zionism was forged. With a great deal of effort, moral values, which were transformed into personal and common property, were assembled and determined. From being takers and the recipients of influence, we were transformed into givers and disbursers of influence, and on the Jewish street a trend for basic changes in cultural values came into being and many people began to weave their life in the movement framework, full of enthusiasm and a powerful faith.

One after another, types and figures of the Jews of the *shtetl* pass through my mind, the public and individuals, they and their life, their conversations, talks and worldviews, their actions, achievements and failures, the week-days and the Sabbaths. This wonderful gallery of figures and institutions against the colorful background of all the sectors, the poor people, the tradesmen, shopkeepers and merchants, property owners, professionals and regular scholars and just plain Jews. All this was embraced by the life in the *shtetl*, which sparkled and aspired to national and general human redemption – a *shtetl* that was destroyed along with the other holy communities. Thus was the magnificent strand of pearls that beautified and crowned the Jewish people broken and torn apart. The light was extinguished, the fire of enthusiasm was quenched, the constantly flowing spring of energy, initiative and the mighty Jewish undertaking dried out. Let us hope that we have the ability to bring out just something of the bygone days, in order to perform a real act of grace for the dry bones, and to commemorate and mourn the martyrs, of whom only a small remnant remains here and there as a keepsake.

[Page 167]
Sara Postawski-Steinhardt

Waiting in Line for Bread

Whenever I walk in the street, I am saddened to see bread thrown by the dumpsters. Compounding my normal distaste for this aberrant phenomenon is the burden of the dark days of the Holocaust. During the first couple of months after the German soldiers entered Wierzbnik we were already starting to feel the shortage of bread and the situation became worse with each passing day. Although a coupon system was instituted to provide us with rationed supplies, the coupons proved to be of little help. Those families that depended on them to get their daily bread were unfortunate indeed. Securing the bread was a road paved with unimaginable suffering and hardships, and by the time we received our meager share, we already suffered much beatings and swearing. According to the "order" established by the German authorities, the distribution of bread took place only in one place, at the Polish grocery store, and one can easily imagine the long lines that stretched from both sides of the entrance to the store, practically across the entire street.

Jews were thrown out of line

Since the very act of standing in line was physically challenging, the youths were typically the ones sent, since they were stronger than the old and the infirm. Pressure and distress have worn everyone's nerves thin and the smallest action led to arguments and bitter disputes. There were also individuals who failed to show self-discipline, wedging themselves into line with utter disregard for others. However worse of all were the attacks by Anti-Semites, who would get the Jews kicked out of the line after hours of standing and waiting.

The bread was only distributed once a week, and the quantity distributed never came close to fulfilling our needs. It is no wonder that we were all scared that we might never get our fair share. People would wake up in the small hours of the night, and would go to stand in line in hope that they would reach their desired goal by morning.

Since my family had no sources for bread other than the official distribution, I, the youngest, was forced to wake up early and stand in line for bread. Arriving at 3am I already found a row of people standing, their teeth chattering in the morning cold. I joined the line which grew longer with every passing moment. Time crawled and the distress in my heart made me feel even worse. But I held on to the hope that after bearing the suffering and hardships of this line, my efforts would be repaid and I could bring bread to my family. I was devastated when, a short time before the store opened, several Anti-Semite locals showed up and maliciously started a riot which resulted in the Jews getting kicked out of line. I could do nothing but walk back home empty handed, depressed and filled with bitterness and despair.

Ha Lachma Anya

The distress and agonies which accompanied our efforts to get bread have also made us ignore certain minor details that caused their own fair share of trouble and grief. Those in charge of bread distribution purposefully forced the administrative arrangement of the distribution in a way that would abuse the consumers. This precise order of business – where to come in and where to leave – was to be maintained by all and woe unto he who stumbles during these "foot drills".

We stood in line regardless of the weather, of course, and if it was raining people simply got completely drenched. And anyone who managed to be among the happy ones who got their portion of the bread would have cringed at its look and taste under normal circumstances. It was black as tar, burned and hard on the outside and entirely unbaked on the inside, in other words – actual dough.

The Jews are to blame for the war

I sadly recall one of those nightly journeys to the line. I was standing for hours waiting for bread and saw with my own eyes the store open at 8 a.m. and the start of the anticipated distribution of bread. I stand gripped with immense inner tension, thinking of nothing but the big question: will the bread last until it was my turn? My emotions fluttered every time the line before me grew shorter, bringing me closer to the entrance to the store. One moment I was embracing hope and the next I was feeling pessimistic and verging on panic.

Time went by. The time is 9:30; at 10, my sister Rivka comes to check up on me, because this was unusual. Distribution was usually over by 9. However when she saw that I was close to the entrance to store, she not only realized the situation but was also encouraged by my "achievement", which was nearly realized. I too grew more optimistic upon seeing my sister. We exchanged short hopeful looks and treasured the awaited moment in our hearts. My sister was standing a short distance from the line, because the supervisors ordered no one to come near for fear of disrupting the queue. The rays of the sun rising to the sky are shedding some warmth and brilliance on all of us. Only a few more minutes and a few meters left. There's a woman ahead of me in line, and there I am inside the store! The big moment is upon us! But no, fate is cruel. As if from under the ground an anti-Semite showed up and started raging and swearing at all of us, blaming the Jews for the war. A riot started, the atmosphere soured and all the anti-Semites lifted their heads hoping to make a catch. This intentional havoc resulted in all the Jews being driven out of the line. My hurt and grief were entirely understandable. I was broken and despairing. I cried all day and could not calm down due to my grief and distress.

In time, the distribution process was passed unto Jewish hands and certain locations in the ghetto. As far as the distribution was concerned things became easier, but the new hardships that came upon us that made the previous ones pale by comparison...

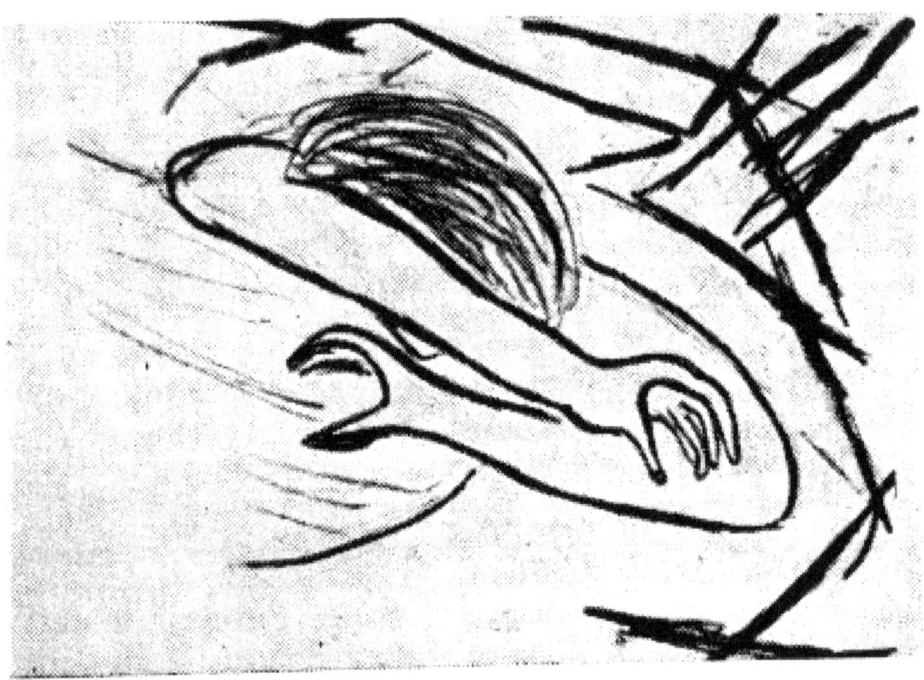

[Page 169]
Sara Postawski-Steinhardt

The First Murder

It is only natural for primal deeds to be carved into memory. Such is the case with events and phenomena that delight the human heart, let alone with things imbued with sadness and tears.

During the years of the holocaust we knew bloody terrors, suffering and hardships that are unlike anything in human history, not even in the tragic history of the suffering Jewish people. But the first murder committed by the damn Nazis in our town was carved into my soul and I recall it as if it was yesterday.

He was called "Neizl" because of his unique nose, which bent upwards and made his nostrils flare abnormally. But his fame came not from these "anthropological" markings, but from his insatiable murderous, bestial attributes. This archvillain had a habit of wandering the streets of our town neighboring the Jewish ghetto, seeking a victim he could use to quench his blood thirst.

This tale took place during the initial establishment of the ghetto, when the Jews were ordered not to leave it under penalty of death. But at the time, the danger has not yet penetrated the minds of the ghetto's residents, and here and there people tried to leave and fell prey to those who sought to harm them. It was noontime when I went down to the yard and through the fence saw the "Neizl" leading a young Jewish boy through the street near the ghetto. Since the Nazi's sadistic reputation was already common knowledge, I was anxious for the young man, although it was hard to suspect his horrific intents based on the way the two walked and talked. In time we unveiled the cunning of this murderer, who used to lower the victim's guard with sweet talk before carrying out his evil schemes.

Further down the road, I saw them arrive at the police building and go into it. I waited a long time in the yard and saw the Neizl leave the building alone, realizing that the young man was incarcerated within. I followed the Nazi on his prowls through the streets, until finally I lost him. The next day he went hunting again, and managed to satisfy his murderous lust yet again. Three Jewish fellows who walked from the city of Iłża to Starachowice ran into him at the entrance to town and were arrested by him. At first he pretended that they must accompany him merely as a formality, because they were strangers, and the four freely chatted on the way, in an impeccably amiable manner, typical of this executioner. He brought them to the police building and while they were waiting there he brought out the fellow that was locked up the day before and then led the four of them, again without significant protest, through Koliowa Street and toward the forest. I happened to be in the yard again and my eyes caught a vision much like the day before: the Neizl is walking with four Jewish youths in the street outside the ghetto, talking to them in earnest, without arousing their suspicions. When they arrived at the river he had them stand on the bridge and shot the four of them. Following this treacherous murder he went to the ghetto police and ordered the policemen to go pick up the bodies.

Later, we have learned that this Nazi acted in the same brutal manner towards the Poles as well, and they repaid him for it. Eventually, they ambushed and killed him.

Testimonies

[Page 171]
Malka Cohen (Leopold)

Wierzbnik, Auschwitz, Bergen-Belsen

On the day the war broke out, we had a strange feeling: we have prepared all this time for a prolonged gas war (father even prepared gas masks), and suddenly events were unfolding in a rush. We expected long battles over the munitions factories in the area and we also feared aerial bombardment. That is why we were surprised when the Germans suddenly walked into our town.

We were a family of seven. My sister has wed later on and left the house, but when the situation grew worse, she returned to us with her husband and baby. That night we escaped to Ostrowiec, to my brother-in-law's parents, to consult with them about what we should do and where we should run to.

We owned a grocery store, among the largest in town, and it was hard to accept at first that we must suddenly abandon it all. Therefore it was decided that only the women would escape, while the men stayed behind, to take care of business. We stayed in Ostrowiec for two weeks and when the situation stabilized a bit I returned home to Wierzbnik, to learn what was going on. When I arrived, my world has shattered! My father was gone and so was my brother-in-law, the two of them hiding with other Jews in fear of being beaten up by the Germans, an event that practically became a daily phenomenon. That was my first "opportunity" for contact with the Germans. Apart from its front door, our store also had a "back" entrance, which was a typical feature in stores and allowed us unload cargo without interfering with the course of business. When I entered the area where merchandise was stored, i felt my heart break. The place was a mess; the merchandise was pillaged by the Germans and gentiles in the area, who spent the two weeks on a looting rampage. While I was standing there shocked with grief over this loss, I was surprised by a few Germans who came from behind me and demanded coffee. Their sudden appearance shocked me and I murmured I was merely going to fetch it, but in fact I was planning on escaping them. I ran away and watched them from afar as they continued their theft of our merchandise. We were powerless to resist their brute force. Desperation turned me apathetic. A young Anti-Semite gentile stood outside and signaled to every German car passing him that there is something here to loot… After a while I found out where my father and brother-in-law were hiding and I made efforts to meet them.

As time went by things became worse and worse and the hunger started to bother us more and more. Everything was scarce and rationed. I remember going to stand in line for a piece of bread. All we ever got were tiny rations. For Shabbat we only had herring…

The German looters were insatiable. Merchandise at the store practically ran out, but they continued to search it mercilessly, sacking and looting anything they could put their hands on. We were all scared. And since at the time we were living together (in the same building) with the Gmina, the Jewish community board, we had many visits from the Germans and perhaps felt their oppression more than any others.

The girl with the nuts

With mixed feelings I recall today a very depressing experience, when a young innocent girl was used by the banes as a means of trapping us in wrongdoing so they can later unleash their murderous fury upon us.

Cunning and lies have served the Nazi beasts as sure and tested means of planning their destructive work. Not only was it part of their general policy, it was also carried out in a small-scale in various places. As I already mentioned, the robbing and looting continued for several weeks and most of the stock we had at our big store was stolen.

Nevertheless, we managed to hide some essentials for a rainy day. The Germans, for their part, suspected everything and were eager to bleed us dry. Always demanding more, they heard us say who knows how many times that there is nothing more to give, and so they decided to use a ploy: they sent a young, innocent hungry Jewish girl over and even gave her some money so she would come buy nuts from us.

When she appeared in our store, we were tempted to sell her some nuts, but the Germans followed her and the results were soon to follow. They came immediately, charged us and beat us all brutally.

In 1940 we received a shipment of close to 1,000 Jews from Lodz, who arrived during the night and were distributed among the local Jewish homes. They were followed by a shipment from the town of Płock. The first refugees could find an acceptable place for themselves, but there was no room left for the refugees from Płock and the housing and living conditions were bad.

Establishment of the ghetto

From time to time we heard various rumors from other Jewish towns, about cruel pogroms, edicts and oppression. In our town, a curfew was instated from 6 a.m. to 5 p.m. and we were all forced to wear the mark of disgrace on our sleeves. Rumors started circulating about a population swap, a change of residence and so on. As time went by, Jews were ordered to live on certain streets. Our family was not forced to move out, however, because we lived in the quarter that was designated as the new ghetto. But the stir and crowdedness that resulted from this order have left their depressing mark on residence conditions and our entire lifestyle.

The eviction

By 1942 we no longer had any commodities or merchandise left. We managed, however, to hide some valuables "for dark times". We had an old Polish acquaintance, a sympathetic and trustworthy man who was a customer of ours for years, and we gave him certain valuables – accessories, Jewels and so on – in return for news and perhaps even some assistance. On the night before the eviction he showed up at our place, but he was too drunk to tell us anything useful about what was going to happen.

The next day, the Germans swarmed every building and drove all the Jews to the center of town, a place called the "Rinek". We were forced to run as fast as the bikes trailing us... and those who fell suffered a bitter fate. When I met my father at the camp, I learned that my brother-in-law stumbled and fell while running and was shot to death when he couldn't get up quickly enough.

His wife, that is, my sister, knew nothing of the disaster and hid with her baby among the gentiles to whom we gave our valuables.

After a while, the Germans and their servants started pressuring and threatening anyone who would hide Jews with a death sentence. This threat was naturally effective, and the family that was hiding my sister grew afraid and refused to hide her any longer, forcing my sister to take her baby and flee to the town of Wolbrom, where she found no assistance either because the situation was similar to that in Wierzbnik. She had no choice left other than returning to Starachowice, where she gave the baby to a missionary house and took up a job at the lumber-mill.

She innocently gave up the baby, hoping to save his life, but reality was tragic. She only managed to visit the child a few times before the disaster struck, and the Germans took all Jewish kids in that place to Szydłowiec and viciously murdered them.

At the camp, I had various small chores in the kitchen. While working, we received from time to time secret packages from the gentile to whom we gave our jewels.

In 1944 we were all sent to Auschwitz, and had to bid farewell to my father and brother, as I was taken with my sister to the women's camp. We entered the camp in despair, certain that we were brought there to be murdered. We walked in silent lines with tears in our eyes, none of us saying anything to the others. We were ordered to take off our clothes and our hair was shaved. Some Jews were walking around, claiming that we weren't being transported to death. We were given a numbered camp uniform and taken to blocks, where we lay on multistoried bunks. The camp followed a regular schedule. At 3 in the morning a reveille, during which we were lined up outside while they read out each person's number. From there we had a long walk to work. It was just hard, pointless physical labor. We also suffered from the cold and damp and sometimes we got wet to the bone and had to carry our wet clothes until they dried.

One day I fell asleep in the cabin and didn't come out. The German block supervisor forcefully dragged me out and I fell and hurt myself badly.

The liberation from Bergen-Belsen

The next day we were deported to Bergen-Belsen and taken to a new camp, which was even worse than the last. At first we did not work, but later they gave us small tasks to do. The routine was much the same as in the last camp, but we all had some hope because we sensed that the end of the Germans was near. I prayed only that we will hold on. And that hope became a reality. After a year long stay in Bergen-Belsen, we were liberated by the British, in 15.04.1945.

[Page 174]
Sarah Brodbeker

On this Day They Shall Mourn

I was born in Starachowice and lived there until the day we were driven out. I was still young and remember little from the time before the war, but the tragic events that transpired during the Holocaust were carved deep into my mind and left a scar which cannot be erased upon my soul.

I will never forget the prophetic words of my dear mother, who predicted the terrible calamity that was threatening us. While most of the Jewish public deluded itself that the oncoming storm will somehow pass it by and still failed to grasp the scope of the disaster swiftly approaching, my mother realized the nature of the murderers straight away and understood their intentions. On the day the Germans entered our town, mother said "children, I can hear every family in Israel cry 'Eicha Yashva'", referring to the Ninth of Ab, the mourning day of the Hebrew prophet who lamented the destruction of our people. And she was right. Her words became a cruel reality. Crying, bereavement and sorrow became our daily bread, and the turbid current expressed itself first as financial demands, "contributions" and ransom payments, then as forced labor abductions, and the noose tightened around our necks from year to year and month to month.

When the persecution started in the form of "contributions", which many thought to be their price of penance, my mother said "I wish that would be the end of it", because her intuition told her this was only the beginning... and since she felt that we are going to face countless more hardships and tragedies, she wanted to strengthen us mentally, so we can face this trial. When the Nazis ordered us to wear the mark of disgrace, she told me: "You may be young but you must wear the yellow patch with pride, because it is not a crime to be a good Jew."

Indeed the events of those dark days cannot be measured by the standards of normal human relations, and during this terrible time I have witnessed with my own eyes such social phenomena that weighed on me and made me ask the important question: what happened to the proud Jewish people?

I received my answer only years later, in the independent State of Israel, where the Jewish people live and fight bravely to defend their homeland and the best of national and humane values.

[Page 176]
Menachem Mincberg

In the Jaws of Destiny

Following the events that afflicted our community I ended up in the camp and worked at the top floor of the munitions factory. I usually worked shifts of 8 and sometimes 12 hours, inspecting 152mm shells. First we would inspect the shells lying on the table, and then we would pile them and imprint them with a serial number, indicating that the shells passed our inspection. On the aforementioned night I was working a 12 hour shift. During the evening, policemen arrived from the camp accompanied by the department supervisor, a man named Weinberg, who signaled me in secret so the others won't understand. He made exaggerated hand gestures as he spoke, pretending to point at the piles, while hissing at me the details between his teeth – that the camp was surrounded by Germans and that there was no point for me to go to the residence camp in the factory area. Since I was partnered with another Jewish guy from Bodzentyn named Schechter, I passed the information along to him as well. In the meantime, the policemen ordered us to go down to the courtyard by the guard room, and then left. At that moment, my friend told me "Come with me to the smithy," because that was where his brother worked and together, the three of us could devise a plan of action.

We did not tarry but went directly to his brother and the three of us decided to run away, at any cost!

We came to this decision because we knew what was about to befall us, in light of the events that have already taken place in our town and those neighboring towns we heard about. We had no detailed plan, but our first priority was escaping the jaws of the Nazi beast. We walked out the front door, since the working conditions allowed us to wander around the factory, and headed directly for the fence. We jumped over it and were outside the factory.

When we crossed the fence, two others ran after us: one was called Meir Geller and the other Eli Zvuliner.

A municipal road stretched a few meters from the fence. We crossed the road and kept walking. It turned out, however, that we crossed it near one of the factory gates, which was well guarded, and while crossing the road we were noticed by a Ukraine policeman who opened fire on us. The cover of darkness was the only thing that hampered his aim and saved us from being shot.

In the Sieclenice Labor Camp, in the Konsom cooperative

After running a short distance away from the factory we took a short rest, making use of the dense foliage as cover while we recaptured our breath. We slowly recovered our strength and started talking amongst ourselves. We consulted with each other – what next? What should we do? The Schechter brothers said: "We should go to a village 20 kilometers from here, by the town of Bodzentyn, where we have friends, a Polish family, villagers who might be willing to take us in until the storm blows over." The year was 1944, the Russian-German front line was approaching us and we were hoping that if we could survive this, we might yet be saved.

Instead of wasting time, we decided to continue walking through the night. We had no food but did not feel its lack yet. We crossed the Kamienna River and passed by a populated area, but we did not know the direction to the village. We had no choice but to turn to one of the houses and knock on the window. When they asked who we were, we told them we were partisans. When they opened the door for us, we asked them for directions. It was a woman, and she pointed the way for us. From here on we continued walking along the main road. Suddenly we heard shouts of "Halt!" coming from afar. As soon as we heard them we left the road and headed into the field, and immediately heard the sound of gunfire. We realized we could not continue on our way and so we escaped deep into the forest. Dawn was coming, preventing us from continuing on our way, and so we stayed in the forest all day long and resumed our march when darkness fell. We walked all night, grew hungry and stopped at a farmer's house where we received some bread. The Schechter brothers were already familiar with the area and in the morning we arrived at the village that was our destination. At first, we went into the cemetery, hiding inside one of the open graves. One of the Schechters went to pay their friends a visit and we waited for the results of his reconnaissance. After a brief conversation with the landlady he returned to us and the three of us went to the house and promised the woman that we will pay her for the favor she was doing us after the liberation. We settled in the cowshed's attic, where she arranged a hiding place for us and another Jewish guy who was already staying with her.

The woman treated us well and brought us food and drinks from time to time, but the days grew long and the liberation never came. The woman expected the Russians to arrive within a couple of days, putting matters to rights, but three weeks have passed and the liberation we longed for was yet to come. The woman grew anxious and started hinting that she was unwilling to continue the "game". The Schechters also consulted with each other and explained that they were willing to go someplace to get money. They left while I stayed with the other guy, but then the landlady came to me and told me outright that she could not hide us there any longer. She added that there was a hole under the barn, which was far from the house, and that if I am interested I can hide there because it would no longer put her at risk. We had no choice but to hide in the hole.

We lay there for a day, then we lay there for a night, and as time passed we grew hungry. We had no money, only a watch. I gave the woman the watch so she could sell it and bring me some food, and she did so; but that food ran out as well. And so I decided to get out and head towards Wierzbnik, where I had gentile acquaintances. A day later I arrived there and visited a gentile named Zhorwitz, who promised to help me. He gave me some money and I went back to the woman who was hiding me earlier.

I went to the bushes, where I was supposed to rendezvous with the other fellow, but I could not find him. I went to the hole and saw that it was filled up. This horrified me. I went to the woman and said that I wanted to talk to her. She was sympathetic but begged us to leave the place, because partisans arrived the night before and murdered the guy and one of the Schechter brothers who came back and was hiding with her. I decided to leave, of course, and she gave me a slice of bread as supply for the road. I did not want to walk by day so I hid inside a bale of straw in the field and after nightfall I left and returned once more to Wierzbnik, to the acquaintance who helped and encouraged me earlier. I overcame many hardships before I managed to make my way to him and he lived up to my expectations.

He had strong ties to the resistance and arranged a false ID for me, but the picture was missing and without it, the ID was worthless. I had no choice but to go to a photographer in town at noon, pretending to be a Christian and asking to have my picture taken. He agreed and took my picture, because he didn't know I was Jewish. After taking my picture he told me to come back two days later, but I saw suspicion in his eyes. I left him money and told him that I will come on time to collect the pictures. This was naturally a deception on my part, to prevent him from reporting me. In truth, I went to another photographer, told him I needed a picture immediately and he made me one on the spot. When I left his business I had to cross the Rinek, where some brats were standing selling newspapers. When they saw me they started shouting "Jude, Jude!" after me.

The reason they were yelling was the two gendarmes who stood nearby. Luckily for me, the two were off duty and unarmed. I panicked, and froze, and then a gentile acquaintance of mine came towards me, pushed me and cried "Run!" I took off running, crossed a railway and took a long winding path back to my acquaintance. He got me the ID and I used it to look for work as a Pole. I moved away from the town and entered a village in the area of Iłża. I entered the house of a farmer and introduced myself as a refugee from Poznan County, looking for work. The farmer hired me because another worker left him the day before and I started to work there. Unfortunately, the old worker came back a few days later and the farmer fired me, giving me the address of a place in Iłża that needed a worker.

I followed his recommendations and went there. It was the time of harvest, when workers are in greater demand than usual, and I was hired as soon as I arrived. I had to do many different chores, such as caring for the horses, the cows and so on. No one knew that I was a Jew, of course. The family I worked for was composed of an elderly couple and a son who used to be a senior county clerk but returned to the village during the war. They were fervent anti-Semites and I often had to listen to their slander of Jews. I remember how the old woman said once, during breakfast: "Mr. Michalski (that was my alias), you live like a Jew, never praying or visiting church. Her words made me uneasy. I feared they were suspecting me. I didn't know whether the old woman based her words on conjectures or was merely guessing, but to be on the safe side I started the very next morning to make the sign of the cross and mutter something. I was working alongside another Christian and was forced to join the walk to church next Sunday. When we came back the old woman beamed with joy and her attitude towards me improved considerably.

The tale of the straw sheaf

Christmas was also coming at the time, and we started preparing for the holiday – decorating a tree and so on. But a new calamity almost befell me. One of their old customs was spreading a sheaf of straw on the table, commemorating the birth of Christ on straw… I was therefore sent to fetch the straw, a task that confused me because I did not understand the situation. I was debating whether I should bring a little straw, or a lot, and I was leaning towards bringing plenty of straw, because it would be possible to get rid of some if I turned out to be wrong. The straw was over the cowshed in the attic. As I already mentioned, I thought that I should bring plenty of straw and was about to make a mistake, because we only needed a token amount. But uncertainty made me hide the ladder instead and turn to the neighboring house of a young man I befriended, whom I told: "Look, I don't have a ladder, climb my shoulders and get some straw for the sake of custom." Luckily he suspected nothing, climbed my shoulders and brought down a little straw, saving me from a major calamity…

By the well

This family also owned some horses and from time to time they were ordered to drive senior clerks or Germans to all sorts of places. I have managed to dodge this task a few times, but eventually the circumstances made it impossible for me to avoid, forcing me to serve as a driver for some senior clerks, headed to Wierzbnik of all places… I was naturally terrified that someone might recognize me, and my fears came true. The clerks got off the wagon and went into the office, leaving me with the horses. I went to the nearby well to draw water for them. At that moment, a local who knew me well approached me and started talking to me... but he promised to keep quiet. The clerks came back and we continued on our way to Starachowice. When we passed the Ukrainian guard house, one of the Ukrainian guards named Paschkewitz came out, stopped the wagon and asked where they were going. They answered "To the county headquarters" and he asked for a ride, taking a seat next to me. My heart started beating like a tractor, but he left us before we arrived in town. And fortunately, he did not talk to me.

The clerks left the wagon again and went into the office by the Gestapo, while I stayed with the horses waiting for their return. In the meantime, the friend who got me the ID passed me in the street and waved me hello. I was worried that if I returned his wave I would get caught, and he understood my silence and ignored me.

After all these adventures we safely returned "home". On the way back I was wondering "How come no one recognized me? There are many gentiles who knew me in the town where I was born and raised and still I was not exposed..." after the war I learned that many recognized me, but kept their mouths shut.

Driving SS officers

The place I was living at was near Pakosław mansion, which was awarded during the war to a German "loyalist". On Christmas, the SS units camped in the area were invited and my landlord was ordered to use his horses and wagons for transporting the Germans. I had the misfortune of driving two SS unit commanders... I went where I was told and waited. A cry in German came out of the house: "Where is the driver?" When I went there, the Gestapo commander came out and told me to go up to his room. He was already dressed but without his shirt on. When I entered, he took out a glass, poured the two of us some vodka then called for the other officer to join us, and the three of us shared a drink... immediately afterwards we went back downstairs and I drove them to the mansion. On the way we were joined by other wagons carrying the rest of the SS squad. "God," I was thinking, "the devil must be toying with me, sending me to drive an SS squad whose members could kill me thrice each in a second..." There was a hall there and they had a big party. When they were all drunk, the commander came out looking for me and called out "Where is the driver, give him something to eat!" During the whole drive back they acted drunkenly.

Time passed and eventually we started hearing the sound of cannons and exploding shells as the front line came closer, prompting everyone to hide in the cellars. Then the shooting stopped and the Russians conquered the town. When I heard about it, I dared go to the center of town. I stayed with this family for a few days longer, until I learned that the entire area was conquered, and then I headed to Wierzbnik. When I got there I found a few other Jews who managed to survive this hell, a mere 5 or 6 people.

[Page 180]
M. Magen

Diaspora

The battles that followed the outbreak of the German-Poland War 1939 and the unique conditions in town (the presence of munitions factories) made the Jews of Wierzbnik flee to nearby places, while the changes in regime and the conquest of the entire region by the German army made those people who first left the town flow back to Wierzbnik, some of them having no reason to stay away and others accepting the new reality.

But the sudden increase in persecution, oppression, edicts and "spontaneous" murders by German soldiers and their vile assistants, made the people of Wierzbnik ponder and plan their escape from the noose that was tightening around their necks. The problem was that this thought occurred only to a few, farsighted people whose intuition allowed them to sense what was coming or those who had the benefit of experience due to special circumstances (such as visiting other regions, where the Nazis already carried out their evil plans against the Jewish population with the help of the local anti-Semites). Only they knew what the future held and drew their conclusions on time.

As I have mentioned, there were but a few, either individuals or small groups, who drew the far-reaching conclusion, grabbed their traveling staff and left on a difficult road, to seek their escape under God's sky. They traveled a winding path, some of them hiding in town, among the gentiles, in bunkers, attics or cellars. Others went into the nearby forests or crossed the Russian border – where they kept on wandering, the warfront and the soldiers of the enemy at their heels.

But unfortunately, during the first stages of the Nazi occupation the majority of the Jews in Wierzbnik could not fathom that the horror the Germans were plotting is even possible. Like most of the Jewish people in the European countries conquered by the Nazis, the naïve Jews of Wierzbnik could never imagine that, in the 20th century, innocent people – men, women and infants – will be taken and murdered. And when they started realizing what was going on around them to some degree, it was already too late, because in the meantime the possibilities of breaking out of the straights have narrowed down to the point where they were trapped inside.

From that point onward, the only options left were the daring escapes of individuals through the closed perimeter of the ghetto, which was closely guarded, or leaping from the death trains. Both options resulted in endless wandering from place to place and from town to town, until finally they rejoined the great stream of people sent to the camps.

Others were more successful, if they managed to cross the field separating the camp from the forest, wade through the drops of leaden rain showered by the German pursuers and penetrate the depths of the woods.

They have faced additional adventures and dangers down the road as well, encounters with the devil's henchmen in the form of the Vlasovs, or Ukrainians, Lithuanians and other such quislings. Equally dangerous was running into Polish partisans, who also betrayed and murdered Jews by the droves.

Finally came the last stage of the "Diaspora", which the Germans falsely named "The final solution"; the Jews of Wierzbnik went on their final journey, to the death Diaspora of the camps – Auschwitz, Birkenau, Treblinka, Ravensbrück, Bergen-Belsen and others – the final stage of the terrible tragedy. In the following chapters, the lone survivors describe the various directions that "Diaspora" took them in, their nature and their unique circumstances.

[Page 181]
Menachem Efrati

On the Road to Treblinka

The train by which the Germans took the last of the Jews in the ghettos of Radom County to Treblinka left on January 13th 1943 from Szydłowiec.

My daughter Chava (17 years old at the time) and I were among the five thousand Jews crammed into the train's fifty freight cars. After an 8 hour long ride, we jumped off the moving train. The first Pole we met told us that we are in the vicinity of Łuków. From another Pole we learned also that there are still Jews in the ghetto in Łuków. When we heard that, we risked our lives time and again until we managed to infiltrate the closed ghetto and joined the remaining Jews of Łuków and the area.

In Yatkova Street, at the edge of town, stood a group of wooden houses collapsing with age. Their roofs were rotten through, their walls were worn and their windows reflected a terrible anguish. Before, under normal circumstances, they housed two hundred tenants; now, they housed 2,800. The place was so crowded that during the day, the Jewish residents of the ghetto were forced to look for room to breath between the huts and the barbed-wire fence surrounding them. But there were no complaints about the size of the place, because the question on everyone's minds was – what might happen when the Gestapo arrive, and when might they arrive?

Today is 02.05.1943, the time is 4 in the morning and they are already here! That says everything. The cruel implication of these news was instantly clear to all. Our worse fears have come to pass. Treblinka was no longer a secret by then, especially for the Łuków ghetto. First of all, most of the transports headed to Treblinka passed through Łuków, and secondly, the distance is short, a mere 100 kilometers. In addition, we also had "live mail"; Jews who were not put into the gas chambers were ordered to load the clothes of the victims who were already cremated. Some of them managed to hide in the car, under the piles of clothes, and when the train returned with the cargo on its way to Germany, they jumped from the car and sneaked into the Łuków ghetto, hoping to find some shelter.

This led the Dayan Petachyah to instruct us all to say Kaddish for the dead, while other ghettos were still uncertain of the fact. I can never forget the occasion: on Shabbat, a hundred prayers would stand together in low-ceilinged room and all of us, without exception, would say Kaddish, each for families or whole towns.

Treblinka was indeed no secret to us. The Gestapo too knew that the Jews were aware of the situation, and used every means possible to ensure that none of the 2,800 people under siege will escape the trap. A moment later we were all on our feet. A few, mostly old residents of Łuków, have prepared underground "bunkers" and were now hurrying down into them. The rest, however, the majority including my daughter and me, came "out" when ordered.

The ghetto is surrounded by the Gestapo. The assistants of the Einzatsruppen, Latvians and Lithuanians armed to their teeth, receive the order from the SS to enter the ghetto. They concentrate us at the large empty lot in the ghetto and command us to sit on the ground. While we are sitting, nervously waiting for things to come, we hear gunfire all around us – the work of murderers sating their malicious obsession with innocent victims. Those of us sitting on the ground are ordered to rise and line up in ranks of five for the last march.

Escorted by armed guards the Jews of the ghetto are marching through the wide streets of Łuków. The Germans are meticulous to the extreme… they make sure no one strays from his quintet. Those of us marching feel like a single body, carrying itself through its own funeral… marching on its own feet to its grave.

Suddenly I felt curious to see and observe the entire "procession" of Jews walking slowly, heads bowed, as if escorting themselves on their last journey; I look at our "handlers", I look at the regular German soldiers who are standing on the sidewalks and watching this strange vision curiously, I see the Polish citizens who are standing on the sidewalks by the houses, those houses that many of those marching used to live in…

Suddenly, I recall the annihilation of the ghetto in Szydłowiec, when the voices and the screams mixed with endless gunfire were deafening.

Oh! Not a single shot missed its mark, nearly 600 Jews, men and women, fell before our eyes and were left wallowing in their own blood.

But here the picture is altogether different. Not a single shot sounds. The procession moves "normally", quietly, like a solemn parade…

The sentries are all dressed in new uniforms. The cuffs brightly colored, decorated with blossoms and flowers. The guns seem more like accessories than killing machines. All is quiet around us. Everyone is looking and thinking quietly. The air is clear and pure.

If only we could soar like eagles… the skies are remarkably clear. Not a single cloud, not even a small one. Is this meant for us, to ease our last way? Or maybe to keep out of the sun's way, so she can also witness what is happening "in broad daylight!"

My train of thought is derailed by the voice of a woman marching next to me. "The gentile maids dressed up to see our plight". After a long march, we arrived at the train station. The Jewish residents of Łuków, who are familiar with the area, determine that the cars haven't arrived yet. In the meantime, we are ordered to "Sit!"

We sit on the ground and wait. After an hour people start whispering: "The train is coming." I turn my eyes toward the railroad tracks. The locomotive is making a noisy approach. The chimney is decorated with a birch tree sapling. The "guards" among the locomotive crew are watching us. We look back at them: humans! Sons of mothers, husbands of wives and fathers of sons! Can you believe it?

The cars decorated in greenery pass us by, but behind the grilled portholes we see the desperate eyes of Jews. Again a whisper: "Miedzyrzec, the Miedzyrzec ghetto. The last two ghettos in Poland."

The cars roll on. The next ones are empty. Their doors are open. They are meant for us… and immediately we are hit by shouts coming all around us, "Rise, march, one by one, 60 in every car." There aren't many Jews anymore.

I am struck with a new concern. I pray that I am not number 60 and my daughter 61… if they separate the two of us, all my plans are in vain…

My time to board the train draws near. The SS man numbering the prisoners whips my back and spews the number 51 from his murderous maw, giving my daughter the number 52. We are no longer at risk of being separated; the two of us are in the same car.

The train is moving, the wheels are turning rapidly but I am in shock. I do not hear the moaning of the men and I do not see the women tearing their hair and crying bitterly. I do not even feel my daughter clinging to my arm with both her hands. But when the mists of bewilderment cleared they left a single question behind: "What is going on here?"

And suddenly, like an electric shock, I recall the words that I heard when we were sitting on the ground before we boarded the train: Miedzyrzec, the last two ghettos..."

It is all clear to me. This is the Devil's grand finale, the victory of annihilation. Satan is celebrating his victory over the 3 million Jews of Poland, who embodied the accomplishments of 50 generations and are now no more than dust and ashes.

Constantly jumping off

Gunfire reminds me that we are on the way to hell. Guns and machineguns spit fire from the roof of every car. It is now clear to me that the silent obedience with which the Jews of Łuków reacted to the commands of the Gestapo was not the result of despair. On the contrary, it seemed that every person was preparing for action. As soon as the train cleared the town, they started jumping off. In some of the cars there were men with tools who easily opened the doors, while the people who had no tools – me among them – had to jump through the portholes, which could be opened with nothing more than bare hands and courage.

The train keeps going and people are jumping even though the Lithuanian guards are raining ceaseless fire. The game is clear: the Jews know where they are being led and the murderers know that we know... hence our daring, which borders on desperation.

We pass the Szydłowiec station, following by Sokołów and Kosów, only 7 kilometers left before the hell mouth and the train is quickly closing down the distance. I am determined not to enter the furnaces of Treblinka no matter what! I have faced hardships so far, and it would seem that I must accompany the last of the ghetto Jews on their last journey to the very gates of Treblinka... 4 kilometers are left, 4 minutes from the furnace. Jewish hands lift me (then my daughter) to the porthole. Saving souls is their last act before they are themselves martyred.

I jumped and fell! The "welcoming" blow I receive from the ground runs through my spine and into my brain and I feel like I shattered into a million pieces. Instinctively I turn my head towards the train – it is still moving while I am sitting here unharmed! I rolled into the ditch by the tracks and pressed hard against the ground... and when the train passed I got up and started running after it. I must meet immediately with my daughter; we agreed that I will run after the train and she will run in the opposite direction. I kept running and every moment seemed like eternity. Suddenly I noticed a figure running towards me; I pick up the pace and yes, it's her... "Chava! Chava!" I cry. "Father! Father!" She answers. Thank God, the two of us are safe and sound. We draw closer, 50 meters, 30 meters, 20 meters... we hold out our hands for a hug, but suddenly hear "Halt!" A Polish gentile is already holding me by the throat and his friend holds my daughter. They are taking us off the tracks and to the side. There are two other "kidnappers" there, holding two Jews and a woman. I understand the situation and realize that we have only moments to act, because if the German gendarmes come it would be too late...

I turned to the kidnappers using short but poignant words. I did not beg them but spoke proudly. I tried to stir their respect for the young girl and the woman who carried out such a heroic act. Real Poles would respect such an accomplishment, I told them, and felt that one of them in particular was persuaded by my words. I turn to the Jews. If any of you have money, give it to me. They do. I add all my money (29 zloty) to theirs and give the money to the peasant who was more impressed by my words than the others.

We start running – where to? About half a kilometer away there is a small copse. "We have to run fast", I told my daughter, holding her hand. They are busy splitting the loot for now, but it is not enough to satisfy them. They might pursue us. We run as fast as we can and are already halfway to the copse when we hear "Halt!" again. I turn my head back and see one of the "kidnappers", wearing a white coat, following us. We ignore his repeated orders to "halt", and continue our dramatic escape. He is naturally faster than us and keeps closing the distance... suddenly he was gone, along with the voices. At first we were amazed, but the volleys of bullets shot at us from German machine guns make our situation crystal clear: the gendarmes from Kosów have arrived. We immediately started crawling and made our winding way to the copse.

Their attack on us continues into the forest, but the generous trees offer us cover and protection. The battle continues until the desired reinforcements arrive... darkness falls and the Germans retreat.

This was the first time during our hard journey from Treblinka to the camp I defected from that we found sanctuary from the human beasts – among the trees of the copse just outside of Treblinka. These trees bore silent witness to the thousands of trains that passed by filled with Jews and came back empty, among them the train bearing the last of the Jews from Łuków and Miedzyrzec, on May 2nd 1943.

[Page 185]
Rivka Greenberg (Mincberg)

My Journeys Through the Valley of the Shadow of Death

On the day the war broke out, we were all home – my parents, both my brothers, my grandfather on mother's side and myself. We were listening to the radio and heard the Polish government announce that a war broke out. This news report that struck us all dumb said also that the Polish army has fended off the German invasion and was even advancing towards Germany. At first we trusted these news but when we saw the German planes flying over our town and bombing it unhindered, we realized that the announcements made by the Polish government are false, leading to immediate panic and a massive rush of people escaping to the nearby villages.

Our entire family left as well, heading on foot towards Ostrowiec, where we had some relatives, intending to continue east.

On the way we managed to acquire a wagon and the entire family drove on to the village of Adamów, where we paid some gentiles for lodging.

The next day we heard that the Germans were advancing on the village so we continued by wagon to Ostrowiec. By the time we arrived, the Germans were already there and we went to our aunt.

In the meantime we learned that other Jews continued fleeing toward the Wisła River. An extended flight was out of the question since we were accompanied by my elderly grandfather whom we did not wish to leave behind, and so we decided to stay in Ostrowiec until the Germans left.

In the meantime, we heard rumors from nearby towns that the Germans were abusing the Jews, kidnapping them to do hard labor, shaving their beards and so on. In Wierzbnik, however, everything was quiet. We therefore decided, two weeks later, to go back home. A few days later we arrived back home and found that the local gentiles have broken into our apartment and looted it. While we were still shaken by the sight, we were struck by a new disaster. A few days after our return home, the Germans took 20 hostages and demanded a contribution of 20,000 guldens or else the hostages will be executed.

Since my father was known as a Zionist activist, the relatives of the hostages came to him and asked him to negotiate the release of the abductees in return for the contribution with the Germans.

My father went and begged for the lives of the hostages, but the Germans insisted on getting paid. We had no other recourse but to collect the necessary sum, because we naively assumed this will be the end of the calamity. The money was raised quickly and delivered to the authorities, and the hostages were released. But the persecution did not end, it grew worse and worse.

As time passed, they started kidnapping people from their homes to do hard labor, abusing and humiliating them in the process. Once they took a few people, my brother among them, to a place by the train station and ordered them to carry large planks, tree trunks, while sadistically abusing them. They were told to lie on the ground and anyone who got up would be shot. In some cases they murdered a few people and ordered the others to dance.

On New Year, the Jews started organizing holiday prayer meetings. A Minyan was gathered on Koleyova Street, at the home of the Rubinstein family. While the people were communing with God, the Germans came and dragged them outside, beat them up and sent them to work at the train station, still wearing their tallits. Bearded folk had their beards shaved until their faces were bloody and raw. A few managed to hide, but it was only for a short while because the Germans conducted searches and pulled all those who were hiding out, beating them viciously.

Every day brought a new edict, leading to complete chaos. People once again turned to my father, who had contacts among the local authorities, but when he went there, all the clerks, who were former acquaintances of his, pretended they did not know him and even gloated at the fate of the Jews.

Germans were popping out like mushrooms after the rain and it turned out that many of them have been acting as spies for years, planted into the munitions factories in our town.

Since the edicts have grown too heavy for the people to bear, they once again turned to my father, asking him to form some kind of organization that would try and help them. Naturally there was very little they could do since the Germans already had detailed plans, directing the course of our lives towards the goal they have set, using vile trickery and cunning. At first the Jews thought that the war would be over quickly and everything will blow over, but it was a false hope. On the contrary, things became worse with each passing day.

Famine and diseases

Time passed and the ghetto was established, the people ordered to move into a specific residence area. The place quickly became crowded, filled with famine and disease. Winter offered its own share of natural disasters, which were felt even more keenly this time. We felt cold to the bone and suffered greatly, because there was no way of getting heating supplies (lumber or coal).

A short while after the establishment of the ghetto a typhoid plague broke out. Two rooms, taken from one of the families, were dedicated to treating the sick, and I worked there as a volunteer nurse. I pitched in despite my lack of experience in this field and together with Mrs. Chava Singer I arranged hot meals (a little porridge and hot soup), cooked by my mother, and served them to the sick that lay in the "isolaterium", as the place was called. Most of the patients were refugees from Płock who came to us earlier.

Sanitation in this place was terrible; the people lay on bare bunks, while we collected some blankets to cover the patients. Medical aid was scarce; there was no medicine, just aspirin. Risking my own life, I washed the sick, put ice on their brows, deloused them and did everything a child like me could do, while hiding our actions from the Germans whom we feared.

Aside from the diseases, we were also heavily burdened by hunger. Getting what little food we could was a daring operation, involving great risk and low odds of success. The Germans have set up a military camp where our plywood factory used to stand, taking away our livelihood. I had dropped out of school at the time, but a group of children banded together and we continued studying as much as we could.

Fortunately, the Germans required a cheap workforce to operate the munitions factories in town, and so they hired the Jews and paid them a meager wage that somehow allowed us to "keep our heads above the water".

The summer of 1941 showed the first signs of the Russo-German war, since the military camps were nearby and we could sense them stir, increasing their activity and readying their weapons. This event marked no respite for us, and perhaps made things worse. The German victories on the front lines improved their position, a fact that undermined the Jewish moral.

The eviction

During October 1942 the number of shipments of Jewish refugees to our town increased and rumors started circulating about the extermination camps. We felt our end was drawing near but we were helpless to resist since there was no place to run to; the surrounding area was hostile and offered no hope for sanctuary. We all prayed for a miracle, but the miracle never came.

In its stead came the black day. The disaster struck on 27.10.1942, a day that will live in infamy. Early in the morning we could already sense an increased activity around the ghetto. We saw armed Lithuanian soldiers with their steel helmets in front of our house, circling the ghetto. At dawn, we heard earsplitting shouts – "Juden Raus!"[1]

People started leaving their houses and hurrying with their belongings to the Rinek, as ordered. The Polish chief of police, Chamiltzki, came into our home that morning, accompanied by two gendarmes, and ordered father to go to town while we were ordered to leave the house in a hurry. Father went, leaving us behind in hope that he could do something.

We were left alone, with an ill grandfather lying in his bed, and mother decided not to leave the house and stay with him. Through the window we saw our relatives, the Lichtensteins, and as they passed by we asked them "Where to?"

We children wanted to go as well but mother forbid us from leaving grandfather's sickbed, while he only turned his head and cried. I went to him, kissed him and forcefully pulled my mother outside.

From that point on we merged with the stream of our townsfolk. We dragged our feet through the shoving, the threats and the shouts, until we arrived at the Rinek, where we were all ordered to stand in ranks of five.

The Lithuanian policemen, the Polish gendarmes and the SS made sure the lines were straight and orderly. The children held their parents' hands, frightened, and despair and fear were written on the faces of all. Gunfire cut the air in every direction and on both sides of the road we could see corpses lying in the gateways and alleys, and hear moans and gasps.

On our way to the Rinek, we saw Chanoch Biderman leave his house wearing a Tallit and walking alone. When most of the people have already gathered at the Rinek, the men in charge demanded to know who had a certificate and placed them in a separate queue.

The people who had certificates and were placed in that queue were later taken to work at the factory while the others were led to Koleyova Street. Both my brothers were sent to the munitions factory while my mother and I stayed for the time being at the Rinek, with about 60 other people. The Germans debated what to do with us, and then sent us to the factory camp as well.

At first, our entire family was at the Strzelnica camp, but later we were separated. My brother and I were sent to Majowka while my parents remained in Strzelnica.

To Auschwitz

On the night before 29.7.1944, the Germans and Ukrainians encircled the camp and people felt something was about to happen. Knowing that they had nothing left to lose, they decided on a desperate act that offered a glimmer of hope. About 200 people broke through the camp fence, trying to escape to the woods, though they didn't know exactly where they would go. But the guards opened fire on them and killed many. Those who managed to escape entered the woods and joined the partisans.

On the next day, the Germans ordered us to leave the camp and enter the railroad cars that stood on the tracks by the factory. We thought we were being taken to Treblinka but the signs we passed along the way – Katowice, Częstochowa – told us we were going in a different direction. After three days of travel, with no food or water, we reached Auschwitz.

Our first impression was terrible. At dawn we were ordered out of the cars, lined up in fives once more and marched to the baths, where they separated the men from the women and ordered us to give them any money or Jewels we had. Fortunately, our shipment was not taken to the incinerators, but sent to the women camp at Birkenau. I saw my little brother wave his hand at me and that was the last I saw of him.

In Auschwitz I worked in the same commando as my mother and we were given all manner of hard tasks, pushing wheelbarrows full of rocks, doing construction work, in the mud, in the cold, under terrible conditions. We were in Auschwitz until January 1945.

On 18.01.1945 I was separated from my mother and sent to Ravensbrück camp while my mother remained in Auschwitz. She was also sent to Ravensbrück later on, and we haven't met since.

From this camp we were sent after 3 weeks to Neustadt-Glewe which was called "Krappirungs Lager". There were approximately 5,000 women there, only 600 of whom survived. This camp had a single purpose – there was nothing to do there, no work at all, only wait for a horrible death by starvation.

During these dark days I too faced a terrible experience, when I lost a friend who was like a sister to me, Tobcia Tenser, who came down with dysentery and died by my side.

One day we witnessed a rebellion of Russian prisoners. My cell contained 40 women, most of them Russian, and I was the only Jew among them. They brought iron bars with them and hid them in their mattresses. I noticed that they were organizing something and although I didn't understand "what was going on", I was ordered to keep silent.

They used the bars to loosen up the grille and waited for their chance. When they noticed the German jailors taking off their uniform and the echoes of the front line coming closer, the Russian prisoners burst out and started escaping from the camp. I was left sitting on the floor because I couldn't move. Some male prisoners came later and told me we were free.

1. Jews, out!

At Umszalagplatz (the deportation place)

[Page 190]
Hanna Tenzer

On the Edge of the Abyss

The day after the war broke out, a bomb fell in town. Classes were cancelled, so we had to continue our studies in private. The munitions factories in town made us assume that we would be bombed, and almost everyone started fleeing to the neighboring town of Iłża. Our family – father, mother, my sister and I – also fled. We took only our personal belongings, silverware, Jewelry and so on. I remember that some Poles came to us, asking us to donate all manner of valuables "for airplanes".

We spent about two weeks in Iłża, staying with friends, the Zylbersteins, who owned a grocery store.

To save our lives we went with the Zylbersteins to a building by the town hall, which was sturdier than most. We stayed there for a few hours; people were praying, lighting candles, and suddenly a bomb shell fell inside the building! A panic broke out and people started running out, gunshots were heard and many have died, among them the town's rabbi. We were scattered, but my parents finally found me. We stayed there for a few more hours and then returned to the Zylbersteins, until the Germans came in. Upon their arrival, a rumor spread that we should escape to Russia and the youths started swarming eastward. They also turned to my father and told him "Come with us," and he liked the idea and decided to join them. Since he was a traditionalist, he first picked up his tallit and his tefillin and then started bidding us goodbye. But his decision agitated so much that we started crying, and he changed his mind and stayed. All of us therefore stayed for a while longer in Iłża, with the Germans. Later, we got a wagon and went back to Wierzbnik. We had to earn a living and show resourcefulness and adaptability. People went to the big city of Lodz and brought supplies from there. I remember that there was a severe shortage of yeast (this was The supply to have), and there was also no bread. There was a bakery next to our house, whose owner was called "the Kielcer Baker", and we would all stand in line there to get some bread. Things continued in this fashion for a few months and life "got back on track," until one day came the order to wear the mark of disgrace on our sleeves. About two months later the streets were classified and the Jews were forbidden to live in some of them. Whole families had to move to a new place, and since we had a large apartment we had many relatives and friends staying with us.

A while later, a labor camp was established in Wierzbnik, next to the munitions factory, and Jews sent to Wierzbnik from various places were employed there. They told us about the ones who were not so fortunate and were sent to the concentration camps instead. At first we thought that it would never happen to us, but eventually we realized that the scourge will not spare us. Every person prepared packages and people sowed gold coins into hidden places in their clothes, to serve as emergency funds. Tensions intensified day by day.

A German soldier was found dead at a certain house, and all residents of the house (all Poles) paid dearly for it. The Germans demanded that the local authorities provide ropes and recruited all butchers in town to serve as executioners. The next day, every resident of the house, man or woman, was taken to the center of town and hanged for an entire day (it was on a Sunday, and most of the Poles went to church).

It was not long before the Holocaust was fully upon us. With a loud clamor the Germans, Gestapo and SS, came and drove all the Jews – men, women and children – to the town's commercial center, the Rinek. After a brief wait, most people were led to the train station and crammed into the waiting cars, to be sent to Treblinka. Only a few of them were sent back to Strzelnica and others to Majowka. Most of our family – my father, my mother and I – was sent to Strzelnica and my sister to Majowka.

We walked for about 4 hours, tired and sweaty. We were forced to throw away many things along the way, while the gentiles stood by the sides of the road, gloating and gathering valuables at their leisure. When we arrived, we were told to hand over all the gold we had and throw it on the pile. Some secreted their valuables in various hiding places while we naively gave away everything we had. From this place we were led to our new "living quarters". We settled in cabins and started a "new" way of life: my father did physical labor in the camp along with others while my mother and I worked in the kitchen.

Cherinska fought like a lioness

This is a tale from those days:

A lady doctor named Cherinska, who arrived before the war, was living with her elderly mother and her daughter named Natasha. During our eviction from town, they wanted to take away her daughter and leave her, but she refused. She fiercely held on to her daughter Natasha and fought for her like a lioness until the Germans realized they could not separate the two. Finally they gave up and added the mother to the shipment....

After a while, we were transferred from both Strzelnica and Majowka into one camp located next to the factory, and the people continued working there, manufacturing munitions and doing hard labor. The most common task was manning the furnaces at the munitions factory. It was very hard work. People worked three shifts. Things continued in this manner for about a year and a half, until one day we heard the scream of wheels on the railroad tracks by the factory, a sound that made us all shudder. Our hearts told us that those cars were meant for us. People started fleeing, although the place was fenced and patrolled by Ukrainian guards. During the night, they broke through the fences and escaped. Some of them reached Russia and survived while others were shot down by the guards. In the morning, we found the bodies of the dead in the yard, along with the wounded crying for water, but the Germans refused to let us approach them. Fearing that we might try to escape again, they took away our shoes.

During this time, my father came down with partial paralysis. Unfortunately, there was no medicine and we paid much money to a Ukrainian who brought us some leeches. At first it seemed to help, we noticed some improvement in his condition and were happy that he was feeling better, but after a few days his condition deteriorated and he became completely paralyzed. My mother had to feed him and he continued to suffer until he finally passed away. We covered him with an overcoat and buried him in Strzelnica.

The next day, the Germans ordered us into the cars, but after a significant number of people already went in, the Germans decided for some reason to call them back out. A few days later, they drove us back into the cars, separating the men from the women. Our family was also a part of this turbid flow this time. The cars were so crowded there wasn't room left to fit a needle. We received no food or drink during the entire journey while being forced to listen to the terrible cries coming from the cars. Gradually the voices fell silent and everything became quiet. At dawn the train arrived at a station called "Auschwitz". People outside opened the cars and told us to get out and wait by the cars. My mother, my sister and I stood together. When the rest of the cars were opened, especially those of the men, we saw that one of them was filled only with dead people, who suffocated from the crowdedness and lack of air.

We looked around horrified. We saw electric wire fences and behind them people who looked more like skeletons. We thought this to be a madhouse; a jumble of languages assaulted us on every direction and we didn't understand a word.

To the bathhouse

We stood there for about an hour before our entire shipment was marched on foot to the Brzezinski camp, to the "bathhouse" (sauna). Before the entrance to the sauna was a trench 50cm deep, filled with water, and every person had to walk into this trench with his shoes on, for reasons I never learned. From there we proceeded to a large hall where a few men were walking around and they ordered us to take off our clothes. They shaved our heads, tattooed a number on our arms and dressed us in slips and dresses – "camp uniforms" – and wooden shoes (clogs). The same number that appeared on our arms was also on our dresses.

This entire process shocked us, because we didn't know what was going on. They took us outside, where we met the men. They were dressed the same way we were, and it was impossible for people to recognize each other, even among husbands and wives. The sheer absurdity made this perhaps the only moment when a person might smile...

The women were all taken to Birkenau, and placed in a large cabin numbered 25. We lay on bunks that were attached to the wall in special grooves, two stories each. Every bunk was shared by 10 women and we had to sleep "head to toe" because there wasn't enough room. The place we were put in was considered "quarantine", no one comes and no one goes. We sat there for hours, knees bent, with nothing to do. From time to time we were taken out for a few hours.

In the morning they conducted a lineup before the cabin and while we stood there, they gave each line soup from the same bowl, which passed from mouth to mouth. There was nothing to launder since we only had one dress, but the women used every spare drop of water for laundry and because we had no other clothes, we had to walk "dressed" in the wet clothing until it dried.

The nightmare reached its peak at night, because we could see the incinerators from afar.

At the end of the quarantine period, they took us to work loading stones on cars. This was very hard work even for men, let alone for starved, exhausted women, but the suffering was greatest when a car derailed and had to be put back on track. It was unbearable.

Weiselcommando

We also worked by a river whose name I no longer recall. During the cold winter, we had to make coal from the wood of a tree called "predator", while another group would leave camp to work among the reeds. The women would alternate between the three groups. I recall that when we were working in the "out" group that went to collect reeds, we would pass by a band which was always playing the same tune, "Rosamunde". The walk lasted 4 hours and those who fell behind were severely beaten. I was feeling particularly distressed because I was part of the last quintet in line, followed closely by the SS with their hounds... some women used the opportunity to make the reeds into a broom, which they sneaked into the camp and traded for some food. I wanted to make such a broom once but failed to hide it. The Germans at the gate caught me and beat me up.

"Researches"

One day while we were standing before our "block" we were approached by two prisoners who worked at the infirmary. They wrote down our numbers and told us that we must report to the infirmary on Sunday. Needless to say that any deviation from our routine filled us with dread, and when we told the block manager she said this was bad...we already considered this a bad omen, but the supervisor's words stunned us. Our lives became nothing more than stress and anticipation of that special day, knowing that whatever will be, will be. When the ill-fated day came I bid my mother and sister goodbye and went to the infirmary with the rest of the women so ordered. When we got there we were sent with an escort to camp Auschwitz, inside the city, and there we were led to a big structure that served as a hospital. When we went inside we saw men walking around wearing white coats. From the waiting room we moved to a room that was filled with stretchers covered with white sheets. We already knew that the Germans were experimenting on prisoners and figured this to be the torture awaiting us, leaving us dispirited and desperate. Before long, someone directed us each to a special, separate room, sitting in wheelchairs. Everything must have been prepared for us, because the same number that was on my arm was also on the chair's armrest... but to my astonishment, no experiments were conducted on me; they merely took shots of my head from every possible angle, the same as they did with the others.

We never learned the meaning of this act, but we can assume that it was necessary for their insane research into matters of race and so on.

After the strange photo session we were taken back to "our" block, and life returned to normal.

Selection

And then one day we heard the sound of a whistle followed by the order: "Block 25, line up! We're going to the sauna!" We lined in fives and started marching toward the "bathhouse". There was a great mayham by the building. Fear and desperation mingled. People were whispering: Eviction or the gas chamber... it's all over, there's no escape!"

And while we were all panicking at the thought of the death waiting for us, we were approached by the shiny uniform of Dr. Mengele, "the doctor", the hangman who murdered millions of innocent people. He came in person to continue his murderous work. He was tall, his eyes glittering with authority and his demeanor full of pride and a sense of Prussian superiority as he stood before a pathetic group of defenseless, naked women...

His face showing his shameless satisfaction at carrying out this diabolical role as his elegantly gloved hand rose slowly and with the slightest gesture of a finger pointed out who would live and who would die. Who would go to the gas chamber and who would merely be evicted.

My mother's turn is drawing near. "Good lord," I whispered, "Have mercy! Protect her! Don't let her die!" Another second, and my heart is pounding, I am trembling. My breath is caught in my throat! I want to close my eyes, but they refuse to listen to me... the gloved hand rises apathetically and points towards the gas chambers... I cannot bear to see this!

I was shocked, my head dizzy...

My life lost all meaning that second.

My turn came, and my eyes were already devoid of life. The light that flickered in them a moment ago died. I apathetically stared at the hand of the murderer move, but to my surprise, the finger "said" eviction this time.

I could not accept my bitter fate, the separation from my mother. I decided – it is all over, I cannot return to life. If my mother is doomed to die I will die with her! I moved...

The sadist noticed my hesitation. His stare measured me from head to toe and his bored voice echoed through my ears: "How old are you?"

I do not recall my answer anymore but I suppose I told him I was younger than my 14 years. When I answered he smiled, took a whistle out of his pocket and whistled shortly, a sound that meant: put me with my mother!

I sighed with relief. I no longer cared about my fate so long as I foiled the attempt to separate me from my mother.

At the end of the selection, the SS monitors whipped us to hurry us along – "Dress up!" The supervisor came quickly and read out our numbers. With every reply she crossed out a name from her list, the entire process carried out with meticulous German order. As far as she was concerned, we were crossed out from the book of the living.

When she finished the process of reading and crossing out names, we were ordered into rows and marched toward the gas chambers; gas! We trembled at the sound of this word. For three years we avoided it and now we are led like lambs to the slaughter. We felt alternating despair and rage. "Alas! If only I could attack this sadist, this villain, this devil!" I thought in my heart, "if only I could claw his eyes out!"

But what could I, a poor, defenseless girl, plot and dare?

Time was also against us, events were unfolding rapidly. The end was urging, leaving no room for thoughts. We left the sauna, approached the fence and crossed it into the second yard.

The SS women were leading us to the gas chambers. This is the last chance to run! But where to?!

We arrived at another building and formed a long line before the door. We were ordered into the barracks-like house and the monitors pushed us inside, a total of 120 women one after the other, hitting and cursing us.

I don't know where I suddenly got the idea from that I should help the other women present. The entrance was narrow, so I tried to take the door off its hinges, but my efforts were in vain.

When we were inside, all hope was lost, as if the end was drawing near, and utter despair spread. Suddenly I spotted a ventilator in the wall, like a glimmer of hope. I formed a plan immediately – to break the ventilator during the night, get out through the hole, crawl to camp "A" and reach block 25. This was naturally a false hope, a kind of sweet illusion, merely a figment of my imagination. Weak and exhausted, I fell down. I couldn't cry anymore, my eyes were dry, my heart turned to stone. My fear of what was coming gave me no rest. From time to time I awoke from this nap of oblivion. My eyes measured the hall and in the darkness I noticed a nail-studded plank on the ceiling, a rope hanging from its center reminding me of a gallows, and here and there were piles of rags and hair, seated by "living corpses". This was the gate of Hell, at the edge of perdition! Closed cars came here to be loaded with those condemned to death and take them to the gas chambers.

I sat next to my mother and hugged her. We tried to comfort each other, but suddenly my mother grew angry at me for choosing death of my own free will. "Why did you do it?" she asked me "Hanna was crying, you are so young and have your whole life ahead of you!" She seemed to try and comfort me when she added "Life in this world is but a corridor. Our real life starts in the next world. We will meet your father there." But despite her harsh words, I was glad that I didn't forsake my mother. I was at peace with my decision.

Suddenly, the door opened and my blood froze at the sound of the devil's footsteps. At the door was the SS supervisor. She put her hands on her hips, tilted her head back domineeringly and asked loudly: "Well! Who among you is willing to be in charge? Who wants to be a kapo?" But when she saw our confusion she added, true to the deception policy: "Sort out the rags and after you finish you will go to camp C while the rags go to the incinerator." She was saying the exact opposite of her true intentions. In truth, she meant for the rags to go to camp C while we would go to the incinerators. She left the room after hitting my mother and me.

We had no choice but to cling to any shred of hope, and so we rose and started "working". We deluded ourselves that this might help us, but in our hearts we felt it was the end. Outside we heard orders, shouts, cursing, and I was jealous at the people outside who were "only" getting beaten… suddenly the light went off and the ventilator stopped working. The door opened and two SS men wearing gas masks entered the room.

One of them threw an open canister filled with a white powder into the room, and while we instinctively drew away from this canister, they left the room, shutting the doors behind them. We sat quietly and apathetically, waiting for death to come. I was sure these were my last moments, and my entire short life passed before my eyes. But nothing happened. I suppose they were trying to unnerve us again. From behind the doors came the sound of loud laughter and the song "Rosamunde".

After a short time, the spectacle repeated itself. The same sadists came in again, holding guns. "Are you still alive?" they mocked us and asked "Where is the gun?" pointing at the floor. We didn't understand what they wanted from us but they gave us five minutes to "find the gun", threatening to shoot us if we couldn't find it. Eventually it turned out that they meant the box they threw into the room earlier and we were left like this for 48 hours without a drop of water and with no bread.

We recovered a bit during that time. When they brought us into the room, we thought we would die immediately, but the postponement of the execution gave us some small hope. Might we live a little longer while our loved ones are certain we are no longer among the living? Dear God! Could we be luckier than our millions of brothers and sisters, who perished in the gas chambers?!

Suddenly we heard a whistle, the call for a lineup! The doors opened, the block supervisor showed up and screamed: "Out!" in an inhuman voice. The date was November 2nd 1944.

Tired and weak we left the place after 48 hours of hunger and fear. At first I was looking suspiciously for cars that will take us to the incinerator, but no, the supervisor of block 4 told us briefly "You are free".

We all surrounded her, hugged and kissed her. We were then taken to the "recuperation" block. In time we solved the riddle of our survival: it turned out that the battle on the front lines, which were drawing closer, forced the murderers to destroy the incinerators and evacuate the prisoners.

[Page 197]
Rachel Laor (Dreksler)

To the Wilderness of the Taiga

Unlike many of our townsmen, we have not fled the city despite the risk of military activity due to the presence of munitions factories in Starachowice. I do not know if this was the result of confidence or fatalism and acceptance of fate, but the fact is that during the first three months after the Germans moved into our town, we stayed put despite all the changes.

A common funeral

Only at the end of that period did my parents come to the conclusion that staying there could doom us, leaving no chance of escape in the future. It was therefore decided that we will cross the Wisła to "the new world", that is, the Russian side.

My father rented a wagon and we left in the morning, accompanied by many Jews who considered our actions a sort of public event and being tied to my father in thousands of different ways, saw fit to accompany us for a while.

We were not alone at the start of our journey from town, although in retrospect it is truly regrettable that only 20 people, most of them youths, traveled with us, while most of the Jews in town stayed behind.

The road was hard and arduous, and we were not used to this kind of "mobile" life. In addition to the physical hardships involved, we had suffered at the hands of people, local anti-Semites who took every chance to torment us.

The border between Russia and Germany, that is, the areas that the two countries have snatched from Poland, was marked by the Bug River, which was our closest destination. But before we could reach it, we had to cross a bigger river, that is the national river of Poland, the Wisła, and this natural barrier posed a major problem. These were not normal times and we were not normal citizens, who could travel safely, but rather Jews, second rate citizens, and facing the unknown at that. Any bridge we crossed would most certainly be guarded by German soldiers and it was uncertain whether they would let us cross. On the other hand, we didn't know if there was another way of crossing. But lady luck has smiled on us this time, and when we reached the river, we found a barge and used it to cross.

Have you no shame?

We were now somewhat relieved. After overcoming this first obstacle, we continued eastwards in the direction of the Bug. Ahead of us traveled another Jewish refugee family in a wagon, with two young girls. A German patrol was slowly advancing towards them, then stopped by the wagon and ordered the girls to get off. Not only that, but they ordered the two to undress…

It is easy to understand our panic as the Germans led the two naked girls into some yard and returned to the road without them. It was now time for our wagon to advance towards them, and my parents feared that they would do the same to me. I decided to resist them no matter what! But fortunately for me and my family, things did not get that far. When our wagon approached them they indeed stopped us and when they heard where we were headed they started swearing angrily, complaining that we were headed for the Russian pigs. Then they turned their eyes to me – part in question, part in doubt, and asked "And what is she doing with you?" My father, who could act in a calculated and wise manner even under pressure, showed his resourcefulness at this point; he immediately responded that they "picked me along the way". This answer implied that I was not Jewish, and the Germans appeared convinced as they started chastising me: "Have you no shame that you are riding with these Jews?" I pretended not to speak German and the situation absolved me from answering them.

Advance scout

After this exchange of "compliments" they let us pass and slowly we made our way to the Bug River. Here it was decided for some reason that I must cross first to the other bank, like some kind of advance scout, and find out what was waiting for us there.

While doing so, I met on the bridge a girl from Wierzbnik named Yehudit Fishman (today Landau, living in Israel). She was alone and the two of us continued together to the other side of the Bug River, while my parents stayed on that side of the river waiting for a signal from me.

Luck was on our side this time, and no one stopped us from crossing – on either side of the bridge. After we saw that everything was well, we continued to walk toward the city of Łuck, where we hoped to find aid on our arduous journey. My father had business ties with a mill-owner who lived in that city. My father also told me when I headed that way that the town's rabbi was a relative of ours and that I should go to his house, and ask for help or at the very least some advice. My friend Yehudit also had her share of addresses to turn to and so we split up, each going her way.

I easily found my way to the rabbi's house, because everyone knew where the rabbi lives, but instead of finding advice and support I was disappointed. The house was locked and deserted, nothing around but silence. On the door I found a notice saying "A feudal lord lived here, and we sent him to Siberia".

The people standing by the shop window

I required no further explanations, everything was clear to me. But my long journey and the disappointment both showed their marks. I could not continue on foot and went to rent a carriage that will take me to the second address.

While riding through the streets of Łuck I looked to the sidewalk, where a man and woman were standing by a shop window and looking into it. My heart seemed to leap in my chest. The people standing before the window were so familiar to me that I could recognize them even from behind. Another second, no, a fraction of a second and I had no more doubts! They were no other than my brother and my sister-in-law, standing here in the center of Łuck, looking casually at a shop window.

With one empathic gesture I stop the carriage and jump into the arms of my relatives. How? What? How did we end up here all of a sudden? We pause for a moment and take a long breath, and the mystery is quickly solved: like me, they had the rabbi's address, walked to his home and when they found the notice mentioned earlier, they turned back and intended to go to the same address I had... and to pass the time, they were looking at shop windows.

We therefore continued together, and on the way I was told by my brother that about 20 people from Wierzbnik have gone to the rabbi and are now scattered across town. I also learned that the people waiting across the Bug grew tired of waiting for the results of my patrol and decided to take a risk and cross.

Three more days passed before my parents crossed as well, practically the last people to cross the border. Now that all the people from Wierzbnik were in Łuck we tried to decide what to do next.

Going to Siberia

We decided to go to the town of Łuniniec. Why? Because we had a "contact" there in the form of a teacher who used to work at the Tarbut school. The man was very popular and was considered an important part of town and those facts made us hopeful. Therefore, the whole group from Wierzbnik headed to Łuniniec and the home of the teacher, Lupta. Our hopes came true as the teacher welcomed us, willing and eager to help!

We settled in town and slowly started to familiarize ourselves with the new place. The Russians considered us an unknown factor that required definition, and gave us questionnaires to fill out. Among the more routine questions was a significant one: Where would we like to go: Germany, Russia or Palestine?!

Since we were dealing with a new and unfamiliar regime and considering the difference between the Germans, who sought to kill us, and the Russians to whom we fled to escape the Nazis, we trusted them and never even suspected their intentions. My father therefore decided to answer the question with the word "Palestine."

Our disappointment came swiftly. A few days after we submitted the forms, a Russian who seemed important came to see us and unofficially announced that my parents would be deported to Siberia, suggesting that I hide so I could stay. I have naturally refused him, and he left as he came. And indeed, the following night we were visited by policemen who took our family to the train station. We were surprised to see other residents of Wierzbnik there, such as Sola Kleiner, her future husband Wiesenfeld, and others. We were loaded into freight cars and rode the train for a long time, until we reached a station near the town of Arkhangelsk, by the primeval forests, where we were ordered to disembark. After a brief wait, during which we were counted, we were led into the forest and succinctly told the famous Russian word "Stroits", meaning that from now on we had to get by, that is to live and work here.

Everyone on horseback

There were cabins inside the forest, ready to "welcome" us, and 50 people were housed in each. We were not incarcerated, we were free to go as we pleased, but the odds of leaving the place were close to none, both because the it was forbidden by law and because the geographic conditions and the climate made it all but impossible.

The temperatures dropped as far as -50c, and even lower on the wild taiga, and the amount of food we received was minimal, a slice of bread a day and nothing more.

Nevertheless, my father was optimistic. On the way to Arkhangelsk he already had a kind of prophetic vision, which eventually came true.

While the rest of us were depressed about heading to Siberia, my father claimed that we were going to Israel. We were astonished and wondered how that was possible, but he insisted that we were destined to end up in Israel. He preached patience, and said that the road will be long and winded but we will end up in Jerusalem.

Time went by and we started working because the bread we received was not free. We worked in the forest, cutting down trees. After a while, my father and brother were given wagons and charged with transporting the lumber. I was given a horse as well, and the entire Dreksler family turned into carters. We were hungry and needed more food to sustain us. Whenever we visited the nearby kolkhozes, we tried to trade items for food. Since I excelled at my work, I was given another job, coordination of the work groups, and our situation slightly improved.

As time went by, the Polish general Sikorski struck a bargain with the Soviet government and we were released as part of this agreement, along with thousands of Poles and Jews who were Polish citizens before the war.

After our release we traveled to Middle Asia, where we crossed the border to Persia in orderly fashion and from there to Israel. It was the fulfillment of the vision my late father had during those dark days.

[Page 200]
Chava Faigenbaum (Shraga)

Going to Palestine

It was not enough for the Nazi murderers to plot the annihilation of the Jews in a systematical manner, using calculated and detailed procedures. Nor did they settle for the help of their villainous, venomous, anti-Semite servants among the local populace, who were eager and willing to help them carry out this mass murder.

In addition to the aforementioned methods, the Germans also relied on vile lies, diabolical plots, trickery and cunning, to distract people from the terrible danger that lurked behind the wall.

Knowing about the affinity of the Jews to Israel and that Zion is forever inscribed in their hearts ("As long as the Jewish spirit is yearning deep in the heart, with eyes turned toward the East, looking toward Zion"), they cruelly decided to exploit this deep affinity for the sake of their annihilation plans.

There were two stages to this scheme: first they started to collect the Jews from neighboring towns in Szydłowiec. They were not part of the local population but the remnants from various places, who the Nazis had no time to kill or send to the death camps. Since their mass murder was no longer a secret by the time this took place, the Nazis were weary of surprises and decided to disguise their actions from now on. They therefore named the concentration zone in Szydłowiec "Judenstat", that is "the Jewish State", supposedly hinting that there was some kind of "plausible plan" behind this transfer and concentration.

The next stage was even more cunning and despicable: posters suddenly covered the town, announcing the organization of a collective journey of Jews to Palestine, and that those who wanted to go should come and register.

The snow turned red

This act of trickery managed to mislead people, drawing into their web even those who managed to go into hiding and bringing them one day to the lot by the train station.

When we arrived there, the tragic meaning of the "operation" became dreadfully clear to everyone. The human mind refuses to grasp the terrible event which took place there. First, we were forced to stand for days on end, with no food or water. Every once in a while, someone was pulled out of the ranks, just like that, and murdered on the spot.

Their cruelty was even greater when it came to children, infants, and babes. The Germans would throw babies against the walls of houses, killing them. I can never forget that horror.

The days were days of winter, and the snow that covered the area turned red with the blood of the victims. Among those murdered were some from Wierzbnik – Jechiel Weintraub and his wife, Blumenfeld, Yaakov Kornwaser with his wife and daughter.

At the end of these 6 terrible days came the order to "March" and after walking for 2 kilometers we arrived at the railroad tracks, where the cars were waiting, ready to "receive" us.

Three trucks were also brought to this station, pulling trailers full of Jews dressed in rags and paper bags, all of them exhausted, half-dead and yellow faced. The shipment from the trucks was murdered on the spot, practically to a man, while we were loaded into the cars and the train took off towards Treblinka.

Would they kill healthy people?

My father's contacts in the resistance afforded him extensive knowledge of the German plans, and he knew that we were doomed for certain death. Therefore, he started planning our escape the moment we entered the car. He explained the situation to everyone and instructed them how to jump from the train. Unfortunately, he was faced with the ignorance of people who could not or would not believe. They simply refused to believe or understand that we were all being led to the slaughter.

I remember a couple named Herschman that was in our car. The woman answered my father's explanations by saying "I can't believe they would take strong, healthy people like us and kill them. I don't believe it and I don't want to jump".

Seeing that it was pointless, my father ceased his efforts and focused on instructing those who showed understanding, teaching them how to jump from the train.

After we covered some distance, my father jumped from the car with me right behind him, and for a time we were safe.

[Page 202]
Avraham (Moshe) Minkowski

In the Claws of Death's Minions

It all happened suddenly. Despite the unusual activity and the tension in the air, people refused to believe that it could happen so quickly. And then the bombs fell. We feared the bombardment would continue, because there was a munitions industry in town, and so we fled, my brother Avraham and me, to Słupia, a small town with no industry where we had an uncle. We went to him and he welcomed us, so we stayed there for about 10 days. During that time, we were cut off from our town and didn't know what was happening there, although the army movements we saw made us feel at war. There was a prison for political prisoners sentenced for life in Słupia, and during those days they were evacuated by the police and taken elsewhere. The day after their evacuation the Germans moved in, both regular and armored forces, and we stood in the streets and watched the gentiles welcome them with flowers. The Germans, however, started abusing the population indiscriminately, burning down even the houses of Christians.

I stayed with my uncle for a few more days then went back to Starachowice since I was in German occupied territory anyway.

When I came back home I heard that the Germans kidnapped certain dignitaries and forced them to do physical labor – mostly heavy lifting. Next they started abducting Jews off the streets and taking them to do dirty work at the train station. My father was a sales agent for the Singer sewing machine company all his life, but the Nazi occupation forced him to quit his position because the gentiles refused to pay. After a time, the Germans organized workplaces for us and my father, my brother Aharon and I all went to work for them chopping wood for heating. We would ride the German trucks to the forest where we would chop down trees and bring them back to town. In return we received coupons that were worth a small amount of food that had to be enough for the whole family. This lifestyle continued more or less until 1941. At that point, the Germans ordered us to wear the mark of disgrace on our sleeves. Until that time we worked at a bakery, and worked hard until the late hours of the night, but after the edict concerning the mark of disgrace was issued we could no longer work there, because Jews were not allowed to wander around at late hours. We, on the other hand, were interested in working longer hours to get more bread. Despite the desperate situation, we decided that the risk involved in refusing to wear the mark of disgrace was worth earning a little extra food. Fortunately we were never arrested or inspected. There were others, however, who did not wear the mark and were caught, earning harsh punishments: beatings, abuse and so on.

A while later, the Germans ordered a curfew and limited the time Jews were allowed to stay out of the house.

In 1942 they built a camp at the "Starachowice Mining Factories" munitions factory, and sent many Jews there to do hard labor, but we stayed put for the time being.

In the meantime, German terrorism was escalating with every passing day. I remember a time when they hanged 12 men, young and old, at the center of town, because they shot a German. We were later ordered by the Germans to take the hanged men off the gallows. I remember this case in particular; when we arrived there, they laid all the convicts on the ground, their arms tied behind their backs, exhausted and beaten and desperate. None of them were in any condition to resist, of course. When we were ordered to take them down from the gallows I approached and saw some familiar faces among them, which made things even worse for me. Later my father and I were taken to the main warehouse, to do all sorts of tasks, while the rest of our family was sent to the death camp in Treblinka and never heard from again. We stayed in this camp until my father fell ill and passed away. Afterwards I was taken along with the other prisoners to Auschwitz.

Evicted to Auschwitz

When we arrived in Auschwitz we were directed to the gypsy camp, where I immediately underwent a selection "orchestrated" by Dr. Mengele, before being transported to the "Buna" factories where I worked in construction, in the 105th commando, until January 18th 1944 when the camp was abandoned because the front line was getting closer. The Germans were unwilling to risk leaving us behind and forced us into the infamous "Death March" in the harsh winter cold, to the point where people were falling around us like flies and the snow ran red with the murders carried out by our SS escort. First we went to Gliwice, where we worked at a brick kiln, and later we were loaded on trains but it turned out that the trains had nowhere to go and so they unloaded us set us marching again. We crossed a forest, rushing on because we suspected that they planned to kill us there. Suddenly a shot was heard and panic broke out. We started running while our escort opened fire on us. A few moments later, an officer arrived on the scene and said "Those who are alive must get up, and no harm will come to them." When we rose to our feet we saw that many have died during the shooting. We were ordered to line up and started marching again, for a whole month. The only food we got was a little bread and coffee. Throughout the journey we stayed in public buildings, until we arrived at the city of Landshut. There was no place to house us in this town and they had to put us inside a big tunnel that only had one entrance. After a short while we realized that there was no air in the tunnel, although there was light. A riot started, with everyone pushing their way towards the entrance, and people chocked to death and got trampled, while some committed suicide (the barbers who had shaving tools). In the morning, when we were let out of the tunnel, we learned that dozens have died. This bloody event was followed by a short investigation and they decided to give us two days of rest as a reward. Later we were housed in cabins that used to house French prisoners who were evacuated, and the Germans announced that we will be leaving the place in two days. But since I did not trust the Germans I decided to escape.

Escape

Five of us have banded together. One day I told them about my plan to escape. They encouraged me, because I was exhausted and had no chance of going on. That night, after we received our food in the courtyard, I entered the cabin with some tools and built myself a hiding place made of lumber inside, by the window that also served as an entrance to the cabin. My friends piled lumber on top of me and I lay there until 6 in the morning.

At that time we were called out for a lineup, but I stayed put. The SS conducted an inspection and those who couldn't walk were taken to a cabin and killed. During the inspection, an SS soldier came into our cabin and stood on the lumber piled over me. I held my breath so he wouldn't notice me but I was mortified by the notion that the dogs might smell me.

Half an hour later everyone left while I stayed for several hours under the lumber. Then I went out of hiding and saw that no one was around. I was wearing camp uniform, clothes dangerous to be seen in, but I had a blanket that I tore up and used to cover my pants. I turned out my hat and walked dressed in this manner. About 200 meters away was a cart shed that had a barrel of tar in it. I took some of it and smeared it on my prison uniform to mask my identity. I noticed a cabin in the distance and entered it, and when I found out it was empty I waited there until nightfall. I was hungry and infiltrated the house of gentiles, but when I took off my hat they realized I was an escaped prisoner. I said I was hungry and got some food.

At night, I heard the sounds of cannon shells and realized that the front lines were drawing closer. I concluded that I shouldn't stray far but wait until the danger passed. I prepared for my stay: I found a cement storehouse, built myself a kind of tunnel, and collected some food that I took from German houses. After a while, I met a German woman who asked me: "Do you want clothes?"

I said I did and climbed a tree, afraid that she might try and trick me. Fortunately, she proved me wrong and brought me a bundle of clothes. I was now dressed like a French forced-laborer and could walk around. People gave me food but bid me to go away, because it was still dangerous. Unfortunately, they were proven right before I had the chance to listen to their advice. One day a peasant came and took a bed from the cabin. He was followed by four SS soldiers who asked me "What are you doing here?" "Making bread", I answered, but they didn't believe me and discussed what they should do with me. In the meantime, they made me stand between the fences and then they decided to harness me to a wagon like a horse and made me pull it until I collapsed. At that point they started interrogating me, beating me and demanding that I tell them where the gold is hidden… And then they harnessed me to the cart again and made me pull it.

The night of their departure arrived, but no orders came for them. The block supervisors wanted to know what was going on "outside" so they "fought" to keep me. I came into the block and received some food. The next day they harnessed me again and the show repeated itself for four days.

Then the order arrived, to head for the anti-tank trenches. All of them left, but I was forbidden to leave and placed in a cabin under guard. There I sat until May 5th 1945, when the Russians came and freed us.

After the war I went back to Wierzbnik but didn't stay long in that vale of tears. I crossed the border to Czech and immigrated to Israel. I arrived in Israel aboard the ship Altalena, as a kind of finale for my dramatic adventures during the years of the war.

[Page 204]
Pinchas Hochmitz

In Desperation

After the Death March to Auschwitz I arrived at camp Mauthausen and a few days later at camp Ebensee in Austria, which turned out to be one of the worst we have experienced. We worked hard in the stone quarries there, and dug tunnels for the German arms industry.

My situation was very harsh. Among other things I worked at shoveling snow off the roads and bridges near the camp, and my limbs froze from the cold and caused me indescribable pain. During the nights I put cold water compresses on my feet to prevent them from warming up, which made me feel sharp pains like the prick of needles. In the morning, my friends would help me walk my first few steps and slowly I could resume my work. This spectacle repeated itself day after day, causing me indescribable agony. After a while, I went to the infirmary and they wanted to send me to the hospital, but I knew from experience that staying at a Nazi hospital meant a certain death sentence and so I waved this "privilege". Fortunately, I got some advice during my visit to the infirmary, from a Yugoslavian doctor who told me to rub my fingers in the snow or keep my feet in cold water for a while.

I continued putting a kind of compress (rags) on my toes to keep them from warming up but to no avail. One night, when the cabin was warmer than usual and the pain became unbearable, I was squirming in pain and finally gave up hope. in desperation, I decided to rid myself of this suffering once and for all, by escaping. I was burdened by my condition, as well as the war and the hardships and the dark future awaiting each of us there, and so I decided to end my wretched existence. At that moment, I saw in my mind's eye the image of the people entangled in the electric-wire fence and I decided to follow them. To give you a full picture of my situation I must add that I was also sentenced to 25 lashes, which were hanging over me like the sword of Damocles. I had nothing to lose, because I felt that in my condition the flogging would be the end of me anyway. And so I used the last of my strength to drag myself out of the cabin and headed for the fence. Although I could not see the distant fence when I left the cabin, I sensed my way towards it. I covered some distance and could already notice the fence. The night was wintry and cold, and snow covered the ground and was still falling. Suddenly, someone grabbed me from behind and fervently called my name, saying: "I know where you are going and I understand your reasons, but promise me you would not go further and would not repeat this attempt. Swear to me that you would not do this again, or I will do the same and our family will have no remnants left, not even someone to tell what became of us." It was my uncle, Shlomo Weisbloom, who was with me the whole time.

He continued, saying: "The war would have to end eventually and if we held on so far, there is no reason to despair at the last moment, which we know is has come." He also reminded me of the registration for immigration to Israel that had taken place when we were at the camp in Starachowice, and said: "Our brothers are waiting for us there," because he had 2 brothers and a sister in Israel. He convinced me and we returned to the cabin together, where I promised to heed his words.

When we arrived at the cabin and after I recovered from the ordeal, I asked how he found me there in the field and he told me that while he was sleeping on his bunk he dreamt that I was marching toward the electric fence in despair, and when he awoke and saw I wasn't next to him he jumped, ran out, saw my footprints in the snow and ran as fast as he could until he saw me.

The next day I turned to the local infirmary and for a time we were separated. Later we met at the same infirmary with him exhausted and in very bad shape.

He was suffering from a terrible disease that filled his mouth with sores and prevented him from eating, making his condition even worse. I turned to an acquaintance of ours, Feldsher, and asked him to help my uncle, but our efforts were in vain, and he passed away in my arms a day before our liberation.

[Page 206]
Malka Bittan Weisblum

The Death March from Auschwitz

Winter was in progress, the cold penetrating the dried and shriveled bones of the exhausted prisoners and prickling their living flesh like a thorn. Only in some hidden corner of the heart was a flicker of hope: maybe the miracle will happen? Perhaps we will reach the day we waited for!

During the earlier days, we never entertained such thoughts, of crossing the bloody, hellish maelstrom of Auschwitz and surviving. But now, with the echoes of the mortars on the front lines reaching the ears of the prisoners, telling them that the time for redemption is near, something was awakening in our hearts.

But then again, the danger is felt even more keenly: will the wolves accept their fate? Won't they strive with all their diabolical vigor to wipe out the evidence of their horrible crimes and leave no witnesses alive?

Those fears came true quickly and dreadfully. Without a second thought, the Germans decided to take all the Muzelmans[1] and transfer them to Germany. And since they didn't have any trains left to use, the skeletons would be forced to walk, even if they could barely move a limb. Most of them would probably fall along the way, but that was not a snag but rather part of their main plan – to get rid of those Jews…

Of the residents of Wierzbnik in Auschwitz, only a few remained, among them Mrs. Pola Wajzer, Gucia Singer, Esther and Regina Weisbloom, Lea and Yocheved Rosenberg, Pola Unger, Hanna Tenenbaum, Mania Goldstein and others. It was no use begging, people were ordered to march in the cold, in the snow, wearing rags, hungry and thirsty, with the Germans threatening and forcing them to pick up the pace. It was only natural that most of them succumbed to exhaustion while those that held on continued until we reached some station where railroad cars were waiting on the tracks. They loaded us into those cars, ignoring their limited physical capacity. Every car, suited perhaps for holding 35 people, was crammed with over 100 people and our ride was an indescribably crowded one. The result was easy to fathom, its full cruelty revealed when we reached Bergen-Belsen, which was our last stop.

Many have suffocated on the way, and when the doors of the car were opened their have corpses spilled out. The few who remained alive were ordered into a ramshackle cabin and settled on its dirty bunks.

The death of fair Helena

Among the residents of our shack was girl named Helena Tenenbaum, who was known in town for her beauty. Little of her beauty remained now, but she retained her pleasant voice and despite the harsh conditions she started singing, breathing hope into the rest of the prisoners, so they would gather the last of their strength and fight the despair. In this way she would disperse the gloom that covered the "block" we were imprisoned in every day.

One day, the girls in the cabin no longer heard her voice and when they approached her bunk, they found her lying lifeless. A brief look showed that she died of starvation. Her death saddened even those people who were staring death in the face on a daily basis, like an old acquaintance.

Fair Helena's corpse was taken from the cabin and tossed on the pile of corpses in the yard. Cars came around and "cleaned" the area.

Sadly, she passed away only a short time before our liberation, but she was not the only one. A similar fate, crueler than anything imaginable, was shared by thousands of women, including my own sister Lala, who were monstrously locked up by the Germans with no food or water, until they perished.

1. Prisoners in a state of near-death

[Page 207]
Gershon Rosenwald

A Mountain of Corpses in Korenwasser's Yard

The entire picture is still before my eyes in all its gruesomeness, and I ask myself: could I have gone through this? Where did we find the strength at that time to bear this? This year the 16th day of the month of Heshvan falls on a Tuesday. Twenty-eight years ago on a Tuesday in 1942, it was then "Black Tuesday", the darkest day of our lives. That was the last time we saw our dearest ones. The Wierzbnik survivors remember it despite all the assurances of the *Judenrat* [Jewish Council] that Wierzbnik would escape deportation because the Wierzbnik Jews were useful Jews, who worked in the Hermann Göring Works.

Jews from other cities came and paid all their money and valuables in order to receive a work card and the *Judenrat* assured its validity. Black Tuesday showed this to be false. The people in the ghetto were awoken at dawn from their exhausted sleep after a whole day of hard labor, with shooting and shouts telling them to run quickly to the market. The terrible moment, that we didn't want to believe, had arrived. The city was surrounded by Germans, Lithuanians and other drunken murderers, who had been provided with drink throughout the night, when the *shtetl* knew nothing about what was going to happen. The crying of children and screams mixed with shooting broke our hearts. Everyone raced to the market. At 9:00 AM the marketplace was filled with Jews. The older ones, who couldn't run quickly, were shot. I suddenly saw that there was already a mound of corpses in Kornwasser's yard. Children whose parents had a few days previously handed them over to good Poles for large sums of money were abandoned by the latter in the market that morning. It was a nice fall day, the sun was warm, but in our eyes everything was dark and bleak. Jewish blood flowed like water in the center of the market.

The Poles were walking home from work and with a smile on their faces watched how in one fell swoop Jewish life became completely forfeit and the world kept silent.

From the rows (which had to be 5 in a row) they removed the healthy to one side, and the parents who were holding their children were permitted by the murderers to remain with all those intended for deportation. I believe that none of those who remained ever forgot how the Lithuanians beat them on their heads, and everyone remembers how those who had been taken out to work looked at those who remained with a feeling of pity, and those allocated to the transport were accompanied only by tears. The parents only blessed their children who were standing on the work side and in their eyes could be read the words "perhaps he'll survive", and be able to avenge us and tell the world what the murderers did to us…

The road of those who remained to work was a terrible one. Starvation, epidemics. I was also among those who remained and could still withstand cold and warmth.

[Page 209]
Natan-Neta Gelbart

We Ate Grass and Coal

In memory of my unforgettable brother – Shmuel Gelbart, of blessed memory

From his earliest years, Shmulik was active in sports (football, ping pong, etc.) and excelled in it. Always in a good mood, happy, looking to tell good jokes, he was really loved by all his friends. The Christian youth also took him into account, because they knew that he would react to every insult – and it wasn't worth starting up with him…

The time of his blooming youth flowed without worries. A year before the outbreak of WWII, Shmulik married Manya Kazimierzski. When the war broke out, Shmulik, like many other young people, was also drafted into the ranks of the fight against Hitler's Germany. He took part in many battles and endured a great deal, but he nevertheless came home whole.

When the Polish defense system was broken down and Hitler's Germany had overrun all of Poland, the persecution of Jews immediately began. Confiscations, robbery, forced labor, etc. Fright and panic ruled everywhere, not knowing what tomorrow would bring. Many young people were immediately dragged off to Lublin for forced labor. In the sadly famous square on Lipowa 17, where among others Shmulik, Avraham Goldstein and the writer of these lines spent two weeks, the prevailing frame of mind was heavy, with bad conditions and bad food. Thanks to the intervention of the *Judenrat* in Wierzbnik, we were freed, but the forced labor didn't stop. At the direction of the Gestapo, a labor office was opened, which demanded that people go to a variety of jobs. Every morning young people marched in long columns, accompanied by the policemen of the *Ordnungsdienst* [Jewish police] to various jobs. Shmulik and the writer of these lines went to work at the Wielki Piec. In this way the young people became worn out and defeated. The poor nutrition on one hand, and the sense of being lost on the other. Life without hope made the situation worse every day, both materially and morale-wise.

In 1942 news began to arrive that in various cities deportations were taking place, with the Jewish population being transported to Treblinka, Majdanek and Auschwitz, and that there men, women and children were being gassed and incinerated in the crematoria. However, none of us wanted to believe it. We didn't permit the thought that such a thing was at all possible.

To the Umschlagplatz [Gathering place for deportation]

The cracking sound of weapons was already freely heard. Men, women and children with packs and bags with food, a bit of clothing, etc. were dragging themselves to the *Umschlagplatz*. Jews who had been shot were already lying in the streets, and everyone was looking death in the eye. The Gestapo murderers ran around with automatic weapons and revolvers – to murder anyone they pleased. Money and jewelry were robbed under threat of being shot. The Gestapo took away sacks full of money and jewelry from the *Umschlagplatz*. The people fit for work were led away to the work sites, but the majority of men, women and children were placed in railway cars and taken away to a place from which no one ever returned... The most terrible picture to be seen was when each person in that huge mass of people, with a face filled with fear looked for an opportunity to escape from being deported with the "death cars." It was a nightmare that I will never forget. In July 1944 the evacuation of the Wierzbnik Jews began, as they were shoved into freight cars to be taken away to the death camps. Those who were afraid of a slow death from hunger and thirst poisoned themselves. There were also those who jumped off the cars and were killed on the spot. The trains arrived in Birkenau concentration camp filled with corpses: poisoned, starved, smothered, and those who remained alive were humiliated, apathetic, resigned. Much has already been written about the selections and crematoria in Birkenau and there were few who could endure it, but thanks to my brother Shmulik, of blessed memory, who with great risk organized food and shared every bite with me, I was able to hold out in Birkenau concentration camp, despite the hardest physical labor.

In January 1945 the directors of Birkenau tore up and demolished the crematoria, and evacuation of the camp began. The prisoners fell on the food stores in order to supply themselves with a bit of food for the unknown march. My brother Shmulik, of blessed memory, had also managed to organize some provisions, with which we fed ourselves during the Death March. People who had been shot were lying on the road from Birkenau to Breslau (Wrocław), and we saw large bloodstains on the white snow. Those who didn't keep up were cold-bloodedly shot by the SS. The majority of the prisoners reached Mauthausen frozen, dying of thirst and starving. Those who remained alive were sent to a cold bath, when everything around was frozen, and silent snow fell as though everything surrounding us in nature was pastoral and nothing had changed... My brother Shmulik, of blessed memory, before being chased off to bathe, had still managed to hide a gold 20-dollar piece, to use it to buy a piece of bread at some time. Unfortunately, the SS examiners found it on him, and as punishment broke a thick stick across his back...

From Mauthausen they sent us a few days later with a transport to Melk, to work with great physical exertion in stables. Within a short while our strength slowly left us and we grew weaker and weaker from day to day.

In April 1945 we were transferred to Ebensee Krapierungslager [punishment camp], with a daily provision of 40 grams of bread mixed with sand, peels from a potato soup and a little black coffee. Not human beings wandered around Ebensee camp, but devils. All sources of life were used up. We looked for something to eat with our eyes, but we didn't find anything. People said that there were those who cut off human flesh from dead bodies, and ate it...

The writer of these lines ate grass and embers!.. Under such conditions we were still pushed to work in Unach-Fichheim to repair damage after the bombardment by the American army...

Once, coming back from work, I lost all my strength; I fell over and couldn't get back up. My brother Shmulik, of blessed memory, with his close friends carried me into the camp this way and laid me in a corner. I felt that I was an immediate candidate for the crematorium...

One day later, Shmulik, of blessed memory, came running with a face gleaming with unexpected joy, saying that a white flag had been hung onto the camp!... The Germans had surrendered and we were free!

The prisoners' shouts of joy were wild and incomprehensible, as all the sources for life had dried out, only the energy to remain alive kept up our strength.

That was May 5, 1945, when the American army marched into Ebensee camp and liberated us. That was the day of rebirth for millions of worn out, enslaved, prostate and depleted lives. The better nourishment, which we received after liberation, was detrimental to many people; they came down with dysentery, from which many died...

After three months we gradually regained our strength and decided to travel to Poland, in order to get something out of the Poles. We believed that we would get something back from what we had left with them. The welcome from the Poles was very cold and they warned us to immediately leave the town of Wierzbnik, because the Jews that were coming back from the camps were being shot, i.e. there was a reign of murder and terror. Consequently we returned to Łódź on the same day.

At the end of 1945 we left Poland forever.

In 1948, when the major immigration from Germany to Israel began, Shmulik and his family were on the first transport. A short while after their arrival, the War of Independence broke out. Being a trained lock mechanic, Shmulik worked somewhere with defense equipment. At that time Tel Aviv was bombarded by the Egyptians and he left his place of work in order to hide somewhere, when shrapnel tore up near him and stole his young, blooming life...

He fell at his post – at the age of 31. His last words were "my wife, my child..."

[Page 212]
Moshe Weintraub

Only Graves Remain

The years since 1939, when I left my home, have flown by. I will never forget the day when the Nazis marched into our *shtetl*. My parents, my brothers and sisters, and also all our friends and family were frightened and confused, because we knew that the Jews would suffer the most.

A few weeks after the Germans entered our town, they immediately demanded that Jews go to work for them and I was among the first of those who were selected for this. This happened just as I was discussing with Bina Markowicz, my girlfriend, that we should flee from the Germans. We arranged to meet in the market, and there to make a plan of where to run. However, we didn't manage to do so, because while we were meeting, German soldiers arrived and took us for work. Bina was dragged away with other girls and they took me to work in a bakery, where they ordered me to load baskets of bread onto trucks.

I wasn't a big hero, and the baskets of bread weighed more than I, so once when I picked up a basket of bread, I tripped and spilled the loaves of bread onto the street. When the Nazi who kept guard over me saw what had happened, he first beat me and then took his bayonet and slashed my left hand, in which I was still holding the empty basket. My blood was flowing and my heart was filled with hatred for these murderers. When the bleeding didn't stop, he took me to the Starachowice hospital, where they bandaged me and told me to go home. I was terribly afraid. Before I reached home on Drilzer St., I again encountered a couple of Nazis who were guarding the street, and they beat me some more and told me to run away quickly, shooting at me over my head, so that I would be even more frightened.

When I barely entered the house, half dead with fear and the loss of blood, I found my parents and my sister Leah also very frightened, because they feared whether they would ever see me again alive in their lives.

My brother Yossl had gone out a few days previously to buy some bread, and they really never did see him again; my brother Shlomo was taken into the army when the war broke out; my brother Mendel went with his wife. Her father and family fled to Lipsk, but they encountered their tragic fate there. When the German thugs set fire to the house and shot into it, they also killed my brother. Some of the family managed to save themselves and they fled into the forests, but when my brother Mendel tried to jump out the window, the Germans shot him.

Off to Russia

Afterwards the peasants of Lipsk took over the half-burnt house. I could no longer bear it, seeing that there was no longer any hope for us Jews under the Nazis. I decided to save myself from the Germans by escaping.

I went to Lvov and smuggled myself across the border to the Russian side. In Lvov I encountered many people from Wierzbnik and we suffered greatly – having nothing to eat nor anywhere to sleep. Therefore I registered to go deep into Russia and work at manual labor. There I encountered Shlomo, the *melamed*'s [teacher of young children] son, and Nahum, the miller's son. It was in winter, and we had no warm clothing, even though the cold in Russia was extreme, and could not be borne. We worked outdoors, quarrying stones, like prisoners.

Shlomo and Nahum fled back to Wierbznik, because I had received a letter from my parents saying that they had returned home, and that the situation was bearable. My brother Yossl was alive and working for the Germans; my brother Shlomo was alive and living in Radlice with his wife. I received hope that I would see my family again, and enlisted in the newly-founded army of Polish units that were in Russia.

After all my trials and tribulations, hunger and suffering, when the war ended I returned to Poland and the Poles told me that I should not go back because no one remained alive and I would find only graves and no Jews, and that the Poles would kill me, because they would think that I had come back for my inheritance…

More than once I have cried over the bitter fate that my parents, together with millions of Jews, suffered throughout their entire lives in Poland, living in constant fear of the Poles, struggling to eke out an existence, and added to this they also had to be burned by the Germans in their crematoria, for no reason whatsoever...

[Page 214]
Abe Zukerman

Where No Birds Fly

My family was a large one, like many other families in Wierzbnik, but out of seven children I alone survived. My Mother, may she rest in peace, was born in Radom and I remember nothing whatsoever about her because she died when I was too young to understand what was happening to her. Alone and with small children, my Father, may he rest in peace, married Hadassah, the daughter of Yechiel-Meir Bluestein from Slupia. My Father had a dry goods store and actively participated in Jewish life along with all the other Wierzbnik merchants.

For some time he was also a Municipal Councilor. I remember that my Father used to go to the Town Hall near our house to testify on behalf of Jews. Who does not recall how Polish citizens required that Jews be vouched for at every step. There was no way to avoid it, no such thing as giving excuses such as not having time. Such were the Jews of Wierzbnik, always ready to do a favour for one another. I remember well the nearby *gmiles-khosodim*, the Free Loan Society. There was no need to go there and beg like a pauper. A child could be sent to fetch what was needed, without signatures, without guarantors. When the time came to repay the loan, again it sufficed to send a child.

Unfortunately, I cannot write much more about the good qualities of the Jews of Wierzbnik, because I lived in that town for only a short time. Returning on all the holidays, I would witness incidents that clearly reflected the colourful life of the Jewish population of Wierzbnik, with its various organizations and activities.

In 1937-1938, I served in the Polish Army in Warsaw, and there I encountered the tremendous hatred of the Polish Anti-Semites. The Polish scoundrels, who later became the loyal helpers of the Nazis, despised the Jewish soldiers. Well-versed in Jew-hatred, they felt quite comfortable with the murders perpetrated by Hitler.

In 1939, when the war broke out, I had to report to Pzemysl to be mobilized. The rest of the members of my family had already prepared to go to smaller towns and villages in the belief that they would avoid the bombing. They abandoned all their possessions in order to save their lives. I went to the train accompanied by some relatives and friends. Because I was being sent to the front, I wondered if I would ever come back home again. Not for one second did I imagine that the opposite could happen, that I would return home and find no one left... it was beyond anything we could have imagined at the time.

To my great sorrow, that is what happened. All of my relatives and the entire Jewish population of Wierzbnik shared in the fate of the six million murdered victims. Yes, such a terrible bloodbath is beyond reason, and no human mind will ever comprehend it.

Sent to Archangelsk on the train to Pzemysl, I met a few Wierzbnikers: Hershel Goldberg, Pinchas Kris, and Milman. At the time when Stalin and Hitler had divided Poland between them, I found myself in Lemberg, and from there "Stalinist Saviours" sent me to a camp in Archangelsk. It was far away beyond, "the hills of darkness" where there was not the slightest trace of a human footstep to be found and no sign of human civilization.

There in the virgin forests, under the constant surveillance of the N.K.V.D. with their trained dogs and rifles at the ready, I quickly became an expert woodsman to the extent that I knew how to escape a falling tree. It often happened that out of ignorance, people ran in the wrong direction and were crushed by falling trees.

Working from early morning until late at night in the deep, dense forests, and enduring so many hardships, I imagined that if I survived and returned home, I would have much to tell about the harsh conditions of my wrongful exile. Even in Siberia, aside from fear, the surroundings were cultivated and not as incomprehensibly primitive and uncivilized as in Archangelsk. Apart from forests I saw nothing, not even a bird. In these faraway forests in the middle of nowhere, we who were able-bodied did the work not only of machines, but also of horses and oxen. Besides the daily physical toll of hard work, hunger and cold, at night, lying on bare boards we anguished over the question "why".

Not knowing that worse could exist, that the devil could be even more terrible and take on more gruesome forms, we were constantly tormented by thoughts about justice that broke our spirit, and undermined our general health more than the heavy physical work. If we heard someone preaching equal rights, we understood it to be the propaganda of the "Russian paradise", that in reality it was the opposite! Where was the truth? Thinking about this cost us many hours of badly needed sleep, but we could reach no conclusions.

On my return to Poland, when I crossed the former Russian-Polish border and discovered the Holocaust, there was no point in relating my experiences. I soon realized that pain and suffering had no limits, and that everything I had endured had been child's play compared to the torture and humiliation my relatives must have suffered up to the final moments of their lives.

No One Survived...

It was hard for me to grasp the horror. Like an eye getting used to the darkness, I reacted slowly when I met people who had survived Hitler's inferno and learned that only a negligible number of the great Polish Jewry had survived. I thought that the few who had managed to escape must be talented and capable people, among them my brother (Moniek) Mordechai-Pesach, may he rest in peace. It did not take long, however, before I realized how very naive I was. My illusions quickly evaporated. Hitler's Angel of Death did not care about a person's fine qualities, was not afraid of the righteous, had not spared the sick or the innocent children. The fact that a few remnants of European Jewry had survived, that some Jews had managed to escape the clutches of the sadistic murderers was sheer luck and not a result of decency or cleverness. The specially trained murderers were extremely talented. My fervent hope that someone from my family had survived turned out to be an empty dream, sheer fantasy. I am utterly incapable of expressing in words how devastating it was for me to make this discovery and come to terms with the fact that not a single member of my entire family had survived. They had all perished. Even my sister Gitshe, may she rest in peace, who had been on a visit to Poland from Palestine, was also destined never to return. I was now certain that I could no longer remain on Polish soil. The tragic disappearance of all who were dear to me convinced me that the strong ties that bound me to my place of birth had been severed. I decided to leave Poland forever.

Where no birds fly

[Page 217]
Pinchas Helstein

Father, I am Going to the Crematorium

During our time in the vale of tears, while our lives were in the balance, we went through such suffering and hardships that can scarcely be described in words. A single drop of the ocean of blood and tears that drowned our lives would be enough to send a shiver through your bones.

And although walking through the valley of the shadow of death, threatened every step of the way by oblivion, has almost became second nature to us, there were moments that could darken days and years and were carved into memory forever.

After the Death March, the remnants of the large host that started out on this path of agony arrived in Buchenwald. Here the demonic dance started anew, as if the hell we have been through never happened and we had to begin anew. And according to Nazi customs, the daily routine starts with a "selection". Considering our condition after the deadly journey and the standards of the SS doctors, we were all fit for death, but the Nazis love order beyond anything else, and the extermination process must take place according to the "rules" they have established for this "game". And so a selection would take place and determine the fate – who will live and who will die – of the exhausted, the starved and those barely standing on their feet, all according to the standards of the executioners. For a long time, I managed to share the fate of my son. Being together was the only flicker of hope during our bitter ordeal and it gave us the willpower to overcome the pain and hardships of this road. And then, not long ago, we were separated and since then I have been trying to keep an eye on him. I followed my son directly and indirectly, anxious for his fate, and now that which I dreaded came to be.

When I heard the dreadful news about the selection I ran out of the cabin, to make sure that my son was not swallowed by this dreadful whirlpool leading to the abyss. For some reason I thought that I could save him from this edict. But my heart whispered once more that the footsteps of the angel of death are echoing closer. Like a gale I jumped from my bunk and rushed immediately outside, frantically making my way to the selection yard. My way was paved with obstacles, and those who broke the rules were sentenced to death, because there is no other punishment in the death camps. And in the meantime, the devil has already completed his work. The lines were already drawn, who will go back to the cabin and who will head to the crematorium. I was right, the place and the circumstances were telling me that my son was in danger and my skin was prickling, I felt my mind slipping, the nightmare raising beads of sweat on my forehead. The lines start moving, the column heading back breaking up while the other continues marching. I look for my son among those returning and I do not see him. It is twilight and I can't see well, but straining with all my might, I notice him and he sees me and damn my eyes! The column draws away and I am stunned by the sight, while my son's voice echoes from afar "Father! I am headed to the crematorium!"

That was the most horrible moment in my entire life.

Quickly I ran to the camp's doctor and offered him the remainder of my money to save my child's life. He probably would have angrily refused me but at my heels came one of his townsmen, whose relative was doomed by the selection as well, and begged for his life. I know not how they were related but the executioner in the white robe consented and went and erased two names, that of the man's relative and that of my son. Unfortunately, by the time my son was saved miraculously from the Holocaust, the terrible years already took their toll on him. His health deteriorated and after his liberation he fell ill and passed away, despite our best efforts.

We will always remember him with endless love.

[Page 218]
Zvi (Hersh) Unger

From Wierzbnik to Mauthausen

On the day the war broke out, German airplanes appeared in the skies of our town and we recognized them, but I was a child and knew nothing of war at the time. I ran to watch the anti-aircraft cannons that were mounted by the steel factory and immediately there was an alarm followed by cannon fire. Some bombs fell by the factory later. It seemed the Germans had no intention of heavily damaging the industry, since they were certain they would inherit it. I ran home and found everyone debating what we must do. Finally it was decided that we should defect to the village of Wąceniów, located 30 kilometers from Wierzbnik, because we had relatives there.

When we arrived at the village we found the place calm, and our relatives welcomed us and shared their home with us, even rented a room for us because they were a large family of 13 people. Other refugees, from our town and other places, have also been arriving there.

"Vive le France"

After staying there for three days, the Germans came into the village and a bizarre event took place. The villagers thought for some reason that those were the French, and sympathizing with France they welcomed the German soldiers warmly, with flowers and cheers of "vive le France". At some point a German motorcycle from the front unit stopped and the rider shouted loudly "Vorwärts!"

I grew scared and told our relatives that the soldiers that came to the village are German. When they heard that, the streets were quickly cleared of people and everyone shut themselves in their houses. In light of this situation, my brother decided to leave and head towards the Russian border, because he felt the danger was drawing near, and he left the place with a group of friends from Wierzbnik. When they arrived in Ostrowiec they found more Germans there, decided there was no point to continue, and returned to us.

My father and my sister Polcia decided to go back to Wierzbnik and learn what was going on there, while the rest of the family stayed in the village for the time being. Two weeks later, my father came from Wierzbnik to take us all home and so we did.

Upon our return, we found the courtyard (it was a large courtyard named "Mysliborski" after my aunt's family, which owned the entire row of houses on this street) full of Germans, who set up camp there while residing at the town courthouse. The conquering regime issued a curfew between 8 at night and 6 in the morning, but since the courtyard was big you could go from house to house through it. As time went by, the Germans forbade that kind of thing as well. The situation grew difficult because we couldn't get any water and had to plead with the Germans from time to time to allow us to get some water. Sometimes they agreed, but mostly they refused. Going to the toilet posed a considerable problem, because although you could store water, you still needed to use the toilet from time to time... and that posed some major complications. As a boy, I managed to endear myself to some of the soldiers and their affection allowed me to help people. Among other things, they allowed people to come pray at our house. We already knew that it would be impossible to pray at the synagogue on the New Year of 1941, because the Germans have forbidden it, and so a Torah Scroll was brought to our house and a Minyan was organized, with the permission of a German sergeant and at the cost of a few small favors.

During those days, a cousin from Yugoslavia called Shmuel Unger was staying with us. He was a cantor, and led prayer during the high holidays.

On the eve of Yom Kippur, people were praying at our house again and the German who authorized the prayers came in during Kol Nidrei and asked that we pray quietly because it was very dangerous. We did not understand what he meant, but the next day the great synagogue was burned down. The thing I remember most from those days as a boy was the heartrending prayer that sounded, in anguish and heartbreak.

A change of lifestyle

The conquest regime started to affect every aspect of our lives, especially work and livelihood. The limitations and edicts forced many to change their profession. People started using up their savings, sold property to the gentiles, traded in the black market and risked their lives going to the villages and selling valuables for food. But when the Germans started abducting people to do hard labor, mostly demeaning, unnecessary tasks, it became impossible to get anything from the villages. A famine started and grew worse with every passing month.

People tried at first to avoid the abductions to work at the factories, but the hunger forced them to turn to those very workplaces, since they were the only sources of food to sustain the body.

The Jewish council

After a while, we learned that the Germans have appointed a council composed of town dignitaries and known public activists, and ordered it to assign people for the different workplaces such as the Czerwonka iron mine and others. This council had trouble securing the necessary quota, because people refused to obey them; and so the Germans sent a squad to attack the council and everyone they found was beaten senseless, among them my relative Romek Singer, who was beaten until his head was bleeding and then ordered to show them where other Jews live. The Germans didn't even allow him to bandage his head and clean off the blood. As a boy, I ran to him with a bowl of water and a rag and when the Germans entered a particular house, I used the opportunity to wipe his face and head.

We were then forced to show them every Jewish house. We were so afraid that we even led them to our home. They gathered a large group of Jews from those houses and threatened that anyone who refused to work will look like Singer. Our lives became a little more organized then; institutes such as the employment office were established, and the Germans considered them a way of extorting money. From this point on, Jews were sent to work at the various factories. Every man aged 17-45 had to be registered with the employment office, which would direct people to their various jobs.

In April 1940 the Gestapo and their leader, Becker, showed up for the first time. They conducted a search for traitors based on false information, but found nothing.

The establishment of the ghetto

A while later came the order that all Jews must live in places and houses specifically designated for them. The zones that were allotted us were one street in the Rinek, as well as Krotka, Niska, Visoka and Radishveska Streets. These streets were all adjoined and made it easy to enclose the Jewish residents within a specific area.

Our family moved to Krotka Street, at the corner of the Rinek, where we had a fairly good apartment because we traded our old one with some gentiles. Seven of us lived in that apartment.

One day, I believe it was on Shabbat, I went down to the street and saw a car full of Gestapo, Commander Becker among them, pull over by our house. They approached me and asked: "Jew?" The Jews were already supposed to wear the mark of disgrace at the time, but as a young boy I was not obligated to do so. I answered that I do not understand. One of them spoke Czech and asked me in Polish if I was a Jew and I answered I wasn't. He continued asking if I lived there and I said I did. He continued: "Where do the Jews live?" I showed him a house where Christians lived, hoping to buy myself some time to warn the Jews about the situation. I tried to escape them but failed. In the meantime, a Christian girl came down and they asked her if I was a Jew and she said I was. Becker lifted his stick and hit me over the head. I started running, and since I feared pursuit I escaped to the Rinek and hid in a yard. My head started swelling but I managed to reach my relative, Gucia Singer, who lived at the Rinek and she bandaged my head. In the meanwhile, the Gestapo found themselves a prostitute and stayed with her.

As the danger grew, some people organized an escape attempt and headed east. Some of them managed to leave the war behind and survived. Our own situation became worse and worse, especially in the field of housing, as refugees flowed into town from other places and the Germans started evicting people. One morning in 1942, the Germans broke into Jewish houses early in the morning and drove the people toward the Rinek. Our family was also among those evicted. We had factory worker certificates and we thought they granted us some privileges, but we were disappointed. When we arrived, no one knew what would happen to us. We thought that we would be taken somewhere to work. The Germans were selecting people for work regardless of the certificates. My brother was missing and only my father, my mother and my sister were with me. I was a child at the time, but when the Germans examined me and asked for my age, I innocently gave myself a few more years and said I was 18. One of them wanted to put me among the evicted and the other mentioned that I was rosy-cheeked and could still work. Later I found out that only my father and my sister Pola were chosen for work, while my mother and my other sisters – Lutka and Ruszka – were put with the group of the people who would be evicted and later sent to Treblinka.

From there we were marched to Strzelnica, which was a fenced labor camp surrounded by sentries. When we arrived in this camp they confiscated everything we had, left us bare and naked and assigned us cabins. There were three-storied bunks in those cabins, which were very crowded and dirty. We worked at the munitions factory for 12 hours a day and the only food we received was a slice of bread and a spoonful of soup. The regime in camp was very strict, and every escape attempt resulted in death. Even during our march to the camp a German was running among our ranks threatening: "Anyone who takes a step out of line would be shot on the spot." To make good on the threats, they fired into the crowd and killed some people, among them a man named Rosenberg who was walking in the row before me. After a short while, a typhoid plague broke out, resulting in its own casualties. My sister was among the first to fall ill and I stole some flour from the kitchen in order to get her some food, but I was caught with the flour and taken to the guard room where I received a beating, some 70 lashes. After the beating I was ill myself and they suspected I was down with typhus. Plague victims were assigned a special cabin, number 5. I didn't want to go there because I knew I didn't have typhus, but some of the other patients refused to go unless I did as well.

Saved from certain death

The man in charge of camp police was a hard and brutal man, but he showed me some kindness, perhaps because I was a friend of his son, and kept me from going to the typhus patient cabin. The horror took place the very next day, when the Gestapo went into the cabin and shot all the patients. After a while, they carried out an "action" in the camp and took some of the people away, among them the sick and the feeble. The beating I received made me weak enough to be part of that group. At some point one of the Germans winked at me, signaling for me to approach him. I approached him, trembling, and when he asked why I was shivering like that I said that I was cold. He ordered to dress me up and I returned to my place in line. Then I was ordered to run, and those who couldn't keep up were taken away. Suddenly, someone in front of me tripped and I fell on top of him. A German ordered me to leave the place and get in a car. I did as he ordered, got in the car and then right out the other side, then hid in a potato warehouse for about an hour and a half. After they loaded all the sick people into the freight cars, including my cousin, Efraim, they drove them to the Bug River and murdered them to a man. I went back to camp and continued my arduous life. In 1943, the camp in Strzelnica was abandoned and everyone was moved to a different camp, Majowka, a barren and rocky place. The regime at the new camp was the same as before.

Another selection was carried out and some people were sent to Firlej, an area near Radom, where they were murdered. We stayed in camp Majowka until 1944, when the camp was abandoned and the people were transferred to the camp of an actual factory. It was here that people started organizing an escape attempt. Two such attempts were made, the first of them at night: a group of people broke through a wooden fence and crossed it but were discovered by the Germans, who lobbed grenades at them, killing some of them. Others succeeded in escaping, and we never learned their fate. The next day, the Germans confiscated our shoes and conducted a lineup. A short while later, another escape attempt was made. Some of the people managed to escape despite being discovered by the Germans, while others were killed. The day after the second escape we were loaded on cars and taken about 1,500 kilometers away, to Auschwitz. On the way to Auschwitz, my brother tried to escape from the car; the window was broken and he and several others threw themselves out, but the Germans noticed and killed them.

Another selection was carried out in Auschwitz, to determine who will work and who will go to the gas chambers. My father was taken to work and I was sent to my demise by Dr. Mengele.

I stood in line that day, and when I realized where I was being taken I managed to run and hide in a toilet. I heard a rumor that they were looking for craftsmen and I was already desperate enough to take a risk. A German in civilian clothing was standing there and I introduced myself to him as a mechanical locksmith, but he answered me sarcastically that there were no mechanical locksmiths in Poland... "How old are you?" he asked. I said I was 20. When he heard that, he took me. This act saved my life, because they would have taken me to the crematorium otherwise. I was taken to the town of Œwiętochłowice by Katowice and conditions there were pretty good. We worked at a cannon factory. We stayed there until January 1945. Then we were transferred to Mauthausen and our conditions deteriorated again.

In March 1945 we were taken again to Gensenkirchen in Austria. This was strictly a death camp, with nothing to do and nothing to eat – dying was the only option. People died there like flies, we had to split a single loaf of bread among 14 people. There were people who didn't even get their share... And that was where we stayed until the Americans came and freed us.

[Page 221]
Yaffa Barkai – Rosenwald

A Gruesome Reality

I was eleven years old when the dark nightmare of the horrific bloody days spread like a specter and covered the bright horizon of my childhood and clouded over the present and future of my beloved family; my father, mother and younger brother Mordchele.

I was too young then and I understood little, but seeing the worry and fear of my beloved parents, hearing the terrible news of Jews being grabbed for slave labor, and other troublesome edicts, I understood that we were living in bitter times.

The situation grew worse from day to day; it wasn't enough that we remained without any income, without businesses that had been robbed, and without all our possessions, but our lives themselves became forfeit. And thus we quickly had to leave our home and move into the crowded ghetto.

I recall that in those difficult days we received news from my mother's sister, Sara Goldfarb from Zwoleń, that their house had been burnt down, and despite all the difficulties, my beloved, blessed father managed to send them pillows and bedding. Sharing the last bit was deeply rooted in our family.

But the Nazis weren't satisfied with limiting the Jews' rights and utterly humiliating them, but their devilish plans thought up an *"Endlösung"* [final solution] to the Jewish question and they were bloodthirsty and demanded the annihilation of the Jews. So in my most blooming years, I was torn from the possibility of enjoying peace and education, development and freedom. My eyes saw only pain and horror, and all my education and knowledge consisted of drawing from the strength and endurance of family sources, which were permeated with so much love for humanity.

I suffered greatly until I was rescued from that hell and I am simply not capable of gathering my thoughts without describing the ghastly reality of despair, apathy and danger, until the downfall of our foe. And as the prophet Ezekiel says (16:6) *"And when I passed by you and saw you struggling in your own blood, I said to you in your blood, 'Live!' Yes, I said to you in your blood, 'Live!"* – From this blood you must find the strength and energy to rebuild a new life, and give it new content.

Thus we plant and re-forge the chain of our beloved parents in our own homeland, so that such a catastrophe can never recur, so that we will never again be helpless and unprotected. This is our revenge on all our enemies in the whole world.

[Page 222]
Esther Zukerman-Zilberman

Sorrowful Reunions Tragic Encounters

Very soon after the outbreak of war in 1939, when the German murderers had completely taken over our town Vierzbnek, we could already foresee the tragedy that would befall the Jewish people.

As the situation became increasingly intolerable, people found various ways to escape. If they could not save their entire family, then perhaps they could save a child. Whoever had Christian acquaintances they considered trustworthy, gave these Christians all their possessions, hoping for the best, in the way a drowning person grasps at straws...

We accuse!

In his youth, before leaving Poland for Paris, my brother, Pintshe Zilberman, had a good relationship with the Christian Kshishznovski. He was known in Vierzbenek as a person with liberal views, a man with a secular outlook in contrast to the majority of Polish Anti-Semites. To this Christian, my brother Pintshe and sister-in-law Manya (née Shift) entrusted the life of their child, believing in the conscience of their good Christian friend but at the same time hoping for a great miracle.

The Christian sent their child to his sister somewhere in Galicia, where there would be less suspicion, and the risk of hiding a Jewish child would be much smaller. As for himself and his wife, my brother had an agreement with another Christian who lived on the road to Mikhalov by the name of Mazuranov, that they could hide with him if the necessity arose. They paid him well for this. This was the same place that my late husband Beniek and I had chosen to hide our two innocent children, for which the Christian received a large sum.

Polish Betrayal

On the terrible day of the round-up, amid the heart-rending screams and the horrendous confusion, my brother and sister-in-law were separated. Unable to find his wife in the dreadful commotion, my brother ran to Masurov and hid in the attic, thinking that this wife would also make her way there. He waited for her in vain. He never saw his wife again, because she was immediately rounded up and sent away on her last journey.

After a few days of sitting in the attic, the Christian's wife told my brother to leave, choosing to forgo the large sum of money she had received. During these critical moments she revealed the treachery of the Christians, even though she had been paid well.

Sitting in the cramped attic, my brother Pintshe heard how this couple turned away my child Meyishi (Meyer), sending him to his fate. It is easy to imagine my brother Pintshe's tremendous grief and heartbreak lying in his hiding place, unable to protest the inhumanity, treachery and brutal treatment of the child by these heartless Christians. Under the cover of darkness, my brother made his way to Kshishznovski.

I knew nothing about all this, and had no idea where my brother was. To find out where he had disappeared to, despite the danger, I began to make inquiries among certain Christians, but alas without results. I also went to Kshishznovski to see if I could get any information there. I risked my life to do this because I had to sneak away from the commando taking us to conduct forced labour and then later sneak back into the same group as it was returning to the camp. With bitter tears, I begged Kshishznovski to tell me if he knew anything about my brother Pintshe. I appealed to his conscience, telling him that I was the only one left of my entire family, and that now my only hope and consolation was that my brother Pintshe was still among the living. I also explained to him that I was no longer safe, and that something could happen to me at any moment. Every day Jews in the camps were being shot and murdered for no reason. I kept begging for his pity. I let him know that all our possessions had been distributed among various Christians, and if my brother Pintche was still alive, he could help himself to these things. I also let him know that what we had given away to Polish "friends" was worth a lot of money. I still hoped and believed that if he knew anything, he would help me. We had enjoyed friendly relations with him for so many years and my brother Pintche had been a close childhood friend of his.

A "Warm" Christian

Only when I was about to leave, did my deep despair and many supplications move him, but only to the extent that he uttered these few words, "Don't worry about your brother Pintshe, he is in a good place, he has a place to eat and sleep in a clean and warm house."

The Christian emphasized the word "warm", because it was a bitterly cold winter. Other than these few words he would say nothing. But I recognized that even these few words had cost him great effort. Moved by my suffering and desperation, he did not want to let me leave with nothing and he wanted to reassure me. Hearing these few words, I left the house partly consoled, thinking that perhaps it was really true. I felt a spark of humanity in his words.

A few months later my brother Pintshe suddenly appeared in the camp by sneaking in with work commando. Only then did I discover that when I had been at Kshishznovski's house, he had been in the same room hiding under the table and had heard everything I had said. Hearing my sad report, he was choked with tears but could not call out and reveal his presence because it had to remain an absolute secret, even to his own sister. My bitter situation broke him mentally and physically, so that he fainted under the table and did not even hear me leave. My brother also told me that after I left, once he had regained consciousness, Kshishznovski told him that he could not have behaved otherwise. Even though Kshishznovski sympathized with our sorrowful situation, he was afraid that I might confide in someone else and something would be said that could endanger both my brother and himself.

My brother Pintche was miserable once in the camp. He was hounded on all sides because he had not registered himself and was there illegally. This was especially dangerous at roll call. The count had to be accurate, no fewer and no more. If someone were missing, a relative of the missing person was held responsible and threatened with being shot. It was also a problem if the number was too high. Therefore my brother was constantly persecuted.

On the other hand, not informing them of his presence had a positive side. My brother could go in and out of the camp whenever the opportunity presented itself, and thus he could move around freely. Sometimes this "freedom" became the object of envy by those who without logic considered it unfair - why he could come and go, as he wanted and why was he able to return to the world of so-called freedom. One time my brother came into the camp sick with typhus. This was especially dangerous because in addition to the disease itself, if one of the two big murderers, Shrot or Becker, ever were to come in and ask who was lying there, he would be shot on the spot. I am referring to the two-blood??thirsty Nazi murderers. The two cold-blooded sadists, who are now on the prisoners' dock in Germany for their important role in the torture of our people, have the gall to deny all their horrific crimes. However, my brother was saved from the murderer's clutches and they never noticed him.

Just Like Hell

As soon as he felt better, he left the camp. For a long time I did not know where he was. At the same time I also got out of the camp, but I was plagued by guilt that someone else would be held responsible. At that time two cousins of mine were with me in the camp - Tobche Wolfovich (now lives in Canada) and her sister Rochel Lipman (now lives in Israel). When I came back, Feygele Rabinowicz was very disappointed because she was supposed to follow me to the same place. She had wanted to cry out: "Don't you see what is happening? They are transporting us from here!" In the camp it looked just like hell. People were falling as though they had been poisoned. Everyone was so upset. There was a foreboding about tomorrow.

Although no one knew exactly what awaited us, we still felt that the earth was burning under our feet... but we did not know why. Suddenly it became very quiet and camp life returned to so-called "normal". The rumour that we were about to be deported evaporated.

Again I wanted to establish contact with my brother Pintche, who was somewhere in hiding. One day I overheard Sarah Steinhart (Pastavsky - now in Israel) telling a Ukrainian guard to let her out and she would bring him back something. Hearing this, I ran over and left the camp with her. She had also distributed many possessions among several Poles.

This was in the evening after work. We arranged to meet in a certain place when we were ready to go back, and whoever got there first would wait for the other. We parted, each going to a specific Polish friend to take back some of our belongings. Sarah Steinhart was done sooner. Not finding me in the agreed spot, she set out to find me. It did not take long before we found each other. Telling each other about the "miracles" that happened to us, Sarah asked me if I had seen my brother Pintche. I said, no, that everywhere I went I asked about him, but no one had anything to tell me about him. Then I noticed that Sarah suspected that I was not telling her the truth. 1 could even see that she resented the fact that had it not been for her, I would not have had this chance. However, when I reassured her that I was not hiding anything from her, that I really had no idea where my brother Pintche was, she grabbed me by the arm and said: "Come, I will show you where your brother is." She explained that while she was looking for me, she remembered that I was at Kshishznovski's. Passing by there by coincidence she noticed my brother Pintche from a distance. With my heart pounding, I went back there with her.

As we approached the Christian's house, I froze and simply could not move. We noticed a curtain on a cellar door slowly opening and out crawled my brother very carefully. Shocked and upset, I stood there until he had crawled out completely. I hardly recognized him. He had a frightened face with long whiskers like some Poles used to wear. His appearance reflected the sad and difficult conditions he was struggling with day in and day out. His face and frightened eyes revealed the anxiety and insecurity of his life. We all quickly went into the cellar so that no one would see us. I was still bewildered, unaware of what was happening. I had just been at this house where I was told that no one knew anything about my brother, and now suddenly we were standing face to face. At that moment I stood and wondered whether this was reality or a dream. When I regained my senses, and had calmed down a little, my brother explained that the Christian must not know that we had discovered this hiding place, or he would make my brother leave the cellar immediately.

We could not stay with him very long because we did not want to return to the camp late at night. However, I did arrange with my brother that, if possible, I would come to him the following day. Indeed the next morning, when I went with the commando to work, I broke away from the line and went straight to my brother in the cellar, where we spent the entire day together because I knew when the people in the commando were supposed to go back to the camp. It is hard for me to describe the time we spent together. We had to be silent and keep to ourselves the tremendous pain of our dark fate, not daring to allow ourselves even the smallest sigh.

After a few hours I had to leave the cellar. We parted with tears in our eyes but could not allow ourselves the luxury of crying together. We exchanged glances filled with pain and sorrow and a large question mark. Neither of us knew what would happen next.

In the Hands of the Furious Murderers

Although we could not cry, our parting was so tragic that I cannot describe it in words. A short time after I visited my brother, the Christian received an order to vacate his house. The Nazis requisitioned his house. Forced from his cellar hideout, my brother returned to the camp and this time the camp council registered him. He was then so badly beaten by the Nazi murderer Shrot, that my brother became very sick. As soon as he had recovered somewhat and could walk again, my brother left the camp. When the Nazi murderers and their helpers were informed about this, they immediately arrested me. The scoundrel Shrot beat me and set his dog on me who tore everything off me. He tortured me to find out where my brother went. He wanted to extract from me my brother's hiding place. If not he threatened I would be shot. I keep on shouting that I did not have the slightest idea. I summoned all my strength to survive this ordeal. Despite the dreadful torture at the hands of the infuriated murderer I did not break down. By a miracle I escaped certain death. I never set eyes on my brother Pintche again, and did not know what became of him. I never again had the opportunity to make contact with him because soon afterward we were sent to Auschwitz.

After the war I was in Vierzbenek and saw Kshishznovski who told me that when the Germans requisitioned his house, Pintche came out of the cellar and went to Vanatsie where a few so-called "good" Poles lived. Kshishznovski saw him there once and then lost contact with him. He also knew that my brother left there to go to Mietelitsk. Kshishznovski even advised me not to go around asking questions, reminding me of the slaughter by Polish Anti-Semites, the faithful servants of the Nazis. Kshishznovski also advised me to go to a larger city, and the sooner the better.

I did not follow his advice, but went to make inquiries in Vanatsie. In one house I recognized many household items that had belonged to my brother and sister-in-law Manya. But no one had anything to tell me about the disappearance of my brother. On the way to Vanatsie, I noticed Russian soldiers in the distance. As we came closer, I suddenly froze in my tracks and could not believe my eyes. One of the soldiers turned out to be my cousin Jacob Sheiner, who had run away to Russia, fought with the Red Army, and now lives in Israel.

Mindel Binstock (now lives in Toronto, Canada) told me that while she was hiding in the house of the Christian Plasse, she once heard the voice of my brother Pintche begging to be let in, but his pleas fell on deaf ears. It seems that he fell into the hands of Polish murderers. His constant vigilance, his daring courage and speed had saved him from the clutches of the Nazis but were not enough to help him escape the cunning Polish Anti-Semites. Whenever a few Poles with a spark of humanity and morality wanted to help him, there always were many more Polish murderers, servants of the Nazis, who were constantly persecuting him until he finally succumbed to their bestiality. His bones lie in an unknown grave.

Sorrow will remain forever in the hearts of his family, his brother Antshl, his son Claude, and his sister who wrote these lines.

[Page 228]
Anonymous

Wierzbnik's Lament

When I take my pen in hand to chronicle that gruesome period, I am overcome with trembling and horror. I can't find the words to express and describe that sad and tragic time. The extent of the tragedy is too great to possibly describe the terrible suffering that individuals endured in that vale of tears. Perhaps with time a general picture of the disaster will be produced, which will grow into a monumental work that will transmit the terrible limitations of humanity and its culture.

Among the hundreds of cities and towns in Poland, in our *shtetl* Wierzbnik the Jewish population was also composed of small shopkeepers, merchants, craftsmen, etc. The majority of Jews were religious, believers, who used to go to public prayers every day in the "*shtiblech*" [small one room prayer halls of the Hassidim] and the synagogue. Jews with beards and ear locks, dressed in long capotes, with round Jewish caps on their heads. The youth, on the other hand, were mainly modern and wore European clothes. There were also some young people that were religious and studied in the study area of the synagogue. The specific melody of the Gemara [part of the Talmud] could be heard from afar and resounded all day long until late in the evening.

Everything went along in this way until 1939, which will be recorded as the year in which the commercial situation of the Jewish population reached its culmination.

The anti-Semitic economic battle against the Jews was waged in every way and with all possible means. Because of these circumstances, the Jewish youth were early on burdened with earning a living, in order to provide themselves with a basis for future existence. But disregarding the worries of earning a living, the Jewish youth in Wierzbnik were not behindhand with their nationalistic education and aspirations. This all found expression in the active Zionist activity, and the main thing – in the collections for the Jewish National Fund and Keren Hayesod [United Israel Appeal].

A Sad Date

The date of September 1, 1939 will remain a dramatic event in general human history, but for Jews it will remain in their memories forever as a ghastly specter that causes every Jewish heart to quiver. After the horrible facts, we first realized the terrible calamity later on. We Jews saw what a weak political sense we had, what our political orientation was. We were sunk in a hoo-ha of daily life, in trade and business. We served the "golden calf" and other idols, and we didn't want to see the reality, and that is truly why we didn't foresee the sad future.

It was Friday, September 1, 1939: the whole *shtetl* was encompassed with trembling, some sort of weird nervousness pervaded everyone. The tension grew, mixed with fear and terror. People absentmindedly ran to each other, running in fear, not knowing where to. The events weren't long in coming. Everything occurred like split lightning. The heavens and the earth all spewed fire; panic and pandemonium ensued. What could we do?

In the evening the terror became even greater. The artillery, bombs and shells cut through the air and our hearts became heavy and our souls were filled with gloom. As though purposely to upset us, the dawn irritated us with its bright sunlight, but the birds sang sorrowfully, as though they were mourning the fate of our doomed *shtetl*. Movement in the *shtetl* became feverish; each person looked at the others with questioning looks; what's happening?

We very quickly discovered that the Polish army was not withstanding the push of the attacking German army, and it was quickly withdrawing. The cut off army increased the panic and the nervousness and tension grew. Everyone wanted to run. People took their things; the psychosis of running encompassed the entire *shtetl* and people ran around in a frenzy, not knowing where to, without a specific goal. The confused running around presented a sad picture. Frightened men, women and children ran without a goal. Several days later everyone realized that the running was senseless. The German beast, which was motorized, caught up with everyone and sowed destruction and death at every step. However, it didn't take long, and the blood-soaked days set a terrible fear into motion. Everyone remained at home. Men didn't show their faces in the street at all, and at night we didn't undress to go to bed. Large groups of families gathered together.

How Do We Avenge Ourselves

The sleepless nights and days dragged out in this way, filled with horror and fear. Everyone sat at home, not daring to stick their heads out, and outside a glorious sun shone. The world was filled with light, but for the Jews it was dark and bitter. Many Poles sprung up from below the ground, who immediately collaborated with the Germans. The enemy began to abase the Jews, transforming them into animals, taking away their human worth, and the Poles laughed, enjoying the Jewish pain.

When you reflect on the wild acts of the Nazi murderers, the blood congeals in your veins, your heart bursts from anger and you are encompassed with only one desire, how do you take revenge.

Our entire two thousand-year old history of martyrdom, in which every page is full of horror and fright, blood and tears, pales in comparison to what the Hitler-cannibals did and thought of. World history contains stories about wild Huns, grim Tatars, Roman emperors, Torquemada inquisitions, but what the *Herrenvolk* evinced in the twentieth century, exceeds everything...

Calculated and planned, with a variety of tricks and deceptions, they broke up Jewish life in all its aspects: spiritually, physically and in morally, accompanied by distress and aggravation, hunger and cold, naked and barefoot with savage beatings and inhuman conditions, through defilement and sadism, which increased from day to day.

That is how the Wierzbnik Jews suffered along with all the Jews in other places and cities, until 1942, which brought with it the atrocious total destruction of the entire Jewish community. Life became more and more precarious, murdering Jews became a "normal" daily occurrence. Everything was confiscated and taken away; the murders took on a mass character; the ghettos become filled with fear and it felt as though dark clouds were approaching.

Extermination

The deportations of the time were characterized by absolute annihilation and extermination. Terrible news about fire and blood traveled all over Poland, and everyone was seized with the fear that the mass-murder was coming closer and closer.

Jewish possessions were robbed and plundered – they took away houses, money, jewelry, furniture, linens, all valuables collected by the Germans and their collaborators; even the hair of the Jewish mothers and daughters, the beards and ear locks of the religious men were collected. The Christian Poles helped the Nazi murderers destroy the Jews; they uncovered the tracks of every hiding place and bunker, even though they themselves were an object of German hatred. Thus the desolation and pain of the Jewish population multiplied. Death and fear prevailed everywhere.

The darkness in the Jewish hearts had no limits; everyone was engulfed with fear, and the air was saturated with bloody tears, groans and desperation.

The bloody drama was so great that it was almost impossible to grasp. Yes, writers, musicians and composers, masters of the language of the soul, creators and thinkers of human culture – Schiller, Goethe, Hegel, Kant. Bach, Mozart, Beethoven – look how low your people has fallen! They went beyond the cannibals, the barbarians and the wild Huns.

You created models of the highest poetry, heavenly sounds of music and singing, that heal hearts and souls, and the beasts created compositions of blood, tears, pain, distress and suffering. Their culture is Auschwitz, Sobibor, Treblinka and Majdanek! Their poetic creation is the Horst-Wessel song ("When Jewish blood spurts from the knife"). In one fell swoop they burned up all the cultural values and achievements of hundreds of years!

That is how the new martyrdom history of the Jewish people ended, who with all their strength clung to the existence of something that didn't exist. When we recall all this, our soul weeps within us and an eternal sorrow remains in our hearts, which will never leave us.

We will always remember our *shtetl*; our fathers and mothers, brothers and sisters, our dearest ones, who were destroyed because they were Jews, will always remain in our memory.

I remember you my *shtetl* Wierzbnik, I see the traces of that former life, which was extinguished from the Jewish entity that reverberated in you.

The laughter of the Jewish children is no longer heard, the *Gemara* melody that was carried from the synagogue and the *shtiblech* has been silenced; you no longer hear the voices of the people at prayer in the synagogues and *shtiblech*; everything has disappeared forever! The song of hope and longing of the former Jewish youth – the *Hatikvah*, the song of Zion and redemption, has been torn off – take comfort my *shtetl*. All those who survived will always carry your memory in their hearts. You were also a victim together with us all. You also donated your share to the bitter total of six million Jews.

Yes, the little band of survivors is the most tragic generation in the Jewish history of martyrdom. They drank from the bitter cup of tears until the end, and on their shoulders they bore the entire horror of the destruction and annihilation. But at the same time, they belong to the luckiest generation, which dreamt and yearned for redemption and freedom, and who always directed their aspirations and hopes to the rebirth and reconstruction of the Jewish people in its historical old-new land.

They are witnesses of the destruction and extermination but also living witnesses of the "revival of the dead". The enemy did not succeed in annihilating us and from the ruins of Europe emerged a free people and a free country – the State of Israel.

[Page 232]
M. K.

Memorial Candle

I stand silent before the inscribed tombstone, the monument for our town, Wierzbnik, which was destroyed and no longer exists. There is pain in my heart, my eyes tear and I have no words for it. Human lips cannot express the agony and sorrow.

My hands trembling with awe, I light a memorial candle for my birthplace in foreign lands, the fountain of love, a source of vibrant life that was destroyed and silenced forever.

In memory of our dear, devoted parents, who were cruelly tortured in the unholy land and perished as martyrs.

In memory of our brothers and sisters, the holy, pure, innocent, honest and kind people who faced all those horrors, who were murdered together, proud trees that were cut down and uprooted in the vale of tears.

We will lovingly carry their holy memory in our aching hearts and will never forget them.

May these words serve as a perpetual light and the tears of a bereaved nation over unknown graves.

Yitgadal Veyitkadash...

*

Malka Weisbloom

Bar Mitzvah in the Forest

"Where are you running to?" shouted the girl to her brother, who was running toward the forest.

"It is better to die," answered the brother.

"What would a child like him do alone in the forest?" thought the sister, and started running after him. During their fateful run they heard the murderers chasing after them. Theirs was a supreme effort. After a dramatic and dangerous chase, they managed to reach the forest and after the murderers were gone they felt the terrible weariness and their wounded feet while the forest sheltered them.

They fell exhausted, and the quiet forest sang them a lullaby that put them to sleep for hours.

Then came days of suffering, hunger, fear and cold. Winter came and covered the forest with white fur. The brother and sister dug a bunker in the ground and sat there for many days. From time to time, they would separate to find food and then rejoin each other. Suddenly they heard motion among the branches! "Could it be the murderers?" they thought.

But a few anxious seconds later, it turned out to be some animal passing by, disrupting the tranquility of the forest. Soon it was quiet again. Hanukkah was approaching, and they had to celebrate the brother's birthday. Tamar got a candle and divided it into 4 pieces, because her brother was born on the fourth day of Hanukkah. She lit four candles and the two sat in their light and reminisced.

[Page 233]
Pinchas Hochmitz

We were Ten Brothers

Many used to hum the popular Jewish tune "We were ten brothers", its humorous nature in sharp contrast with its tragic content, as only one brother of the ten survived their numerous adventures. Only one...

But while content and form were distinct in the song, our tale is unequivocally sorrowful and dark. It begins in sadness and ends in bitterness: after being evicted from the labor camp in Wierzbnik, only a few of our relatives remained with us and it was only natural that we kept close to each other. Our entire great family was down to three: Shlomo Weisbloom, his sister Esther (in Israel) and I. Two harsh days after we were all loaded on the dreadfully crowded freight cars we arrived at the camp in Auschwitz. We did not know the significance of our new situation yet, but it was clear to all of us that this did not bode well. Therefore, we strove with all our might to stay as close as we could to our brothers, relatives, friends, acquaintances and townsmen. I no longer had any close relatives like parents, brothers or sisters, and after they separated the men and women there were others of our town who found themselves in a similar situation. Ten of us, townsmen of Wierzbnik all, decided to make ourselves relatives by going under the same name, Weisbloom. We did it to be classified under the same letter, allowing us to stay under one roof. We carried out our decision and it turned out to be the right one; for a time, we remained as a group.

Arriving in Birkenau

Reality has changed so drastically when we arrived in Auschwitz that at first I felt as though we have landed on a different planet.

We arrived early in the morning, and through the mists of dawn we saw before us fields fenced with two lines of barbed-wire and upwards hooked pickets. On the other side of the fences wandered skinny people wearing striped "uniforms" which looked like pajamas, marching this way and that to a military beat and a marching band, while screams in every tongue sounded from all directions. It all mixed into an unnatural nightmare and for a moment I felt as though we found ourselves in some kind of huge insane asylum. But the screaming and the orders brought us back down to the gloomy reality in which we found ourselves, and we had no time to think because we were lined up and ordered to forward march.

We crossed the camps, barbed-wire fences on both our sides. After a short march we arrived at a building used as a bathhouse and dubbed by the prisoners in camp a "sauna." When we were ordered to go into the bathhouse, many panicked and refused to approach the door. Our fear was heightened by the signs on the wall, which said: "To the wash", because when we were still at the labor camps we heard about the extermination of Jews in the camps and the various means of trickery and subterfuge used, and upon seeing those signs we recognized them from the stories we heard. Nevertheless, members the commandos called "Canada" approached us and started soothing and convincing us. As proof, the people in the front rows were led to the other end of the sauna, where the exit was, and were shown the people that were coming out at the end of the wash. After seeing that, we started entering the building, although our doubts were not completely erased, because we were filled with fear and suspicion. Inside, we were ordered to undress and leave all valuables behind. A few prisoners who served as barbers showed up and started shaving every hairy place on our bodies. They were using old, rusty tools and carried out their work in a hasty and rough manner that left stings and pain. This activity took place in a kind of "waiting room" and after the "haircut" we were ushered in groups into the bathhouse itself, where they barely sprayed us with a bit of turbid water before hurrying us into another room. At the exit stood two prisoners holding paint brushes with Lysol, which they spread over the bodies of the people as they left. The liquid was very pungent and burned our eyes for a long time, since we had no way of washing it off. Instead of returning our clothes, we were taken to a pile of prisoner uniforms and handed the striped "pajamas". Unfortunately, we received mismatched clothes; a tall man would receive short pants and vice versa...

Settling scores

While we were receiving our prisoner uniforms and dressing up, the people from the Canada commando came to us and asked us who were our leaders or policemen in the ghetto. At first we didn't understand the reason for their interest but we soon learned that they were eager to "settle scores" with people who cooperated with the Nazis, although they were doing the same vile thing here. Somehow they found someone who pointed out our townsman Langelban, who served as a kapo, and one of the Canada people asking the questions approached him. He was a tall, large man whose appearance was frightening under these circumstances. In a hypocritical, cunning manner he announced loudly: "I heard that my uncle Langelban was among you, where is he?" The man he was talking about brightened up when he heard that, thinking that he found a family member, but when he approached the big man the latter started beating him up and refused to stop until he sated his twisted urges. This event, added on top of everything we have seen and suffered thus far, brought our morale even lower.

After we got dressed we were led again to an encampment of cabins fenced with barbed-wire, which was known as the "gypsy camp".

The ten Weisbloom brothers

Here we were ordered to stand in single file and the registration process began, taking on a unique air as it turned us from people with human form and characteristics, with first and last names, into mechanical creatures whose sole feature was a number. The entire process took the form of a ceremony: every person was forced to pass by a registration desk, where the clerks wrote down necessary facts before handing him over to a tattooist who used a special needle and ink to carve a prisoner's personal number into his left arm. This number bore a great significance, as we learned later on: it made it easier for the supervisors to track the prisoners and made it harder for prisoners to escape from camp. In time, the identification number also gained a unique "value", allowing people to estimate the seniority of the prisoner, which sometimes granted certain advantages.

For me, however, the personal number had a special significance, saving me from certain death.

While standing in line waiting for the numeration process to take place, ten of us from Wierzbnik decided to give Weisbloom as our surname, hoping to receive similar numbers. Naively we assumed that it would allow us to stay close to each other for the time being. From this point on, it became a routine: each of us approached the table, but when my turn came I did something that mattered later on. After I was tattooed with the number 19866A, I stepped aside, turned my back and tried rubbing the letters with my finger to see if we could ever be rid of this number once we left this place. As fortune would have it, I started with the last numeral, "6", and when I succeeded I stopped. Nevertheless, rubbing the number changed it a little, enough for a cursory glance to mistake it for "0" and require a closer examination to identify it as "6". I myself never noticed this fact except under unique circumstances, which I will describe below.

Staying in quarantine

At the end of the tattooing process we were transferred to the quarantine cabins. We started feeling the pressure of life in hell in full. The various supervisors would scream us awake at 4 in the morning and we had to quickly get off our bunks – covered with mattresses that were nothing more than sacks filled with some straw – And after every group of prisoners shared a bowl of foul, runny soup we were ordered to line up in the courtyard. Standing there during the cold dawn was a nightmare in its own right. The report had to match the Nazi records and if someone failed to report because he was ill, or because he died and no one realized it, we had to stand there until the loss was found.

After the "apple" came the next stage of torment: military foot drill. We were taught to march in ranks of five and keep our hands at our thighs to make sure we moved as a unit. They literally beat this exercise into us with fists, clubs and sticks. They also devised a drill of taking off one's hat as a show of respect to officers, which also had to be carried out in uniform military fashion. This torture, taking off our hats and putting them back on repeatedly, continued until we carried out the drill to the satisfaction of the Nazis. Anyone who carried it out sloppily received a beating on the spot and was watched in the future.

Another part of the abuse was "sports". The prisoners were forced to run barefooted over a gravel covered lot or jump with their hands up and perform other such exhausting tricks.

Another "apple" was conducted at noon, and after we were given our noon soup we were made once more to carry out certain sports exercises while singing German songs. Sometimes they would punish people by making them stand holding their hands up and anyone found to lower even a single arm, was beaten up mercilessly.

During our two weeks in quarantine, we never left or did any work and every day was a reflection of the last, with its routine of torture, suffering and hardships.

At the Gypsy Camp

After two weeks we were moved from quarantine to the Gypsy Camp. The transfer itself was a gloomy, sad event. With our own eyes we saw the cabins evicted of their previous residents, the gypsies, who were taken for extermination at the gas chambers in the incinerators' area. The smell of charred flesh and the licks of flame seen at night left no doubts concerning the final fate of people in this place, and the fact we have taken their place emphasized what the future held in store for us.

We were put in cabins lined by three-storied wooden bunks, with a 1.5 meter wide passage between them. There were no windows in the cabin because it has originally served, we were told, as a stable. Only up, by the roof, could we see a bulge with some ports. There was no floor to the cabin either, merely damp, pitted earth; when the rain got in, it formed muddy puddles. The blocks were surrounded with boggy mud, and wading through it on the wooden clogs we were given was a hard and exhausting business. We suffered a severe shortage of drinking water; there were many people and only a few faucets that were always crowded. SS soldiers would show up at times, and when they saw the prisoners crowding around the water faucet they used the chance to beat them brutally.

Going to work

From this camp they started taking us to work, which divided into two general kinds: there were groups who worked outside in factories, construction, paving roads, draining swamps, dismantling airplanes, digging trenches and so on. Others worked inside the camp, in the kitchens, warehouses, laundry and so on.

My ten "brothers" and I, along with a few others from Wierzbnik, worked outside the camp, dismantling airplanes. A unit assigned with a specific task was called a "commando" and divided into groups of 100 prisoners or less.

Every morning we would stand for half an hour in the dark after the reveille, while they assembled a commando that would go to work. We would head for the gate in ranks of five and stop there for inspection. They counted the ranks on every side, and everything had to match the Nazi records. While we were crossing the gate, the marching band would play marching tunes and the prisoners were ordered to march to the beat and take off their hats until they reached the other side of the gate. On foggy days, the commando was detained at the gate until the fog has cleared so no one will take advantage of it and try to escape. The work day was 12 hours long and if you add that to the time required to march to the workplace and back, then during the summer we worked from dawn to dusk. Work was hard and strictly supervised; we had a single, short lunch break during the entire day, when we were served a bowl of thin soup. Each group had a secretary, a "Schreiber", who would show up at the workplace every half an hour, and a "Vorarbeiter" who was in charge of ten people had to sign for all those present. If someone went missing, he had to inform the kapo about it immediately.

As aforesaid, the working conditions were very harsh but we were comforted by the fact that for the first time, we had the chance to hamper the Nazis. Tasked with the dismantling of airplanes that were damaged during the battles, we made sure that those parts we found would be entirely beyond repair. Had this kind of sabotage been discovered, the results would have been unquestionable… therefore, we were very careful and each of us did the best he could, without any organization or common enterprise. Each of us felt and knew what he had to do and that encouraged us and gave our suffering some meaning.

Famine

We were always hungry, because we only received a minimal amount of food and our work offered no chances for more food. Food was constantly on our minds because we never ate enough, and hunger chased away other considerations. Our distress was twofold; not only did we suffer constant hunger, but the lack of even minimal nutrition was slowly destroying our physical ability to face these hardships and led to certain demise.

In theory, we were supposed to receive 350 grams of bread a day by order of the camp command, but in practice we only received 250 grams of bread and some jam or a piece of cheese, because some of the food was usually stolen by "machers", who were called "prominents" at the camp. The thefts and robbery of prisoners' food was carried out with the knowledge and approval of the SS, and anyone who dared to complain would become a victim himself. The bread was distributed among us upon our return from work, when hunger was at its peak, and most people would swallow it immediately and go hungry until the next distribution. Hunger also caused all sorts of diseases and as time went by there were more and more people, some of them from Wierzbnik, whose body could not survive this trial of hunger and hardship. They became "Muzelmans", candidates for extermination in the next selection.

The saving number

A selection was conducted in camp from time to time, the worst of the nightmares that haunted us on a regular basis. This disaster would strike unexpectedly, like a bolt from the blue. Between selections we heard rumors about the date for the next selection, and so we lived under terrible stress. At some point, the order "Blockshpre" would be heard all of a sudden, and everyone would head for the selection, where the Muzelmans were the first in line to be disqualified.

Auschwitz: "Drill" in the torture field

We have faced several selections since I first arrived in Birkenau, but I was lucky enough to survive them. But during the event I am about to describe, my luck abandoned me and I was put to the test of life and death. Unfortunately for me, a long time of hard work and constant hunger left me completely exhausted, a certain candidate for doom. And indeed, as I passed by the beast sentencing the prisoners, he unerringly pointed at me over to the side of the condemned. I tried to object, I pleaded with the angel of death claiming that I was strong enough and could work for a long time, I even showed him my meager muscles, but to no avail. The "secretary" demanded that I raise my arm so he could see the number and as I lifted it, and I "helped" him by reading out the wrong number... I have realized I could do this earlier, while receiving a bonus for my hard work in the form of a cigarette pack. After I received my reward, they wrote my number Wrong. I used this opportunity to get back in line and receive another pack of cigarettes – this time using my true number. Now that moment flashed through my mind and had a critical impact on my future. Our elders said that a person can determine his whole future in an hour, while I bought my whole life in a second, or perhaps a fraction of a second.

As custom dictated, this registration was followed by an execution that night. And indeed, a freight cat stopped before our cabin that night, while we were lying on our bunks, and the block supervisor walked in, accompanied by SS soldiers, and read the numbers of the prisoners sentenced to death during the selection. A prisoner whose number was read had to take his blanket and get in the car. When it was my turn, I stayed put, because they read the aforementioned wrong number. They repeated the number twice and thrice and when no response came one of them announced "there will be one less today". I heard his words as if coming from a long way off, because I was extremely anxious. When they left, I couldn't believe that I was still inside the cabin; I felt my body and suddenly burst out laughing and crying alternately. My uncle, Shlomo Weisbloom, held me and put his hand over my mouth, ending my loud outburst, and that was the end of it.

[Page 238]
Malka Weisbloom

The Deception: "Work Sets You Free"

Wierzbnik, my town, was once a blooming community and was destroyed completely. The pages are copied to a time of doom and anger in the shadow of the furnaces, to the human skeletons who were shivering from cold and hungry for bread. Many from Wierzbnik have died in Auschwitz, Bergen-Belsen, Treblinka, Majdanek and other such places.

Yocheved and some of our friends from Wierzbnik, who miraculously survived, describe life in camp at the beginning:

The camp commander made them run around the courtyard for hours, barefoot over a ground covered with gravel. They were constantly screamed at and hit in the head and stomach with fists, sticks, iron bars and rubber clubs. The superiors in the women's camp were women as well, German whores and criminals.

The extermination camps were surrounded by double electric-wire fences, four meters tall. Every hundred meters stood a guard tower equipped with machine guns and searchlights to scour the darkness. Hounds were guarding the perimeter. Over the gate of the camp was a slogan, spelled in capital letters: "Work Sets You Free"... Newly arrived prisoners would cling to the illusion: perhaps there is a grain of truth to this slogan? But soon they realized that only **Death** frees you from Auschwitz. The cabins were like stables. There were no windows. The rain leaked in. there were no floors, and the puddles that usually formed turned the ground into mud. The prisoners slept on three-storied bunks. The boards that made up the first floor were placed directly on the bare ground and all three stories amounted to 2 meters in all. Outside stood armed SS soldiers, who welcomed the prisoners with shouts, curses and blows. When the selection started – no man who underwent this manner of classification would ever forget the image. The cold, stony figure judged you with a wave of its hand – left or right, life or death. The prisoners learned to fall into fives and march stooped, to jump and dance with their hands over their heads or run barefooted around the gravel covered courtyard. Many fell exhausted and the SS troopers would take the weak out of the line and execute them with a shot. They were also taught German songs, and those who didn't sing were punished, made to stand to attention at the plaza from evening to noon the next day, their hands behind their necks. If they fainted, they were doused with cold water and revived with blows. The prisoners at the camp were always hungry. Hunger stabbed them before and after their meals, at every hour, day or night. Every cell in their bodies cried for food. The thought of food was always on their minds, and they secretly went through the trash looking for leftovers. Every person was covered with barely healed wounds. The wounds were numerous and caused by the beatings and from walking long distances wearing wooden clogs. The body suffered regularly from loss of blood, and had no strength left to overcome the wounds. Those who had a fever were sent to the gas chambers. There was no interest in children in the camp. Every infant that arrived with a shipment was sentenced to death on arrival. A friend who arrived as a child told me how he entered into the camp: his transport consisted only of children, who were all sent to the gas. He took an opportunity to escape the lines and when they were ordered to move he hid among the older men. The hardships made the children of the ghettos and the camps mature quickly. Eight year olds seemed like little adults, looking at you with the eyes of a hunted animal. They never had enough to eat, never knew the freedom of a field or the smell of flowers, and never had a taste of free play. They lived their lives crammed between the crowded gray cabins and the barbed-wire fences. They didn't understand what they did wrong. They only knew one thing – that they were Jews and a great evil was hounding them. The life of a child was many times harder than that of an adult. The child had to work. His soft body suffered from the cold, the beatings, the filth and especially the hunger.

The fall of the camps into the hands of the Red Army

The train workers informed us that the Red Army was approaching, but our hearts refused to believe. The knowledge spread and hundreds of people went out into the streets. Large quantities of food and clothes were distributed. A hidden storehouse yielded plenty of food after a thousand days of hunger. The attempt to break our hunger was merely an illusion. It only caused a plague of diarrhea and thousands died from overeating. The body could not contain the fats crammed into it. The shriveled digestive organs were unused to strained work and thousands paid with their lives. Nevertheless, those were joyous events: behold, the Germans are fleeing! It was worth suffering to get to this moment. The scouts of the Red Army arrived. The soldiers looked at the twisted human skeletons. And perhaps they understood better than anyone the purpose of this war.

[Page 240]
Yoseph Honigsberg

Echoes from the Valley of Tears

On my father's side (Honigsberg), I am descended from Kelph and my family wasspread among the towns of Poland – Radom, Ostrowiec and so on… my grandfather Shlomo and his wife Gitl had three sons and a daughter. The name of the daughter was Reizl and the sons – Melech, Ber and Yoseph.

I remember little about my mother's side (Dizenhoiz). My mother had a stepmother and a stepbrother named Berl Dizenhoiz, who lived nearby in Wierzbnik. After my parents Reizl and Yoseph were married, they moved the town of Łagüw where they built their house by the river.

Father made sweets and life was peaceful. The children learned at the little Heder... a large stove made of clay stood in the corner. The children sat around a rectangular table made of rough wood and the good rabbi taught them the Torah.

It was probably the difficulty of making a living in such a small town like Łagüw that pushed my parents to immigrate to a more dynamic town – Wierzbnik – where my father made a living as a painter. The Poles in the area were anti-Semite and hostile. The lives of Jews in Polish residence areas were unbearable. It was only natural that we sought a way out, especially since our family was tied emotionally and religiously to Israel. As a result, we considered immigration to Israel.

Our family was young and in full bloom, filled with happiness: three sons and three daughters, aged 6-10, the joy of all who see them. I can never forget the laughter of the eldest daughter, Bilha, her coal black hair, her strict dress. She was a lively girl, unlike the hostile environment she was born into. Her younger sister, Lea, lived up to her name; gentle in body and soul, with dimples in her oft smiling, pale, typically quiet, thoughtful and beautiful. The youngest was 6 when she perished, the joy of her family. She seemed to understand the burden of Jewish existence and grasp her situation. We called her Zerka, or Zerka'le in endearment.

My experience with the Germans at the concentration camp during the war left me unable to let go of the terrible image of my mother and the four young children with her, caught helpless in the jaws of the murderous Germans. We were tricked apart – the men to temporary "labor camps" and the women and children to other camps, after the prolonged period of starvation and humiliation that preceded the eviction. And so, our paths separated forever.

My father, my older brother Moshe and I were taken into a "labor" camp in Starachowice. My mother, my younger brother Mordechai and my sisters were separated from us. To this day I cannot forget the terrible moment, remembering my brother Mordechai fight for his life, his heart telling him what was coming; how he sought with all his might to join the men... my mother knew in her heart where the separation led. Her last words were spoken quietly, in terrible distress: go, my children, perhaps you would be saved. I am not young anymore, I lived long enough. And she turned her head. How little I knew about my mother: a proud, simple and noble woman. She could see her coming death and the destruction of her family.

My father, my brother Moshe and I went through "labor" and extermination camps, always together, despite the impossible. Striving to survive no matter the odds, and believing that we will meet the rest of our family again...

My father was a Hasid, a pleasant man versed in both scholarship and physical labor who carried the heavy burden of his large family all his life and never saw his family prosper.

The noose tightens

When the war started and the aerial bombardment commenced, the Germans did not distinguish between military-industrial sites and civilian residences. The Jews were the first to scatter, unsure where to or why here and not there. The youths traveled east in hope of saving themselves.

The poor lost their meager livelihood. The community fell into disarray. The religious community that met the daily needs of the Jews, did not know how to organize for such an emergency.

And so an organized havoc formed within the small settlement of Wierzbnik. Slowly and thoroughly, the Germans tightened the noose of destruction around the Jewish settlement – whether by cutting off livelihood outside it or through abuse, intrigues and deception. They cunningly used the generations old Jewish tenet: Nezah Israel Lo Yeshaker. The war continued on the front lines while on the home front, the Nazi murderers starved the Jews and systematically exterminated them. Rumors spread that the situation was not so bad, that there is hope of finding work and that nothing would jeopardize our physical existence. These rumors found willing ears in the Jewish community, although the future was already fairly clear. And so we missed our chance to save many lives, let alone the chance to form any resistance on a national level during the first stages of extermination.

In our new home, to which we were evicted from our apartment in the Polish quarter, lived two families to a room, a total of 12 people crammed together. The hunger was unbearable. I remember my parents, helpless to feed all those little mouths. They were running through the house as though it was a cage, while the children looked at them silently, hoping for a potato to calm their hunger.

The last Shabbat

When we men (and, as we later found out, quite a few influential women) arrived at the "labor camp" in Wierzbnik, we were surrounded Ukrainians who lusted for both our blood and money. They ordered: "Anyone who has money, Jewels and valuables would put them on the pile, or die." To ensure our understanding, they immediately followed their words with a demonstration. As a hungry boy, I realized that those without means would die. I was thinking about fighting for my continued survival and paid little attention to the immediate threat. I therefore collected whatever means that the others wanted to be rid of at any cost. Later, these means helped us quite a bit.

There seemed to be a certain purpose to this camp: to exterminate as many as possible, as quickly as possible, while providing the munitions factories with as many workers as possible. This explained why we could not become sick, or rather, get well. Work at the weapon factories was hard: we worked 12 hour shifts and had to walk to work and back to camp. Nutrition was inadequate: a puny slice of bread and a bowl of foul soup. Plagues broke out in camp and those who were not strong enough to go to work were doomed. Who can walk to work suffering from typhus and a 40-41c fever? Once, while my father was sick and unconscious, we were told that all those who were strong enough should get out, and the sick will remain in the cabins. We realized the trap. My brother and I dragged our father out. Suddenly, we heard gunfire. We were forced to run between two rows of armed Germans and Ukrainians, who were shooting at the fallen. Those who fell were shot on the spot. Suddenly we realized we were out of the firing range. When the chaos died down, we dragged our father back to his bunk and what did we see? All those left in the cabins were shot in their bunks.

Some attempts were made to escape from the camps, but very few succeeded. Those who escaped the Germans fell into the hands of the Poles. The small Jewish minority found itself surrounded by bloodthirsty, hateful beasts. The constant German propaganda against the Jews fell on fertile, hateful ground. The evictions and murders were carried out without any protest or guilt from the Poles, who never lifted a finger to try and stop the spilling of blood.

The temporary life afforded to the Jews working at the camps was seemingly pointless: the war seemed endless; the border to the lands of freedom was just a dream. The deaths and the killing whittled down the town that used to be Wierzbnik. After a while, we were transferred to a new place and a new reality. Eventually, we learned that we were brought to Birkenau-Auschwitz.

We were mostly surprised by the encounter with Jews from different countries, with strange customs. We realized that we ended up in a harsh place, living in constant abuse and in fear of burning in the furnaces, whose smokestacks towered over the camp. We were well guarded: electric fences and deep trenches, constant headcounts... Inside, the organization was in the hands of German prisoners serving their time, while outside the place was run by SS soldiers. When we arrived at the camp there was no room for us. Whole families of Gypsies, women and children, were quickly sent to the incinerators, crying in anguish. Only the smell of burnt flesh lingered over the camp for a long time after they were taken.

Next was a series of selections by the infamous German "doctors". While we, who lived through the hardships of Wierzbnik, were already immune to new horrors, we were also too weak to face a strict examination and hope to be found fit to work. This was our chance to use the guile we acquired in the past while fighting for our lives, as opposed to the Jews recently brought in from Hungary and a more normal reality.

As a boy-child slight and pale, I had no hope pf avoiding the incinerators. But we burned with a great will to live, driving us to be uncannily shrewd and resourceful in our attempts to evade the doctor who prescribed our deaths time and again.

After staying at the Birkenau death camp for a few weeks we were transferred on foot to the labor camp "Buna". On the way to the new camp we were marched, whether on purpose or not, through a reality that was new to us: incinerators, huge stacks of lumber and the lime pits. It was terrible, but we were disciplined and didn't cry out... only offered the occasional prayer to God. When we passed all that we sighed in relief and felt revitalized, because we were going to live, we were going to overcome our haters, our murderers. During the hardships that found us in the different camps, I never saw a man commit suicide.

Buna was run with typical German efficiency. Like the previous camp, the internal regime was in the hands of German convicts and the external one in the hands of the SS with their black, skull-bearing berets. Sanitation, order and the constant selections for the incinerators were a matter of routine. Public executions were part of the routine – taking place on the drill ground. What was considered a crime? I have vivid memories of an event we participated in: an alliance bombardment caused mayhem in the kitchens. We were tempted to take some vegetables. The person who got caught was hanged and the entire camp was marched past the gallows as a lesson.

At this time, we felt the front lines approaching us. We concluded that the German progress eastwards was halted and that they were even being pushed back. Airplanes paid daily visits to the factories we worked in, delivering a harsh bombardment. We rooted for them in our hearts. It was the first time we saw the Germans in distress. But we bitterly mourned the fact that those airplanes refused to bomb the incinerators, the camp fences, or the SS barracks, and the camps continued working, undisturbed, until the last moment. We played no part in the strategies of the allies. The Jews apparently had no part in any humane or legal category worth fighting for.

When the eastern front approached, we were evicted from Auschwitz and taken to Buchenwald. We were probably considered useful by Hitler's Reich, but no means were allocated for transporting us. Therefore, we were marched to the border of Germany by day and by night we "rested". The winter was harsh: snow storms accompanied us along our way. We were wearing the famous striped uniforms, with no underwear or jackets, only wooden clogs on our feet. By the time we arrived in Buchenwald, countless of us fell from the hunger and the cold. Our German escorts were assisted by German prisoners and criminals, and the latter assaulted the marchers, abusing the fallen to death. Our rest stops during the nights mostly took place in rural areas, around some shed or stable. The strong and the quick claimed a safe area. The weak slept on the snow, under the sky. And so, cowering beside each other and waiting for a new day, we closed our eyes, hungry and tired, and tried to gather our strength and get through this. New hopes fueled the hearts of our people. We had many chances for escape, but only few of them were seized. My father, my brother and I kept in constant touch. Individuals had better odds for survival and hiding in this anti-Semite region than a group such as ours. We were guided by the notion that since we overcame so many hardships to get here together, there was no reason why we couldn't survive this together again, with the end in plain sight.

We made a long stop in Gliwice and new selections took place. This time I was separated from my father, who was weakened by the prolonged journey, the cold and hunger. He was probably doomed for extermination. My world shattered and I didn't know what to do. I thought only about saving him, and I was able to do so by almost killing myself. The only important thing was that we were together again, and we continued our journey to Buchenwald on a coal train, that is, crammed standing into open cars and guarded closely.

This trip was worse than the last. The frost and snow continued to bother us as before but there was no chance to sit, let alone lie down. We received no food for ten days! Death struck mercilessly. The bodies were thrown out, so that eventually we had room to sit.

One of the beautiful things etched into my memory was the sacrifice of the Czechs, whose country we crossed through. People were standing on bridges over the railroad tracks and throwing down food to us under gunfire from our escorts. Women were crying. For the first time in years, we witnessed humanity.

During one of our stops (I later found out that it was in Bratislava) I did something that ensured our continued existence: I sneaked out with a can that we always kept with us toward the train station where the SS officers standing in line received food from a big cauldron. Under the cover of darkness I managed to sneak there unnoticed and to the astonishment of those in line I dipped my can into the hot gruel, filled it up and allowed darkness to swallow me again! In the car, a fight broke out over the food (which offered a little more life).

In Buchenwald we were welcomed by the famous smokestack. Our first question was whether people were being burned here... we were glad to hear that only the dead were being burned here. But other horrors took place in this place. People were strung feet up to die in the middle of the living cabin. Their crime – getting caught stealing or some such... Here we learned for the first time about cannibalism. People ate each other to save their own lives.

When we arrived, we were put through a warm bath and disinfection: they were worried that we would infect their home, Germany, with plagues. After the bath we were taken outside wearing our meager covers, exposed to a harsh snowstorm. We stood like that for hours. Next they put us in a stinking lair filled with four-storied bunks covered in rotting straw. Feeling joy mixed with suspicion of the unknown, we were transported from Buchenwald, this time in hermetically sealed railroad cars each guarded by two armed Germans. During one of the stops along our journey, (the guards told us it was Frankfurt) the train was brought into the open country outside the city, after an alarm sounded. This was the start of an indescribable slaughter carried out by alliance airplanes: the cars were closed and the pilots never knew what they contained. In the cars whose German guards were killed people started breaking open the doors and running out into the open field. The pilots, who presumably realized the nature of the cargo, stopped their attack. The sight was terrible: people who lost their legs and other organs were crawling, trying to get away from this deathtrap. The locals brought first aid, and for the first time we saw the faces of this nation: women and children came bearing drinks, medicine and bandages for the SS – while scornfully charging us like shepherd dogs herding cattle, so we will not escape in the commotion. They never even dreamed of offering help to our wounded!

At the end of this journey we were brought to the worst of camps. This place was full of tunnels leading to the factories at the bottom of a mountain. The place, called Langer Stein, was located near Halberstadt. Here, our eyes were drawn not to a smokestack but to something we haven't encountered so far: huge piles were stacked in the middle of this mountainous camp. We soon realized that they were carefully made of frozen human bodies, stored in this manner during the winter. Death was made tangible here at all times. Hundreds fell every day, but new prisoners arrived at the same rate. Work was grueling. Working underground, we haven't seen the sun for months. Hunger was unbearable. Food was provided once a day, at midnight, and consisted of a slice of bread and some foul soup, cooked from the peels of the potatoes eaten by the Germans. We had to subsist on this food while working hard, excavating and carrying rocks, in the dark. As soon as we received our food, the bread robbery would start – if you didn't swallow it in time you were robbed. After a couple of days, we could see our end near.

This camp enforced the following routine: wake up at 3 in the morning. Standing for hours in a lineup; then marching out for 14 hours of work without any food; marching back; food distribution at midnight and sleep in doorless, windowless cabins. We slept on a floor dirty with mud and snow. A ghost camp filled with skeletons, shambling and collapsing aimlessly. Then we marched again. The front lines were approaching but they did not leave us alone. There was an onion store in camp, and every person received a few onions. And so we marched, escaped, robbed a food train and got recaptured losing my brother in the process (I met him again after our liberation). My father died a day before our liberation, starving and sick, and was buried in an unmarked grave in the Christian cemetery in Sandersleben.

Our liberation was as bitter as the wait for it: countless people died within a few short days. Suddenly we had plenty of food, provided by the American army to the living corpses that were walking around aimlessly. Suddenly they didn't know what to do, where to turn? Their past was irrevocably shattered; their homeland has vilely forsaken them. Their future was unknown. Their minds were equally foggy. Their hearts were hardened like stone, homo homini lupus est... six years of killing and brutality turned them apathetic to human emotion, to any standards of behavior among people. Confusion was widespread, joy and sadness mixed in their pained souls.

You could see them fill the railway stations, hoping someone would direct them. For years they have been conditioned not to think, not to make decisions, not to be masters of their own fate. Some returned to their homelands and paid with their lives for clinging to the illusion that they might rebuild their lives there or find any of their dear ones where they once lived...

We, recalling our old home, felt the old yearning that was nurtured by our family, the great love for the land of the sun, the date and vine. With all our might we strove there, and indeed, a few months after our liberation, we managed to fulfill our heart's desire, to immigrate to Israel, and assured ourselves that our feet will never again set in those murderous lands.

[Page 245]
Sara Postawski-Steinhardt

Aiding Children in the Holocaust

A tragic and bloody chapter was reserved for the Jewish youth during the terrible Holocaust, twice the share of adults, and I would like to tell the story of the young girls of Wierzbnik from 1941 to the bitter end.

When the German soldiers entered Poland, they started evicting people from many towns, and the flow of refugees flooding into our town increased daily. The women of our town, led by Mrs. Yocheved Cohen, banded together and collected food and clothing for those poor souls.

As great as the plight of the adults was, the plight of the children was tenfold. Therefore all the young girls in town banded together, regardless of their social status or ideals, with a single purpose – to help the children a little. A committee was established that included Sheindl Herblum, Rivka Mincberg, Malka Cohen and the author. This group formed under a woman called Kalman-Singer. The operation was called "Milk Drop"[1].

Every Friday, the girls on duty would pass among the other members and collect food or money. Every girl gave what she could and even more. I will add that at times, I gave my last slice of bread because I knew how vital the cause was. Such a deed can only be appreciated by someone who knew the conditions we lived in and how hard it was to get a slice of bread...

At seven in the morning on Shabbats, the children of the needy refugees on our list would come and receive a cup of coffee and a sandwich. The joy of the children knew no bounds, but there were also tears.

We did not provide the children only with food, but also played and sang to them to make them feel a little better.

From time to time we gathered some of the talented children in town and put on plays to amuse the children. When the children were happy, they showed initiative of their own and some of them proved to be very talented.

Not many knew about this activity, because we did everything on our own, without asking for help or advertising our activities. Our actions were carried out with humility. We used for this purpose the house on 17 Koleyova Street, which served as the kitchen of the Jewish school in the ghetto. We girls gathered there every Shabbat afternoon and the girls on duty reported the events of the morning and offered improvements.

On the last mid-holiday of Sukkoth (1942) we organized a big rally and many of the town's dignitaries were invited because we wanted to expand our activities and provide greater aid for the needy children, especially warm clothes for the winter.

This reminds me of a major rally participated by Simcha Mincberg and Y. Singer, who served as representatives of the public, and the impressive play the children put on during it. The event's organizer was naturally Eva, who explained our organization's situation and spoke of things that were unknown before.

As time went by, the situation improved a little, but sadly, just when things were looking up, it was all destroyed.

I was a member of the committee, and visited every Shabbat morning.

The last Shabbat

I remember the last Shabbat: I gave a little girl a cup of coffee and a sandwich as usual. She drank the coffee and was holding the sandwich in her two little hands when her older sister, who was not among the lucky ones, came towards her holding a slice of bread of her own. The girls were hesitant to bite into the bread while their mother was watching them, with great sadness on her pale, noble face. Her clothes, although ragged, told of better times. The mother looked at the two girls and wiped the tears streaming from her eyes.

I was standing next to Hanna Guterman, who witnessed the moving moment with me, and once the mother realized that the two of us were looking at her, she turned and disappeared. This moved me and I told myself that I had to find out who the woman was and add the older girl to the group next Shabbat. Those were very dark times; each of the rumors spreading was worse than the last and our town was among the last ones "still standing".

When I expressed my intention, Hanna answered me with sad eyes: "I hope we would still be here next Shabbat."

Our fears came to pass. That very Shabbat noon marked the arrival of Jewish refugees from Wąchock. The usual Shabbat afternoon meeting never took place because we already knew that we were doomed. Those were the last days before our eviction and the events that followed it.

Every year, as I light the memorial candle for all my dear ones who perished, I see in my mind those nice and innocent children, as if it were only yesterday.

1. A term synonymous with infant welfare

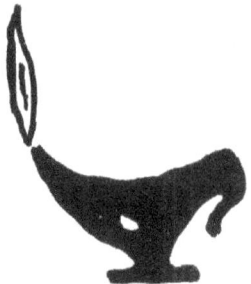

As I light a memorial candle – the precious, innocent children stand before my eye

[Page 247]
Esther Zukerman-Zilberman

The Little Orphaned Shoes

When the war broke out and the first bombs fell on our little town, I fled with my husband Beniek Shiezinger, my sons, Meir Avram (Meyish), who was then eight years old, and Alexander (Alush), who was still a baby of two, to Mietelitsk, hoping to avoid the bombing. My mother joined us in our flight.

Once there, we heard constant shooting. As it turned out later, the shooting took place in Drildz (IIza). Many Jews lost their lives in the great massacre that took place there, among them people from Wierzbnik who had gone there in the hope of saving themselves. A short time later German soldiers marched into Mietelitsk and the nightmare began. They grabbed people from the street, including Shiezinger, my former husband, and sent them to an unknown destination for hard labour. The children and I remained alone. Now that the entire area was under German occupation and the situation was tense, there was no point in remaining there. I returned to Wierzbnik with my mother and children.

The children asked many questions. Why had their father been taken away? Where had they sent him? I assured them that he would come home soon. In fact, a few weeks later he did return. I will never forget the moment he came into our apartment, the children ran to him and refused to let go of him. They were afraid that he would be taken away from them again.

At the beginning of the Nazi occupation we thought that only men would be sent to hard labour. We thus sought a way for them to avoid it. My husband Beniek and his two brothers, Hilek and Heniek, and Heniek's wife and child, decided to cross the Russian border illegally, as did many other Jews. But at the last minute my husband felt guilty about leaving me alone with the children and he came back to Wierzbnik. He also thought that we should all try cross the Russian border. Due to my Mother I could not make up my mind to do so. Of my husband's two brothers, only Hilek survived. Today he lives with his wife and three sons in Haifa.

After a while the Germans sent Jewish refugees from other towns and villages to Wierzbnik. The Jewish community undertook a large relief effort and every local family took in the newly arrived refugees. The Wierzbnik Jews shared their homes and whatever else they could with the new arrivals. The Ziskind family from Lodz, a couple with two small children, moved in with us. When the school year began, Jews were prohibited from sending their children to school. However, Jews made every effort to educate their children. Rushke Laks taught my son Meyish to read and write and every day he went to learn Jewish subjects from the son of the former Rabbi Regensberg.

The Fiddle is Lost

When we received the order to leave our house on Starachowice Street, we moved in with the baker lady from Kielc where the Ziskind family had already been living. Of the Ziskind family, only the son Jerzyk, survived. After the war he was brought to Canada by the Canadian Jewish Congress together with other Jewish orphans who had miraculously survived. He grew to be a well-known Professor of Statistics and is now in the United States. He is married and has two small children. Who knows how many brilliant minds were among the million Jewish children who were murdered by Hitler.

We were given 24 hours to leave our house and move in with the baker lady from Kielc. We could only take a few things with us from home. Firstly, we did not have any means of transport. Secondly, there was not enough room in the already crowded house where a few families were already living. My children immediately noticed that among the furniture and belongings we left behind were Meyish's violin and Alush's sled. The very next day Meyish took Alush to our former home to get their valuable possessions. On arrival they were shocked as new occupants were already living there and refused to let them in.

The children went to their old house almost every day with their straightforward and just claim that the new owners return to them their treasured possessions. Each time they returned empty-handed and broken-hearted and unable to understand such cruelty. This was such a great tragedy for them that it was very difficult for me to convince them that going there so often was extremely risky. They tried crying and complaining, in hope that I could help them. However, after seeing it was hopeless, they resigned themselves to their fate. Meyish gave up any hope of getting back his violin. He had been taking lessons from Yakov Vigdorovich for a few years already. Little Alush also understood and was resigned to the idea that he would never again see his little sled, which was not just thrown together with a couple of boards, but made with the finest bent wood.

Seeing my children's pain caused me much heartache. My helplessness caused me so much distress that for a moment I forgot the problems that lay ahead which were becoming more evident and worse with each new day.

Bitter Times Begin

Very quickly and almost overnight, my children were transformed into adults. As they rapidly matured, they lost their childlike naiveté. Meyish in particular began to think and act like a grown-up, assuming responsibility for the whole house. He was suddenly forced to learn what the new realities dictated. Whenever there was something to buy he was one of the first to stand in line. He always hurried home to bring good news about any new item that could be purchased with ration cards. With a satchel in each hand, just like a grown-up, he went to Starachowice to bring home some coals or a few potatoes. Already aware that it was dangerous to look like a Jew, he quickly learned how to look like a non-Jewish child.

Soon we had to move again and leave the house of the baker lady from Kielc. More and more Jews kept arriving from other places. Due to the lack of housing, the Jewish community could no longer help people find a place to live. They had to fend for themselves. After much searching, we finally found a place for ourselves at Rotbard's grandson's, where the entire house consisted of one room with a kitchen. We could already see that bad times awaited us, and we began to think of ways to save the children.

On the way to the Michalow Forest lived a Christian woman called Mazurova to whom we had given many of our belongings with the idea that it might help us. Soon after moving in with Rotbard's grandson, we began sending Meyish to stay overnight at Mazurova's home so he could gradually get used to this arrangement. There were my Mother, brother, and sister Idel, her husband and five children. We were all subjected to the constant shouting of those in charge, "Five in a row, including children!" The shouts to line up in orderly rows went on for a long time. To this day they reverberate in my ears.

We tried to figure out how we could all remain together. Meyish stood in a row with his Father and myself. Alush was with my Mother and sister Idel with her husband and small children. A passing German foreman recognized Beniek and took him away, saying he needed him for work.

The shouts and cries of the large crowd of people being hit over the head with whips created indescribable panic. In the noise and confusion we lost our places, and I suddenly found myself in a completely different row. When they began to chase us to "shtshelnitse"[1]*, I thought everyone would be taken there and sent away in boxcars. As it turned out some were taken to "shtshelnitse"[1]*, while others were sent to "mayuvke"[1]*. The rest were taken by the murderers to the station and like animals loaded onto boxcars and sent to Treblinka.

A few days later I met up with my husband. We no longer had our children and we did not know what had happened to my Mother and my sister Idel. From that time on we were sick at heart. Beniek soon after contracted typhus and died in the camp. I remained alone, a shadow of my former self, completely broken emotionally and physically.

A Deep Wound

We had given a Christian man the two leather satchels that Meyish had used to supply the house with a few coals and the necessaries of life. He was to make a pair of shoes for each child from one of them and keep the other as payment. The Christian was a good man and kept his word. Yet, by the time he sent the two pairs of shoes to me in the camp, I no longer had any use for them.

Very often in my dreams, I see my two children. I have recurring nightmares where I see them ragged with torn shoes. That incident of receiving the two pairs of children's shoes from the Christian man had embedded itself deep in my subconscious and left a tragic wound that will stay with me for the rest of my life.

1. This was the name of a location in the town even though the Polish word has a specific meaning.

[Page 251]
Mindl Rosenwald-Farbman

Like Dark Clouds

Never forget and don't forgive the murder-nation! My hand trembles as I pick up a pen to relate something of my memories from that ghastly, horrible period, and what I lived through in the dark years of 1939-1945. There is simply no language, there are no suitable expressions to describe the tragedy that we went through. Even now, from the perspective of decades after those bloody days, when I recall the wild acts of the Nazi murderers, my blood congeals in my veins and my heart bursts with pain and anger, my mind stops thinking and only one wish encompasses me: revenge against the German beasts. Our entire two thousand-year old Diaspora history is permeated with pages of horror and fright, blood and tears, inquisitions and deportations – but all this is nothing and pales in comparison to the aggravations and murderous acts of the Hitler-Haman people. Even the poet and writer in his work "Inferno" was unable to depict such a racehatred, and such means of death as the *Herrenvolk* developed and transformed to use against the Jews, the highest degree of sadism.

At the age of eighteen I encountered the misfortune, the outbreak of the Hitler war. At the age of twenty I was kidnapped by the Nazi vandals while walking in the street in my hometown of Drilecz, and was torn away from my parents, brothers and sisters, from my dearest and most beloved ones.

Without a why or when, like a dark threatening cloud they fell on the streets, grabbed Jews and threw them into prepared freight cars, not knowing where they were being taken. The fearful panic and fright that prevailed then is indescribable. Jewish property and Jewish life were forfeit.

Yes, thirty years have already gone by since those sad days, and the picture has remained with me the entire time. The echo of that bitter crying, pain and groaning of my near and dear ones, who didn't know where I had disappeared to, and who were so tragically separated from me, constantly resounds in my ears. A chain of wandering and harsh experiences began for me, and I was then taken away to work in the Hasak ammunition factory in Skarżysko.

Sleepless nights and days of horror, pain and fear, of hunger and distress, dragged out thus, but in the depth of my heart glowed the hope, the aspiration, to survive the nightmare and to reconnect myself to my stem, with my dear parents.

Unfortunately, to my regret my hopes were dispersed after liberation, not finding any trace of my beloved and extensive family.

And at the moments of despair and apathy, the two angel-emissaries, Rosenwald and Avraham Frimmerman came to me, and consoled and encouraged me to control myself and renew my life struggle, to build a Jewish home, to restore all the traditional values that were so dear to our parents, who died as innocent martyrs.

May their memory be blessed

[Page 253]
Simcha Minzberg

The Beginning of the Downfall

With the outbreak of World War II, nervousness and tension grew, and because of the extensive bombing we all began to run, not knowing where to. My family and I went off to Ostrowiec, and the first victim that we saw fall there was Berele Herzog from Wierzbnik. Near the time of the High Holidays, turning back to Wierzbnik, Haim-Tuvia Tennenbaum, who was a refined Jew with a Jewish heart and one of my best friends, perished on the road. We were very shocked by this occurrence and brought him to be buried in Wierzbnik.

The confused running without a goal created a panic and tragically affected everyone.

Among the Jewish refugees that ran to Dzielce, the teacher of the town, Reb Mendel Tennenbaum, fell a victim to death.

Several days before Yom Kippur, we came back to Wierzbnik and we smelled the fetid atmosphere introduced by the Nazi beasts. On the first evening of Yom Kippur the synagogue was set on fire, and sleepless nights and days of horror and fear began. Nevertheless, there were clandestine *minyanim* [quorum of ten men required for prayers] for services, among them a *minyan* in the home of Reb Avraham-Mordechai Rotbart.

Yom Kippur, while we were at services and wearing our prayer shawls, and as usual – only socks, the Nazi scum entered, surrounded all the praying people and led them away to the train station, forcing them to unload cars of coal.

Weak from fasting, the Jews carried out the forced labor with the last of their strength, and afterwards they had to smear themselves with dirt and mud, in order to abase themselves even more. My Mendush was among them.

Several days after Yom Kippur the dark days of fear and suffering began. Jews were kidnapped in the streets and were dragged off to hard labor, which was accompanied by humiliation. These occurrences strongly affected and actually paralyzed our entire life, because we could no longer show ourselves in the street.

Then various property owners turned to me for advice on how to control the difficult situation, so that we could move around and slightly ease our hard lives. At the request of the public I undertook an extremely daring step; I sneaked out to the mayor's office by a back way, approached the mayor Sokol, begging him for help, but he informed me that he was powerless and no longer had a say in anything.

I then gathered courage and went in to the German commandant and with a bitter heart explained to him the difficult situation the Jewish population was in because of the kidnapping for forced labor. He agreed to organize Jewish groups that would be allocated to work in various places. He also allocated me a clerk from the municipality, and together we composed a list of the Jewish population, from which I was told to every day allocate a certain number of workers. He promised me that they would no longer grab Jews for work, other than the allocated number. That is how it was; every day a group was sent to work in various places, and the kidnappings stopped. The Jewish population could finally move around freely in the streets and life was a little bit easier. In this way the people who had means also paid the poor people who were willing to go work in their place.

That is how the first winter went by. I, being the initiator of this change, moved freely in the streets and wore an armband with German lettering: "Member of the municipal government".

Until a certain day, standing there in the street organizing the work, a German officer went by and seeing the sign on my arm he gave a shout; "A Jew – member of the municipal government?!" He tore the armband off and gave me a few strong blows. I went to the commandant to complain, but he said that he couldn't help me.

Refugees

Sleepless nights began, and days of horror and fright. The persecutions increased from day to day, and the first edict about the obligation to wear a badge with a Star of David arrived.

The atrocious reality became unbearable and frightful news arrived that created great panic.

On a certain day, we received word to prepare to receive a transport of refugees, Jews from Łódź.

We immediately got organized to await the transport at the train station.

The arrival of the refugees made a shocking impression; the frost was terrible and the Jews – broken, physically and mentally exhausted, wearing two yellow badges on their front and on their back.

We immediately tore the yellow badges off them. Some of them were transferred to neighboring towns in the area, and the majority were housed by us. There was a large aid action, and we collected clothing, underwear, bedding and also money for that purpose, because most of them arrived naked and barefoot and frightened and starving. We created a soup kitchen and little hospital for the sick, and saw to medicines, so that the refugees' situation improved.

However, it didn't take long and the edicts and aggravations became constantly harsher and more unbearable. Right from the start, when the German mayor took over he removed all the members of the city council, and also the mayor, and the first edict was to pay a payment of ten thousand zloty within three days, and if not – the ultimatum was – many people would die.

A short while later a contribution of forty thousand zloty was placed on us, accompanied by severe threats and repressions.

Forced Labor

Afterwards came the new order with regard to forced labor by the Jewish population from 14 to 60 years of age. At the same time a transport of homeless Jews from Plock arrived. It is hard to describe the shock that encompassed everyone; such a poor *shtetl*, with such hard conditions, and added to that another 500 sick, broken men, women and children arrived, after we had just recently taken in 150 homeless people from Łódź.

Nevertheless, despite the great difficulties, individuals or whole families were housed in nearly every home. The soup kitchen was greatly enlarged, and in that way the fate of the poor, sick refugees was eased. But the situation of the people from our town was also not much better, and from day to day life became harder and worse. And then suddenly a specter loomed: in the winter, when it was extremely cold outside, on the Christian Christmas day, a new edict came out, that all Jews had to hand in all their fur and leather clothing.

It is hard to describe the mood introduced by this edict. People had to give away their last possessions, the furs and the warm clothes, even tearing off the children's fur collars.

Within two days two large looted freight vehicles were filled with furs, and we all escorted them like a funeral. In the morning, we first felt the signs. People went around with torn and worn out clothes and young children shivered from cold.

At the same time, the grabbing of people in the streets for work became a daily occurrence, and there were Gestapo men to be seen everywhere and various other policemen and gendarmes, who treated the Jews very brutally, as though they were of no account.

Ghetto

However, one of the gravest edicts was the creation of the ghetto for Jews. It is impossible for the normal mind to conceive how they could take a population of 3,500 local people and an additional 1,000 homeless people and pack them into such a small area of a few narrow streets!

People were squeezed together like herrings, but the will to live was so strong, that even in these terrible circumstances we again had to forge the chain of the daily battle for life.

I will recall two important episodes here, which took place before the creation of the ghetto.

One Case

On a certain day, an engineer called Hajdukewicz was murdered by the Polish underground resistance. This led to a major action and arrests among the Polish population, and especially among the Jews. Thus the Gestapo arrested 23 distinguished Jews and sent them off to the Radom prison. It is clear that the tension and resentment were very great, not knowing what would happen to them. However, thanks to the tremendous steps and intervention of a few community members, we were able to free all of them and bring them back to the city.

The Second Case

A few days before Rosh Hashana 1940, a Gestapo expedition arrived in the city from Radom, which herded all the Jewish men into a single place, and after severe beatings and humiliations they took out 120 young men and sent them off to work somewhere in the area of Lublin. We learned that this same action was also carried out in other towns in our region. The fear and suffering that the deportation aroused in the Jewish population is impossible to describe, especially in the broken-up families. Then I, together with my friend Yossl Tencer and a few others, decided to make an effort to rescue them. We went off to the Central Bureau in Radom, and after major efforts we received a letter from the powers that be for Lublin. I recall that it was a Friday and we went to see the rabbi of Wąchock, Rabbi Yossele (the father of our Rabbi Rabinowicz), who gave us permission to ride to Lublin on the Sabbath and also gave us his blessing.

We finally arrived in Lublin and met with our people, who were still in the transit camp on the infamous 7 Lipowa St., which had a dreadful reputation.

I remained in Lublin until after Succoth, searching for various ways to rescue our people. I also visited my relative, who was a prominent man of action in Lublin.

And suddenly there was a police raid on Jews at night and among others they took my cousin, me and Yossl Tencer in the middle of the night and threw us unto freight trucks and dragged us off to the camp on 7 Lipowa St. What we went through that night was terrible; it was extremely cold and we had to lie face-down on the bare bricks, until daylight. A selection took place in that camp to send people to various places of work, but thanks to the great efforts made on the outside, my cousin was freed together with me and Yossl Tencer. Being free, we renewed our efforts to liberate our people, until we succeeded and all 120 of them were freed. Walking with them in the street many of them were amazed and filled with wonder at the fact. I would like to take this opportunity to give honorable mention to the distinguished member of the Lublin community Reb David Werber, of blessed memory, who assisted us greatly with the liberation of the 120 men, and saw to it that two freight platforms were specially attached to the train, and we all rode directly back to Wierzbnik. Everyone was extremely happy. Unfortunately, later on these people also didn't escape the bitter fate of all Jews.

I have only recalled these two specific incidents in order to show that also in the most difficult times of fear and torment, of arrests and deportations, thanks to the intervention of several community activists, many of the harsh edicts were overturned, and many times life was made a little easier.

At the end of the summer of 1942, a few weeks before the general liquidation, the Germans set up a labor camp in the ammunition factory, which was called by an abbreviation of *Juden Lager* [camp for Jews], "Julag", and it was supposed to take in 2,500 Jews. At that time the camp consisted of two parts. One was erected in the forest, the so-called Szczelnice-Lager, and the other was called the Majowka Lager.

Death

Then the last days of the community's demise actually drew nearer, even though no one imagined that the liquidation was so close. Everyone looked for a way to save himself, some through finding a place of work, others through hiding, and others handed over young children into Christian hands, in order to rescue them from death. The tension grew from day to day, and on the last Sabbath before the liquidation we still managed to gather a *minyan* at the home of Yankel Rubinstein, among whom were Henech Biderman, Yankele Mandelzis, Yehiel Lerman, Leibish Rubinstein and others. While I was reading the Torah portion, panic was created with the arrival of the news that all the Jews of Wąchock (700 people) had been brought to Wierzbnik. This served as a sign that the liquidation was advancing.

Even though it was sensed in the air that the repression and annihilation were coming nearer, deep in our hearts a spark of hope still glowed, that it would perhaps be possible by various means to elude or abolish the sentence of annihilation. I recall that one night before the liquidation I still made various efforts in that respect, but unfortunately with no success, because the entire city was already surrounded by the murderous military formations. The bloody day, the 16th of Marheshvan, October 27, 1942, is inscribed in my memory as the fatal date of cruelty and brutality. Early in the morning the shuddering cry resounded "All Jews out," and from all sides tormented Jews streamed to the marketplace: men and women, old and young and little children to the assembly point. Within a short time the market place was filled with five thousand Jews, composed of the Wierzbnik population together with homeless Jews from other places.

The entire mass of people stood there surrounded by angels of destruction, with the infamous murderer and leader of the SD, Becker, at their head, holding a revolver cocked to shoot. Dozens of Jewish men and women were shot to death that day by those murderous hands, and their names are remembered and commemorated in this Yizkor Book. The victims of that bloody day were given Jewish burial by our compatriot and friend, Leibish Herblum. After that, the majority of the Jewish population was driven to the train station, from where they were sent on their final journey in an unfamiliar direction. The remaining Jews, who were divided up, were driven off to the large camp in the forest, which was called Szczelnica Camp. While they were pushing the beaten Jews to the new camp, Yosef Rosenberg, the son-in-law of Reb Shmuel Cohen, was shot on the way. The gates of the camp were immediately locked, and the first reception was to hand in all our private, hidden, last valuables, under threat of death. All our clothes, sacks and packs with our last remaining things were immediately collected, and people remained with what they were standing up in.

And under these hard, inhuman conditions, we continued to bear the yoke of work, hunger and torment for another nineteen months until the end of July 1944.

It is impossible to describe all the seven sections of hell that each of us went through in the camps, and only a very small part is related here and there in the Yizkor Book, because every day had its bloody story.

Acts of Aggravation and Horror

Thus on that same Christmas eve, a freight truck arrived in the middle of the night and a shout was heard "*Eine Minute – alles raus!*" [Everybody out in one minute]. This happened in the Szczelnica camp, and everyone ran madly and wildly to the only gate, and people with a fever of forty degrees, all on a bright moonlit night when the infamous murderer Althoff ordered everyone to run around the camp as fast as possible. Afterwards he shouted out "*Eine Minute – alles schlaft*" [Everyone asleep in one minute]. That was a "Christmas play" accompanied by death and humiliation.

The grim life dragged on in this way, filled with despair and fear. Exhausted and starved, the people were pushed to hard physical labor, and afterwards lay in the barracks on the bare boards covered with dirty rags and without the minimal sanitary conditions, not knowing what the morrow would bring.

Understandably, in such circumstances people became weak and there were outbreaks of various diseases, especially a typhus epidemic, which encompassed a large proportion of the people. Suddenly an order was received to construct a bunker and to isolate the women and children with typhus in it.

But the isolation was just an excuse, and it didn't take long until the murderer Althoff showed up in the middle of the night and shot all the sick people in the bunker, and afterwards ordered us to bury them in the forest. But typhus continued to prevail in the camp, and sick people were again isolated in a special bunker. But the will to live was so strong, that despite the terrible conditions and the minimal medical help, some of them nevertheless revived and regained their health.

The second mass murder took place when the vicious Althoff together with Meyer entered the barrack and shot right and left and so horribly murdered all the sick people.

Mass Murder in the Bogaj Forest

So the grim days dragged on in the cold winter, from one mass murder to the next. Only several weeks had passed when the bloodthirsty murderer Althoff again entered the camp with Gestapo men and ordered us to assemble outside, where he selected 120 people and led them away to the Bogaj Forest, where deep graves had already been prepared previously by Jews, who didn't know what they would be used for, and there all 120 Jews were bestially killed. That was the so called "Bogaj Action". After that Purim drew near and a small clinic was set up in the camp, where the sick received some medical help, to the degree that it was possible, and the people caught their breath a bit from the terrible actions. When Passover arrived, the mood was calm, and then with the help of my friend Leibish Herblum I undertook to create the opportunity of eating matzos on Passover. A little flour was smuggled in through the people who worked in the factory, and Leibish Herblum, being a craftsman, put together an oven from bricks and other things, and using bottles as rolling pins the women kneaded the dough and prepared the matzos. In this way, in spite of the hard conditions, we were able to eat matzos in the camp, which served as a symbol of redemption, because the entire time was bitter enough.

But the Szczelnica camp was liquidated immediately after Passover and the remaining people were transferred to the Majowka camp. That is how the summer of 1943 began, and we thought that in spite of everything many people would survive and live to experience the victory. But the Hitler beast that searched for different ways and means to destroy all the Jews, to the very last one, thought differently. On a certain day, it was when the uprising of the Jewish fighters was taking place in the Warsaw ghetto, the wild Huns again entered the camp, herded everyone together and again removed a number of people and led them off to Firlej, near Radom, and a day later we learned that they had all been brutally murdered there. Thus the camp was sifted through from time to time, through brutal actions and deceptions, until the leading away to death.

The sinners of Edom

To Prison in Radom

On the night between June 5 and 6, 1944, while in the barrack, more or less a month before the ultimate final liquidation, the infamous camp commandant Schratt came in and said that I was being called to the works guardhouse. From then on what happened to me is to this day a mystery to me and also to all the other people in the camp. I entered the works guardhouse and there encountered two Gestapo men who led me out of the camp gate, shoved me into a vehicle that was waiting outside, and accompanied by the Gestapo men we drove in the direction of the forest. Understandably, at that moment I thought about the worst of all. But after driving for a certain amount of time, I suddenly found myself in the Wierzbnik jail, where I was locked up in a separate cell. This frightened me greatly, and my thoughts became very scattered and hopeless. But very early, when day dawned, a Polish policeman who knew me from before the war whispered through the keyhole that I was being taken away to Radom.

And that is what actually happened. At 7 AM two armed works guards came and took me and chained me to a Polish criminal, to take me off to Radom. Then something happened. At that moment a well-dressed Jewish woman entered the jail, carrying a suitcase. It was Avraham Zukerman's sister (Kosowski). I asked her what she was doing there, and she answered me briefly that while she was in the Heller's sawmill camp, she was told to put on her best clothes and take her things with her, and thanks to the efforts made on her behalf abroad, she was being liberated, with the goal of going to Israel.

Walking thus to the depot, accompanied by the "skins", with my free hand I helped her carry the suitcase with her things. When we boarded the train they separated us and I didn't see her again. In Radom I was immediately taken to the headquarters of the SS head of police and placed into a dark cellar prison, where about forty Christian arrestees were already sitting. The conditions were very bad, and we were under constant guard. Right in the morning I was taken into another room, where two higher Gestapo officials began interrogating me and asking various questions, such as how many Jews there were still in the camp, what they did and which Jews thought about running away from the camp. I shrewdly answered them that if anyone thought about running away, they kept it a secret to themselves. In this way I sat with my hands cuffed, and they wrote everything down in the record, and afterwards they took me back to the prison. For three days, from Wednesday to Friday, they hassled me this way with questions, and returned me to the prison, and to this day it is a mystery to me what it meant, and how I remained alive.

I believe that only thanks to Divine Providence was I able to bear all these trials, so that I would survive and be a witness who together with all the Jews saw and suffered the bitter torment until the downfall of the enemy. Otherwise it is impossible to grasp it logically. The terrible impression made by my sudden disappearance from the camp on my sainted wife and children, who remained in the camp, is impossible to describe. After they finished the interrogation, I was again returned to the prison on Warsaw Street, and the infamous cannibal Koch was already waiting for me, and did such terrible and painful things to me, which, because of the respect due to the Yizkor Book, I can't repeat.

The Day of Liberation

I suffered for five weeks in the prison until June 11, 1944, when I was sent off to Gross-Rosen camp. After spending several days there, I heard them asking who among the people was a clerk. I immediately responded and I was taken away to another camp, "Fünf Teichen" [Five Lakes], where I worked in the factory. I would like to mention the Yom Kippur eve which has become deeply etched in my memory. It was a night when I and an additional group of Jews lay sick and weakened, and quietly murmured the holiday prayers and with broken hearts called out "In distress I called out to you, O Lord."

And I also recall a Hanukah evening, when I was in a *revier* [infirmary] with the rabbi of Sępienko, and we were able to carry out the mitzvah of lighting Hanukah candles in the dark infirmary. This happened just a few weeks before liberation. From then on the Sępienko rabbi, who now lives in Israel, and I became good friends.

I was liberated from the infirmary on January 23, 1945.

Before I relate the rest of my experiences after liberation, I consider it necessary to mention Mrs. Kosowski (née Zukerman), who unfortunately did not live to reach Israel, the country which she dreamed of coming to, and she died in the eternally cursed Auschwitz, where she yet encountered her daughter Rivka, and told her about her sudden meeting with me on the road.

[Page 262]
Simcha Mincberg

Days of Misery and Ruin

When the war broke out, anxiety and fear escalated. The harsh bombardments made everyone panic and flee, not even knowing where. My family and I moved to Ostrowiec and the first victim we stumbled across in that town was Berl Hercig, from Wierzbnik.

Before the high holidays, we decided to go back to Wierzbnik accompanied by a few other families. On the way, we suddenly lost Chaim Tuvia Tenenbaum, a warm, kindhearted Jew and one of my closest friends. His death came to us as a great shock and we had to make an effort to provide him a proper burial in Wierzbnik.

The very act of escape made the situation unbearably tense, and resulted in a fare share of casualties. The same could be said about the escape to nearby Iłża, which resulted in the death of local teacher Mendel Tenenbaum.

As I already mentioned, a few days before Yom Kippur we returned to town, where we keenly felt the tense atmosphere that resulted from the Nazi invasion. The night of Yom Kippur, when the synagogue was set on fire, signaled the beginning of many sleepless days and nights, of threats and regular murders. All of which never stopped the Minyans that gathered for prayer, including one at the home of Avraham Mordechai Rotbart.

On Yom Kippur, in the middle of prayer, while those gathered were standing wrapped in their tallits and pouring their hearts before God, German soldiers burst into the house, dragged all the prayers and led them to the train station, where they were ordered to unload heavy cargos from the cars. The prayers were weak and tired from the Yom Kippur fast, but they made superhuman efforts to carry out this forced task. This proved inadequate in the eyes of the villains, who forced them to sully their clothes with mud and slime, hoping to humiliate and daunt them. Among them was also my son, Mendel.

A few days after Yom Kippur, the times of fear and suffering started anew. Jews were captured in the streets and carried off to do hard labors involving indescribable humiliations. These events were naturally very disruptive, completely paralyzing Jewish life, because people dared not leave the house; we practically locked ourselves in. During those mad days, I was approached by several of the landowners and asked to find a way of overcoming the intolerable situation and make it easier to move around without a risk. I could not refuse them and so I made a rare, risky move. I sneaked out and somehow made my way to town hall. I found several members of the city council there, including mayor Sokul and the senior Nazi officer representing the government. I turned to the mayor, explained the situation and asked for his help, but he explained to me that he could not do anything to help because he had no control over matters. After receiving this answer I risked my life and introduced myself to the representative of the military regime. I explained to him that the lives of the Jews in town were made unbearable by the partisan abductions of Jews walking the streets for forced labor. During our conversation he accepted my offer to organize Jewish teams that would be assigned for work in the different areas, according to a daily schedule. We formed a list of candidates for work with the help of a certified town clerk, and every day we sent a group of Jews out to work according to that list, bringing a stop to the abductions in accordance with the representative's promise. The Jews breathed a little more easily, more Jews were seen on the streets again and life went back to normal. Furthermore, Jews of means paid others to go to work for them.

Things were slow during the first months of winter. I, being the initiator and organizer of this activity, was free to walk around the streets, with a ribbon on my arm saying "city council member" in German. One day, a German officer passed me by and seeing the words "city council member" started swearing at me, tore the ribbon off and beat me severely. When I went to complain before the representative, he told me that he could not intervene in such matters.

The dark days and nights of fear returned. The persecution escalated from day to day until finally we were told that every Jew must wear a mark of disgrace in the shape of a David's Shield embroidered on a piece of cloth and worn in a highly visible place. Life became harder and harder and the rumors that started spreading were terrible and made the public anxious. After a while, we were ordered to prepare for a shipment of Jewish refugees from Lodz. We immediately made preparations and waited for the newcomers by the train station. The arrival of the refugees left a shocking and depressing impression on us. The weather was cold and the Jews who arrived were exhausted, scared and physically and emotionally broken, covered front and back with yellow patches.

First we removed the yellow patches of disgrace from them, and then some of them were sent to towns nearby while the majority settled among us. We immediately started an extensive aid drive, collecting clothes, linen and money, because most of the refugees were torn, ragged and hungry. We opened a soup kitchen and a minute hospital to offer the aid necessary to the sick, making the lives of the refugees more humane under those conditions.

Life continued in this manner while we were looking to the future with anxiety. Strict martial law was declared in town, but the Gestapo murderers were not seen yet. Shortly after, we were struck left and right with edicts, the noose tightened around us and life became unbearable. It should be mentioned that when the Nazi officer took control over city hall, he removed from office all the chosen members of the city council, including the mayor, and his first edict was that the Jewish public must pay a collective ransom of 10,000 zloty within three days or else lives would be lost and blood would be spilled.

Raising that much money was impossible for us at the time, since most of the Jewish population was poor and bereft of financial means. We made great efforts and were able to raise a significant portion of the tax and postpone the deadline.

This was not enough for our nemesis, and a few weeks later he levied us with another payment of 40,000 zloty. No doubt the enemy knew it was an impossible demand, but he was looking for an excuse to spill blood and kill Jews. We made superhuman efforts to collect the necessary sums and thwart his plans.

Another decree required the entire Jewish population of ages 14-60 to provide forced labor, while at the same time we were told about an incoming shipment of refugees from Płock. It is hard to describe the anxiety that struck the Jewish public, poor people who were forced under such horrid conditions to take in 500 refugees – among them women and children, sick and infirm – in addition to 150 Jewish refugees that came not long ago from Lodz. Nevertheless and despite the hardships, we made every effort possible to house individuals or entire families with local families, cramming them together. The soup kitchen was expanded and the destitute refugees joined our townsmen, whose condition was bad enough to begin with.

Forced labor

These events took place in the middle of winter, while the weather was cold and accompanied by frost and snow. And then, on the cold eve of Christmas, came a new edict ordering us to give the Germans all our furs and warm clothes and stipulating that Jews found in possession of such clothing would be killed. The stir this edict caused was unbelievable. People gave whatever they had, furs of every kind and warm clothes, and our hearts ached seeing the fur collars and covers taken off our children and given to our enemies. Large trucks collected warm fur coats for two days and every one of us took part in this funeral, as if it was for the dead. The next day, we felt and saw the terrible results of this operation, which left children, women and men bereft of warm clothes, dressed only in rags and shivering from cold.

And then the abductions resumed, and Gestapo and other uniformed Nazis were everywhere, treating the Jewish population with lawless brutally. But the height of persecution and torture was the creation of a crowded residence area for Jews called a "ghetto". To this day I cannot fathom how anyone could force a population of 3,500 locals and about 1,000 refugees from other places into a crowded area consisting of a few dark, narrow alleys. People were stuffed like sardines. But the urge to live was so strong, that even under these inhuman conditions we all did our best to hold on.

I would like to describe two events that stirred the public and bred fear and panic among the Jewish population even before the establishment of the "ghetto".

The edict was withdrawn

One day, the Polish engineer Hidukewitz was murdered by the Polish resistance, an act that resulted in the persecution and arrest of many Jewish and Polish suspects. The Jewish suspects arrested were 23 men of means and dignitaries, and they were sent to the prison in Radom. The arrest caused much grief to the Jews in town and bitterness, fear and despair gnawed at their hearts. But through various means and efforts, we managed to have this edict withdrawn, release our people from jail and bring them back home.

The second event happened a few days before the New Year in 1940, when a delegation of Gestapo came to Wierzbnik from Radom, ordered all the Jewish men to gather, and after beating them up and swearing at them they took 120 youths and sent them to the labor camp in Lublin County. Later on we learned that this event repeated itself in nearby towns. It is impossible to describe the despair this act caused us, and particularly the sorrow of the families of the ones snatched away.

It occurred to me that we must try and fight this. Along with my friend Yoseph Tenzer and a few other friends, I decided to try and save them. We drove to the local central bureau that was located at the time in Radom and after many efforts received from the military authorities in Radom a letter, addressed to the military bureau in Lublin County, ordering the release of the abductees. I remember that it was Friday when we talked with the rabbi of Wąchock, Yoseph (father of Rabbi Rabinowicz of our town), and asked for his permission to travel on Shabbat to Lublin to save lives. The rabbi gave us his blessing and wished us luck in our task.

When we arrived in Lublin we found that our people were still all at the infamous transfer camp in Lipowa Street no. 7. We tried various ways of reaching the top ranks of the government and stayed there until after Sukkoth. I was staying with a relative who was one of Lublin's dignitaries when, one night, the Germans conducted a hunt for Jews. They took my relatives, myself and Yoseph Tenzer out of the house, loaded us on trucks and took us to the same infamous camp on Lipowa Street no. 7. The cold was terrible; we felt horrible and were forced to lie face down on the cold floor until morning. A selection took place in camp and people were sent to work in different places in Poland. However thanks to the efforts of various people on the outside, we were released from custody – my relative, myself and Yoseph Tenzer as well. As soon as we were out again, we renewed our efforts to free all our people and our efforts met with success. Upon their release, we walked together in the streets of Lublin to the amazement of its people. I would like to take this chance to mention the extensive role played in the release of our people by an important public activist of the Lublin Jewish community, David Werber, who not only freed those 120 men but convinced the authorities to add two freight cars to the train that was carrying us directly to Wierzbnik. The joy of the release brought us new hope, but sadly none of them escaped from the bitter fate shared by most of the Jews, and they died later under tragic circumstances.

I mentioned these two events to prove that even during those harsh days of persecutions, abductions and attempts to annihilate us, we were occasionally saved by the efforts of our people, which made our dark lives easier to bear. We must take into account that during those days, every Nazi hoodlum was as good as a governor and the Jewish population suffered scorn, ridicule and abuse.

Annihilation draws near

Towards the end of the summer of 1942, a few years before the annihilation, the Nazis built a labor camp called "Yulag", which was supposed to house about 2,500 Jewish workers and was split into two different places: one that was called "Strzelnica" and the other "Majowka". No one knew the purpose of those two camps, but when the Germans started recruiting people to work and registering them, everything became clear.

By that time, we already knew we were headed for things unlike any before. Every person sought to find refuge, either by getting a "safe" place to work at, or a place to hide. Some paid Polish acquaintances to adopt their little children in hope of saving them from extermination, as there was no longer a way to escape and the fear of future events was mounting. During the last

Shabbat before the annihilation, we still managed to gather a Minyan for prayer at the house of Yaakov Rubinstein, including people such as Chanoch Biderman, Yankel Mandelzis, Jechiel Lerman Leibish Rubinstein and myself. We were reading the portion of the week, with an empathic, bitter intonation, when we heard a racket. We learned that all 700 Jews of the nearby town of Wąchock were brought to Wierzbnik. It was a sign that our complete annihilation was drawing near.

The dark days of grueling work, abuse and insults continued, but in our hearts there was still a spark of hope, that we might somehow delay and prevent the complete extermination of the remaining Jewish public. On the night before the annihilation we made many efforts to delay the threat, but we failed because the entire town was already surrounded by murderous squads.

This bloody day, 27.10.1942 was carved into my memory as a dark, bitter day, a day of cruelty and murder. As soon as dawn broke, we heard the screams: "All Jews out!" and humiliated, tortured Jews flowed out, their feet buckling under them and their faces stricken, men, women and children all headed to the place of gathering. A little while later, the entire town square was filled by nearly 5,000 Jews, locals and refugees alike.

The place was surrounded by bloodthirsty brutes, led by Becker who was brandishing a pistol. Dozens of Jews, men and women, were killed on that accursed day, and their names are carved in this Yizkor book. These victims were buried by our townsman, Leibish Herblum. Of those who lived, some were considered capable of working and were ordered to the labor camp in the forest called "Strzelnica". The rest, the majority of our people, were led toward the train station, where they were loaded on the death cars on their way to annihilation.

The march to the labor camp claimed a victim: Yoseph Rosenberg, son-in-law of Shmuel Cohen. When we arrived at the camp, the gates were locked and we were ordered to surrender all personal effects and valuables in our possession, or die. Piles of personal belongings formed quickly and people were left literally naked and barefoot.

Running in a circle

Our lives continued, filled with fear, despair and destitution and bereft of both sustenance and hygiene. A hellish life of suffering that lasted for 19 months, until the end of July 1944. It is hard to describe all the terrors we suffered daily at the hands of the Nazi devil. I wish like to focus my memories and review the daily lives of the Jews in both labor camps – Strzelnica in the forests of Starachowice and infamous Majowka.

One night, in the middle of Christmas Eve, we heard the rattle of a car followed immediately by a hysterical scream: "Everyone out in one minute!" This happened in Strzelnica and we all ran out in a panic, including sick people who suffered from a 40c fever. It was a clear, moonlit night and at the center of camp stood the infamous oppressor Althoff, who ordered us all to run around the camp. After a while he screamed: "One minute and you're all asleep." To him, this was a "Christmas game" spiced with mortal dread and humiliating abuse.

Life continued in this manner, filled with despair and anxiety, hunger and destitution, slavery and harsh physical work all day long. At the end of the work day we lay on ragcovered wooden bunks that lacked humane sanitation, uncertain of what might happen to us on the morrow. These crowded conditions that lacked even the most rudimentary hygiene were naturally a hotbed for various diseases, especially the typhus plague that spread and infected many in the camp who were too exhausted and weak to overcome it.

One day, we received an order to prepare a special "bunker" to quarantine the sick women and children, but it turned out to be merely an excuse. The master butcher Althoff eventually murdered everyone inside the bunker, and ordered the bodies buried in the forest.

A few days later, as the number of sick people rose again, it became necessary to allocate a special cabin for them. Even under those conditions, the survival instinct was so strong that people recovered from the disease and regained their strength without actual medical help. After a while, however, the oppressors Althoff and his assistant Mayer returned. They went into one of the cabins where the sick lay and murdered them all.

The murder at the Bugai

The days of murder and the days of reprieve continued alternately and time moved on. The cold, the sickness and the murders left their marks on all. And then one day, the bloodthirsty Althoff showed up again, accompanied by a gang of Gestapo murderers, and ordered everyone to gather outside. He pulled 120 people out of the ranks and led them in the direction of the Bugai forests, where special pits were dug for them in advance by other Jews, who did not know their purpose. They were all brutally murdered on the spot and tossed into the pits.

This premeditated mass slaughter received the name "Operation Bugai".

Things calmed down a bit before Purim. A small infirmary was set up in camp, a place that provided the sick with whatever minimal aid possible. Sanitation, hygiene and cleanness were all observed more closely. The public breathed more easily for a while, and tensions slackened a bit.

By the time Pesach rolled by, the camp was in a state of relative relief, affording us time to plan our celebration of Pesach and the matzahs. My friend Leibish Herblum and I started organizing things; the people who worked in the factory outside camp managed to sneak in some flour and Leibish, who had experience with baking, built an oven from broken bricks. The women kneaded the dough and used empty bottles as rolling pins. Our resourcefulness allowed us to uphold the commandment of eating matzahs in camp despite the oppressive regime, symbolizing our strong yearning to go from darkness to light, and from enslavement to redemption.

Camp Strzelnica was abandoned immediately after Pesach, and those who remained were transferred to the labor camp Majowka; and so the summer of 1943 began, with a faint hope in our hearts that we will be saved from annihilation. But the Nazi beast refused to let go of its prey and thoroughly planned the destruction of us all. On the very day of the uprising against the enemy in the ghetto of Warsaw, the Nazi hounds showed up in our camp, took away some of the people and led them to Firlej, on the road to Radom, where they murdered them. In this manner they thinned down our ranks from time to time, sowing death and oblivion everywhere.

One night, between the 5th and 6th of June 1944, I was in our cabin (a few weeks before the camp was abandoned) when the murderer in charge of the camp, Schrott, came running in and ordered me to report immediately to the "Werkschutz" guard. This event has remained a mystery for me to this very day. When I arrived at the Werkschutz, I met two Gestapo soldiers who led me out of the camp, put me in a car that waited outside and accompanied me to the forest. All kinds of thoughts were racing through my mind at the time and I was certain of my doom. But after a long drive, we arrived at the prison in Wierzbnik, where they locked me up alone in a cell. I was desperate and helpless and didn't understand the meaning of this incarceration. In the morning, a Polish officer standing guard, who knew me before the war, whispered to me through the keyhole that they were taking me to Radom, which was indeed the case. At 7 in the morning, two armed soldiers came into my cell, handcuffed me to a Polish prisoner and led me from the place. At that very moment, an elegantly dressed Jewish girl came into the prison, holding a small suitcase. She was the sister of Avraham Zukerman (Kosovski). I asked her what she was doing here and she replied that she was at camp Heller**Error! Bookmark not defined.**, where she was told to dress in her finest clothes and take her precious belongings because efforts made abroad allowed her to leave Poland and go to Israel. We walked together toward the train station, accompanied by armed guards, and I helped her carry her suitcase with my one free arm. By the train we were separated, and I never saw her since (unfortunately, we later learned that Mrs. Kosovski, whose only wish was to reach the safety of Israel, was deceived and led instead to the gas chambers in Auschwitz. There, in the vale of tears, she met before her death with my daughter Rivka and told her about her sudden encounter with me at the prison in Wierzbnik).

In Radom I was led to the SS commander and put in a dark prison cell that already held about 40 Polish prisoners. The conditions there were very harsh and a special guard was watching over us. The following morning we were taken out of the cell and put in another room, where a couple of Gestapo interrogators asked me all kinds of questions such as: "How many Jews are still in the camp? What are they doing? Who among them are considering escape?" I told them that I had no idea about any escape attempts, because if someone was planning such a thing he wouldn't tell the others to keep the secret safe. And so I sat with my arms shackled, while they wrote the protocol. When the interrogation was over, they put me back in prison. This cross-interrogation followed by my return to prison repeated itself for three days, from Wednesday to Friday. To this very day I do not understand what their purpose was and how I managed to survive. It must be Providence that saved me to serve as a living testimony of the torment suffered by the community of Wierzbnik and to observe the fall of the bane. My sudden disappearance from the camp made the atmosphere there even gloomier, and particularly shocked my dear wife and the children who remained at the camp. At the end of the interrogation, I was taken from the jail and transferred to the renowned prison on Warsaw Street, where the infamous Nazi serpent Koch waited for me and tortured me in ways that I dare not mention in this book.

I suffered through five weeks of torture until 11.06.1944, when I was moved to camp Gross-Rosen. I was there only for a few days when I heard that they were looking for a civilized person to serve as a clerk. I volunteered and received the position in another camp, Funf Teichen ("five lakes"), which housed a large munitions factory. Memories come and go, and I recall one Yom Kippur Eve that was carved deep into my heart: most of the Jews were sick and weak. We sat and whispered the holiday prayer with broken hearts and called "Min hametzar karati Yah", but our liberation failed to come. I also recall one Hanukkah Eve when I was with the rabbi of Săpânța and the two of us humbly observed the commandment of lighting Hanukkah candles. We became true friends from that night onwards (the rabbi resides today in Bnei Brak in Israel). These things happened mere weeks before our liberation and on 23.01.1945 came the day we hoped and longed for, the day of liberation and salvation.

[Page 267]
Zvi Unger

Mengele's "Promise"

Another indication of our helplessness before the life and death regime implemented by the Nazis in the extermination camps is perhaps the cynicism and whimsicalness with which the various superiors treated the life and deaths of the prisoners. These whims pushed us to oblivion at times, but sometimes also gave us a ray of hope…

I am living example of this fact: while taking my daily walk down the paths of death and despair in camp, I suddenly discovered a spark of light that never would have expected. It was during my first days in camp, before I was dressed in my "royal garb", and I was still wearing my Shabbat suit, the only suit I had left after all my travels, the persecution and the hardships I have been through. One day, while I was walking to work, I was stopped by a Ukrainian camp guard, who bluntly demanded that I take off my suit and give it to him. I begged, saying that I could not walk around naked, but he ignored my pleas and grew even more aggressive and impatient. I realized that he was looking for a quicker, "simpler" solution to this problem, and that he was going to kill me, because under those circumstances my life had less value than the life of a fly, which one commonly squashes to be rid of its buzz…

I had no choice but to take off the suit and continue walking naked to work. But when I arrived I immediately attracted the attention of the German overseer. Surprised, he asked why I came to work dressed in this manner, and I told him what happened to me on the way. The latter immediately ordered to line up all the Ukrainian guards and asked me if I could identify the person who stole my clothes. I was naturally afraid to do such a thing, because the Ukrainian guard or his friends could easily take revenge on me and murder me.

I voiced my fears before the German supervisor, saying that I could identify the man but was afraid of doing so… when he heard my concerns he promised me that nothing would happen to me if I pointed out the man, giving me "his word as a German".

I was already caught in the loop of these events and so I agreed to identify the Ukrainian guard. We walked along the lineup, looking at the faces of the guards. Unfortunately, I was too nervous to remember what he looked like (they all seemed alike to me for some reason) and I found myself helpless. I told the German that I cannot identify the man, but he refused to give up. He ordered the guards to bring their belongings, bags and suitcases and so on, line up in a row and place those belongings before them. He then ordered the bags and suitcases opened and we looked through them. Finally we discovered in one of the suitcases a suit that matched the description I gave to the German when I reported the case. He took the suit and returned it to me, threatening the guards that should something happen to me, they would be held responsible. The threat seemed to impress the guards, because they stopped harassing me.

Another kind of cynical behavior that I remember from those terrible days was associated with the archvillain who once swore to save human life and instead did everything in his power to end it, the infamous Dr. Josef Mengele.

He was in command of the Selections that determined the fates of thousands and tens of thousands – who would live and who would die. The flick of his thumb this way or that was a final, absolute verdict. One day, I was standing with my father in line for selection and Mengele's finger nudged me towards the abyss, while my father was allowed to continue his agonized existence. An innocent boy, I made a daring move; I stepped aside a bit and with a yearning for life in my voice I begged Mengele to let me go with...my father. He did not beat me up for my "insolence" as usual, but smiled cynically instead, while his lips whispered softly: "Don't worry, you will all meet there..."

[Page 268]
Beniek Zukerman

Polish Cooperation in the Extermination of Jews

I am sitting down to write this contribution to the memorial for the martyrs (kehilas koydesh) of the Jewish community of Wierzbnik with mixed feelings of "yirashakoved", great respect, and hatred.

Perhaps it seems paradoxical. How can a person have two such extreme opposite feelings at the same time?

Yet, this really is my state of mind as true as the Five Books of Moses.

For someone who was not in the territory of the Holocaust during the annihilation of our people, it will be difficult to understand such emotional turbulence. This spiritual turmoil is such a flood of associations and memories about the frightening catastrophe that befell our people.

However, driven by an inner impulse to memorialize our nearest and dearest while at the same time to carry out their last wishes of not to forget and not to forgive. I cannot formulate my thoughts other than with Kaddish for their holy memory, and curses against their barbaric murderers.

Thirty years have already passed since that dark day of October 27, 1942 the 16th day of Cheshvan, when the savage Nazis and their bloody collaborators destroyed our hometown. Three decades have passed, almost a third of a century, more than enough time to have an historic perspective and provide an objective assessment of the horrific genocide of our people.

Now, in 1972 it has become obvious and there is no doubt whatsoever that it was not a geographical coincidence that the fiendish Adolph Hitler, may his name be erased, chose the land of Poland for his concentration camps and death factories. Today, in 1972, after witnessing the historical fact that Communist Poland under Wladislaw Gomulka completed the job of exterminating the Jews, which the fascist National Socialists began in the "general government" under the leadership of Hans Frank we need no clearer indication.

Yes! Hitler's experts deliberately chose the accursed Polish earth as the best location for their gas chambers, crematoria, and the production of soap from the bodies of Jewish children.

No! It was not mere coincidence that Auschwitz was in Poland, Treblinka was in Poland, Belzec was in Poland, and also Maidanek, Sobibor, and others as well. The Nazi leadership carefully studied the Polish mentality and came to the conclusion that the majority of Poles would remain indifferent to the extermination of their Jewish neighbours. A greater number would even happily participate in the killing them and only a few would have the will and profound humanitarian desire to save Jewish souls.

Therefore, the opinion of this writer is that while we are publishing this memorial book, a monument to our murdered town, we must not hide from history or from the sad truth about the Wierzbnik Poles, who so willingly cooperated with the German beasts in liquidating the centuries old Jewish community.

Let those criminal Poles, who conspired together with Hitler's wild beasts like sly hyenas and jackals with drooling mouths waiting impatiently for their plunder, be placed on the same pillory as the murderers.

Let this be a hellish enlightenment for those naive and often cynical questioners who cannot grasp why we, "went like sheep to our slaughter."

No, ladies and gentlemen! Jews did not voluntarily go like sheep to their death! They were treacherously dispatched to their deaths by Polish swindlers and "shmalstovnitses". Those Poles, who for two kilos of sugar per head, handed over Jews to the Gestapo. If Jews had only been forced to contend with external German hatred, they would perhaps have had a chance. But to fight on two fronts, against an external occupier on the one hand and an internal enemy on the other, was too difficult to accomplish.

Chief of Police and Loyal Servant of the Gestapo

The name of Wierzbnik's Chief of Police was Chmielevski, a typical Polish name with a "Chmie" in the front and a "ski" at the end. A tall and boorish man with a swollen crotch and belly, he personified the local authority, the keeper of law and order. In truth he was a corrupt degenerate and bribe-taker, who without any hesitation at once put himself at the disposal of the S.D. (security service) and the Gestapo, instructing his underlings to be completely loyal to the builders of the "new Europe".

He did this with deceitful joy over the fact that now, under the wing of the satanic Reich's eagle, he was in full control over the life and death of his Jewish subjects and could do what he wanted with them.

One only had to observe his proud entry into Jewish shops and houses, asking with mock concern, "How are our Jews?" One would then know that this glutton and guzzler with the red face and drunken eyes would cause a great deal of trouble for the Jews.

And so it was! Soon, in January of 1940, he diligently went on his first mission to gather Jewish hostages. Accompanied by his Polish policemen in their dark blue uniforms, he entered Jewish houses and with vicious brutality dragged out twenty men, the crème de la crème of the Jewish population, and threw them into the commissariat.

Among those arrested was my father Shmuel Zukerman, the dentist Dr. Kurto, Dr. Kramazh, Hershel (Shuhat am'sh), Yudel Tchatchke and others.

In the evening after coming home from work and hearing what had happened, I, a 17-year old boy, went to the police station to find out why they were detaining the prisoners and what they would do with them.

Chmielevski received me without standing on ceremony. He sarcastically asked me if I was Zukerman's son, and upon hearing my reply he simply grabbed me by the collar and threw me into the cell with the others and added with a laugh, "The more the merrier."

A few hours later the Gestapo came and Chmielevski handed over his catch, while in the freezing weather they began to load us onto sealed trucks.

We arrived almost frozen at the Radomer Gestapo Criminal where we sobered up with special welcome exercises, and after we were black and blue from the sticks they used on us.

For almost two months we endured gruesome tortures at the hands of black uniformed guards with skull and cross bones on their caps. As though deaf and dumb, they never exchanged a word with us, never said what we were charged with or how long we would be held or what would become of us. But every night in the middle of the night, we were wakened from our sleep and forced to do Gestapo-style gymnastics, leaving every part of our bodies bruised and battered.

Fortunately, when the Radomer Judenrat found out about our isolated "quarantined" existence and of course this was before the infamous Wansee Conference on the final liquidation of the Jews, they immediately contacted the Wierzbnik community leaders. With some pull (proteksia), great pain and effort, and most importantly a heavy amount of ransom money we were released, only to be later recaptured and share the fate of all Jewish victims.

City Student Denounces Me to the S.S.

In the meantime, anti-Jewish antics grew more pronounced and menacing. Extortion of money and belongings became a daily event. The Germans always needed something: boots, manufactured goods, clothing, furs, down blankets, curtains for their lodgings, furniture, pianos, and leather valises in which to send home the plundered goods.

A new symbol appeared, the 9-centimetre band with a blue Star of David, which we had to wear on the right arm to designate ourselves as Jewish "untermenshen" and candidates for all the dirty work in and around town.

Grabbing Jews for work became a new reality. "Jew hunting" became a popular German pastime and indeed also an unlimited source of unpaid labour for the master race.

We walked the streets with our senses heightened, in constant terror, and looking in all directions for somewhere danger was lurking. There was the real danger of being invited for hard labour rewarded by physical insults and beatings.

The Germans knew how to identify a Jew by the Jewish armband he wore or by his beard or an especially Semitic appearance. But I, being a young man with fair hair and an Aryan nose, most of the time managed to avoid the humiliation of being kicked in the behind like a football onto a waiting truck. Until one late summer day, suddenly, as if out of nowhere, I caught sight of an S.S. man not far from Pzshititshki's store on the magisterial side. For a moment, busy with the other people who had been caught for work, he did not notice me. In that moment, I decided to take off my armband and continue walking in his direction as though nothing had happened with a carefree expression on my face, like a real non-Jew.

"Hey you! Are you a Jew?" He stopped me with a fierce roar.

My head instinctively began to move from side to side, which he interpreted as a no and he let me continue. Unfortunately for me, however, at that same moment a young Polish student was walking toward us, who recognized me from my Father's men's clothing shop, or from school and on principle did not tolerate Jewish liars. In a giddy voice he began to shout to the S.S. man as he pointed at me with his finger, "Pan! Jew! Jew!"

The furious Nazi, red with rage, called me back and punched me so hard! First with his fist and then a rod hit me and within seconds most of my teeth were lying on the sidewalk. Blood flowed from my split lips and torn gums to the obvious enjoyment of my informant, who was holding his sides in laughter.

The spectacle was not yet over. With a theatrical gesture of sympathy, the Nazi Scoundrel took an apple out of his pocket, wiped off the dust and politely passed it to me, telling me to chew the fruit with my bloodied gums... an old, inquisitorial practice of giving torture a touch of the grotesque, the comic he was.

My young Polish compatriot, perhaps raised in the Christian spirit of compassion, stood and took true delight in the fact that he had delivered a Jew into the hands of German justice.

I, doubled over in pain, looked at him and thought: My G-d, this is not an ignorant peasant, but an educated urbanite, which like the majority of Poles hated the damned Germans. But when it came to the Jewish question, he was an accomplice in their devilish deeds and prepared with the same cannibalistic cruelty to take an active part in their beastly anti-Jewish excesses, including the taking of lives.

Late at night, while going home from Starakhavitz, where we cleaned outhouses and washed trucks, I read the underground revolutionary slogans on the factory walls: "Poland for the Poles, Palestine for the Arabs, Jews to the scaffold!"

Poles Begin to Inherit Jewish Property

A human being is stronger than iron, yet a Jew is stronger than steel!

Life went on despite the ever-increasing persecutions. Polish commissars and socalled trustees (Treuhandler) were placed in all Jewish businesses and factories. This is how Poles from Posen and Silesia suddenly and painlessly found themselves the virtual owners of Jewish property, which they officially managed.

The Nazis devised this system of piracy as a brilliant strategy to accomplish two objectives in one stroke. First, to create for the Poles an image of the Germans as Robin Hoods who steal from the Jews, but give to the Poles! Secondly, to serve as an explicit and clear message to the Jews that their careers as merchants were definitely over. To reinforce this message, signs were posted all over town stating that all Jews, men, women and children were forbidden to walk in the town under threat of the death penalty.

Survival became a daily struggle even for a piece of bread. Middle-class Jews and former merchants lived by selling their hidden merchandise and risking the confiscation of their last valuables. Ordinary Jews simply gambled with their lives by going to the villages to exchange their personal belongings for something to eat. A new industry sprang up for the poorest. They presented themselves for forced labour in the place of the well-to-do folks, who would pay someone else to do the heavy labour of cleaving rocks, loading coal, and to endure the customary accompanying beatings.

Nevertheless, there was not one case of suicide. Never. Jews stubbornly made every effort to survive the bitter times and used every ounce of Jewish genius to outwit the German barbarians. With Jewish mills requisitioned and flour a forbidden item, Jews invented hand mills out of baskets and secretly ground their own flour at home. In truth, this product was not first class. But we would no longer die of hunger. In the ghetto we did not expect white challah. A fresh piece of black bread was also delicious.

The German rulers could not comprehend Jewish vitality and the mysterious power to adapt to the most inhuman conditions. Despite all the laws and orders, threats of shooting and concentration camps and under the very noses of the Germans, Jews smuggled in animals and slaughtered them. Grain merchants in small numbers, of course, sold sacks half full of corn and wheat. Tailors remade clothes left and right and tinsmiths found new, cheaper ovens, which cooked and heated with sawdust.

Together with oppression came the ability to resist and immunity to problems. Jews even organized their own medical services and with every means at their disposal, tried to save the sick. Soup kitchens were created for several fugitives and those no longer able to sustain themselves.

So, another year of Jewish survival went by challenging the German policy of Jewish annihilation until June 22, 1941, when things took an unfortunate turn for the worse. The outbreak of war with the Soviet Union was a signal for the authorities, once and for all, to solve the damned Jewish problem according to the Fuhrer's (leader's) wishes.

The deportation chapter was accompanied by the outbreak of typhoid fever and typhus. Jewish villagers were brought into the town. Moreover, transports began to arrive from Plotsk and Lodz with Jews who were forcefully shoved into overcrowded Jewish dwellings. The living conditions were truly unbearable. Jews began to sign over property, orchards, houses, gardens and land outside the ghetto in exchange for occasional provisions needed to sustain life. These Christian "friends" gladly accepted the officially transferred property with all kinds of promises, which turned out to be empty. The famous Polish proverb, "The houses are yours, but the streets are ours" was now changed to, "The streets are ours, and the houses are ours also!" The phase of final extermination of the Jews had begun.

Animals of Prey in Human Form

Feverish days came to Wierzbnik. What the Nazis were preparing to do with the Jewish population was clear beyond any doubt. The angel of death could be felt in the air.

Polish railroad workers began to talk about cattle cars, in which Jews were being brought from all over Europe to mass killing places. On walls and billboards appeared caricatures from Geobbel's Folkischer Beobachter and Stretcher's Stiirmer. A poster showed a Jewish butcher in a skullcap with a beard and side locks grinding rats into meat for the Christian population. In another, a Jew with a hooked nose covered in lice from head to toe knowingly spreads the infectious disease. The posters would say things such as, "The Jew is a spider which must be eradicated. The Jewish Communists provoked the war. The Jew is responsible for all the evil which exists."

On the streets one felt that a pogrom was imminent. It would not have taken much for the Poles themselves to send a lynch mob after the Jews. But, the Germans loved order! After the hate propaganda came more moderate bureaucratic requirements for every Jew to wear a yellow armband and each Jewish landlord had to post a list of all his tenants and subtenants, including their birth dates and occupations on the gate of his building. The intent of these orders was obvious to everyone; the Nazis wanted comprehensive statistics for technical purposes in the event of a deportation so that no one would be able to escape.

Disorder and confusion beset many families. Some believed that young people would be taken away immediately and should not be put on the list. Others were convinced that one should avoid, at any cost, listing people over sixty years of age whom the Nazis considered useless bread-eaters.

A mania for building bunkers and hiding places gripped everyone. Under floors, between double walls, in cellars, under roofs and even in doorways, hiding places were built in the most fantastic ways.

Worrying about a place of work became another psychosis, which lasted even after the liquidation of the ghetto.

New occupations arose with hastily acquired qualifications. For example, my sister Chaya-Sara Nisker (now Lentshitsky) became a "fire putter-outer" in the cafeteria of the Starachavitser Hermann Goering Werke. Her task was to watch that the small pieces of coal lying around did not catch fire. Others quickly became experts on wood and went to work in Vanatsia in Helem's sawmill which, provided boards and veneer for the Wehrmacht. Tradesmen, tailors and shoemakers went to the "Consum" to sew uniforms and make boots for the military elite.

In the many departments of the Starachovicher munitions factory, Jewish slave labour was used for producing explosives, ammunition, pressing machines, locks, as well as in the foundry, smithy, and the smelter. The most punitively difficult labour later turned out to be among the columns of people transporting ore to the great oven (gikhta). The worst and most dangerous place among the workers, who were later placed in barracks, was the former rifle range built up with barracks for Jewish workers encircled with barbed wire and watchtowers. That was where the sadistic German blackguard Althof (Obersturm-Wachfuhrer of "Werk-Schutz" in charge of the factory guards) used to walk around and suddenly shoot in all directions as his own personal way of maintaining a suitable work environment. The revolver is a cure for everyone, he would pontificate. It cures laziness and eliminates unwanted elements and above all illnesses. True to his "revolver philosophy" he once came into a ward full of Jews suffering from typhus and shot every one of them to death.

The sound of bullets exploding in Jewish bodies became a frequent occurrence and in the neighbouring but not yet emptied Jewish towns and villages as well. In Ostrovste, the two infamous arch murderers, Peter and Bruno went into a Jewish courtyard on Stodolga Street and arbitrarily shot a large number of Jews. In Tsoysmer (Sandomierz) the gendarme Lesher, may his name be erased, victimized and took Jewish lives.

Everywhere there were punishing angels (malakhey habole) ready to fill the quota of Jewish victims.

Terrible news also arrived from the largest Jewish ghetto in Warsaw, about an Umschlagplatz on Stavki Street. From this spot thousands of Jews were transported every day in locked freight cars.

Once again Polish railroad workers brought gloomy information about the mysterious Treblinka and Auschwitz, where the giant Jewish transports were taken and disappeared as though into the abyss. To lend credence to their news, they described the terrible smell of burning human flesh from huge smoking ovens.

A death decree for all the Jews was approaching with giant steps. Every day was full of new job-like stories about Jewish slaughter. Local Poles began to talk business and urged the Jews to hand over their personal property for safekeeping, volunteering to become the unpaid guards of Jewish labour. Others were more forthcoming and not shy at all about their larcenous eagerness to appropriate Jewish belongings by appealing to the Jew's logic, "You, Moshke! Your officer's boots are no longer of any use to you. Better give them to me! Why should the Kraut take them?"

The highest point of Polish villainy and greed for Jewish property I witnessed was on the day of the "resettlement" (the deportations). Only a great poet like Bialik could properly convey the scene of how our own landlord Spitkovsky of Drildz Street near the pond, broke down the wall between his apartment and ours and like a wild animal, still in our presence, began to grab everything that was left.

As long as I live, I will not forget the 27th of October 1942 at 5 a.m. The outside of the ghetto was surrounded by S.S. Lithuanians and Latvians armed from head to toe and preparing themselves to complete the aktsie. I stood with my Father, Mother (Brindl Yankev Bzizhers-Golombiovski), my sister Chaya-Sara and her 9-year-old son Yankev who was already dressed in several pairs of underwear, layers of suits and dressed in sweaters with backpacks and yet still shivering with fear and trepidation. The "gentleman" who had taken a fortune in key money from us for his rented room and kitchen was selecting with predatory composure the silver spoons and forks as well as linens and tablecloths. Working quickly he pulled out drawers looking for jewellery. He didn't deny himself pieces of furniture, which he dragged with the help of his daughter to the other half of the house!

In the moments of Jewish destruction this was the behaviour of a Pole, a produce dealer, a churchgoer, an upright citizen of the town of Wierzbnik.

But this was not yet the highest level of Polish abomination and plunder.

In another part of town, a much bloodier drama was playing itself out where the thief of Jewish property was a member of the intelligentsia, neatly dressed and an official of the pre-war municipal justice system.

His name was Tomchik, a secret agent by profession and educated man. He had just sent three Jewish children he had hidden in his home aged 5.5, 7.5 and 8.5 into the marketplace where they were shot. Rose Millman (now Heriing), the owner of the bakery, had given this vile "secret agent" everything she had in exchange for his promise to save her children (Manyele, Chaim-Yosele, and Roche-Pesl). The murderer took the money and the gold and sent the children to their deaths.

However, Polish anti-Jewish banditry was not limited to businessmen and the intelligentsia. Yitzhak Rosenwald had hidden himself under an oven in the foundry. A simple worker, an ordinary proletarian that noticed this handed him over to the Ukrainians who gave him a bullet in the head.

In the surrounding forests, Polish soldiers who had organized the A.K. (Armia Krayava) settled their own accounts with captured Jews by cutting off their heads as though with a guillotine, to once and for all to free the Polish fatherland of the "yids."

Soon after the war they [the Poles] reinstated this patriotic heroic tradition of throatcutting when they chopped off the head of Abraham Kadishevitch for the Jewish chutzpah of selling a house. What kind of ideological motive made them savagely murder two women survivors, Wolfovitch and Anisman or to kill three children and throw Rifka and Marmele Silvemian from a moving train remains a secret mystery and a matter for a study into the pathological Polish hatred of the Jewish people.

Let these stories of the deceit of Polish blackmailers, collaborators and hangmen be forever recorded in our memorial book! Let future generations know that during the massive slaughter of the Wierzbnik Jewish community, Poles were murderers and profiteers.

Resistance and Rebellion

[Page 281]
Zvi Faigenbaum

Led Like Lambs to the Slaughter

Much has already been told about the demise of a third of our people, the tortures and agonies they faced and the hell they suffered through on their way to annihilation.

But the scope of this terrible Holocaust often raises the question: How could this great disaster take so many lives and within such a relatively short time? This question begs the equally distressing question: Is it because no resistance was shown? In other words – were we led like lambs to the slaughter?

There are two answers for this question:

The first concerns the circumstances, the processes and the methods used by the Germans during each stage of the extermination; the second is a fact that might not be very evident, but bears a historical significance under those terrible conditions, and that fact is – that there was resistance! The terrible persecution met with resistance!

This phenomenon took various forms in various places:

Organization of groups and individual resistance, rebellions and warfare, daring deeds and glorious heroics could be found practically everywhere, although they seldom left their mark because the Nazi bane has permanently erased any sign of those heroic efforts.

Mr. Zvi Fajgenbaum provides us with a living testimony of the attempts to reject this reality and of the active resistance shown by the people of Wierzbnik, within the town and its area:

The summer of 1942 was already upon us when we started hearing rumors of Jews evicted from their homes and sent to the camps. First we heard about Lublin, and then about Radom. Many considered those to be mere rumors, of unclear and perhaps untrustworthy sources, but I had reason to accept them as unquestionable facts.

For a while, I had covert ties to members of the Polish resistance, who listened regularly to Radio London for updates concerning our situation. But since these broadcasts were meant not only to provide people with information but also to raise their moral, the news concerning the war efforts and the acts of the enemy were sometimes exaggerated. Members of the Polish resistance would therefore come to me often with full lists of the news they have heard listening to those broadcasts, asking for my impressions and interpretation, since they realized that I could provide them with a balanced picture that proved true in retrospect. I provided them with a simple analysis of the situation based on whatever information I received, and extracted the truth from the layers of words. It seemed that they had much faith in my opinion and therefore honoured me with repeated visits, which kept me informed of events around us at all times.

One clear morning I received an underground newsletter from them, detailing the shipments of Jews to the camps, which included whole communities of Jews who were taken to Sobibor and never came back. When I linked this piece of news with the evictions and shipments from the nearby towns and cities, I no longer had any doubts about the terrible, tragic meaning of these shipments. I felt that the end was near and that we could no longer trust blind fate, which held only one thing in store for us – the angel of death that was certain to come for our souls. I knew these were our last moments and that something must be done to prevent the worst from coming true, and done right now!

I consulted with a few likeminded youths and we started making plans to rebel. We decided to act, to resist and to fight, instead of walking like lambs to the slaughter. We considered joining with the partisans, or organizing our own fighting groups. However these considerations made us instantly aware of our gloomy reality and the fact that rebellion would require weapons, which we did not have. Bereft of even the bare necessities, we had to plan our actions carefully, because as soon as we were discovered we would be helpless to resist and doomed for immediate extermination. The second problem we faced was the sacred tradition of our people, succinctly expressed by our elders: "All Jews are responsible for one another". How can a whole group escape into the forest or some other place, putting the rest of the public at risk? We knew that the Germans would take revenge against the entire public. This meant that we had to escape individually.

We were familiar with the ways of our haters-oppressors, and we knew the kind of calamity that would result from any event that could indicate resistance. We therefore put much thought into our plans: escape itself was meaningless unless it had a chance to succeed. And since success could only be achieved by force of arms, we had to get weapons no matter what. But where would we acquire weapons? The Germans were the only ones who had them; therefore, we had to kill a German and take his weapon. And if a German was found murdered, the result would be the mass-slaughter of hundreds of Jews... what would the people say then? Won't they blame us for helping further this bloody deluge?

Another obstacle, of a different kind, was facing us. While talking to different people about our attempt to escape and join the partisans, we formed a kind of silent agreement concerning these matters. All of us except for two, who were terrified of the Germans. We worried that fear might push them to become snitches... one of them even showed clear signs of his wavering loyalty and we needed to "remove" him to be rid of the risk. This kind of action, planning the murder of a fellow Jew, was well and truly beyond us.

Finally we feared our own official representatives, who were made responsible by the Germans for everything that happened among the Jews. Their fear of a brutal reprisal could also make them act against us before we did anything.

There were other reasons that prevented us from organizing any operations, and the idea was delayed by all the obstacles in our path. But we drew one conclusion from all our conversations about taking action, and some resented me for pointing out even that much: that the Jews in every town and city in Poland were destined for a single fate, and anyone who thought that Wierzbnik-Starachowice would be spared by the Germans because the people here are vital for work at the factory was utterly mistaken.

We purposefully explained this reality to the people, in order to make them realize that only action could save them from the certain doom awaiting. But despite everything, it was not time to act yet.

We postponed the actual organization of partisan activity for the time being, but the notion came up time and again, every once in a while.

The bitter day

Unfortunately, our dark predictions all came true: on October 27th 1942, at the break of dawn, screams were heard on the Jewish street: "Raus! Raus!" and the uniformed Germans, accompanied by their local assistants, started driving everyone to the Rinek, which became one of the infamous "Umschlagplatz". The sick, the elderly and others who couldn't leave immediately – were shot on the spot. Nearly 80 men and women were killed this way on that day. 2,000 people survived this pogrom, some of whom already left for work and were staying at the factory. It should be noted that the number of people who went to work was greater than usual, because the Jewish council heard about what was coming and bribed senior officers to order more workers. Families were torn during the eviction, with the men staying behind at the factory while the women and the children were evicted and vice versa. Our family shared this cruel fate; my wife and six of our precious children: Moshe-Baruch, Hanna, Yitzhak Meir, Tzipora, Libe and Sarah were sent to Treblinka, while I remained with two of the girls, one of whom was later taken to a hospital when she came down with typhus and murdered by the Gestapo along with 140 other patients.

How to get a certificate

When I arrived at the camp in Starachowice I realized there were no bounds to this evil. Even our previous situation was better than what I saw now. It was hard to imagine people being kept under such inhumane conditions. The camp was composed of small cabins, and inside them, against the walls, were three-storied bunks with no mattresses, just a little sawdust scattered over them. The camp was surrounded by a barbed-wire fence and watch towers. Upon our arrival, whether by pure coincidence or design, a child came close enough to touch the fence and was shot on the spot. Such horrors and their likes were henceforth the lot of anyone who ended in this camp. I felt that the Germans intended for the inmates to starve slowly to their bitter end, and decided I would refuse to go like a lamb to the slaughter. I was yearning to do "something" and my mind was constantly plotting and scheming.

"A person's mind is full of thought." There were two camps for prisoners in the area, one on the hills and the other in the valley. Using bribes, the people who had work certificates from the factories received permission to leave the camp and join one of the groups headed for work. I had no certificate that would make me a member of one factory or another and so I could not leave the camp. On the third day, I met two people who wanted to leave but dared not go. They turned to me and asked if I was willing to join them. After I agreed, we decided to act. We bribed some of the camp personnel and left at night. At the gate, we were stopped and asked where we were going. We answered that we worked below and they sent armed guards to escort us. On the way we bribed the guards and continued on the hard road to the factory, where we briefly stopped for rest, before turning to the "Zeork" power plant, again using bribes. The situation we found there was different than the situation in the other factories. People were allowed to bring beddings and other belongings from their homes. There was a special area for women and children and it was possible to live here. But to do so, I had to overcome another obstacle. The people here were all known and had their own place, while I had no certificate and was prone for all kinds of unpleasant surprises.

I was lost, but the people who lived there suggested that I hide for a time, while a "contact" who was in touch with the authorities bribed them into entering me in "the book of life", that is, adding me to the happy workers of the place. There was only one problem; my benefactor told me it would cost 2,000 guldens, while I had no money at all. Everything I had was taken from me back at the Umschlagplatz. While we stood there, we were ordered to empty our pockets and give the Germans any valuables we had: money, gold, Jewelry and the like. As usual, the demand was accompanied by the threat that anyone found hiding something would be shot! I gave them everything I had, believing the valuables to be worthless in this hell and regretting not the loss of my possessions but that of my dear ones, whom I will never see again. And here I am, faced once again with the conflict – blood or money!

But not all was lost; I was among my people, and Jews, as you know, are a compassionate people. They started looking for a solution, and at least 20 people, some of them my acquaintances, were willing to donate 100 guldens. They needed time to gather the necessary amount, but I was seeing a light on the horizon.

Organizing a partisan group

As I mentioned earlier, I was constantly thinking about the need to act against the German bane who was determined to destroy our people and was actively carrying out his diabolical plan anywhere he set foot. I thought about it from time to time, whenever I could recover for a while from the constant danger. Now that I was waiting for people to arrange my stay in this place, I had some time to think. I became acquainted with some of the youths in that place, and two of them became my close friends. Our friendship was not coincidental but a purposeful one. One of the two, Shlomo Drajnudel, was a former officer in the Polish military and was also trained in partisan warfare. The other, Leibish Nojman, was leader of the Jewish communists in our town, and was familiar with matters of conspiracy and resistance, while I have already decided to pave the way for partisan activity. We quickly found common ground, and made plans to start our activity. We discussed matters, and based on what we knew about the Polish and Ukrainian partisans, who abused Jews, we decided not to join any other gentile groups but to form an independent group, and we started recruiting people.

This naturally required utmost caution, because every "slip" could lead to death. We were ordered to maintain complete secrecy and walk on tiptoes, so that no unreliable ears would hear of our actions. Nevertheless and despite our efforts our secret leaked and became known to all 84 residents of the camp. Confusion, laced with fear and resentment, spread quickly. People felt safer here than in any other place, and now the guest they considered a good, God-fearing man started inviting trouble and bringing danger... They needed to get rid of me at any cost, and the sooner, the better. They did just that: they hinted to the person who was supposed to try and add me to the list of locals that he should cease from his efforts. A short time later he came to me: "Mr. Hershel, I'm very sorry," he stuttered with embarrassment, "There's nothing I can do... it's impossible..." and after a brief pause he added, "Here are 1,000 guldens, to help you on your way."

Since I knew the reason behind his actions, there was no need for further explanations and I accepted my fate and the need to leave.

Using an alias

Next to the power plant where I tried to "acquire citizenship" was a lumber-mill that also employed about 50-60 Jews under relatively good conditions. Those who were in charge of the Jewish workers were also in touch with them and could be bribed to add people to the list of workers, claiming they were necessary for the factory, which in turn worked for the German war industry. It was only natural that I was drawn to this place. When I came to the fence surrounding the factory I noticed a woman I knew and asked her to help me become a resident of their factory. She took my ID to arrange my inclusion in the list. For the time being, I returned to my hiding place in Zeork, until I could get my "legal certificate". However I only had a single night to dream about a more peaceful existence, because early next morning, the place was surrounded by police cars, Gestapo and armed and frowning SS troopers. As soon as they got out of the cars they started bellowing orders – "Gather everyone!"

I was faced with another quick decision. Soon, they would start checking certificates, and then deciding who shall live and who shall die. I was not registered among the workers, which meant I had to act before it was too late. I "sneaked" away as quickly as I could, and entered a nearby warehouse filled with scraps and thick cables. I hid among this trash, planning to stay there until the storm blows over, and saw parents bringing in their unauthorized children.

But after gathering all the Jews in the courtyard, the Germans started searching the place for people in hiding, and eventually arrived at the warehouse I was hiding in. A German stood with a drawn pistol and screamed: "Raus! Raus!" and the children became frightened and made noises that told the Germans there was someone hiding there. The officer jumped on one of the pylons and when he noticed me, he aimed his pistol directly at me... Fortunately, I didn't panic; I distracted him for a few more seconds while I helped a child cross a hay bale he couldn't climb over on his own, and used the last fateful seconds to escape. The policeman managed to hit me over the head with his nightstick, but I ignored my pain and continued running until I joined the rest of the gathered people. In the process, I burned all my certificates to make it less obvious that I was a stranger.

We anxiously waited there for a long time until finally we were led to a big courtyard and ordered to surrender money, gold, Jewels and other valuables. I had nothing left and the orders didn't apply to me.

Next came the interrogation, carried out by the head of the Gestapo in Starachowice, a man named Becker. He asked the factory manager such questions as: "Under whose authority are all these Jews employed here?" and the latter answered that he knew nothing, because he was merely standing in for the manager of the factory, Mr. Starker, and carrying out his orders. When the Gestapo commander heard that, he ordered the guards to keep us there while he went to clear things up.... We stood there for hours, afraid of the unknown future, until the latter returned in the afternoon with orders from the Radom County Gestapo that said: "Those who are here legally will stay, while those that are here illegally will be shot!" The atmosphere around me became charged, and the people who knew of my presence looked at me in consternation and then reached the conclusion I was a dead man...

This marked the start of a race against the angel of death. Minute by minute, name by name, they read the names off the list, one reading and the other translating. Whenever they would read a name, the person would answer, and everything was done in alphabetical order, because the

Germans insisted on order. People answered when they heard their name called, and went running to the other side of the courtyard. The reading and the migration continued; one rank was growing shorter and the other longer. Another name is called, and suddenly, a pause! There's no answer. Someone's name was called and no one answered... my heart is beating hard and my head is dizzy, I can't miss this opportunity, I gather all my strength and answer a single word, "Here", and immediately cross to the other side of the courtyard. And then I was again among Jews and muttering "Hagomel".

But no crime goes unpunished, and just as it seemed that things were going smoothly, something happened to make me feel uneasy. Among the residents was a boy of 17 named Adler, who broke his leg in a work accident. He was therefore unable to reach the courtyard on time and when he finally arrived, he drew the attention of Gestapo commander Becker, who ordered him killed on the spot because of his disability.

This vile murder depressed us as we stood there in the courtyard until nightfall, when we were each allowed to return to his or her work. As for me, it was clear to everyone, myself included, that I should not remain there, because the fact that I was not on the list put them all at risk. And so I decided to leave as soon as I was registered at the lumbermill.

We heard that Zeork needed workers in other places as well, especially around Skarżysko, where they were putting up power lines and needed 11-20 additional workers. I joined the small group that was headed there, and started working at a new place.

Joining the partisans

As I mentioned earlier, whenever I was out of immediate danger I was faced with that fly buzzing around my brain, demanding that I refuse to accept the situation, rebel, oppose!

During our brief stay at the small camp we had repeated visits from the bloody Starker, who was filled with a sick lust for torture and murder. Whenever he showed up he would ask about a random person: "What does he do, is he a good worker?" and when the work inspector gave a positive answer, he drew out his gun and shot the victim. He was constantly up to such bloody, sadistic tricks.

News came to us that partisan groups in the area included several Jews from the town of Iłża. Since some of the camp dwellers came from that town, they eventually made contact with their townsmen among the partisans. At first I knew nothing about it but when I learned of it I went to one of the Jews and asked "Why didn't you tell me? My heart is set on joining the partisans!" The notion of active fighting and joining those battling the Nazi enemy was always foremost on my mind, like a fire in my veins. "Wait," they told me, "in a few days, representatives of the partisans would come here and then we can introduce you, and see what happens".

From that moment on I could not sleep. I found no rest at night, and waited anxiously for them to come...

One day, or rather, one night, some Poles arrived in wagons and said: "Anyone who wants to join – can come with us." Without hesitation, I told them I wanted to join, and so did some of the others, among them my friend Shlomo Drajnudel. A total of eleven people, most of them young, have left with the Poles.

Disappointment for the Jews

We left in secret, under the cover of night, and marched in a route that offered some cover from hostile eyes, among trees, bushes and copses. Our destination was not far from the town of Szydłowiec and near Skarżysko. After we marched for about 15 kilometers, we arrived at the edge of a nearby forest, but here we faced an inexplicable surprise: we noticed that the Poles' wagon was gone and while we were wondering about this mystery, we were told by the Poles us that they would be leaving us here, and we should go into the forest where we will find everything we need.

These events made me suspect that we were being set up and I started considering the best course of action. It soon became clear that I was not the only one entertaining such doubts, but though we were united in our doubts concerning the situation, we differed in our estimates of our position. The majority argued that if we were determined to join the partisans, we had to follow this through, even if unexpected dangers were involved, while the minority, which I sided with – claimed that we had to go back. Either intuition or cold logic told me that we were being set up.

Convinced that I was right, I claimed that we must not allow the routine to dictate our actions. I stated simply that it takes courage not only to walk forward, but also to pull back.

Others sided with me and our discussion became heated, until finally we decided to split up: seven continued walking toward the forest and four, including me, headed back. I repeated time and again that we must not be fooled and that we should strive to carry out our original plan and establish a partisan group of our own. But my words fell on deaf ears. Those who decided to continue refused to listen to me and even voiced their disappointment of me...

I was hoping that I was wrong, for the sake of those who left, but regrettably, my intuition proved tragically true and sooner than I expected.

The four of us arrived in camp at dawn, exhausted by our nightly adventures, but the people considered us "deserters". One man named Yeshayahu Stern expressed their disappointment and sorrow by saying: "What have you done to us, Wierzbniker butcher? Yesterday we considered you a bold hero, and your actions warmed our hearts and fortified our spirit. We all thought of following you and now you return to us, as people who make lofty speeches and take back what they said when they stumble across the harsh reality..."

I answered them: "Hear me, my friends; this is not a matter of cowardice as you might believe. Going and coming back, each involved a risk. Nevertheless, we were excited about the idea, walked with determination and marched in a row in military fashion. Next to me in line marched my young townsman, Mendel Brodbeker. Our spirits were high. Outside, snowflakes were falling, mixing with the moist earth and clinging to the soles of our shoes. I turned to my neighbor and asked him: Mendel, do you know how to read foot writing?"

"What do you mean?" He answered, surprised.

"Look," I told him, "look at our footsteps, exposing the purity of the earth under the whiteness of the snow. What does it remind you of? It is as though our feet write paragraphs of respect for our tortured, abused people." And indeed, we felt like we were rebelling against the cruel reality, that we are not walking 'like lambs to the slaughter', as the villainous murderers intended.

However our hopes were dashed when we realized the evil scheme of our Polish "associates", who wanted to turn us over to the German foe."

I saw that my explanation was received and added: the lesson we learned from this is that we must not trust others and must only rely on ourselves, if we could assemble a group of Jewish partisans – I'd be first to join!

My words convinced them and the notion met with a willingness to act. We started organizing and managed to acquire two guns, but the German schedule spoiled our plans and took us by surprise.

The next day, when we came back to camp from work, we were suddenly told that we won't be leaving for work anymore because the whole camp will be moved in the morning to the "Judenstat" in Szydłowiec...

The new situation split us into two groups: some said we should go to the forest and join the partisans and the others came to me, to ask my opinion. I told them I was going to Szydłowiec.

Around midnight came wagons that took the belongings of those going to join the partisans. Although I didn't side with their decision, I naturally wished them luck on their way, while I joined those who decided to walk to Szydłowiec.

Most of the partisans were murdered

After many hardships we arrived at the ghetto in Szydłowiec. Three days later arrived one of the 11 who wanted to join the partisans and later split up. He was among those who continued into the forest. The man arrived running for his life, after surviving terrible dangers and narrowly escaping the claws of the angel of death, carrying the tale of that group's fate. According to him, they managed to find the Polish partisans, but the deception was soon revealed. The entire forest was suddenly surrounded by SS and Gestapo, armed and accompanied by bloodhounds. The Poles left the forest, individually or in pairs, and each of them headed home. The Jews, however, had nowhere to turn and had to stay in the forest. The long arm of the Nazi murderers quickly caught up with them and they opened fire on them from state of the art weapons. The Jews only had about 30 rifles, which were by no way a match for the German firepower, and most of them fell in combat.

Other groups of Jews went to the forest, numbering about 150 people in all, and 120 of them were murdered by the Germans when the forest was surrounded while 30 managed somehow to get to the ghetto. While we were making efforts to welcome this group, we suffered another blow. The day after their arrival, the ghetto was surrounded by armed SS troopers who immediately started screaming "Juden Raus! Raus!" we all had to come out and line up in two opposed rows in the big courtyard of the factory, while the Germans aimed their weapons at us.

Line-up

After we lined up as ordered, they pulled a Jewish boy out of a nearby car, and I immediately recognized him as one of those who joined the partisans and never came back.

You may recall that I was among the ones who came back, while this boy was among the other group. He was dragged by two SS troopers who were leading him along the rows as if it were a lineup and telling him to identify. No one was sure what he was supposed to identify and in what context, but based on our common past, I could guess. He faced every man, looked at him, "measured" him and moved on. When he stood before me, he looked at me with glassy eyes and I too pretended I was made of stone. He walked past me with hardly any delay, as though he didn't know me, and I realized that he didn't want to give us away. He therefore moved from one person to the next, until he reached the end of the line with no results. But this fact annoyed the Germans, who started threatening that if he didn't tell them what they wanted to know, they would kill him. Then they ordered everyone to take off their hats and the lineup was started anew. Their threats worked this time, the boy cracked and started pulling people out of the rows – one, two, three. He was coming towards me, stood before me looking, raised his hand towards me and my blood froze in my veins. The seconds tick by and I refuse to panic. Knowing that any movement I make will seal my fate, I remained standing motionless...waiting to see what will happen next. The guy touched my arm and motioned for me to step aside, so the man standing behind me could come out of the line... As soon as the man stepped out of line, the SS asked: "Is your name Langer? When did you become a "bandit"?

When I heard that I was certain they were looking for partisans, because the Germans commonly used the term "bandit" when referring to the partisans. The guy was still young, about 16, the nephew of Jedlinker from Iłża who was among the first Jewish partisans and carried out many heroic deeds during the war against the Nazi enemy. The Germans, who wanted to take revenge against all the people of Iłża, had him pointing out people from Iłża, whom they led to the cemetery and murdered there, in addition to those murdered in the forest. This was the tragic end of the Jewish partisans who left camp Skarżysko and reached Polanka forest.

[Page 288]
Chava Faigenbaum (Shraga)

Hell's Dungeon

The summer was coming to an end, the eldest leaves started falling and a light breeze told of the coming of fall. It was twilight when I put my coat on and headed toward the second street, near our house. Suddenly the gendarmes appeared behind me, accompanied by their local assistants, grabbed my arm and ordered me to come with them. I realized I was being kidnapped to do forced labor, a phenomenon that became common over the past few months. About 20 other girls were abducted that day, and all of us were incarcerated. In the evening they took us out of jail and led us to camp Lavortzia, where they divided us into two groups, one packing ammunition and the other working in the kitchen.

Beaten over a barrel

The camp's staff was composed of Germans, who had the senior positions, and Ukrainian subordinates who nevertheless had complete control over the prisoners, which they exercised with great cruelty. They considered anything to be an excuse to abuse and beat the Jews, and often they did it with no reason at all.

One horror that was carved into my memory during those dark days I will never forget. We were standing in a lineup, an event which repeated itself twice a day, and they dragged a barrel to the center of the courtyard and then dragged out a Jewish resident of our town named Wajman and ordered him to lie on the barrel, while one of the hangmen beat him with all his murderous might. When the beating was over the man fell exhausted and I never learned his fate because we were ordered to disburse.

On 08.12.1942 they abandoned camp Lavortzia and we were taken on foot to the town of Szydłowiec, where the Nazis established a kind of concentration camp for the Jews who remained in various places, mockingly naming the place "Judenstat". Conditions here were no worse than what we faced before, but I was pleasantly surprised to learn that my father and sister are alive, and I met them a short while later.

In a shipment to Auschwitz

After a while we realized that the German talk about a Judenstat was meant to trick the Jews and cover up the preparations for "the final solution", that is, the transportation to the death camps. As usual, the Germans made their preparations in secret and then came one day and took us from Szydłowiec, led us to the train station and crammed everyone into the cars. Although many were still uncertain about the purpose of this transport, we no longer entertained any doubts. But we were wrong about the direction we were going in.

Thanks to his contacts with the underground, my father knew where the transport was headed: to the furnaces of Treblinka – to doom.

My father has already organized a group of people who would jump from the train during a previous transport, and the two of us joined them. After breathtaking, blood curdling adventures we arrived at the Łuków "Judenstat", hoping to find refuge for a while, but four months later we were threatened again with annihilation and had to repeat the dramatic stunt of jumping off a moving train headed to Treblinka (See Zvi Fajgenbaum's article).

Our adventures continued for 21 nights before we finally arrived at the camp in Starachowice, where our first wish was to see my sister, Faiga. Unfortunately, we were gravely disappointed. We learned that on March 5th, Adar B 28th 1943, the villainous murderers took a group of sick people from the camp, my sister among, led them to the nearby Bugai forest and shot them to death.

We "settled in" quickly at the camp in Starachowice and our friends tried their best to help us. We found work at the Hermann Göring Werke factory and even received special treatment, because people considered us the survivors of an inescapable planet.

In the meantime, the front lines approached us rapidly, and the Germans were in constant retreat, under the pressure of the attacking allies. It was the end of 1944, and the Nazi defeat was starting to bud, but we were still in peril, and could die any day.

It was not long before the camp in Starachowice was abandoned. The ground was burning under the feet of the oppressors and they have decided to relocate the camps away from the front lines. It was under these circumstances that we ended up once again on the train to extermination.

A different direction

Since we already had a reputation for jumping, we were ready to do so again. I dressed up as a man, so I could be in the same car as my father. We managed to stay together and as soon as the train started moving, we prepared to jump. Most of the people in the car (which was open) did likewise, but our plans were hampered by the guard nearby. This fact ended up saving us, because the people who managed to jump off this train ended up in the murderous hands of the Polish "partisans" lurking in the area and they savaged those Jews like wild beasts.

This transport contained as many as 300 people from Wierzbnik and Starachowice and the first thing that shocked me to the core was being separated from my father. Men and women were separated in that camp, and the moment I took off my hat they realized I was a girl. After making us stand and wait for a short while, they led us to the "sauna" and then to the quarantine cabins. We spent a whole month in those cabins, without going to work, but the lineups and the hunger weighed heavily on us. One day Dr. Mengele came into our cabin, selected 84 women and told them to come out. We were immediately taken to a hospital called "Royer" and given a blood test. If the test showed that one of the girls had the blood type they were after, and they took blood from her. I was among those whose blood was taken. When it was over, they returned us to the quarantine cabins where we stayed for about two more weeks before we were moved to Block 24. Transports of Jews from Lodz arrived while we were in quarantine and were sent directly to the gas chambers and the incinerators. When we entered block 24, our schedule changed. Up to that point we had to suffer the various hardships and persecutions associated with prison life, the abuse, the cruelty, the constant hunger and the pressure of the stressful living conditions. Now they were compounded by the burden of hard labor, as part of "AuserCommando 212". Every morning we walked about four kilometers from camp and worked at paving a new road. First we had to uproot bushes with our bare hands and next to pull carts full of earth to even the ground. We worked in any weather, in the cold and in the rain, and our meager clothes offered no shelter from the elements. Many have naturally fallen ill that under these conditions, myself among them. For a time I hid my sickness, because any sign of sickness could cost a person his life, but when my fever rose I could hold out no longer and was sent to a kind of hospital called "Royer". Every patient in this place was in great need of heaven's mercy, because this was where the hangmen came on occasion to select victims for extermination. I somehow managed to escape this peril, because the Germans were starting to change their policy concerning the concentration camps in the eastern regions of Germany. The Russian front was drawing closer and the Germans feared that this "treasure" would fall into the hands of the allied forces, exposing their crimes to the whole world. Therefore, they started evacuating the prisoners from the various camps and Auschwitz' turn was soon to come. This allowed me time to recover a little and I was added to the transport that left on foot for the town of Gliwice.

Hell's Dungeon

We did not stay in Gliwice. We were taken to the local train station, loaded into freight cars and taken to a small, unknown station. After a brief stay there we were ordered out of the cars and lined up in fives before starting a grueling two day march without food or water, until finally we arrived at the camp in Ravensbrück. Our sufferings reached new peaks here, because our ability to endure the harsh conditions passed beyond the point of breaking and into doom and nothingness. We arrived in the middle of the night, hungry, tired, spent, and were nevertheless forced to stand for long hours in the cold of night. Thirst burned in our throats to the point of suffocation and our bodies were simmering with an inner fever. We stuck out our tongues and licked snowflakes off each other to slacken the deadly thirst.

Our path so far was not padded with roses, but the horrors we encountered in Ravensbrück made every event that preceded it in the Nazi hell pale by comparison. If Auschwitz was a prison, Ravensbrück was its dungeon, the worst hell on earth. The prisoners were housed in wooden cabins, but the cabins were all full and so we were put in a tent. Two thousand women in a single tent. At the edges of the tent stood four-storied bunks and the place was so crowded that we had to climb each other to reach our place. The women in charge were cruel, brutal Russian prisoners. They swore at the prisoners and beat them whenever they had a chance. Our meals, which consisted of a small amount of soup, were given to us at a late hour and posed a unique risk. The bunks at the edges of the tent lacked not only mattress but sometimes planks as well, and some prisoners would steal planks while a woman left her place to get her food. We therefore had to post guards over our planks. We had no drinking water, and couldn't even bathe. Soon we were dying, slowly but surely. The incinerators burned not far from the tent, and their maws seemed to wait for us, like prey lined up. The daily mortality rate was staggering and we felt that none of us would leave this place. But an event that should have hastened my doom has in fact saved me from the noose. The inhuman conditions afflicted me with dysentery and the disease invoked the compassion of those around me. This fact gave me the courage to overcome my death throes and recover a little. In the meantime, those who could still stand were pulled to their feet for a new death march to camp Malkov. Here, we were put in a big cabin that served as an outdoor theatre in the past, and made to lie on the bare floor. The place was too narrow to contain all of us and women had to lie on top of each other. I was still sick, but there was a Hungarian woman next to me who nursed me and helped me face my terrible suffering. A few women died every day from hunger and diseases. We spent almost three weeks in this place, until we were taken to the town of Leipzig. From there on we traveled away from the approaching front lines, until one night all the guards and policemen disappeared from the camp and in the morning we were liberated.

[Page 291]
Abraham Shiner

The Policeman Shot and Missed

In the year 1939 I was staying at the town of Stanisławów in Eastern Galicja and when the war broke out I was caught in a situation that I could not easily escape. Under those circumstances I witnessed the first stages of the persecutions, the oppression and the murder of the Jewish population (in Stanisławów itself and the neighboring towns) both by the German soldiers and the local farmers – the anti-Semitic Ukrainians.

The attacks and pogroms were already extensive at the time and I was determined to escape at any cost. After many efforts and much hardship I managed to escape Galicja and reach my home town Wierzbnik. Although the atmosphere and the lifestyle I found there differed completely from the place I escaped, I was certain that this scourge will reach us sooner or later, because I already realized that the murders and abuse of Jews were not random and spontaneous acts but a measured policy dictated from the higher ranks down, and it will not skip any place where Jews live.

In time, I received a letter from an acquaintance in Stanisławów, who wrote to me in code because she feared unfriendly eyes. The most important sentence in the aforementioned letter was phrased thusly: There was a very big wedding, everyone went and didn't come back."

The meaning of this sentence was immediately clear to me in light of everything that I have seen while I was staying in Galicja, and I became anxious and worried about things to come. I was forced to go into hiding to keep my presence a secret from the German authorities, because they killed anyone who came from the eastern regions without their official permission.

After two months my father rest his soul got me an ID certificate and I started working at the lumber-mill. Nevertheless I was did not feel at ease, because I could foresee the next stages of the tragedy approaching and knew that this was my chance to do something, to organize and initiate action that may save us from the doom about to befall us.

I had some gentile acquaintances that were in touch with the partisans, and from them I first heard about Treblinka and its horrors. I found it easy to believe the terrible tales about the things taking place in that camp because I have already seen mass murders carried out by the Germans and their profane supporters. Therefore I tried to have words with some people at work, to share the news about the bloody plots of the Germans and find a solution, a way to get weapons, to fight and resist the Nazi murderers and their villainous supporters.

But to my great dismay, the people did not realize the danger and its tragic, menacing extent. Their replies were empty, mocking, often indecisive, and some were even amazed and resentful, asking "are you crazy?"

I mentioned the subject to them again and again, describing the news and the facts known to me, but the people showed remarkable disbelief and my efforts were in vain.

Eventually I gave up on them and stopped bringing the subject up before others.

An axe under the bed

Although faced with the indifference and incomprehension of the others to the extent that I despaired from acting in that direction, I refused to accept this fate and be led like a lamb to the slaughter. A while later, something happened in our family. The Nazis have abused my sister, and the fact sealed my opinion of them. When I had nothing else to do, I made an axe my constant companion, intent of using it in time of need to give myself a chance. I carried it hidden under my coat to work as well. Only when I went to bed I removed it from under my clothes and put it under the bed instead. I knew in advance that my axe is unlikely to make a major difference, being the act of single person, but I was determined not to accept the situation.

The rest of my family knew about the matter but they did nothing to stop me because they knew my stand on the subject. In time I bore witness to the murder of helpless Jews by German soldiers, but I could never understand or accept the fact that the people did refused to resist or rebel against their criminal acts.

To the home of Kocharzow

The persecution and abuse grew from day to day, and reached their peek during the first eviction of Wierzbnik's Jews to Treblinka. Nearly two weeks after the eviction I learned that my father is at the Strzelnica labor camp and that people there are starving. My situation was better and I wanted to give him some food and money. At night I snuck out of the lumber-mill where I worked and went into the streets of the ghetto. The night was very cold and I considered entering one of the houses and taking some blankets from it. I headed to an area I was familiar with, near our home, but when I entered the apartment I was so anxious that I could not touch anything. The place still felt "warm", that is, as though the residents just left, and I could not make myself take anything and left empty handed.

My next concern was getting something to eat that I could give to a Jewish policeman who would pass it to my father, but as I was wandering the streets I noticed German gendarmes and quickly hid in the post office building so they will not find me. When the danger passed I headed to the home of a Polish policeman named Kocharzow, an old acquaintance of ours, who was keeping certain items hidden for us. I reached his house and knocked on the window. It wasn't long before the lady of the house came out in a hurry and told me that I cannot come inside because she has guests. She motioned for me to wait and then came back out with half of a big loaf of bread, and armed with these provisions I turned around and headed back towards the lumber mill. On the way I stopped at the Jewish police building to give the bread to a policeman that would take it to my father, but I couldn't find the man and turned back to "my" camp.

During both legs of my trip I ran into no obstacles except for the momentary appearance of the gendarmes. But when I got back to camp, I was stopped at the gate by a policeman who demanded identification. I gave him my certificate and he examined it thoroughly then asked "You are a Jew?" when I answered that I was, he continued asking "So what are you doing here?" meaning "since you know you're not supposed to be here at this hour."

Turn around

I told him the truth, that I left to get some food for my starving father and here is the loaf of bread that I got from my friends. I was hoping that he would show understanding and leave me be, but I was gravely disappointed. He was not only unsympathetic, but clearly prepared himself for some important event. Another clue to this lay in the fact that before my arrival he already stopped a Pole who worked at the lumber mill and was checking papers, but when he decided to "take me in" he muttered at the Pole that he may go, gave him back his ID and indicated that he can leave.

My sixth sense was already telling me that I am headed into trouble, but I did not realize just how bad my situation was until the latter unsheathed his claws, hissing ominous words between his filthy teeth: "You're not getting out of this alive!"

When I realized who I was dealing with, I understood that any word I say would only make things worse and so I didn't respond. He ordered me to turn around and I immediately guessed his intent. He was armed with a rifle and wanted to shoot me in the back so he could make up an alibi and claim that I fled and he was forced to shoot me...

I naturally refused to do so but he ordered and pressed me to turn around! I continued to defy him, thinking "Does he really intend to murder me in cold blood? I did nothing to anger him, did nothing to him. Perhaps," it occurred to me "he wants money?" And since I had nothing to lose I told him, "Look, if you let me go I'll pay you." Sadly, his reaction was even worse than before. "I'll kill you in a second," he muttered furiously, and to make good on his threat he unslung the rifle from his shoulder. The name of this policeman was Wolczek, and he was a handsome but infamous youth. He searched for hiding Jews murdered many of them with sadistic glee. One of those cold blooded murders could shock anyone but the heatless: he arranged Rosa Milman's children in a row so he could kill all three with a single bullet...

Now, as I recalled that monstrous crime and saw him unsling the rifle from his shoulder I had no doubt what his vile mind had in store for me. I was thinking desperately of ways to escape him. In truth, I could take him in a fight. I was young and strong enough to fight him evenly. But I knew that my victory would be paid for by dozens of Jews, perhaps even all the Jews in camp. Therefore, I had to abandon any thought of an active, violent escape and save myself by fleeing him.

I dove into the river

I started coaxing him again, this time without real intent. I wanted to distract him and use the chance to escape. When he trained his rifle on me I decided to position myself in a way that would keep me unharmed if he suddenly decided to pull the trigger... I repeated my earlier offer of money and appealed to his conscience: "Look," I told him, "I'm a Jew and you're a Pole, and the Germans are our common enemies!" for a moment I thought I managed to sway his stony heart, but I was sorely mistaken. He didn't even let me finish speaking and before he started screaming "Turn around! Turn around!" and landed a serious blow to my face. I felt my face covered with blood and after recovering my senses I realized that any delay would only make things worse and started running as fast as I could. A shot was fired immediately, but he missed me. This encouraged me and I kept on running without slowing down. I ran like mad, because I realized that my life depended on it. As I ran on I grew hot and felt the weight of every pin, so I first threw off my coat and then the bread, although getting it landed me in trouble in the first place. Since I heard no more gunshots I suspected that he was chasing me, and when I turned my head back I saw that he was indeed on my heels. The race was already sealed. He was healthy and strong and well fed, while we Jews lived on bread of affliction. It was no surprise that the distance between us grew shorter by the minute. I was already preparing for the worst, but suddenly a thought occurred to me that could stave off the immediate danger. I was running next to a ditch and it occurred to me to enter the water. I went down into the ditch while the policeman stopped, because he was too lazy to climb into the ditch, and started shooting at me. The river water served me as cover and the bullet did not hit me. After that I would occasionally bring my head out for air and then dive back in, but the "game" could not last long because I was running out of strength. I therefore got out of the water, climbed the other bank, and fell exhausted. Seeing my condition, the policeman decided that there was no need for him to cross the river and get me, because lying on the ground I was an easy target for his bullet, a sitting duck. He acted on these thoughts, raising the rifle and leisurely taking aim, moving the barrel this way and that occasionally. But the distance seemed too much for him. A shot rang out, but it hit a little ways from me. He wasn't satisfied with the result, adjusted his aim and fired again. He missed again, but this time in the other direction. The villain refused to give up and aimed his rifle at me for the third time. Several minutes passed and I managed to recover some of my strength. I told myself that if I would be lucky once again and he would miss me, I will make an effort to get away. I will try to fight for my life again. Two or three more minutes passed and another shot was heard. He missed!

Breaking contact

As soon as the shot was fired I bolted up and started running as fast as I could towards the camp. The distance was not great, but I deliberately took a winding path to make it harder for the fiend to chase me if he decided to persist. During my renewed flight I crossed the Kamienna River and managed to break contact from the enemy, until I reached a spot near the camp. I could hear the name Kocharzow shouted from afar, the name of the policeman whose wife gave me the bread. I did not know what the shouting was about and I was running out of strength again and had to lie on the ground and rest for a while. A few minutes later I started crawling back into camp, but then I started second guessing myself: it occurred to me that after everything that just happened, they are bound to look for me here and so I must stay away from it for the time being. Therefore, I started edging away until I left the camp. I was facing many hardships, because I could not go out in the open. I waited for things to settle down. I will never know if they did, but I grew weary of being a hunted vagabond with no roof over my head, food or water, so I took a risk and returned to camp.

[Page 294]
Pinchas Hochmitz

A Hole in the Floor of the Railway Car

Two days before the final eviction we could feel plenty of tension in the air and the Jewish police commander, Wilczek, shouted suddenly: "Guys, why did you leave the tools outside the camp, bring them in!" He meant that if we were all doomed for eviction or extermination, one way or another, then the tools can serve us as weapons in the absence of alternatives. Hearing the harsh words of the police commander, the people left quickly to bring the tools and placed them in the camp, next to the cabins.

The people stayed up all night. No one could sleep because we felt that something was about to happen. That night they brought in the Jewish workers from the lumber mill and later we had an outbreak followed by an escape attempt.

The next morning there was a lineup, and officer Herblum (who was shot and wounded during the escape, then captured and brought back) was accused of organizing the escape, sentenced to death and shot on the spot.

During the lineup, the wardens made it clear that this was the last case. I noticed some people holding whispered conversation by the fence, near the food store, and assumed they were planning an escape. I was instinctively drawn to the idea, grabbed the arm of my uncle, Shlomo Weisbloom, and told him my intentions. He objected to this line of action because he was afraid that the Germans would take revenge on his sister, Esther Weisbloom, who we would have to leave behind because we couldn't find her at the time. I therefore agreed with him and accepted the situation.

My suspicions were realized. The group by the fence broke through it and a massive escape started in broad daylight. Many managed to reach the forest that offered temporary safety, but others were shot by the Germans and never made it. Many have fallen, among them Steinbaum and his sons, Moshe and Laibke, officer Kornwaser, who threw his police cap away and jumped over the fence, and others. When the Germans realized what was going on they disbursed the lineup and ordered us into the cabins, where we could hear the echoes of gunfire for a long time.

The Germans also took precautions against a second escape, and ordered us to take off our shoes, piling them next to the cabins. When the situation calmed down, every person went and took back his shoes.

The train arrived in the evening, coming to a stop by the gates of the camp, and we were ordered into the cars. Only a few cars were loaded when the surprising order to unload us came. We were still wondering about the meaning of this when we received new orders, to get back into the cars, while the camp was being surrounded by Ukrainian policemen and cavalry.

This time the train headed in an unknown direction while we, about 120 people in every car, stood pressed against each other. The lack of air in the cars made everyone try to stand as close as possible to the little ports. We prepared for this event in advance and sneaked some tools into the car, which allowed us to break out of the train. I carried a fireman's axe, another had a wood drill and so on. We were ready for this moment and as soon as the train started moving, we started realizing our own plans, first ripping a toilet hole in the floor of the car.

Many hoped that we would be lucky enough to be attacked along the way by partisans, or a by one of the Russian army units that were fighting not far from there, allowing us to make an even more daring use of the hole and escape. And indeed, that night, when the train passed by the forests of Œwiętokrzyż, we heard constant gunfire that inspired us and gave us the hope that salvation was near, but our hopes were in vain. We later found out that the source of the gunfire was completely different. People in other cars tried to escape through the portholes, but were shot by the armed German guards who escorted the train. We thought there might have been partisans shooting at the train as well, but we never found out the truth.

The next morning we arrived in Częstochowa, where a train worker told us that our train was headed for Auschwitz.

[Page 295]
Zvi Faigenbaum

We Jumped from the Railway Car of Death

After about 100 people were crammed into every car, and there was no room left, the train started moving. We were all standing, crowded and stuffed, with no air to breathe. We left the train station in Szydłowiec at 4 in the afternoon and an hour and a half later we arrived in Radom. Ten more cars were added to our train there, meaning 1,000 more Jews. We had no doubts concerning the direction we were headed, we already knew that all transports arrive in Treblinka and the end of that line means extermination. Therefore we thought about doing something, acting immediately to save our lives at the last moment from this terrible fate waiting for us. I personally felt that however things turned out, we must not walk willingly into the blazing furnaces!

Having read the publications of the resistance for a long time, I knew what was going on and had no illusions concerning the intentions of the Germans. As soon as we entered the cars, I started planning how we might save ourselves by escaping. Although it was not easy, I have taken the first steps of preparing for the fateful operation during the first stage of my planning. As soon as we shared our plan with others, it became clear that some of them disagreed with it. Some were afraid that the Germans would count the passengers later, and would pour their wrath on those who remained behind, who would be murdered by these predators that never missed a chance to kill or destroy. I managed to calm them down after a tiresome argument, and even acquired some accomplices.

First, the candidates approached the window, which was nothing more than a small porthole, and mentally prepared themselves for the operation. Then we considered the physical aspects of breaking out.

Overcoming his hesitations and the sense of looming danger, the first person pushed through the porthole and immediately jumped from the train. He was followed by two others who jumped one after another, while the fourth suffered from a panic attack after he already managed to squeeze past the porthole, and refused to jump. We had no choice but to pull him back inside, difficult as it was.

But that was not the end of it. My turn was next, but when I was about to climb to the porthole he blocked my way and said that he regrets his decision and wants to try again. We saw the man was insecure and showed compassion. He climbed to the porthole again, crossed it and this time he gathered his courage and jumped! Unfortunately, he was so nervous that he got entangled, failed and fell on the ground...

This event discouraged us, and being the next in line to jump, I was not only discouraged but also frightened.

In the meantime, the train was fast approaching the town of Dęblin. The information we had led us to assume that this place was crawling with Germans and I told myself it was a bad time to jump, because we might fall right into the hands of the murderers. "It is best," I told my daughter who was standing next to me the whole time, "for us to travel a while longer and then jump." As I spoke, I noticed that we were crossing an area lit by great lamps, indicating a major settlement. The light shining through the tiny porthole was dim and brief, but it was enough to tell us that we were passing by a station, although its name and size remained a mystery since we had no idea where we were. The circumstances left us puzzled and doubtful, compounded by tension, fear and anxiety to the point where I thought that we already missed... the train, meaning that we were so close to the camp that there was no longer a chance for escape.

Nevertheless I was guided by the notion that we had nothing to lose and that this was my final chance – I shall escape no matter what! I followed that thought through, telling my daughter: "This is the moment, follow me!"

I bid farewell to the people nearby, asked them to lift me to the porthole and carefully flung my feet outside the car then flung my whole body after them, pulled myself out and clung to the wall.

These events took place in wintertime, and the surrounding area was covered with thick white snow. This fact greatly encouraged me and after standing pressed against the wall of the car for a few seconds I jumped, as if unto a mattress...

The pastimes of my youth availed me, because I learned how to jump when I was eight years old. A train used to cross the part of town where I lived, and whenever it would stop to pick up passengers, the children had a chance to play at jumping on and off the train. We became skilled jumpers by practicing under different circumstances, mostly while the train was already in motion, reaching rather high levels of expertise. At the time I never imagined that such expertise could ever be useful or play a part in saving our lives.

Met halfway

My daughter jumped right after me, but we couldn't find each other because the train was moving quickly and we were separated by a considerable distance. Before she jumped, we agreed that I would walk in the direction the train was headed and she would walk in the opposite direction so we would eventually meet.

I was eager now to meet my daughter. I started running ahead without looking in any other direction. Every moment seemed like an eternity to me. I ran as fast as I could, as if driven, until I noticed her approaching figure. After five minutes of running we met.

There was no time to lose and we immediately started putting some distance between us and the railroad tracks, because it was dangerous to stay there. We walked blindly, wading through the deep snow while the frost seeped into our bones. We were worried that we might fall into a hole or even a lake, because the whole area was covered by deep snow and there was no telling what might be lurking under it in the open field. Eventually we arrived at a barn, stopped and waited next to it.

After a while, a second train has arrived, pulled over on the tracks in front of us and bathed the nearby area with searchlights. Three SS troopers came out of one of the cars, singing loudly, and when they came in our direction we moved to the other side of the barn so we wouldn't get noticed. We stood all night long in the frost, until dawn broke.

Knocking on the door

In the morning, we approached the outermost house in the village and knocked on the door. When they answered: "Who's there?" I said that I was there with my daughter and asked them to take pity on her and give us some hot water. The Polish owner must have realized who he was dealing with and refused, saying that he is afraid because there were still guards by the tracks and they will capture all of us. His refusal to help and his fear convinced me that we had nothing to lose, and so I asked: "Could you at least tell us where we are and where we might go?"

"You are near Łuków", answered the voice on the other side of the wall, and continued: "Across from us there is a village, go and you will find shelter there."

We took his advice and started walking toward the nearby village. When we arrived there an hour later, we approached the first house and entered it without asking, merely greeting the owner when she welcomed us with a frightened scream: "What are you doing here?!"

We showed her the items and money we had and she mellowed. We sat down and asked for something warm. Money seemed to be the answer for all our problems, because a few moments later the woman set some bread and coffee on the table. Her husband arrived as soon as we finished eating and before he could say a word the woman explained the situation to him, hinting that we had money... his behavior indicated that he took the hint, because he never questioned our presence in his house. The situation was self-explanatory and we could get down to business. We needed clothes and they craved the money we had, so we bought some things from them, including an old fourpointed Polish army hat they found somewhere, a great find that could prevent my immediate identification as a Jew. I bought a peasant scarf for my daughter as well, to replace her silk scarf that was very typical of traditional Jewish garb.

After we disguised ourselves with these clothes that afforded us a Christian appearance, we asked the Poles about the nearest ghetto and started walking in the direction they showed us.

The road was long and arduous, steeped with natural obstacles and unforeseeable hardships. Eventually we overcame it all and arrived at the Łuków ghetto. For a time we were safe, but only "for a time"...

[Page 297]
Jerachmiel Singer

Aba Kumetz Dared to Swear

After long hours of anxiety, selection and the horrors of the Rinek, where families were torn apart – some for the camps and some back to work at the factories – our group arrived at the Strzelnica camp, where we were led into a broad ditch, while the German and Ukrainian soldiers stood over us rifles aimed and ready.

We stood there for a long time, depressed and worried for the loved ones that were recently separated from us and for our own fate, which also hung in the balance. And as we stood there and waited for the next decree, some of the SS troopers guarding us came down and ordered us to give them any valuables we had, including money.

This order horrified us for two reasons: first of all, we already learned that the looting and pillaging were generally accompanied by additional calamities and served as warning of oncoming brutalities such as eviction, killing, murder and so on. Secondly, this order followed previous acts of robbery and we were already "fleeced" on several occasions, so that most of us had nothing left – only a few managed to save a little as a last refuge. I myself was bereft of any valuables.

It is no wonder then that the order caused panic in our ranks and a deep silence spread across that vale of tears, broken by the sound of cocking guns. Suddenly, a terrible roar tore the air, shaking hearts and stunning all the people in the ditch, as well as the armed guards standing over us.

The voice carried unnatural anxiety and came from the throat of one of our townsmen, who had the courage to start swearing at the Germans, their leaders and their unholy land that committed this bloodbath. His fury made his last words an incoherent babble but the things he said were enough to shock us all.

For a moment, no one reacted, because the scene was too surreal. But the Germans quickly recovered from their shock and turned crimson with fury. We expected them to react at any moment, because we could see murder in their eyes and when they aimed their weapons at the man swearing, the people standing next to him instinctively drew away. And then came the shots from Althoff's gun, ending the loud protest and the life of the brave man, Aba Kumetz, the son of Moshe Kumetz.

Active Resistance

During the time of the Nazi conquest, individuals and groups among the people of Wierzbnik have taken part in the active resistance against the cruel enemy, joining whatever armies and fighting organizations that would take them in, for many have refused to do so.

Many of these attempts have met with failure and some even resulted in casualties.

The Jews of Wierzbnik joined the partisan units based in the nearby forests, as well as the ranks of the Soviet and Polish armies and fought alongside them against the common enemy.

We have room only for a few of their stories, each the tale of an active warrior in one of the three branches of resistance mentioned above, whose actions and sacrifices represent those of many other Jews from Wierzbnik-Starachowice, their comrades-in-arms who risked their lives and fought for their oppressed people.

[Page 301]
David Sali

In the Woods of Wierzbnik (With the Partisans)

After many wanderings, I arrived together with my younger brother in Mansera to work there. My sister reached this place some time before. I did all kinds of manual odd jobs there.

On the 24th of June 1944, the Gestapo arrived and encircled the Camp on three sides with the "Gmina" flowing on the other flank. Their purpose was to supervise the transfer to the bigger Camp in Starachowice, and from there to the railway sidings with the ultimate destination, Auschwitz.

The Germans came in the afternoon, whilst I was working with the second shift. When we heard of their arrival, their intentions were clear to us and it didn't take much time for us to decide on the spot, to try and flee to the woods.

The windows of one side of the factory, where we worked, looked over the river. We broke the windowpanes and jumped into the river. The noise of the break and excitement of a few groups of people aroused the Germans, who started firing at us with rifles and machineguns. We crossed the river at all possible speed and in this attempt many of us were hit by the German's bullets.

All this happened so quickly that I did not even have the time to say goodbye to my sister.

Having crossed the river, we ran to the woods and divided up into smaller groups and individuals as not to present an easy mark for our pursuers.

On our way we had to cross the busy urban road leading to Ostrowiec and Skavzysko. We passed this highway without any mishaps and finally arrived in the adjoining forest.

Everyone ran his own way and when I arrived in the forest I found myself alone. After half an hour or so I met two friends from our town, Meir Sternkrantz and Moshe Pinchevsky, who had also fled at the same opportunity. Meanwhile, the sun had set and a deep darkness cam over the forest. We were still wet from the river crossing and we suffered from the cold. Because of the darkness amidst strange surroundings, we stopped marching and "encamped" on the spot. The whole night we spent beneath the trees and talked about the happenings of the past and especially about what was awaiting us and how to go on. Needless to say, we didn't sleep a wink the whole night but we had made our first decision. We were to make our way further into the depth of the forest because we were too near its outer edge and all the dangers that ensued.

We continued another few miles and stopped at a densely wooded spot, which provided better cover against any unwanted peeping eyes.

At this time we were still under the deep impression and excitement of the recent events and didn't miss not having food. After two days of not tasting any food and taking into consideration the physical effort of our forced marching, hunger began to harry us more and more. We came to the conclusion that we had to provide ourselves with this important item, food, were we to continue this way. Whilst this was on our minds, we noticed through the trees the peasants carrying vegetables and milk products (cheese, butter, etc.) were on their way to town. We decided to approach them and ask for some food. To our pleasant surprise, they gave us some, although not from goodwill but from fear, taking us as Partisans.

These same peasants, returning from the market, told the Partisans who were quartered in their village of their meeting with Jewish Partisans who had so-called robbed them on the way. The Partisans, who had apparently taken upon themselves the "protection" of the peasants, were angered and began looking for us.

Having stilled our hunger, we were once more on the march deeper into the forest. On the way we met a small group of Jews, who had fled from our Camp and from other places. Altogether we numbered already 48 men.

Since our ranks grew, our self-confidence increased somewhat and we fixed our encampment in a certain spot in the forest. Without any tools or material at our disposal, we obviously were unable to put up tents or any other structures for that matter. We simply encamped on the spot as we were whilst patrols were sent out in different directions to discover any Partisans.

Within our enlarged group, discussions started as to our immediate goal but soon it became clear that we could not rely on ourselves since we were not self-sufficient. Our only possibility was to join on of the Partisan's units, which was not unfriendly to us. This will explain the reconnoitering parties and probing towards the end.

Encounters with Polish Partisans

At night some men were sent to an adjoining village, Ratkowice, to get some food. I was chosen together with my friend Pinchevsky, to be the leaders of these expeditions to the village. One of these excursions I remember especially well. At dusk we both set out and carefully made our way to the house of the village chief who lived with a Jewish woman as his wife. Without the villagers knowing her real identity and with her help, we gathered the necessary food products. The village chief realized that we were Jewish but chose to ignore this because he himself was living with a Jewish woman.

One day, armed members of the A.K. encircled our group, and warned us not to go near the village anymore and not to demand food from the villagers. They threatened that they would kill us if we did not comply.

We asked them, "Where will we get our food supplies to stay alive? After all, we want to join the Partisans."

David Sali, at the extreme right, among the officers in the ranks of the Polish army

Their response was, "Do come and join us." Most of us declined this invitation, because we were wary of the A.K. people and questioned their real intentions and did not feel at ease with them. In spite of the majority's decisions, six men joined the A.K. and went with them.

Four days later we found their bodies, all six of them murdered in cold blood, not far from the village.

Shortly after this episode, another group of Polish Partisans, who were associated with the P.P.S party, wearing the party's initials on their armbands, stopped nearby.

We went out to meet them and expressed out wish to join their ranks. Their reaction was to order us to undress, it was futile to resist since they were armed and we had no weapons. Then they searched our clothes and took all the money they found. After the search and robbery they simply marched off, explaining that they were only a pioneer company and that the bulk of the unit with the commanders would shortly appear and that we should apply to them.

Yaakov Shnir (Shiner) with his comrades, the officers of his unit

In fact, the next day the whole Partisans unit appeared. Again, we repeated our request before the commanders. They listened patiently and heard the story of the robbery that was perpetrated by their men the day before. They took full particulars from each of us what was stolen, promised to look into the matter and to return us the stolen money.

Yet, they rejected our pleas to join them and had the stupid and bad-hearted excuse of asking us, "Why didn't you flee the Germans a few years earlier?" Then off they went...

Amongst the commanders we recognized a few who were from our town. One of them I knew personally well since he was imprisoned before the war, as a Communist together with my cousin. I used this "kinship" to urge him to use his influence at least to see to it that the stolen money be returned to us.

Our money was returned to us in full a few days later. Looking back, I cannot help but draw the conclusion that in spite of their correctness about the return of the stolen money, their refusal to admit us to their ranks stemmed out of deep-rooted "principles" by being Anti-Semites, they did not want any Jews amongst them.

Shortly afterwards we met another big Partisan unit and once more we tried our luck. After some negotiations, one of the officers-in-charge announced that in principle they agreed to accept us, on condition that we proved ourselves in deed as well as in words. "Procure yourselves arms and we will accept you as a group within our ranks."

He advised us how and where to put our hands on German weapons, upon which we decided to take up the challenge for lack of another choice.

The unit was stationed in the forest some distance away from us. After they had left us, we drew up plans and decided upon a course of action as told hereafter.

The Acquisition of Arms

According to the information we had, the Germans used to come down to a village once a week in order to collect tax, which they gathered in food, meat, chickens, etc. Usually five men arrived with a cart, and our plan was to overcome the German who was left in charge of the cart, steal his rifle and then to deal with the rest.

At noon, the following day, five men Pinchevsky, Mats the cobbler, may his blood be revenged, another two men whose names I don't remember and myself marched down to the village. Nearing the place we watched and waited the German's arrival. From afar we saw four soldiers going to the first farmhouse, it was them that we ran unseen to the remaining guard and tackled him from behind. He was taken completely by surprise, which left him aghast, and he didn't utter one word. Two of us remained to guard him, whilst the rest ran up to the house.

Newly armed with the German's rifle, one of us took up position near the window and the other two entered the house. The one outside the window ordered the Germans to put up their hands, which they did without resistance and our men collected their weapons.

With our precious charge, a revolver and four rifles, we made off at all speed to the forest. We returned to our group, whose joy knew no bounds, and we were feted like heroes.

After the excitement had subsided we decided to send a delegated and present our newly acquired arms to the headquarters of the Partisans.

They were impressed by our achievement and the commander announced his decision on the spot that he was ready to receive our group within their ranks. On hearing those words, we hurried off to the rest of our group to announce to them the good tidings. Next morning, we moved to a new encampment nest to the Partisans.

Our group consisted, at the time, of 37 men and 3 girls, one of them I remember was Tamara Weisblum, and may her blood be revenged.

The swearing-in ceremony was held at a general parade and the commander stressed in his welcoming address the ultimate command not to leave any arms on the battlefield. "Rather return without your head than without your weapon..."

All of us were equipped with arms; some of us got rifles whilst the rest received sub-machine guns of Russian make.

The man who negotiated with us and was responsible for our initiation into the Partisans was no other than Mitchlev Motzar, who today is the deputy Prime Minister of Poland.

We were all integrated within the different platoons of the unit. I was posted as runner at headquarters. From then on we were part and parcel of the Partisans, and we took part in all their activities and operations.

The First Encounter

In an adjoining village to the forest was an informer, who used to keep us posted on the German's movements. One day we were warned that the Germans intended to make a comb-out of the forest. Usually they avoided the forest and when they did venture into the forest they used Mongolian P.O.W. for that purpose.

I was sent together with my friend Pinchevsky to try to substantiate this information. It was in the early evening when we arrived at the outskirts of the forest and a deafening noise of chains reached our ears. We advanced about 100 meters when suddenly we heard the Germans command "HALT".

Darkness had set in already; we stopped in our steps and looked around to find out where the voice came from. About 200 meters in front of us there was the silhouette of a tent where the guard was. Instinctively, we threw two hand grenades in that direction to cover our withdrawal. We certainly needed no further confirmation, since the facts spoke for themselves.

The explosion of the grenades invited a volley of fire from the village. The bullets shrieked around us and found their mark in the trees. We reported back to headquarters, where preparations were being made for the forthcoming encounter.

The fighting tactics in a forest are different altogether. Trenches are not dug and only the big trees provide the ample camouflage and cover against bullets. We prepared to meet the German onslaught.

The night passed relatively quiet, although from afar we could hear the German's movements. We had posted lookouts near the outskirts of the forest. Next day hoards of Mongolians under German command reached the outer ring of the forest, marching upright and shouting battle cries.

The Partisans outmaneuvered the Germans, attacked them from the rear and broke through their lines. Battling their way through, they succeeded in getting to another part of the forest where the Germans encamped. We suffered casualties, dead and wounded.

Two days before this battle, one of our friends was injured. We got medical help to him, who could do little to help him but dress his wounds. He could not be moved. With the enemy approaching we decided to hide him in the forest. I was told to stay close to him, thereupon I climbed a high tree and settled under its crest and remained in observation there the whole time. I had a few hand grenades and a rifle, and had made up my mind that if worst came to worst, I would throw the grenades at the Germans and put an end to my life. Fortunately, the Mongolians passed by me without discovering my presence, although they did find our wounded friend and loaded him on a cart. I was unable to come to his help since the overwhelming enemy numbers. Shortly afterwards we found his body and buried him. He had been shot through the head.

After the Germans had gone, I climbed down the tree and started looking for the unit. On the way I met other members who had dispersed during the fighting, together we walked until we finally found the new encampment.

The Germans continued these comb-outs on and off every few weeks.

Besides these defensive actions, there were planned operations by our unit. Our unit was a mixed crowd, there were Poles, Jews and escaped Russian P.O.W. from German prison camps who had joined us. Amongst them were many minorities: Tartars, Gruzinim, Azbedjanim and white Russians. We had radio contact with the Partisan command in Kiev.

From time to time planes appeared overhead, usually at night, and parachuted arms and men. The parachutists constituted a unit of their own and they operated apart, without anyone sharing their secrets. I approached this unit once and got friendly with them; imagine my surprise to hear some of them talking Yiddish. It appeared that there were some Jews amongst them, a fact that strengthened our morale.

One day a unit was detailed to blow up an ammunition train on its way to the front.

For this operation the unit was made up of Poles, Russians and one Jew, Israel Rosenberg. The action was a success, all of them returned without any casualties, but the Jew was missing. We learned later that he was murdered by the Poles, his "brother-inarms" who had participated in the operation with him.

The whole story came to light when his body was found in the forest, some time after the action. The Poles had reported that he had been killed in action, but we had serious doubts about the truth of this statement. We knew them [Poles] as they were, rabid Anti-Semites, and decided to bring the matter to the attention of the commander, Motzar, who ordered an immediate inquiry.

Two of the Poles were found guilty of the murder and were sentenced to death and executed the 7th of November, Revolution Day. Together with them, a number of spies and provocateurs that had been planted by the Germans within our ranks, went to the firing squad.

The blowing up of trains and railways were frequent actions that Jews participated actively.

Provision of Food

At some distance there was a big farm estate that belonged to a Polish landowner and which the Germans had confiscated. The Partisans used to "pay them a visit" from time to time to get food supplies for the whole unit. Since the Germans guarded the place, these excursions always entailed bitter fighting.

A Story About a Cow

During the German comb-out we were obliged to leave our encampment and leave behind our food provisions in wooden cases, which we couldn't take with us. The Germans carted them away.

When I returned to the place I saw a cow attached to a tree. I reported this to my unit commander who detailed a few men to go with me to guide them to the place, and to examine whether it was a trap or not.

There were six Tartars who did not want to go out of laziness and fright. On the way they told me, "If there won't be a cow, then you too won't be…"

I began to fear that the cow wouldn't be there anymore, perhaps someone had forestalled us because we were a few miles marching distance away. When we finally got there, tents had been put up and we saw two Mongolians in German uniforms with rifles, but there was no sign of the cow.

We lay down on the ground, "my" Tartars pointed their arms in the direction of the Mongolians and ordered me to go in towards them whilst they covered me. I had no alternative, the odds were one against six, and so I started out.

Meanwhile, the Mongolians had observed me and gave sign that they had no intention of fighting. When I got to them they told me that they were deserters who had deserted the Germans during the comb-out and wanted to join the Partisans. We took them with us to our headquarters. But "my" Tartars kept on bothering me and asking, "Where is the cow?"

I was confused and didn't know what to answer, when to my great surprise help came from an unexpected quarter. Hearing the question about the cow, the two Mongolians confirmed that they too had seen the cow and that a farmer from the village had taken her away half an hour earlier.

On our return journey to the unit, the Tartars led us a different route. When we arrived on the open space where arms and ammunition were usually parachuted, they told me to go in front. I noticed they had lowered their rifles from their shoulder straps, which aroused an immediate suspicion within me. I had a feeling they intended to kill me. It was then that I took advantage of the fact that there were many water shoals on the way and started to jump as if to avoid the water. I was running in my underpants and suddenly started to flee as fast as I could, assuming that I would be out of range already before they could point their rifles.

I didn't have to wait long before the first shots rang out; my forebodings had come true. I ran on into the deepness of the forest and had escaped from my fate at their hands. The distance to the unit being still considerable, I decided to spend the night in hiding. Next day, I made it to the vicinity of the unit, where I met a Jewish friend of mind who was on his way to fetch water. I told him of my adventure and asked him to bring me food and clothes and also to report the whole story to the commander. He sent for me, and it became evident that the Tartars had forestalled me with their version and had reported that the story about the cow was pure invention on my part and that I had fled.

The commander heard me out and upon my accusation ordered an inquiry.

Once more the two Mongolians saved the day for me, as they had done so earlier. The Tartars got their due punishment of continuous guard duty for a whole week.

The Day of Liberation

We were now in winter 1944, the Germans were in full withdrawal from the main front and our region filled with large German troop units that had retreated. The time had passed when small units could be of any use and the front line was rapidly coming nearer. In these circumstances, we were told to cross the lines and go over to the Russians. The front was about 60 miles away, near Sandomir. We marched the whole night through and before dawn we had neared the lines. In every village on the way we picked up a local guide who led us through the German concentrations. We heard the explosions of shells and small arms fire.

We marched in Indian file, Pinchevsky and I went up the rear. It was our duty to cut the German communication wires.

The whole area was covered in a deep layer of snow and had apparently one line, when suddenly we found ourselves before barbed wire guarding the trenches.

The order was given to storm the trenches and we opened fire. The Germans replied in kind and we continued fighting until we had crossed their lines. We were now in no-man's land.

The Germans opened up mortar fire. We suffered many casualties whilst crossing the lines and now from this infernal fire.

We were left without officers or guides, nor did we have a compass so we didn't know in which direction to run. Firing continued with rockets falling on all sides. We were afraid that the Russians, perhaps in the immediate vicinity, would suddenly open up fire against us not knowing our identity. Therefore we kept on shouting the whole time in Russian, "We are Partisans" in the hope that our voices be heard and to avoid the danger of being caught in crossfire.

It appears that we had crossed the first Russian lines without having been observed, nor had we observed them for that matter. In the meantime, dawn began to appear and we found ourselves again in an empty space, uninhabited so to speak. Once more we were in a quandary which way to turn. All was quiet, no longer did we hear any shooting and we continued marching towards a forest without knowing what fate had in store for us there. We were tired, exhausted and in despair.

We had already reached the forest when we noticed a sign posted to a tree in Russian, "Injured to the Hospital" and underneath was an arrow pointing the way. Needless to say, we took that turn and came upon a concentration of gun emplacements and tanks that abounded there.

Here, for the first time we met Russian soldiers and our meeting was overwhelming. We conversed together and they took us to their headquarters. We recuperated there for some time from all our troubles and looked over our ranks. We had suffered heavy casualties. From 320 men who started out to the front, only 68 survived. The rest was killed with five Jews amongst them.

Here ends the accounts of the Partisan activities by the Jews of the Wierzbnik region.

[Page 307]
Yaacov Snir (Shiner)

Fighting the Nazi Conqueror

When the War between Germany and Poland broke out, I took my Mother and sisters to Ostrowiec, where my uncle lived. By the time I returned to Wierzbnik for my grandmother and a few necessary items, the Germans have captured Ostrowiec and I was forced to change direction and head for Ilza. When we got there, the Polish authorities sent word for all the young men to travel to the other side of the Wisla River, where the main defense against the German invaders will be staged.

Hitting the Road

During those horrible days, a newspaper article my Father once read to us kept coming to back haunt my mind. In the article, Hitler claimed among other things that should a war break, all Jews would perish from the face of the earth. The meaning of that announcement was clear to me and I was determined to flee the danger of coming face to face with the Nazi threat. Therefore, I had a constant urge to leave places that were about to be invaded, both during the Germany-Poland War and during the Russo-German War of 1941.

Innocent as we were, we went to great lengths trying to cross the Wisla and join the Resistance. When we got there, we were faced only with disappointment. There was no line of defense, neither an Army nor any kind of fighting force and not even someone to talk to. I continued on my way toward Lublin, and got caught in a Luftwaffe bombardment. I survived through sheer luck. I realized that the place was far from secure and decided to leave the city for the time being. At that point, I ran into other people from Wierzbnik for the first time since I left my home. Among them were the Freemerman brothers, Zeev Killman, and others. We found ourselves bicycles and rode them toward the new USSR/Germany border, along the Bug River where our bicycles were confiscated which forced us to proceed on foot to the nearest town of Vladimir-Volinsky. Here we parted ways and each of us went his own way. It wasn't long before I met other former residents of Wierzbnik, such as the lawyer Shtramer's family, who asked me to join them.

I traveled with the Shtramers to Lutzk, accompanied by the sounds of German bombardment and the waning Polish Resistance. There were abundant rumors about a treaty between Russia and Germany, which later became known as the Ribbentrop-Molotov Treaty. According to the rumors, the Russian were to return to pre-World War I borders and that meant our town of Wierzbnik would be in Russian territory. Embracing that rumor we waited for ten days and then decided to take the initiative and return home. We got on a train bound to the Wierzbnik region, but stopped short when the news declared the new official border was the Bug River.

Those were the days when world order came apart and entire states fell under an almighty German-Nazi conqueror. The roads were full of refugees, tattered Army units and chaos and despair reigned supreme. My Father was in the Polish Army by then, and from time to time I received word from people who met him. Looking for him brought me to Kovel in Volin, where I met to my surprise a group of Wierzbnik youths such as the Goldgrub brothers, Wilenchik, Nudelman, and others. My search for my Father was not going well and I had to decide what to do next. As a young man I was interested in agriculture and in preparations for immigrating to Israel,

I wanted to apply at the Agricultural School of Baron Hirsh Foundation near Kolomeya. That did not work out.

Therefore, I decided to apply at the Agriculture School in Slobodka-Leshna, and after a harsh journey I enrolled at the school. Despite being a fugitive, I succeeded this time. We lived in boarding-school conditions. In December 1939, I met my brother Abraham, who fled Wierzbnik and crossed the Russo-German border. He knew my whereabouts from letters and food packages I sent home with as much money as I could get by working at the Food Conservatory and as a farmer.

Rumors of a Pogrom by the Ukrainians

After the Russo-German War broke out in June 1941, the Soviet teachers and the entire school management left suddenly at night. The students were left behind and everything crumbled. The local students returned home, and the others were left dumbfounded. Rumors spread about a pogrom about to take place, and we spontaneously formed a Resistance. We barricaded one of the halls, armed ourselves with rocks and clubs, and set watches. The Ukrainian attackers seemed to lose interest as they learned of our preparations, and after a few days the whole affair was forgotten and the Jewish pupils, boys and girls alike, were sent home. A day before the German Army came with cannon blasts and exploding shells echoing all around, I left the school along with two friends and we headed east toward the old border on the river Zbruch. We suffered aerial bombardments and machinegun fire from the German airplanes the entire journey. We crossed the Russian border toward Kaminitz-Podolsky. Food was not easy to come by and most of the time we went hungry, finding only scraps of this and that left in the fields to settle our hunger. For a short time we joined a Russian unit on a retreat and walked 40 kilometers a day. We mostly walked after dark and after several days we reached Kirovograd. When we were close to the city, something spectacular happened. As the nightly bombardment was commencing, the whole city lit up despite the blackout making the Germans' job a whole lot easier. German agents also infiltrated important places and signaled airplanes with colorful flares and rockets.

A Burning Mosaic

As we left the city we saw a wonderful vision. The city was burning with all the colors of the rainbow. Several factories that contained the various kindling that burned with colorful flames such as fuel reserves, wood stoves, spirit factories, and gas reserves each burned a different color. It was quite a spectacular show for such a horrible and deadly event. We left in a hurry, walking all night and reaching the city of Vinniza. We didn't have a place to stay, and had to sleep outdoors at public parks and other such places. We also had no food but there were refugee help centers, which supplied food for the needy.

I decided to join the Red Army and after a short inquiry was sent to Uman. When I got there I faced repeated rejections, based on the fact that they did not want to recruit people from the Ukrainian provinces conquered in 1939. I found out that they were looking for volunteers and people who would stay in the captured territories and perform acts of sabotage against the enemy (the organized Partisan movement was still unknown in those days). I was rejected for similar reasons. A rumor spread that the German forces were advancing toward us, and the rumors were further substantiated when the authorities gave the Military orders to open its stores and supply food and clothing to the population. Many left the city, making haste, and I was caught in the crowd heading east.

We walked day and night, 128 long kilometers of harsh terrain. We were exhausted and without food or water. I don't remember the exact route we took, but I remember passing Piervomaysk, then entering a small woodland area to rest a while. We were certain that 150 kilometers left us far enough from the advancing German forces. As we sat down we heard the echoes of the German bombardment and the Russian Retaliation and knew that we were mistaken as the front lines were catching up to us. We sat in that clearing feeling trapped, explosions on all sides of us. We gathered our strength and began marching east, hoping to avoid capture.

Near the village of Virzovka we ran across railroad tracks. My schoolmate Israel Verthime (from Rava-Ruska) and I decided to stay and wait for the train because we figured that the race between the walking refugees and the mobile German Army would be a futile one. We managed to board a train delivering coal to Dnierpropetrowsk, where life was still untouched by the war except for food rationing and recruiting for both the Army and various arms factories. We stayed there for three days until the German bombardment began. Then we tried crossing the Dnieper River by train. This required a special license given only to high-class citizens, but we snuck aboard the train and hid under the benches. When the conductor discovered us, we presented our Agriculture student cards. We didn't think the student cards would save us because they were quite meaningless during the War, but luckily the conductor's son was an Agriculture student as well. He spared us. We got to Kharkov, and later learned that our train was last to pass the river Dnieper before Russian demolition squads destroyed the bridge. We got off the train in Kharkov and went to a refugee center, which was opened to help the refugees from western regions of Russia. We received food coupons and a place to sleep in a public building. A few days later we turned to the Ministry of Agriculture. Our school was branched to the Ministry and we got assigned to an Agriculture school 100 kilometers west of the city. We began studying there, again in boarding school conditions.

Venomous Jewish Hatred

The school was filled with a strong Anti-Semitic atmosphere. The other students did not know we were Jews and thought we were Poles, but all their talks and conversations were full of scorn and mockery of Jews. Ironically enough, the Anti-Semites did not know that the schoolmaster, whose name was Fania Naumovna, was Jewish. They were so full of hatred. The students went to Kharkov and worked hard digging anti-tank trenches because they heard that Jews were working there and wanted to make fun of them. Upon their return, they spent days and nights telling about the behavior of the Jews they met and mocking them.

We didn't study much because the German's advance accelerated and we had to join the refugees moving east, this time in a more organized fashion. We traveled in a freight wagon with other students and personnel who chose to leave.

Short on Money

The harvest was good that year. The storerooms were full of grain and students were sent out to sell the grain before the German Army arrived. My friend Israel Verthime and I collected an amount of 30,000 rubles for the grain. When we arrived to deposit the money at the school's office it had already closed and the teller we consulted told us to just, "Leave the bag in the corner". We did as she said. While we were now on our way we had no money to buy food with. We told the schoolmaster about the 30,000 rubles we collected and left at the school office. She was shocked at the amount and gave us some money to buy food.

We traveled for a month, passing through the mountains and valleys, towns and cities, crossing republics until we reached the foot of the Ural Mountains at the border between Europe and Asia. We arrived at the Autonomic Republic of Bashkiria, populated mostly by Muslims, Bashkir and Tatars. We got off there and were assigned to continue our studies at the Agricultural School of Belibey. The rough Russian winter was coming. The season was late autumn and everything was covered with rime and the temperature was dropping below 25 degrees Celsius. Unaccustomed to the cold, bereft of proper clothing and given poor food we suffered and were forced to resort to ploys that would get us more food. The locals who dressed in furs used to mock us and claim that we were cold because we were not used to the weather.

I soon spoke fluent Russian and was able to mingle with the locals and thus get us adequate conditions in order to survive. Anti-Semitism was uncommon here since few Jews ever lived in this place before. After two months, we heard that a volunteer ski-squad was being assembled and destined to strike behind enemy lines. Since we wanted to start fighting the Germans, my friend Israel Verthime and I went to sign up. We were rejected, allegedly because we weren't members of the Komsomol (despite the fact that other applicants, also not members of the Komsomol, were accepted). We were deeply disappointed.

To Officer Artillery School

Meanwhile, a Ukrainian officer who worked in the Mobilization office heard we came from Ukraine and seemed interested in helping us. He scoffed at the ski-squad idea and instead advised us to go to an Officer Artillery school. After some consideration we were on our way to the Military Officer School in Ural. We studied there for a year. After graduating I was sent to further my education at an Artillery Officers' Reserve camp.

It was there that I met a Russian Captain named Milstein who surprised me with his knowledge of the Hebrew language. I was resting when he came over and started speaking Hebrew to me. I was confused and wasn't sure what to do. I wanted desperately to answer him, but feared it was a trap of the Russian secret police. I decided to play it safe and told him I didn't understand him. He said he spoke Hebrew, "ancient Jewish", as he called it, which he had learned from his grandfather, an enthusiastic Zionist who also taught him Torah and Gmara as well as "Palestinography". His surprising confession convinced me of his sincerity but I was still afraid. Was this a provocation? I'll never know the answer, but it was a revelation of Russia's great Jewish heritage, which produced the foundations for Zionism.

After six weeks at the reserve camp I was assigned to an Artillery unit. The conditions in the new camp were harsh and the limitations on food and clothing being so strict that people were actually looking forward to being sent to the front lines. After a short regrouping, we were sent to fight near Kharkov at the Ukrainian front. It was during the time shortly after the German's great defeat in Stalingrad from which they could not recover and retreated.

They retreated over a long distance, stopping briefly then moving once more. Yet, they didn't pose much resistance because they lacked the time to form a stable and organized line of defense. The process repeated itself all the way to the Dnieper River. We traveled by foot and by vehicle, moving day and night and pausing only to crush any resistance, which we encountered.

There were places, especially near towns and cities, which the Germans used for their natural defensive potential. Bitter battles were waged there and sometimes degenerating into street brawls. I specifically remember the conquest of Poltava that was won through the clever strategy of sending cavalry to the rear of the German forces. The successful battle and the conquest of the city opened the way for the continued advance of our forces toward the Dnieper River. When we got there, the natural obstacles used by the Germans to form a well-fortified defense line stopped us short.

Crossing the Dnieper River

The night before the attack that was supposed to allow us to cross the river, we turned on the headlights of all vehicles and exposed all the areas down to the river. From my high perch, I saw a scene that had a tremendous psychological effect over the enemy. During the night, small teams crossed the river and although they were discovered and came under fire, they managed to form a bridgehead allowing infantry, artillery and armored vehicles to cross over. The bridgehead expanded and we broke through the German line that very day. We proceeded toward the border between Russia and Poland passing on our way small settlements, towns and cities like Kremenchug, Zhitomir and Berdichev, which had a mostly Jewish population, but not a single Jew was left in any of those places. The gentiles told us about the tragedy that befell the Jewish population. The road was lined with razed settlements and only the chimneys left standing were proof they were once full villages and towns as the Germans employed a "scorched earth" retreat tactic.

The Korsun-Cherkasy Pocket

Our front lines had marched far ahead while at our rear large numbers of German soldiers, approximately 60,000, remained surrounded. The German High Command moved two armored divisions out of France to rescue these forces. The German troops broke through the Russian lines but stopped short about 5 kilometers from their trapped comrades because they were afraid of getting caught themselves. The small Lishanka River separated them and they called for the captives to make a break toward them. When they received the transmission, the Germans tried to storm the blockade. Tide after tide of wounded and exhausted soldiers started moving. We opened fire and they suffered many casualties but kept coming at us. We received orders to cross the river and dig in on the other side. On our way to the bridge we were ambushed and those who didn't make it to a nearby trench lost their lives. When we crossed the river we came upon stranded tanks. A General began searching for drivers, while the rest of us manned the machine guns. When the Germans appeared we opened fire and killed nearly all of them. Those who tried to cross the river further downstream were met with ambush and were killed. German casualties of the Korsun-Cherkasy Pocket, also nicknamed "Little Stalingrad" were very high. Nearly 18,000 killed, 3,000 wounded and thousands more captured. The commanders of this operation were Marshals Zhukow and Konev.

Warmed by Burning Deutsche Marks

On February 16, 1944 the morning following the battle it was very cold. We were staying in a deep ravine hiding from the frozen winds. During the battle we captured the treasury vehicle full of Deutsche Marks, which we burned to warm ourselves. The Russian units continued to advance south towards Romania, while inflicting heavy losses on the Nazi army.

In Romania, I participated in battles to free Bessarabia after crossing the River Prut. We stopped for protection in the city of Yassi. It was then that the Red Army High Command issued orders to send all the Polish-speaking soldiers to Moscow to be reassigned to the Polish army units being formed. I traveled to Moscow to the Artillery Army personnel management. At the personnel management, I met a clerk who helped send me back to a Russian unit because I did not wish to serve in the Polish army that was highly Anti-Semitic.

So, I was sent to a Russian unit that was forming in Belarus. Following the liberation of the city Baranovich we advanced north-west and at the border crossing of Poland-Lithuania-Eastern Prussia. We stumbled across a powerful German defense force that took advantage of the deep ravines near the cities of Eidkunen and Vilkovishki and entrenched themselves. The strong fire opened on our forces stopped the progress of our units and the High Command decided on defensive entrenchment.

Meeting General Chernikhovsky

Days drifted by until we received a visit from the Frontline Commander (a rank which during those days was second only to the High Commander of the Army and the Chief of Staff) General Armai Chernikhovsky. I had special interest in him, for he was not only Jewish but also one whose name inspired connotations in every Jewish heart. I awaited his arrival and prepared my soldiers for the important visit When he entered my bunker, I gave him a short review of the situation then he asked me a few questions about the state of my men and their morale and in a more personal tone, about my origins. He was an impressive man of great stature that inspired awe beyond his rank (there were at the time four or five Frontline Commanders such as Zhukow, Konev, Rokosovsky and Bharmian, who later on were all promoted to Marshals). I was thrilled to be in the presence of this man, a Jew who reached the peek of Military office. I don't know whether the other Commanders of the Red Army, whom I didn't get to meet personally, made a habit of visiting frontline outposts. Yet, General Chernikhovsky, after his brief stay at my bunker, walked straight to the front line where he checked the conditions of the soldiers and battled himself.

He Perished Shortly After His Visit

His visit left a mark in all who met him. Shortly afterwards, with the visit's memory still fresh in our minds, he died in an accident.

It turned out his visit wasn't merely for show but a probe before the great attack, which was set into motion with massive artillery fire and infantry assault. The enemy line was breached and we pushed forward with all our might. The enemy made a fast retreat and our forces were having a hard time catching up.

Everything had to be done with haste and with a dazzling speed; based on the fact that the faster one moves the harder it is for the enemy to regroup. So, speed would save casualties or in military terms, "the more sweat, the less blood". The only negative result was that our rush caused a traffic jam near a town. The Germans had abandoned six barreled mortars not far away, so you couldn't miss them when you came down the road. Some soldiers, including my own, took interest in those horrible weapons. For some reason, I can't recall why, I didn't let my soldiers near the things. Later that day, General Chernikhovsky and his entourage passed by that field and took interest in the mortars. The first person to touch the weapon set off a big blast, killing them all. The mortars were booby-trapped and General Chernikhovsky was among the fallen in that fatal accident. His death made me feel very sad and downcast.

The Battle Over Kenigsberg

This time our progress was much slower as the Germans had a large concentration of troops in that area and every step of the way bought with it blood. The enemy saw they were losing men without being able to maintain the defense line, and decided to surrender the region and rescue the fighting force via sea. But the closer they got to the shore, the more they were pushed into a narrow land strip. We opened fire with all our weapons at the Germans trying to board the escape barges that were supposed to bring them to safety. My artillery crew played a substantial part in "softening" the enemy there and with its complete annihilation opened the road to the great city of Kenigsberg (whose named was later changed to Kaliningrad).

From that point on, our advance was hindered only by minor problems until we reached the city, where we stopped to refresh ourselves before the upcoming grand assault. After a while the artillery started "softening" the enemy and the charge started at the first few blocks. There was substantial resistance and we suffered many casualties. Massive fire was opened on us and we had to fight for every house and yard. In those close-quarters situations, the artillery was made useless, as it had to make its winding way out into the open.

It was then that I was separated from my unit and found myself a target for German snipers hiding up in the high stories of buildings. I glanced up and saw a German aiming his rifle at me from the window of a house across the street. I realized that whoever pulled the trigger first would win, so I aimed and fired. I saw the gun fall out of the window, but other snipers took aim at me. A German soldier suddenly appeared and tried to lob a grenade toward me. I shot him and he fell on his grenade, absorbing the blast. I was like an acrobat, jumping here and there to avoid being hit. I felt alone in battle, fighting to keep myself out of danger's clutches every step of the way. I clung to the building wall, moving forward and saved by pure miracle from a rifle shot. A new miracle every minute, no, every second! I reached the corner of the building and flung myself around it, hoping for salvation but the fire was every bit as intense there as well. I heard footsteps behind me and then saw a German soldier running toward me. I realized he had cover and started running away. I ran along walls and between houses until I saw a crevice in the wall. I squeezed myself into it and as the German passed by, I shot him with the last of my ammunition. I kept maneuvering toward our forces but all the twists and turns left me out in the open, with a wall blocking my path. I couldn't go over it because it would have exposed me to the marksmen, so I turned back and crossed the street with a sudden leap. There I was protected from most of the fire and able to advance safely until I reached my unit, exhausted but alive.

I arrived just as our forces were preparing to storm the center of town. Massive artillery "softening" began, followed by infantry charges. The German's resistance wavered and after being pushed out of some key positions they abandoned the city and headed out to sea.

The German High Command meant to rescue the forces by sea, much like the allies did at Dunkirk at the start of the war. But before they could evacuate their men, we surrounded them and pushed them towards the ocean. Unable to organize their evacuation in time, our artillery wreaked havoc and killed many. They were called to surrender but refused and so their fates were sealed.

The Germans suffered a great defeat there. By doing my duty of fighting the evil will of the Nazi enemy, I felt more satisfaction than a common soldier would.

The Battle of Berlin

After two days of fighting in the streets, the city was purged and our forces continued their march west. My tattered unit was sent to the rear to recuperate and fill in the missing ranks, a process that normally took a month, but in those days with the end of the Nazi beast seeming to draw near we were back on the front lines within a few days. This time we went south to Kotbus, a city on the road to the beast's lair, Germany's capital of Berlin. Indeed, we traveled quickly by foot and by vehicle and reached the city's entrance. You could feel the preparations for the final battle all around. Both sides gathered massive forces and every kind of weapon. It is not my place to describe this historical battle, but I have a drop of it to call my own in that vast sea of battles.

The major attack began at night, with thousands of Russian projectors blinding the enemy while artillery and aerial bombardment pounded at them.

Two Against Four

The main charge came at dawn. After breaching enemy lines our forces flowed into the city, while the Germans were in shambles. There was chaos at the point of resistance. Retreating German infantry occasionally mixed with the fleeing civilian population. Waves of refugees were pouring into the maelstrom of blood and lead. Men, most of them elderly, women and children were in the midst with all with their packages, a sight that can only be explained by a common phenomenon of the horrors of the war.

Our cannons were stationed near a big building and we started firing at points of resistance. The war split into two parts: one above ground was the fires of battle, the shots, guns and cannons and the other one below ground where a population was in hiding while waiting for the battle to end.

Under those circumstances, some contact was made between local citizens and the conquering Army. A German civilian came to tell us, for his own unknown reasons, about German officers hiding in his apartment nearby. Full of confidence forged in the heat of battle, I told my driver to come with me and we went to the apartment. The door was locked and chained and my demands to open it were not met. I ordered my driver to fetch a crowbar and we broke through the meager fortifications. A gunshot was heard inside, and only once we entered did we solve that mystery. One of the five men in the room had taken his own life. They were dressed like civilians, but wore military boots. When I cried, "hands up" one tried to flee through the nearby kitchen door and another tried to reach for his pocket. I opened fire and so did my driver and they fell. The four "civilians" turned out to be S.D. Officers and we found a large weapon cache hidden in the sofa.

Such cases of Army-Guerrilla warriors increased. When one day, the communication line between the heavy artillery units and the scouting teams went dead. I sent two men to repair it. When they did not come back, I sent others who reported on their return that the first two were ambushed by Germans and tortured before being killed. It was amazing how the Germans, even on the verge of doom, refused to give up their lust for blood and cruelty. It was like the elders said, "evil men will not repent even at the very gates of hell."

When the city finally fell, on May 2, 1945 and the war was almost over, our unit climbed the stairs to the Reichstag where we took a triumphant group photo.

[Page 316]
Moshe (Michael) Samet

In the Ranks of the Polish Army

Two days before the German invasion I have fled to the neighboring town, Iłża. The newspapers and the rumors gave me a clear picture of the plans the Nazis had for us Jews, and I was determined to get out of Wierzbnik before their arrival and avoid any contact with them. I have heard that the Nazis abuse and humiliate Jews, and those who refused to accept these horrors and showed resistance have all met with the same fate: murder! As a man of dignity, I knew I could not survive under such conditions and concluded that I had to disappear, quickly and at any cost. I had an acquaintance In Iłża, a wealthy Jew who bought the two of us bicycles, which we used to leave town. After a few hours of pedaling we stopped for a short rest, and two Polish soldiers in uniform approached us and confiscated our bicycles. This daylight robbery has forced us to continue on foot.

When we arrived at the town of Sarna, we stumbled into a heavy German bombardment. People panicked and sought refuge and in the confusion I was separated from my friend, who I never saw again. A while later I met a Jewish girl in the street. She realized I was a refugee and invited me to her home. Her parents were very courteous and allowed me to stay with them until the danger has passed. I wanted to repay them with what little money I had, but they would not hear of it.

In the meantime there were unexpected developments on the front line and we heard rumors about the Ribbentrop-Molotov Treaty and the unopposed advance of the German army eastward toward Rokitno and from there to the town of Robno. The situation in town roughly mirrored the weather. It was the mid-autumn and already possible to hear the footsteps of winter drawing closer. The Polish army suffered a complete defeat and what was left of the regular forces crossed the border to Romania. The large army storehouses were full of food and uniforms, and after the units have left, the rear guard distributed these uniforms on demand. I too have arrived there and received military garbs. Since I was still young, the uniform was too big for me.

To my surprise, I stumbled upon a group of people from Wierzbnik who used to serve in the Polish army and were now like sheep without their shepherd. Among them were: Vigdorovich, Taichman and Moshe Shiner. The latter I knew well, because I was friends with his two sons, Avraham and Yaakov, and the three of us belonged to the Beitar movement in Wierzbnik. This group numbered a total of eight people, and after a brief discussion we decided to go home. I joined them and became the youngest member of the group.

We headed out on foot, because we had no private means of transport and public services were completely paralyzed. We intended to head for the new border between Russia and Germany, cross it and take the shortest route home.

Along the way, we were fortunate enough to get rides from random vehicles that were headed in our direction. After walking and riding for three days, we reached the town of Zamoœæ, which lay on the border between the two countries. We managed to hire a carter to smuggle us across the border, and he did just that.

After the excitement of crossing the border, we decided on a short rest. We were relieved to have this experience behind us. After a short while, we got up and continued marching. A few miles down the road we met four German soldiers, who were walking in the opposite direction. They stopped us and asked: "Where are you going?"

They seemed to be one of the patrols in charge of securing the area. We told them we were headed home and they let us go. We walked another four or five kilometers before we stumbled into another German patrol, but this time we weren't as lucky. Instead of letting us go, they seemed to consider us "a catch", and without further ado they marched us back to Zamoœæ, where they stopped by a church and took us inside.

The church was full of people, perhaps 2,000 in all, and all of them captives from the defeated Polish army – soldiers and officers of every rank – including quite a few Jews. Assessing the situation, I realized that we were considered prisoners of war. This seemed like an mistake to me, because I was far too young to serve in the army and was only wearing a military uniform by coincidence.

I tried explaining the situation to anyone who would listen, but no person of rank would listen to me despite my desperate pleas. I offered documents that would prove my age, but they wouldn't even look at them. Therefore, I had to stay at this church with the Polish prisoners of war, even though I was never a soldier.

Conditions in that place were very harsh. The only food we received during the day was one loaf of bread for every four people, and a bit of coffee, and people were rarely allowed to step away and relieve themselves.

Things continued this way for three weeks, and then freight trucks have arrived to take away all the Polish soldiers, leaving behind only the Jews and the sick, who had to march by foot. This march was particularly hard for the sick, but the Germans terrorized anyone who showed signs of resistance and we were forced to continue marching, escorted by armed guards and watchdogs.

The atmosphere during our stay at the "prisoner church" and the march that followed it made it clear to me that the future held even greater dangers, and I started thinking about escaping.

I discussed the matter with Mr. Shiner but he opposed to the idea, worrying that I might get hurt or die.

I was swayed by his personality and public standing and postponed any escape plans for the time being. After a day's walk we were brought to a rural settlement and crammed together into a stable. This place was by no means fit for so many people, and grew more and more crowded by the moment until there was no air left to breathe. People were begging for a little air, cried out and pleaded with the Nazi guards, but the guards reacted to the contrary. They threatened to kill us all if we did not shut up immediately...

We already had enough contact with the Nazi army and its heralds to take their threats seriously. People hushed and accepted their terrible suffering despite the tight situation, with a silence that "cried" to the heavens.

The brutality of the German guards tested our endurance; the prisoners were not even allowed to leave the stable to relieve themselves, resulting in things that I am prevented from describing. The captives were tortured in this manner for another day and then we were all taken to the Wisła river and shipped across it on barges, near the town of Ostrowiec, about 28 kilometers from Wierzbnik. We were put in a temporary detention camp prepared for us and rumors quickly spread that we would be transferred to Germany from there.

Escape from the detention camp

This place was supposed to hold us for an extended period of time, and therefore it was run in the same way as a prison, which meant specific visiting hours.

People from Wierzbnik started arriving looking for relatives, and among them was Pola Shiner, accompanied by a man I didn't know. They brought me news from home, which slightly cheered me up.

I was facing a hard decision. I was constantly worried about the fact that I was too young to serve in the army. I was afraid that my "crime" would be exposed, and imagined that the punishment I would receive from the Germans would be harsh. On the other hand, the fact that my random capture was never recorded or documented gave me hope of escaping under the proper circumstances. This situation seemed like a chance to carry out my plans. It occurred to me that I could get rid of the military uniform, mingle with the visitors and go back with them to Wierzbnik.

I told Mr. Shiner about my plan and he approved of it, giving me his blessing and some money "just in case". When visiting hours were over, the Germans started urging people to finish their visits and leave the place. People hugged and kissed while the Germans screamed, resulting in mayhem that afforded me the chance to quickly take off my uniform, and stay wearing only the civilian clothes under them. I followed the example of the other visitors, hugged my acquaintances and waited for the policemen to urge me out. The moment came and I left the place, nervously holding the arms of Pola Shiner and the man who came with her.

Going to Donbas

We walked back to our town, Wierzbnik, and went our separate ways at the suburbs, each of us heading home. While I was walking, meeting acquaintances along the way, I heard news that people were being abducted off the streets to do forced labor. The youths, who were likely candidates for these abductions, went into hiding and I immediately entered the house next to me. The place turned out to be a cobbler's workshop and realizing that I was still wearing combat boots, I exchanged them for normal shoes so they would not betray my recent adventures, to the joy of the old cobbler. I stayed there for a long while, waiting for the danger to pass, and then went out to the street again, but after taking a few steps I realized that the danger was not gone yet. I saw a barbershop and entered it, asking for a haircut. Several people were inside, talking about a prisoner who escaped from the camp in the neighboring town...

I listened to them and realized that they were talking about me. As it turned out, the Germans were fanatic about order, and although I wasn't processed properly and my presence wasn't documented, the Germans knew the total number of prisoners and discovered my escape the first time they took count again.

In time, I learned that they have conducted an endless number of censuses and lineups to determine whether this was the result of an escape or a miscount.

After getting my hair cut, I went back into the street and had the misfortune of bumping occasionally into Germans in uniform on my way home. Some of them stopped me and inquired about my business, but I managed to escape those situations unharmed. There was no way of escaping them completely unscathed, however, and one incident deeply shocked me. In one of the streets, I saw Germans stop people and inquire about Nachum More, a known madman; they wanted to know whether he was truly insane or merely trying to fool them. The people they asked were afraid that the Germans might take offense at his behavior, leading to inevitable retribution. They innocently replied that the person in question was indeed mentally ill. The Germans faced him against the wall and shot him.

Finally I arrived home, and after a few natural moments of excitement I realized the scope of the disaster and the depressing situation of the Jews. The lives of Jews became very hard, and the oppression and abuse kept escalating. With my own eyes I saw them grab the butcher who lived in our street, a God-fearing bearded man, and shave him using a sword. Another time they grabbed a gentile who looked like a Jew and beat him soundly. And to top those acts, they continued abducting people to do forced labor occasionally, myself included.

The situation urged me to escape to the Russian side. Encouraged by my earlier success, I pleaded with my close friends Yoseph Wilenczyk and Yitzhak Kerbel to escape. One day we left, headed for the train station. We got ourselves Polish student caps and thus disguised we boarded the train and traveled all the way to the town of Przemyœl, where a river crossed between Germany and Russia.

We found Jews in this town who directed us to professional smugglers who took us over to the Russian side that very night.

We faced no obstacles this time and continued walking until we encountered a Russian border patrol. They stopped us for interrogation and then ordered us to return to the German side. We refused to go back, no matter what! They seemed familiar with this phenomenon and didn't press the matter, convinced that even the harshest punishment won't convince us to return to the Germans. They brought us to a refugee camp, where we found people who took care of us. As a matter of fact, we were free to do as we pleased and so we decided to go to the city of Lvov. We made a living doing odd jobs, and finally decided to travel to Donbas, to work in the coal mines.

After a few months in Donbas I traveled to the southern districts of Russia, where I joined the Polish Army, under the command of General Berling.

Part of the army later crossed into Iran, led by General Anders (eventually reaching Israel) while the rest stayed behind and participated in the war against the Nazi conqueror. I was among those warriors, and after receiving basic training I earned the rank of officer and even took part in the battles near Lenino. At the end of the war, I was discharged from the army.

[Page 319]
Hania Kuper (Reichzeig)

He Died on the Way to Freedom

The ghastly fate of my family already began in our native city – Krakow, from which we were driven out by the Nazi murderers. We then came to Wierzbnik and shared the difficult wartime conditions with the local Jews. We had to begin everything anew. My father began to work as a postman, but not for long, because the long murderous arm of the devilish German powers reached us there as well.

In 1942, the general annihilation of the Jews of Wierzbnik began through *"Aussiedlung"* [deportation] to the death camps, and my parents also met their horrifying death in that blood campaign.

At that time I was in the Starachowice camp with my brother Israel. He was younger than I and I felt that from then on I was responsible for him and I did everything that I could to keep him alive. I gave him my last piece of bread, everything that I possibly could, so that we would make it through the day together, because I hoped that we would one day live to see liberation, and that we would yet be able to live like normal people. That gave me the strength and the energy to keep myself going with the last of my strength, to hang on by the nails to every sign of life, just to survive and live through the dreadful nightmare.

However, my brother had a different point of view; he didn't believe that the Germans would leave anyone alive. He understood that the death sentence was for everyone, for the entire Jewish people. Because of that he maintained that we mustn't passively await death, but should do something to escape from the enemy's murderous hands. When a small group of people who had decided to cut through the barbed wire of the labor camp and run away to the partisans in order to join their ranks came together, he threw off the bridle of enslavement together with them.

With complete audacity and readiness he threw himself at the barbed wire with the other Wierzbnik Jews, in order to break through a way to freedom, but unfortunately, his way was obstructed by Satan. The murderous bullet of a Ukrainian gendarme reduced the last gleam of hope to nothing.

May his eternal memory be blessed.

[Page 320]
Zvi Faigenbaum

Shmuel Dov Faigenbaum Fell in the Line of Duty

A quiet, humble person, Shmuel-Dov was not very prominent among his friends in Agudath Israel Youths. An educated, kind and mild-mannered man, he spoke calmly, worked hard and conducted himself with dignity.

Shmuel, (as he was commonly known), was born in 1908 to a family of Hasidic merchants. Even as a child, his life was filed with hardships. World War I broke out when he was only six years old, bringing its share of misery and hardships. When the war entered its second year, and our town was caught between the two fronts, it was stormed in the middle of the night by Russian troopers, who forced all the Jews to leave in the dark and abandon their property to the looters.

We spent two months as refugees in the county town of Radom, until it was conquered by the German army. Then we learned that half our town was burned down. Our apartment and store both turned to ashes. And that was how Shmuel spent his childhood.

His father, Moshe Baruch, who was a kind Yeshiva student, fell prey to the hardships and cruelties of the war; he caught a cold and his illness lasted for three years before he finally passed away, leaving behind six orphans, 12 years old Shmuel among them.

His mother, Esther (daughter of David Yehoshua and his famous righteous wife Rivka Zisl), kept her wits about her even after becoming a widow. A capable woman, she put her trust in God, tried her hand in trade, provided for her young children and raised them according to Jewish custom. Shmuel served as her right hand and helped her run the store, and when he came of age he married Ms. Chava, daughter of Yehoshua Morgenstern from the nearby town of Wąchock. A year later she gave birth to a cute baby boy who was named Moshe, after the father. They earned enough for a living and were content with their lot. Everything was going well until... World War II broke out.

Shmuel was 31 years old when he was drafted into the Polish army. He went and never came back. It is common knowledge that the Polish army was unable to hold off the invading German army. The ranks fell apart and a panicked retreat started. More and more soldiers came back home every day, but Shmuel wasn't among them. Each of the returnees passed word of friends who were on their way home. But anyone who asked about Shmuel met with silence. His wife Chava, her son in her arms, visited the returnees hoping for news, but they all maintained their silence.

Time passed. In the morning one would say, "O that it were evening!" and in the evening one would say, "O that it were morning!" Suddenly, I saw people whispering! I told them: "Tell us what you know, it is unwise to hide something like this. The wife...the son..."

A few moments of thunderous silence passed before they told me to go see Jermiahu.

Jermiahu Waigman lived in Piłsudskiego Street, in the home of Avraham Radkowizer. "Go to him. Say that. He will tell you".

I called the father of my sister-in-law, Yehoshua Morgenstern, and suggested that the two of us should go and ask for a clear, specific testimony.

The road was very dangerous. A battalion of soldiers set up camp in the spacious courtyard of the old lumber-mill. We entered the apartment. Jermiahu welcomed us quietly, and seemed to be expecting us. He gestured with his left arm at a couple of chairs for us to sit in. He left his right arm at the hospital in Lodz. And this was his tale:

"We were in the same battalion. During all our travels and retreats, we watched out for each other and kept in touch. On Tuesday, September 5th, we were in the same trench on the front line. It was by the town of Lusk, not far from Lodz. The Germans started bombarding the trenches. A shell fell into our dig and we were both wounded. We started bandaging the wounds when suddenly the Germans showed up over the trench. They could see we were wounded and their commander pointed at Shmuel and said 'This is a Jew, kill him!' He was shot and killed on the spot. Before he passed away, he said to me: 'Tell Chava and my Moshe that I was thinking about them during my final moments.'

Members of the Red Cross arrived two hours later and mistaking me for a 'Pole' they took me to the hospital in Lodz. Now I am back, but with only one arm.

Though Shmuel fell on the front lines of the battle against the Nazi beast, he was murdered by the villains in a most foul way, while wounded, merely because he was a Jew."

When we heard the terrible news we all cried bitterly over the man who was taken in his prime.

We headed back. After finishing our straw-cutting quota, we finally arrived at the house, where everyone was waiting to learn: what, how, where, when. Everyone was crying. A mother lost her precious son; Chava was a young widow, and Moshe, an orphan... the father who loved him so much will never come back... I could not cry yet, because I was petrified with shock.

I signaled for his mother to come home with me. We went home in silence, surrounded by an air of anguish. No refreshments were served. We remained standing. I said: "We know where it happened, near Lusk, if we hurry we might be able to find out where he was buried and give him a proper Jewish burial." Someone had to go there. There was no doubt that the Jews of Lusk would help if they could. But who will go? The men won't come back alive, Chava, his wife was in no state to leave Moshe, she was not strong enough and the trip itself was dangerous for a young woman...

"I am going immediately, tomorrow morning," said the mother decisively and without fear. It was only then that I started crying as well, loudly.

We all cried together – my mother, the sister-in-law, the relatives, the neighbors who gathered to hear about Shmuel and myself – over our precious, noble Shmuel Dov who was gone...

"They saw he was wounded and killed him because he was a Jew."

His mother carried out her role faithfully. She arrived in Lusk, asked and inquired but learned nothing. She returned as empty handed as she went. We never learned the location of his grave. But we knew he would not come back. We knew he was the sole victim... because we never imagined, couldn't imagine, that he was only the first victim among the many who followed... we didn't know that three years later he would be joined by his mother, Chava and Moshe, as they burned among the other martyrs of Wierzbnik, among the six million martyrs, who were sentenced to death "because they were Jews".

[Page 322]
Tzipora Snir (Faiga Lustman)

Hela Sacrificed Her Life
(In memory of Hava Kleinberg z"l)

I had a friend in my hometown, named Hela. She was a pretty girl, clever and gentle and devoted to her family, and she worked hard at home taking care of her three brothers, the youngest of whom was still a baby.

After the war broke out and our town was conquered by the Nazis, she shared the same cruel fate as her people: oppression, abuse and annihilation. I still carry with me a horrible event from those fateful days, one that was carved into my memory and which I can see as though it were yesterday:

During the great action we were all gathered at the Rinek, where they carried out the selection – who would work and live, and who would die in the incinerators.

16 years old Hela was standing in the row next to mine, beside her little sister and younger brother and holding her baby brother in her arms. The German commanding the selection marked her among the able – which meant she would live. He tried to pull her out of the line, but Hela would not budge. Lithuanian soldiers approached her and tried to drag her forcefully out of the line and even tried to convince her with words, knowing that this young girl would be part of the "work force" that serves them. They urged her to leave her spot and join the living. The townsmen around her told her to leave the baby and be saved, but Hela would not budge.

In light of her disobedience, she was approached by a cruel, homely Lithuanian soldier: his round face, his pink cheeks, and his brutal actions all indicated a person unfit to be called a man, having lost his humanity. He stopped next to her and forcefully and maliciously struck her face with the barrel of his rifle. The rifle cracked her jaw and slashed her chin in two. Then he told her again to leave the baby and join those who could work.

Hela stood there, bleeding, with Luba, her brother and the baby in her arms, bathed in her blood. She never shed a single tear. Her ruined face never flinched. She was decisive, stubborn and courageous. And she went with the rest of them, refusing to leave her brothers and save her own skin.

I survived the war and saw far more terrible scenes, people becoming beasts, suffocating, burning, murdered. But during this entire hard journey, I was accompanied by the image of Hela at the marketplace, during the action. The image of the girl who sacrificed herself. And this girl gave me the strength to keep fighting, hoping that there some noble human ideals worth fighting for still existed. It was the heroic sacrifice of a vivacious, youthful and vigorous life for beloved brothers.

[Page 323]
Jerachmiel Singer

Guta Blass-Weintraub Snatched the Gun

By the end of 1944, the lead-colored skies over tortured Europe started to clear and the scales of battle against the Nazi beast tipped more and more in favor of the allies battling the conqueror. The allied armies pressed the armies of fascist Germany in a pincer movement, east and west, liberating towns and villages that suffered for a long time under the heel of the retreating conqueror. The free world slowly started to breath in relief and we could already sense the coming fall of Hitler and hear the footfalls of the freedom to come.

But for the residents of the concentration and labor camps, those events were like a noose tightening around their necks, because we knew that the Germans would do anything to eliminate those who witnessed their horrid crimes…

It was as we feared. When the front lines drew closer, the Germans started concentrating prisoners from various areas into central places, making it easier to transport them to "safer" places. One day they took all the residents of the camp over by the lumber-mill and brought them to our camp.

These actions made us live in despair and fear of the Germans' next move, because we all considered them to be bad omens. But the boldest among us was a girl named Guta (the wife of Leon Weintraub, currently residing in Charleston in the US), who came from the camp by the lumber-mill. Before she could be captured, she assumed that everyone taken into the camp would be killed there and then, and decided to resist this cruel fate with all her might.

Schrott, the German commander, was standing by the gate to the camp, his terrible gaze sweeping over those crossing the gates, expecting nothing unusual. He was merely toying with the vision before him. And while he was feasting his eyes with satisfaction on the events taking place by the gate, Guta turned back and charged him, biting and snatching his gun from its holster.

This girl's rare and daring act has stunned everyone around her, and even the German was shocked.

Guta, on the other hand, took advantage of the confusion and under the cover of night's darkness she ran away with the gun. A few moments later the German recovered and started chasing her, but she managed to outmaneuver him and hid under one of the cabins, in the space between the floor and the ground.

Since he could not catch her, the German returned to the camp gate embarrassed, desperate and confused.

Although this event has badly hurt his image, he seemed to have some appreciation for the Jewish girl's courage.

He asked the people around him to find Guta and tell her that she will not be harmed if she returned his gun.

Some were naturally eager to earn his favor, and were willing to do this, and they convinced the girl to return the weapon.

It should be noted that the German kept his word, despite being otherwise known as an unscrupulous murderer.

[Page 324]
Gershon Rosenwald

In the Shade of the Thick Forest

Our shtetl Wierzbnik was attacked right at the beginning of the war because there were factories and military industries and ammunition works there. Moreover, concealed German spies and agents , who had been planted there in advance, signaled all the details that interested them to the airplanes.

I myself was preparing to go to Brazil and had even already arranged all the necessary papers, but the war destroyed all my plans and I remained at home and together with my mother and brother continued working as a retailer.

As soon as they began to kidnap Jews on the street in order to send them to forced labor, I ran away to Słopiec and I hid there with other acquaintances, because the Germans were not yet there at that time.

In the meantime, after a short time I saw that the Germans were advancing, so that there was no point in being away from home, and I returned to Wierzbnik.

Meanwhile, times had become more difficult and worse and many people came to the decision that there was nothing to be expected from the Germans and that we had to save ourselves by fleeing. People began to cross the border onto the Russian side.

Thinking it over, I and my brother Moshe and Avraham Unger also decided to sneak across to the Russian side, and on a beautiful morning we set out and walked to the train station. We had made many preparations. We hid just a little money in the soles of our shoes, to have for a rainy day. We boarded the train and rode to the city of Przemyśl. As we had been previously informed, a certain woman lived there, who engaged in smuggling people to the Russian side, and we went to the address we had received.

Time passed slowly, everyone was absorbed in thinking about the hard times awaiting us in a strange place, away from our own people. A depressing mood prevailed, but nevertheless we were already waiting impatiently for the moment when we would be able to escape from the German hell and save ourselves momentarily from the Nazi danger. And as we were worrying and lost in thought, two Gestapo men suddenly showed up and with revolvers pointed began asking us menacingly whether we had money, jewelry, valuables, etc.

They demanded that we immediately hand over all the above-mentioned items to them, and if they searched us and found something on anyone that he had hidden, they would shoot him on the spot.

Our friend Avraham Unger was frightened to death and told them that he had money in the soles of his shoes. Consequently, the Gestapo man forced him to remove the money with his... teeth.

It was a horrifying picture to see, Unger woefully torturing himself with the sadistic idea of the Nazi murderer. His teeth were bleeding and he was sweating profusely until he managed to rip the soles off his shoes and pull the money out from them. However, on the other hand the scene made such a terrible impression on the others, that we no longer dared to say that we had money – despite the danger – and we kept silent. In this way our money stayed with us.

After they had satisfied themselves with the robbery, the Gestapo men left, and because in the meantime it was already late at night, we didn't wait much longer, but left the house and began walking to the water.

We arrived at about one o'clock at night to the San River, which throughout the years had divided the city into two parts, and this time into two countries, and one could even say – two worlds. We were supposed to be taken across to the other side in a boat, and we had paid for that. But it turned out otherwise, because the peasants who were supposed to row us over not only didn't do it, they also took away all the packages from the Jews, robbed all their goods and told us to cross the water... on foot.

The river was deep enough, the water sometimes reached our mouth and it was a miracle that we didn't drown. We reached the bank barely alive.

On the Russian Side

We didn't run into any guards there, and after catching our breath after all that we had gone through up to then, we began to move farther away. At first we crawled carefully on all fours and afterwards we permitted ourselves to walk. After we had walked several hundred meters, we suddenly overheard a voice saying in Russian: "*Stoi!*" [halt]. We immediately stood still and a pair of Russian soldiers quickly came up to us and brought us to the city of Przemyśl.

After a short hearing we were placed in a closed house where almost fifty of us sat in a room. There was a big crush there and a serious lack of food, and we were extremely hungry. Nevertheless, we were lucky that five days later they let us go. Leaving that internment, we thought that we were doing well, but we discovered that we were extremely mistaken. Nothing was better in "freedom". Hunger raged without mercy. We also had no decent clothing, even though winter had already arrived. We all shivered, our hands and feet froze from the bitter cold and we suffered greatly.

Back to Wierzbnik

Looking at all those devastating problems, we began to feel regret over running away from home, because we saw that we would not be able to endure the situation there, so that there was nothing to lose. From day to day we were overcome by deep despair. At the end, we decided to turn back towards Wierzbnik.

Going back wasn't so easy, and we had to endure a great deal until we managed to get back to Wierzbnik. But we had apparently gone from the frying pan into the fire. We had just returned, when the Germans began to oppress the Jewish population. They abused people brutally, pursued and badgered innocent victims.

In the meantime we also had to worry about a minimal income, so I traveled to Słopiec to sell something on the black market and earn a few cents.

However, I had no luck and was caught. A certain SS man called Kiel, caught me, beat me severely and took away all my goods. The same criminal also once caught my mother in the street when she was trying to sell a little butter – and he beat her severely and took everything away from her.

At the same time my two sisters came to us from Łódź and we cried together.

Oppression at Each Step

Over time I began to work in the Majowka, together with my brother. My work was to be a sanitation worker in the bathhouse, i.e. I worked at disinfecting clothes. What remains in my memory from that time is connected to an episode when we bribed the commandant to agree that during the disinfection they wouldn't shave off the religious Jews' beards.

That was a time when we still had illusions that the situation would change, that conditions would improve, and that whoever worked would be able to survive the hard times. So Jews really worked hard, we tried to do more than we could. There were even many people who worked two shifts, but in reality it was just the opposite.

Money Fines

The situation kept getting worse. They began to oppress us at every step. The Germans placed various contributions and monetary fines on the Jewish population via the *Judenrat*. Whoever didn't pay, sometimes because he didn't have the money, was taken by the police to the police station. Afterwards he was fired from his job and replaced by someone else who had paid them well, sometimes people from out of town, because there were many refugees in Wierzbnik at that time.

Ghetto

Later on they set up the ghetto. A few streets were designated and it was decreed that Jews could only live in these places. It obviously became very crowded and miserable, several families had to live together – and the sanitary conditions were beneath all consideration. We went to live together with the Feigenbaum family and we suffered greatly from crowding.

The ghetto was guarded on all sides by armed guards and anyone who wanted to sneak out was risking his/her life.

Also in this situation of oppression and affliction we thought that we had already reached the highest level of suffering and pain, hoping that it would at sometime come to an end, but the suffering continued and every day brought new edicts and troubles.

It reached the stage that when we discovered that someone had died a natural death, we envied him for not having fallen into the hands of the Nazi hangmen.

Aussiedlung **[Deportation]**

Despite everything, we didn't imagine that things could be much worse, and that the situation could deteriorate into such a tragedy, one that common sense couldn't grasp. We couldn't believe that in the twentieth century such a catastrophe as the one the murderous Germans planned and afterwards began to implement, could occur.

The last stage in the realization of their murderous extermination plan had begun, which envisaged the obliteration of the entire people. The sadly infamous deportations began.

To tell the truth, we had already received news, from here and there, that transports packed full with Jews from the neighboring towns had been sent away, and that they wee going somewhere... We just didn't want to believe that it was in fact their last journey...Even less did we believe that the Jews of Wierzbnik would have to suffer the same fate, because we had military factories and they needed the manpower.

That thought was even reinforced when the Germans kidnapped Jews from neighboring towns and brought them to Wierzbnik for forced labor. Some of the kidnapped Jews afterwards ransomed themselves through the *Judenrat*, but the whole process highlighted the importance of our city as a work center – and it was on that that we built so much...

But as was later revealed, these were just illusions. We ourselves lived not far from the train station and we saw the freight trains, which traveled closed and sealed, without doors or windows, and from inside could be heard the pitiful moaning of the innocent victims who had been sentenced to death – men women, old people, children and babies, who had barely seen the world.

[Page 327]
Reuven Shuali (Lis)

Memorial

Wierzbnik-Starachowice, a town as beloved as a mother
I shall not stand over your ruins;
Thoroughly were you destroyed by villains;
Only the memory continues beating, like a pulse.

Jews, men, women,
Boys, girls and infants,
Lived in you for 400 years.
Like a raging river;
Workshops, stores, markets,
Merchants, craftsmen, carters,
Rabbis, butchers, teachers,
Lumberjacks and water-drawers,
A Jewish community.

Life offered few pleasures
Many were poor
But your residents were men of faith
Of torah, virtues and prayer.
You were lost during the days of the Holocaust
Like thousands of our nation's communities
In the great Diaspora
I shall make this book your memorial.

Malka Weisbloom

We Wished to Die as Heroes

They come, they come
The accursed Gestapo
Shivers ran across our body
Because they were so cruel to us

We were young and wished to live
Because we were only nineteen, twenty
Our lives have barely began
And the murderers decreed our end

Many quick thoughts in our mind,
How to save our lives and souls
And though our death may come tomorrow or a year from now
I know for certain that I will die
We wished to die as heroes
And so we made our way to the forest

[Page 328]
Avraham Shiner

Flames Rose from the Steam

After many adventures, hardships and agonies, I was put to work at the central steam machine at the lumber-mill. This was a fairly routine task, but my mind was restless. The noisy, steady machine stood in contrast to my mind, which worked quietly but frantically. I never accepted this cruel fate thrust upon me. I constantly considered refusing it, resisting, rebelling against the situation to the best of my ability. And now the circumstances gave me something to cling to, room for action. Day after day I stand by the machine, thinking and planning, scheming and plotting. My machine is part of the great war-machine built by the Germans to carry out their plots against people and nations. The blood of millions of victims was necessary to grease their great machine, while my little machine in the lumber-mill needed actual grease to work properly.

Even without seeing its products with my own eyes, I would have known that it was working for the warmongers, because it was clear beyond a doubt. The machine makes crates for munitions, for those deadly weapons that will be used to kill any person who dared to rise against the wild beast, as well as the innocents. I wanted more than anything to silence the beast, to stop it from its vile work, to disable it, if only temporarily. Those were my thoughts as I stood before it, day after day.

It was not a simple matter. I must keep a low profile, because I would be the first suspect, the trail will lead to me! I must not act directly, I had to use trickery, subterfuge... but I could not wait any longer, some greater force encouraged me to end things and whispered to me: "Do it, as soon as possible!"

But in truth, my path lay not in action but rather in inaction, meaning that I had to sit and do nothing. Since I was ordered to grease the machine every day, I now had to refrain from doing so.

One day, I did not pour the grease... and waited with baited breath for the results that were certain to come shortly. As a matter of fact, those moments seemed like an eternity to me. Stress and anxiety mingled. I wanted to learn whether my actions would bear any fruit, and I was afraid of getting caught and being punished for my "crime".

And then, as I was waiting eagerly for some sign, flames erupted from the machine and towered higher and higher. Confusion and panic broke out all around me, because the people were afraid that the entire lumber-mill would burn down. The fire was constantly spreading further and further.

It is therefore no wonder that everyone took part in the efforts to put out the fire, pouring sand, throwing rags and so on. I too had to pretend to fight the flames, to draw suspicion away from myself.

And although I managed to generally divert the attention of the Germans and their local flunkies away from myself, there was no way for me to escape this unscathed.

Every failure requires a scapegoat, and a defenseless Jew is the easiest person to blame. Although they never imagined the part I played in starting this conflagration, my responsibility for the steam machine was enough of a reason for them to blame these events on my "negligence". My punishment was naturally mild, and the matter was settled after I received a beating from the Polish workers and was locked in the dungeon for seven days by the Germans.

But it was easier to bear my punishment this time, because I was satisfied by the results of my actions, which have disabled the entire lumber-mill for several weeks – and this was my reward.

[Page 329]
Rivka Greenberg (Minzberg)

Knives by the Crematoriums

I was acquainted with Ruszka Liebeskind in Wierzbnik because she organized our Zionist youth movement. She used to come to Wierzbnik often, and that is how I got to know her. I served as secretary and instructor in our branch, and so I was directly in touch with the leaders of the movement, including Heniek Yaffe, Dolek Liebeskind, who later became a renowned partisan warrior in the area of Kraków, and Ruszka, Liebeskind's wife. Since I spoke Hebrew very well, I could talk to Ruszka in the language of the past.

When the war broke out we lost touch, but a year later, around the summer of 1940, I received an unexpected letter and was happy when I recognized the handwriting of Dolek Liebeskind at first glance. The letter has arrived in mysterious ways, which was only expected because it spoke of a youth movement being organized in Warsaw, called "ZOB" (Jewish fighting organization) and called for Jewish youths everywhere, in every town, to form similar organizations that would fight the plots of the Germans who seek to destroy us.

This letter also told us about the plans of the Germans, and although the conditions in our town were not as bad yet, we put our trust in this new information. When we considered the rebellion mentioned, however, it seemed like a fanciful idea. "How," we asked ourselves, "could we organize an active resistance against such a powerful force as the German war machine, which conquered nearly all of Europe?"

But the letter was so important to me that I kept it safely hidden, fearing it might one day fall into the wrong hands...

Later, when the Germans started searching our homes as an excuse for looting furs and other valuables, I hid the letter in a box and buried the box under some dirt in an abandoned stable in our yard.

That was the last contact I had with her, until I arrived in Auschwitz.

When we arrived in Auschwitz we underwent a life and death selection, and then had to assemble in groups of five and wait by Brzezinski for hours, without food, water or knowing what was waiting for us. Suddenly we were approached by some of the veteran prisoners in camp, nicknamed "Canada", who were wearing red handkerchiefs. They asked us where our shipment came from. We answered them, and they left. An hour later, another young woman showed up wearing a red handkerchief and a prison uniform, her hair cut short, and I immediately recognized her as Ruszka. She recognized me as well, but never betrayed the fact. Instead, she hissed at me out of the corner of her mouth: "Which of the other girls survived?" She meant, of course, the youths who were active in the movement she organized in Wierzbnik. I told her that 20 or 30 of the girls she used to know were here. After that she left, but she came back an hour later and brought us a few slices of bread, telling us to distribute them among the girls. She seemed to have contacts in the camp, because she already had news and told us that we were headed to camp A, block 25, which meant that we were going to live, for the time being. She added that once we arrived there, we should talk to a girl called "Elsa" who was in charge of the "block" (big cabin). When we arrived there, I passed Ruska's message to her. To disguise her subversive actions, the girl acted in a harsh, even rude manner, but she also did her best to encourage the prisoners, with food and other kinds of help.

On Yom Kippur Eve, we were told that the Nazis are planning a big selection, and she put us into a closed block. Ruszka arrived in the evening and they used some sheets and mattresses to make a table of sorts, with perforated potatoes serving as makeshift candlesticks. We lit memorial candles for Yom Kippur and sang "Kol Nidrei" together, quietly.

It was a very moving sight, a group of over 1,000 women singing, or more accurately crying, a heartbreaking, collective dirge.

They also sang the famous song "Our town is burning" by Mordechai Gebirtig, as well as the song of the partisans.

A few weeks later, Ruszka showed up again and secretly brought me a knife, saying that if I found myself in a desperate situation and all was lost, I should shove it into the body of a Nazi – or in her own words: "Don't walk alive into the crematorium, kill at least one of them".

The search for the victims' remains who were murdered in the Myowka Camp, and gathering them into a communal grave. The native of the city, Gershon Rozenwald, was among those involved in this holy task.

This was a matter of utmost secrecy, because getting caught with such a weapon was dangerous, and so she never told me who else received a knife, but I'm sure she gave them to other girls as well. I hid the knife in the shoes that I also got from her, and walked in those shoes despite the pain it caused me, keeping the knife in my possession until the day of our liberation. I still have it, to this day. For some reason, this knife gave me confidence, as if it were a real weapon.

[Page 331]
Malka Weisbloom

Saved by Finkelstein's Sacrifice

Early in the morning, people started whispering that the Gestapo were coming. "Run, as quickly as possible," we all thought. The labor camp of the lumber-mill lay by the Kamienna River and Jews from the entire region worked there. Eventually there was a great break out attempt, and those who had the chance tried to flee across the river, chased by the shots of the murderous guards.

The Germans noticed that the Jews were escaping and started giving chase. The river turned red with the blood of victims. Among those fleeing was a brave lad from the town of Płock, called Finkelstein. When he saw that the Germans were gaining and all the escapees were likely to be recaptured, he decided to defy them. He filled a bottle with sand and threw it at the Germans, right in the eyes! The confusion which ensued briefly halted the pursuit, and by the time the Germans have recovered, the rest of the escapees managed to cover some distance. The fellow himself had not escaped, and fell before the murderers. Among those who managed to escape and hide in the forest until the danger passed were Mendel Rybak, G. Rosenwald, Weisberg, the brothers Arie and Israel Rosenberg and their sister Tamar and another guy called Shmuel from the village nearby.

Conditions were harsh in the forest; the A.K. partisans harried the Jews, disarmed them and then murdered them. Rybak and Israel Rosenberg were brutally murdered by the A.K. and their sister Tamar had to see her brother lying at her feet like a butchered bird. She dug his grave with her bare hands and never recovered from the ordeal. The escape attempt generally came to a tragic end. Most of the people were killed and very few survived and are here in Israel with us.

The Heroism of Esther Manela

She was a young girl, born to a well-respected family, and only 20 years old. Her parents had a metal shop in Wierzbnik. One sunny spring day, while nature around us was coming to life, the accursed Germans rushed people to the train station, on their last journey. Among these multitudes of men, women and children, walked the girl, Esther Manela, followed by the Gestapo with their guns and clubs. By the time they arrived at the train station, the people were left breathless.

This station was typically filled with expectant people, happy to welcome guests arriving for the holidays or bid farewell to someone who was going to Israel. The people always waited with joy, but this time they stood brokenhearted, holding their breath. Hearts were pounding loudly. Suddenly, there was a long bellow of a horn, the sign that the train was coming, and everyone froze, unable to move or talk. Suddenly, the silence was interrupted and the Gestapo started pushing people into the cars using their guns and clubs. Esther refused to budge. The policemen yelled and ordered her into the car, but she stood tall, unmoving. They started beating her but to no avail. She resisted with all her might, yelling: "Kill me, I want to die in our town! In our station! I will not move from here! I do not want to see my loved ones destroyed, shoot me in the head, why would I go far away I want to die here!" "Verfluchter Jude," yelled a Gestapo officer and added, "The bullets are too precious, and we have cheaper means of exterminating you." He started pushing her inside but Esther held on for dear life and refused to go in. finally they had "no other choice" but to shoot her. Her last words were: "I beat you". She fell down on the train tracks. We all watched and cried.

[Page 332]
Avraham Shiner

Avraham Sheiner in the uniform of a Polish captain

A Gap in the Fence

The day of July 19th 1944 did not at first glance seem different from those before it. Everyone got up at the designated time and prepared to go on the second shift at the Arms and Ammunition factory in Starachovitz. The factory's name was changed by order of its new masters to "Herman Goering Werke". All of a sudden, something happened which hadn't occurred since the Germans invaded. It was almost too good to be true as work in the factory had stopped and the workers were ordered not to go on the second shift but to remain in the camp.

Although stopping the work was surprising, the reasons for it were quite clear. The Germans were suffering defeats on the front. One after the other and they began to retreat in haste from the towns of Poland and its conquered villages. The Jews imprisoned in the camp wanted to exploit this and to untie the shackles before the retribution came. There was great fear that with time running out as the Germans wanted "to get rid of" the Jews, in order to erase any traces of their terrible crimes.

That same night many Jews decided to escape. My former neighbour, a lad by the name of Shmuel had prepared himself for the eventuality of an escape by setting aside some pliers. A good effective opportunity to use them arose. He eventually cut the wire fence surrounding the camp and once a gap was made, hundreds of people crowded around it and started pushing to get through to freedom.

However, like Satan in the way, stood the Ukrainian Guards of the camp. Once they saw the huge crowd next to the fence they opened fire and threw grenades at the escaping people. They brought down many fatal casualties. In the end, a small group succeeded in avoiding the shower of lead and had escaped for the time being.

The next day, no one went out to work again and it was now very clear that the Germans intended to move. The amount of traffic on the road grew increasingly and the plan to escape strengthened in urgency while on the other hand a sense of danger intimidated all of us. The vigorous thinking and scheming found us planning things that we would have never considered in the recent past. We even thought of grabbing arms from the Germans and discussed all the trouble that could cause. However, when I approached the Ukrainian Captain of the Guard whose name was Shrott, in order to take his cocked sub-machine gun from his hands, he warned me not to get closer than 4 metres from him or he would shoot me. My attempt did not succeed, although I was not yet in despair. I searched for some substitute in the form of an iron bar or something like it so that I would not give up my life without a fight. This thought of not going to my slaughter willingly but to retaliate against persecutors and killers was always with me. My thoughts were, "Let me die with the philistines." All the time and at every step I searched to implement an escape.

In the meantime, the order was to dig deep holes, something, which had only one meaning and our hours were numbered. Therefore, there was no time to delay I had to act immediately. At first, I planned to escape through the fence opening that was torn open the previous evening, but I was forced to abandon that plan. It was too close to the place where the Ukrainian guard stood and a Germany soldier guarded the opening in case prisoners should escape through it again.

I turned around in time without them seeing me and I searched for another spot through which it would be possible to break out. When I got to the rear of the huts, a spark of hope rose in me. It appeared that the hands of G-d were there to help me because precisely during those seconds the Guard on the tower at the corner of the camp was about to change. Therefore, I waited impatiently until the one lot had descended and their replacements ascended so meanwhile, attention would be drawn from me to them and I would be able to vanish.

Finally, the fateful moment arrived. I took my life in my hands, mumbled a prayer quietly to the Lord saying, "Master of the world who ruled when no living creature had yet been created...in his hand I entrust my soul...G-d. G-d is with me and I shall not fear."

I turned my head back and forth looking around and waited a while. I noticed a little gap in the fence and bent the wire. I stuck my head through, then my body and I stood before the second fence of planks. I climbed it without being stopped and I was out...almost! It appeared that there was another obstacle! A stumbling block, which had to be moved out of the way and a wire fence above the fence of planks. I climbed it without trouble. I ascended up and leapt down. Thank G-d, blessed be He. I passed through the barrier of fire. The way was open to the dangers of the forest and the horrors of persecution and within them the hope of being saved.

[Page 334]
Gershon Rosenwald

Deep in the Forest

The town of Wierzbnik was hit early in the war, because of the factories there, and the secret agents who passed every detail to the Germans. I was planning to go to Brazil and already prepared a passport, but the war disrupted my plans and forced us all – my mother, my brother Moshe and myself – to stay at home and continues working in retail. When the abductions for forced labor started, I escaped to Słupia and hid with our relatives, since the Germans haven't reached that far yet. The Germans continued their conquests, however, and so I returned to Wierzbnik. Two months later, Jews started escaping for the other side of the border, to the Russian side.

One day, Avraham Unger, my brother Moshe and I all set out. We hid money in our shoes, boarded the train and traveled as far as the town of Przemyœl. There was a woman there who smuggled people, and we got her address and paid her a visit. When we arrived, we found three rooms full of people and were told to wait for nightfall. While we were waiting to cross the border, the Gestapo suddenly arrived at midnight. They asked if we had any money or Jewels and threatened that if they found anything hidden, they would kill us. Avraham Unger got scared and said he had money in his shoes. The German forced him to take out the money with his teeth. After witnessing that, we kept quiet and kept our money. The next day, we crossed the river at night and the peasants took all our belongings and forced us to cross the current, which was so deep the water reached almost to our mouths. We crossed the river, reached the bank and crawled until we ran into a Russian patrol that arrested us and led us to Przemyœl. Fifty of us were put in a single cell and then released five days later. We were greatly disappointed. Although we escaped from dangers and hardships, we now faced hunger, the lack of clothes and a harsh cold. Despairing, I decided to return to Wierzbnik. The persecution has already started and the Germans were abusing our people. I sought to earn some money for a living and traveled to Słupia to smuggle something, but failed. I was captured by an SS officer called Kizel, who beat me and took everything I had. He also caught my mother selling some butter and beat her up. A while later, two sisters from Lodz came to live with us. Later still I started working at the Majowka factory along with my brother. I was appointed as sanitarian and my job was to sanitize the clothes at the bathhouse. We used the money we earned to bribe the manager so he wouldn't shave the beards of Jews.

We lived in hope that things will change for the better. We didn't expect the extermination. We believed that work would save us, because everyone worked at the factories, some even two shifts. The Germans fined people, and if someone couldn't afford to pay a policeman would come and take him to the police station, replacing the poor workers of Wierzbnik with workers from other places who bribed them. The entire factory was a melting pot of people from various places, such as Vienna, Lublin, Kalisz and Płock, were sent there to do forced labor only to be replaced by others later.

Next came the establishment of the ghetto and we moved in with the Fajgenbaum family. Life was very bitter and the situation was harsh, to the point where we envied those who died of natural causes and thus escaped the clutches of the Germans. Terror reigned at night, the

Germans and the Volksdeutsche were looking for people, there was nowhere to hide and so it all continued until the eviction.

The eviction

As I have already mentioned, we hoped that the people of Wierzbnik could be saved. Although we already heard about the extermination of Jews in other places, we thought it wouldn't happen to us. The Gestapo would go to other towns and kidnap people to do forced labor in Starachowice, and our Judenrat tried to ransom them. People came to us to get work certificates from places that had no factories of their own (from Opatów, Bodzentyn, Słupia, Wąchock, Iłża and elsewhere). A railway crossed our town and we lived next to the station and heard the trains go by, full of people, the sound of their moans coming from the cars. We knew the cars were full of prisoners, because Yaakov Kleiner and I used to read the newspapers published by the resistance, which said that Treblinka "swallowed" half a million Jews already. We lived next to the Judenrat and we started worrying about getting work certificates, because we already heard about the transports. My brother Yitzhak worked at the furnace in the factory and was able to provide work certificates for his relatives. One night, however, we heard something happening in the street. It was the night of 26.10.1942. I got myself two certificates, one for the "Zeork" power plant and the other for the lumber-mill. That night, it was no longer possible to leave the ghetto. It was dark and we heard gunshots. The town was surrounded by SS troopers, Polish police and Ukrainians as well as Lithuanian policemen. My brother-in-law, Kopel Maslowicz, a father of four, was still at work at the lumbermill and my brother Yitzhak and his children were at the factory in Starachowice, where they were prevented from returning home. Suddenly, the Germans showed up along with their villainous assistants, broke down doors and ordered everyone to leave town. I told my mother to hide our few remaining dollars, to sew them into her dress, and explained to her that we were merely going someplace else, although I knew what was going on…

A little girl, the same age as my sister, came to us with tears in her eyes saying her father never came back home. Their twins were also left behind and we all headed for the Rinek, where we were beaten and shot at. My mother and I were joined there by the brother, Berl Niskier, and his wife Hanna who stood next to my mother. They lined us in fives. Every single member of that murderous machine was drunk. I stood next to my mother when I was approached by Althoff, the German commander, who told me to get out of the line or he would kill me on the spot. I didn't want to move but my mother told me to do it, so there would be someone left to tell the tale.

My brother-in-law Maslowicz, on the other hand, despite being at the factory, ran with his children to the Rinek, found his wife Sheindl and his other children and joined them. I never saw them again. I was among those who were forced to run to Starachowice, while those who refused to run were shot on the spot. They brought us to the firing range, where we sat down with our belongings. That night, they put us in a cabin and I was lying in the bunk above Leibish Kerbel. My brother Yitzhak was also there. After seeing the people lying there, I joined a group of people who were taken to the Stalownia, accompanied by Ukrainians. The lumber-mill was nearby and I escaped from the line and sneaked into the lumber-mill through the fence along with Noah Fryd. The people brought to the lumber-mill registered and so did Fryd and I. The following night I recalled that all my stuff was left at "Zeork", across the fence. I crossed the fence and got captured by a Gestapo officer, who brought me into the office where the Polish commander informed him that I wasn't on the list. Since I wasn't on the list they called for Becker to kill us. In the meantime, the people at the lumber-mill heard they were planning to kill me, so they begged Piatek to save me. After a long while he arrived and saw a German soldier guarding me. He told the guard he needed me for work and saved me from certain death.

The sons of Moshe Koznitz

I continued working at the lumber-mill for several months, until the Germans announced the founding of a "Jewish State" in Szydłowiec. They wanted to send me there, so I hid under the lumber. They found me anyway and sent me to the munitions factory. The manager, a Polish "Volksdeutsche" called Novak (they were two brothers) was very cruel to me.

In the meantime, three people escaped from camp. This fact was announced in the morning, before we were all lined up. An SS officer called Becker arrived and announced that the relatives of the escapees must stand aside. The leader of the Jews was a man from Płock called Dr. Blum. In addition to the relatives, they were going to kill every tenth man. Dr. Blum stood with us, and Becker went up to the cabin to make sure that no one remained behind. There was a false partition in that cabin, and behind it we hid two children, the sons of Moshe Kopf, and another baby. Their mother worked in camp as a cleaner while the baby was born there and the mother took care of these children. The baby belonged to a man called David. When Becker went up there he found the baby, and asked Dr. Blum why he left the baby upstairs. The latter answered that he cut the cord and then told him to send him to the machine if he can't be a doctor.

In the meantime, they returned every tenth man back to the line after chastising them. I worked double shifts, in the garden and the lumber-mill. Diseases and plagues broke out. Our manager extorted food from us, although he didn't kill people. He had a secretary named Lotz and she told the Gestapo about the sick people in camp. The soldiers came to camp and took four people: the son of Moshe Cukier, Avraham Goldstein, Magister Lublinski and the carpenter Ash. They put them in quarantine and I was among those chosen to carry the sick.

These people have almost recovered when they were told they were going to a hospital. They dressed up and even took some money. On the way we were told not to look back or we would be killed. When we looked back, we saw that there was a man walking behind us carrying shovels. On the way we also realized we weren't headed to a hospital but to a cemetery. When we arrived, we were told to put the men on the ground, and then they shot them all. Among these people was Cukier's father. They told us to cover them and took us back to camp. One of them was buried alive...

I continued working there until 1944. Some of my friends (Yaakov Kleiner, his son-inlaw David, Shmuel Yitzhak) and I had contact with the resistance and we learned from them that half a million Jews were killed in Treblinka. We saw there was no way out. We despaired.

Escaping to the forest

The Russians started advancing and when they entered Galicia they captured the gas mines, paralyzing the factories in Starachowice. We realized that the Jews will not remain at the factories and started planning ways to defect and hide. I had no means, but I learned of various ways of escape and we heard that several people escaped from camp. At one time we had to carry munitions crates to the train and saw words inscribed inside the car: "We, the last Jews from the ghetto of Vilna, were murdered in Treblinka – avenge us." Since the people pushing the wheelbarrows alternated constantly, many have seen the writing.

People continued working at the mill. The Germans promised that no harm would come to us, but we didn't believe them. One day I was working in the garden while the others have already finished their work. Wooden planks were placed overhead to dry. I saw a truck arrive, full of Gestapo troopers armed with bayoneted rifles. I went up to the "sushernia" and cried to the others that they came to take us. Then I decided to escape. I pulled down a short plank. I jumped over the fence, crossed the water and found other people. We continued running. As soon as we were discovered, they opened fire! We ran through the wheat and found other people: Mendel Rybak, Brodbeker and others. I ran, and when I reached the forest I found four other men: David Kerbel, Shmuel Brodbeker, Yaakov Weisberg and a fifth person whose name I no longer remember. Night was falling and we decided to spend it there. We fell asleep at dawn and when we woke up, we noticed a man. We approached him and asked where we are and he told us. We continued walking, left the forest and found other people. Later, we met a gentile who gave us bread and asked us to leave. We returned to the forest and found the ranger. He gave us directions how to approach the partisans. We found Bolek, the leader of the partisans, who welcomed us and told us not to run around the forest, mentioning a girl he met there. I thought it was my cousin, but I was wrong. The partisan group was small and composed of Poles. Later, we found out that the forest ranger was a snitch but they didn't kill him, threatening instead that if he kept providing information about them, they would burn down his house. Bolek couldn't take us in, because he didn't have weapons for us, so we left. We needed to eat, so we spread out to try and get food from the peasants. Sometimes we got some, and sometimes we didn't. When we met partisans, they told us to line up. I recognized some of them as people who worked at the factory in Starachowice. They demanded money, items and all sorts of things from us. They said they were communists, and that it was wrong for one person to have money and for another not to have any. They said they couldn't take us in because we worked for the Germans. I told them they did too and they slapped me twice and immediately we went to the village again to look for food. In one of the villages, a gristmill was seized by a group of Gestapo troopers. A Jewish girl lived in this village. From time to time, one of us got killed. Once I was with a group of five. We met a man on a bicycle, who said: "I have some bread for you, come with me to the gristmill." We knew it was a trap so we escaped back to the forest. That was how we lived. We went to the fields and gathered potatoes. The peasants ambushed us at night and beat us up. Once, we arrived at the village at night and found a lot of partisans, who captured us and took us to their headquarters. The commander told us he couldn't take us in, but gave us grenades for self defense and meat. When we arrived at the forest we stumbled again across the Polish partisans, and one of them killed Rosenberg for his suit. After a while we met another group of Polish partisans who took the rest of our Polish money. I recognized one of them and told him that they took our money, and the commander went, gave us back the money and took in three of us – an accountant, a barber and one other. Next we crossed paths with mounted partisans who asked if any of us served in the army. Some people who served in the army followed them, never suspecting a trap. The next day they killed them all.

A Hasid came from camp Majowka, the brother of Hershel Wajzer. He looked like a monk, tall and thin. His only possessions were a pair of tefillin, which he wore devoutly, no matter the circumstances. He spent a long time hiding under straw and eating grain.

How could the trees remain standing?

A few days later he arrived at the forest, but he would not eat any of the food there, which wasn't kosher, save for potatoes. He knew how to calculate the Hebrew calendar and determined when Yom Kippur should fall. He prepared the prayers himself. On the night of Kol Nidrei he led prayer and we stood among the trees and prayed Kol Nidrei, wailing bitterly in a voice that could scare every living thing in the forest. Our cry for mercy could tear a heart of stone. We cried out until we collapsed. I am amazed that the trees remained standing.

A new group of Russian partisans appeared later on, and they taught us how to use rifles. After our training was completed, we followed them. About two weeks later, the Germans besieged us and captured Itche and some guy who was scarred by a grenade that exploded once in his pocket. The partisans escaped and we found the dead chopped to pieces. A few days later, another group of partisans arrived, and we joined them and server under a regiment commander called "Pioter".

They didn't give us any weapons, assigning us service duties like pitching tents and so on.

Once, commander Pioter gave a speech and said that we were all equal before assigning the various tasks. The two Goldberg brothers went at night to the village, found two Germans with the mayor, disarmed them and brought them to the forest, where they played around with them for a bit and then shot them. Then we were besieged and the entire partisan group escaped, but the Germans kept up the chase and we split up and regrouped later. One night, they said we were going to cross the front line. I was sick and had trouble walking, and they wanted to leave me behind, but David Kerbel refused to leave me. I tied my shoes to my neck with a rope to keep them from falling apart, but along the way I had to throw them away and walk barefoot. One of the guys, named Moshe, killed himself. We stopped by a village and hid in an attic. We learned that the passage is narrow and many would have to go back. So we split up, because we didn't want to go back. They threatened us that if we came back, they would kill us. On the other hand, they promised that if we stayed in the forest, they would come to save us later.

Shlomo Enisman

One of us wanted to leave. He left us some money and took off, and we went into the forest and stayed by the stream, where we were told to wait. We went into the village, stole some leather and tried to trade it for food. After a while, we noticed the Germans laying telephone lines. They didn't see us, so we decided to go back and went the other way around, so they wouldn't find our tracks. We had grenades and decided that if the Germans captured us we would blow ourselves up. We were besieged and some of us were captured and killed. I found myself alone, started walking and found a corpse. I immediately recognized it – Itche Greenberg. Then came a commander, gathered all of us and said we were heading for the front line. By that time, Enisman has returned to the forest and said he was coming with us. We started walking and reached the front line on the third night. Then Enisman told me: "Let's go back, I have some money, we'll get by," but I refused his offer. On the way we stopped for rest and the first in line remained sitting and died. We all stopped because of him. Then we continued walking. We were told that when we arrive at the front line someone would give the order and we would all shout "Ora!" and charge. And that was what happened. We crossed the lines, and by the glare of the rockets fired I saw Germans in the trenches. They opened fire on us. We ran. Shells exploded before us. We ran all the way, until we reached the Russian unit.

[Page 338]
Avraham Shiner

Hunted and Murdered by Polish Partisans

It was as though the change we yearned for was already in the air. The Germans and their supporters seemed more and more worried. The closer the Russian-German front drew, the more tense they became, while we started having mixed feelings about the matter. The near future seemed to hold both chance and risk: on the one hand, we hoped for release; on the other, we feared that they would seek to eliminate us at the last moment, to cover their tracks.

This was the reason that many decided to beat them to the task and leave before the Germans could carry out their plot. One night, nearly 200 people broke through the fence and started escaping towards the forest. The Germans fired at them and killed many, but some of the escapees have managed to reach the forest.

The next day the Germans ordered us to dig holes. Since there was no reason or cause for such holes to be dug, I realized that their sole purpose was to serve as common graves for the entrapped Jews. I felt that the ground was burning under our feet. Therefore if I was going to escape, the sooner the better.

After brief preparations and a tour of the area, I have chosen several paths and finally snuck unseen, crossed the inner fence and the outer fence and started running towards the forest. It seemed that the Germans did not notice my escape because no shots were heard, and after a brief dash I reached the edge of the forest. Here I ran into a cow herder. I circled around him because I didn't want any contact with anyone out in the open and entered the forest. A few dozen meters later I noticed a German army camp. Instead of continuing in this direction I doubled back the way I came, to get away from the danger I almost ran into.

While I was walking in the forest, I must have swerved from my original track, and finally I reached a clearing, not far from the German camp. A group of people, hard to distinguish from a distance, sat there. They were sitting in a semi-circle, which had me convinced that they are partisans, but when I approached them I noticed that they are Jews, the same Jews that escaped from our camp the night before. Some were wounded from the shots of the Germans who chased them.

I told the Jews about the army camp I ran into in the area and urged them to leave the place as soon as possible, but they refused to listen or leave before it grew dark.

I joined them anyway. I sat next to them and we started talking about the bloody night before. After a short while, while we are talking or listening to each other, we suddenly heard gunshots from the direction of the camp, the sounds amplified by the bullets hitting the trees. We all ducked low to avoid the flight path of the bullets. But when we raised our heads, we saw dozens of Jews running from the camp toward the forest, with the Germans firing on them ceaselessly. The fire grew heavier and people started scattering and running in aimlessly! People panicked and ran away in every direction, unsure what waited for them down the road. I ran as fast as I could as well, and after a while I was seeing fewer and fewer people around me. When I finally stopped, only two remained next to me – Arie Lustgarten and Helstoch. They were wearier than I was and couldn't go on, but I begged them not to stop for rest and encouraged them to keep running until we reached someplace safer. They accepted my words and after a short rest we continued running and walking alternately, until we reached the region of the town of Iłża. At night we slept in the forest and in the morning we tried to delve deep into the thick undergrowth that covered us from unwanted eyes.

And so we remained trapped within the forest, unsure what to do next. After a while, we grew desperate for food. Everything we had was gone, and we were faced with the need to get some food at any cost. We knew that we would be putting our lives at risk, but we had no choice and tried to approach the villages near the forest. Our fears came to pass. The villagers not only inhospitable and refused to sell or give us anything, but informed the Germans of our presence in all manner of cunning ways, and then we would be chased and shot at, barely escaping with our lives. Nevertheless, we did not give up and attempted to return to village to get some food from time to time, because in the forest we were doomed to starve.

Sometimes we got lucky, and managed to find something to satisfy our terrible hunger, but more often we failed.

The first encounter with the partisans

Since approaching the village meant risking discovery, we tried to avoid making too much noise. Therefore we refrained from walking in groups and preferred to sneak in ones and twos. One day, as I walked through the forest on the way to the village, a Pole popped out of thin air with a rifle aimed at me and ordered: "Hands up!"

I was unarmed and so I obeyed him, and led to his partisan camp. Later I learned that it was an A.K. unit.

There were six other Jews in the place we arrived at, lying face down on the ground. My "escort" pointed at them and told me in Polish to lie on the ground like them. I asked him for permission to speak with their commander first, and after permission was granted I approached him and told him that I wanted to fight with them against the Germans, emphasizing that I am willing to go first into battle. While talking to him I looked this way and that and noticed that were some gentiles from Wierzbnik among the partisans, former classmates of mine. I give them pointed looks, but they pretended not to notice and the commander dismissed me as well. Eventually I was forced to lie down next to the rest of the Jews, face down.

We lay there miserable and affronted for a few hours until we were pulled to our feet and the commander chastised us for our supposed negative actions. "The villagers," he said, "have been complaining about you, saying that you rob them and steal things from them. I warn you that if I ever hear anything like that again, I will kill you."

We knew that there was no truth to this tale and they were merely looking for excuses to abuse us, so there was no point in arguing with him.

Next they ordered us to run away, and shot at us as we did until we were gone, leaving us unharmed only by God's good grace.

Between a rock and a hard place

A few days after the unpleasant encounter with the A.K. partisans we ran into another partisan group, this time part of the NSZ organization. We naively believed they might treat us better than their predecessors, but we were sorely mistaken.

As it turned out, this organization of so called partisans was noted particularly for its cruel treatment of Jews. Its policy concerning Jews was identical to the acts of the Germans, and like them they murdered Jews whenever they found them.

This time they were going to execute us without qualms, and only a ruse that occurred to me at the last moment saved us from this calamity. I told them that on the way there we noticed a group of Vlasovs (Russian defectors who joined the Germans) from a distance and by my estimate they should be nearby. If they heard shots they were sure to locate them, "And then", I added, "we would all be doomed". They seemed to believe me, because they quickly fled to their village to get their people and cattle into the forest before dark and left us alone.

To Abraham's grave

Not only were these encounters troubling, the severe disappointment also made us despair. We based all our hopes on the notion that once we escaped the German prison we would join the partisans and fight with them against the common enemy and avenge our murdered brothers, and here we find ourselves at risk of being murdered by the partisans themselves, a fact demonstrating acutely how alone we were, trapped in a malicious and hateful place. We took care not to hit such "snags" again, but they too made their way in the forest by stealth and so we ran into yet another calamity.

While crossing the road from the forest to a village, we were jumped by two partisans who aimed their rifles at us. They had a wagon hitched to horses and they ordered us to climb in. On the way they started harassing us with anti-Semitic scorn. When we told them we wish to join them and fight the Germans together, they laughed out loud, cutting into our wounded souls like a scalpel through living flesh. Without being asked they sarcastically told us "We are taking you to Abraham's grave." Now we started fearing that mockery will not be the end of this, and they had something far more wicked planned. In light of our previous experiences, we were already bitterly familiar with the Polish partisans and we made our minds to escape at any cost.

While driving, we reached a steep slope and the horses were having trouble pulling the wagon. They ordered us off the wagon and had us walk behind it.

But God was with us. After a long journey on even ground, we reached a mountain slope. After we reached the top, we started down a steep incline. The horses started running, and we took advantage of the situation. Instead of following them, we also started running, in another direction, to right, so we quickly gained some distance from them and had a chance to disappear.

I wish I was a dog

Three times we faced death, twice by partisans from the ONR and A.K., and once by common murderous bandits. By God' grace we somehow managed to escape them every time through flight and deception. We didn't know, and neither did the gentiles, how close the front line was. The German presence in the area was at its peak, and given the situation every gentile considered the killing of Jews to be his first commandment. We were hunted for our lives to the point that once, I envied a dog I saw: "How lucky you are, you dog! I wish I was a dog like you!"

In the meantime, we heard about the murder of Jews who like us escaped no long ago from the camps. My goal was therefore to escape this oppressive place, where death lay in wait for us every step of the way. I wanted to go east, to the front lines, to cross them and get to the soviets. I was familiar with the area, and already close to Poland's border. Days of light, unending rain came upon us. We had no cover or shelter from the endless rain. We had to sleep on the wet ground, and our bodies were sodden. Once the rain stopped my chest and back were so swollen that you couldn't see the bones, but the greatest inconveniences were the swelling in my knees and the wounds on my feet, inside the torn shoes. Our third member, Helstoch, joined four Jews we met in the forest. I continued traveling with Arie until I could go on no further. The hunger of a weak body that suffered from malnutrition for years, the rain and damp and the lice that ate us alive, the effort of running, the fear and the rest of our hardships got to me. My health was so poor that I could no longer walk. I felt my pulse and estimated that my temperature was over 40 degrees high. I was barely conscious, and felt that I was dying.

The noble Yezierski family

And then, like in a dream, I saw the image of a young man standing on a hill before me and addressing us kindly: "Dear Jews, beware, the nearby village (some 500 meters from us) is filled with a German soldiers, take heed. When it grows darker, come to us, you can sleep in the barn. Here it is," pointed the man, "the first house in this direction. Would you like some bimber?" He showed us a bottle of home made vodka, came closer and offered us some. Arie took a sip and brought the bottle to my lips. I couldn't even resist, but I could not drink. I never thought I would sleep under a roof again, and the possibility gave me strength. By evening I could already enter the gentile's yard. We were invited in by the one of the proprietor's many sons, who welcomed us with true affection. They offered us a hearty meal. I will never forget that first evening in years that I sat in a private house without the nightmare of persecution hovering over my head, out of the Germans' direct reach.

The owner of the house himself was happy, proud of the good deed he was able to do, but my condition worried him. His wife realized my condition and started taking care of me. Among other things, she covered my bloated body with horseradish leafs, which warmed my skin until the swelling went down and the fever broke. Over the next few days Arie started working in the field, but I was exhausted. I lay all day and all night in the stable, hidden from the Germans. These good gentiles covered me with their furs, washed my clothes and boiled them, and slowly I came back to myself. Only my wounded feet have not fully healed yet. The older boys loved us.

Once, the gentile sent us both away when they feared that two young men who noticed us in his house might burn down the house and everyone in it. One night, I was separated from Arie. I came back to the gentile and found him there. The gentile sheltered us again, until the Germans started visiting his house often and he asked Arie to explain to me that he could not hide two. But before I left he came, apologized and gave me enough money for the road, and asked me to come back if I was in trouble. One of the boys instructed me how to find a contact of the A.L. partisans, who guided me to the Russian partisans.

After the War

[Page 343]
Simcha Mincberg

After my Liberation

After my liberation I remained in camp for a few days to regain my strength and recover from the illness I suffered during the last weeks of our captivity. Then I left, hoping to go back to town and find my loved ones, my friends and townsmen. I plodded along on foot until I arrived in Częstochowa, which according to rumors was the gathering place of many refugees from various camps.

From Częstochowa I continued walking until finally, on the eve of 16.3.1945, I reached Wierzbnik, which was now both in ruins and alien to me. I sneaked across the Rinek and stumbled suddenly into our townsman, Gershon Rosenwald, who couldn't believe his eyes when he saw me and exclaimed: "Baruch mehaye metim," since everyone thought I was already dead.

A few families were already in town by then. Some came back from hiding or the forests, and most were survivors of the death camps. Since they greatly feared the anti-Semite Polish population, they banded together. Most people lived at the home of Leibish Brodbeker, because most of the Jewish houses in town were already taken over by the Poles and even going out on the streets alone was dangerous.

It is hard to describe my meeting with the survivors of our town, especially since I found my son, Mendel, among them. Our meeting was indescribable: the crying and shouting, the tears and joy mixed together, and we were all very emotional.

I stayed there for a few days before my son and I moved to the apartment of Avraham Frimerman, since the Brodbekers' apartment was too crowded. We started looking for ways to settle back in, but upon reflection, bearing in mind the bloody past, I came to the conclusion that we could not build a new life on the ruins of the Jewish community.

Before leaving the place, I felt the need to visit all the killing grounds where our martyred loved ones lost their pure lives. Naturally, I turned to the labor camps and searched the area for Jewish graves, but my efforts were in vain. There were no familiar markings in the area. I entered the remaining cabins, which were drenched with Jewish toil and suffering, and suddenly I found on one of the shelves authentic lists of all the Jews ever to go through the camps, written with typical German meticulousness. I took the notes with me, because I considered them evidence of the years of slavery, torture and destruction, written by the hangman himself to serve as an indictment against all the leaders who silently accepted these actions, which no doubt helped the Nazi devil carry out his diabolical scheme.

In addition, I handled the proper Jewish burial of the dozens of victims who were murdered on the day the camp was abandoned and were temporarily buried next to it. This was a hard, complex task, because there were Poles among the dead. It took many efforts before we received permission to dig two common graves, one for Jewish victims and one for Poles. I therefore went with my friend, Leibish Herblum, to a Polish tombstone maker and ordered a nice tombstone. The news spread around town and Leibish took upon himself the holy task of transporting the bones of the martyrs to the new common grave. The Poles did the same for their dead. The entire Polish population gathered for the ceremony, along with our few survivors, and I went on stage and delivered the tear-filled, bitter and wrathful eulogy. I was closing the lid on the remainder of the town's glorified Jewry.

A monument was erected after the liberation. Simcha Mincberg delivering a speech.

More bereaved, orphaned, widowed and childless people came back every day, broken and tired, in the vain hope of finding some relative or friend. And as I have said before, they banded together out of fear of the Polish persecutors.

One night, members of the A.K. have attacked the home of Leibish Brodbeker, where several of the Holocaust survivors have settled. The residents of the house, among them Wolfowicz's wife and her children and Enisman's wife and her child who miraculously survived the crematoriums of Auschwitz, tried to flee and climbed to the roof, but fell before the Polish murderers. Only Mrs. Enisman's little daughter, who was covered by her mother's slain corpse was saved and lives today in Israel. It is only natural that this terrible slaughter encouraged the survivors to quickly leave the bloodied city that turned into a deathtrap. I, along with my son Mendel and others, traveled to the town of Lodz, where many survivors have already gathered after escaping from all corners of Poland.

The Organization of our Landsleit

Our ambition and hope was to get to Israel, although arranging the necessary certificates involved much bureaucracy and took a long time because many were waiting in line for them. In august 1949 I left Poland forever, headed for Israel, but we were delayed for several months in Paris and only on December 9th 1949 did we arrive at our goal, Israel. Slowly we settled in and started meeting the remainder of our townsmen, especially my fellow Zionist activist, Yoseph Dreksler, who arrived before me with his family from the plains of Russia. As time went by, I felt that we had to organize our townsmen and arrange for some kind of social activity. But the hardships of striking root and the need to learn how to plan our actions delayed our activity, because we had to form first the infrastructure on which we will develop social organizational activity. And so the idea of immortalizing our community and all its aspects was born. The original idea came from my friend Yoseph Dreksler, as well as Hershel Fajgenbaum, Jerachmiel Singer, Hershel Wajzer, Moshe Kerbel and others, and it started winning the hearts of many survivors. First we needed to create the framework for an organization of our townsmen and to establish contact with them. Most importantly, we started to hold annual memorial rallies to commemorate our martyrs. And so we turned the 16th of Marheshvan into a memorial day and a time of gathering for the survivors, and every year we commemorate our ruined community and our martyred loved ones who perished in the terrible Holocaust. During one of those annual memorials came up the notion of publishing the "Yizkor" book to commemorate the annihilation, telling the story of our community from its days of glory to its tragic, reckless doom.

To carry out this idea we talked to the survivors in Israel and abroad. We circulated letters telling them how important this piece would be for future generations. At first, I was assisted by Yoseph Dreksler, Hershel Fajgenbaum, Jerachmiel Singer, Avraham Shiner and others. But the cooperation we received from the other survivors was limited.

Apathy and disinterest ran rampant and no actual activity took place.

Memorial book

And then, about three years ago, we were fortunate to have our distinguished townsman Moshe Sali-Kerbel take part in the annual memorial service and join the book committee, taking over the position of secretary. His initiative and enthusiasm worked wonders and the idea started taking shape. He kept in constant touch with people, offering convincing explanations of how important this enterprise is and sending hundreds of letters and requests regarding the subject to our scattered townsmen, shaking them out of their complacency and convincing many of the need to publish the book. A small editorial board for the book gradually took shape, comprised of Moshe Sali, Jerachmiel Singer, Hershel Fajgenbaum and myself, and we started moving at full steam ahead. We quickly saw results as the first memoirs flowed in: articles, notes and pictures, along with substantial monetary donations. The committees formed in Toronto and New York both excelled in raising funds for this purpose. We tightened our relationship with our landsleit abroad and interest in the publication of the book was slowly catching among our townsmen everywhere.

And so our work has continued for several years, through complex, daily efforts that required strength, vigilance, initiative and patience. Most important of all were the conviction that this task could be completed, as well as sharing this conviction with others and gaining their trust. The expanded committee meets from time to time to discuss current affairs and receive a report on the work carried out. As chairman of the organization, I keep daily contact with our member Moshe Sali, who is the life of this enterprise, and we meet once or twice a week to discuss and determine future lines of action, to guide and direct the system and keep in constant touch with the rest of the survivors.

I also meet our townsmen at the home of my daughter, Rivka Mincberg-Greenberg, which became the home of the book committee and a meeting place for all our foreign townsmen visiting Israel.

And now we can clearly see that thanks to the dedication of individuals in Israel and abroad we will soon be able to realize our desired goal, the publication of a "Yizkor book" for the glory of our unforgettable community of Wierzbnik-Starachowice, commemorating the martyrs of our town who died as saints. May the lord avenge them.

[Page 349]
Moshe Sali (Kerbel)

Yizkor…

Before World War II, immigrants coming to Israel did not assemble according to their hometowns. The term "Landsmanshaft" was foreign to a country that nurtured the ideal of merging the immigrants into a single people. Jews who came from small towns would blur their origins by naming a renowned city in the region they came from.

The situation changed completely in the aftermath of World War II, whose flames devoured the roots of the lively European Jewry, for whom Poland served as a kind of pyre (auto de fe).

As a result of this terrible reality, any memory of Jewish Poland suddenly became invaluable. Every city and town, every village and settlement where Jews lived before the Holocaust suddenly became precious After the annihilation, any place where Jews lived and worked became a sacred archeological site. It is therefore no wonder that the residents of every city and town, even the smallest ones, started invoking the name of their town in awe, respect and longing. Every person who lived there suddenly became so familiar, and anything created in the town, every memory, became sacred. These reasons motivated certain activists to form a social framework for the residents of the town, to build a memorial in the Holocaust Cellar on Mount Zion and hold an annual memorial service on the day commemorating the terrible Holocaust.

A host of our townsmen come every year to this Memorial Day, to commemorate the martyrs of our town and take part in the precious past that was so tragically expunged and decimated. They are drawn, as if by invisible strings, from near and far, to that place of friendship. They stand in groups and pairs and whisper. A torrent of memories floods them when they see each other, and the place buzzes like a beehive.

It is pleasant to walk among those groups, to linger here and there. To look and listen, and turn those scattered words and glances into threads that weave images from the past. My soul is aquiver and I feel warmth bathing me during those moments, as I see my dear parents and the entire community of my sacred town. Our Hair may no longer be black, taken over by silver, but the precious memory remains, as if according to the song:

"Days go by, the year changes, But the tune remains the same"

And once again we return to those beautiful years, when we were young dreamers. Our hearts still tremble recalling those days that teased our imagination and slaked the thirst in our souls. We argued with youthful passion and ignored the daily hardships and the hatred that clouded the town. The yearning for salvation echoed in us and we were aware of everything happening in Israel and the world. The activity for the national funds, the blue box and the Zionist spirit, all gave us fortitude. We are filled with sadness seeing how few we are. Our brave loved ones, who drank the ideals of the movement, worked for Zion enthusiastically and waited by its cradle, were all taken before their time, so tragically and callously, without seeing their work bear fruit in the form of a Jewish state for the Jewish people.

This reality is sad and hard to swallow. I look at the survivors of the Holocaust and although they have suffered years of torment and hardship I see a flame that burns within their collective hearts, the secret memory of the town that is no more.

They cling to each other, with words and looks, immersed deep in the memories of their youth, the war, their neighbors, their livelihood or their activism. Silence spreads, a mysterious sense of expectation, eyes watching the burning memorial candles. Filled with sadness and sorrow, heads bent, we commune with our townsmen, touched by the voice of the cantor: "El Male Rahamim..."

Our hearts stir, you hear scattered sighs, eyes tear like fountains and the heart cries in silence.

"Land, never cover their blood."

[Page 350]
Perele Brodbeker-Unger

Murders – After Liberation

I will never forget that day. It is impossible to forget.

The great day of May 8, 1945 arrived, the day of liberation. My sister and I were in Theresienstadt camp. At the first moment of liberation, the urge to go home was aroused in us; perhaps we would find someone there.

With great effort we managed to get on the train that was going to Poland. Throughout the entire journey we had illusions, but when we arrived at the Starachowice train station, we received a fright – how bare and empty it was!

Where were the former Jewish merchants, the carriers, the *droshkys* {carriages]? Everything was empty and silent. We walked by Kaliowa Street, where we had built a large house in 1937. Here also – silence and emptiness. We could no longer hear the beautiful melody of Heniek Biderman's studying.

When we reached the market we encountered Leibish Broidbeker (now in Canada), the late Haim Broidbeker's son. He invited us into his house saying that "all the Jews from the city are in my house." We were delighted at his invitation and went along with him.

In his house we encountered 25 people, among them Shlomo Enisman's wife and two daughters, Yerahmiel Wolfowicz's wife and two children, and all the others were men.

After a long while we went out to the market. Looking around we stood as though turned to stone. The city looked like after a tragedy. Everything was empty, closed, all Jewish shops were empty, the streets without a living soul, and fear blew from all sides.

My sister and I decided to go to the Jewish cemetery to look for the grave of our beloved dead father, Moshe Broidbeker, of blessed memory. On the way we met Christian acquaintances who greeted us with wonder: "You're alive?" they asked us in astonishment. "What are you doing here?" "You are risking your lives!" they warned us further.

We didn't understand all that. Now that we were liberated from the Nazis, did we also have to be afraid? Was danger threatening us now too?

We nevertheless continued walking. When we arrived at the cemetery we again saw the great destruction that had befallen us. Even the graves and gravestones had suffered it. All the gravestones were broken, strewn around or carried off. You couldn't see a sign of the *"ohel"* [elaborate grave of distinguished people] belonging to the former rabbi of the city; no sign of the hedge around the field.

We recognized our father's grave by various signs. We covered him with pieces of stone, cried thoroughly and left.

On our way back to Leibish Broidbeker's house, it was almost nighttime. We looked around – where would we arrange to sleep. In the meantime, Binie came along and asked us to come sleep at her place. We immediately agreed and went with her. Binie had a two-room apartment for herself on ¯ecke St. and we prepared for sleep there. As soon as it got dark, we heard a knock at the door. We were again frightened to death. We recognized the voice of Leibish Broidbeker and opened the door. "Are you alive?" he called out in fear, and then gave us the terrible news that that night there had been a terrible slaughter of the small handful of Jews in his house. The bloodthirsty Polish thugs attacked them, killing the women and children, only one of Shlomo Enisman's daughter's was wounded (now lives in Israel).

Four fresh victims in the *shtetl*. Innocent Jewish blood was spilled again. This happened twenty-four hours after liberation.

We gave the victims a Jewish burial with deep sorrow and a weeping heart. My sister and I immediately left our former hometown forever, leaving behind nothing but memories of what once was.

[Page 352]
Chava Fajgenbaum (Shraga)

The Nazis' Followers

After the defeat of the Nazi beast, when the world could finally, after many bloody years, breath easy once again, there were still people – scum whose bloodlust was not yet slaked – who continued the dreaded work of the Nazis by murdering Jews, whether individually or as organized groups .

In the aftermath of my liberation from the death camp near the end of the war, I arrived after a long and arduous journey at my home town Wierzbnik. Everything I found only made me more certain of the things I assumed based on the tragic chain of events I have witnessed myself. Everything was destroyed. A wasteland surrounding me and in my heart.

The few remnants who survived the hellfire started gathering, and since there were only a few of them, they clustered in two houses: one group in the apartment of the Krongold family on Starachowice Street and the second group at the home of Chaim Brodbeker at the Rinek.

Sad and despondent, I walked in the streets of our town, where I spent both the beautiful years of my youth and the dark days of the Holocaust. With no family or relatives, I decided to visit the Wykrota family, non-Jewish friends who were once our neighbors, and headed for Visoka Street, no. 16.

Murdered everyone

They welcomed me and even expressed their grief over everything that happened. We talked about the tragic events that befell the Jews and I told them about my fate during those dark days. While we were talking, as the wife got up to bring me refreshments, the family's young son came in and as soon as he saw me he gave a loud and joyful exclamation. He was glad and excited that I survived, and wanted me to join him for drinks. Alcoholic beverages soon appeared on the table and he poured me a glass, urging me to drink. His mother saw my discomfort and quickly offered me without his notice a glass of cold water, as colorless as the vodka, and I drank to his complete satisfaction. He had plenty to drink himself, an as he became inebriated he suddenly cried "Run away from here, because they murdered all of them!" At first I didn't understand what he meant but after he repeated himself again and again, and after hearing my neighbor's explanations, I realized that I was in danger and there are still malicious anti-Semites among the local populace who attack and murder Jews. The son didn't wait but continued: "Run away from here, quickly, before they kill them all!"

Then he suggested that I go to his sister, who was living in a more remote area, where he said I would be safer.

My neighbor started crying, sensing how low her people have sunk. But my tears have dried long since and cases such as this required me to make a quick decision. I got up and left. The son accompanied me a short distance to protect me from harm. Halfway there he bid me goodbye, thinking that the rest of the way would be safe. But as soon as I arrived I could clearly hear gunfire, and later I found out these were the fatal bullets fired at the murderous hands of the Polish A.K. into the hearts of the Jewish survivors who lived at the home of the Brodbekers. I haven't stayed long at the woman's place, because I felt the ground was burning under our feet. I escaped to my aunt and together we boarded the first train and fled once again from our hometown, looking for sanctuary and salvation in other places.

[Page 353]
Yitzhak Kerbel

The Encounter in Munich

The war was over and those who survived the Holocaust started wandering – some in search of relatives and some hoping to build a new life.

This terrible period was naturally followed by one of the most wondrous periods townsmen lending each other help wherever they met.

In my search for the remnants of my family I arrived in Lodz, at the home of Simcha Mincberg, and from him I received information about our surviving townsmen. And indeed, as soon as they heard I survived, they came looking for me. When they found me, they gave me with everything I needed to move quickly to Berlin, where a large group of our townsmen was gathered.

When I arrived in Berlin I was welcomed warmly and further equipped for the road to the infamous Bergen-Belsen. This encounter was practically festive, because I never imagined that a substantial number of our townsmen survived. I also learned that my sister Sarah was in the regions controlled by the Americans, and there were also rumors of my brother David. I traveled to Munich to track them and the most unpredictable thing happened:

Before my journey to the city where my sister Sarah was supposed to be, I sat in one of Munich's public gardens, musing to myself. Suddenly I thought I saw a familiar face pass by, looking very much like my brother David. I was uncertain, because it has been five years since I left the house. He was still a boy at the time, and now I see a man before me, wearing a Polish army uniform!

I do not know if I did it intentionally, but I whispered, as if to myself, "David!" and through some miracle he heard me and turned around, and indeed it was my brother, who only escaped from Poland to Germany a day earlier, looking for relatives.

The joy of our encounter is unimaginable, and naturally we remained together until we immigrated to Israel.

The next day, after finding and meeting our sister, we went to Bergen-Belsen and my brother was among the first to immigrate to Israel using one of the 100,000 certificates given to Holocaust survivors through the intervention of United States president Harry Truman.

[Page 354]
Dvora Rubinstein-Erlichsohn

It Began on an Autumn Day

I will never forget the fall day when the Nazi murderers drove us out of our homes to the marketplace. I stood with my sainted parents and waited in the rows...

Then my sainted husband Hune Rubinstein came up to me with a German, pointing at me to indicate that I was his wife. The German gave me several blows to step out of the row. Then my parents turned to me and begged me to go, to flee and save myself, that I was still young and would still be able to survive, because my child was with Christians and would still need me.

Thus I disappeared from my dear father and mother, and never saw them again...

Especially in the tragic time of the war did we, the children, feel what dear and devoted parents we had, but unfortunately, they were horribly torn away from us and perished in Treblinka.

My two brothers and I later encountered each other in the labor camp and my youngest brother went off to Russia.

We lived thus in the camp for several years, until murders and shooting also took place there, and one day during such shooting everyone began to run to wherever they could. And so my two sisters and my husband ran away and my little sister was hit by a bullet and fell to the ground. To this day I don't know what happened to me; I only remember that I suddenly felt that someone was pulling me strongly by the arm. It was my beloved brother Eli.

After liberation I met up with my two brothers in Łódź. My third brother, Fishl, died in my arms in Bergen-Belsen – two days after liberation, and his last words were: "Thank God that you are still alive," and with those words he ended his young life.

I also don't know how my sainted husband and my sister Sheinche perished. Only my youngest sister, who was barely 17 years old, received a Jewish burial thanks to our respected public activist and friend – Simcha Minzberg. After the war he was among those who worried that all those who had perished be given a Jewish burial.

From the many memories that are permeated with blood and tears, I am not in the condition to relate more of my unforgotten suffering in the tragic years of the Nazi nightmare, until the happy day of the liberation of Bergen-Belsen, April 15, 1945.

Page 355]
Yitzhak Edison-Erlichsohn

I Ran Away and Returned Home

In the fall of 1939, I left my hometown of Wierzbnik, and I returned in 1944. I am now trying, after such a stretch of years, to recall those two days: the tragic day when I decided to flee from our *shtetl*, which was already occupied by the Nazis, and the awesome day, when – after imprisonment and deportation in Russia – I returned to the deathly silent *shtetl*.

Our *shtetl* Wierzbnik lay in a valley and was surrounded by pine-covered mountains. The sharp and pleasant odor of the trees accompanied all my childhood years.

Through the *shtetl* flowed a little river, the Kamienna, in which were reflected the bits of sky between the surrounding mountains. But the Kamienna was not just a little river, but also a divider, which divided the two sections of the city. The right side was inhabited by Poles, and the left side by Jews.

The right side was called Starachowice, and was full of factories and mines. It was an industrial city with dozens of factory chimneys that rose to the sky and covered the city with perpetual smoke.

Wierzbnik, on the other hand, was a Jewish *shtetl*, one of those *shtetls* of which the large Jewish community in Poland was comprised.

In the middle of the *shtetl* was a market with its usual impurity, which especially on holidays cast something sinister on the Jews.

Only a small number of houses in Wierzbnik were made of brick. The rest were wooden, poor little houses, in which ninety percent of the Wierzbnik Jews lived. Just like in all the other provincial towns, the Wierzbnik Jews engaged in crafts – Wierzbnik Jews were tailors, cobblers, carpenters. Many Jewish children began working at the age of twelve. Children were sent to "learn". The learning years were very difficult ones and the later prospects of earning a living from the trade learned were very poor. The government factories on the opposite bank of the river were closed to Jews. The Polish directors made sure of that just as well as the Nazis later on.

Wierzbnik was surrounded by pine-covered mountains, the scent of which filled my childhood years.

But what nature provided so plentifully was spoiled for us by people... For a Jewish child lying on the sand by the river or wandering in a forest was dangerous, because Wierzbnik was a stronghold of the Polish ND. The Kamienna River not only separated the Jewish part of the city from the Polish side, but it also represented a river of anti-Semitism, which created a barrier between the two groups of residents of the same city.

There were also honest Poles, who didn't surrender to the dirty stream. There were also a number of workers who belonged to the socialist party, who opposed the dark influence of the racists. But as always, the honest elements were passive, while the pugnacious hooligans were active.

The house in which I lived with my parents had the biggest yard in the *shtetl*. It was inhabited by 39 Jewish families and the only Christian was the caretaker.

The house had three owners, but it was called Yudel "Miszleborske's" house. One of the three owners was Itcze Singer. He had three children, who all attended the *gymnasia* [high school] in Radom – Polcze, Gutcze and Rachmiel. Polcze, who now lives in New Jersey and whose married name is Funk, was my history teacher.

Another owner of the house was Shmuel Kleiner, who had four children. His daughter Sarale finished middle school in Kielce and he himself was a lumber merchant. My father worked for him in the forests as a clerk, spending weeks in the forests. When he used to come home, he brought the aromatic air of the forest with him into the house, the freshness of the branches, of green leaves, the glorious resinous smell of the trees and the wide range of far off, unfamiliar areas.

My mother was my father's opposite – both in figure and in character. She stemmed from an ultra-religious home – and day and night was occupied with Jewishness and every Sabbath she used to read the *Tzena Urena* [a religious text in Yiddish that was used by women, who didn't know Hebrew] to a group of women.

Across from us lived a remarkable Jewish type – Shlomo Neiman. He had already been arrested in the time of the Tsar for socialism and had been deported to Siberia. Later on – in independent Poland, he received a government pension, because he had once been an ally of Józef Piłsudski and he was the first to fly the banner of the Polish marshal "the first brigade."

It was possible to live one's entire life in our yard and never need to go out, because among the residents were a tailor, a cobbler, a dental technician, a doctor and all kinds of shops and merchants. Yes, and there was something else in our yard, which definitely made us an "independent republic": our own well!

The residents didn't have to carry water from distant pumps, because we had it at hand, and the entire *shtetl* envied us for it. Wow! "Water under our nose..."

The Outbreak of War

When the Polish-German war broke out on September the first, my older brother was already in the army, stationed in the city of Sanok. My older brother had completed his military service and then, as a reservist, received a mobilization notice to report to Przemyśl. The first air raid alarm went off at 6 AM; when the second alarm went off at 9 AM, the first bomb fell on the marketplace.

On the third day of the war a poster appeared on the city hall, stating that the town was about to fall into enemy hands and that the powers had ordered the young people to leave the city and go eastward.

The factories in Starachowice stopped working. The next day the Nazis were already in Cęstochowa, 60 kilometers from Wierzbnik. Then the last chapter arrived – the entry of the Germans into the city.

The entire market was filled with Nazi soldiers. The following day the persecution and torture of Jews began: kidnapping them for work, frightful beatings, robbery of Jewish possessions, and the laughter and ridicule of our neighbors of a thousand years – the Poles.

At times we heard that the Russian armies had crossed the border and occupied part of eastern Poland. That immediately made us think: away from Wierzbnik, where the hell had begun to take on even more atrocious forms, and to flee to that legendary land, where "everyone is equal", where justice and honesty prevailed for everyone – no matter who…

Leaving the City

I quickly consulted with the leader of *Hechalutz*, Kalman Kanner, who was an energetic fellow. He had only been living in Wierzbnik for two years, having arrived from Chmielnik in 1937 with his parents.

Despite the short time, he was the heart and soul of our *Hechalutz* move- ment. We quickly discussed the situation and unhesitatingly decided to leave the city.

It was early in the morning, when the first rays of the sun stole in through the blinds. Without waking anyone in the house, I quickly dragged myself outside, where Kalman was already waiting for me.

We greeted each other silently and immediately set out on a back road to the highway that led to Ostrowiec. Both our hearts were squeezed and we didn't say a word to each other. I looked around for the last time – Wierzbnik in the melted gold of the rising sun. The rows of little houses emerged from the sunny mist like small, glowing islands. I tried to stifle my sorrow, thinking that I was only leaving the *shtetl* for a short time and would shortly be returning. But somewhere in a corner of my mind lurked the fear that even if that came to pass Wierzbnik would no longer be what it had been.

[Page 358]
Abe Zukerman

A Memorial Stone in Toronto
Dedicated to the Wierzbniker Martyrs

Once those of us, who survived the war, came to Toronto we were immediately welcomed and brought into the Wierzbnik Society to witness the many good workings of the Society. Together with our Toronto landsleit, we discussed the problem of how to perpetuate the holy memory of our loved ones, the Wierzbniker martyrs, whose innocent blood was spilled by the most barbarous Nazi murderers.

Those familiar with the Wierzbniker Society, knew the President, Joseph Naiman, well, who was also one of the founders of the Society. For him, everything that had to do with Wierzbnik was among the most important things in his life, as he was totally dedicated to the Society and the landsleit. Dealing with anything to do with Wierzbnik was a continual and necessary part of his daily life. Naturally, the home of Joseph (Yosef) Naiman and with his beloved wife Hanka had a welcoming open door policy to all the newly arrived Wierzbnik landsleit. Day and night, this devoted man felt the need to fervently help everyone and everything that had to do with his former home of Wierzbnik. Even their children, although born in Canada, were so imbued with the lifestyle and stories about Wierzbnik that they too felt a deep connection to Wierzbnik. The Naimans and their children were fully able to find commonality among the newly arrived landsleit. During a holiday their house would be full of landsleit with whom they rejoiced.

Joseph (Yosef) Naiman was instrumental in welcoming to the Society many of the newcomers and involving them in the many different projects of the Society. The newcomers were introduced to the proposal to erect a monument in the Wierzbnik Cemetery. This monument was to honour the murdered Wierzbnikers and those in the surrounding area. During countless meetings and get-togethers, Joseph (Yosef) Naiman would point out with great earnest and deep heartfelt feelings the need for this holy project. He would explain that it was our responsibility and our duty to forever memorialize the hallowed memory of our loved ones and our martyrs who perished in the Holocaust, even though they will forever remain in our hearts and thoughts.

Many discussions were held to determine the date of the final destruction of Wierzbnik. It was discussed with the Barzechiner Rabbi Avrum Shmuel Zvi Zylbershtein who had a reputation as a Torah Scholar. Rabbi Zylbershtein had an abiding love for the Jewish people in that entire district and was a Father-in-law to our own Rabbi Ben Zion Shlomo (son of Rabbi Yosef Eliazer). Our Rabbi and the Rebbitzin Gittle (daughter of Rabbi Avrum Shmuel Zvi) were the leaders of the Wierzbniker community. Both of them performed many good deeds. Any city or town should be fortunate enough to have such good people as leaders. They put the wellbeing of others before themselves. After many meetings with Rabbi Zylbershtein and Rabbi Mendel Kirshenblatt a Yahrzeit date for the Kedoshim was decided. The date was to be the 16th day of Cheshvan.

[Page 360]
Abe Zukerman

The Wierzbniker Society in Toronto

It was in 1934, when several former residents of Wierzbnik in Toronto got together under the leadership of our respected compatriot, Yossl Neiman, of blessed memory, who called them together.

The following people participated in the first meeting, which took place on October 14, 1934: Hershel Neiman, Sam Kleinberg, Benny Kleinberg, Yosef Neiman, Yossl Levin, Fishl Beker, Yehoshua Eisenberg, Yossl Absbad, Yehosua Riba and Benny Gold. At that meeting they discussed the question of how to organize the former residents of Wierzbnik to share a common interest in being connected to the situation of those in Wierzbnik, especially to help those who needed help. The problem was extensively discussed; first it was decided to create an organization. A Wierzbnik Men's Social Club was founded and also a Ladies' Auxiliary. The mission of both organizations was to achieve various undertakings. First of all, a yearly banquet was arranged, at which a fundraising campaign for the Jews in Wierzbnik who needed help was implemented. They also carried out other activities with the purpose of raising money, which was raised with the help of the Women's Auxiliary (quite a few dollars). Then the question arose – who would have the right to decide on the proposals for support. A proposal by Y. Neiman, seconded by Fishl Beker was accepted, to write to Wierzbnik to those whom we knew as upright people and to state our business to them, telling them that we had a certain number of dollars to assist those who were needy, and that they should put together a list there and send it to us.

A large group of Wierzbnikers in the house of Avraham Zukerman of Toronto

We did indeed receive the list with approximately 120 poor families with young children.

We didn't have overly large amounts of money, but it was decided to send whatever there was directly to each family.

This is what was done – until 1939. We held the yearly banquet afterwards, at which we raised money for those who appealed to us in any country whatever.

The same applied to the Wierzbnik Ladies' Auxiliary, whose mission was to help in any way possible. The first chairlady was Mrs. A. Besbaum.

The Wierzbnik Men's Society was founded on Sunday, May 15, 1935. At a general assembly, a committee of the following members was elected: chairman – Sam Kleinberg; vice-chairman – R. Goldbach; secretary – Y. Neiman; treasurer – Y. Jacobs; hospitaler – H. Eisen; trust – A. Kleinberg; members of the executive – P. Beker, P. Kleinberg, B. Gold, M. Riba, J. Kelmanson.

Relief Committee: M. Manheit, Y. Absbam, H. Kirschenblatt and S. Kleinberg. The following were added from among the first members: Y. Jacobs, M. Manheit, Y. Goldbach, Murray Eisen, P. Kleinberg, Y, Neiman, J. Kelmanson, Arish Kleinberg, Y. Eisen, B. Gold, Izzie Einer, S. Kleinberg, P. Beker, Y. Absbam, M. Riba, Haim Bienstok and H. Kirschenblatt.

The organization was very active, especially under the leadership of Yossl Neiman. In 1939 an action was carried out by the Wierzbnik *Landsmanschaft* [society of people from the same town], which initiated a fund to help needy members with loans. The main leaders of this action were Benny Gold – president, Izzie Eisner – treasurer and H. Linzon – financial secretary.

In 1938 an organization was created by the Wierzbnik Men's Club that was called the Wierzbnik Friendly Society, which accepted members up to 45 years of age. The society's mission was to make sure that all the members were insured with a doctor in case of sickness, and also when a member was ill, Heaven forbid, he would have the right to receive a certain sum for eight weeks. The society also bought a plot, i.e. when a member died, he would have a right to Jewish burial. The same applied to the member's family.

The Wierzbnik Friendly Society also takes part in other benevolent activities in the Jewish world, such as assistance for the Jewish hospital, Hebrew schools and old-age homes. Special help is donated to Israel.

The present administration of the Society in 1970 consists of the following people:

Levi Brodbeker – chairman, W. Kirschenblatt – vice-chairman, H. Milner – correspondence and financial secretary and Arish Kleinberg - recording secretary.
S. Kleinman
Y. Sachs
Benny Zagerman – Financial Entity
S. Kleinberg
Y. Sachs – Hospitalers
A Diet Committee
L. Brodbeker
A. Kleinberg
Benny Zagerman
Members of the executive: Moshe Neiman, N. Kornwasser, H. Lepek, S. Eisenberg, Y. Segilim and A. Zukerman.
Social Committee: S. Klowenman, H. Lepek; directorate: L. Brodbeker – chairman, S. Kleinberg, A. Zukerman, M. Gotlieb, S. Eisenberg, S. Kleinman. L. Weisdorf and A. Kleinberg.

[Page 363]
Abe Zukerman

Last Impressions of my Native City

When I decided to leave the tainted country of Poland forever, I began to be perturbed by the thought of whether I would ever forgive myself if I didn't first go to my native city of Wierzbnik to at least take a glimpse at what everything looked like.

Although I knew very well that unfortunately and to my great sorrow no one from my entire family was still alive, neither the relatives or friends that I had left behind when I was drafted into the Polish army before the war, and I had even already abandoned all hope that anyone close to me was still to be found there, nevertheless something instinctively drew me to at least take a look at the place where I was born and raised.

Perhaps it was an internal urge, or a call from my subconscious, to at least say goodbye to the earth and stones on which we trod for years – day in and day out – and now it was all saturated with innocent blood, which will never dry out, and permeated with the indescribable pain and suffering that the martyrs of Wierzbnik suffered until their horrible death.

Abe Zukerman, [193-?]. Abe Zukerman collection, Ontario Jewish Archives, Blankenstein Family Heritage Centre, accession 2017-9-1. Not in the original Yizkor Book.

Isn't it normal for a person to pine for even the dry worthless stones and wood that his house and home, to which he was tied his entire life, was made of?

It was this normal urge that governed me at a given moment. It didn't help to take the logical advice of my fellow townspeople that I should forget about Wierzbnik, because the city was no longer what it used to be. And in addition, they informed me that it was simply dangerous to go there, because right after the war Polish fascists had killed the remaining few surviving Jews that were drawn home, just like a bird that has been driven away returns to its disturbed nest.

Nevertheless, I couldn't alter the decision to go to Wierzbnik and take a look at it for the last time.

On a certain evening, when I was in Łódź (where I lived) I went to the railway station and provided myself with a train ticket. The train arrived full, and immediately became completely packed with Polish faces, which simply increased my fear.

There was no thought of getting into a car; I immediately saw that I couldn't expect a comfortable journey here, but I didn't waver for even a minute because of this, to let the discomfort keep me from reaching my sole goal at that time.

I went up the stairs along with other Gentile passengers, made my standing position comfortable, just as though it was one of the normal classes that a passenger obtains for himself in advance. At a sign from the conductor the train began moving, and I became a normal passenger. After a short time standing pressed against the car, I became very cold, because the wind began to ceaselessly blow in my face, and my hands began to feel as though they were frozen to the iron handrails. This was part of the rights that nature has over a passenger who chooses to travel in the last and lowest class in the train. However, the feeling of discomfort soon diminished, when I thought for a second what my present crowded state meant when compared with the way my near and dear ones were dragged into the cars on their final journey...

The locomotive huffed and puffed and while speeding along let out a resounding noise every few minutes, as though it wanted to remind me not to nod off and fall off the stairs. My eyes were very strained in the utter darkness, which was only broken by the flying sparks given off by the locomotive.

After riding all night, the train approached Starachowice – Wierzbnik's sister city. I knew the region very well and everything looked exactly the same as it used to. Nothing had changed; you couldn't see any difference, as though in the entire time that I was absent no terrible or dreadful nightmare had occurred.

We stopped in Starachowice for a short while as usual, at a train station, and the wheels immediately began moving again.

The thought that in another 5-10 minutes I would arrive in Wierzbnik caused me to perspire and tremble throughout my entire body. My mood became more and more dejected and my doubts grew ever greater. I though to myself how different my present arrival in Wierzbnik was: I was coming to the graves of my ancestors, or more correctly, to the graves of my family, although I expected nothing, not even the sign of a grave, because the Nazi murderers, may their names be blotted out, saw to that too. They did everything possible to wipe out every trace and not to leave a single reminder of their shockingly horrible acts of murder. The sadists carried out their barbarity with such exact precision, that only the devil in the form of a person could have thought of.

After a ride of two minutes, the train suddenly stopped in the empty field. I was bathed in a cold sweat from head to toe – what did this mean? We knew that it quite often happened that Polish fascists stopped trains and dragged off Jewish passengers and killed them. However, what could I do expect to rely on fate and pray to the Lord that if something had to happen, He would give me the courage to take some of them with me, like Samson when he brought down their temple on the Philistines.

Every second seemed like eternity to me. I strained my ears in all directions, so that perhaps I would hear the reason for the abrupt stop from one of the surrounding passengers...

But my ears were as though they were plugged. Just as though they had lost the ability to hear. I was simply not in a condition to make out a single word.

Eternity disappeared and the train began moving. This short event meanwhile left a mark on my heart and it was a miracle that it didn't stop beating, just as though the train itself was infected with the poison of anti-Semitism and wanted to frighten me for no reason.

By a Miracle I Avoided the Kielce Pogrom

We Jews are anyways only living through miracles now. How long ago was it, that only by chance I avoided the Kielce pogrom? I lived in the same building in which the slaughter took place. A day before the terrible event, I left the city of Kielce with my friend Yehiel-David Spiegel from Łagów, without any reason, and went to Łódź just for a day or two, with the goal of perhaps encountering someone we knew.

The trip hadn't been planned even one day in advance, but as soon as we decided on it we took the first train going to Łódź, without taking the few things that made up our "fortune" with us, as we planned to return immediately. That is how we only by chance avoided being among the almost 100 victims, of blessed memory, that were slaughtered there in broad daylight by the anti-Semitic Polish murderers, right under the nose of the Stalinist overseers, whose quarters were a five minute walk from the building in which the victims struggled with the murderous attackers for several hours.

There is no doubt that just the appearance of one of the worthless saviors, would have ruined the murderers' sinister plan. Therefore their absence and silence must indicate their agreeing with the grisly murder-pogrom.

A Weird Alienness

After another few minutes of travel, the train stopped and the conductor called out the words I knew so well – " Wierzbnik Station". Trembling and with a feeling of longing I got off the train steps and there I was in my home! – Yes, I say "home", because how else could someone call the place where he was born and grew up, a place in which my extended family had lived all the years that I can remember?

Off the train. I walked through the depot with the entire mass of Polish passengers. For a moment I thought – what a change has taken place between now and the war, when I still had a home?...

As soon as we came out of the depot, everyone used to be surrounded with a sense of a pleasant atmosphere. But today – this was missing, because the sweet feeling had disappeared together with all the Wierzbnik martyrs, and you didn't need to have a special sense in order to feel it. I felt a weird alienness and extremely uncomfortable, more than up until then...

Where do I go and with whom do I exchange a word? I started walking to our house, Rynek 13. I walked the same way I used to go, going through Jatke St. to the market. I felt my heart beating stronger and faster. It trembled. I was afraid to discovery the sad reality that everything was empty and bare with my own eyes, that absolutely no sign remained of Jewish Wierzbnik, where a vibrant and colorful life used to exist. Since I knew well, based on various testimonies, that Wierzbnik was completely without Jews, I imagined less about what our town looked like now; although I had no illusions that I would still find one of my dear ones, I could previously not perceive to the smallest degree what my psychological reaction would be when I saw it all with my own eyes.

I walked up to the market and stopped to stand in the very corner, by Jastal's house near the tavern. Standing in that place, I found myself across from Szlang's house, where my sister Rochcze lived with her husband and their dear children, of blessed memory. The Szlang building already had a history of murder from before the war. There a Polish anti-Semite, a murderer, entered Yerahmiel Rabinowicz's, of blessed memory, shoe shop and shot my friend Moishele Rabinowicz, whose life was cut off so young by the murderous bullet. When his brother Yaakov-Yitzhak, of blessed memory, chased the anti-Semite, he also took a bullet, and he suffered for a long time to recover from his wounds. My eyes were turned in the direction of the building and couldn't turn away, as though I was waiting to see someone from my sister's house there, or from among the former Jewish residents. However, I didn't dare go nearer, for fear that someone from among the new criminal heirs would recognize me.

The Well of Tears is Dried Up

From there I went in the direction of our house. Approaching the place, I only walked along and stood still, looked at my house from outside and was afraid to go in, lest the new owners discover who I was. What I was not in a position to see with my eyes, my memory, and also my imagination, helped me see, as though I was looking at every corner of the house from inside. When I was already in the market, at the threshold of my house, a weird thing happened to me. I had been bothered by a constant fear the entire time, that when I came into factual contact with the naked and terrible truth, the truth of the lying world, I would probably break down and cry a lake full of tears. However, the actual case was otherwise. The fear that something would happen to me in the emotional moments, which would certainly have been an absolutely normal occurrence, showed itself to be false. Just now, when I was standing face to face with the sad and grim truth, just now when my understandable falling apart reached the highest culmination point, now when I was looking at my home and the smallest thing that I saw with my eyes looked as though it was talking to me, or perhaps the opposite, that I wanted to forcefully talk to it, just now when the reality of my gruesome tragedy could reach no higher, when the infected blister was on the verge of bursting – in that same pain-filled moment, I couldn't find even a hint of a tear in my dried out eyes, as though they had absolutely no ability to flow.

Because of the blatant facts, I stood as though turned to stone and stopped reacting like a normal person should, and as the result of this, my well of tears froze.

I wandered around thus in my native city, feeling as though I was in a cemetery. My steps were weak and not very sure, as though I wanted to avoid stepping on a Jewish grave. I really didn't have anyone with whom to exchange a word, but everything that I passed seemed to me to be dumb witnesses, pressing to relate everything they saw. Every house, every place reminded me of something. Especially since I found myself in a muddled, confused state, spiritually and physically broken. I was absolutely not in a condition to think about the so recent past. Nevertheless, a few memories stole into my passing thoughts, when I passed by all the former Jewish houses.

While I crept around, I stood for a while and thought with a special feeling about Haim Brodbeker's house, may his memory be blessed, and a shiver passed through my bones. Here in this building, the Polish anti-Semites, the former assistants of the Nazis and now their faithful heirs, murdered the few Jewish residents of Wierzbnik that had miraculously survived. It was already after the war, but Jewish life was still fair game, and the shedding of Jewish blood still didn't bother or move anyone. It didn't help the weak and worn out residents to seal themselves up and hide themselves well, and the murderous scum forced themselves into the apartment and attacked the powerless martyrs with axes and rifles.

They had evaded death many times, but this time the "miracle" of being rescued, didn't want to appear and almost all of them died gruesomely.

Here their sad fate came to an end, and this time they didn't manage to escape the claws of the Angel of Death and remain alive.

Not wanting to spend the night in Wierzbnik, I began to walk back to the train station, in order to take the train to Ostrowiec, where life seemed to be a bit safer.

When I was already in the depot, I again thought over everything that I had seen in Wierzbnik, and this time I properly understood the meaning of the statement "Hearing is not the same as seeing" [original in Hebrew].

The roar of the oncoming train broke into my thoughts. I was luckier now because the cars were not so packed and I got into the train quite easily. As soon as I was inside I immediately stood by the window in order to get a last glimpse of my hometown Wierzbnik, which I was now leaving forever.

Without moving my lips, just with my pain-filled heart, I silently inside myself murmured *Yitgadal Veyitkadash*" [the prayer for the dead], and paid my respects to the holy memory of all our near ones and the entire community of Wierzbnik.

The train had already gone quite far from the station, had even passed by the large stone at the edge of the Michalow Forest. The stone that everyone knew and on which so many names of our Jewish Wierzbnik citizens were inscribed.

We had already gone quite a bit of the way, but my eyes were still turned in the direction of Wierzbnik, and at that moment, when I could no longer see our city through the train window, my heart and memory immediately replaced my eyes and took over the picture of my hometown Wierzbnik. Everything that I saw for the last time and the impressions I felt will remain there, until the final moments of my life.

[Page 368]
Sarah Postawski – Steinhart

To the Cemetery in Wierzbnik

Workers placing flowers at the grave of the fallen heroes of the battle against the Nazi beasts.

Several months after liberation, when I had recovered a bit, I made the long and difficult journey from Bergen-Belsen camp to Łódź, in order to encounter someone from my family. Regretfully, I didn't find anyone, because all of them had been murdered by the Nazi murderers and I had nothing left but my father's grave in the cemetery in Wierzbnik.

That is why I decided to go to the cemetery there to visit the grave of my father, who had been the ritual slaughterer of the community.

I arrived in Wierzbnik on a Monday morning, at the beginning of November 1945. I was shocked when I came face to face with the terrible destruction that had taken place.

The streets were the same streets, the houses were the same, only the Jews weren't there, and a wild, oppressing emptiness prevailed everywhere.

Nothing remained of the Jewish community, even the synagogue had been burned. Only the cemetery remained. But even there – much had changed. The iron gate with the wooden fence was no longer there. It had been robbed and plundered. Many gravestones had also been disturbed. The *ohel* [lit "tent", a mausoleum-like grave for prominent people], which was close to the entrance, had disappeared. My father's grave wasn't far from there, but I barely found it, because everything had changed.

At a memorial of the Wierzbnik natives in Toronto, Canada

In the meantime I sensed that angry eyes were spying on me, and I began to be afraid – not of death, but of the living two-legged wild animals...

I quickly went away from there and went to see some Gentiles I had known. Wherever I went I was received with "Hello – you're alive?" And then they immediately began to interrogate me about why I had come. At this "opportunity" they also told me that certain Jews who had come there to retrieve their property, had been murdered by local criminals. Their words pierced me like poison, and aroused my will to run away from there – the faster and the further, the better!

I could no longer bear the oppressive air and the polluted ground, that was saturated with Jewish blood. There was only one thing I still wanted to do: as I would never be coming back there again, I wanted to take my leave of my deceased father...

The next morning I again went to the cemetery and approached the grave. There I was standing in front of him and thinking ... I had thought that if I came there I would cry out my heart, weep a sea of tears, because I wasn't just standing at my father's grave there, but at the grave of all of Jewish Wierzbnik. But not a tear fell – the well of my tears had dried up... I stood as though petrified and frozen, and couldn't even bring out a groan from my throat. I was completely struck dumb! Perhaps it was because I didn't know for whom to cry first? ... For my father, who died "in time" and received a Jewish burial, or for my mother, sisters and brothers and their families, who were murdered and no one even knew where their bones were lying?

And as I stood there writhing in pain and agony, a Gentile who had been following his cows that were pasturing in the area, sprang up, as though from under the ground. The cows had wandered into the cemetery and he had come after them, strolling between the graves, and when he suddenly saw me, he caught fright and crossed himself... His appearance roused me and interrupted my contemplations of a lost world. I looked around and saw an entire herd of cows pasturing in the cemetery, and all around were cowherds, who had been observing me the entire time.

In a heavy frame of mind I moved away from there and went back to my former hometown. I walked through the streets that were so familiar to me, each little stone, each blade of grass said something to me, and nevertheless felt alone and alien Walking along Starachowice Street, I was noticed by the photographer who lived across from the pharmacist, and she invited me into her house. She was truly the only one who behaved like a real human being! Nevertheless, I couldn't remain in her home very long; something drove me from there. Some kind of unknown force pressed on me and impelled me to leave as soon as possible. And right on that same day I left Wierzbnik with a broken heart – this time forever.

[Page 370]
Yitzhak Kerbel

The Town Elder Lied Deliberately

The migration from the town has actually started immediately after the fire.

I remember coming back from the nearby village, Ostrożanka, and seeing the terrible spectacle: the burning of the great seminary, which was elegantly restored before the war with the donation of the famous Heller family, owners of lumber-mills and plywood factories.

The Germans carried out this criminal act with detailed precision, because the synagogue and the Talmud Torah building nearby were the only buildings in the area touched by the fire.

Pain gnawed at us: so many memories were linked to these buildings; it felt as though a precious part of our lives was just destroyed.

A few of us guys gathered in secret and decided that we were determined to free ourselves of the Nazi beast's conquest. Actions followed words: the next morning, November 5th 1939, we departed toward the eastern border, though none of us knew where the journey would lead us or that some might never return from it.

Among those of us who left were Moshe Samet, Yoseph Wilenczyk, Moshe Binstock, Yitzhak Lustgarten, Avraham Manela, Chaim Yankel, who was called "the carter's son", the son of the hunchbacked bath attendant whose name I forgot but who is no longer among the living, and perhaps a few others that the years passing by erased from my memory.

The road was dangerous, and the Polish informers made it necessary to lay low and take hidden paths, sometimes walking dozens of kilometers by foot, across forests and fields.

We were also burdened by the clothes we each wore, 3-4 shirts and two suits at the least.

Along the way, we had a chance to glimpse the camps of Czechoslovakian Jews scattered past the city of Sandomierz. Those were supposedly only refugee camps, but as a matter of fact they were the first camps intended for "the final solution".

We reached the town of Rozwadów, where we were arrested because someone informed the authorities about us. The Germans incarcerated us at the town's synagogue, which they have turned into a stable.

We lived in uncertainty for a whole week.

Nevertheless, a week later we were taken to the SS headquarters and from there we were led to the river, under heavy guard, and ferried across it.

The Ukrainian boatmen constantly abused us, going as far as tipping the boats over into the water while the Germans fired shots over our heads.

I remember arriving on the other side wet to the bones and wearing only my socks, because my shoes fell into the water. I had to run shoeless for many kilometers until by nightfall we arrived at the town of Grochów, on the side conquered by the Russians.

From there we went, by train and without any complications, to the city of Lvov, where a number of our townsmen have gathered.

This was not the end of our travels, however. Some of us ventured deeper into Russia, some changed their minds and went back to the German occupation, where they perished with their parents and the rest of their townsmen.

Our travels also spanned camps in Siberia, in Middle-Asia, the Far East and the rest of Great Russia.

We were completely cut off from our homeland, our town and our families. We received no news about events there until January 15th 1944, the day the Russian armies swept over the entire county and conquered by storm the towns of Ostrowiec, Iłża, Wierzbnik, Wąchock, Skarżysko, Końskie, Szydłowiec, Kamilnik, Ożarów, Opatów and so on.

A letter from the town elder

One time, I was among a small group of friends in a camp and we were listening to the radio in secret when we heard news about the liberation of our town by the Russians. When I heard that, I fainted. The friends who revived me didn't understand what came over me, and only after coming back to my senses I told them that it was my town. Someone pulled out a bottle of vodka (distilled by the resistance) from somewhere and we celebrated the liberation. But from that moment onward I kept wondering: did anyone survive? Will I ever see my parents, my brothers, my sisters?

I remembered that before the war, my parents lived in a village next to our town and I wrote to the village elder, asking for news of their fate. A month later I received his reply, as follows (translated from Polish):

"Your father, Leibish Kerbel, was taken away by the Germans in 1940. We have no idea what they did with him. In any case, he is no longer here."

I keep this document with me to this day. Was the elder really oblivious to what the Germans "did" to my father or any other Jew? It was simply easier for him to lie.

The news made it obvious, however, that I had nothing left to look for in my town and so I continued my travels. I knew that my sister was taken to Sweden, along with a group of other boys and girls. One of my brothers was somewhere among the partisans or with the Polish army, and that was all I knew.

Arrested by the Russians

I continued traveling westward, hoping to reach Israel. Along the way, at the Russian-German border, I ran into trouble. Someone informed the authorities about me, and this time I was arrested by the Russians. They started to cross-examine me during the nights, according to the best of KGB traditions.

I decided to tell them the truth. I told the interrogator that I was a Jew seeking to reach Israel, the only country where I can live as a Jew.

He was stunned and outraged by my answer. "You would trade an eagle (meaning Russia) for a cuckoo (meaning Palestine)?!"

Fortunately, they made a different decision than the one he threatened me with, and I was told to "go to hell" with the prosaic addition "You can wander until your pants fall off and you will never reach Israel."

But fate decreed otherwise. The strange prophecy of the Russian interrogator never came to pass and I live as a proud, free Jew in my free country to this very day.

[Page 372]
Moshe Neiman

Hunted to Extinction

Right after the German hordes marched into our *shtetl*, they immediately began to rob and plunder Jewish possessions. They introduced a new "custom", to take the shops away from the Jews and place a "trustee" in them.

The Nazis also placed a dog of theirs, in the form a *Volksdeutcher*, in the shop of my parents, Hershel and Hanna Neiman, who for many years had run a shop selling rawhide. Obviously, this meant a terrible blow to my parents' morale, because they suddenly felt the ground sinking beneath their feet.

But it not only hounded their morale, it also physically had a very acute effect. The payment that they received for their work in their own shop was so minimal, that it couldn't suffice to support a home and six children, of which our family consisted.

But the German oppressors cared very little about that. They only thought about one single thing – how to send as much leather as possible to Germany.

Aggravations and Horrendous Acts

Later it was revealed that all these cases of robbery and theft, were only the "prelude" to what followed.

Over time the cases of attacks, sadistic bullying and oppression at every step began.

They began to kidnap people from the street and houses and send them away for gruelingly hard labor. We lived near the city hall, and so our fate was hard, because we were among the first victims and also exposed to danger.

My father was, in fact, the first one whose beard was forcefully shaved off. They also did it in a mocking way, so that they only cut off part of it, and my father had to afterwards search for someone to shave it off completely, so as not to be an object of derision.

Refugees

Suddenly the Nazi murderers began to force masses of refugees from Płock and Łódź to us, and we had to support the people so they wouldn't perish. At that time we voluntarily took a family into our home and shared everything with them, even though we were already suffering from great poverty. There is a proverb that says that "A friend in need is a friend indeed," and the Wierzbnik Jews' hospitality and willingness to make sacrifices was revealed to the refugees in crowded conditions as an example of moral values and the eternal commandment: Love they neighbor as thyself.

Kidnapped for Work

Afterwards a new phase of brutal terror and oppression progressed. All of a sudden the Nazis began to grab people off the street and also from the houses – and send them off to forced labor. My father also met this dark fate and they grabbed him and sent him away.

I personally heard about the deportations in time and hid. Nevertheless, the Jewish community was informed that if there were married men with children among the deportees, they could be "ransomed" – if people wished – by sending young unmarried men in their place.

My mother, already knowing where my father was, worriedly prepared a full knapsack with various things for me and escorted me on my unfamiliar way with a broken heart and eyes filled with tears. And so I left my native city with a knapsack on my back and a yellow badge on my arm and set out on my way.

As soon as I arrived at the appointed place, the Nazis attacked me with blows and beat and tortured me for so long that I stopped feeling the pain and the blows.

They did let my father out and left me in his place. They did the same with many other young people, who came to ransom their parents.

Sent Off to Lublin

After a short time, they sent me and a group of other people away to the Lublin region, near the places that they had occupied on the Russian border. My father came to Lublin six weeks later, and after great exertion was able to free me from the Nazi yoke, from the forced labor, and we returned to Wierzbnik together. When the deportations took place I was working at the large furnace, and I was temporarily not taken. Afterwards however, I suffered through all the seven stages of hell until I was liberated by the Americans in 1945. Of my whole family, only my brother Wowe, who had fled to Russia in time (and now lives in Toronto) survived.

The others – my parents and four sisters, were bestially murdered together with all the Wierzbnik martyrs. Their holy memory will always remain in my heart.

[Page 373]
Zvi Magen (Hershel Pancer)

From Slavery to Freedom

The Jews of Wierzbnik-Starachowice, like the Jews of every town in the Diaspora, have been retailers and craftsmen. There were also lumber-mills in the area, as well as a plywood factory that employed Jewish workers. My father, Zeev Welwl Pancer, earned a livelihood working as a salesman for the leather merchant, Eizik Najman.

We were four sisters and two brothers. My father was a devout Jew and we received a strict religious upbringing at home. When I turned 16, I became a companion for Reuven Lichtenstein, one of the town dignitaries, whose eyesight was diminished with old age. I would help him during his various travels and visits. During times of leisure, I would read him chapters from the torah and the Bible, while this wonderful Jew taught me the Hebrew tongue, which he knew fluently.

When the Germans entered our town, they immediately forbidden Jewish trade, confiscated property, pillaged shops, declared a residence area that Jews were not allowed to leave and decreed that every person over the age of 16 must do forced labor. These were the first stages of the ghetto.

Because of the Germans' forced labor edict I worked since 1940 at the brick kiln. We worked two shifts, and every day we were led to our workplace under Ukrainian guard at a specific hour in the morning, and then back to the ghetto at the end of our shift.

We worked for 10 hours or more every day, and the wage was so low it wasn't even enough to buy bread.

In the autumn of 1942, the town filled with rumors that the Jews were going to be transported to concentration camps, and the rumors spread more and more every day. And then one day, in Heshvan 1942, we heard a rumor that our eviction was drawing near. I remember working the night shift that day, and when evening fell and it was almost time to go to work, the house was in uproar. My mother started crying, because she could sense the danger coming and that this would be a final farewell. Knowing well what would happen to me if I didn't show up for work, I tried to calm her down with the help of my father, who claimed that I must not be late for work. And so I left the house with my sister, who was also headed for work at one of the factories in the area. I remember a special incident from that night. I was walking along when I met an officer of the Jewish police, Jermiahu Wilczek, who was a friend of my family. He invited me to come and attend the wedding of his daughter that night. They already knew that the town was doomed and wanted the children to meet their fate as man and wife and not as bride and groom. This delay made me arrive at the factory a few minutes late, and the Ukrainian gentile standing guard at the gate swore at me, shoved me into the guard room and knocked me down, beating me soundly with his club. Grunts of pain, moans and screams erupted from my throat and the terrible cries summoned the manager of the factory. Seeing me lying beaten and bloodied he commanded the guard to let go of me and so I was saved.

We would normally finish our night shift at 6 in the morning, when the next shift arrived to take our place, but this time dawn brought with it the echoes of gunfire. We didn't understand the meaning of it but we knew in our hearts that something bad was happening, and as the sun came up the shooting escalated. We waited impatiently for the second shift to arrive, but at 6 we were surprised to see the work manager Korczinski, who said that he can't let us go as long as the next shift hasn't showed up. Then he left the hall and went to the office to contact the Gestapo. A few minutes later, he returned with an order that we must go back to work and continue through the next shift. We realized that something was going on and that some disaster struck the town. We were depressed and agitated, while the Poles working with us gloated. At 2 in the afternoon came through the gate a small group of young men from the town, ordered to take our places. From them we learned that early in the morning the ghetto was surrounded and all the Jews – old men, women and children – were taken out of their houses and herded to the market square. A selection has separated the young from the rest. The young were taken from the square to the labor camps and the others were led somewhere outside of town. After two days of work, we nightshift workers were led into a fenced camp by the factory and imprisoned behind barbed-wire fences. Our first jobs in this camp were to pitch those barbed-wire fences and clean the stables that served as our quarters. From that day onward, I never left the concentration camp until our liberation in 1945.

Camp Majowka

The only thing I knew about the fate of my family after I left them was that they were sent to a camp called "Treblinka". In time I learned that my remaining sister was in one of the nearby camps, working with other Jewish girls at the lumber-mill. One night, after dark, I risked everything sneaking out of the camp to try and find my sister. I reached as far as the camp gate and pretended to be one of the Polish workers, who were allowed to come and go, and fortunately no one stopped me. My sister was astonished to see me, and didn't believe her eyes because she thought me long dead. Those were the only moments of solace I enjoyed throughout my time at the concentration camp.

Hundreds of Jews were imprisoned in camp Majowka, many of them from neighboring towns. The number of prisoners kept rising and falling. From time to time we faced a selection; the sick and ailing were taken and transported elsewhere, but later we found out they were executed. I remember one selection in particular. We were lined up in the courtyard. Every block supervisor had to report the number of people present and the number of people missing. But a girl was found hiding in the attic supervised by Wilczek's son-in-law. They brought her down to the commander and executed them both, the girl and the supervisor, Wilczek's son-in-law whose wedding I attended on the night before the eviction.

Breakout attempt

In June 1944 they announced that all the prisoners would soon be transported to another, unknown camp. This announcement filled the hearts of people with dread. Another rumor spread at the time, saying that during one of the nights a partisan unit will approach the camp and cut a hole through the fence, allowing anyone who wished to escape to do so. And indeed, one night we discovered a hole in the fence and people from every block started a panicked stampede towards it. Unfortunately, the guard towers opened fire on them before they had a chance to go through and about 200 Jews were killed by the bullets of the murderers.

The road to Auschwitz

The next day we were all ordered to line up at the courtyard. They distributed the food left in the storehouses among us and took us to the train station, where a row of freight cars stood waiting. We were crammed into those cars and locked up inside, with no air to breath.

After hours of waiting the train moved in an unknown direction, and days later we arrived at the "famous" gate of Auschwitz. The train stopped by a secondary block camp and the doors opened. The filth was unbearable and there were suffocated corpses in every car. From the cars we were led to the shower cabin. We were ordered to leave all our clothes and our belongings behind. We were marched under a cold drizzle to where the tattooists sat and tattooed every arm with a number. From that moment on I became number A19517, wearing the infamous striped Auschwitz uniform.

The gypsies

The camp kapo informed us of the gypsies prisoners imprisoned across from the cabins we lived in. In the middle of the night we heard suspicious movement and had no doubt that something was afoot. And indeed, at dawn we found out that the gypsies were taken away during the night and led to the gas chambers and that we, the survivors, will do their jobs in camp, working at all hours. It was not long before I was transferred from this camp to another.

Evacuation and escape

On the morning of April 9th 1945, came the order that all those capable of walking can leave the camp. This was the evacuation march and we headed out, accompanied by guards. The march continued for four days. We were forced to march in the driving rain, thirsty and hungry. It was then that I decided to run away no matter what. I looked for an opportunity and when night fell, I convinced one of my friends to join me and the two of us left the convoy and hid in the thick bushes along the roadside. Once the convoy passed us by, we started walking and after a few hours we arrived at the suburbs of the city of Keln.

We passed by German army units retreating from the city in a panic. We met two Germans and they led us to a house where people from various countries who ended up here lived, and they welcomed us. On April 16th 1945 we learned that American soldiers were approaching the town and the time of our liberation draws near with their coming.

I left the house and saw a beautiful sight, lines of American soldiers passing me by, carrying me with them to freedom.

After years of suffering and unbearable torture, enslaved and humiliated and tumbling like a leaf in the wind, I regained my humanity. I was free.

[Page 376]

M. S., Zvi Faigenbaum

The Miraculous Journey of Mr. Hershel Wiser

Mr. Hershel Zvi Wajzer was considered one of the most respected and renowned character in the community of Wierzbnik. Fortunately he is with us in Israel and bestows his presence upon the visitors of our annual memorial meetings.

Hershel Zvi was born in the town of Przytyk. His father, who served as a kosher butcher in this town, was known as a sharp scholar and admired by his friends; as one of the Warka Hasidim he loved his fellow men, adhered to the torah and yearned for our ancestral homeland. According to these ideals he raised his son, Hershel, until the boy came of marrying age. Hershel arrived in Wierzbnik to wed the daughter of the head of the Kornwaser family, Mordechai David.

It was not long before Hershel Wajzer has proven himself to be a great person blessed with many virtues, supporting every charitable enterprise and kind to all, a generous and hospitable man.

His pleasant voice gave great pleasure to the listeners when he took up the role of cantor.

When I was a boy, we used to live next door to the Wajzer family, whose house was a warm Jewish home filled with devout, fundamental Jewish tradition. His singing talent passed to his entire family, regardless of sex or age.

On Shabbats and holidays, when the family was gathered by the table, the songs sang by this choir of boys and girls echoed far, spreading a unique Jewish experience.

He cherished the prayer "May it please you to bring us happily to our land, and bring us to your city of Zion in joy and to your Temple of Jerusalem", and felt a yearning for our homeland. He dreamt about Israel and considered it his heart's desire, a kind of commandment that a faithful Jew is bound by. He raised his own children according to these ideals – torah and scholarship, a love of the Israeli people and the land of Israel.

And so he ruled his house peacefully until the early days of the 1930s, when the skies of Poland's Jewry grew dark with clouds. And although no one imagined the Holocaust yet in those days, he decided to leave the Diaspora and immigrate to Israel, and was determined to make this decision a reality.

Forerunners

His first step in realizing his dream was sending his eldest son Shmuel to Israel, to lead the way. He got him a certificate from the first batch of immigration certificates secured by the group Shmuel was a member of, "Agudath Israel Youths". He married Sarah Boim from Łęczyce, who worked as a teacher at the Beit-Yaakov school in Przytyk, and after receiving proper training the two arrived in Israel in 1935, to build a home in the chosen land.

Upon their arrival, they faced a harsh and grey reality, and countless obstacles stood between them and their goal. Their letters to their parents were not very excited. But none of this swayed the strong will of Hershel-Zvi, who was filled with the vision of the end of days.

Eventually we learned that Hershel's boundless yearning for Israel made him so determined to immigrate that he was willing to consider illegal means (second Aliya).

His family was shocked to learn that he took actual steps in this direction. They couldn't understand how such a respected Jew could choose such an adventurous and dangerous path?! But when they realized they could not dissuade him from realizing this worthy goal, they urged the grandfather, Yoseph Chaim from Przytyk, to dissuade his son from acting recklessly. They also asked the help of the Admor of Warka, a man he respected and followed. Together, the two managed to dissuade him from taking an illegal path.

Hershel immigrates to Israel

After he agreed, they wished him a quick and legal immigration. And indeed, at the request of religious circles, the mandate government has granted in those days a number of certificates for rabbis, and one of those certificates was given to Hershel Wajzer, who immigrated to Israel with the blessing of the rabbi, his father, his family and all the Jews in town.

This was a cold fact. Hershel Wajzer has immigrated to Israel; he was not merely taking a trip to assess the situation but actually immigrating and settling there. He arrived in 1936, with four of his children – Esther, Mordechai, Lea and Hanna (a year later they were joined by the daughter, Rachel). His wife Rivka, a capable woman with a sense for business, claimed that something new must bud before you could rid yourself of the old, and she temporarily stayed in Wierzbnik with three of the girls and continued running the business until the time came.

The slow liquidation process and the separation of the family continued until World War II broke out, and the women were trapped in the vale of tears and shared the horrors and the suffering of Europe's Jews.

Those who remained in the Diaspora became martyrs while those in Jerusalem survived... two of his daughters became martyrs while the mother Rivka and the daughter Hinda were among the few survivors who managed to join the family in Jerusalem and start a new life.

Starting anew

In Israel they were naturally forced to rebuild, and suffered more than a few economic hardships, but Hershel Wajzer never looked for the simple life that a man of his means could have. He wished to work for a living, like he did in Wierzbnik, and so he worked hard from dawn to dusk until his retirement, along with his wife Rivka and his family. But despite all these concerns, he always left himself time for torah and study.

Despite his humility, he was known to many who came in contact with him and recognized his virtues.

Indeed, he was a colorful, patriarchal figure, dignified and possessing of a Jewish tranquility and an aura of nobility.

As Hershel and his wife reach old age, we wish them many blessed years of life, health and joy from their offspring, Amen.

[Page 378]
Gershon Rosenwald

To Mention – Through Allusion

At the request of the Toronto committee of the Wierzbnik Friendly Society, we here present a synopsis of the correspondence between our compatriot Gershon Rosenwald and the "*Tog Morgen Journal*" [a Yiddish newspaper] in Toronto!

"In your column by Dr. Klarman you mention Yizkor Books in which the publishers were requested to expunge the names of members of the *Judenrat* as well as other Jews who collaborated with the Gestapo.

Since we are also facing a similar problem I would like to ask:

I stem from a small city in Congress Poland, where 700 Jewish families lived. When the dark days and nights began, when all Jews were incarcerated in a ghetto, a Jewish administration and a Jewish police force, which were composed of local Jewish leaders and several public activists, were appointed to head the ghetto.

Taking charge of the ghetto, some of them unfortunately behaved mercilessly towards their brethren. They personally decided who would work in the ammunition factory. And since it was thought that whoever worked would be able to save himself, everyone wanted to work and for the privilege gave away the last of their possessions.

Many years have already gone by since that dreadful period. We are now, the survivors of our city, in Canada, in America and in Israel. We are united into a society, and are active in all Jewish areas. Our society has decided to publish a Yizkor Book in order to perpetuate the memory of our destroyed life, our martyrs.

In the meantime there are differences of opinion among us. Some of us think that the names of the Jewish administrators and their actions, as well as the names of the Jewish policemen and how cruelly they behaved towards their brethren, should also be mentioned in the Yizkor Book.

Others think the opposite: since the book will be a book of the martyrs, we mustn't defile it with the names of the Hitler collaborators, even though before the war they were distinguished Jews and even public activists.

I personally, who have prepared a wealth of material for the Yizkor Book, cannot decide how to act. After all, before the war they had been Jews with a good reputation and perhaps they did it in the hope of saving their own skins, and that is why they received their judgment.

We would like to know how to act, whether we are allowed to mention the names of the administrators, or should we keep silent?"

Reply

Dear Mr. Rosenwald,

As we can see, you yourself considered it necessary and didn't mention the name of the city, because you have a sentimental feeling for those who became tools in the hands of the Gestapo.

Unfortunately, this occurred in many Jewish ghettos. To make matters short, our opinion is that they can be mentioned, by alluding to them, without defiling the holy Yizkor Book with their names.

Dr. A. Klarman Tog Morgen Journal

Avraham Zukerman, One of the two chairmen of the United Jewish Fund of the Wierzbniker organization presenting a check to the chairman of the eneral Jewish United Fund, Gordon Mendele, with the other chairman of the organization of the united fund, Max Nolman, looking on. Present as well was the chairman of the Wierzbnik Organization, Sam Stern, and vice president Willy Kirshenblatt, as well as members of the executive.

In Memory of the Missing Ones

[Page 383]
Moshe Kerbel

Reb Mordechai Mendel Zilberstein, of Blessed Memory

Mordechai Mendel Zilberstein was one of the most distinguished property owners in the *shtetl*. A fine figure of a Jew, he was respected and esteemed by Jews. He was famous in the entire city as one of the best *mohelim* [ritual circumciser], and every family considered it a great privilege to obtain him as the *mohel* for their sons.

Reb Mordechai Mendel was a traditional Jew, a pursuer of justice and a God-fearing man, who was noted for many virtues. He was a man with a sharp mind and deep logic, and also had an excellent memory. It was an absolute pleasure to chat with him. He used to include many proverbs and much humor in his conversations.

He was a nationalistic Jew and at the same time he was extremely tolerant of the younger generation, and well and truly understood their aspirations and ponderings.

I still recall how many years ago Reb Mordechai Mendel used to come to pray in the Talmud Torah on every Sabbath and holiday, accompanied by his sons – Avraham, Noah and Yaakov.

He used to devote a lot of time, energy and work to the Talmud Torah, and also other community institutions. His house was of a Zionist bent, and his sons were respected members of the Zionist organization.

Reb Mordechai Mendel had a warm heart, and he especially loved little children, and so it was clear that during the holidays, when the portion "All the youths" was read – the privilege of covering all the children with his *tallis* [prayer shawl] belonged to him.

His wife, Reizele, was a quiet and modest woman, who loved to give charity (anonymously), and was utterly devoted to her home and children.

His daughters Sheindl and Sara were accomplished girls and occupied themselves with the housekeeping and also loved the tranquil atmosphere of home.

In contrast, his daughter Hannale was the embodiment of energy and courage, socially very developed and active in various cultural institutions and youth organizations.

Thus the life of the patriarchal family was woven. The children married, the family grew, and everything streamed with satisfaction and joy.

Until the sudden waves of the Hitlerite ocean of blood arrived and destroyed everything - the trunk and the branches. The only branch of the family that survived is the daughter Hannale, who has been living in Toronto for many years. She was married to the talented, active young Wierzbnik man, Yossl Neiman, who passed away in Toronto.

But the twig, the little plant of Hanna Neiman-Zilberstein, grew deep new roots and branched out. All the children and grandchildren are instilled with the holy values of her beloved parents, who were not privileged to see them in life. And the Jewish chain is forged anew.

May God take revenge!

And you – the survivors – remember – and don't forget!

[Page 427]
Yitzhak Kerbel

Shmuel Morgenstern, of Blessed Memory

A great distance separates the quiet humble *shtetl* of Wierzbnik, which was located on the banks of the Kamienna River, surrounded by old mountains and thick pine forests, and the big and noisy city of Caracas in Venezuela. If you need to unfold a tragic life of wandering, dreams that were shattered, aspirations that weren't fulfilled, then the biography of Shmuel Morgenstern can serve as a clear case of such an occurrence.

He himself didn't move in the front rows of society and his family didn't belong to those that sat at the "eastern wall" [a place of honor in the synagogue]. But the father of the family, Reb Shlomo, of blessed memory, who was better known as Reb Shlomo the Beadle (who served the rabbi of the city and his school and synagogue), was an honest and upright man, a scholar, respected and loved by all, goodhearted and ready to do a mitzvah with great devotion.

If I am not mistaken, they lived in an attic apartment, in the house of the Tennenbaum family in the middle of the market, and earned money from a stall that sold haberdashery. This "little shop" was run by Shmuel's mother, a very modest, goodhearted woman whose name I can't remember, but I recall that they called her "the Beadle's wife" – and every child in the *shtetl* knew her by that name.

Shmuel was born in 1912 and went to Łódź when he was young, and learned carpentry there, working and spending his youth there. He had two brothers and a sister. One brother, Efraim, was a clerk in the one and only bank in our *shtetl*, and his other brother – Leibish – was one of the most outstanding young people in the Young Agudath Israel movement.

His wandering began immediately after the Germans entered Wierzbnik. Together with Sara Kerbel, whom he later married, he left for Russia. As happened there with thousands of other Jews, they were arrested there and deported to Siberia for many years.

After the war they were released from the camp and traveled to Poland, and then via the illegal ways of the *Bricha* they illegally crossed the border into Germany, from there to France, and their last stop was Caracas – in Venezuela.

The first tragedy happened to him while still in Siberia, when their only daughter died. This was a terrible blow for them, from which Shmuel couldn't recover, probably because after that they had no more children.

Desolate and alone, he wandered around the world, because none of his family survived. He actually had a distant uncle in Israel, but only in 1964 did he have the opportunity to see him during a visit to Israel, and indeed, from then on the relations between them grew closer. However, how tragic and impossible to understand are the ways of nature. Exactly one month after Shmuel passed away, his uncle in Israel passed away as well.

Shmuel had dreamed of settling in the Jewish country; he had even visited it a second time after the Six Day War, visited the new territories and the holy places, stood thrilled and wondering in liberated Jerusalem. Nevertheless something bothered him, something depressed him, perhaps his serious illness, and possibly things we don't know about. He was very refined and dignified, never bothered anyone, quiet and unassuming. After his death at his cousin's home in Holon, an entire chapter came to an end, and the branch of the Morgenstern family of Wierzbnik was chopped off.

May these lines be a memorial candle in memory of his holy spirit.

May his soul be bound up in the bond of eternal life.

[Page 385]
His Daughter Esther

Mr. Noah Citrinbaum

My father, Noah Citrinbaum, was a wonderful and rare blend between a devout Hasid and a true lover of Israel.

I remember sitting in my father's lap every Shabbat while he told me in a voice full of yearning wonderful stories about Israel, the land of his dreams, ending them with the words: "One day we would make it to Israel..."

He instilled his love of Israel in his children as well. His sons, Yoseph and Zisman, volunteered to serve in the Haganah as soon as they came to Israel. When my father received his first chance to leave for Israel (his son Zisman sent him a certificate) he never hesitated, and we were among the first families in Wierzbnik to pack up and immigrate: he, my mother Gitl and myself, his youngest daughter. A dark affair cast a cloud over his happiness in Israel: his daughter Sarah, her husband Avraham Yitzhak and their daughter Hanna all remained in Poland and perished in the Holocaust. Avraham Yitzhak finished a training course of Agudath Israel and their immigration was guaranteed to follow ours. Regretfully, they were preceded by others and remained behind in the vale of tears.

Yoseph served at the time in the Polish army, and upon his release my father spared no effort or expense and managed to bring him to Israel. Out of deep love for the fatherland he offered his military experience to the Haganah, dedicating much of his time and energy to this sacred cause, as one of the organization's commanders.

Our path in the new land was strewn with hardships and obstacles, but my father accepted it all with love, since he always believed that God will provide. Father never wanted to be rich and was content with what he had. He lived his entire life with such innocence and integrity. While we still sat among the gentiles in Wierzbnik, he was praised by many of our gentile customers for his business integrity, while in Israel he set a personal example for many of his townsmen.

When we arrived, my father found work at an orchard, wishing to thank God for our immigration. He wanted to work with something that gave the holy land its unique character, such as citrus fruit. His coworkers from those days surely remember him standing at the top of the ladder and picking the golden fruits lovingly, singing. He was filled with admiration and joy for everything he saw in Israel, an inner joy he retained even after losing his sight... and our home was always filled with song. His children and friends were encouraged by his strong stance and our admiration for this amazing person, who was like a model to us, only grew with time.

His virtues, his integrity, his modesty, his love of God, man and town, are all carved into the memories of the residents of Bnei Brak, the town he loved so much during his 35 years of residence, and they offer some consolation for the loss of a father and such a dear a friend.

My father, rest his soul, passed away on Marheshvan 10th 1970 and was buried at the Poniewież plot in Bnei-Brak where he found eternal rest.

[Page 386]
Yaakov Katz

Hershel Froyman

Of all the humble and righteous saints and unique people that our town was blessed with, and who perished tragically without a trace, one who springs to mind is Hershel Froyman, also known as "Hershel Got"[1].

I remember him as a man who spent all his time studying the torah and debating it. His devoutness and thirst for religious knowledge stemmed from his faith and a deep desire to delve into the issues and glean pearls of knowledge and justice from them. Day and night he would read the Talmud and its supplements, and his face would shine with an otherworldly glow, as if he had no worries and was happy with his lot.

He also liked giving for charity, collecting donations of clothes and food from our people to distribute among the needy. All done in secrecy, so the needy would no feel shame.

But in truth, he was as poor as a church mouse and barely managed to provide for his family, a burden that often fell to his wife. He owned a small grocery store and his humble wife cared for both the house and that sore, providing them with a living. It was as if they divided the chores between them, he would take care of higher things such as torah and good deeds, while she took care of livelihood, the family and raising the children.

Their house was small and the family members numerous, yet no one complained and the children were raised to be humble and modest, accepting everything with love and never opposing the will of God, who maintains the whole world.

In order to give an example of the humility and innocence that characterized Hershel, I would tell you how he got the nickname "Hershel Got".

Rumor has it that once, while he was talking to the students at the Beit Midrash, someone asked him, part in earnest part in jest: "Hershel, how come you are such a great and handsome scholar, while your wife doesn't suit you at all?"

And he answered, "My wife may not be pretty, but surely it is the will of God." Ever since he was known in town as "Hershel Got", rather than by his true name, Froyman.

1. Yiddish for God

[Page 387]
Abe Zukerman

Israel Reisler, of Blessed Memory

Israel Reisler, know to the people of Wierzbnik as Srulu, suffered greatly during the horrible nightmare of the Hitler years, and in his relations with the survivors his presence was clearly felt, from the aspect of helping in any way he could. He spared neither money nor time. More than once he left everything behind and took me with him to Ottawa, where the Canadian central immigration bureau is located, in order to personally settle the formalities required for bringing over a relative, or just any survivor of the Nazi extermination.

He approached the act of assistance, which he considered a mission, with complete sensitivity and dedication. That is why he accelerated the immigration process for all the Holocaust survivors that he brought over to Canada, and afterwards also helped them get settled and begin their new lives.

When any former resident of Wierzbnik showed up in Montreal, (Srala) Reisler immediately engaged himself with him, just as though all the compatriots were in the physical sense a large surviving family. Possessing a broad vision with regard to the future in anti-Semitic Poland, he left Wierzbnik in 1921. After a short time, when he had saved the few dollars and it was just sufficient for a boat ticket, he immediately brought his younger brother Haim, of blessed memory, to Canada. He planned to do it one by one with the rest of his family, but unfortunately, it was already too late. The war intervened and all his near and dear ones also died as martyrs. To our great regret, our compatriot, to whose help and dedication many things can be attributed, was torn away from us at a very early age, dying suddenly, and a year later his brother Haim, of blessed memory, also suddenly passed away. Both of them left behind their own families, in whose hearts they will remain forever, and the Wierzbnik Society in Canada will always bear them in its memory.

[Page 388]
David Plonsky

Shmuel Gelbard

His heart burned with a love for Zion even as a young boy. Before the last World War broke out, he planned to immigrate to Israel, settle there and build it. But the coming of the war has forced him to remain in Poland. He suffered greatly. In 1947, he managed to leave Poland and immigrate to Israel. Here, he immediately joined the ranks of the Haganah, and carried out his assignments with devotion. He perished in the malicious Egyptian bombardment during the war.

Loved by those who knew him, he was 31 in death and left behind a wife and a year old child.

May God avenge him.

Moshe Sali (Kerbel)

On the Grave of Yosef Citrinbaum

Heads bowed, consumed by grief, we stand on your newly filled grave, your kin and family, your townsmen, your relatives and your friends.

You were a gentle soul, honest and spirited. A blameless scholar, blending religion and literacy. A conversationalist, kind and virtuous. You loved the torah of Israel, the people of Israel and the land of Israel. Even while you suffered, you never complained and accepted reality for a fact.

A man dedicated heart and soul to his family and yet always willing to listen to others, assisting and helping in their time of need. Even when the suffering and stress were evident on you face, when the disease was already nesting within you, you would ignore your situation and pay attention to the suffering of others.

You were among the activists of our organization, one of the surviving townsmen of Wierzbnik in Poland, and you felt the pain of the terrible Holocaust that visited the Jewry of Europe and your townsmen among them. Recently you have managed to write for the Yizkor book of our community a moving commemoration of the town's martyrs, your friends from youth, who perished at the hands of evildoers – and suddenly you were taken from us before your time. We cling to the holy task and will strive to hasten the publication of the book containing your thoughts about the Holocaust and its results.

The pain is great and I cannot express it well enough. "Vai Lehai Shefra Devli baerea".

May your soul rest among the saints.

[Page 389]
His Sons, David and Amos

Yoseph Citrinbaum (Harari)

Father liked to watch and take part in an experience personally, because physical participation was part of his world view.

These characteristics made him realize that the Diaspora is not the place for Jews, and despite the news from Israel during the 1930s that life was hard, he chose to immigrate because he believed that a Jew belonged in Israel. He therefore encouraged and pressured his parents into immigrating to Israel, even though he himself was serving in the army at the time. And indeed, as soon as his service in the Polish army ended in 1938, he immigrated to Israel.

When he arrived, he volunteered to the Haganah and served as an active member until the foundation of the state, when he enlisted with the Israeli Defense Force.

Membership of the Haganah was a sacred thing for him and he was willing to give his life for it. His humility prevented him from telling of his adventures, but from time to time, when a similar topic came up in conversation, he would tell of events from his time with the Haganah, events which often put his life in danger. He wrote down about some of his time with the Haganah.

His innate intelligence and the desire to know pushed him to study, although he never received formal education.

In Poland, he studied in the Heder and the Yeshiva, where he acquired religious education and learned some Hebrew. In secret, without the permission of his parents and despite their active objection, he studied Polish and became fluent in it. In Israel, despite the hardships of earning a living, he studied English and became fluent in it, and naturally he knew the Hebrew language through and through.

Reading was his sole source of general education. He read many books and was glad to find a job at a publication house. Authors and poets whose books were published there became his dear friends because they found him to be an avid reader.

Father loved to tour the land, to travel the country on foot before 1967, and he quickly became familiar with the liberated territories. He was fond of trips and tours of the holy places, Jerusalem, Bethlehem and Hebron, which he considered links to the glorious past of the Jewish people. During the last days of his illness he was planning a trip to Sinai once he got well. He believed in Greater Israel and argued this position passionately.

He faced hard times but never complained or asked for favors. He knew how to keep his suffering to himself, and share joys with friends.

Mother and father took great care to educate their children. They spent their energy ensuring that we, their children, had a proper education that would guarantee our future. Our parents taught us that we must prepare for the future, and helped us as much as they could. We regret that they found so little happiness.

My father observed the fifth commandment, showing his father and his mother full respect. He spent many hours doing their bidding.

Father passed away on Tamuz 7th 1971 (26.6.71), at the age of sixty. On his tombstone, at the cemetery in Zichron Meir in Bnei-Brak we have inscribed:

A man of Integrity
And of modesty
Poet and warrior
Participated in the Haganah to found the country
Blameless and sincere
Concerned with the education of his sons
Forever beloved
His deeds and his memory would never be forgotten
May he rest in peace.

[Page 390]
Zvi Faigenbaum

Rabbi Moshe David Rothschild

One of the interesting characters in our community was Rabbi Moshe David Rothschild, who came from Kielce.

His father, Yehuda Hiskiyah, was a scholar and a noble man, one of the students of the Admor Gaon Rabbi Avraham Borenstein from Sochaczew.

His house was scholastic-Hasidic in the full sense of the word and Moshe David was raised in this atmosphere. To supplement his religious-Hasidic education, he also studied at the Hasidic house of Gur in Kielce. We should also mention that the two, father and son, were among the most important of the Gur Hasidim.

To Wierzbnik he arrived as a husband to Libale, daughter of one of the oldest landowners in the community, Mendel Zukerman, sister of Yaakov Zukerman and sister-in-law to Simcha Buchbinder.

As customary in the days before World War I, they received financial support from Libale's father-in-law for a few years ("kest") before opening a store for iron and construction materials. During the first few years, the business was managed by his young wife Libale, who acquired business experience at home, while her husband assisted her. But Moshe learned quickly and became an expert iron merchant.

The reconstruction of the town following the battles of World War I turned the store into a success. Nevertheless, the two never considered their success a personal advantage. They participated generously in every charity enterprise, especially those concerning the Hasidic house of Gur. Moshe David became a member of that shtibl and held many parties at his house on holidays. He also took part in public affairs and was chosen chairman of Agudath Israel in town. During one of his occasional visits to the Admor of Gur, he was offered Rabbi Yitzhak Goldknopf, one of the finest Gur Hasidim in Warsaw, as a husband for his eldest daughter, Hitzi Yochit. The grand wedding took place in Wierzbnik and from that day onward there was a new aspect to the religious and Hasidic life in the community of Wierzbnik, because Yitzhak quickly proved his spiritual wealth in matters of torah, morals and the world. Many youths who wished to study the torah gathered around him and listened to him, learning and debating. The only survivors among them are Zisman Citrinbaum, Jechiel Brodbeker and David Cohen.

I remember that the righteous Admor Yeheskel of Ostrowiec used to study the torah in secret with Yitzhak, who was considered a great man by all. Moshe David and his wife were naturally pleased with their son-in-law, who earned the respect of all. They did not pressure him into earning a living and his wife Hitzi Yochit helped her parents at the store while Yitzhak taught torah and morals and shared his personality with his students.

In the middle of the 1930s, Moshe David was among the first to see the coming darkness, and headed to Israel with Zvi Wajzer, to build the country together.

Upon their arrival, however, they separated in search of a living. After securing his livelihood, Moshe David innocently believed that he would soon bring his son-in-law Yitzhak (who meanwhile took part in managing the store) and his daughter Hitzi Yochit, along with the daughters, the granddaughters, the younger daughter Gucia and his brother Reuben, who joined the family by marrying the daughter of Simcha Buchbinder. Those were his intentions, but he was outraced by the terrible events. The war broke out, the armies of Hitler stormed Poland and the communities of Israel fell into the hands of the devil, which slaughtered and destroyed them.

It should be noted that during the dark days before the destruction of the community by the murderers, it seemed that the young men could be saved from this plight by signing up for work at the factories in Starachowice. Those who listened to Yitzhak came to ask him what to do and he told them his opinion: don't leave your family, we cannot defend ourselves from this cruelty by being cruel to our family (wife and children)...

And so he went with the martyrs, pure in mind, to accept judgment as his body was burned and his soul ascended into the heavens.

Moshe David spent the rest of his days in Jerusalem, at the court of the Admor of Gur, as a reader of the torah at the great Gur synagogue in Jerusalem. He considered his reading, which impressed all his listeners, to be a great privilege which inspired him to survive the ocean of hardships he waded through.

The rabbi was very close to him. He came to visit him from time to time during his illness. When he passed away, the rabbi lead his followers after the late man's bed, escorting him to Har Menuhot where he and his wife Libale rest.

The only survivor from this family is his young daughter Gucia, who immigrated to Israel and made a new home. May she live long (and prosper).

[Page 391]
Leibl Rabinowicz

I Cry for Them

My father Yerahmiel Rabinowicz, of blessed memory, was a grandson of the "Holy Jew" of Pechishce.

He had lived in Wierzbnik since 1925 and was an active co-worker in the city Talmud Torah, as well as in the Merchants' Union. In the month of Sivan 1935, a murderous Polish hand shot my youngest brother Moishele, of blessed memory, to death, and gravely wounded my brother Yaakov-Yitzhak.

After this tragic event, happiness disappeared from our life, and the glimmers of energy and hope were extinguished.

In October 1942, my father and my mother Sheindel-Leah, of blessed memory, along with other martyrs, were deported to their terrible deaths. Blessed be their memory.

My son, Eliezer Mordechai, of blessed memory, was born in 1938. When the news of the deportations reached us, we prepared to hide the child with a *Volksdeutsch* acquaintance, but as soon as the search for hidden children was intensified, the child was handed over to the missionaries in Wierzbnik, which was supposed to be a place of rescue for the unlucky children. But on a beautiful morning we received word in the camp that the murderers had taken the children who were with the missionaries and had sent them to the assembly point in Szydłowiec, from where they were afterwards taken away to be exterminated.

My brother-in-law Yashe Rosenberg, of blessed memory, was a student of the Ostrowiec rabbi, of blessed memory, and an activist in the Ostrowiec Young Agudath Israel, and also a periodic writer in a Warsaw daily newspaper. He participated generously in all public undertakings. He never lacked the time or money to do favors for people.

He took the destruction of the Ostrowiec Jewish community and the loss of his own child Tuvia-Yehiel very much to heart, and filled with despair he walked to the market place and marching from there on the way to the Starachowice camp, he fell at the hands of a Ukrainian-Hitler murderer.

May his soul be bound in the bond of life.

[Page 392]
Yehoshua Jerry Rolnizki

In Memory of my Beloved Ones

My father Reuven and mother Reizl ran a respectable home and lived a traditional, modest life. We stem from a large extended family, and in our family alone there were six children, five brothers and one sister.

In 1938, I, the oldest son in the family, went off to America with the intention of afterwards bringing over the whole family, but unfortunately, the World War broke out in 1939, and brought a halt to all my plans and hopes.

When the war began I enlisted as a volunteer in the American army, and took part in the battles against Hitlerism in Europe.

After the Hitler war, out of my entire big family only one brother, Aaron, who now lives in America, survived. When he was liberated in Begen-Belsen, he consisted of skin and bones, a real skeleton, and he had to be taken to Sweden to save his life and put him back on his feet.

Now, the two of us, my brother and I, have, thank the Lord, created new families and raised our children in the spirit of our parents. Our sons study in well-known yeshivas and colleges, and our daughters in Beit Yaakov [school system for religious girls].

I will never forget one of the first letters I received from my brother Aaron after liberation, because it incorporates the anguish and torment of our martyrs by the Hitler specter.

This is the content: "Dear brother Yehoshua, your letters affect me like the best medicine. I didn't believe I would survive the bloody nightmare and still live to hear from you. When I was in sorrowful Bergen-Belsen, where hundreds and thousands of people lay in the gutters and putrefied while still alive, so that the stink could be smelled for miles, people risked death for a bit of potato peel. I once positioned myself and grabbed a potato, and the people attacked me like wild animals, and afterwards the Nazi police came and shot at us. Beside me many people fell, and I miraculously survived. Yaakov Kamec, Yehiel Lerman, Yosef Zawner, Yaakov Meir Krystal, Kalman Kornwasser and other people from our town dropped dead before my eyes. I can't believe what I witnessed, and to this day I haven't been able to recover. When I was liberated, I weighed 35 kg., they carried me like a little child. We didn't have an easy time in the previous camps either. The lice ate us alive, and many typhus and dysentery epidemics broke out from time to time.

Those who didn't die of typhus, were shot by the wild German Huns. Our cousins died in this way.

I myself also became very ill, but this time more than half the camp was very ill with typhus and the Germans were afraid that they would be infected with the typhus, so they no longer entered the sick-bay barrack, and stopped shooting us.

When I was back on my feet, I went to work in the well-know ammunition factory. I went around hungry and naked, and the work was grueling.

The situation was saved by the Russians, who were then carrying out strong offensives by the Wisła. Then the Germans sent us off to Auschwitz, from Auschwitz to Austria and afterwards to Bergen-Belsen camp, where we were finally liberated.

Your brother Aaron."

I considered it necessary to submit this letter for the Yizkor Book. To commemorate the memories and to remember and report the Hitler hangmen's devilish and cruel methods and plans to exterminate the Jewish people.

But just as "The Eternal One of Israel doesn't lie", so the Haman had his downfall, like all the other enemies of Israel in the history of Jewish martyrdom, and the Jewish people has re-forged its future in the State of Israel and in the Diaspora.

[Page 393]

In Memory of our Family – Sternkranz Family

Yehezkel Sternkranz

With great pain and deep sorrow we commemorate the memory of our beloved father, who perished on the way to Auschwitz.

Our father was not only loyal and devoted to his family, but he was also well known as a Zionist and social activist, who contributed a great deal to the national revival and the development of the Zionist ideals.

Sara Sternkranz

Our beloved mother was a quiet, modest woman, a real Jewish mother who worried, suffered the pain and endured the fight for life and lived to come to Israel. Unfortunately, the vestiges of that hard time left her terribly injured in body and soul, which caused her premature death, and she passed away in 1967.

Elka Sternkranz

Our beloved sister, who was brought up in the spirit of beautiful ideals, was instilled with the best virtues of a Jewish child and dreamed of a bright future. Unfortunately, cruel fate tore off the thread of her life and she perished tragically in a concentration camp in 1942.

Yankel Sternkranz

Our dear brother was born in 1932 and had barely begun to grasp the meaning of life, when the dreadful Nazi catastrophe advanced on Jewish life. He was murdered by the Nazi beasts during the deportations in 1942.

We also recall our relatives and family members who tragically perished in the Nazi hell.

We honor their memory.
The sorrowing survivors,
Sima, Zehava, Hava, Binyamin and Meir

[Page 394]
Moshe Sali (Kerbel)

The House of R' Shmuel Kleiner

This house was famous in our town because of its unique charm. Any person who needed moral or material support could find it there.

The house was quiet and peaceful and popular among the folks. A Zionist house, radiating a distinctive sense of nobility. A house of scholars and educated people.

The head of the family, Mr. Shmuel Kleiner, was a believer in Jewish tradition, a pleasant, kind man, tall and always elegantly dressed.

He was known as a philanthropist, whose house and heart were open to the needy. He was among the most prominent members of the Mizrachi and took active part in every Zionist enterprise and especially in the collection of funds for Keren Hayesod. In 1940 he passed away unexpectedly from terror of the terrible acts of the Nazi beasts against the Jews.

The mother, Mrs. Sheindl, was a model "Yiddishe Mama". With limitless humility and dedication she cared for and nurtured her home. She was kind and offered unconditional love. Her main concern was providing the children with traditional education about their people and their land.

And indeed, the children grew well, a source of pride to their parents, and the house was filled with life and creation. Unfortunately she was not spared by the Nazi soldiers, who murdered her brutally.

The eldest son, Fishel, was a true genius, schooled in "fine print" and trade, full of knowledge and aware of events around him.

He married a girl from Kielce and moved to her town. He settled there with surprising ease and secured a respectful place for himself among the activists of "Mizrachi", who excelled in social and public activities. Cruel fate has decreed that he, his wife Golda, his daughter Rivka and his son Baruch all perished at the hands the Nazi beasts.

The second son, Yaakov, was a lovely lad, full of life and open of heart and mind, schooled in trade and barter. He was always an activist of the Zionist Organization and later became a pillar of the revisionist movement in our town. He was also murdered by the villains and only his wife and daughter survived and reached Israel after many travels.

The familial harmony at their home was perfect, there was an air of mutual respect and even more so of respect for father and mother. Over the years, the sons helped their father manage the business. The children grew up and married, raised families and moved to other places, but always remembered where they came from and often visited their family, until the Holocaust.

The ones who survived the Holocaust, having suffered through the camps, were the daughter, Sarah, who married lawyer Leon Wiesenfeld, and the son Yoseph, who married Ruszka Kerbel. Both raised lovely families.

A glorious tree was cut down, but the offshoots and branches that grew from this strong trunk follow the ways of their ancestors, imparting Zionist and universal education to their children. The legacy of the parents has forged and given the children the strength and desire to impart ideals of culture, tradition and knowledge, a truly comforting fact.

May our loved ones, who were burned at the stake, rest in peace among the pure martyrs.

Magnified and sanctified may His great Name be...

[Page 395]
Moshe Sali-Kerbel

At the Mass Grave of our Brethren

We will eternally remember and sanctify our compatriots from our city who so tragically perished in anguish at the hands of the most atrocious cannibal, devourer of Jews, that History has ever known, in the dark period of Hitlerism. We won't forget that many of you did not receive Jewish burial, and that your bones are sown and spread, without a sign or a vestige.

We have therefore decided to perpetuate your memory and that of all the martyrs in our memory, hearts and souls. For this purpose, with tears in our eyes and trembling hands we have gathered together your holy names, so that in the future they will be turned into a written, worthy tombstone, which will be a symbol of your heroic fight for life and of your death.

In this way your names will be rehabilitated, will receive eternal meaning, and your souls will be inscribed in the Book of Life of all the souls who perished as martyrs in "sanctification of the name" in the Diaspora and also in the State of Israel.

With the publication of the Yizkor Book in the State of Israel, we have symbolically and visibly given you Jewish burial and have erected a verbal monument, which will remain as a memorial for generations. With deep sorrow and broken hearts we stand beside the mass grave and together say *Kaddish – Yitgadal Veyitkadash...*

[Page 396]

For Eternal Memory

With a mournful silence, heads bowed and hearts filled with sorrow and rage, we hereby commemorate the pure souls of our townsmen, who were brutally murdered by Polish criminals after the Holocaust.

And these are the names of the victims:

Sarah Wolfowicz, her son Fishel and her daughter Rivka

Rivka Enisman, the wife of Shlomo Enisman

Miriam Zylberberg, daughter of Avraham Zylberberg

Rivka Pszytycki, daughter of Jechiel Pszytycki

Noah Kornwaser

Bronia Cipis, daughter of E. Kalmanzon

Chaim Binstock, from Wąchock

Avraham Kadyszewicz, son of Godel Kadyszewicz

Noah Enisman, from Bodzentyn

[Page 397]

Conclusion

Dear Townspeople,

After many doubts and hard, financial and human efforts, and after such a long wait, we are finally done and the Yizkor book for the community of Wierzbnik was published along with testimonies and memories dear to each and every one of us.

For years we have debated how to immortalize the town, its Jews and lifestyle. And while we were debating, a few started gathering the material, filled with a holy sense of duty, to remember and preserve the memory of those tortured to death, and offer the next generations a truthful testimony of this time of horrors. It was not an easy task, because the publication of a Yizkor book is not an easy project. The book is therefore the result of a collective effort, made mostly by people who put their thoughts, feelings and memories into writing for the first time. But therein lays the advantage of such writing, which is true honesty.

Every line, every letter, every name and every fact related to our memories are likely to stir the hearts of our town's survivors. Every one of them will feel from this book the air of the time and place that wove the threads of their past and connected them with those who are no longer among the living and whose memory is as precious as life itself – the lives of their families, relatives and friends. And while leafing through the book they would realize its value and scope. Now, in a time when the patterns of the past are being destroyed and the belief in ideals and high moral values is collapsing, when religion and tradition have ceased to serve as the most important elements in Jewish society, now of all times we need to present youths with the spiritual and moral light, the way of thinking that characterized the Jews of our town and their lifestyle that was filled with sacred values and deep religious and national sentiments, which offered succor in the hardest of times.

This Jewry has spun a thousand sentimental threads of love for Israel, the people of Israel and its eternal ideals. This spiritual milieu, which sheltered generations, and this atmosphere of deep affinity to legacy, national calling, spiritual and moral values, have given us many of the finest thinkers of our national rebirth. Without them, who knows if we would have reached this far.

It is natural and unavoidable that some of the details would be incorrect or lacking, and for several of the articles to repeat or offer alternate versions of the same events. After all, the book is nothing but a reflection of the rich reality of old, which was gone with most of its people and is no more.

We hope that this memorial enterprise will be an ever-burning candle among the burning candles of Israel's communities, creating together the flame that lights the unique milieu and existence of this magnificent Jewry.

This memorial book, which is a memorial candle for the souls and memories of martyrs, will also serve as a torch lighting the path of the living for the young generation and the generations that will follow it, because their light will be ours.

Yizkor book committee

Wierzbnik Necrology

Wierzbnik Necrology
Translated by Jerrold Landau

Translator's notes:

1. The necrology section of the Wierzbnik book has no page numbers in the original. Therefore, I have numbered these pages based on the Image number from the scans of the New York Public Library (https://yizkor.nypl.org).

2. At the top of each memorial page, there is a verse fragment from Lamentations 1:16. "My eyes, my eyes, they drop water," and "For these do I weep." These fragments alternate every two pages, starting from from scan 435.

3. The numerous photos are generally uncaptioned. In most cases, I was able to surmise the identity from the content of the memorial dedication.

4. Spelling of names is always an open question. I used Hebraized forms of first names. I generally used Polish forms of surnames for the victims, and Anglicized forms for the perpetuators.

[Scan 433]

Please note that the following pages are numbered "Scan" because in the original Yizkor Book these pages were not numbered. On the PDF of the scan of original book available from the National Yiddish Book Center web site, the pages are identified by the scanned page number.

Yizkor

In eternal memory on Mount Zion in Jerusalem

In memory of the pure and holy souls

Elderly and youths, children and women

Of the community of Wierzbnik-Starachowitz and the region

Who were hauled to the furnaces of Treblinka

On 16 Marcheshvan, 5703 (October 27, 1942)

And who were murdered by the impure Nazis and their helpers

In any place during the Holocaust

May G-d avenge their blood, and may their souls be bound in the bonds of eternal life.

[Scan 434]

Yizkor by Yaakov Katz

Remember everyone who was buried, in quiet secrecy.

Without a grave to visit, without a monument to remember them, we cannot find comfort.

Remember… The people in the pits of corpses, when their souls ascended to the heavens.

We swore then to remember their names, to never forget them until the end of the world.

Hear Oh Israel; You have been adjured by the mouth that was strangled, and whose sprit died,

Oh G-d, oh G-d, why have you abandoned us, without You I have nobody to bequeath.

Please remember all the souls that have been listed by our hands

Those pure souls that dwell in Your house.

The souls of the holy and pure House of Israel

Who light up the Garden of Eden with the flame of their souls.

O, souls in the Garden of Eden, please listen, the sons of the nation of the Torah will never cease

They were murdered, strangled, and burned in the lands of murder, but their flame was not extinguished.

The burnt parchment will not be erased, and the eternal writing stands opposite truth,

The broken, shattered tables please remember, there is a continuation for the nation, and it exists.

The survivors of the furnaces, brands plucked from the fires, we weep with floods of tears,

To bring forth the hidden light and light up the vale of darkness.

We will cleave to the traditions of our mothers and fathers with greater strength,

To ensure the renewal of our days as of old, and the coming of our redeemer and redemption.

Adela (Idel) Lewkowicz-Shlesinger, husband Dov Shlesinger, and their children Meir, Abraham and Alexander, Wierzbnik, 23 August 1937. Abe Zukerman collection, Ontario Jewish Archives, Blankenstein Family Heritage Centre, accession 2017-9-1.

(This image was originally on p. 458 in the Hebrew edition.)

[Scan 435]

In Eternal Memory

The rabbi of our community, a scion of the dynasty of Admorim [Hassidic leaders] of the "Holy Jew" [1] may the memory of the righteous be a blessing.

Rabbi BenZion Shlomo Rabinowicz, may the memory of the righteous be a blessing.

Who perished along with the members of his community in the furnaces of Treblinka

His wife, the **Rebbetzin Gitale**, the daughter of

Rabbi Avraham Shmuel Tzvi Zilberstein, may the memory of the righteous be a blessing.

The rabbi of Bodzentyn, Wierzbnik, and Toronto

Their daughters: Rivkale and Bracha

[Photo: Rebbetzin Gitale]

The survivors of the community of Wierzbnik

Daughters: Racha, Dina, and Hashia, of Toronto

[Scan 436]

In eternal memory

I hereby perpetuate the holy memory of the dear family members

My father: the rabbi and gaon, **Rabbi Menachem Mendel Tenenbaum**, rabbi and rabbinical judge of the community

My brothers: **Yaakov** and **Zadok**

My sisters: **Chana** and her sister **Yosef Avrech, Hadassa, Rachel**, her husband and their children

[5 photos: Upper left is likely the father, and the four on the right are likely the siblings]

Minka Benno Tenenbaum

[Scan 437]

[Right side]

A memorial candle

To holy martyrs

There was a righteous man:

Rabbi **Chaoch Biderman**

A scion of the family of the Rebbe of Ger

Blessed with a prominent wife: **Rivkale**

May their memories shine forever!

May G-d avenge their blood

Tzvi Morgenstern

[Left side]

A memorial candle

To the holy memory of our dear martyred family

Father: **Reb Yeshaya Guterman**, a scion of the Radzymin dynasty

Mother: **Zelda**

Brothers: **Yisrael-Yaakov**, his wife and children

      Yosef, his wife and their children **Moshe** and **Levi-Yitzchak**

Chaya Guterman

Libtsha Guterman

[Scan 438]

[Right side]

In eternal memory

Of the memory of my dear family members

Father: **Yosef Unger**

Mother: **Frania**

Brother: **Moshe**

      [Photos: two photos, likely of the father and mother]

Sisters: **Leah**, **Roza**, and **Paula**, who died in Cyprus and were buried in Israel

Their memory will never depart from our hearts

Tzvi Unger

[Left side]

In eternal memory

Our or dearly beloved parents, siblings, and relatives

Father: **Pesach Ajzenberg**
Mother: **Rivka Ajzenberg**
Brother: **Mordechai**, his wife **Chaya**, and daughter
Sister: **Chaya Zisel Reisman**
Relatives: **Moshe Kuperman**, wife **Tova** and son
    Sara Rubensztajn and son
    Shmuel Brandmesser, wife **Reizel** and family

[Photos: 2 photos, the father and mother]

Meir Eisenberg
Sam Eisenberg
Zev Reisman

[Scan 439]

[Right side]

In eternal memory

Of our dearly beloved

[Two photos: the father and the mother]

Father: **Reb Shmuel Isser**
Mother: **Rivka-Yehudit**
Sisters: **Sarale, Tzipa, Chaya**
Children: **Chaim-Yosef, Rachel-Pesil, Manya**
Relatives: **Sara Milman**

[Family photo with parents and 4 children]

Roiza Isser-Herling

[Left side]

In eternal memory

With great awe and honor, I perpetuate the memory of my dearest

Father: **Avraham-Natan Baumsztajn**
Mother: **Chana Baumsztajn** (Lichtman)
Brother: **Baruch Baumsztajn** (lived in Paris)
Sisters: **Pesel**, her husband **Moshe Waldman**, and two children.
        Ita, husband **Zelig Zilberman**, and two children

[Family photo: parents and three children]

Shlomo Baumstein (Sam Stein)

[Scan 440]

[Upper right]

In sorrow and pain

I perpetuate our dearly beloved

Father: **Yechiel Ajdelkopf**
Mother: **Esther**
Sisters: **Malka** and **Yona Brojt** and children
        Sara-Lea and **Yosef Brojt** and children
        Golda and her husband **Jablowski** and children
        Rivka

Chana Korenwasser-Ajdelkopf

[Upper left]

With awe and honor

I perpetuate my dear

Father: **Moshe Baranek**
Brother: **Yechezkel**
Relatives: **Ben-Zion, Lea, Dova** and her husband **Avraham**

Michael Baranek

[Lower right]

In deep sorrow

And a weeping heart, I perpetuate
The memory of our unforgettable
Husband and father

Ben-Zion Baranek of blessed memory

Wife Sara (Sala) Baranek
Daughter Necha Markovitch (Baranek)

[Lower left]

In eternal memory

With honor, awe, and a holy obligation, we hereby perpetuate

The memory of the martyred residents of our town

Shimshon Bornsztajn
Chana Bornsztajn
Meir Stajnbaum, his wife **Rucha Stajnbaum**, and their sons **Monek** and **Leibcha**
Who perished in the terrible Holocaust, may G-d avenge their blood
Guta Blom-Weintraub
Noach Blom, and their son Moshe

[Scan 441]

[Right side]

In eternal memory

Of my dear

Brother: **Manela Binsztok** [photo]
Sister: **Rivka-Rachel** [photo]

Miriam Binstztok-Shulman

[Upper left]

In eternal memory

Of my dear

Father: **Leibish Binsztok**
Mother: **Rachel**
Brothers: **Akiva, Avraham**
Sisters: **Dvora, Neche, Chana**
Aunt: **Esther Malka Kacman**
Father: **Abba Kacman**
Relatives: **Leibel Wajnman** and children
        Yitzchak Tropper and daughter

Mindel Binstock

[Lower left]

A monument

To the graves of my dearly beloved

Father: **Leibish Bekermaszin**
Mother: **Hinda**
Sisters: **Matela, Yentale**
Aunts: **Dina, Golda, Rachel**
Uncles: **Tovia Tenenbaum, Mendel Rubin, Baruch Rubin, Leibish Rubin, Shimon Lipszyc**

Baruch Bakermaszin

[Scan 442]

[Upper right]

In eternal memory

Of my dearly beloved

Relatives: **Perl Furman**
Feiga Furman
Rachel Furman
Reizel Furman
Reizel Najman, nee **Rozenzweig**
Fishel Najman
Moshe Najman
Shmuel Najman

Luba Bar-Birenzweig

[Upper left]

In eternal memory

Of my dear parents, brother, and sister

Father: **David** the son of **Reb Yaakov Shlomo**
Mother: **Tzirel** the daughter of **Reb Yaakov Nisker**
Brother: **Menachem**
Sister: **Bracha**

Yosef Brodbeker

[Lower right]

In eternal memory

Of our dearly beloved martyrs

Father: **Yaakov Birenzweig** (died before the war)
Mother: **Rachel**
Brothers: **Mendel, Hershel, Moshe-Leib**
Aunt: **Hinda Mendelson** and her husband **Pinchas**
Relatives: **Avraham** and **Moshe**, the children of **Mendel Birenzweig**

Luba Bar-Birenzweig
Ida Brechin-Birenzweig
Feiga Weisman-Birenzweig
Sara Monstein-Birenzweig
Yosef Birenzweig

[Lower left]

In eternal memory

Of my dear martyrs

Father: **Chaim** the son of **Mendel**
Mother: **Freida** the daughter of **Avraham Meir**
Brothers: **Kalman, Yaakov, Lipa**
Sister: **Dvora**
Aunts: **Neche, Tzipa, Chaya**
Uncles: **Yosef Shmelki, Moshe, Naftali**
Relatives: four children of our brothers and sister – **Mendel** and **Hershel**

Levi Brodbeker

[Scan 443]

[Right side]

In eternal memory

Of our dearly beloved

[Two photos: the father and mother]

Father: **Moshe HaKohen Brodbeker**
Mother: **Malka**
Brother: **Mendel**, his wife **Tzipora** and son **Moshe**
Sister: **Rivka**, and children, **Menachem, Feiga, Shlomo**
Uncles: **Eliahu Brodbeker** and family
Miriam, Berish, Michael, and **Leibish Rosenblum** and family
Relatives: **Rivka** and **Dvora**

Perla Brodbeker-Unger
Sara Brodbeker-Rubin

[Upper left]

In eternal memory

Of my dear martyrs, tragically killed

Wife: **Sara** the daughter of **Zalman Rozenbaum Brodbeker**
Son: **Shlomo-Zalman Brodbeker**
Daughter: **Chaya-Rachel Brodbeker**

Yitzchak Brodbeker

[Lower left]

In eternal memory

Of our dear martyrs, tragically killed

Father: **Yaakov Goldgrob**
Mother: **Chava**
Brothers: **Pinchas**
        Shlomo – died in Brazil
Sister: **Mintzia**

Moshe and Meir Goldgrob

[Scan 444]

[Right side]

A memorial candle

In holy memory of our dear family members

[Photo: the father]

Father: **Fishel** the son of **Reb Yosef Goldsztajn**
Mother: **Chaya Rachel**
Brother: **Avraham**

Dov-Berish Goldstein
Chana Perl Weintraub-Goldstein
Shmuel Weintraub
Mania Kaufman-Goldstein

[Left side]

A memorial candle

To the holy memory of our dear, pure martyrs
Who shine as the splendor of the firmament

[Photo: the father and mother]

Father: **Dov-Berish** the son of **Reb Yeshayahu Guterman**

Mother: **Esther** the daughter of **Reb Yosef Goldsztajn**

They died in the United States

Our brother **Zalman**, and sister **Itka** who perished in the Holocaust

Yitzchak and Moshe Guterman

[Scan 445]

[Right side]

An eternal light

For the graves of my dear ones

Father: **Baruch Gold**
Mother: **Gittel**
Brother: **Shmuel**

[Two separate photos: the father and the mother]

Yisrael Gold

[Upper left]

In eternal memory

Of our dearly beloved martyrs

Father: **Ezriel Glatt**
Mother: **Shprintza**
Son: **Dov (Berl) Hercik**
Daughter: **Perl**, husband **Eli Gincburg**, and children
Grandfather: **Shlomo Hirszhorn** and grandmother **Feiga**
Aunt: **Blima**, husband **Zalka Klajnmic**, and four children
Uncle: **Fishel**

Chana Glatt

[Lower left]

With great pain

I perpetuate the memory of my dear

Father: **Moshe Leib Glaser**
Mother: **Tzirel**
Brothers: **Avraham** and wife **Chaya**
        Aharon and family
Baruch Yehoshua Weintraub

Leah Glaser

[Scan 446]

[Right side]

Let these lines in the Yizkor Book serve as a monument for the unknown graves of our dear

Father: **Yaakov-Ahron Gelbard**, murdered in Szydłowiec

Mother: **Leah**, died in the ghetto

Brothers: **Yisrael**, murdered in Auschwitz

Tzvi Hershel, wife and two children, murdered in Treblinka

Edzia (of the **Holcman** family) with a two-year-old son **Dudu**, murdered in Treblinka

Brother: **Shmuel (Shmulik)**, who fell in the War of Independence in 1948

[Family photo]

Honor their memory!

Nathan Gelbard

Froma Gelbard-Maslowitz

[Upper left]

In eternal memory

Of our dear family members who perished in the terrible Holocaust

Father: **Elimelech Gruber**

Mother: **Miriam**

Brothers: **Shimon** and **Shmelke**

Sisters: **Sara** and **Luba**

Uncles: **Yosef, Yaakov, Moshe** and their families

Grandmother: **Dina**

Aryeh (Leibel) Gruber

[Lower left]

A monument

To the unknown grave of our dear

Yosef Grynhaut   [photo]

Wife: Ameila Gynhaut

Children: Tina and Zigmund Dinfeld

Sala and Zeev Kilman

[Scan 447]

[Upper right]

In eternal memory

Our or dearly beloved

Father: **Reb Meir Dawidowicz**
Mother: **Rachel**
Brother: **Moshe** and son **Yechezkel**
Sisters: **Sara-Rivka, Chana-Roiza**
Relatives: **Leah Baranek, Dvora Puterman**

Helen Weisblum-Dawidowicz
Savka Rusak-Dawidowicz

[Lower right]

A memorial candle

To the memory of my dear family members

Father: **Chaim Drajnodel**
Mother: **Rivka**
Brothers: **Shlomo, Mendel, Yitzchak, Hittel**
Sisters: **Chana, Ita, Perl**
Uncles: **Avraham Kadiszowicz, Moshe Drajnodel**

Yosef Dreinodel

[Upper left]

A memorial candle

To the holy memory of our dear family members

Grandfather: **Fishel Dreksler**
Grandmother: **Golda**
Their children: **Shmuel, Yosef, Sinai, Simcha**
Their daughters: **Mindel, Hendel, Rivka**, and **Rachel**

Yeshayahu Dekel (Dreksler)
Rachel Lauer (Dreksler)

[Lower left]

In eternal memory

Of my dearly beloved

Father: **Sinai Dreksler**
Mother: **Freindel**
Brother: **Chaim-Eli**
Sister: **Yocheved**

David Dreksler

[Scan 448]

In eternal memory

We hereby perpetuate in this Yizkor book of the community of Wierzbnik-Sarachowitz the memory of

Our dear parents who died in Israel

Father: **Yosef Dreksler** of blessed memory
Mother: **Chana Dreksler** of blessed memory

[Photos: Yosef and Chana]

May their souls be bound in the bonds of eternal life

Yeshayahu Dekel (Dreksler)
Rachel Lauer (Dreksler)

[Scan 449]

[Upper right]

In eternal memory

In memory of my dear parents, brother, and sisters

Father: **Yosef** the son of **Yisrael Honigsberg**
Mother: **Reizel Honigsberg** (nee **Disenhaus**)
Brother: **Mordechai Honigsberg**
Sisters: **Bilha, Leah**, and **Sarahke Honigsberg**

Their memory will never leave my heart

Meir Honigsberg (Ginnosar)

[Lower right]

In eternal memory

Of our unforgettable son

Mondek [photo]

Who went through all seven levels of the Nazi hell, but unfortunately was unable to bear the wounds of the tragedy, and fell after the liberation.

Parents: Pinchas and Rachel Helstein

[Upper left]

In eternal memory

Of our dearly beloved

Father: **Fishel Hilf**
Mother: **Esther-Malka**
Brothers: **Yaakov** and **Yitzchak**
Sister: **Rachel**

Chaim Hilf

[Lower left]

With great pain

I perpetuate the memory of our dear

Father: **Gershon Herblum**
Mother: **Tzipora**
Brothers: **Hershel**, his wife **Dvora**, and daughter **Tzipora**
Sister: **Feigele**, husband **Tanchum Lajtajzen**, and children **Gershon** and **Rivkale**

Sheindel Herblum-Burman (Toronto, Canada)

[Scan 450]

A monument

To the unknown graves of our dearly beloved

Father: **Yosef-Leib** the son of **Chaim** and **Sara Herblum**
Mother: **Sheindel** the daughter of **Avraham** and **Miriam-Leah**
Brothers: **Shalom, Aharon-Meir, Nachum, Yaakov-David** and family
Uncle: **Gershon** the son of **Avraham**
Grandfather: **Chaim Hilf** from Kinew. Grandmother: Sarah

[Photo Upper right: A family photo]
[Two photos on left: Probably the parents]
[Two photos on bottom: Probably two of the brothers]

The families of Gershon's daughter
Yehudit from Salitz
Leibish Herblum

[Scan 451]

[Right side]

In eternal memory

We hereby perpetuate the memory of our holy and pure family members

My wife **Yocheved** the daughter of **Dov-Ber** [photo]
Daughters: **Sheindel, Yehudit, Chaya-Rachel**
Son: **David Ber**
Daughter of my wife's sister: **Chaya Reizel** daughter of **Aharon**
My sister: **Sarake** daughter of **Yechezkel**
Her husband: **Elyakim Getzel** son of **Dov Yaakov HaKohen**

Leibish Herblum
And his children Yaakov and Miriam

[Upper left]

In eternal memory

Of my unforgettable parents and brothers

Father: **Tovia Herling**
Mother: **Feiga-Malka**
Brothers: **Shlomo, Yitzchak-Meir**, and **Shmuel**

Moshe Herling

[Lower left]

In eternal memory

May these words serve as a source of tears for the unknown graves of my dear

Father: **Meir Weinberg**
Mother: **Esther**
Sisters: **Pesi** and **Shrintza**, with their children **Liba**, **Ratza**, and **Rachel**
Grandfather: **Eliezer Rolnicki**
Grandmother: **Tema**

Yosef Herling

[Scan 452]

[Right side]

In eternal memory

With a pained heart and feelings of honor and awe,
I hereby perpetuate the memory of my dear parents

Father: **Yosef Hochmitz**
Mother: **Rivka Hochmitz**

[Two photos: **Yosef** and **Rivka**]

May their souls be bound in the bonds of eternal life

Pinchas Hochmitz

[Left side]

In eternal memory

With a pained heart, honor and awe, we hereby perpetuate the memory of our holy and pure parents, brothers, and sisters

Father: **Tovia Weisblum**
Mother: **Yehudit**

[Two photos: **Tovia** and **Yehudit**]

Brothers: **Leibish** and **Shlomo**
Sisters: **Rivka** and **Chaviva**

[Two photos: the two brothers]

May their souls be bound in the bonds of eternal life

Shaul, Binyamin, and Esther Weisblum

[Scan 453]

[Right side]

In eternal memory

Of my dearly beloved

[Family photo]

Father: **Yehoshua Weintraub**
Mother: **Chaya**
Brothers: **Yosef, Mendel**, and **Shlomo**
Sister: **Leah**
Aunts: **Chana, Gittel, Sara, Genendel, Esther**
Relatives: **Matos, Yeshaya, Hershel, Yisrael**

[Photo: likely the three brothers]

Moshe Weintraub, Montreal

[Left side]

A monument

To the graves of our dear

[Photo: the mother and father]

Father: **Shmuel Weisblum**
Mother: **Gitele** (nee **Silverman**)

Rivka Shabaton
Zeev Weisblum

[Scan 454]

[Right side]

In eternal memory

Of our holy martyrs

Father: **Leibush Winograd**
Mother: **Sara**
Brothers: **Yerachmiel, David**
Grandfather: **Kalman**
Grandmother: **Gitel**

[Family photo]

Zahava Proviner
Leah Hopfeld

[Left side]

In eternal memory

May this notice serve as a floral wreath over the unknown grave of my parents, brothers, sisters, and relatives

[Photo: the mother and father]

Father: **Kalman Winograd**
Mother: **Gitel**
Brothers: **Shmuel, Shlomo, Leibush**, and **Nathan**
Sisters: **Gela** and **Miriam**

May their souls be bound in the bonds of eternal life

Tzvi Winograd

[Scan 455]

[Upper right]

In eternal memory

May these lines serve as a monument over the graves of our dearly beloved

[Photo: the father]

Father: **Yaakov Wilenczyk**
Mother: **Rachel Leah**
Brothers: **Yosef, Pinchas (Piniek)**
Sisters: **Sheindel**, **Lubba**

Eli Wilenchik

[Lower right]

In eternal memory

Of my dearly beloved

Father: **Leibka Weichandler**
Mother: **Perl-Bluma Weichandler**
Brother: **Shmuel**
Sister: **Gittel**
Aunt: **Gittel Weisglas**
Uncle: **Pinia Weisglas**

Chaim Weitzendler

[Upper left]

A memorial candle

To the holy memory of my dear family members

Father: **Shlomo Zalman**, the son of **Reb Yehuda Aryeh Wicznik** of Siedlow

Mother: **Feiga Sheindel** the daughter of **Rabbi Yissachar** of blessed memory

Brothers: **Avraham** and **Elazar**, sons of **Shlomo Zalman** [2]

Sisters: **Chaya-Sara, Rivka-Leah**

Yissachar Elimelech Weichnik

[Lower left]

A memorial candle

To the precious memory of those dear to me, beloved and pleasant, who are unforgettable

Husband: **Reb Tzvi Shmuel Zeinwil Zoberman**
Sons: **Mordechai, Yitzchak Meir Moshe**
Daughter: **Hinda Goldele**

Rivka Zoberman

[Scan 456]

In eternal memory

With great sorrow and pain, I recall my dearly beloved

[Family photo: father, mother, and a child]

Father: **Nathan David Zachcinski**
Mother: **Chaya Tova-Esther**
Sisters: **Sheindel, Roiza, Golda**, and **Malka**, with their children

[Three bottom photos; three of the sisters]

Never forgotten! Never forgotten!

Yair Zachcinski

[Scan 457]

[Right side]

A monument for the dear souls

Who perished in the terrible Holocaust

Father: **Avraham Mordechai** the son of Chaim **David Zylberberg**
Mother: **Reizel** the daughter of **Reuven Herblum**
Sisters: **Miriam** and **Esther**
Brothers: **Chaim-David** and **Yeshayahu-Yona**

May G-d avenge their blood!

Leah Silberberg-Rosenthal

[Upper left]

A memorial candle

In memory of my dear family members who were murdered by the Nazi enemy and their criminal assistants

Father: **Moshe Meir** the son of **Yechezkel Zilberberg**

Mother: **Esther**

Sister: **Rivka**

Uncle: **Yechezkel**

Bluma Albert-Silberberg

[Lower left]

With great sorrow

I perpetuate the memory of my dear

Father: **Simcha Ziskind**

Mother: **Dvora**

Brother: **Dov-Berl**

I will never forget you!

Professor Yosef Avigdor Ziskind (Joszek Ziskind)

[Scan 458]

In eternal memory

Of our dearly beloved

Father: **Avraham Silberman** [photo]

Mother: **Chana-Riva** [photo]

Brother: **Pinchas** and his wife **Miriam**

Sister: **Eidel**, husband and children

Dov Schlesinger and children **Meir, Avraham,** and **Alexander**

[Photo Lower right: probably the brother]

[Photo bottom left: a family photo]

Esther Zukerman-Schlesinger
Anshel Silverman

[Scan 459]

[Right side]

In eternal memory

Of our dearly beloved

Father: **Mordechai Mendel Silbersztajn**

Mother: **Reizel**

Brothers: **Avraham**, wife **Chana**, and children **Chaim**, **Zlata** and son **Shmuel**
      Yaakov, wife **Esther**, and daughter
      Noach, wife **Sheindel**, and family

Sisters: **Sheindel**
   Eli Zuker, and son **Shlomo Yechiel**, and families

[Photo: Mother, father, and two daughters]

Chana Neuman-Silberstein

[Left side]

A monument

To the graves of my dear, unforgettable parents and brothers

Father: **Yosef Jabner**

Mother: **Tova**

Brothres: **David**, **Yisrael**, and **Chanoch**

[Family photo]

May G-d avenge their blood

Esther Jabner

[Scan 460]

[Upper right]

An eternal light

With grief, I perpetuate the memory of my dear father

Shlomo Tobman

Who was murdered in the Nazi hell
May G-d avenge his blood

Manya Zylberberg-Tobman

[Lower right]

A monument

To the unmarked graves of our dear

Father: **Avraham Chaitan**
Mother: **Sara-Gele**
Sisters: **Rachel, Golda, Freda**
Aunts: **Sara, Ruchama**
Uncles: **Nathan, Leibush, Shlomo, Shmuel**
Grandfather: **Kalman**
Grandmother: **Gitel**
Relatives: **Sarel, Halen Kirszenbaum**

Yerachmiel Chaitan
Yaakov Chaitain
Yisrael Chaitan

[Left side]

In eternal memory

Father: **Mendel Toman** [photo]
Mother: **Chana** the daughter of **Moshe Tenenbaum** [photo]
Brother: **David** [lower right photo]
Sister: **Dorka** [lower left photo]

Miriam Rosenkrantz-Toman
Tova (Yona) Perl-Toman

[Scan 461]

[Right side]

In eternal memory

With a pained heart and subdued spirit, I hereby perpetuate my martyred dear ones

Father: **Yosef Tencer** [photo]

Mother: **Guchia**

Sister: **Tova**

May their souls be bound in the bonds of eternal life

Chana Tencer

[Left side]

In eternal memory

We hereby perpetuate the memory of our dear

[photo of parents]

Father: **Avraham-Yitzchak**, murdered by the Nazi enemy

Mother: **Keila**, died in Wierzbnik on July 12, 1939

Paula Funk
Guchia and Moshe Tencer
Ada and Yerachmiel Singer

[Scan 462]

[Upper right]

A memorial candle

To the memory of our honored dear

Reb Yosef the son of **Avraham Taubman** [photo]
Who died in our Holy land, may his memory be blessed

His wife – Chana Taubman
His daughters – Miriam Lublin-Taubman, Tova Amir-Taubman

[Lower right]

In eternal memory

I hereby perpetuate the memory of my pure and holy martyrs, whose souls should shine like the splendor of the firmament

Father: **Avraham-Elimelech** the son of **Reb Shmuel** of blessed memory
Mother: **Dvora**
Brother: **Moshe**
Sisters: **Esther, Leah, Chayah-Sara**

Yaakov Katz

[Left side]

In eternal memory

I will remember these, lament, and pour out my soul. Immersed in mourning and agony, to the memory of my family – in accordance with the words of the prophet Jeremiah, which give deep expression to the feelings of my soul.

Would it be that my head is water, and my eyes are a source of tears, I would weep day and night for the victims of my people [3]

And for my murdered wife

Wife: **Bracha**, nee **Troper** [photo]

Son: **Eliezer**

Father-in-law: **Peretz Troper**

Mother-in-law: **Sara-Beila**

Brother-in-law: **Chaim**

Sister-in-law: **Chaya**

May their souls be bound in the bonds of eternal life

Yaakov Katz

[Scan 463]

In eternal memory

We hereby perpetuate the memory of our holy and pure dear ones

Father: **Shmuel** the son of **Reb Tovia Yechiel HaKohen** [photo]

Mother: **Yocheved** the daughter of **Reb Mordechai David Kornwasser**

Brother: **Avraham** and **Eli**

Sister: **Esther**

Grandfather: **Tovia Yechiel HaKohen**

Grandmother: **Feiga Leah**

Aunt: **Sara**, her husband **Feivel Fricher**, their daughter **Taba** and son **Vovche**

Aunt: **Libtshe**, her husband **Dov Skurnik**

Uncle: **Leibel Sapirsztajn**

Brother-in-law: **Yosef Rozenberg** (killed on the way to the camp) and his son **Tovia Yechiel**

[Lower right photo: probably the father and mother]

[bottom left photo: One of the brothers or uncles]

Tova Zweig-Cohen

Malka Leopold-Cohen

David Cohen

[Scan 464]

[Upper right]

A memorial candle

To the memory of our father and mother who died in Israel

Father: **Avraham** the son of **Meir Zeinwil** of blessed memory [photo]

Mother: **Manya Lichtensztajn**

Their daughter: Rania Levinson-Lichtenstein

Their daughter: Dora Cohen-Lichtenstein

Their son: Binyamin Lichtenstein

[Lower right]

In eternal memory

Of our dear family members

Father: **Yerchamiel** Mordechai the son of **Reb Shlomo Lipsztajn**
Mother: **Rachel-Rivka** the daughter of **Moshe Grosman**
Brother: **Shlomo**
Sister: **Frumet**
Relatives: **Chaim** the son of **Moshe Grosman, Sara Lipsztajn**

May their memories be a blessing

Basha Lipstein
Gitel Rubenstein-Lipstein

[Left side]

To the holy memory

Of our dear parents

Father: **Tzvi (Hershel) Lichtensztajn**
Mother: **Miriam (Mania)**

[two photos: Tzvi and Miriam]

David Lichtenstein
Chana Levita
Rivka Shnir (Sheiner)

[Scan 465]

In eternal memory

*In memory of our dear ones who perished in the terrible
Holocaust at the hands of the Nazi murderers*

Father: **Mordechai Lis**

Mother: **Reizel**

Brother: **Mendel**, who was murdered by the Polish partisans

Grandfather: **Yona Rosenberg**

[Top photo: probably the grandfather]

[Bottom 3 photos from right: probably Mordechai, Reizel, Mendel]

May their souls be bound in the bonds of eternal life.

Reuven Lis-Shuali

Eliezer Lis-Shuali

Chaim Lis of blessed memory

[Scan 466]

[Right side]

In eternal memory

Of my dearly beloved

Father: **Akiva Czepla**

Mother: **Sara-Gitel**

Brothers: **Yaakov, Kopel, Eliezer**

Sisters: **Chaya, Hinda, Freindel**

Aunt: **Shprintza**

Uncle: **Idel**

Relatives: **Hershel, Kopel,** and **Bina Goldberg**

[two photos: likely the father and mother]

Yitzchak Czepla

[Left side]

In eternal memory

With great sorrow, we perpetuate the memory of my dear

Father: **Yirmiyahu Levinson**

Mother: **Freida**

Brothers: **Fishel** and **Dov**

Sisters: **Miriam** and **Rachel**

Relatives: **Malkiel Lusternik, Yeshayahu-Yona Szarpharc, Sara-Rivka** and **Fishel Szarpharc, Rabbi Yisrael Szarpharc,** the shochet and his wife **Kreindel**

Beila Frimerman

[Scan 467]

In eternal memory

Of our dearly beloved, who were murdered by the Nazi murderers

Yitzchak-Meir the son of **Shmuel Zeinwil Manela**

Isser-Yehuda the son of **Yitzchak Meir**

Feiga the daughter of **Yitzchak Meir** the wife of **Yitzchak Rosenwald**

Pesel the daughter of **Yitzchak Meir** the wife of **Avraham Unger**

Sara the daughter of **Yitzchak Meir** the wife of **Yaakov Goldfarb** and his son

Yitzchak the son of **Mottel Rosenwald**

Sheina the daughter of **Avraham Unger**

Mordechai the son of **Yitzchak Rosenwald**

Idel Manel

[Top photo: probably Yitzchak Meir]

[Bottom photo: family photo]

David and Rivka Mandelaum

[Scan 468]

[Upper right]

In eternal memory

With these lines of mourning, we hereby perpetuate the memory of my unforgettable husband and our father.

Nathan Lustman, may G-d avenge his blood [photo]

Murdered by the Nazi murderers, may their names be blotted out

His wife: Esther Lustman

His daughters: Tzipora Schnir and Tova Saguy

[Lower right]

A memorial candle

To the holy memory of those dear to my soul

Father: **Reb Kalman Leibman**

Mother: **Rachel** the daughter of **David Yehoshua HaKohen Brotbeker**

Brothers: **Tzvi-Dov, Pinchas, Leibel**

Sister: **Rivka**

Sara-Liba Leigman Kahana

[Left side]

In grief and agony

We weep over the untimely death in a strange place

Of my dear wife and mother

Mrs. **Leah Liber-Rosenthal**, daughter of **Reb Avraham Mordechai Zylberberg** of Wierzbnik

May her memory be blessed, and may her soul be bound in the bonds of eternal life.

Her husband: Yitzchak

Her son: Avi

[Scan 469]

A memorial monument

To the soul of our family members who gave their lives in sanctification of the Divine Name during the Holocaust, and those who died before and after the war.

My father-in-law and our dear grandfather: **Reb Moshe Pinchas** the son of **Reb Meir Zeinwil** of blessed memory Lichtensztajn

Mother-in-law and grandmother: **Riva** the daughter of **Reb Nechemia Potok** of Zawiercie

My wife and our dear mother: **Machla** the daughter of **Reb Moshe Pinchas** of blessed memory

My son and our brother: **Nechemia Yehuda**, cut off in his prime in Buchenwald

My sister-in-law and our aunt: **Sheina** the daughter of **Reb Moshe Pinchas**

My brother-in-law and our uncle: **Gershon** the son of **Reb Moshe Pinchas**

My sister-in-law and our aunt: **Shifra Gorfinkel** the daughter of **Reb Moshe Pinchas**, her husband and their children – perished in the Holocaust

May their souls be bound in the bonds of eternal life, and may G-d avenge their blood.

[Five photos: unclear who is who, but upper left is likely the father-in-law / grandfather]

Simcha Mincberg
Rivka Grynberg-Mincberg
Tzvi Menachem Mincberg

[Scan 470]

[Right side]

In eternal memory

Of my dearly beloved who were murdered in a brutal fashion

Father: **Yitzchak (Isak) Laks**
Mother: **Pola**

[Photo: Yitzchak and Pola]

May their souls be bound in the bonds of eternal life.

Rozhka Laks Lerman

[Left side]

In eternal memory

Of my dearly beloved

Father: **Yaakov Mandelzis**
Mother: **Sara-Gitel**
Brother: **Mordechai (Mottel)**
Sister: **Tzvia** and husband **Aharon Melman**
Aunts: **Dina, Chaya, Rachcha**
Uncles: **Hershel Brodbeker**
       Eliezer Yechiel Lerman
       Yosel Kornwasser
Relatives: **Moshe** and **Yechiel Brodbeker**

[family photo]

Shmuel Mandelzis, Montreal

[Scan 471]

In eternal memory

A memorial candle to the pure memory of my family members who perished during the terrible Holocaust. I will never forget my dear ones.

[Top photos: mother, father, and brother.]

Mother: **Dvora Morgensztern** nee **Biderman**

Brothers and sisters: **Reizel**, her son **Yosef** and daughter **Racha**; **Yehuda Leibish**, his wife **Sara**, their sons **Yosef, Yaakov, Elimelech, Shmuel**, and their daughters **Freidele, Rachele, Tuchi,** and **Golda**

Relatives: **Yisrael-Isser, Yechezkel** and wife **Nechama** and their sons **Yosef, Yitzchak; Avraham-Yitzchak Weksler; Henik (Chanoch) Weksler**

Aunt: **Rivkale** daughter of **Reb Shmuel Frajdman**

[Two family photos]

Tzvi Morgensztajn

[Scan 472]

[Upper right]

Forever Remembered

I perpetuate the memory of my dearly beloved

Father: **Yaakov-Yitzchak Milman**
Brother: **Chaim Yosef**
Sisters: **Rachel, Pesl, Miriam, Sara**

Rivka Levenstat (Milman)

[Lower right]

A memorial candle

To the holy memory of my dear family members

Father: **Pinchas Manela**
Mother: **Chana** nee **Zilberman**
Brother: **Baruch**
Sisters: **Esther, Sara, Rivka** and husband **Yerachmiel Liberman** and their daughter **Bracha**

Leah Greiber (Manela)

[Left side]

In eternal memory

Of our dear, beloved martyrs

[Photo: father and a son]

Father: **Nathan Minkowski**
Mother: **Sheindel**
Brothers: **Aharon, Yerachmiel, Mendel**
Sisters: **Naomi** and **Chaya**

[Bottom photos: a brother and a sister]

Yechiel Minkowski
Moshe Minkowski

[Scan 473]

In eternal memory

Of our dear, beloved martyrs

Father: **Hershel Najman**
Mother: **Reizel**
Sisters: **Hinda, Chana-Liba, Esther**
Aunt: **Chaya Golda Gryn**
Uncle: **Leibish Najman**
Grandfather: **Izik**
Grandmother: **Perl**

[Top photo: likely the mother]
[Bottom photo: family photo]

Moshe (Max) Naiman
Wolf Naiman

[Scan 474]

[Right side]

A memorial candle

To the holy memory of our dear family members

Mother: **Leah Markowicz**
Brothers: **Yechezkel** and **Peretz**

[Photo: the brothers]

Sisters: **Bina** and **Tzipa**

[Photo: one of the women]

Uncles: **Berl, Yudel**, and **Yosef Goldberg** and his family
Relatives: Grandfather and Grandmother **Goldberg (Ilja)**

Yosef and Aharon Markowicz

[Upper left]

A memorial candle

To the holy memory of my dear family members

Father: **Shimshon Goldman**
Mother: **Tzirel**
Brothers: **Sender, Shlomo,** and **Avraham**
Sisters: **Malka, Roiza,** and **Rivka**

Shmuel Goldman

[Lower left]

In eternal memory

Of our dearly beloved

Father: **Shlomo Goldman**
Mother: **Chaya**
Brothers: **Berish** and **Hershel**
Sister: **Toiba**

Peretz Goldman
Esther – Nota's wife

[Scan 475]

[Upper right]

In eternal memory

Of our unforgettable, beloved parents and sisters

Father: **Levi Nemed**
Mother: **Bracha Nemed**
Sisters: **Malka, Chaya-Sara**

Bracha Nemed– Kadishevitz (wife of Yechiel Kadishevitz)
Slovieny (Slovenia?)

[Lower right]

In eternal memory

Of our dear parents

Father: Leon Neuman
Mother: Stefa

[Family photo]

Neuman Family
Avraham Neuman

[Left side]

A monument

To the unknown graves of our dear

Mother: **Chaya Neuman**
Brother: **Yitzchak** and wife **Sheindel**
Sisters: **Luba** and **Chana**
Relatives: **Pinchas Neuman** and family
        Yosef Gruner and family
        Chaim Neuman and family
        Feigel Neuman
        Yaakov Neuman and family
        Grubsztajn family

Yerachmiel Neuman, New York
Eliezer Neuman, Germany

[Scan 476]

In eternal memory

We hereby perpetuate the memory of our dear family members

Father: **Shmuel Samet**, perished in the Holocaust

Mother: **Chaya**, murdered by the Nazis

Son: **Shmuel**, fell in the Six Day War

Sister: **Rivka**, perished in the Holocaust

Uncles, **Moshe-David, Yaakov Birnbaum, Yisrael** and **Leah**

Aunt: **Matilda**, perished in the Holocaust

Cousin: **Charna Birnbaum**, perished in the Holocaust

[Photo: Mother, father and child]

Moshe Samet

Paula Kluger

Miriam Glick

[Left side]

In eternal memory

Let these lines serve as a monument to the unmarked graves

of my dearly beloved

Father: **Moshel Enisman** [photo]

Mother: **Shifra**

Brother: **Yitzchak**

Sister: **Gitel**

Children of **Peretz Grinszpan** and **Yachet Enisman**

Miriam Goldberg-Enisman

[Scan 477]

In eternal memory

Of my dear, unforgettable parents, sisters, and relatives

Father: **Dov Farbman**

Mother: **Gitel**

Brother: **Yechiel** and his family **Shmerl**

Sisters: **Eidel** and family, **Esther**

Grandfathers and grandmothers: **Nechemia**, **Chana** and families, **Shmerl**, **Esther**, and families

[Photo of a woman, probably Gitel, photo of 3 people, and photo of 2 men.]

Mendel Rosenwald-Farbman (Drildsz)

[Scan 478]

[Upper right]

Never forget

Let these lines serve as a monument to the graves of my dearly beloved

Father: **Tzvi Neuman**

Mother: **Rivka**

Brother: **Moshe**

Sister: **Chana**, and children **Yerachmiel, Hinda,** and **Gitel**

Sara Mann-Neuman

[Lower right]

In eternal memory

Of our dear husband and father

Avraham Funk of blessed memory [Photo]

Fela Funk-Singer, and son Paul

[Left side]

A monument

To the unmarked graves of our dear

Father: **Yisrael-Moshe Erlichsman**
Mother: **Chaya-Sara** nee **Gliksman**
Sister: **Peshel**
Aunts: **Sheindel** and **Gitel**

[Family picture]

Shmuel, Eli, Yitzchak, and Devora Erlichsman

[Scan 479]

[Upper right]

A memorial monument

To our dear, unforgettable mother

Esther the daughter of **Reb David Yehoshua Brodbeker**, widow of **Reb Moshe-Baruch Fajgenbaum** of blessed memory

Who ascended in the ascent of the pure, holy martyrs in the vale of killing in Treblinka.

[Photo of Esther]

May G-d avenge her blod

Her children: Tzvi Menachem, Ahuva, Simcha Bunim, Yeshayahu, and Moshe-Baruch

[Lower right]

In memory of our dear martyrs

His Wife: **Chava** nee **Morgensztern**

Their dear son: **Moshe Baruch**

    Who went up in the inferno of Treblinka

Our brother: **Shmuel Dov**, who fell in battle as a Jew

Tzvi-Menachem Feigenbaum
Chava Shraga-Feigenbaum

[Left side]

A memorial monument

Beloved and pleasant in their life, and not separated in death, To Rachel, and her seven holy, martyred children, who perished in the Holocaust.

Wife and their mother: **Rachel**, the daughter of **Reb Yitzchak-Meir** (the shochet) **Kenigsberg** of blessed memory

The sons and daughters in order: **Feiga-Rivka, Moshe Baruch Zusman, Chana Matil, Yitzchak Meir Yisrael, Tzipora, Libele.**

[A photo of a young child, and a photo of a baby]

Their memory will never leave us.

May G-d avenge their blood

Husband and father: Tzvi-Menachem Feigenbaum
Daughter and sister: Chava Shraga-Feigenbaum

[Scan 480]

[Upper right]

In eternal memory

Of our dearly beloved parents and sister

Father: **Moshe Pasternak**
Mother: **Beila-Tzvetel Pasternak**
Sister: **Miriam Pasternak**

Bina Rosenzweig (Pasternak)

[Lower right]

In eternal memory

I hereby perpetuate the memory of my dear

Wife: **Rivka** the daughter of **Shlomo Krauzman**, and my son
Who were murdered by the Nazi enemy and their criminal helpers.

David Pinczewski

[Upper left]

In eternal memory

Of our dear

Father: **Mordechai Finkelsztajn**
Mother: **Rachel**
Brothers: **Hersh, Yosef**
Sisters: **Pola, Frania**
Uncle: **Yisrael-Hersch Kasztan**
Aunt: **Feiga**
Cousins: **Meir, Shifra, Bela, Moshe,** and **Yisrael Kasztan**

Dora Botnik-Finkelstein
Zelda Bogdanski-Finkelstein

[Lower left]

An eternal flame

To holy memory of our dear family members

Grandfather: **Avraham-Mordechai Rotbard**

Grandmother: **Chana-Leah**

Father: **Yitzchak Shlomo Fiszman**

Mother: **Nechama**

Brothers: **Yerachmiel, Yaakov,** and **Aryeh**

Sisters: **Esther, Sara,** and **Rachel**

Uncles: **Ben-Zion, Isser**

Aunts: **Naomi, Golda**

Yehudit Landau – nee Fiszman
Moshe Fiszman

[Scan 481]

[Right side]

A memorial monument

To the graves of my dear family members

[Photo: Two young women]

Father: **Shmuel Yeshayahu Feldman**

Brothers: **Moshe**, his wife and children

    Avraham, and his wife

Sisters: **Sara-Hinda**, her husband **Tovia Tenenbaum**, and their children **Chaya-Ita** her husband and children

    Freda, and her husband **Baruch-Rubin**

Yechezkel Feldman

[Upper left]

A memorial monument

To my dear ones who perished in the Holocaust

Father: **Shmuel** the son of **Menachem**

Mother: **Chava** daughter of **Sheva**

Brother: **Tzvi**

Sisters: **Freidel** and **Sara**

Hyman Flantzenbaum, New York

[Lower left]

In eternal memory

With great sorrow and deep agony, we perpetuate the memory of our dear

Rachel Fruchtman

Roza Fruchtman

Yaakov Kac and his family

The Kuperman Family

Michael Hernik

[Scan 482]

[Right side]

A monument

To the unknown graves of my dear family members

Father: **Meir** the son of **Yaakov Maslowicz**

Mother: **Tzirel**

Brothers: **Kopel-Berl, Fishel**

Sister: **Aidel**

Uncle: **Yosel Maslowicz** and his wife.

[Photo: a brother and sister]

Mordechai Maslowicz

[Left side]

In memory of our dear ones

Who perished in the Holocaust

Father: **Chaim Asher Heilblum**
Mother: **Malka**
Sisters: **Rivka, Sara, Tzipora**
Brothers: **Efraim, Yehoshua**
Uncles: **Gidel** and **Idel** (**Mora**) with their families
    Yosef Eidelkopf with his family
    Shlomo Marmorek with his family
Aunts: **Reizel** with her children
    Finkelstein and family

May their memories light up the holy, pure heights

Yaakov and Alex Heilblum

[Scan 483]

[Right side]

In eternal memory

Of my dearly beloved

Father: **Shimshon Frimerman** [photo]
Mother: **Rachel-Malka** [photo]
Uncles: **Naftali** and **Moshe**
Aunts: **Chaya, Leah,** and **Tzvetel**

Tova Steinman-Frimerman

[Left side]

In eternal memory

Of our dear parents, siblings, and relatives

Father: **Yaakov Aryeh Frimerman** [photo]
Mother: **Malka** [photo]
Brothers: **Hillel** and **Chaim**
Sisters: **Chava Frajdman, Chana** and her husband and child (**Sztszensliwaj**)
Uncle: **Betzalel Frajdman**
Relatives: **Yaakov** and **Renia Frajdman, Mindel** and her son **Yaakov-Aryeh Frimerman**

Avraham Frimerman
Moshe Frimerman

[Scan 484]

[Upper right]

In eternal memory

I perpetuate my dearly beloved

Wife: **Mindel** nee **Kornwasser**
Children: **Avraham, Moshe-Yitzchak, Zalman, Doba**

Meir Frenkel

[Upper left]

In eternal memory

Of our dearly beloved

Father: **Pinchas Cytryn**
Mother: **Yocheved**
Brothers: **Tzvi, Menashe,** and **Yosef**
Sister: **Chana**

Rivka Cytryn

[Bottom]

In eternal memory

I hereby perpetuate my dear ones who were murdered in the Holocaust

My sister **Sara**, her husband **Avraham Kornwasser**, and their daughter **Chana** may G-d avenge their blood.

[Three photos of Sara, Chana, and Avraham]

Esther Cytrynbaum

[Scan 485]

In eternal memory

Of our dearly beloved, who were murdered in a tragic fashion during the terrible tragedy of the Jewish people.

Father: **Yaakov** the son of **Menachem Cukierman**

Mother: **Chana Bracha** the daughter of **Tzvi Najman**

Brothers: **Mordechai, Pesach**, and wife **Feiga**

Sisters: **Rachel, Yocheved**, and their familes. **Gitel Kasawaska**

Uncles: **Avraham-Idel** and his wife **Chaya Cukierman** and family, **Simcha** and his wife **Chaya Buchbinder** and family, **Zalman** and his wife **Golda Kirszenblat** and family

Aunt: **Hadassa** the daughter of **Yechiel-Meir Blusztajn**

Honor their memory

[Photo right: two sisters]
[Photo left: family photo]
[Photo bottom: family photo]

Avraham Zukerman (Toronto)

[Scan 486]

[Upper right]

In eternal memory

With deep pain, we perpetuate the memory of our dear

Rabbi Yechiel and **Rachel Przytyki** and family

Chanatshe, her husband **Moshe Najman**, and their children

Rivkatshe

Who were murdered by the wild, criminal Polish murderers in the city of Gdynia in Poland, already after the war.

Their relatives: Rivka Zoberman, Chava Shraga (Feigenbaum)

[Lower right]

An eternal flame

To the holy memory of our dear family members who perished in the Holocaust

Father: **Yeshayahu Cukierman**

Mother: **Leah**

Brothers: **Idel** and **Shmuel**

Sisters: **Rachel, Mirmel, Hene-Tobe**, and families

Uncle: **Leizer Cukier**

Relatives: **Moshe Richtenberg, David Yeshayahu, Leizer Sztarkman** and his son **Avraham**

Baruch Cukierman (Zukerman)

[Left side]

In eternal memory

Of our dearly beloved martyrs

Grandmother: **Sheindel**
Grandfather: **Mendel Feldficer**
Grandfather: **Yaakov (Brziszer) Golombiowski**
Grandmother: **Gitel**
Father: **Shmuel Cukierman**
Mother: **Breindel**
Aunts: **Miriam, Esther** (from Siedlowice)
Uncle: **Shaul Cukier**

[Family photo]

Chaya-Sara and Shmuel-Leib Lencicki (Lang)
Beniek Cukierman (Zukerman)

[Scan 487]

[Right side]

In memory

Of our dear martyrs

Father: **Moshe Kamec**
Mother: **Chava**
Brothers: **Abba, Simcha, Eliezer**
Sisters: **Chancha, Sara**

Pesach Groda-Kamec

[Left side]

In eternal memory

Of my dearly beloved

Father: **Moshe** the son of **Mendel Kogut**
Mother: **Rachel** the daughter of **Eliezer** and **Dvora Cuker**
Brothers: **Chaim**, **Feivel**, and **Shimon**

[Family photo]

Rachel Wajtceken-Kogut

[Scan 488]

[Right side]

We will never forget

Our dearly beloved

[Family photo]

Father: **Godel Kadiszewicz**
Mother: **Sara-Leah**
Brothers: **Avraham, Eliahu, Feivel**, and **Moshe**
Aunts: **Sarake Najman, Ita Kadiszewicz, Tzipa Hoffman**
Uncle: **Chaim Najman**
Relatives: **Chana** and **Avraham Kadiszewicz**

Yechiel and Akiva Kadiszewicz

[Upper left]

In eternal memory

Of our dearly beloved

Father: **Avraham-Moshe Kornwasser**

Mother: **Rachel**

Brother: **Moshe Reuven** and wife **Rivka**

Sister: **Chaya**, husband **Mordechai**, and children **Moshe** and **Miriam**

Aunts: **Guta, Fove** and **Noach Gutwajl** and children

Uncle: **Reuven** and wife **Sara**

Relatives: **Hinda** and **Moshe-Yosef, Yechiel** and **Rivka, Yerachmiel** and **Esther**

Naftali and Yaakov Kornwasser

[Lower left]

A memorial candle

To the holy memory of my dear family members

Father: **Yaakov** the son of **Meir Kornwasser**

Mother: **Rivka**

Brother: **Avraham**

Sisters: **Mindel Frenkel, Miriam (Feigele)**

Yosef Kornwasser, Meir and Rachel

[Scan 489]

A memorial candle

To the memory of our dear family members who died before the war and who perished in the Holocaust

Grandfather: **Mordechai David Kornwasser** of blessed memory

Grandmother: **Sara** [photo]

Aunt: Dvora, her husband **Leibel Sapirsztajn**, their children **Esther**, **Malka**, **Pinchas**, **Rivka**, and **Leah**

[four photos of family members]

Tova Zweig-Cohen

Malka Leopold-Cohen

David Cohen

[Scan 490]

[Right side]

A memorial candle

With agony as deep as the sea, we hereby perpetuate for eternal memory in this memorial book of the community of Wierzbnik our dear daughters

Beila

Genendel

[Photos of the two daughters]

Who were murdered by the Nazi enemy

Their parents: Tzvi and Rivka Weizer

[Upper left]

In eternal memory

We perpetuate the memory of our dear

Neche-Feiga, wife of **Reb Nathan-Nota Kornwasser**

Daughter: **Bracha**, her husband **Yaakov Guterman** and children

Sons: **Eliahu-Meir Noach**, and **Mordechai-David**

Yaakov Yitzchak Kornwasser and family

Hinda Teitelbaum

[Lower left]

In eternal memory

With great sorrow and deep agony, we hereby perpetuate the memory of our dear martyrs who perished in the Holocaust

Esther-Mirl, wife of **Reb Noach Meir Kornwasser**

Their sons: **Nathan-Nota, Yosef, Avraham, Yitzchak, Moshe**, and their families

Their daughters: **Ahuva (Liba) Brodbeker** and her family; **Rivka-Rachel Anisman**, her husband **Shlomo** and their children – who were murdered after the liberation by the murderers of the Polish A.K.

Hentshe and Yaakov Kornwassser

[Scan 491]

[Upper right]

In eternal memory

*Let these letters engraved in the memory book of our community
serve as a monument to the holy memory of my dear parents*

Father: **Rabbi Chanoch (Henech)** the son of **Reb Yisrael Yitzchak** [photo]

Mother: **Miriam** the daughter of **Reb Davi Yehoshua HaCohen Brodbeker** [photo]

May their souls be bound in the bonds of eternal life

Sons:
Mordechai Kaufman
Meir Kaufman

[Lower right]

In eternal memory

*Let this serve as the monument to my dear ones,
etched in the memorial book of the community of Wierzbnik.
Let these letters shout out and give no rest to the human conscience.*

Father: **Yaakov Kaufman** [photo]

Mother: **Chava** nee **Koclowicz**

Brother: **Yosef**

Sister: **Sheindel**

Chana Sendowski-Kaufman

[Left side]

In eternal memory

Of our martyrs

Father: **Yosef David Kaufman**
Aunts: **Chaya, Tova, Esther**
Sister: **Mindel**
Brother: **Yisraelik**

[photo: probably the mother]
[photo bottom: 3 girls]

Golda Bornstein-Kaufman
Yaakov Kaufman

[Scan 492]

[Right side]

In eternal memory

With deep agony and a subdued spirit, we perpetuate the memory of our dear martyrs

Father: **Yehuda-Ber Dov HaLevi Kopf** of blessed memory
Mother: **Beila-Gitel**, daughter of **Rabbi Eliezer HaLevi**, may the memory of the righteous be a blessing
Uncle: **Asher Zelig Celinski** of blessed memory
Aunt: **Sara Hendeles Celinski** (nee **Kopf**) of blessed memory
Relatives: **Dvora** and **Avraham Puterman**

Rachel Lipman (Kopf) Tel Aviv
Tovchia Wilfowicz (Kopf) Toronto

[Left side]

In eternal memory

May the memories of our dear martyrs be etched in the memory book of the community of Wierzbnik-Starachowice

Father: **Henik-Chanoch Kazimirski**, died before the war [photo]

Mother: **Gustava** nee **Zylberberg** [heart shaped photo]

Uncle: **Moshe Silberfenig**

Aunt: **Bronia Kalmanson**

Grandmother: **Tova Kalmanson**

Grandfather: **Eli Kalmanson**

All perished in the Holocaust – may G-d avenge their blood

Sister: **Sara Polonski-Kazimirski**, died in Israel [photo]

Tania Gelbard-Kazimirski

[Scan 493]

[Right side]

In eternal memory

*With holy trembling, we perpetuate the memory of
our dear family members, pure and holy,
who were murdered for no iniquity by the Nazi enemy*

Father: **Yosef Reuven Lichtensztajn**, may G-d avenge his blood [photo]

Mother: **Gitel**, may G-d avenge her blood [photo]

Grandchildren:
Rania Frimerman – Eva Singer
Zev Kilman, and families

[Left side]

In eternal memory

*With holy trembling, honor, and awe,
we perpetuate the dear memory of my unforgettable
family members, who perished in the terrible Holocaust
that took place to the Jewish people.*

Father: **Leibish Kilman (Yehuda Ari)**
Mother: **Sheina Kilman**

[Family photo]

Paula and Zeev Kilman
Eva and Yerachmiel Singer
Rania and Moshe Frimerman

[Scan 494]

[Upper right]

In eternal memory

*With great agony, honor, and awe,
I perpetuate the memory of the martyrs*

Father: **Shlomo Zalman** the son of **Ovadia Kirszenblat**
Mother: **Golda** daughter of **Yaakov Menachem-Mendel**
Brother: **Tzvi-Hershel** son of **Shlomo Zalman**
Sister: **Leah** daughter of **Shlomo Zalman**

Rabbi Yaakov Menachem the son of Zalman Kirszenblat

[Lower right]

In eternal memory

Of our dearly beloved

Mother-in-law: **Moshe** the son of **Tovia Gutman** from Slipia

Her children: **Beila, Sara, Aryeh, Tovia, David**

Uncle: **Efraim Finkelsztajn** from Slipia, wife and sons: **Avraham, Leibel, Yitzchak**, and their families

Cantor Moshe Yitzchak Kleinberg, Toronto

[Left side]

In holy memory

I perpetuate in this Yizkor Book of the community of Wierzbnik, our dear parents and siblings

Father: **Hershel Kleinberg**

Mother: **Sima**

Brothers: **Yitzchak, Antshel**

Sisters: **Reizel, Feiga**

Uncle: **Yisrael Kleinberg** and family

Relatives: **Helsztajn** family

[family photo]

Chaim Kleinberg
Arish Kleinberg

[Scan 495]

In eternal memory

Of our dearly beloved

Father: **Shmuel Kleiner** [photo]
Mother: **Sheindele**
Brothers: **Yaakov, Fishel**, and families [two photos – the brothers]

Yosef Kleiner, Venezuela
Sara Weisenfeld Kleiner, Venezuela

[Scan 496]
[Right side]

In eternal memory

Of our dearly beloved martyrs

Father: **Berl Baum** [photo]
Mother: **Miriam-Reizel** [photo]
Brothers: **Ben-Zion, Meir, Yisrael, Fishel**, and **Yaakov**
Grandfather: **Yosef Baum**, his wife **Rivka**, and their family

Nechtshe Kleinberg (Baum)

[Left side]

In eternal memory

Of our dearly beloved

Mother: **Chaya Kirszenblum-Krauzman**
Brother: **Refael**

[family photo]

Luba Chaitan Kirshelblum

[Scan 497]
[Right side]

With Deep Agony

I perpetuate the dear martyrs

Father: **Reb Yosef David** the son of **Baruch Abramowicz**

Mother: **Reizel** daughter of **Reb Yitzchak**

Sisters: **Esther Zelda**, her husband **Chaim Nachman Markowicz**, and their daughter **Golda**

Chaya Sara, her husband **Moshe Tzvi Delewkowicz**, their sons **Shimshon** and **Menachem-Mendel** and families

[Photo: father, mother, and a daughter]

Pinchas Yitzchak Abramowicz, Rio de Janeiro

[Upper left]

We bring forth the memory

Of our dear parents

Moshe Tzvi the son of **Yosef David Abramowicz** of Wierzbnik, died on 25 Marcheshvan 5732 (1971) in Rio de Janeiro

Sara Malka daughter of **Yitzchak Izak**, died on 29 Marcheshvan 5732 (1971)

Son: Baruch and his wife Zlata Abramowicz

Daughter: Golda and husband Benno Nisenbaum

Daughter: Ita and husband Shimon Breier

Brother: Pinchas Yitzchak Abramowicz and wife Tova Rucha

Rio de Janeiro

[Lower left]

We perpetuate

The memory of our dear father

Nachman Abramowicz the son of **Yosef David** of Wierzbnik, who died in Rio de Janeiro

Son: Yitzcak
Daughter: Dina and husband Yaakov Manela
Daughter: Brucha and husband Yaakov Warsewski

Rio de Janeiro

[Scan 498]

[Upper right]

We perpetuate

Our dear parents

Father: **Yaakov Bursztajn**
Mother: **Perl Nisel**
Who died in Rio de Janeiro

Son: Yitzchak
Daughter: Dina and husband Yaakov Manela
Daughter: Bracha and husband Yaakov Warsewski
Rio de Janeiro

[Lower right]

We perpetuate

The memory of our dear ones

Yechiel Yaakov Hilf the son of **Menashe** and **Tzetil**

Who died in Rio de Janeiro

Wife: Chava

Son: Yitzchak

Daughters: Perl and Hinda

Brother-in-law: Yitzchak Kornblum

Rio de Janeiro

[Upper left]

In eternal memory

For the unknown graves of our dear ones

Shmuel and **Fishel Hilf**, who perished in the Holocaust

Chava Hilf and children Yitzchak, Perl, Hinda
Rio de Janeiro

[Lower left]

In memory of our dear ones

Father: **Moshe Tzve Delewkowicz**

Mother: **Chaya Sara**, the daughter of **Yosef David Abramowicz**

Brother: **Shimshon** and family

Brother: **Menachem Mendel** and family

Daughters:

Golda Ita and husband Menashe Loterman

Perl and husband Yehuda Tenenbaum

Son: Yehuda Aryeh Zelekowicz

Grandchidren: Asher Zelig, Malka, Chana

Rio de Janeiro

[Scan 499]

[Right side]

In eternal memory

With great pain and deep agony, we perpetuate the memory of our dear, pure martyrs, whose souls shine like the splendor of the firmament

Parents: **Reb Dov David (Berl) Tenenbaum** [photo]

Dovra of blessed memory (died in the year 5691 – 1931)

Uncles: **Mendel Tenenbaum** and family, **Leibel Tenenbaum**

Aunt: **Sara Tenenbaum** and son **Yosef**

Grandfather: **Reb Avraham-Chanoch Tenenbaum**, may G-d avenge his blood

Hershel Tenenbaum

Mendel Tenenbaum

Dvora Kaminer

[Left side]

A memorial candle and monument

In memory of a noble woman

Dvora-Chaya (Dorka) Tenenbaum of blessed memory, daughter of **Reb Yirmia Levinson** of Optatów, may G-d avenge his blood, who died in her prime in Toronto Canada [photo], on 28 Tishrei 5632 (October 17, 1971).

The pain and grief are great among all who know her

May her soul be bound in the bonds of life, and may her memory be blessed forever

Hershel Tenenbaum

Sons: Benny and Meir

Daughter: Ruth

A cup of comfort

To her husband, our friend and acquaintance, **Reb Tzvi**, may he live, to their dear children and the entire family – comfort.

May the L-rd comfort you amongst the mourners of Zion and Jerusalem, and may you no longer suffer

The Organization of Wierzbnik Natives in Israel

[Scan 500]

[Right side]

In eternal memory

Of our dear

Stepmother: **Hadassa** the daughter of **Yechiel Meir Cukerman**

Children: **Yechiel-Meir** and **Ben-Zion**

Uncle: **Avraham-Yudel Cukerman**

Aunt: **Chayale** and family

[Photo: possibly the uncle]

Avraham Cukerman (Toronto)

Bracha Schetland (Toronto)

[Left side]

An eternal light

For the elevation of the souls of our dear ones

Father: Reb Shmuel Dov the son of Yehuda Tenenbaum

Mother: Rivka-Alta the daughter of Peretz Troper

Sister: Rachel

Brother: Moshe

Yerachmiel Tenenbaum – Rome

Chaim Tenenbaum – Brazil

[Scan 501]

[Right side]

With great sorrow

I perpetuate the memory of our friend

Esther Zukerman of blessed memory [photo]

Who was so suddenly taken away from us

Avraham, you should find your comfort in your fruitful work for the benefit of the community, and your various efforts to make the publication of the Yizkor Book possible.

Committee members in Toronto: Hershel Tenenbaum, Gershon Rosenwald, Max Neiman, Chana Neiman, Leibel Rabinovitch, Beniek Zukerman, Levi Brodbeker, and Tobcha Wolfovich

[Left side]

Esther Zukerman of blessed memory

Fate was cruel to her, and she did not merit to see the fruition of the memorialization about which she dreamed so much – the publication of the Yizkor Book. It is appropriate to note her name in memory of her children and her relatives who lost their children in the Holocaust, and her townsfolk who were murdered in such a tragic fashion. Esther was known for entertaining guests, and turned her home into a place of communal gathering for all natives of the city. Her smile never left her face, even though blood was flowing from the depths of her heart over the grief of the loss of her children, two young children, who perished in the Nazi inferno. She dedicated herself to her life's work, to memorialization of the natives of the city. She spared no means to see it to fruition.

She excelled in the goodness of her heart, in her fine traits, in her modest spirit, and her efforts to nurture a traditional, warm, home.

We will continue on with doubled energy to fulfil her final desire, and we will attempt to the extent possible to hasten the publication of the book of memorialization, in memory of the martyrs of our city, and to her eternal memory.

[Three pictures: the top two would likely be her deceased children.]

Gershon and Mosheke

[Translator's note: I am unsure if these are the perpetuators – or if these are the names of the deceased children – and the perpetuator was the society in general.]

[Scan 502]

A monument

*To the unmarked graves of our martyrs,
who were murdered in the Nazi hell*

Father: **Tzvi Zimmerman**

Mother: **Sara**   [Photo, Tzvi and Sara]

Brothers: **Michael, Shlomo-David**

Sisters: **Yochet, Chana, Golda, Fela**

Grandfather: **Efraim**

Grandmother: **Sara**

[Two photos on bottom: right one may be the parents again, and left one probably one of the sisters]

Perpetuated by Peretz Zimmerman

[Scan 503]

[Upper right]

In memory of

Our dear martyrs

Father: **Moshe Komec**
Mother: **Chava**
Brothers: **Abba, Simcha, Eliezer**
Sisters, **Chancha, Sara**

Pesach Groda-Komec

[Lower right]

In eternal memory

Of our dearly beloved

Father: **Yaakov Kopf**
Mother: **Pesia**
Brother: **Chaim-Ber**
Sister: **Bronia** and husband **Moshe Dawidowicz**, and child
Aunt: **Leah Baranek**

Moshe Kopf
Aryeh Kopf

[Left side]

In eternal memory

*Of our dear, pure martyrs whose souls
shine like the splendor of the firmament*

Father-in-law: **Yisrael Kaner**
Mother-in-law: **Leah**
Daughters: **Eidel, Esther**
Sons: **Shmuel, Kalman-Yosef**

[Family photo]

Leibish Kaner

Yaakov Katz

[Scan 504]

An eternal light

*To the eternal memory and elevation of the souls
of our parents and family members*

Father: **Leibush-Pesach** the son of **Moshe Kerbel**
Mother: **Hinda** the daughter of **Zusha** (nee **Weisberg**)

[Photo: the father and mother]

Brother: **Avraham (Omek)**

Uncles, aunts, relatives, and family members

May their holy memory not depart from our hearts
May their souls be bound in the bonds of eternal life

Moshe, Yitzchak, David, Shmuel, Yisrael, Shifra, Rozhshka, Sara – Venezuela

[Scan 505]

[Upper right]

I perpetuate

My dear martyrs

Father: **Avraham Eli Klikwaser**
Mother: **Rachel**
Brother: **Yisrael-Moshe**
Sisters: **Rivka, Chaya, Paula, Mina**
Grandmother: **Sheindel**
Grandfather: **Mendel Feldpicer**

Yosef Klikwaser

[Lower right]

In eternal memory

Of my dearly beloved

Father: **Nechemia-Menachem** the son of **Dov Rosenberg**
Mother: **Feiga-Alta** the daughter of **Yehuda**
Brother: **Levi-Yitzchak**, his wife **Henia**, and children **Avraham, Yosef,** and **Tovia**
Sister: **Rivka**, her husband **Yitzchak-Zeev**, and their family
Aunt: **Rachel** and her husband **Yehuda**
Uncle: **Meir-Eliezer** and family
Relatives: **Yechezkel** and family

Bella Rabinovitch-Rosenberg (Toronto)

[Left side]

In eternal memory

With great sorrow, I perpetuate our martyrs

Father: **Reuven Rolnicki**

Brothers: **Meir**, **Nathan-David**, and the youngest brother Leibishle, who was only two years old

Sister: Sara

[Family photo]

Yehoshua and Aharon Rolnicki (America)

[Scan 506]

In eternal memory

Of our dear martyrs

Father: **Yerachmiel Rabinowicz**

Mother: **Sheindel**

Brother: **Yaakov-Yitzchak**, his wife **Malka**, and their children **Moshe**, **Elimelech**, and **Eliezer-Mordechai**

Aunts: **Hindel, Dina, Chaya**

[Photo: A group of Hasidim with the Komarner Rebbe. Sitting first from left is Reb Yerachmiel Rabinowicz, of blessed memory.]

Leibel Rabinovitch (Toronto)

[Scan 507]

Standing at the market square, together with my beloved mother in the rows of those being deported, she said to me, "Go over, my son to the rows of the worker groups. Perhaps you will survive until the end, and remain alive. You will be able to tell how they tortured us." Indeed, this is everybody's command and duty toward our relatives: to tell! To remember and not forget!

In eternal memory

Of our dearly beloved parents and relatives

Father: **Mordechai Shraga** the son of **Reb David** – died [a natural death]

Mother: **Freda**, the daughter of **Yaakov Nisker**

Brother: **Yisrael-Yitzchaka** the son of **Reb Mordechai Shraga**, his wife **Feiga**, and their son **Mordechai**

Sister: **Sheindel-Leah**, her husband **Kopel Maskowicz**, and their children **Beila, Mordechai, Feiga, Yaakov**

Aunt: **Miriam Kac-Rozenwald**

Sara-Dina Finkelsztajn-Rozenwald and children

Uncle: **Berl Nisker**, his wife **Chana**, and their four children **Yisrael, Yitzchak, Yechiel,** and **Leibel**

Relatives: **Idel Nisker**, wife and children

[Two photos: left, the father and a son, right, the mother.]

Gershon and Moshe Rosenwald (Toronto)

[Scan 508]

[Upper right]

In memory of my dear ones

*Who were murdered by the impure Nazis
and their criminal assistants*

Zecharia the son of **Mordechai Gimpel**

Chana Feldpicer the daughter of **Kreindel**, and her son **Zecharia**

Simcha Rubensztajn the son of **Gimpel** and his family

Kreindel and **Dvora Yiti, Leah** and **Shmuel**

Gitel the daughter of **Dvora**

Avraham Zeev Rubinsztajn the son of **Mordechai Gimpel** and his family

Menashe the son of **Zev Komarowski**

Baruch Rubinstein

[Lower right]

A monument

To my martyrs

Father: **Moshe Rubinsztajn**

Mother: **Reizel**

Brother: **Chanan** and his family

Aunt: **Gitel Bekermaszyn** and his family

Uncle: **Leibel** and his family

Esther Nudelman-Rubinstein

[Left side]

In eternal memory

*I hereby perpetuate the memory of
my holy and pure dear ones*

Avraham Rubinsztajn the son of **Elchanan** (**Avrahamele** the tailor)

Chana, his wife, daughter of **Zecharia Rubinsztajn**

Nachum Grynbaum (daughter of **Esther-Malka**)

His wife **Gitel** daughter of **Zecharia Rubinsztajn**

Their daughters **Breindel, Reizel, Feiga**, and **Ita-Leah**

Their memory will never leave my heart

Yerachmiel Rubinstein

[Scan 509]

[Right side]

In eternal memory

*Of my dear ones who were murdered
in sanctification of the Divine Name*

[Photo: the father and mother]

Father: **Chanan Rubinsztajn** son of **Gimpel**, died in Israel

Mother: **Yocheved Rubinsztajn** daughter of **Esther**

Sister: **Ita Rubinsztajn** daughter of **Yocheved**

Aunt: **Esther daughter** of **Devora**

Grandfather: **Efraim Zimmerman** son of **Mordechai**

Relatives: **Golda Zimmerman, Frimet Zimmerman, Simcha Rubinsztajn**, and **Sara** daughter of **Devora**

Golda Biderman-Rubenstein

[Left side]

In eternal memory

Of our dearly beloved, who were murdered in a brutal fashion

Father: **Yaakov Rubinsztajn** [photo]
Sister: **Sabina**
Aunt: **Priva**
Uncles: **Yosef, Yaakov** and **Moshe Herblum**
Grandfather: **Leibush**
Grandmother: **Esther-Perl**

Miriam Rubinstein-Hendler
Malka Rubinstein

[Scan 510]

[Right side]

In eternal memory

With a heart full of agony and grief,
we perpetuate the memory of our dear,
pure martyrs who perished in the Holocaust

Father: **Dov Rosenberg**
Mother: **Yehudi**
Brother: **Yisrael**
Sisters: **Leah** and **Tamara**, may G-d avenge their blood

[Family photo]

Malka Weisblum-Rosenberg
Yocheved Bialik-Rosenberg
Aryeh Rosenberg

[Left side]

In eternal memory

In memory of my dear family members

Father: **Avraham Moshe Ribak** [photo]
Mother: **Chana-Gitel**
Brother: **Mendel-Noach**, **Shmuel**, and **Avraham**

[Photo: two brothers]

May his soul be bound in the bonds of eternal life

Sara Miriam Ribak

[Scan 511]

[Right side]

A monument

To the graves of my dear

Father: **Reuven Reisler**
Mother: **Malka**
Sister: **Chana**, her husband **David Nowicki**, and children
My husband **Yisrael Reisler**, who died in Montreal

[Two photos: probably the father and mother]

Freda Reisler (Montreal)

[Left side]

In eternal memory

I hereby perpetuate the memory of our dear martyrs

Father: **Avraham Reichzeig**
Mother: **Leah**
Brothers: **Baruch, Yisrael, Menachem**
Sisters: **Pnina** and **Chava**
Aunts: **Rachel Farbman, Chaya Miller**
Cousins: **Chava** and **Perl Miller**

[Family photo]

Henia Kupfer (Reichzeig)

[Scan 512]

[Right side]

A memorial candle

To the memory of my dear ones

Father: **Yosef Krausman** (died in Israel)
Mother: **Sara** (died in Toronto and buried in Israel)
Aunts: **Chana-Ruchtsha, Priva, Miriam, Chaya**
Uncle: **Moshe**

[Photo: likely the mother]

Chaya and Max Neuman (Toronto)

[Left side]

In eternal memory

With great sorrow, I perpetuate the memory of our martyrs

Father: **Yaakov Meir Krisztal** [photo]

Mother: **Chana** [photo]

Sisters: **Miriam Gitel, Perl-Malka,** and **Chaya**

Aunts: **Rivka-Rachel** and **Chana**

Uncles: **Avraham-Eliezer, Shlomo Teichman**

Feiga Krisztal-Mondik

Shmuel Krisztal

(America)

[Scan 513]

[Upper right]

In eternal memory

Of our dearly beloved

Father: **Elazar Rubinsztajn**

Mother: **Neche**

Brother: **Moshe** and family

Sisters: **Chana Jablonski** and family, **Genendel Komarowski** and family, **Sara Gorfinkel** and family

Rivka Roizman-Rubinsztajn

[Lower right]

In eternal memory

Of my dearly beloved

Father: **Shmuel Konowicki**
Mother: **Chaya Gitel** (nee **Tuchszeler**)
Brothers: **Tovia** (**Tulek**), **David, Pinchas, Zalman** (**Zenek**)
Sister: **Leah Zisel**

May their memories be a blessing

Yaakov (Kuba) Konowicki

[Upper left]

In eternal memory

Of my dear, holy family members

Father: **Zeev** (**Velvel**) **Pancer**
Mother: **Liba-Gitel**
Brother: **Berl** (**Dov**)
Sisters: **Breindel, Beila, Pesia-Leah, Miriam**

Tzvi Pancer

[Lower left]

In eternal memory

In memory of my dear family members

Brother-in-law: **Yechezkel Morgensztern** and his wife **Nechama**
Nephews (sister's children): **Yosef** and **Yitzchak**
May their memories be a blessing

Rachel Rubin

[Scan 514]

A monument to the dear souls

Father: **Reb Moshe-David Rothschild** [upper right photo]

Mother: **Libale** (both died in Israel) [upper left photo]

Sister: **Itzi Yachet** [middle photo], her husband **Rabbi Yitzchak Goldkopf** (middle right photo], and their two children [middle left photo]

Uncle: **Reuven Rothschild** [bottom photo] his wife and their children

Gitel Rothschild-Szprung

[Scan 515]

In eternal memory

Of our dearly beloved

Father: **Yechezkel Szternkranc** [upper left photo]

Mother: **Sara**

Brother: **Yaakov**

Sister: **Elka** nee **Tenenbaum** and her child

Aunt: **Rachel Wagman** and family

Uncles: **Moshe Binsztok**, **Mordechai Binsztok** and their families

[Bottom photos: two photos of a woman, and a family photo]

May their souls be bound in the bonds of eternal life

Chaya Galili-Sternkrantz

Sima Scheinwald-Sternkrantz

Zahava Sandman-Sternkrantz

Meir Sternkrantz

Binyamin Sternkrantz

[Scan 516]

[Upper right]

A memorial candle

To the dear memory of

Father: **Moshe Kalman Najman**, died in Rio de Janeiro

Daughter: Yetta

[Lower right]

In eternal memory

Of our dearly beloved martyrs

Father: **BenZion** the son of **Yechiel Sztarkman**
Mother: **Matil**

Daughters: Miriam Roichert-Starkman
Bina Kleinbaum-Starkman
Mirel Berber-Starkman

[Left side]

In eternal memory

Of our dearly beloved

Father: **Mendel Brodbeker**
Aunt: **Bashe**
Cousins: **Meir** and **Naomi Brodbeker**, **Alter Brodbeker** and family, **Chaim Brodbeker**

Avraham and Yaakov Sheiner

[Scan 517]

[Upper right]

In eternal memory

Let our dearly beloved be noted in the memorial book of Wierzbnik

Father: **Avraham Mordechai Sztarkman**
Mother: **Chaya**
Brother: **Yosef** and family
Sisters: **Reizel, Golda, Perl, Blima**, and families

Feiga Hochberg-Starkman
Menashe Starkman

[Lower right]

In memory of our dear ones

Grandfather: **Yitzchak Izik Najman**
Grandmother: **Perl**

Their grandchildren:
Avraham and Liba, grandchild of Moshe Kalman
Baruch son of Moshe Tzvi
Golda daughter of Moshe Tzvi
Ita daughter of Moshe Tzvi
Rio de Janeiro

[Left side]

In eternal memory

Grandfather: **Reb Chaim Zeifman** of blessed memory [photo]

Grandmother: **Rivka Zeifman**, may G-d avenge her blood [photo]

Yaakov Shnir (Sheiner)

Avraham Sheiner

[Scan 518]

[Upper right]

With great agony

I perpetuate the memory of our dear

Father: **Elimelech Sztreitman**

Mother: **Feigel**

Brother: **Yechiel-Michel**

Sister: **Yochet**

Peretz Streitman

[Lower right]

In eternal memory

With great agony and deep sorrow, we perpetuate the memory of my parents, brother, and sisters

Father: **Reb Tzvi Hershel Sztajnhart**, shochet from Serlo

Mother: **Feiga-Ita** daughter of **Meir Shmuel**, shochet

Brothers: **Avraham** and his wife **Libele Tajtelbaum** nee **Krausman**, and their son **Hershele**
    Shaul and his family

Sister: **Rivka**, her husband **Moshe** the shochet **Rosenblum**, and their son

Sara Steinhart-Perstovsky

[Left side]

A memorial candle

In holy memory of our dear family members

Father: **Moshe Szeiner** [photo]
Mother: **Miriam (Manya)** [photo]
Sisters: **Chana** and **Tova**

Sons: Avraham and Yaakov Sheiner

[Scan 519]

[Right side]

In eternal memory

I hereby perpetuate my dear family members

Father: **Anshel Szerfer**
Mother: **Leah**
Brothers: **Binyamin, Moshe,** and **Shmuel**
Sisters: **Ita Gotlib** and her children, **Golda Szerfer**
Uncles: **Moshe Baruch Leibush, Ozer Kogut**
Aunts: **Chaya, Rivka, Rachel,** and **Yenta Kogut**
As well as the families of the aunts and uncles

[Family photo]

Yechiel Sherfer

[Upper left]

In eternal memory

With deep sorrow and great pain, I perpetuate the memory of my dear, unforgettable parents, brother, and sister, who were so tragically killed by the hand of the murderers.

Father: **Yehuda-Arhey (Leibush) Szpagat**
Mother: **Mirl Szpagat**
Brother: **Matityahu Szpagat**
Sister: **Gitel Szpagat**

Moshe Spagat (Toronto)

[Lower left]

With sorrow and agony

I hereby perpetuate our dear martyrs

Father: **Yitzchak Szapir** of Starachowice
Sisters: **Sara**, her husband and children
Ruchama Turkeltaub, her husband and children
Brother: **Meir**, his wife **Tova**, and children

Rachel Shapir-Binstok
Tema Shapir-Knobel

[Scan 520]

I will never forget and never forgive

The criminal, murderous deeds of the Polish murderers that were perpetrated after the war

Noach Anisman from Bodzentin

Rivka, wife of **Shlomo Anisman**

Chaim Binsztok

Sara Wolfowicz, daughter of **Fishel**, and daughter **Rivka**

Miriam, daughter of **Avraham Zylberberg**

Rivka, daughter of **Avraham Zylberberg**

Bronia Cypis, daughter of **Eli Kalmanson**

Avraham, son of **Godel Kadiszewicz**

Noach Kornwasser

And many others whose names are unknown

May G-d avenge their spilled blood

[Scan 521]

[Right side]

In eternal memory

We mourn the loss of our dear one

Chava Dekel-Dreksler (nee **Frimerman**) [photo]

Cut off in the prime of her life

Husband: Yeshayahu Dekel
Daughter: Rachel
Son: Chanan
Sister: Tova Steinman

[Left side]

A memorial candle

*To the holy memory of our dear family members
who were murdered by the impure Nazis and their helpers*

Father: **Yosef Ungar**

Mother: **Frania** [photo]

Brother: **Monik**

Uncles: **Avraham Ungar**, **Shlomo Ungar** and family

Aunt: **Pesia Ungar**

Their son: **Efraim**

Their daughter: **Sheindel**

Tzvi Ungar

[Scan 522]

[Upper right]

A memorial candle

To the memory of my dearly beloved

Sister: **Rivka Rachel**, her husband **Moshe Beker**, and their six children

Brother: **Manele Binsztok**, wife and children

Miriam Shulman-Binstock

[Lower right]

A memorial candle

To the holy memory of our dear family members

Father: **Tzvi Herszman**

Mother: **Pipa Herszman**

May their souls be bound in the bonds of eternal life
Mourner: Leah Nebenzahl-Hershman

[Left side]

A memorial candle to the memory of our dear ones

Father: **Avraham Gotlib**

Mother: **Chaya**

Sisters: **Chana**, her husband **Baruch Kogut**, and children

Esther, her husband **Leibush Zisman**, and their children

Chaya, her husband **Leibush Herblum**, and their children

Brothers: **Gershon Gotlib** and his son **Yaakov**; **Pinchas, Yaakov**

Sister-in-law: **Miriam Gotlib**, and her children **Michael** and **Chaim**

Sisters: **Sara** (nee **Helsztajn**), her husband **Abba Praczownyk**, and their children

Sonia (nee **Helsztajn**), her husband **Yitzchak Wajgszparg**, and their daughter **Klara**

Brother: **Shmuel Mordechai Helsztajn**, his wife **Hela**, and children

Rachel Helstein (nee Gotlib)

Pinchas Helstein

[Scan 523]

A monument

To the memory of the martyrs of the community of

Wąchock

Near Wierzbnik

Who were brought to their deaths along with

the martyrs of our town.

Honor to their memory!

[Scan 524]

[Same as Scan 523. Scan 523 is in Hebrew, and 524 is Yiddish]

[Scan 525]

The Wierzbnik organization

Of New York

Mourns the death of

Six million Jews

Among them,

Four thousand Jews

From Wierzbnik

And perpetuates their

Memory!

[Scan 526]

The Wierzbnik organization

Of Toronto

Mourns the death of

Six million Jews

Among them,

Four thousand Jews

From Wierzbnik

And perpetuates their

Memory!

[Scan 527]

The Organization of Wierzbnik Natives in Israel

Mourns the loss of

Six million Jews

Among them

Four thousand Jews of

Wierzbnik

And perpetuates their memory!

[Scan 528]

A prayer

To the memory of the martyrs of the Holocaust

*Recited at the conclusion of a chapter or a tractate,
as well as at memorial gatherings*

Please, G-d full of mercy

In Your hand is the soul of all living and the spirit of all human flesh. May our Torah and prayers be acceptable to You on behalf of the souls of the six million of Israel, old and young, men, women, and children, who were murdered in sanctification of the Divine name, who were slaughtered, strangled, and burned to ash by the German enemy, may their name be blotted out, including cedars of Lebanon [4], mighty in Torah, holy and pure, heads of Yeshivas and their students, Jewish babies who never tasted the taste of sin, great Tzadikim – Rabbis of Israel with their holy communities, who gave up their souls in sanctification of the Name, as well as of our relatives who perished among them

May G-d remember them for good

Along with the rest of the righteous of the world, and may G-d avenge the spilled blood of His servants, as is written in the Torah of Moses, the man of G-d, "Sing O nations of His people, for He will avenge the blood of His servants, and heap vengeance upon His enemies, and atone for the land of His people." And as is said in the Holy Writings, "Why shall the nations say, 'Where is their G-d,' the vengeance of the blood of Your spilled blood before our eyes shall be known to the nations."

May their souls be bound in the bonds of eternal life.

May they be resurrected at the resurrection of the dead along with all the dead of your nation Israel, in mercy. And send us your righteous Messiah to redeem us from our exile and gather us together from the four corners of the earth to our land. May we speedily merit the complete redemption, Amen.

[Scan 529]

The community of Wierzbnik natives in Israel

Bows their heads in deep sorrow

Over the graves of the dear children

Descendants of Wierzbnik natives

Who gave up their lives in the battles of Israel

And sacrificed their lives for the revival of the nation

And the state, its existence and independence,

So that there will never be another Auschwitz,

Bergen-Belsen, Treblinka, or Majdanek – a second time

We will bind their holy members in our hearts!

[Scan 531]

Yosie (Yosef) Kilman of blessed memory [photo]

He was born in the Bergen-Belsen Camp after the Second World War, thereby symbolizing the end of the era of destruction and atrocities, and the transition from darkness to light.

He made *aliya* to the Land with his parents in 1949, when he was eight months old, aboard the Atzmaut ship.

He displayed unusual talents already during his early childhood, and excelled at school with his elevated traits. He was graced with musical talent and organizational skill from his youth, leading to successful musical endeavors. He set up a group of amateur musicians, and dedicated himself to it with heart and soul, attaining significant success in its performances.

He was drafted to the Israel Defense Forces in 1966. He passed a leadership course and served as a class commander in the Golani Brigade.

His unit fought in the north region during the Six Day War, and Yosef of blessed memory participated in the battles of the conquest of the Golan Heights. He was injured by shrapnel at an early stage of the battle, but did not abandon the battlefield. He continued to fight, and reached a fortified bunker with his comrades during a difficult, bloody battle. They stormed the bunker at the risk of their lives. Yosef was hit and fell there in the line of duty.

In his letter during the time of preparation, Chief Private Kilman wrote to his parents: "There is no choice, we are forced to fight – so that there will not be another Bergen-Belsen for the Jews."

From the words of the Minister of Defense

"Yosef of blessed memory was injured in his hand during the battle. He bandaged himself, and despite the order of his commander to not remain – he continued to move with the forces until the destination.

After his commander was injured, Yosef took the initiative and ascended the heights along with several soldiers. He fell as they were cleaning out one of the bunkers.

The memory of Chief Private Yosef Kilman should be holy, and preserved with pride in our hearts.

With appreciation

Chief of Staff Moshe Dayan

Minister of Defense

[Scan 532]

Lieutenant Shmuel Kluger of blessed memory [photo]

He was born in Stockholm, Sweden. He made *aliya* to Israel when he was still a baby with his parents – Paula (nee Samet), and Yaakov Kluger on the Negba ship. After studying in elementary school in Zichron-Yosef, and in Achva, he began his studies in a public high school in Haifa, and graduated with excellence.

He was drafted to the Israel Defense Forces in 1967. He took part in the Six Day War, participating in the battle of the Golan Heights.

He concluded a captain's course in 1968, and served as a captain in Bika and Ramah.

He was posted in the district of El-Hama in 1969. He participated in the battle against terrorists in his duty as commander, and fell on the 14th of Iyar 5729 (May 2, 1969).

Lieutenant Shmuel was respected by those under his command, and served as an example, displaying the finest of human traits, thanks to his generous character and upstanding abilities.

When he fell in battle, a dear son who was the pride of his parents was lost. A young lad, dedicated to the nation and the homeland was lost. He was the choicest and best of our youth, a true and dedicated friend to all his relatives, friends, and acquaintances.

We will bind his holy memory in our hearts with pride.

From his parents

We are not saying goodbye, for you still live within us...

And the Heart does not Grasp

If a person has something dear to his self and his thoughts, it is those moments in which he ponders and attempts to recall his childhood, with its happenings and events, and everything that succeeded in enriching his treasury of experiences.

As I write these words, I know that someone was taken from us, and the strands connecting many threads of thought were torn. The pillar of our internal treasuries connecting to childhood experiences has been cut off while still in its youth.

It is hard for me to get used to the fact that he is no longer. The thought of his death cannot yet be grasped. It is difficult to understand, and hard to come to terms with it.

However, an example of the finest of human nature will remain etched in the memories of all of us, forever.

To the parents and the family, we say: Be proud of Shmuel, who was so dear to all of us, and know that his memory will never leave our midst."

May his soul be bound in the bonds of eternal life.

A friend of his parents

Reuven Shuali

TRANSLATOR'S FOOTNOTES

1. Hayehudi Hakadosh, Rabbi Yaakov Yitzchak Rabinowicz, was the founder of the Przysucha (Pshishcha) Hassidic dynasty. See https://en.wikipedia.org/wiki/Yaakov_Yitzchak_Rabinowicz
2. It is unclear whether this is one person or two people, as the word "brothers" is plural, but there is no comma between the two names.
3. Jeremiah 9:1, included in the Haftarah of Tisha B'Av
4. Often used as a praise for Torah scholars.

English Section

[Page 3]

In Memoriam (Introduction)

Only a few of us have been spared from the hellfire unlashed by the Holocaust and no words can encompass the full extent of what we have irretrievably lost.

Memory grows dim with the passage of time, among those who have been left behind. We are becoming increasingly aware that an era is about to end, that this generation will have gone its way and sunk into oblivion.

We feel duty bound, however, to leave for posterity a record of the immense suffering and bereavement that have been our sad lot. We, the survivors of the town Wierzbnik, have therefore undertaken the solemn task of perpetuating the memory of our town's community and its martyrs who perished at the hands of the Nazi oppressor and his evil accomplices.

The community of Wierzbnik-Starachowitz never achieved any greatness, and its people did not gain positions of prominence or particular distinction. It just consisted of simple, decent Jewish folk who were happy to live and let live.

Looking back to the past, to the days of life in Wierzbnik we still remember the lively activity that went on there – the people rising at dawn for God's worship and the daily labour, workers and scholars alike, each going his own way.

Ever since the founding of the Wierzbnik community, the townspeople had built their life around Jewish devotion, study and honest work, righteousness and brotherly love.

On the Sabbath and holidays, the streets thronged with worshippers on their way to the synagogues, and the air was filled with the sound of song and prayer celebrating a life of goodness and peace.

And on normal weekdays, the down resounded with the noise of everyday toil and trade, the voices of merchants, porters and cart-drivers mingling in the Rynek square – the square which became under the Nazi oppression a last meeting place before transportation to the extermination camps.

Within the mainstream of this life there also grew the new Zionist generation, young people in youth movements and organizations, who prepared for the day when they would realize the age-long dream of the Jewish people: the rebuilding of their own homeland. While cherishing their hopes the Jews of Wierzbnik-Starachowitz kept up a productive activity in all walks of life. They largely contributed to the economic development of the town, built workshops and factories, and established a flourishing trade. Thus the close-knit Jewish community formed an integral part of the growing town.

Although Wierzbnik was not noted for its riches, everyone could make a living, and a spirit of mutual assistance prevailed.

For many generations of the Jews of Wierzbnik-Starachowitz lived in peace and harmony, tending to their affairs, each one with his hopes and dreams.

But all this peace and quiet was swept aside by a fury of bloodshed and violence unprecedented in the history of man or in the annals of the long persecuted Jewish people. All the dreams and hopes were shattered, all good deeds laid to waste.

The Holocaust had broken loose, and death came to claim a heavy toll.

* * *

This book tells the story of the persecution, deprivation and humiliation to which the Jews of Wierzbnik-Starachowitz were subjected, from the time the first bombs fell near the ammunitions plant of the town and up to the day of deportation to the deathcamps. A story of blood and tears, recounted by the scanty few who miraculously escaped destruction. The book also pays tribute to the courage of the men and groups who refused to resign themselves to their bitter fate and endeavored to oppose the monstrosities of the Nazi perpetrators.

Nearly all of these brave men forfeited their lives for any act of resistance, whether passive or active, against the oppressor. The sublime sacrifice they made in order to preserve the honour of their people, shall live in our memory forever.

The nightmare of the war was eventually over, and the world started rebuilding the damages and returning to normal life again.

Only one people were left unable to arise from the ruins, for they had been dealt a blow beyond restoration.

Only an infinitesimal of the once great Polish Jewry survived, with injuries in body and soul that could heal no more. Among the survivors, there are a small number from the community, just a handful of them.

On the banks of Wierzbnik the voices of Jacob's children were stilled, never to be heard again.

Even today, after a long history of bloody persecution and suffering that culminated in the terrible Holocaust in Europe, even now in the state of Israel reborn, we have still not found peace.

This memorial volume has been conceived and put together at a time when Israel again faces the need to fight for its freedom – for its very existence, indeed – against enemies that greatly outnumber it. As in times past, we are once more we are confronted with forces of evil bent upon wiping us off the face of the earth. But how different our situation today, now that we stand secure in our own land, strong in body and in spirit; no longer a fragmented minority within a hostile environment meekly submitting to its fate, but a united nation that knows to fight back and win!

In order to display the profound change that the Jewish people have undergone, it is our duty to inform the younger generation of what the past was like. They must be made aware how insignificant the Jew felt in the Diaspora, how he was treated with contempt and despised as something to be eliminated.

Young Jewish people everywhere should know these things, in order to appreciate freedom that they have attained, and strive to preserve it in the face of adversity. This record is also dedicated to the thousands of innocent victims of Wierzbnik-Starachowitz, brutally murdered by the Nazi executioners together with the other millions of Jews. The pain and sorrow of their loss can never be assuaged.

Great difficulties were involved in preparing for print this memorial book of the Wierzbnik-Starachowitz community. Besides financial problems, we also encountered considerable trouble in gathering factual material on the past history of the community, as we lacked documentary evidence or library records of any sort. We often thought that the project would be beyond our means, but thanks to the unflagging efforts of the sponsors and compilers we managed to overcome the difficulties and finally got the book ready.

We would not claim, however, that we have done a perfect job. It can be expected that the book suffers from some omissions, inaccuracies, and other defects. These are inevitable in a book of this kind, specifically with the limitations on hand.

Nevertheless, we spared no effort in trying to uncover any available scrap of information, so as to present a balanced account of events and make the picture as complete as possible. We are very grateful to all members of our community, here and abroad, who rendered invaluable assistance in the compilation of this book.

We dedicate this book to them memory of our town and its victims. May our troubled past be superseded by a bright future of fulfillment.

*

[Page 9]

Moshe Sali (Kerbel)

Sketches of a Town

My beloved birthplace, Wierzbnik, you haven't expanded their families, raised their children and wholesomeness, attributed to some cities and Jewish communities in the Polish Diaspora. But you [Wierzbnik] were fortunate in having the love of your own people and the respect and appreciation of your visitors, due to your forests, rivers and lakes that surround you and because of the richness and the excitement of your life, your work, trade and production, as well as learning and enlightenment.

You [Wierzbnik] were so much enriched with liveliness and gaiety of youth. Zionist and pioneering spirit prevailed all over you, and lust for Zion bas been veiled over all Jews. That was the popular, humble, Jewish community, orthodox learned but a struggling one, for bread as well as human rights. That was a very earthy community, but very anxious about its spiritual possessions.

Your streets and narrow alleys were without any splendor or beauty. The dwellings manifested the economic standing of your citizens. Nevertheless, adored you as you were. We never took notice of you repellent and faulty spots. You [Wierzbnik] stood for the enterprise of your people, industrious and creative ones, and the intelligence of your Jews who were at the center of your daily life. For two generations Jews used to live there, they expanded their families, raised their children and struggled for their existence at all conditions and circumstances.

I remember you [Wierzbnik] with excitement; I cherish with fondness and admiration your Jews because of their modesty, innocence and simplicity; because of their way of life – pure and relaxed – and the wonderful harmony of nobility, and unlimited love of Israel.

That was a magnanimous and hospitable town. Whenever a stream of refugees reached its boundaries, at times of catastrophes and emergencies, it opened wide its arms and hearts to welcome the victims of fear and sword. You knew to shelter them, to assist them, to support them in their time of stress. Nobody of its people uttered, "there is no room".

The Jews inhabited the center of the town around the main square, the market, and the neighboring streets. Only the remote suburbs at the outskirts were settled by the majority of the Polish population.

Most of the villagers in the vicinity of the town were farmers who lived on the land and workers, while most of the businessmen and the craftsmen in town were Jews (cattle dealers, tailors, shoemakers, upholsters, hatters, carpenters, blacksmiths, and others). Most of the sawmills surrounding the town were owned by Jews and so were the iron and copper foundries and the armories in which thousands of Polish gentiles were employed.

I remember vividly the town's market day. It was actually a day of joy and festivity for the Jews, since it used to provide an endless source of income and welfare for them. Thursday the traditional weekly market day, when the people of the town, of its suburbs and of the neighboring villages used to stream into the central market place from the very early hours of the morning, some walking, some driving in long convoys with their carriers. On one side there stood the counters of tailors, shoemakers, hatters, haberdashers, and others. On the opposite side there used to stand tabernacles, carriages and counters loaded with fruits, vegetables, milk and dairy products, chickens and piles of potatoes. The market place used to be heavily crowded with buyers and visitors. The proceeds came in abundance.

The shops and the inns in the market area mostly belonging to Jews, benefited most. They were crowded with buyers, traders and visitors who would spend lavishly. At the side streets, the blacksmiths and craftsmen were conducting their business and working, income was flourishing too. They were selling kerosene, and timber, as well as haberdashery, and grocery (in addition to foods and drinks). In essence, the market day mainly provided the Jewish people of our town with opportunities, livelihood and support. Only at late hours of the evening the farmers galloped their carriages through the town's streets back to their villages and then the market place was deserted again by thousands of its visitors and the Jews would relax and make a blessing, "...blessed is God daily..."

And today – everything is gone forever. The main square is probably still there, but with a different shape and look. The rumbling of the active Jewish business has become mute forever. Polish murderers took it over, as the prophet said, "...hast thou killed, and also taken possession..."

But in spite of all this, it is impossible to erase the memory of our youth days, which we spent in our town until the catastrophe occurred and turned life into hell, without hope, without salvation.

There are tombstones erected to commemorate fellow man. There are tombstones to mark one's achievements. But the most important of all tombstones is the ad memoriam, the commemoration book which unfolds the life of one generation, its joys and vivacity, is agonies and torment, and its struggles until its last gasp.

I mourn you, my town. A devastating hand annihilated your Jews, your prime source of liveliness and strength. It is all over and done with a community of exemplary life full of excitement and fermentation of culture of knowledge, of trade and of study.

There was a blessed town. She has gone forever.

[Page 12]
Yaakov Katz

The Jewish People Lives!

With awe and reverence, ardently and with a heart quivering with a holy fear, I wish to join in expressing something of the purpose and meaning behind the publication of a memorial book for the Jewish community of Wierzbnik-Strachowitz.

This was a grand community with a long heritage and deep Jewish roots. In her, we first wove the fabric of our lives and futures, and in her foundation of tradition were laid in our souls forever. In Wierzbnik-Strachowitz's synagogues and study halls we imbibed the living Torah. To her came the blood thirsty Nazi beasts and she went up in smoke. The town is gone and only scattered remnants have escaped.

There has emerged therefore, a felt need to establish a lasting memorial to Wierzbnik-Strachowitz. A living monument in the form of a memorial book was conceived. Its pages were to tell of the life and death of this bustling community in whose shade we had been secure, of the war and of the struggles to save her. It would once again advance the contention that, "The Holy One of Israel will not fail."

For each and everyone of us, it is thus a sacred duty to aid and support to the fullest possible extent those engaged in this holy work, as it is written (Exod. 17, 14), "Write this for a memorial in the book." We must be for them "...aiding and supporting brethren."

In this memorial book we must recall from the depths of the past tortures and torments those dear innocents who bore their suffering with exalted courage. But we must also, so far as the human pen is able, record and eternalize the rich tapestry of tradition: steeped lives, of God; fearing and learned men, men of action and labourers, simple persons and seekers of enlightenment. In brief, we must chart the community's life course from its shining dawn tills its sunset. We must memorialize all for the sake of those who were not privileged to witness the enemy's downfall and the consolations of Zion and Jerusalem. We must memorialize for the sake of our dear ones who went up in flames, sanctifying the Holy Name.

Led to slaughter, they breathed their last pure breath on the altar of their will to remain Jews. Sons of a chosen nation, "stiff-necked" people, they chose to guard the spark of Judaism, despite all. We must memorialize too for our own sakes; we, "splinters saved from the fire" a last remnant which has emerged from bondage and been vouch saved a glimpse of redemption. We must memorialize also for the sake of future generations.

Wierzbnik-Strachowitz was a thriving and flowering branch of the splendid, deeply rooted tree of Polish Jewry and an ornamented link in its chain, a fruitful and productive shoot of Jewish stock. But when the axe of the German hangman was aimed at that beautiful tree, even the gentle and wonderful branch of Wierzbnik-Strachowitz was cut in its prime.

Twenty-eight years have passed since the Nazi terror directed its poison darts at Israel, employing weapons and tactics of destruction hitherto undreamed of by mankind. We were (Jeremiah 9,21), " As dung upon the open field and as the handful after the harvestman which none gathereth..."

Even in the long, blood-drenched history of Jewish martyrdom there is no likeness or parallel to those deeds of destruction.

We, the survivors and mourners, will never forget our loss. Our agony must be unceasing for those who, innocent and pure, fell victims at the hands of the scum of the earth. Let us hope that the conscience of an enlightened world will finally awaken, clearly realize the situation and learn the necessary lessons from this unparalleled Holocaust. Even now, we must be on guard against those who call for a new genocide and who deceitfully schemed to uproot us from the land of our Fathers, our eternal homeland since Abraham.

We are thus commanded on the basis of every consideration to kindle an eternal flame of memorial for our fathers, families, and relatives. May it burn before us forever, sanctifying their name in public mind and all the holy of Israel.

For us it is a privilege and a holy obligation to eternalize the history and events of the village, her social and spiritual life, organizations, public institutions and personalities. Only thus can we understand the proud and brave stand of our fathers and mothers, brothers and sisters, blood relatives and dear friends who were brought to the slaughter with lips trembling at the thought of vengeance.

Their last words were of, "The G-d of Israel who is a G-d of Vengeance" of, "The people of Israel which lives and endures." The downfall of Hitler and his cohorts must certainly not be of any less importance or significance to us than that of Amalek, Haman, Pharoah, or any of Israel's enemies throughout the generations. We were commanded to remember Amalek to celebrate Purim with joy and the reading of the Scroll of Esther. We celebrate Passover and tell stories of the Exodus till morning. Doubly so, should it be out holy obligation and that of all Israel to externalize in flaming letters and in public what the monstrous figure of Hitler bode for us. Unquestionably, enormous difficulties will arise in the practical implementation of such a weighty task. Those pioneers who have unselfishly shouldered the burden of this sacred duty will certainly meet many financial and social problems. Most difficult perhaps, will be the patient "ant's work", of collecting the mass of material, connecting its diverse threads and of finally reworking it for publication.

More than once doubts have arisen whether the strength of these pioneers, Jews and non-Jews alike, would suffice to overcome all the difficulties inherent in this invaluable task.

For those working on this particular volume, the scattering of the descendants of Wierzbnik-Strachowitz throughout the wide world, and their differing relations and attitudes towards the nation's spiritual treasures, weighs as a heavy problem. There is also a lack of substantial and reliable information about the history and events of Jewish Wierzbnik-Strachowitz.

Despite all difficulties, however, our great faith in the "Rock of Israel" together with our belief that (Jeremiah 51,5), "Israel is not widowed" have renewed in us the hope that our combined efforts will suffice, "to roll off the stone from the lip of the well." We will succeed. To me it seems as if our requests and prayers have already been answered. After long, fatiguing efforts, we are now finally entering the advanced stages of the projects realization. G-d willing, the book will soon appear in a format which will do honor to those from the town and its surroundings.

We realize that the work cannot be altogether faultless or complete, certain details regarding personages or historical periods may be missing. We may, however, accept such deficiencies, secure in the knowledge that the editors and all those involved in the project have done everything possible to obtain source materials, to encourage participation and to bring to light memoirs and information about events and feelings in the life of the villagers.

Let me take this opportunity to give my blessing and encouragement to all those engaged in this holy task and to all who have given it material and spiritual aid. Special mention must be made of the small group of organizers of the project who have not spared pain or effort to ensure the book's speedy publication. Similarly, we must thank all those who have actively participated in this lofty cause, whether by volunteering information or contributing financially. May they all be blessed!

May the memory of those who are not with us serve the State of Israel and all the House of Israel. May their merit help protect us from those in every generation who hate us and would seek to destroy us.

May the memory of our town and her holy martyrs be bound up with the eternal life of the renewed State of Israel in which we conceive some small consolation for our great loss. May the State be a source of hope and encouragement to all our brothers and sisters everywhere, thus strengthening the weakened ties among Jews. May her influence serve to forge a new link in the splendid, continuing chain of Jewish learning and values in the tradition of the prophets.

Let us say Amen – may such be thy Heavenly Will!

"Again will I build thee and thou shalt be built, O virgin of Israel."

[Page 15]

Gershon Rosenwald

Twenty Years after the Loss of Jewry of the Cities of Wierzbnik and Drilz (Ilza)

Sixteen days in the month of Heshvan, on Tuesday October 27, 1942 the murderous hands of the Nazi snuffed out the Jewish life that existed for man generations. At the same time, twenty years ago, in the early hours of this dark Tuesday morning, the remaining survivors of Wierzbnik and Drilz congregated to remember their dead who were tragically lost before our own eyes, a world still fresh in every one of us, even though twenty years have passed since this bloody destruction. Everyone of us of Wierzbnik will always see before us this frightening picture, the way we congregated with those from other communities in the thousands and in the early hours of this Tuesday morning. While it was still dark, we were brought together from our camped ghetto quarters and brought together into the market place with clubbing and shooting. There were cries of the little children and the wailing of the Mothers looking at their sleepy tots and the children that were lost looking for their Mothers.

At eight o'clock in the morning we were all standing in the empty market place. Our hearts were bleeding; everything was black before our eyes to see the S.S. murderers with their Ukrainian and Lithuanian helpers shooting at the people and telling the Jewish people to drag the corpses into the yards. Rivers of Jewish blood were flowing like water.

Put the pages back twenty years in our life and for us the few survivors it appears just like yesterday. It is difficult to free oneself of this destruction that the murderers made in a few hours. Eleven o'clock of the same day you will remember that we were standing in line when the murderer Althoff and the others selected who is to live and who is to die and not a light death, but the sealed cars they prepared were already waiting at the station where our sisters, brothers, parents and children by the hundreds packed 150 to the car.

Until that day whoever had hidden valuable items could bribe themselves to life, but on this seventeenth day of Heshvan, the dark Tuesday in the annals of Jewry of Wierzbnik, was the end. You all remember that it was a hot day. It was the 27th of October1942. Those who were chased to the factories for a distance of five kilometers, so far beyond the city with our possessions on our backs and only the bare minimum. Many had to thrown some of these bare possessions away because of the heat and the chase of the murderers.

Our town was the last to be annihilated and the murderers said that the Jews of Wierzbnik are useful; they are good workers in "Hermann Gerring's" ammunition factories. On this Tuesday, the children were standing with their parents and as my brother-in-law, Kopel Maslowitz held his twins in both hands; they asked him if he will give away his children so that he can go to the factory and when he refused they permitted him together with his wife and four children and sister to step aside and go to his death in the sealed cars. The seventeenth day of Heshvan, this unfortunate day in our lives, when the largest number of Jewry of Bendzin, Drilz, Wanhatzk, a part of Plotzk and other cities which the murderers brought to our Wierzbnik, participated together in their dark hour by saying their "Shma Israel" (Hear Ye Oh God) with such composure. You all remember the line condemned to death and how their crying eyes looked and how quietly they accepted their verdict of death.

We, the ones selected for labour, well understood their looks; should some of us survive to take vengeance of their murderers. For those who survived a long list of suffering began. Our punishments were such that we envied those condemned to death. Hunger, epidemics, hard labour was the order of the day. Remember the sick in the special barracks. There were many ill with fever and the murderer Althoff shot them all on their straw beds. Think today of your camp with 120 people for whom pits were prepared and thrown in almost alive, men and women together. Remember the Fathers and the Mothers who would not part with their children and perished together.

How gruesome was the picture for all of us to return to the city and find corpses lying in various parts of town. Let us bow our heads for the 107 who perished and on whom we performed Jewish burial rites and buried them in one plot.

Let us remember those who perished and those who survived that Tuesday and put on our prayer shawls for those whom the murderers shot in their houses. Like our neighbour, Mr. Henoch Biderman, a very fine Jew, put on his religious clothes and marched to his death in the market. Remember; remember all of them who fled from the camp into the woods, 800 in all, and the Poles who reported many of them to the Germans.

I remember, every year, those of us who perished. Itshele Weizer, who came to the woods and found a group of Jews and brought with him his phylacteries and prayed on the eve of Yom Kippur and two days later Itshele was found cut in pieces and we buried him. As shivers run through our bodies remembering all this and it is our duty to remember those of us who perished, we shall never forget them and always avenge them. I want to remember my brother, Isaac, may he rest in peace, whom the murderers shot as he was working in the factory. When the police found him, he had a prayer book open in his hands at the prayer, "God Our Lord Take Vengeance From Those Who Spilled Our Blood". April 1, 1944, after a night's work he apparently prayed after completion of his work and the Ukrainian murderer found him doing this and shot him.

Let us remember them all. I want to mention the name of my Mother with whom I was standing in the market place together with my three sisters and their three children, wanting to go together and not to separate from their children. My Mother kissed me and begged me to go to work, maybe I will survive and be able to tell what they did to us; maybe she said, you will live long enough to see their end. When an S.S. murderer came to me and took me by the throat and told me if you don't come to work you will be shot immediately, I did not see my dear ones again.

[Page 18]
Yaakov Katz

Remember, And Don't Forget

The great, classic Jewish authors at the beginning of the 20th Century did a great service to the people by describing as profusely as they did, Jewish life in the villages of Poland and Russia. Never in their wildest dreams did they imagine that those very same writings would come to be seen as the swansong of the Jewish village. After the Holocaust of 1939-1945 their authentic and creative works came to serve as the graveside monument for the European Jewish village.

In the past, Jewish historians writing in the Diaspora had always skilfully immortalized the heroes and heroic deeds of the nation. They described that national heroism which always emerged in times of suffering: from the Babylonian Exile through the Maccabean Revolt, and down to our own times.

Today, over thirty years since the beginning of World War II, a national poet has no yet arisen, whose writings adequately describe the great Holocaust and the terror which accompanied the unparallel devastation of this cruelest of wars.

Certainly the burden is too great for the historian who might aspire to uncover, beneath the ruins of the villages and ghettos, their nameless heroes. Heroic deeds were almost without number.

Many were those who suffered hellish torment before they breathed their last breath in the Nazi ovens. The Nazis left few survivors in any village and even fewer from any family, as it is written, "One of a city and two of a family."

Thus, for the few survivors there exists a holy obligation to eternalize the memory of the pure and holy dead, that it may never be forgotten.

In the book of Exodus, G-d says to Moses, "Write this as a memorial in the book and rephrase it in the ears of Joshua, for I will utterly blot out the remembrance of Amalek from under heaven." ne might think the word "this" unnecessary, were it not that it hints at a deeper meaning. In the original Hebrew, the letters of the word "this" are identical to the initials of the Biblical phrase, "Remember and do not forget." In that phrase the words "do not forget" also hint at a deeper significance. Perhaps, the verse warns not so much against literal, absolute forgetting ("Tishkach") as against a failure to preserve in memorializing and the command is not to tire in effort "Koach" – to remember (Tish-koach). From the above we learn of the duty to remember and the prohibition to forget, as Divine commandments incumbent upon us all," That you may tell in the ears of thy son, and of thy son's son." We, the last generation in the bondage of exile and the first to glimpse redemption, are obligated and commanded to recall the past, this for our own sake and for the sake of future generations. Let them be proud of the stone from which they were quarried. Let them realize that whole nations and peoples have lived and schemed and are now vanished from the earth, but "The Jewish People lives and endures." and "The Eternal of Israel will not fail." These are not mere phrases, but real truths, which have been tested in the melting pot of history. These words are proven; they are engraved with the blood and flames of blameless martyrs consumed by fire.

The village Wierzbnik-Strachowitz, was perhaps only a small speck on the map of Poland, but in the thirties it was my whole world. It was a small village in the midst of the surrounding fields and pastures, forests, lakes and streams. There were no asphalt roads or large buildings. The antiquated wooden houses, which lacked electricity, running water, or built in sanitary facilities were, nonetheless, marvelously clean. The Jew's life was that Jewish way of life that had belonged to his grandfather; yet it was still alive and effervescent. No wonder then that great writers like Shalom Aleichem, Mendele and Peretz saw fit to describe and immortalize the village Jews as he really was. One's own, "everyday" people who would arise before dawn, winding their way through darkness or by lantern light to serve their Maker at the first service in the study hall. From there they would go to their daily affairs, some to stores, some to their small crafts, and some to their merchandising, The village may have been without luster and pomp, but it certainly did not lack scholars, students of the Torah, righteous persons and others who busied themselves with holy matters.

The study hall was not only a place to pray or study the Talmud, but it also served as a meeting place for all pubic functions. Here was the "parliament" where the congregation's policies were formulated with regard to all local or public matters. Here communal workers would wrestle for influence in all matters that they considered within their sphere. Here, from time to time came important public leaders, famous preachers, and public functionaries. Here, for many years Jewish life and affairs were managed peacefully.

From the time of Hitler's ascent to power in Germany, the world, and particularly the Jewish world, began to be shaken by increasingly severe tremors. Anti-Semitism had always existed, and was deeply rooted, but it had usually been masked and furtive. Then, it gradually began to rear its ugly head and show its true colors. The feeling of economic insecurity grew and Jewish youth began to wonder about the future and seek a way out.

As if born on the wings of a violent storm, the magic word "Eretz Yisrael", the Land of Israel began to take hold. Through every Jewish village swept a wave of Jewish youth movements, religious and secular. Inscribed in their banners and in their hearts was the hope for the return to Zion. Clubs were established where the youth could release its pent-up energy. Not easily did the parents accept this rebellious development. Many Jews, however, made a de facto peace with it in the conviction that in time the youth would find the road to their own salvation. Young people had simply found themselves and their mission in life.

Wierzbnik-Strachowitz was blessed with a small number of communal workers who gave of their time and spirit, of their money and support to this holy work. The Zionist movement was a basic and formative influence upon the youth. It educated them towards human and solid values, towards the acquisition of enlightenment and towards a widening of the horizons of Torah and thought.

On the other hand, there also arose an increasing number of youth organizations, which cleaved to the nation's heritage and to the generation old wellsprings of Torah. Their members plowed deeply in the fields of the Talmud and Codes. They found in the depths of traditional methods of interpretation, whether simple or elaborate, a source of support of boundless enthusiasm. Biblical stories about the desired land of the Patriarchs, about the "Beauteous Land" of the Bible, intoxicated with delight.

The town spewed forth their sons and daughters. Hostile Poles joined with theNazi oppressors in an effort to destroy us utterly.

We shall not weep for her destruction, but only for the destruction of human dignity, for lives that were cut off in their prime. For dear ones whose names were sanctified,

Let us memorize this and remember forever.

Remember what the Amalekite Nazi did to you and may his name and memory be eternally blackened!

[Page 20]
Jerachmiel Singer

Dark Days of Horror and Ruin
(The Tragedy of Wierzbnik)

Dark clouds settled over Poland. Day by day, almost hour by hour one felt the oncoming war approaching and becoming inevitable. The skies turned black and threatening over the towns and villages where the Jewish population was concentrated. Every news item on the worsening situation, every runner with a mobilization order increased the uncertainty and fright among the masses.

The fact that there were ammunition and arms factories in town was sufficient to arouse people's thoughts of what was in store for the place once hostilities broke out. They thought, rightly as the events proved later, that the presence of those factories would invite the German bombers to unload their destructive charges on the densely populated area in the very near vicinity.

Fifth columnists knew how to exploit this fact in addition to their other subversive activities, only encouraged the rumours in order to create a panic amongst the people and create difficulties for the Polish army authorities.

Meanwhile the Poles themselves started to dismantle the arms factories with theintention of putting them up in some "safer" place (hear-say mentioned Kubel). This official step only increased the fear of what was ahead. Slowly, the shopkeepers emptied their stores and people prepared themselves to flee to the neighbouring towns and villages, which they thought to be safer. At about this time a Civil Defense was organized under the auspices of the authorities. Among the organizers were also Jews, Isaac Laks, Josef Unger, Yitzhak Singer, and others.

"We are all in the same boat."

I joined the Civil Defense when a neighbour, a cafeteria owner in our neighbourhood, presented himself as the man in charge of our block and appealed for volunteers among those who were free of army service or had not yet been called to the flag. He assigned me for duty on a certain stretch day and night because the blackout was already in force.

About a week before the war broke out the congregants of the Great Synagogue in Wierzbnik were indeed surprised when during the Friday night service no people appeared but the District Inspector of Police, in person. His sudden unprecedented appearance in "Shul" in those troubled days certainly was dramatic. He didn't waste any time and came straight to the point. As the responsible authority of the District including Civil Defense, he asked for volunteers to dig trenches in all parts of the town. To make the point, he stressed the fact that the Jews and Poles were now bound by the same bonds of destiny and in his own words, "We are all in the same boat." No one needed any convincing that indeed we were on the verge of war.

The next morning, in spite of the Shabbat, many volunteered to dig the trenches together with the Poles.

Special mention must be made here of Professor Godel Janisevitz, the leader of the Union for the light industry, who was the first to take an active part in this matter.

The inevitable came…On the first of September 1939, the first bomb fell on Wierzbnik next to the plywood factory of the Lichtenstein Brothers. This was followed in the afternoon by a second one, which fell near the house of Chaim Brodbekker, and although this was expected, it nonetheless shocked the people who became more wary as what was to come.

Next day, the atmosphere became somewhat lighter when the news came that England and France declared war on Germany.

Jews started to leave town, one after the other houses in the "Jewish" streets became empty. Only those who did not have the possibilities of hiring a cart to stack their belongings or those who had an active part in the Civil Defense stayed behind. The big yard of Maschliburski was nearly empty. In this block only my cousin, Josef Unger, my Father, my sister and myself were left.

When we heard that all the offices of the government and the local authority had been evacuated to the district capital and that the town mayor was advising everyone to leave, we too on second thoughts, decided to follow suit. On the 5th of September, we started out on foot, because no more vehicles of any description were available in town. It soon became apparent that more people shared our thoughts and decided on the last moment to leave town, amongst them, our family. Since they were setting out to Vashniew, we joined them.

German tanks crossed the village...

I couldn't leave town without seeing two of my friends, Dr. Jacob Kramacz and Prof. Leon Korta, who were on duty this time of night at the public bathhouse and to warn them of the situation.

When I got there they were asleep. Without disturbing anyone I awakened them and in a whisper told them of my intention to leave town advising them to join me and after some hesitations and upon my insistence, they quietly and without anyone noticing came away with me.

Together, we made our way through the night uneventful. It was only at dawn, upon meeting the local police sergeant, Oupile, who told us that three German tanks had broken through the village down the road, that we became aware of any change.

These tidings greatly upset us. Instinctively we increased our pace until we started running... Thus we continued marching, taking a little rest here and there until at sunset we reached Vasniew. This was a typical Jewish village, which we found half deserted and in turmoil. We decided therefore to continue our flight.

By then we were quite exhausted and after a few hours sleep all of us, except Unger, took to the road again. This time we went in the direction of Ostrowic.

We felt the effort of the continuous marching and the walking became difficult, besides the strafing from the low flying German planes.

We reached Ostrowic in the early afternoon. The streets teemed with refugees, many from our town. Amongst them we met a close friend of the family, Mordechai Lipstein. Tired from our journey, we sat down to rest when suddenly the streets emptied as German troops were marching into the town.

The German Occupation

The Jews were horror struck, and feared of what was to come. Trouble started soon enough. The Germans immediately imposed a curfew from sunset till 6am. A few Jews on their way home from "Mincha – Mariv" prayers were killed by German patrols.

We stayed a few days with friends, Kleiman family. When we heard that the roads were clear, we decided to return to our town. We hired a horse and wagon and soon arrived back to Wierzbnik. The sight that met our eyes was shocking! There were few people around, all the stores had been broken into and looted. Our flat we found as we had left it so was our provision stock intact that we had prepared before the outbreak of the war.

The bakeries were ordered by the German authorities to open and the people, including Jews, were queuing up for bread. Soon the Poles started to point at the Jews, who were then forcefully removed by the German guards. Daily, Jews were being rounded up for all kinds of jobs: to clean German army vehicles, to clear public buildings of materials and furniture, loading, unloading, etc. This work was carried out with beatings and mistreatment.

The night after Yom Kippur, we smelt a strong smell of smoke. We climbed to the roof to see if we could detect anything, but in vain. Next day, however, an awful sight awaited us. The Synagogue in Nieska Street and the adjoining building of Talmud Torah had burned down completely with al the Torah scrolls, religious objects, the furniture as well as the community offices. (The burning of the Synagogue is described in a separate article by D.P.).

As it transpired later, the Germans had perpetrated this act, since this very same night many Synagogues went up in flames throughout Poland. The Germans had apparently intended to commit this arson on Yom Kippur night but were misled by the Jewish calendar. This event left a deep sorrow on the Jewish community in town.

Edicts

A series of proclamations, decrees and orders against the Jews followed one another. To cite only a few of them: the turning in of foreign currency, jewelry, gold, silver and other precious metals. Orders about restriction of movement: It was forbidden to go by train or any public vehicle without special permission, it was forbidden to raise prices as food rationing and new taxes were introduced and etc.

As life became more difficult, so the tension rose day by day. In many cases, Poles so called "Volksdeutsche" betrayed Jewish shopkeepers, whereupon the Germans put through ruthless searches. Not a day passed without a few Jewish families being ransacked. An enormous quantity of material was taken out of the cellars of Yaacov Guterman. The stores of Shmuel Cohen, Josef Drexler and others were completely emptied. The German authorities expropriated the sawing mills and timber yards of Mordechai Lipstein, Yitshak Rosenberg, Uri Helstein, Meir Steinbaum, Moshe Tentzer, Shmuel and Yaacov Kleiner, Weitzman, the father-in-law of Yaacov Zuckerman. The factory and sawmill of Shmuel Pochachewsky were confiscated, as was the plywood factory or Hortzi. Here I have to mention the tragic case of Shmuel Kleiner, who upon hearing the news that his timber yard had been expropriated had a heart failure and passed away on the spot.

The Sign of Dishonor

The current beatings and seizing of Jews paralyzed the life of the Jewish population altogether. And if the Jews still tried to get about in spite of the atmosphere, this became impossible with the latest and most humiliating of all decrees: the wearing of the yellow patch.

That decree caused great confusion amongst us, everyone felt as if he was being branded and a deep sense of shame overcame many. Not surprising therefore that the first days of the decree most of us did not leave our dwellings, but life continues and slowly people started to show their faces outside.

The Poles meeting us on the street grinned and smiled of satisfaction. In their satanic minds they were convinced that all the furor and enmity of the Germans would be directed only against the Jews, whilst they would enjoy special privileges. Whereas to the Germans, the yellow patch indicated a person who could be taken for forced labour without having to account to anyone.

Another order, which caused us great embarrassment and humiliation, ordered us to take off our hats before a Germans in uniform…

Wierzbnik

The local authority was taken over by German officials, and a "Volksdeutche" (a Pole who declared that he was of German origin) was named as its head.

At the same time the Germans set up a council through which they could govern the Jews, and demanded a special contribution for this purpose. This sum had to be handed over within 24 hours, and the people had to collect it within this time limit. With the setting up of the Jewish council, the random seizing of Jews in the streets ceased, but the council had to provide the necessary manpower in accordance with the German demands. Soon there were two groups: those who were always sent out to work on the one hand, whilst the other group comprised of those who paid ransom money.

The community was ordered to draw up a list of males between the ages of 14 and 65, which actually made up the available manpower for them to draw upon. The Germans made a point of it that all those who appeared on the lists underwent a so-called medical inspection. In fact it was a farce since the doctors did not receive any instructions on the subject. Jewish apostates too were forced to register and were included in the lists.

The Death of Engineer Hidokewitch

A Polish engineer named Hidokewitch, was murdered in the beginning of 1940 by partisans who suspected him of cooperating with the Germans in putting the ammunition factory into production again. Following this act, hundreds of Poles were arrested. The Germans were fully aware that Jews were not involved in this murder. Yet, they arrested a number of them. They were held a whole month in the central prison of Radom and were subjected to harsh treatment. Amongst them we count Dr. Leon Korta, Zwi Feigenbaum, Abraham Shmuel Eisenstadt, Beni Zuckerman and his Father, Josef Paflower and son, Meir and Moshe Brodbeker, Yaacov Guterman and others.

Since they did not succeed in finding the perpetrators, they released the Jews, but not before the community paid a decent sum as a special tax for their release.

Owing to transfer of population orders, which the Germans had enacted, Polish refugees of the Furmon region arrived in Wierzbnik. They found refuge in different places in town. In March a train-full of Jewish and Polish refugees arrived from Lodz. The Jewish community went all out to help them and saw to their needs as far as they could. Part of them traveled on to Warsaw, mostly those who had relations and friends there.

A short wile afterwards another train arrived with Jewish refugees from Plotzk, but now the community could not help much considering the previous influx and settling of refugees in town.

Refugees

The great number of refugees spelled out need and poverty, and it soon became necessary to put up a public kitchen, which provided them with regular meals. The community with the help of volunteers supported the kitchen. A great number of women were active, but special mention should be made of the few who excelled themselves in this task: Yehiel Schechman and his wife, Mrs. Avisa Milman-Herling, Mrs. Hochnitz, Yeshayahu Jona Sharfhertz, Haya Brank-Weisblum, Yeheskel Morgenstern and Moshe Feldman.

Most of the refugees belonged to intellectual circles and it was not easy for them to adapt themselves to the new conditions and to the fare of the public kitchen.

A special effort was made to provide additional nourishment to needy children. Every Friday bread was collected for them and at Shabbat they were guests at a communal meal with the family Steinbaum which was always accompanied with song.

Within this framework, my sister Gutzia Tentzer, organized a children performance "The Trial of the Good Mother". The following took part in this performance: Natasha Zirenska, Sara (Slusia) Scharfhertz, Rivka (Regi) Milman and her brother, Hanna Tentzer, Issy Siskind, Mietek Wiegensprech, Mondek Holtzman and Rachel Milman.

The children played their parts with great gusto and the event was no doubt a bright spot in their dark lives.

Quite a number of refugees were ill, stricken by an epidemic of typhoid, which spread amongst them. The community organized a hospital in one of the houses on Ilitzka Street, where conditions were not ideal due to overcrowding and other physical shortcomings.

The Ghetto

If my memory does not fail me, the ghetto was established, like in other parts of the "General Government" in mid-April 1940.

The district governor ordered the Jewish council to establish the ghetto and gave them 3 days time to arrange the evacuation of certain streets and to concentrate all the Jews within the quarter, which had been proclaimed as Jewish. The boundaries of the ghetto included as follows: the streets of Kilinskiego, Nieska, Wisoka, a small part of Rinach (ie. The pavement from the corner of Visoka until the corner of Nieska only, Krotka, Koliova, Jedushveskiego until the Jewish Cemetery, an alley leading from Koliova Street until the house of Miriam Drexler, Ilsetzka Street until the plywood factory of the Lichtenstein Brothers.

And yet there was something particular about the ghetto in Wierzbnik, which as we learned later was the only place where the ghetto was not completely closed up (where none could come or go). One was free to move to and from other quarters in town.

Credit for this exceptional feat is apparently due to the Community leaders who succeeded in influencing and convincing the Germans to demarcate the ghetto as described above.

This allowed the Poles to move freely in the ghetto, a fact that made life easier for us from the aspect of food supplies, as well as for communication with the outside world.

The refugees who had arrived earlier in Wierzbnik from Lodz and from Plotzk were ordered also to move into the ghetto. This meant overcrowding and with it a spreading of the typhoid epidemic.

Since the healing and the prevention measures called for the isolation of sick persons who were infected by this contagious disease, the overcrowding became still greater.

The Germans transferred part of the refugees from Plotzk to the neighbouring town of Bodzentin.

Mistreatment and Beatings

Life became almost unbearable as new decrees and orders followed one another. One of the decrees, which hit Jews most severely, was the restriction on trade. One had to procure a special license for each deal, and so high was the demanded payment that it was almost impossible to bear.

Many remained without making a living, with the setting up of the ghetto, and were forced to look elsewhere for their wellbeing.

Until May 1940, the Germans used the Jewish manpower for a variety of jobs: ie. Log cutting, cleaning of houses and offices, loading and unloading, street clearing, snow clearance, and etc. All this changed when one Saturday in May 1940, hundreds of men were taken from their homes to an iron ore mine at a distance of 12 kilometers from town. There they had to work hard labour. The Jews were not used to such hard physical tasks and this left them in a state of shock.

A few days afterwards saw the sudden appearance of S.S. troops belonging to the "Skull and Cross-Bones" Regiment. They entered the ghetto, broke open the doors of houses, meted out brutal beatings indiscriminately and forced everyone to the streets. From there they were driven in the direction of the metal factories, which were part of the Starachowice plant.

That same day I was in the office of the Jewish Council together with Moshe Feldman, Abraham Goldstein, the teacher Laps and twenty others. All of us had been called upon for secretarial work, when before we had time to settle down to work, the same S.S. men entered the building and started to beat everyone up with their rifle butts. We tried to flee to the other rooms in the building but none were available. They hit us mercilessly. I received a few blows to my head and ran home from there covered with blood. I had to stay for six weeks at home.

About the time of these bloody events, the Germans started to "employ" the Jews at the Starachowice factory. They were organized into working parties and worked in three shifts.

Until this period it was possible to avoid duties by paying ransom money, but now this became impossible and everyone, without exception, went out to work.

Food Rationing

With the entrance of the Germans in Wierzbnik they ordered the rationing of food, which was distributed in small quantities with food cards. When the factory was put into production again, the workers received supplementary rations of bread, marmalade, fish and a small quantity of sugar. The food rations were insufficient and the people turned to the black market that of course was very dangerous. Trading in the black market was punishable, even with the death penalty.

Hard Labour

In spite of the fact that the Jews worked in a factory, which had first priority, all the Jews were taken one summer afternoon and transported to the Lublin region to work in fortifications on the German-Russian border. Working conditions were beyond description, whilst their supervisors were brutal and whipped them.

Most of the men had families, who stayed behind without the minimal economic means of existence.

This happened on Thursday, Tisha Be' Av, with the women weeping in the streets bewailing their fate.

The council of Jews, after many efforts, succeeded in bringing about the release, after four weeks, of the married men. The bachelors were released after the fortifications were completed.

Hanging and Murders

During the summer of 1940 a German patrol was fired upon from a house at the end of the town, were upon all the inhabitants, Jews and Christians alike were arrested. The Germans soon came to the conclusion that the Jews were not guilty, and released them accordingly, whilst the Poles were held in prison. After a few days the Germans put up a scaffold in the middle of the Ring, and the whole non-Jewish population was forced to witness the execution of the arrested. Amongst the executed was an old woman of 67 years and babies.

Midst 1940, a well-known personality, Itzhak Rosenberg, was murdered by a Ukrainian policeman upon leaving his factory under the pretense that he had ignored this order to halt. This event caused great sorrow by all Jews in town, especially on the workers of the factory who had worked with him. He was a fervent Zionist and a staunch supporter of the national funds, to which he was the biggest donator.

The Collection of Furs

The beginning of 1941, the Jews were ordered to hand over all furs to the Germans. All had to bring in fur coats or any other article made of fur to the police station without receiving anything in return of course. Believing that the Jews had not handed in all furs, the Germans started house searches. A funny thing happened when a German policeman came to the house of Hershel Feigenbaum to look for concealed furs. Upon his question of "where is the fur?" everybody kept quiet except a little girl who thought he was asking about the cream of the milk, which in Yiddish has the same expression like fur, "Peltz". In all innocence she answered, "The cat has eaten it". The German chuckled and left the house without further ado.

Resistance Activities

In spite of the threats and depression exercised by the Germans in the ghetto, there were a few who had the courage to resist by all possible means, These activities were not without danger to their lives. Such was the group which members included (among others), Shmuel Cohen, Shlomo Lev, Buslig Melamed, Zvi Feigenbaum, Hershel Herblum, which somehow got hold of a radio set which they hid in one of the cellars. They used to gather regularly to listen to London radio, and afterwards spread the news "underground" from one to the other.

Every week they used to meet in the house of my wife's Grandfather, Josef Reuven Lichtenstein, a well versed and enlightened man, to discuss the political and military situation and to exchange ideas. They somehow got German newspapers and learned to read the truth between the lines, with the help of the radio in London.

What we feared happened when the Germans arrested Shlomele Ben Zelig Melamed and Itzhak Trupa, the son-in-law of Libish Binstock. Their friends were afraid under torture they would disclose all. But Shlomele assured Hershel Herblum, who was arrested by the Jewish police so as to get him in the prison to contact the arrested, that he would never give his friends away, even if it cost him his life.

From prison they were transferred to a concentration camp where Shlomo Lev died soon after his arrival. His wife received notification to that effect. Itzhak Trupa on the other hand, as told by his brother living now in Petah Tiqua, fell one day before the end of the war during a bombing raid.

The Witch Dance Around Work Permits

1942, was the worst and bitterest year fro the Polish Jewry. On Seder night, a relative of Simcha Mintzberg came to us, who had been in Lublin and had succeeded to escape from there during the expulsion of the Jews and had reached Wierzbnik. The girl by the name of Bianca told of the horrors, which had passed in Lublin, and of the expulsion of the whole Jewish population to an unknown direction. At the same time, news reached us of the concentration of all Jews from the surrounding villages of Warsaw, who were subject to expulsion as well. The Poles spread rumours that the Germans were transporting Jews in wagons to certain places in the Lublin region and returned with empty wagons from there. They also told us that German drivers replaced Polish engine drivers at a certain spot and that was as far as their knowledge went, but added that over the whole area hung a sickly smell of corpses.

It became also known that many of these Poles living in the area went down with jaundice.

Unfortunately, very few took these stories seriously and put them down, as pure fantasy since it did not dawn upon them that is was possible to destroy people, just like that, and without any reason.

The rumours persisted and became louder day-by-day, and fear overtook all for the future. The Germans were at the peak of their success at the front and the political situation worried the Jews still more. The Poles on the whole were hostile, and even those who were active against the Germans refused to take Jews into their ranks. When I addressed myself to an old acquaintance of mine, Jankowsky, on this subject, his answer was curt, "Impossible" without any explanation.

In the registry office I met a non-Jewish comrade with whom I had studied together at college in Konske, and he gave me, without any payment, identity papers with Aryan names for my two sisters, my wife Ida Birentzweig. The last two named in fact, hid themselves with the help of these identity papers with Polish families and thus saved themselves.

Beginning of the summer of 1942, the expulsions started in our vicinity: Ostrowice, Skarzysko, Radom, Kolzev and other places. Those who had succeeded to escape reached us and told of what was happening. With all these facts at hand, it became finally clear to the people that danger was approaching. At the same time it was rumoured that people who were engaged in essential work would be exempted from the expulsion order. This brought rise to a witch dance around the procurement of work permits, and all kinds of agents appeared overnight who led a brisk trade with these permits, which sold at exorbitant prices. The permits sold were fictitious and were especially wanted by elderly people. For them it represented a question of life or death and was therefore willing to pay these prices. There were those who acquired permits with their last savings, to be on the safe side, for a few priority factories like Starachowice, the electricity works "Zeorg" and the sawmill of Heler.

The town was full of refugees, and they too joined the market for work permits. This caused the prices to rise further still.

A month before the expulsion, a work camp was put up by the Germans in the Majowka district. The camp consisted of wooden huts and the non-local workers from Starachowice could live there. The Jewish workers willingly went to live there for two reasons. First of all they wanted to make sure that they had permanent employment in a high priority plant and secondly because it offered a certain security.

This plant was divided into two parts, upper and lower. Whilst the work camp in Majowka was intended for those working in the lower part, the other camp called Szczelnica served those working in the upper part.

In October 1942, Gestapo men and German gendarmes "visited" the houses of the "well off" and robbed and plundered all they could lay their hands on with a special eye on precious objects. Early one morning, I was still in bed, they came to our house too and without a word went straight to the cupboards and emptied them.

Seeing what was happening, the Jews tried to sell their belongings, at least what was left, to the local non-Jews. And that was not always easy; so many objects were passed to Polish neighbours for safekeeping.

As the days passed, the first signs appeared of the German's brutal intention of expulsion of the whole Jewish population from the town. Jews from other places like: Wychock, Szidlowiec, Suchedniow and other villages told of the dire fate of the Jews there when all men, women, and children were expulsed to an unknown place. Another fact which supported these forebodings, was the sudden demand of Germans, who had ordered shoes or suits with Jewish tradesmen, for their orders whether completed or not. This was most suspicious since no reasonable excuse was given.

These ominous signs brought dark shadows on every Jewish house. All the elderly feared and infirmed that they would be the first victims of the expulsion with all its consequences. The speculation begun with a logical reasoning that if and when the expulsion started, it would include all those who were within the ghetto whilst the workers who would be at work in the factories would not be affected. Tine was to prove their reasoning to be right. There were even those who tried to work two consecutive shifts at work, so as to spend as much time as possible in the factory and so to save themselves.

The Expulsion

The 27th of October 1942, this date will always be remembered with horror. Jewish police entered at dawn the courtyards of the houses in the ghetto and announced sorrowfully the German order that everyone without exception had to leave his home and concentrate in the Rynek. Everybody understood what it was all about and took with them small parcels of personal effects that had been kept at hand for some time now.

I was among the first who made their way with their families to the central square, Awaiting us were companies of S.S. troops, Germans gendarmes and for the first time we saw units of Lutishim (Latvians) who were the actual executors of the expulsion, They ordered us to line up five abreast. I stood facing Krotka Street.

The Separation of Families

After a short interval, the Latvians went through the lines and demanded that all money and precious objects be handed over to them. By force accompanied by insults they robbed what they could. An hour or so afterwards, they called on all who had work permits to step outside the lines and group up separately. This caused an immediate splitting up of families, since not all the members of one family had a permit. Heartrending were the scenes that took place.

People with work permits refused to part from their dear ones, relinquishing thereby voluntarily the opportunity to be exempt from the expulsion, but the Germans took them by force from their families into the other group.

Having completed the disposition of the groups, those with the work permits were ordered to march off in the direction of the Szczelnica camp at Starachowice under the guard of Ukrainians, who were called "Werkscutz". The distance from the Rynek until the camp was about 7 kilometers uphill, which we had to run with the guard at our heels beating, shooting into our ranks and murdering. Among the victims was the son-in-law of Shmuel Cohen, Josef. I remember this event very clearly because it happened right next to me and secondly because he was a close friend of mine.

Tired and exhausted we were pushed into a trench while Germans with machine guns at the ready towered over us at both sides, and again we were ordered to hand over money, precious objects and etc. At the same time they got a hold of Jacob Rubinstein to take him to the kitchen and asked him whether he had anything of worth in his possession. When he gave a negative answer, they searched him and found some money. The Germans wanted to execute him on the spot. Under the threat of death he begged for mercy and implored them for his life, with difficulty he did save himself. This incident was sufficient for all others to start to dig deep into their pockets and other hiding places and handed over all that was left to them.

Something unexpected happened when a young lad started to curse the Germans loudly. The commander, Althoff, murdered him on the spot. We were taken to the barracks in the camp, which was surrounded by a barbed wire fence and efficiently guarded.

The people who remained in Rynek were again divided into two groups, one group was taken for forced labour in the sawmill or in the electricity plant, whilst the rest were loaded into wagons and transported to Treblinka.

We learned later that 42 people, old and sick who could not or did not want to go to Rynek and remained in their homes, were murdered in cold blood. My wife's Grandfather, Reb Josef Reuven Lichtenstein and his wife Gitel were amongst them.

The Germans went through every house and murdered everyone indiscriminately they found; a young girl, the daughter of Pinchas Manela was among the victims.

[Page 35]
David Sali

In the Woods of Wierzbnik (With the Partisans)

After many wanderings, I arrived together with my younger brother in Mansera to work there. My sister reached this place some time before. I did all kinds of manual odd jobs there.

On the 24th of June 1944, the Gestapo arrived and encircled the Camp on three sides with the "Gmina" flowing on the other flank. Their purpose was to supervise the transfer to the bigger Camp in Starachowice, and from there to the railway sidings with the ultimate destination, Auschwitz.

The Germans came in the afternoon, whilst I was working with the second shift. When we heard of their arrival, their intentions were clear to us and it didn't take much time for us to decide on the spot, to try and flee to the woods.

The windows of one side of the factory, where we worked, looked over the river. We broke the windowpanes and jumped into the river. The noise of the break and excitement of a few groups of people aroused the Germans, who started firing at us with rifles and machineguns. We crossed the river at all possible speed and in this attempt many of us were hit by the German's bullets.

All this happened so quickly that I did not even have the time to say goodbye to my sister.

Having crossed the river, we ran to the woods and divided up into smaller groups and individuals as not to present an easy mark for our pursuers.

On our way we had to cross the busy urban road leading to Ostrowiec and Skavzysko. We passed this highway without any mishaps and finally arrived in the adjoining forest.

Everyone ran his own way and when I arrived in the forest I found myself alone. After half an hour or so I met two friends from our town, Meir Sternkrantz and Moshe Pinchevsky, who had also fled at the same opportunity. Meanwhile, the sun had set and a deep darkness cam over the forest. We were still wet from the river crossing and we suffered from the cold. Because of the darkness amidst strange surroundings, we stopped marching and "encamped" on the spot. The whole night we spent beneath the trees and talked about the happenings of the past and especially about what was awaiting us and how to go on. Needless to say, we didn't sleep a wink the whole night but we had made our first decision. We were to make our way further into the depth of the forest because we were too near its outer edge and all the dangers that ensued.

We continued another few miles and stopped at a densely wooded spot, which provided better cover against any unwanted peeping eyes.

At this time we were still under the deep impression and excitement of the recent events and didn't miss not having food. After two days of not tasting any food and taking into consideration the physical effort of our forced marching, hunger began to harry us more and more. We came to the conclusion that we had to provide ourselves with this important item, food, were we to continue this way. Whilst this was on our minds, we noticed through the trees the peasants carrying vegetables and milk products (cheese, butter, etc.) were on their way to town. We decided to approach them and ask for some food. To our pleasant surprise, they gave us some, although not from goodwill but from fear, taking us as Partisans.

These same peasants, returning from the market, told the Partisans who were quartered in their village of their meeting with Jewish Partisans who had so-called robbed them on the way. The Partisans, who had apparently taken upon themselves the "protection" of the peasants, were angered and began looking for us.

Having stilled our hunger, we were once more on the march deeper into the forest. On the way we met a small group of Jews, who had fled from our Camp and from other places. Altogether we numbered already 48 men.

Since our ranks grew, our self-confidence increased somewhat and we fixed our encampment in a certain spot in the forest. Without any tools or material at our disposal, we obviously were unable to put up tents or any other structures for that matter. We simply encamped on the spot as we were whilst patrols were sent out in different directions to discover any Partisans.

Within our enlarged group, discussions started as to our immediate goal but soon it became clear that we could not rely on ourselves since we were not self-sufficient. Our only possibility was to join on of the Partisan's units, which was not unfriendly to us. This will explain the reconnoitering parties and probing towards the end.

At night some men were sent to an adjoining village, Ratkowice, to get some food. I was chosen together with my friend Pinchevsky, to be the leaders of these expeditions to the village. One of these excursions I remember especially well. At dusk we both set out and carefully made our way to the house of the village chief who lived with a Jewish woman as his wife. Without the villagers knowing her real identity and with her help, we gathered the necessary food products. The village chief realized that we were Jewish but chose to ignore this because he himself was living with a Jewish woman.

One day, armed members of the A.K. encircled our group, and warned us not to go near the village anymore and not to demand food from the villagers. They threatened that they would kill us if we did not comply.

We asked them, "Where will we get our food supplies to stay alive? After all, we want to join the Partisans."

Their response was, "Do come and join us." Most of us declined this invitation, because we were wary of the A.K. people and questioned their real intentions and did not feel at ease with them. In spite of the majority's decisions, six men joined the A.K. and went with them.

Four days later we found their bodies, all six of them murdered in cold blood, not far from the village.

Shortly after this episode, another group of Polish Partisans, who were associated with the P.P.S party, wearing the party's initials on their armbands, stopped nearby.

We went out to meet them and expressed out wish to join their ranks. Their reaction was to order us to undress, it was futile to resist since they were armed and we had no weapons. Then they searched our clothes and took all the money they found. After the search and robbery they simply marched off, explaining that they were only a pioneer company and that the bulk of the unit with the commanders would shortly appear and that we should apply to them.

In fact, the next day the whole Partisans unit appeared. Again, we repeated our request before the commanders. They listened patiently and heard the story of the robbery that was perpetrated by their men the day before. They took full particulars from each of us what was stolen, promised to look into the matter and to return us the stolen money.

Yet, they rejected our pleas to join them and had the stupid and bad-hearted excuse of asking us, "Why didn't you flee the Germans a few years earlier?" Then off they went...

Amongst the commanders we recognized a few who were from our town. One of them I knew personally well since he was imprisoned before the war, as a Communist together with my cousin. I used this "kinship" to urge him to use his influence at least to see to it that the stolen money be returned to us.

Our money was returned to us in full a few days later. Looking back, I cannot help but draw the conclusion that in spite of their correctness about the return of the stolen money, their refusal to admit us to their ranks stemmed out of deep-rooted "principles" by being Anti-Semites, they did not want any Jews amongst them.

Shortly afterwards we met another big Partisan unit and once more we tried our luck. After some negotiations, one of the officers-in-charge announced that in principle they agreed to accept us, on condition that we proved ourselves in deed as well as in words. "Procure yourselves arms and we will accept you as a group within our ranks."

He advised us how and where to put our hands on German weapons, upon which we decided to take up the challenge for lack of another choice.

The unit was stationed in the forest some distance away from us. After they had left us, we drew up plans and decided upon a course of action as told hereafter.

The Acquisition of Arms

According to the information we had, the Germans used to come down to a village once a week in order to collect tax, which they gathered in food, meat, chickens, etc. Usually five men arrived with a cart, and our plan was to overcome the German who was left in charge of the cart, steal his rifle and then to deal with the rest.

At noon, the following day, five men Pinchevsky, Mats the cobbler, may his blood be revenged, another two men whose names I don't remember and myself marched down to the village. Nearing the place we watched and waited the German's arrival. From afar we saw four soldiers going to the first farmhouse, it was them that we ran unseen to the remaining guard and tackled him from behind. He was taken completely by surprise, which left him aghast, and he didn't utter one word. Two of us remained to guard him, whilst the rest ran up to the house.

Newly armed with the German's rifle, one of us took up position near the window and the other two entered the house. The one outside the window ordered the Germans to put up their hands, which they did without resistance and our men collected their weapons.

With our precious charge, a revolver and four rifles, we made off at all speed to the forest. We returned to our group, whose joy knew no bounds, and we were feted like heroes.

After the excitement had subsided we decided to send a delegated and present our newly acquired arms to the headquarters of the Partisans.

They were impressed by our achievement and the commander announced his decision on the spot that he was ready to receive our group within their ranks. On hearing those words, we hurried off to the rest of our group to announce to them the good tidings. Next morning, we moved to a new encampment nest to the Partisans.

Our group consisted, at the time, of 37 men and 3 girls, one of them I remember was Tamara Weisblum, and may her blood be revenged.

The swearing-in ceremony was held at a general parade and the commander stressed in his welcoming address the ultimate command not to leave any arms on the battlefield. "Rather return without your head than without your weapon..."

All of us were equipped with arms; some of us got rifles whilst the rest received sub-machine guns of Russian make.

The man who negotiated with us and was responsible for our initiation into the Partisans was no other than Mitchlev Motzar, who today is the deputy Prime Minister of Poland.

We were all integrated within the different platoons of the unit. I was posted as runner at headquarters. From then on we were part and parcel of the Partisans, and we took part in all their activities and operations.

The First Encounter

In an adjoining village to the forest was an informer, who used to keep us posted on the German's movements. One day we were warned that the Germans intended to make a comb-out of the forest. Usually they avoided the forest and when they did venture into the forest they used Mongolian P.O.W. for that purpose.

I was sent together with my friend Pinchevsky to try to substantiate this information. It was in the early evening when we arrived at the outskirts of the forest and a deafening noise of chains reached our ears. We advanced about 100 meters when suddenly we heard the Germans command "HALT".

Darkness had set in already; we stopped in our steps and looked around to find out where the voice came from. About 200 meters in front of us there was the silhouette of a tent where the guard was. Instinctively, we threw two hand grenades in that direction to cover our withdrawal. We certainly needed no further confirmation, since the facts spoke for themselves.

The explosion of the grenades invited a volley of fire from the village. The bullets shrieked around us and found their mark in the trees. We reported back to headquarters, where preparations were being made for the forthcoming encounter.

The fighting tactics in a forest are different altogether. Trenches are not dug and only the big trees provide the ample camouflage and cover against bullets. We prepared to meet the German onslaught.

The night passed relatively quiet, although from afar we could hear the German's movements. We had posted lookouts near the outskirts of the forest. Next day hoards of Mongolians under German command reached the outer ring of the forest, marching upright and shouting battle cries.

The Partisans outmaneuvered the Germans, attacked them from the rear and broke through their lines. Battling their way through, they succeeded in getting to another part of the forest where the Germans encamped. We suffered casualties, dead and wounded.

Two days before this battle, one of our friends was injured. We got medical help to him, who could do little to help him but dress his wounds. He could not be moved. With the enemy approaching we decided to hide him in the forest. I was told to stay close to him, thereupon I climbed a high tree and settled under its crest and remained in observation there the whole time. I had a few hand grenades and a rifle, and had made up my mind that if worst came to worst, I would throw the grenades at the Germans and put an end to my life. Fortunately, the Mongolians passed by me without discovering my presence, although they did find our wounded friend and loaded him on a cart. I was unable to come to his help since the overwhelming enemy numbers. Shortly afterwards we found his body and buried him. He had been shot through the head.

After the Germans had gone, I climbed down the tree and started looking for the unit. On the way I met other members who had dispersed during the fighting, together we walked until we finally found the new encampment.

The Germans continued these comb-outs on and off every few weeks.

Besides these defensive actions, there were planned operations by our unit. Our unit was a mixed crowd, there were Poles, Jews and escaped Russian P.O.W. from German prison camps who had joined us. Amongst them were many minorities: Tartars, Gruzinim, Azbedjanim and white Russians. We had radio contact with the Partisan command in Kiev.

From time to time planes appeared overhead, usually at night, and parachuted arms and men. The parachutists constituted a unit of their own and they operated apart, without anyone sharing their secrets. I approached this unit once and got friendly with them; imagine my surprise to hear some of them talking Yiddish. It appeared that there were some Jews amongst them, a fact that strengthened our morale.

One day a unit was detailed to blow up an ammunition train on its way to the front.

For this operation the unit was made up of Poles, Russians and one Jew, Israel Rosenberg. The action was a success, all of them returned without any casualties, but the Jew was missing. We learned later that he was murdered by the Poles, his "brother-inarms" who had participated in the operation with him.

The whole story came to light when his body was found in the forest, some time after the action. The Poles had reported that he had been killed in action, but we had serious doubts about the truth of this statement. We knew them [Poles] as they were, rabid Anti-Semites, and decided to bring the matter to the attention of the commander, Motzar, who ordered an immediate inquiry.

Two of the Poles were found guilty of the murder and were sentenced to death and executed the 7th of November, Revolution Day. Together with them, a number of spies and provocateurs that had been planted by the Germans within our ranks, went to the firing squad.

The blowing up of trains and railways were frequent actions that Jews participated actively.

Provision of Food

At some distance there was a big farm estate that belonged to a Polish landowner and which the Germans had confiscated. The Partisans used to "pay them a visit" from time to time to get food supplies for the whole unit. Since the Germans guarded the place, these excursions always entailed bitter fighting.

A Story About a Cow

During the German comb-out we were obliged to leave our encampment and leave behind our food provisions in wooden cases, which we couldn't take with us. The Germans carted them away. When I returned to the place I saw a cow attached to a tree. I reported this to my unit commander who detailed a few men to go with me to guide them to the place, and to examine whether it was a trap or not.

There were six Tartars who did not want to go out of laziness and fright. On the way they told me, "If there won't be a cow, then you too won't be..."

I began to fear that the cow wouldn't be there anymore, perhaps someone had forestalled us because we were a few miles marching distance away. When we finally got there, tents had been put up and we saw two Mongolians in German uniforms with rifles, but there was no sign of the cow.

We lay down on the ground, "my" Tartars pointed their arms in the direction of the Mongolians and ordered me to go in towards them whilst they covered me. I had no alternative, the odds were one against six, and so I started out.

Meanwhile, the Mongolians had observed me and gave sign that they had no intention of fighting. When I got to them they told me that they were deserters who had deserted the Germans during the comb-out and wanted to join the Partisans. We took them with us to our headquarters. But "my" Tartars kept on bothering me and asking, "Where is the cow?"

I was confused and didn't know what to answer, when to my great surprise help came from an unexpected quarter. Hearing the question about the cow, the two Mongolians confirmed that they too had seen the cow and that a farmer from the village had taken her away half an hour earlier.

On our return journey to the unit, the Tartars led us a different route. When we arrived on the open space where arms and ammunition were usually parachuted, they told me to go in front. I noticed they had lowered their rifles from their shoulder straps, which aroused an immediate suspicion within me. I had a feeling they intended to kill me. It was then that I took advantage of the fact that there were many water shoals on the way and started to jump as if to avoid the water. I was running in my underpants and suddenly started to flee as fast as I could, assuming that I would be out of range already before they could point their rifles.

I didn't have to wait long before the first shots rang out; my forebodings had come true. I ran on into the deepness of the forest and had escaped from my fate at their hands. The distance to the unit being still considerable, I decided to spend the night in hiding. Next day, I made it to the vicinity of the unit, where I met a Jewish friend of mind who was on his way to fetch water. I told him of my adventure and asked him to bring me food and clothes and also to report the whole story to the commander. He sent for me, and it became evident that the Tartars had forestalled me with their version and had reported that the story about the cow was pure invention on my part and that I had fled.

The commander heard me out and upon my accusation ordered an inquiry.

Once more the two Mongolians saved the day for me, as they had done so earlier. The Tartars got their due punishment of continuous guard duty for a whole week.

The Day of Liberation

We were now in winter 1944, the Germans were in full withdrawal from the main front and our region filled with large German troop units that had retreated. The time had passed when small units could be of any use and the front line was rapidly coming nearer. In these circumstances, we were told to cross the lines and go over to the Russians. The front was about 60 miles away, near Sandomir. We marched the whole night through and before dawn we had neared the lines. In every village on the way we picked up a local guide who led us through the German concentrations. We heard the explosions of shells and small arms fire.

We marched in Indian file, Pinchevsky and I went up the rear. It was our duty to cut the German communication wires.

The whole area was covered in a deep layer of snow and had apparently one line, when suddenly we found ourselves before barbed wire guarding the trenches.

The order was given to storm the trenches and we opened fire. The Germans replied in kind and we continued fighting until we had crossed their lines. We were now in no-man's land.

The Germans opened up mortar fire. We suffered many casualties whilst crossing the lines and now from this infernal fire.

We were left without officers or guides, nor did we have a compass so we didn't know in which direction to run. Firing continued with rockets falling on all sides. We were afraid that the Russians, perhaps in the immediate vicinity, would suddenly open up fire against us not knowing our identity. Therefore we kept on shouting the whole time in Russian, "We are Partisans" in the hope that our voices be heard and to avoid the danger of being caught in crossfire.

It appears that we had crossed the first Russian lines without having been observed, nor had we observed them for that matter. In the meantime, dawn began to appear and we found ourselves again in an empty space, uninhabited so to speak. Once more we were in a quandary which way to turn. All was quiet, no longer did we hear any shooting and we continued marching towards a forest without knowing what fate had in store for us there. We were tired, exhausted and in despair.

We had already reached the forest when we noticed a sign posted to a tree in Russian, "Injured to the Hospital" and underneath was an arrow pointing the way. Needless to say, we took that turn and came upon a concentration of gun emplacements and tanks that abounded there.

Here, for the first time we met Russian soldiers and our meeting was overwhelming. We conversed together and they took us to their headquarters. We recuperated there for some time from all our troubles and looked over our ranks. We had suffered heavy casualties. From 320 men who started out to the front, only 68 survived. The rest was killed with five Jews amongst them.

Here ends the accounts of the Partisan activities by the Jews of the Wierzbnik region.

Two soldiers, [192-?]. Abe Zukerman collection, Ontario Jewish Archives, Blankenstein Family Heritage Centre, accession 2017-9-1. Not in the Original Yizkor Book.

[Page 43]
Reva Naiman Karstadt

For the Next Generations

As the daughter of Yosel and Chana Naiman, perhaps I, more so than others was brought up on "Wierzbnik". It was a long time before I realized that Wierzbnik was a small town in far off Poland. For Wierzbnik in those dark dismal days of the depression and the ghastly programs there, was a living, vibrant, all-encompassing part of our household. Meetings, meetings, it seemed as if life revolved around meetings to aid our "landsleit", and there was no distinction between the responsibility shared by us children, who were products of Canada and our parents, who were products of Wierzbnik. We were a viable part of Wierzbnik too, as indeed Wierzbnik was of us and our past and our future were bound up in it.

As soon as we children were old enough, we addressed envelopes, cut ribbons and made decorations for the annual banquet; mailed parcels and a host of other jobs for we too were involved with Wierzbnik.

But our emotional involvement went far deeper than the physical acts allotted to us. Not only did our beloved parents relate stories of the life in Wierzbnik, but the constant stream of visitors to our home while my Father was organizing the Society here in Toronto and long after it was established. Besides the friends, relatives and "landsleit" sparked our imaginations with their recollections of the people, their homes, and most of all those wonderful, sad, marvelous, tear-jerking "maises". Many times my sisters and I would listen behind the closed living-room door to the adventures and reminiscences of "our" Wierzbnikers. So, Wierzbnik and its assortment of characters lived in our home and it seemed almost as if we were an island in a foreign land, where Wierzbnik still thrived. My sisters and I were very proud to be accepted and included.

This book is filled with facts and recollections written by those who were there. Perhaps, it will serve some useful purpose to know that as a first generation Canadian-born Wierzbniker, I feel this book is a very necessary part of the heritage we can pass on to our future generations. For how else can our descendants know what it was like when their beginnings started in a remote part of our world that was obliterated from the face of the earth in the 1940's. Where else can they learn about our ancestors, the leadership they assumed and the avenues that leadership took in their tiny "shtettle".

What other source can convey the warmth and comradeship all Wierzbnikers jealously guarded against a hostile world that smote them time and time again? How will they know, except from sterile history books what it was like to be a Jew in the midst of Poland, not just any fellow Jew, but their very own ancestors. What source other than this book, can bring alive in perpetuity those precious accounts and experiences that in the end shaped our destiny and molded our character? These are things that are lost from generation to generation.

How can my children be expected to understand, when it is difficult even for me, to hear that it was necessary to hide "Yomtovdicke" clothes under everyday garments in order to go to Shul unmolested? When here in North America, whole portions of cities literally stop on High Holy Days.

Although each of us knows that we all lost members of our families in the Holocaust, it seems so remote to us born here in North America. They are tragic, heroic figures of another time, remembered at Yahrzeit, except for their immediate family survivors, who never forget. The old, the young, the poor, the sick, the women, the children...yes, those innocent little children who never had a chance to give of themselves to this world and who never shared the joys that abound in life. Only through a book like this Wierzbnik Memorial Book will we, the next generations remember and have some record of a special place called Wierzbnik. I recall how zealously my Father worked for, and how dedicated he was to the erection of a Yahrzeit Memorial Monument to the memory of those beloved Wierzbnikers who perished in the war. So, it would be recorded for all of time that these families existed and should not be forgotten. I recall how passionately his desire to see this dream a reality was and how very much it means to all Wierzbnikers now that it is completed. But a stone memorial isn't enough. This biography will make those names impersonally carved in granite, living, breathing, and responsible human beings worthy indeed of our memory.

My personal involvement goes so very deep. My paternal Grandparents Hershel and Rifka Najman and their family, except for one son, were all here in Canada. But my Mother was the only child of Mordechai-Mendel and D'Vorah Raizel Zylberstein fortunate enough to have been here in Canada at the time of the war. My Mother kept alive her family for us, her many dear brothers and sisters and all those precious memories by recounting tales of them. She keep telling us over and over again who they were and what they were and what they did. I see this Memorial Book as accomplishing the same feat of bringing alive through memories set down on paper, all our families and "landsleit" for all the generations to come.

[Page 45]
Wendy Tucker, Staff Reporter
German Trial Stirs Memory of Horror Camp

Gusta Blass was 16 when she stood beside what could have been her grave.

The Germans had come into Poland and Jews were being placed in a series of work camps. She and her parents and younger brother had escaped from the large textile city of Lodz to her Mother's hometown of Starachowice.

The day came when they were forced into a work camp with about 300 others where the Germans put them to work making such things as ammunition boxes and stretchers.

Even then, she recalls, "Their main purpose was to eliminate as many of us as they possibly could. There was little food and no medicine. Many died."

Then the time came when Jews from small camps such as that one were gathered together at a large camp called Majowka to be shipped off to concentration camps.

It was at that camp that Gusta Blass, her family, the man she would marry and the others almost went to a mass grave. Her actions would be praised for having saved them on a night of horror in late 1944.

The man who planned their execution that night, Erich Kurt Willi Schroth, the leader or "fuhrer", of the Ukrainischen Wachmannschaften who was in charge of that camp, is on trial this month for war crimes in Dusseldorf, Germany.

Gusta Blass, now Mrs. Leon Weintraub of Charleston, was unable to go to Germany to testify. But she has given sworn testimony before a German judge and an attorney in Philadelphia.

She and her husband both survived a series of concentration camps that included Auschwitz, Buchenwald, Belsen and Dachau to be reunited after the war and marry.

They came to Charleston in late 1946 and have made their home here. In addition to raising six children, Mrs. Weintraub has made a career as a dress designer, and has a dress designing and dressmaking shop here.

She tells of what happened on that night in 1944 out of the belief that, "these things should not be forgotten."

"I would like to forget, but I know I shouldn't. My concern is that such things should be a lesson to people. My hope is that if people do remember these things they will not let them happen again. History should not be allowed to repeat itself."

Gusta Blass, Mrs. Weintraub, recalls Schroth as a man who "was known to be very brutal, almost bloodthirsty."

As she, her family and the others from the smaller camp were gathered in a large fenced field area, "two tremendous graves were dug" and each were about 100 feet long and six feet wide.

"They lined us up on each side, with the women standing three in a row on one side and the men on the other."

She recalls, Schroth "stood at the end of the grave, facing us. He said, "These are the last moments of your life. I give you my permission to say your prayers" and he said, "You will be shot."

She was standing in the second row of women beside the long grave. "I cannot describe what a person can feel when you hear words like this. I was standing with my Mother. My Father and brother were standing on the other side," she said.

But standing there at that moment, "deep in me I felt that there might be a spark of hope. I felt that I must do something in this moment. So, I stepped out from the line and I went to him. I started pleading with him to spare us, to send us on to Auschwitz where we would not have much chance anyway. I pleaded with him to spare us then."

She recalls, "Evidently he thought I was attacking him. He grabbed his rifle and with the back of it, hit me in the back of the head and knocked me down. I fell, but I got up.

"At that moment I knew I had to do something more than just plead. I ran and grabbed his arms from behind and held on, trying to reason with him."

Instead, the German officer yelled that, "he would kill us all." While at that moment "everything seemed to be lost," she recalls determining "that at least I would not die, slaughtered like a lamb."

"I couldn't really do anything to him. I had no weapon or anything," she said. But the German guards were astonished, not knowing exactly what had happened, and she and the officer were so close they dared not shoot.

Then, "we both fell."

One of the guards pulled the officer away and cries went up to kill her immediately.

But he decided not to kill her, and that she should suffer first. He used a phrase in German, which she understood, that meant he wanted the grim pleasure of seeing her fight for life.

"At that point I decided no matter what he did, how much they tortured me, I would not give them the satisfaction of seeing me cry or plead," she explained.

She lay still on the ground, not moving. The guards began "kicking me, knocking and pushing me" until she heard a woman's voice pleading them to stop, saying she must have fainted.

At that point the German officer said that if that were the case, "she won't be alive any longer." He stood over her and fired. The bullet grazed her forehead but, "there was blood all over my face, and when they looked they thought I was dead."

She remembers that, "I was thinking very clearly at that moment, more clearly than ever in my life. I was thinking of all people, especially my family and I was still hoping that nothing would happen to them."

Feigning death, she heard sounds then of the people being marched away. Later she would learn that because it was then dark and late, the German officer who was acting on his own rather than from any orders in deciding to kill them chose to let them live for the moment.

She was left on the ground with a single guard to watch her, and then came more terrifying moments.

He searched her first for money or valuables; he then grabbed her arm and then her leg, trying to break them, "to make sure I was not alive. It was so painful; I felt like every bone was broken. But I didn't utter a sound. I knew if I did it would be the end of me."

Before leaving, the guard made a final check, picking up her hand to feel for a pulse. "Still he had no indication I was alive."

After he left, she was able to make her way to nearby barracks, crawling between passes of a searchlight, and hid beneath one throughout the night.

In the early morning the Germans discovered her absence. She had already discovered her people were in the barracks building above her, and they tried to hide her.

But Schroth arrived screaming in German, "Where is the beast?" When he threatened to kill everyone, she emerged and approached him. "I felt nothing at all. All I was concerned about was that they not kill my people. He grabbed me by the arm and pulled me outside to a small enclosed storage area."

She was not killed. Instead, because the German in charge of the city had learned about her and, she learned later, because her fiancé had given a diamond in hope of saving her, she was saved, for Auschwitz.

She learned that her fiancé had been told, "I don't have to kill her; you are all going to be sent to Auschwitz anyhow."

The next day, she and the others were packed aboard freight cars to be shipped away. But after hours, were released.

"Unfortunately, we were finally put on the train and sent to Auschwitz where many of us met immediate death."

"A very small minority of us survived and are still able to tell of the horror of that night, able to testify about what happened."

"Years pass, but these things should not be forgotten. People should be treated as people, not as animals."

"I remember. I know. Other should know how to prevent anything like this from happening again in the future of humanity."

[Page 48]
Yaakov Katz

The Sixteenth Day of Cheshvan
The Liquidation of our Town

It was a dark and gloomy day in our town of Wierzbnik-Strachowitz, when in the morning at approximately eight o'clock; we heard the yelling and shouting of the S.S. beasts. "Get out! Get out!" they screamed unceasingly.

With terrible fear and trepidation, each and everyone left his house for the Square, where the Nazi preying wolves ordered us to stand in numerous Jewish homes. They were murderous shots aimed at people who were not fast enough to leave their houses.

We lingered at the Square until the afternoon, when suddenly, we heard bloodcurdling shouts, "Line up!" Soon after we were forced to march forward on the way to perdition. With tears in our eyes and bleeding hearts we marched in the direction of the railroad station. Suddenly, I was removed from the line of people and ordered to stay in town. My task was to serve in the clean-up force ("Raum-Kommande").

As soon as I realized what my fate held for me, the last parting from my family and my dear friends, I posed to myself this question, "By what merit have I, Leibush Herblum, been chosen to serve in such a holy task, to engage in the burial of our martyrs? Will this be my last privilege?"

I cast a last glance at the martyrs and my dearest, wife and children, my friends and acquaintances...my whole world was to disappear. Bloody tears streamed from my eyes and moistened the death-darkened road. Oh Lord of the Universe, avenge the bloodshed of the holy ones, of the pure and the righteous!

The clean-up force, which consisted of twenty people, including myself was commanded to march toward the Jewish graveyard of the town. There we beheld unspeakable horrors. Every few minutes a new transport of slaughtered Jews arrived, the cherished ones who had died a martyr's death. We counted 48 bodies, 26 men and 22 women, whose bodies were scattered in the area. We were commanded to bury our murdered brethren.

We dug two graves, a separate one for the men and one for the women. While at work one of the young men of the clean-up unit, Eliyahu Sharif of the town of Bazechin, broke his leg. A Nazi shot him on the spot. The bullet pierced his mouth, and while he was fully conscious, we were ordered to bury him alive. It is difficult to describe my feelings at that moment. It seemed to me that the ground we stood upon would give way; the earth would open its mouth and swallow the universe. At the very last minute, somehow the order was changed to place him in our bunk. Even then, his luck was shortlived; the next morning he was killed.

With great awe, and with the sense of performing a holy task, I buried the martyred women. Amongst the murdered were: Dvorele Morgenstern, Miriam Kaufman, Freindel, and wife of Fischel Menashe. Amongst the 26 murdered men were: Yosef Reuven Lichtenstein, Moshe Pinchas Lichtenstein, Henich Kaufman, the son of Yisroel Yizchak, Fischel Drexler, Moshele Kamf, Moshe Krazman, Shlomo Melamed. Three martyrs had prayer shawls (talesim) to cover their bodies. I did all I could and more than it had seemed possible to bury them honorably, with due respect to their holy and cherished memory.

Before our own eyes perished the elite of our town. Our hearts became afflicted, and we were engulfed in darkness. It is fitting to quote in honor of these martyrs the following opinion of our sages:

"One who stands near the dying at the time when he breathes his last, he is in duty bound to rend [his clothes]. To what is it like? To a scroll of the Law that is burnt." (Sabbath 105; Moed Katan 25ff, and Rambam, The Laws of Mourners, chapter 9.

One has to rend twice, once for the sake of the parchment (which implies the body), and the second time for the sake of the script (which implies the soul). Rashi, the illustrious commentator, elucidated thus, "For the commandment is a lamp, and the teaching is light." (Proverbs 6, 23). The soul is called light, for it is written, "The spirit of man is the lamp of the Lord." (ibid. 20, 27).

Further, in the tractate of Sabbath (105b), it is said:

If a sage dies, all are his kinsmen. All are his kinsmen? Can you think so? Rather say, all are his kinsmen, all must rend [their garments] for him; all must bare [their shoulders] for him...for whoever weeps for a worthy man is forgiven all his iniquities... [And] if one sheds tears for a worthy man, the Holy One, blessed be He, counts them up in his treasure house, for it is said, "Thou count my grievances; put thou my tears into thy bottle, are they not in your book." (Ps. 56, 9).

Thus we bewail our martyrs and lament their passing twofold. Once because they were the embodiment, while they were alive, of the best in human qualities and secondly, because we were deprived of their good deeds and the further contribution that they could have made, if they were allowed to live their full natural span of life.

* * *

When I returned from the cemetery, I was met by two S.S. men, and they ordered me to follow them. I obeyed and walked after them to the local police courtyard. There I found two bodies that were shot by the wild beasts. These were the brothers Aharon and Noah Silverberg, the sons of Abraham Silverberg. Outside the courtyard, I found the body of a murdered child whose name was Mordechai David Cornwasser. I somehow dug up a cart, placed in it the martyred bodies, and gave them a Jewish burial. On Friday morning, the third day of the Nazi atrocities, I was led by an S.S. murderer on the road to Boagi and was ordered to bury two young children. These were the children of Reise, daughter of Shmuel Isers.

With a bleeding heart and eyes full of tears, that still remained, I gave these children a Jewish burial. Again, after I returned to the bunk, I was awaited by a murderer who ordered me to bury yet another martyred girl whose body was lying in a room next to the bunk. And again, I was called to drag out a murdered victim from under the bed to give him a Jewish burial. This was the body of Moshele, the son of Naftoli.

It is not in my power to describe and to enumerate all the horrors and the murderous deeds of the Nazi beasts. Too numerous were the victims I was ordered to bury within the frame of the clean-up group to which I was a part of. May their memory be blessed and may the Lord revenge their blood.

These are the facts conveyed to me by one of the eminent citizens of our town, a man of splendid deeds and accomplishments. In the words of the Sages: A fully rounded man Mr. Leibush Herblum. He endangered his life every second of the day in order to fulfill his holy task and to carry out the burial of our martyrs in accordance with the Jewish laws, He thus performed acts of true kindness and to this day he fully lives up to the dictum of "love thy neighbour as thyself." Mr. Herblum is especially dedicated to the welfare of the descendants of our town ("the poor of your town come first') and is responsive to their needs. Whoever knows him extols his praises. It is therefore our honorable duty to inscribe him in this Memorial Volume and may his light shine as the glow of the firmament forever.

[Page 51]
Necha Baranek

It Was a Great Shock

I was born July 7th, 1940 in Wierzbnik, Poland. My parents were Ben Zion and Sala Baranek.

In 1942, just before Hitler liquidated all Jews from Wierzbnik, my parents gave me away to a Polish couple in Warsaw and I took on the identity of Zosha Murofska. I was two years old and spoke perfect Polish.

Two days after my parents gave me away, they were taken to a labour camp in Wierzbnik called Tartak. From Tartak, my parents communicated with the Pole who kept their child. He was to keep them informed about her health and they in turn would pay him at regular intervals, as agreed upon. After a few months, my parents were transferred from Tartak to Myufka and they had no choice but to ask somebody in Tartak to communicate with the Pole on their behalf. My parents gave this person all the information and money to pay for me. When the Pole came, this person paid him and at that time asked him to take the son of Mortry Maslowicz, a little boy who was hidden in the Tartak Camp with him. The Pole agreed and took the little boy to his home.

This, I believe, was a very important step in my life, an actual turning point. The only recollection of this part of my childhood was a little boy walking back and forth, back and forth and I sitting crossed-legged like an Indian for days on end. The Pole was arrested by the Germans and his wife, was in fear of her life, especially since she was hiding a Jewish boy, had no alternative and found us a new home, beside Warsaw.

The Nuns were very good to us and tried to keep us alive with what little they had. I can remember the hours spent on my knees in prayer, the Virgin Mary was taught to be our one and only Mother. I do not know the date, but I remember when again, I had to leave my home. The Germans made the Nuns evacuate their home and we all had to get out within hours. The healthy had to walk the long journey to Zakopany. Babies and the sick rode in buggies. It was winter and those who had no shoes had to walk barefoot in the snow. When we arrived in Zakopany it was Christmas and I will always remember the warmth and light of that very beautiful Christmas tree. My new home consisted of tables for beds, bread and milky soup once a day and devoted prayer.

When the war ended, a Jewish lady took us away from Zakopany. There were five of us: three girls and two boys. It was a rainy night and I can remember being carried out to the horse and buggy that would take us to a new home. From the horse and buggy we went into trucks that had been waiting for us, and it was here that I got my first taste of sugar in cubes. I recall being very sick for quite a long time and then, we arrived at our new home a Jewish orphanage in Bellevue, in the outskirts of Paris, France.

My Father died in Motthausen. My Mother survived and in 1944 she began her long journey in search of her child.

My Mother's search began in Warsaw. It was a great shock to her when she learned from the Polish lady that her child was no longer there, and in fact had no knowledge of my whereabouts. From here, Mother went to the Missing Children's Bureau in Warsaw. Her daughter, Zosha Murofska was listed as one of many children brought to the Convent outside of Warsaw. From here they traced her to Zakopany and then to a committee who had taken out five Jewish children. My Mother's next step was to go to this committee, who informed her that two days before, all the Jewish children were taken to an Orphanage in France. It had taken my Mother one full year to accumulate all this information. She wrote to Miss Keller, who was in charge of the Orphanage and gave her all the information about me. It was another full year before my Mother was able to get all the papers she needed to go to France, and in 1948 she left Poland. She took me out of the Orphanage just a week before all the children were taken to Israel. It was another four months before my Mother could get all the necessary papers to come to Canada. We arrived in Toronto to begin our new life in March of 1949.

[Page 52]
Sam Stein

My Heart Began to Pound Loudly

Sam Stein (in Wierzbnik, Sam Bumstein). My Father was Avrum Pavlavor and my Mother, Chana.

In 1929, my sister Brucha brought me to Toronto, Canada from Wierzbnik. During the Second World War, I served with the Canadian Forces Army, and in 1945, at the tail end of the war, I was shipped to the European Theatre. First, however, I went to England for training and then the camp was all cleared out and we were shipped to the Continent. After much going back and forth, I was sent to Germany, one of 30 Canadian soldiers of the First Canadian Railway Company as reinforcements. I was stationed at Ebenburen, Germany. I spent all my spare time trying to track down the "camps" but to no avail.

While I had been training in the United Kingdom, I had written a letter to my brother in Paris, France as France was now liberated but there had been no reply. While I was in Germany, a letter was forwarded to me from Paris from my nephew. I had to find a French Canadian soldier to interpret the French writing, and he found it quite difficult to understand. The drift of the letter was that my brother had disappeared, leaving no trace, but he, a brother, and their Mother had survived. He had been so long in answering because they had only just returned to liberated Paris, and as my letter was in Yiddish so, he too had difficulty finding a translator.

I was so anxious to see them, and I began to cause a lot of excitement around the army camp. I approached the Commanding Officer for permission to leave and go to France to see my surviving family. Permission was granted and I had an extraordinary first meeting with my sister-in-law, her oldest son who had written to me, and another son who had gotten compassionate leave from the French Forces to meet me.

When my leave was over, I was transferred to the Army of the Occupation and shifted to Baad Tsvishen, near Oldenburg in Germany. I continued again to search for the 'camps" and inquired of everyone and every place I could. Finally, I discovered that there was a "camp" in existence not far from Hannover, which was Belsen. I found out how to get to Belsen and upon my arrival there asked how to get to the camps. No one appeared to know anything about a "camp".

A group of British soldiers were leaning on a building and as a last hope; I approached them and asked for the Belsen camp. But they too said they knew nothing. I argued with them for over an hour, and finally one soldier asked if perhaps I meant the "honey" camp and if so to follow a group of 5 men passing by as they were from the "honey" camp.

I followed the men from across the street and as I listened, I heard Yiddish being spoken. I crossed the street and greeted them with "Shalom". They immediately looked at me with typical inquisitiveness of the Jewish nature and proceeded to ask me where I was going and who I was going to see. My first question to them produced the answers to "Who are you? Where are you from?" They were Ostrowicers, a place not far from Wierzbnik. I then asked them with much courage if there were any Wierzbnikers in the camp and they replied, "The camp is full of them." My heart began to pound loudly, for there was now hope of finding my family. From then on my feet seemed to be made of clay and that last stretch of walking to the camp was an eternity.

Inside the camp we seemed to walk forever, until we came to the Jewish section. We walked along the street and then one of the men pointed out Landsleit of mine: Herschel Feigenbaum and his 18-year-old daughter (Herschel, son-in-law of Yitche Meyer Schoichet). He came over and we introduced ourselves, and I asked about my family. He told me he had been in Chevra Kadisha when my Father died in 1942, and had buried him. From the description given it must have been due to starvation. When I asked what had become of my Mother and my younger sister Pesel and her family; his [Feigenbaum's] daughter replied, "Treblinka." Upon hearing that one word, I felt the earth should open beneath me and swallow me up. I completely lost my composure. It didn't take long to regain it and now that I knew my family had been wiped out, I asked about other Wierzbnikers.

He began sounding off names which tumbled over me in my sense of loss and then I heard familiar names, Chaim Kleinberg, Boruch Zuckerman, Shier Schnieders and these and other names jarred me back to me senses and I asked to see them.

Herschel Feigenbaum sent his daughter to bring my Landsleit. I wasn't there very long when Chaim Kleinberg appeared. He took one look at me, fell on me and kissed me. I assumed he thought I was his brother Yosel who lived in Canada, because of the Canadian uniform. He looked so terrible, just like everyone else and there is no need to dwell on that. Now that my family was gone, these Wierzbnikers were my family and I asked myself, what can I do for these people? I stayed in the camp for a few days and went around seeing others like Roize Shmiel Isses and her daughter. Roize was very ill at that time. Then, I saw Yoinelle Kliman, Romek Zinger, and so may others whose names escape me now. Many are currently living in Israel.

When I returned to my company, I began to try something to help all the inmates of the camp. I found Rabbi Mussman with the United States Forces, a chaplain with an office in Bremin. He and I met and I discovered he was helping these people and he said that anything I could bring is needed. As per tradition, we were 2 Jews and began planning to see what we could do together to help. Pretty soon, I found other Canadian Jewish soldiers, officers, and servicemen whose hearts were also asking how to help. We got together every so often and accumulated whatever we could to bring to the camp, to help make our fellow brethren's life a little better. We turned over the goods to the Jewish Committee inside the camp for distribution to the most needy. I also performed a marvelous postal service for the inmates. I would send letters to my wife to be passed on to families in the rest of the world from the inmates, thus uniting families, which many of whom had given up hope. The answers of course, were sent to me, and when the mail was distributed to us, I always had many letters from all over the world. When I'd return to the camp, I always had a terrific bundle of mail for the survivors. This was carried on until my return to Toronto.

It gives me great pleasure to see so many of those Wierzbnikers I met under such horrendous conditions in the camp, now successful members of our community with families and friends. When I attend their Simchas and see the happiness of these same people, I can't help but look back to 1945-1946, and remember. It does my heart good to see how well things have gone for them. Of course, the memories they carry with them every day of their lives overshadow so much of their lives. But they have done a tremendous job of living with them and adjusting to a new world.

[Page 55]
Yaakov Katz

Jerusalem of Old and Jerusalem the Golden

For two thousand years, Jews all over the world never ceased hoping for a return to the land of Israel. They yearned to rebuild Jerusalem and transform her into the capital of the State of Israel for the people of Israel. As she was in times past when the Temple stood. Thrice yearly, all of Israel would pilgrimage to Jerusalem with songs and dancing laden with the choice fruits of the land and leading choice sheep and cattle.

Great was the preparation for the festival pilgrimage. From all corners of the land, kinsmen would depart together and the roads and paths bustled with pilgrims. The capital prepared to meet them. The Temple candelabrum lit up the surrounding hills, the priests came out to greet the visitors, and the Levites played and sang in their honour. Great was that joy!

To our great sorrow the Temple was destroyed and Jerusalem razed and gone were the joyful years. The nation was exiled. Only the Western Wall remained to recall Israel's past glory. But for two thousand years Israel continued to long for Jerusalem and did not cease to lament her destruction.

On the same date, the night of the 9th of Ab, both the First and Second Temple were destroyed. Thus, "She weepeth sore in the night." Doubly, did Jeremiah lament, once for the destruction of each Temple. "Mine eye, mine eye runneth down with water…" The verse's repetition of the word "eye" teaches us that the shedding of tears was ceaseless, without respite. On this night, year after long year, they sit upon the ground and keep silence, "the elders of the daughters of Zion"; they have cast dust upon their heads and they have girded themselves with sackcloth. They sat, stricken and motionless on the ground as though sunken into it. During the course of the year too, at Midnight Devotions and at prayer time, with tears streaming from their eyes, they turned towards Jerusalem, to that Western Wall known as the Wailing Wall, the Wall of Tears.

As long as the heavenly Gate of Tears was not shut, it was the wall, which drew Jewish prayers. Truly, lamentation was established for all generations, "And all of Israel shall bemoan the great conflagration which Lord kindled."

Moreover, one is required to rend one's garments in mourning upon the sight of the desolate Jerusalem. For Jerusalem our sages held, the customary single rent is insufficient.

Said Rabbi Helbe, as citing Ulla of Berai, who reported to Rabbi Eleazar: One who sees the cities of Judah in their [state of] ruin, recites the verse: "The holy cities are become a wilderness…" and rends his garments. [On seeing] Jerusalem in its [state of] ruin, one recites, "Our holy and our beautiful House, where our Fathers praised thee, is burned with fire and all our things are laid waste", and rends his garment. (Moed Katan, 26).

Similarly, in the 7th chapter of the tractate of Semachot, we read the following:

"These are the rents which may not be basted [when it was done]...for the ruined Temple...on seeing Jerusalem from Mount Scopus... One who sees Jerusalem from Mount Scopus must rend, when he enters [the city] he extends the rent, and if he goes up [again to Jerusalem], he must extend it further.

We may deduce then that for Jerusalem more than one rent is required.

Through all the ages of Jewish history, since the destruction, thousands of Jews journeyed from far off lands to weep over the ruined Jerusalem, to bow before the wall and to kiss it. Aged Jews came to die and be buried in their holy soil. Even those Jews, who never saw the land, felt the love of Jerusalem, which bound together Jews scattered in many different lands. All Jews from Jerusalem all felt a special brotherly closeness. In his poem, "Jerusalem", the poet A. HaMeiri expresses his longing and outpours his soul towards the city:

Peace to you, Jerusalem
From the summit of Mount Scopus
I'll fall on my face before you.
For a hundred generations I dreamt about you,
To be privileged to behold the light of your Countenance.

Finally, finally..."Your sin is ended, daughter of Zion. He will not exile you." The State of Israel was established! Hope became a reality and Jerusalem was restored to her former eminence. As the capital of our state, she contains the Parliament, the Presidential Residence, the Chief Rabbinate, and many other institutions. Torah and learning are wreathed about her every streets. For Jerusalem is no longer in strange hands, she is wholly ours by being deeply rooted in the collective soul of the Jewish people and firmly stamped in our consciousness. Torn in half, during the battle, she returned to us completely in the whirlwind of the Six Day War. In this miraculous and wonder filled whirlwind she appeared to us suddenly. On one hand, her return seemed strange and was dimly comprehended, but one the other it felt as natural as the rejoining of a lost object with its owner. Finally, finally the words of the poet, Saul Tschernichovsky, had become a reality:

A wanderer through all the world you will be,
But your homeland is one,
Forget it not...until your grave.
Even if the day of redemption may tarry...
Don't despair, you prisoner of hope,
Our sun will rise...
My people too, again will blossom forth
On the land a new breed will arise.
Their iron chains will they remove,
Eye to eye will they see the light.
The soul yearnings of 2000 years have found their fulfillment:
Rejoice you with Jerusalem, and be glad with her,
All you that love her.

Happy are we, who have seen the fulfillment of the 2000 year old longing for the land of Zion and Jerusalem!

LISTS

Translated by Yocheved Klausner

Jews who were interned in the Forced-Labor-Camps Yulag-1 and Yulag-2 in "Stchelnitza" and "Mayovka" near Strechowitz (mentioned in the book)

Please note that the page numbers below refer to the page numbers of the original Yizkor book, not the page numbers in this translation.

Go to the end of the book for the Name Index of this translation pagination.

Several weeks after liberation, as the depth of the Holocaust tragedy became clear to the whole world, R'Simcha Minzberg went to his shtetl Wierzbnik – on the hope that he may find remnants of his family, relatives, town people.

What he saw was horrifying – total devastation and annihilation.

Desolated and full of despair in his heart, depressed and humiliated, he walked through the ruins – on the empty pathways where Jewish life once sparkled; all was depressing, bereavement floating in the air, hanging over his head like a heavy piece of lead.

And suddenly, as he entered a barracks in the camp where Jews worked forced labor, he noticed something on the shelf. His heart beating savagely, he approached the place, took the package of written pages and read the names of the "slaves," recorded by the Germans with their characteristic pedantry.

R'Simcha kept this treasure all those years, and thanks to that we are able to include the names in this Book of Memory and Lament.

[Page 58]

[blank]

[Page 59 - German]

The following lists typed up for inclusion in this project by Genia Hollander

List of Names of the Jews in the Camp

Please note that the page numbers below refer to the page numbers of the original Yizkor book, not the page numbers in this translation.

Go to the end of the book for the Name Index of this translation pagination.

Family name	First name(s)	Remarks	Year of birth	Page
MYNCBERG	Symcha		1894	59
BIRENCWAJG	Moszek		1902	59
EJNESMAN	Szlama		1908	59
KAHAN	Szlama		1894	59
LIPSZTAJN	Mordka		1894	59
ARBEITSMAN	Josek		1909	59
BENDET	Froim		1901	59
BINSZTOK	Chaim Sz.		1904	59
BROMBERGER	Bencjan		1890	59
CHAJTON	Rachmil		1914	59
DREIER	Izrael		1908	59
EJCHMAN	Chil		1905	59
FAJNTUCH	Wolf		1917	59
FELDPICER	Jankiel		1927	59
FINKIELSZTAJN	Hersek		1909	59
FLIKIER	Chaim		1910	59
GOLDBERG	Dawid		1883	59
GOLDEWAJG	Lejb		1910	59
GOLDFARB	Szulim		1917	59
GOTLIB	Jankiel		1924	59
GOTLIB	Gerszom		1913	59
GOTLIB	Moszek		1911	59

GATLIB	Szlama Hersz	1899	59
GROSMAN	Ancel	1899	59
GUTMAN	Kielman	1921	59
HELSZTAJN	Michael	1927	59
HELSZTAJN	Pinkus	1901	59
HERBLUM	Lejbus	1911	59
JABLONSKI	Majer	1909	59
KASZTAN	Izrael	1922	59
KASZTAN	Majer	1908	59
KIRSZENBLAT	Eliasz	1912	59
KLAJNBERG	Izrael	1899	59
KOMOROWSKI	Moszek	1913	59
KORENBLUM	Natan	1901	59
KORENBLUM	Wolf	1928	59
KORENWASER	Icek	1923	59
KORENWASER	Moszek	1907	59
LUSTGARTEN	Lejbus	1924	59
LUSTGARTEN	Moszek	1926	59
NUDELMAN	Majlech	1904	59
MUNE	Icek	1895	59
RUBINSZTAJN	Chuna	1905	59
RUBINSZTAJN	Izrael	1910	59
SZYFF	Mendel	1909	59
TURKO	Izrael	1920	59
WALDMAN	Herszek	1915	59
WINOGRAD	Dawid	1927	59
WINOGRAD	Lejbus	1898	59
BINSZTOK	Hinda	1917	59
BINSZTOK	Mindla	1910	59
BROMBERGER	Lonia	1920	59
BROMBERGER	Mania	1925	59
GOLDBERG	Hinda	1919	59
GOTLIB	Fajga	1916	59

HELSZTAJN	Rachela		1907	59
HELSZTAJN	Sura		1926	59
KASZTAN	Bajla		1915	59
KLAJNBERG	Gitla		1903	59
KORENBLUM	Cywia		1897	59
RUBINSZTAJN	Bina		1916	59
RUBINSZTAJN	Dora		1911	59
SZTARKMAN	Mania		1914	59
USZEROWICZ	Fajga		1915	59
WINOGRAD	Laja		1928	59
AJZENBERG	Majer		1924	59
AJZENMAN	Nusyn		1928	59
AJZENMAN	Abram			59
AJZENMAN	Szaja		1917	59
APELBAUM	Szmul		1921	59
AUSDEUTSCHER	Majer		1910	59
BAJGELMAN	Herszek		1912	59
BARAN	Mendel		1923	59
BEKIERMASZYN	Boruch		1925	60
BENEDYKT	Izachar		1922	60
BIDERMAN	Froim		1908	60
BINSZTOK	Abram Majer		1915	60
BIRENBAUM	Icek		1898	60
BOJMELGRYN	Froim	M.G.W.1	1921	60
BLICHER	Abram		1892	60
BIRENBAUM	Rachmil		1925	60
BOJMELGRYN	Icek		1924	60
BOJMELGRYN	Majlech		1898	60
BRODBEKIER	Herszek		1920	60
BORENSZTAJN	Izrael		1903	60
BROMBERGER	Dawid		1920	60
BRODBEKIER	Mendel			60
CHELMINSKI	Chaim		1918	60

CISLOWSKI	Ancel	1926	60
CISLOWSKI	Chaim	1892	60
CUKIERMAN	Boruch I	1926	60
CUKIERMAN	Boruch II	1912	60
CZERNIKOWSKI	Kielman	1922	60
CZERNUCHA	Jakub	1910	60
DIAMENT	Szmul	1905	60
DREKSLER	Josek	1900	60
DYNER	Moszek	1916	60
DYSENHAUS	Lajbus	1914	60
ECHT	Moszek	1911	60
EJZENBUCH	Moszek	1922	60
FARBER	Izrael		60
FELDMAN	Chaim	1922	60
FELDMAN	Chil Szaja	1920	60
FELDMAN	Moszek	1904	60
FELDPICER	Chuna	1927	60
FISZ	Szulim	1920	60
FLOMAN	Szmul		60
FRENKIEL	Ancel		60
FRENKIEL	Pinkwas		60
FRYDMAN	Izrael	1916	60
FRYDMAN	Moszek Majer	1918	60
FRYDMAN	Mordka	1918	60
FUKA	Abram Chaim	1918	60
FUKA	Jakub	1926	60
? ? ?	Icek	1906	60
GOLDFARB	Herszel	1911	60
GOLDFELD	Josek	1925	60
GOLDSZTAJN	Aron	1923	60
GORLIB	Nachman	1918	60
GRABSKI	Aron	1897	60

GROJESKI	Dawid		1924	60
GRYNBLAT	Dawid		1924	60
GRYNBLAT	Jankiel		1918	60
GRYNSZPAN	Moszek		1913	60
GRYNCBERG	Berek			60
GRYNSZTAJN	Moszek		1920	60
GUTMAN	Chaim		1914	60
GUTERMAN	Josek		1892	60
HALSZTUK	Herychem		1916	60
HERING	Chil		1896	60
HERSZKOWICZ	Majer		1908	60
HILF	Mordka		1918	60
HIMELFARB	Szlama		1910	60
HOLEMAN	Chaskiel		1917	60
HONIGSBERG	Majer		1928	60
HONIGSBERG	Mendel			60
JABLONSKI	Chaskiel		1911	60
JARMULA	Abram Icek		1919	60
JUDKIEWICZ	Fiszel		1916	60
JUDKIEWICZ	Moszek		1919	60
KAE	Aron	M.G.W.1	1918	60
KAC	Moszek		1896	60
KALICHMAN	Moszek		1919	60
KALECHMAN	Wolf			60
KALIMOWICZ	Moszek		1910	60
KAMINER	Chaim		1924	60
KAMINSKI	Jankiel		1918	60
KARP	Chil			60
LSHRDL	Wshrdlu			60
KLAJMAN	Josel		1903	60
KLAJNER	Josel		1912	60
KLAJMAN	Kopel		1903	60
KLEPARDA	Chaskiel		1925	60

KLINGER	Berek	1915	60
KLOS	Josel	1923	60
KNOBEL	Chaskiel	1911	60
KNOBEL	Eliasz	1913	61
KOCHEM	Symcha	1918	61
KOGUT	Juma	1925	61
KORALNIK	Mendel	1921	61
KORENWASER	Izrael	1925	61
KORENWASER	Kielman	1922	61
KUPERMAN	Jakub	1916	61
KUPERBERG	Abram	1920	61
KUPERBERG	Motek	1920	61
KUPERBERG	Wolf	1913	61
LAJTAJZEN	Mordka	1910	61
LAUFER	Szymon	1921	61
LEJBGOT	Chil	1924	61
LEWENTON	Piotr	1910	61
LIBMAN	Berek	1912	61
LISSER	Liber	1913	61
LUSTMAN	Pinkwas	1926	61
MACHTYNGER	Chaim	1919	61
MALICKI	Jankiel	1922	61
MAJZELS	Hersz Josek		61
MAINDEL	Chaskiel	1926	61
MANDEL	Majer	1915	61
MANDEL	Symcha	1915	61
MANDEL	Majer	1910	61
MANGORTEN	Lejzor	1913	61
MELCHIOR	Majer	1920	61
MELMAN	Izrael Aron	1915	61
MERSZEJN	Zelig	1922	61
MINKOWSKI	Nusyn	1897	61
MITELMAN	Fajwel	1915	61

MORGELSZTERN	Eliasz		1922	61
MORGENSZTERN	Joel		1913	61
MORGENSZTERN	Srul		1911	61
MOROWIEC	Lejzor		1903	61
NAJMAN	Rachmil		1920	61
ORZECH	Szlama		1922	61
PACANOWSKI	Michael		1922	61
PINCZEWSKI	Dawid		1912	61
PFLICHTENTRAJN	Uszer		1925	61
RAJCHCAJG	Izrael		1922	61
RAJCHMAN	Abram		1909	61
RAJS	Rywan		1923	61
RECHTMAN	Jankel		1903	61
REDLICH	Szyja		1909	61
ROLNICKI	Aron		1923	61
ROZENBERG	Chemia		1909	61
ROZENBERG	Hercyk		1918	61
ROZENBERG	Nuta		1908	61
ROZENBLAT	Samson	M.G.W.1	1921	61
ROZENBLUM	Chaskiel		1911	61
RUBINSZTAJN	Jakub		1908	61
RUBINSZTAJN	Abram		1915	61
SAMET	Szmul		1894	61
SAMET	Moszek		1913	61
SENDOROWICZ	Icek		1918	61
STRAWCZYNSKI	Lejbus		1914	61
SZERMAN	Izrael			61
SZERMAN	Szmul		1891	61
SZTAJNHART	Szlama		1925	61
SZMUKLERMAN	Tanchem		1913	61
SZTAL	Froim		1906	61
SZTRAJTFELD	Jozek		1900	61
SZTROSBERG	Kalman		1924	61

SZUCH	Rafal	1912	61
SZUCH	Moszek		61
SZWARCBERG	Symcha	1913	61
SZFARCFITER	Szlama	1899	61
SZYFMAN	Rafal	1923	61
TENENBAUM	Rafal	1903	61
TENENBAUM	Mordka	1910	61
TENENBAUM	Chil	1923	61
TREFLER	Fajwel	1915	61
TROPPE	Mojzesz	1916	61
TURKO	Chaskiel	1923	61
UNGER	Hersz	1926	61
WAJCHENDLER	Herszek	1924	61
WAJCHENDLER	Hersz	1921	61
WAJNBAUM	Josek	1924	61
WAJNBERG	Chil	1888	61
WAJNBERG	Josek	1923	61
WAJNGORT	Szyja	1913	61
WAJSKOPF	Nusyn	1922	61
WALGROCH	Chaim	1922	61
WAJNSZTAJN	Izrael	1924	62
WAJSBLUM	Wolf	1925	62
WARCKI	Dawid	1905	62
WASERMAN	Chaim	1908	62
WATMAN	Abram	1916	62
WIETRZNIK	Icek	1920	62
WINOGRAD	Rachmil	1925	62
WISNIEWSKI	Icek	1927	62
ZACHCINSKI	Jos	1915	62
ZALCMAN	Ela		62
EETAO	Ashrdl	1928	62
ZELCER	Abram	1923	62
ZELCER	Hersz	1909	62

ZELCER	Icek		62
ZELCER	Chaim	1915	62
ZEJGMAN	Herszek	1921	62
ZYLBERBERG	Chil	1921	62
ZYLBERBERG	Ela	1912	62
ZYLBERBERG	Fajwel	1909	62
ZYLBERBERG	Fiszel I	1905	62
ZYLBERBERG	Lejb	1927	62
ZYLBERBERG	Majer		62
ZYLBERBERG	Moszek I	1924	62
ZYLBERBERG	Moszek II	1924	62
ZYLBERBERG	Moszek III	1885	62
ZYLBERBERG	Nosch	1926	62
ZYLBERSZTAJN	Josek	1921	62
ZARNOWIECKI	Rubin Aron M.G.W.1	1924	62
AJZENBERG	Gitla	1921	62
BRODBEKIER	Perla	1921	62
BRODBEKIER	Sura	1924	62
BLUMENFELD	Chaja	1923	62
BROMBERGER	Rachela	1915	62
DAWIDOWICZ	Saba	1918	62
FINKIELSZTAJN	Zelda	1917	62
FURMAN	Mania	1904	62
GEWERCER	Sala	1922	62
GOLDBERG	Mania	1921	62
GUTHOLC	Rojza	1913	62
GUTERMAN	Lifela	1925	62
KARNISZYN	Anna	1920	62
KAUFMAN	Sura	1924	62
KLAJMAN	Laja	1923	62
KOGUT	Rozia	1924	62
KORENWASER	Malka	1914	62
KRYSZTAL	Rywka	1915	62

NAJNUDEL	Sala		1924	62
NUDELMAN²	Rojza		1924	62
PAPIERCZYK	Sonia		1923	62
PRZEPIORKA	Basia		1910	62
PRZEPIORKA	Maria		1922	62
PRZEPIORKA	Rela		1918	62
RAJCHCAJG	Hendla		1916	62
SZCZESLIWA	Chana		1924	62
SZTERENSZUS	Sura		1922	62
SZTARKMAN	Mirla		1920	62
UNGER	Perla		1924	62
WAJCHENDLER	Zofia		1920	62
WAJCHENDLER	Estera		1922	62
WAJDENBAUM	Genia		1923	62
WAJNBAUM	vel Lewin Mariem		1918	62
WAJNPER	Brandla		1922	62
WAJZER	Hinda		1925	62
WINOGRAD	Golda		1925	62
ZELCER	Bela		1918	62
MANGARTEN	Alta Cywia		1920	62
WAJNTRAUB	Basia	M.G.W.1	1923	62
WAJNTRAUB	Luba		1920	62
ABRAMOWICZ	Gutman		1904	62
ABRAMOWICZ	Jonas		1915	62
ADLER	Jakub		1916	62
AJLENBERG	Majer		1912	62
ALIOS	Wolf		1920	62
ALTMAN	Mordka			62
BAUM	Gedala		1903	62
BAUM	Szuja		1920	62
BIDERMAN	Szulim		1914	62
BINSZTOK	Abus		1910	62
BINSZTOK	Chaim		1897	62

BINSZTOK	Mendel		1924	62
BIRENBAUM	Motek		1925	62
BLATMAN	Ajzyk			62
BLISKO	Majlech		1921	62
BORENSZTAJN	Zelman		1919	62
BRODBEKIER	Izrael		1919	63
BRODBEKIER	Moszek		1920	63
BRYKMAN	Jakub Majer			63
BRYTT	Izrael			63
CHAJTON	Izrael		1923	63
CHAJTON	Jankiel		1919	63
CIECHANOWSKI	Szaja		1907	63
CUKIER	Mordka		1914	63
CUKIERMAN	Gerszon	M.G.W.2	1905	63
CUKIERMAN	Mordka		1906	63
CUKIERMAN	Mordka II		1900	63
CYMRYNT	Chil		1924	63
CYMRYNT	Szmerek		1918	63
CYTRYN	Menasze		1925	63
CYTRYM	Wolf		1920	63
CZARNY	Chaim		1914	63
DELEWKOWICZ	Szymszon		1912	63
DREKSLER	Dawid		1924	63
DRYGANT	Nusyn		1906	63
EJNESMAN	Icek		1898	63
ELBIRT	Eleazor		1922	63
ERLICHMAN	Chaim Juer		1899	63
FELDPICER	Herszek		1902	63
FINKIELSZTAJN	Matys			63
FLANCBAUM	Dawid		1918	63
FRYC	Izrael		1924	63
FREULICH	Kurt		1907	63
FRYSZMAN	Boruch		1920	63

FRYSZMAN	Wolf	1919	63
GANC	Pinkwas		63
GERSZT	Moszek	1919	63
GITLER	Nuchym	1920	63
GOLDBERG	Chaim	1912	63
GOLDBERG	Josek	1922	63
GOLDSZTAJN	Chaim	1909	63
GOLDSZTAJN	Jakub	1922	63
GOLEBIOWSKI	Hersz Wolf	1920	63
GOLTLIB	Chil.	1915	63
GOTLIB	Zachariasz	1923	63
GRYNBAUM	Moszek	1916	63
GRYNBAUM	Pinkwas	1901	63
GRYNBLAT	Szmul	1906	63
GRYNBERG	Abram	1907	63
GRYNSZPAN	Szeftel	1927	63
GUTERMAN	Moszek	1928	63
GUTERMAN	Icek	1924	63
HAJBLUM	Jankiel	1926	63
HAUPTMAN	Abram	1917	63
HERBLUM	Samuel	1924	63
HERZBERG	Wolf	1909	63
HERSZMAN	Nuchym	1916	63
HERSZEUHORN	Jankiel	1912	63
HOROWICZ	Majer	1910	63
JARECKI	Abram	1903	63
JOSKOWICZ	Josek	1913	63
KALIKWASER	Josek	1923	63
KANINSKI	Chaim Lejb	1909	63
KANAREK	Szlama	1909	63
KAPLAN	Iszrael	1905	63
KAPLAN	Moszek	1924	63
KAUFMAN	Josek	1902	63

KESTENBAUM	Moszek	1894	63
KIERSZENBAUM	Mendel	1923	63
KLAJMAN	Jankiel	1926	63
KLAJN	Szmul	1917	63
KNOBEL	Abram	1918	63
KOCHEN	Ela	1924	63
KOGUT	Rachmil	1924	63
KRYSZTAL	Chananiasz M.G.W.2	1925	63
KUPERMINC	Manela	1908	63
KURC	Pinkus	1921	63
LEJBMAN	Herszel	1921	63
LEWA	Perec	1908	63
LEWIN	Szmul		63
LICHTENSZTAJN	Izrael	1924	63
LILENBAUM	Lejbus	1922	63
LIPMAN	Juer	1914	63
LIPOWICZ	Majer	1923	63
LIPOWICZ	Szmerek	1918	63
LUKSENBERG	Nuchym	1919	63
LEGA	Moszek	1919	63
MANELA	Berek	1914	63
MANELA	Dawid	1923	63
MANELA	Majer	1921	63
MANOWICZ	Szlama	1918	64
MARKIEWICZ	Aron	1923	64
MAUER	Jankiel	1917	64
MERSZAJN	Chaskiel	1919	64
MILGROM	Moszek	1918	64
MIODOWNIK	Dawid	1920	64
MORGENSZTERN	Lejbus	1913	63
NAJMAN	Abram	1927	64
NAJMAN	Icek	1918	64
NAJMAN	Lejzor	1916	64

NEUFELD	Szaja	1924	64
NAJMAN	Szmelka	1918	64
NUDELMAN	Mendel	1909	64
OFMAN	Josek	1917	64
OLSZER	Szlama	1909	64
PERELMAN	Jecheskiel	1914	64
PINKUSIEWICZ	Izrael	1909	64
PFLICHTENTRAJN	Icek	1922	64
PRESEL	Erwin	1906	64
RADOLNIK	Eliasz	1898	64
RAJCHMAN	Mordka	1902	64
RAJZLIK	Izrael	1921	64
RAJZMAN	Moszek	1912	64
RUBINSZTAJN	Rachmil	1920	64
RAPSZTAJN	Sandal	1908	64
ROZENBERG	Szmul	1916	64
ROTBARD	Chil	1923	64
RUTMAN	Fajwel	1925	64
SENDEROWICZ	Berek	1929	64
SZAJN	Hejnoch	1919	64
SZTABHOLC	Dawid	1915	64
SZTAJNBAUM	Moniek	1927	64
SZTERENSZUS	Abram	1923	64
SZTERENSZUS	Rachmil	1926	64
SZTROSBERG	Moszek	1914	64
SZYMANOWSKI	Herszek	1911	64
TAJBLUM	Symcha	1912	64
TAJCHMAN	Jarmia	1909	64
TAUBMAN	Szlama	1898	64
WAJCHENDLER	Lejb	1923	64
WAJCHENDLER	Moszek	1904	64
WAJCHENDLER	Nusyn	1925	64
WAJGENSZPERG	Munisz	1926	64

WAJNBERG	Nusyn	M.G.W.2	1904	64
WAJNSZTAJN	Froim		1915	64
WAJNSZTOK	Lejb		1918	64
POMERANC	Szmul		1908	64
WAJS	Szlama		1923	64
WAJSBLUM	Alter		1903	64
WAJSBLUM	Szmul		1898	64
WAJZER	Icel		1919	64
WAKSMAN	Chaim		1905	64
WEJGMAN	Icek		1905	64
WILINSKI	Chaim		1923	64
WLOSZCZOWSKI	Izrael		1924	64
WLOSZCZOWSKI	Moszek		1927	64
ULSZTAT	Icek		1911	64
ZALCMAN	Aba		1916	64
ZAUBERMAN	Mordka		1926	64
ZEJGMAN	Leon		1916	64
ZONABEND	Icek		1916	64
ZYLBERBERG	Chaim		1924	64
ZYLBERBERG	Chaskiel			64
ZYLBERBERG	Mordka		1906	64
ZYLBERBERG	Josek		1921	64
ZYLBERBERG	Rachmil		1896	64
ZYNGMAN	Chaim		1912	64
ZOLNA	Josek		1922	64
ZOLNA	Majlech		1896	64
ADLER	Tamara		1920	64
KUPERMAN	Ruchla		1912	64
KUPERMAN	Sura		1921	64
LEWENSON	Reka		1914	64
LIPMAN	Laja		1921	64
RABINOWICZ	Chasia		1925	64
RABINOWICZ	Dyna		1924	64

RABINOWICZ	Raca		1919	64
SZLEZYNGER	Estera		1912	64
SZTARKMAN	Matla	M.G.W.2	1901	64
WAKSZAL	Basia		1917	64
ABRAMOWICZ	Pinkus		1909	64
ABRAMOWICZ	Pinkus II		1904	64
AJZENMAN	Abram		1925	64
AJZENMAN	Lejb Szlama		1899	65
AJZENMAN	Moszek		1905	65
BAUM	Zelig		1912	65
BINSZTOK	Jankiel		1920	65
BRODBEKIER	Abram			65
BRODBEKIER	Icek		1902	65
BRODBEKIER	Szmul			65
BRONIEWSKI	Szymon		1911	65
BRYTT	Izrael		1898	65
CYPRIAN	Marian		1913	65
CYRULNIK	Moszek		1922	65
CZAPNIK	Eliasz		1924	65
CYTRYN	Hersz		1920	65
CYTRYN	Jonas		1910	65
DREJZNER	Chil		1903	65
FELNER	Pejsach		1921	65
FRYMERMAN	Bendet		1923	65
GDANSKI	Chaim		1924	65
GEWERCER	Moszek			65
GLAS	Chaim		1920	65
GLIKSMAN	Jakub		1923	65
GROBER	Jankiel		1906	65
GRYNSZPAN	Mendell			65
HAJBLUM	Ajzyk			65
HELSZTAJN	Urysz		1903	65
HENIG	Jeszaja	V.V.2	1914	65

KALMOWICZ	Zelig		1915	65
KAMINER	Aria		1917	65
KAUFMAN	Josek			65
KIERBEL	Dowid		1923	65
KLAJMINC	Berek			65
KOCHEN	Jakub		1920	65
KOCHEN	Maks		1916	65
KONOWIECKI	Jakub		1922	65
KONOWIECKI	Tobiasz		1924	65
KRYSZTAL	Abram		1903	65
LAS	Moszek		1907	65
LEJBMAN	Lejbus		1923	65
LERNER	Zelman		1913	65
LEWI	Berek			65
LIBESKIN	Herszek			65
LAJEWSKI	Lejzor		1911	65
MANDELBAUM	Jankiel		1922	65
MANDELZYS	Szmul		1918	65
MILLER	Chil			65
MILLER	Szlama			65
MINCBERG	Moszek		1898	65
PANCER	Herszek		1922	65
PANCER	Szaja		1905	65
PINCZEWSKI	Moszek		1913	65
POZNER	Herszek		1924	65
RADZINSKI	Lejzora		1910	65
RAJZMAN	Rachmil		1913	65
RODOWICZ	Eliasz		1921	65
ROZMAITY	Chaim	SZP.22	1912	65
RUBINSZTAJN	Boruch		1900	65
RUBINSZTAJN	Chuna		1909	65
STRZYG	Mojzesz		1906	65
SZACHTER	Aron		1923	65

SZAJNWALD	Josek		1922	65
SZTAJNOWICZ	Chaim		1921	65
SZWICMAN	Matys		1901	65
TAUBMAN	Liber		1921	65
WAJNBERG	Josek		1926	65
WAJNBERG	Mendel	V.V.H	1926	65
WAJNSZTOK	Towia		1923	65
WAJNTRAUB	Josek			65
WAJSBLAT	Majlech		1915	65
WARDA	Szlama			65
WARGON	Abram		1920	65
WEKSELMAN	Lejzor			65
ZEMEL	Chaim			65
ZYLBERBERG	Icek		1904	65
ANIELEWICZ	Chaim			65
AJZENBERG	Nuchym			65
BAUM	Bencjan		1918	65
BRODBEKIER	Lejbus			65
DERWIC	Aleksander		1924	65
HERLING	Mendel		1925	65
HOCHMINC	Pinkus		1925	65
KAUFMAN	Jankiel		1925	65
KIERBEL	Szmul		1926	65
KLAJNBERG	Chaim		1925	65
MACHTYNGER	Lejbus		1920	65
MILLER	Dawid		1921	66
NAJMAN	Hewek		1893	66
PAJKUS	Szulim		1925	66
RUBINSZTAJN	Boruch		1925	66
SZACHMAN	Jankiel			66
WAJCHENDLER	Ezra		1906	66
WAJNERMAN	Wolf			66
AJSBERG	Nusyn	H.P.B.	1891	66

WAJSDORF	Lipa			66
WAKSBERG	Mendel		1925	66
WARSZAUER	Lejzor		1925	66
ZYLBERBERG	Moszek		1925	66
ZYSKIND	Beno		1923	66
ZYSKIND	Jerzy		1928	66
ZOLNA	Mendel		1926	66
BRODBEKIER	Rywka		1923	66
CYTRYN	Rywka		1920	66
FRYMERMAN	Cypra		1925	66
GLAT	Chana		1921	66
GLAT	Maria		1925	66
GLAT	Sura		1923	66
GROCHER	Chaja		1910	66
GROCHER	Dwojra		1915	66
GRYNSZPAN	Jacheta		1910	66
KAMINER	Golda		1917	66
KAUFMAN	Golda		1924	66
KRYSZTAL	ywka		1920	66
MANGORTEN	Malka		1920	66
NUDELMAN	Estera			66
NISKIER	Sura		1910	66
RABINOWICZ	Chaja		1911	66
ROZENBERG	Toba		1920	66
RUBINSZTAJN	Golda		1924	66
RUBINSZTAJN	Ita		1924	66
RUBINSZTAJN	Krajndla		1923	66
RUBINSZTAJN	Malka		1923	66
TENENBAUM	Chaja		1925	66
WAJSBERG	Fajga		1923	66
WAJSBLUM	Estera		1922	66
WAJSBLUM	Rywka	H.P.B.	1922	66
ZYLBERBERG	Blima		1917	66

ZYLBERBERG	Gitla		1926	66
ZYLBERFENIG	Chawa		1925	66
CIEPLY	Icek		1923	66
CUKIERMAN	Szmul		1903	66
DRAJNUDEK	Icek		1924	66
WAJNBERG	Dawid		1926	66
FRYMEL	Berek		1907	66
GOLDBERG	Szmerek		1915	66
HILF	Chaim			66
KAUFMAN	Symcha			66
KLAJMAN	Chaim		1924	66
KORENWASER	Majlech	E.L.H.	1897	66
LEJBMAN	Pinkus			66
LIBERMAN	Jojne		1923	66
MORGENSZTERN	Chaskiel		1898	66
MORGENSZTERN	Josek		1923	66
ROZENES	Abram		1921	66
SZTULMAN	Boruch		1914	66
WAJNRYB	Aron		1900	66
WAJNRYB	Mordka		1920	66
WAJNRYB	Szlama		1918	66
WAJSMEHL	Lejb		1911	66
CUKIERMAN	Berek		1920	66
SZTAJNBAUM	Lejbus	H.H.	1925	66
DRAJNUDEL	Mendel			66
FELDMAN	Chaskiel		1913	66
FRYMERMAN	Abram		1903	66
RUBINSZTAJN	Boruch		1908	66
TENENBAUM	Dawid		1925	66
TENENBAUM	Herszek			66
TENENBAUM	Izrael		1925	66
TENENBAUM	Mendel			66
AJZENBERG	Chil		1925	66

AJZENBERG	Majlech		1907	66
ALPERT	Rachmil		1910	66
BEKIERMASZYN	Josek		1927	66
BINSZTOK	Icek		1919	66
BINSZTOK	Szlama			66
BOROWKA	Szmul		1911	66
CUKIERMAN	Moszek	H.H.	1924	66
CYMERMAN	Perec		1921	66
CYMRYNT	Fiszek		1928	67
DRAJNUDEL	Jankiel		1914	67
ERLICHMAN	Moszek		1905	67
FELDPICER	Fajwel		1922	67
FELDPICER	Herszek		1924	67
FELDPICER	Moszek			67
FISZMAN	Moszek		1920	67
FISZMAN	Rachmil		1919	67
FRUCHTMAN	Kielman		1922	67
GELBARD	Szmul		1917	67
GRAFSZTAJN	Zelig		1908	67
HERBLUM	Herszek		1911	67
HOROWICZ	Abram		1906	67
HANNA	Mordchaj		1907	67
KLAJNBERG	Chil		1920	67
KURLENDER	Nuta		1910	67
LECZYCKI	Szmul		1898	67
LIS	Lejzor		1921	67
MAJ	Binem		1913	67
MASLOWICZ	Fiszel I		1920	67
MILBERG	Jerachmil		1914	67
NAJMAN	Moszek		1910	67
ORZECH	Berek		1918	67
ORZECH	Icek		1917	67
ROZENWALD	Icek		1901	67

ROZENTAL	Moszek		1908	67
RUBINSZTAJN	Awner		1915	67
RUBINSZTAJN	Szaja			67
RUBINSZTAJN	Zachariasz			67
RUTMANOWICZ	Kiwa		1922	67
RYCHTENBERG	Moszek		1923	67
SMIALY	Moszek		1895	67
SZERAKOWICZ	Berek			67
SZPAGAT	Moszek		1923	67
TENENBAUM	Moszek		1923	67
WAJZER	Izrael		1897	67
ZIELINSKI	Abram			67
ZOLNA	Lejb		1921	67
BARANEK	Sura		1902	67
BAUM	Nacha		1925	67
DAWIDMAN	Chana		1923	67
ERLICH	Rywka		1925	67
ERLICHMAN	Rywka		1925	67
ERLICHMAN	Welka		1924	67
FINKIELSZTAJN	Dora		1925	67
FINKIELSZTAJN	Rojza		1920	67
FINKIELSZTAJN	Sura	H.H.	1916	67
FERSTENBERG	Fajga		1921	67
FRYDMAN	Regina		1921	67
GELBARD	Maria		1916	67
GROSMAN	Pesla		1920	67
GRYNSZPORN	Basia		1924	67
GRYNSZTAJN	Ruchla		1917	67
HELLER	Anna		1901	67
HELSZTAJN	Fania		1909	67
HOLCMAN	Rozia		1915	67
JANKIELOWICZ	Gina		1902	67
KAUFMAN	Chana		1924	67

KAUFMAN	Chaja	1924	67
KILMAN	Ewa	1915	67
KLAPPER	Frania	1924	67
KOPER	Sura	1914	67
KOPF	Ruchla	1923	67
KORENWASER	Malka	1921	67
LAKS	Pola	1924	67
LISIEWICZ	Mindla	1919	67
LOMSKA	Maria	1924	67
LUSTMAN	Estera	1905	67
MENTLIK	Chaja	1912	67
NAJMAN	Chawa	1921	67
NAJMAN	Szewa	1906	67
OSTROWIECKA	Ruchla	1918	67
PRZYTYCKA	Rywka	1920	67
ROTFOGIEL	Luba	1920	67
ROZENCWAJG	Rywka	1908	67
ROZENWALD	Szajndla	1925	67
RUBINSZTAJN	Rywaka	1920	67
SAMET	Cypra	1922	67
SAMET	Maria	1924	67
SCISLOWSKA	Nacha	1923	67
SZAJNER	Perla	1920	67
SZPAGAT	Gitla	1923	67
SATRAJTMAN	Chaja	1923	67
SZUCH	Mala	1909	67
TAUBMAN	Estera	1904	68
TAUBMAN	Malka	1926	68
TRAJSTER	Miriam	1922	68
WAJNBERG	Chaja	1921	68
WAJSBLUM	Tobka	1917	68
WISLA	Cluwa	1908	68
ZAUBERMAN	Rywka	1905	68

ZYLBERBERG	Laja		1917	68
ZYLBERSZTAJN	Estera		1908	68
ZYLBERSZTAJN	Mindla		1922	68
ZYLBERSZTAJN	Pesla		1916	68
ZABNER	Rajzla		1923	68
BARANEK	Bencjan		1909	68
DREKSLER	Alter		1921	68
DREKSLER	Moszek		1919	68
GUTERMAN	Berek		1895	68
GUTERMAN	Icek		1921	68
GUTERMAN	Moszek		1927	68
GUTERMAN	Lewa		1926	68
KAUFMAN	Majer			68
KAUFMAN	Mordka			68
KIERBEL	Lejbus		1897	68
KIERSZENBLUM	Abram			68
KRYSZTAL	Szmul		1924	68
LEWA	Abram		1912	68
MENTLIK	Abram	Martin	1913	68
MORGENSZTERN	Icel		1926	68
TENENBAUM	Rachmil		1926	68
WAJCHENDLER	Lejbus		1888	68
ZYNGER	Rachmil		1912	68
CUKIERMAN	Izrael			68
CYMERMAN	Samson		1899	68
GOLDBERG	Chaim		1912	68
GERTLER	Nusyn		1921	68
GERTLER	Josef		1897	68
GRYNSZPORN	Abram		1926	68
GRYNSZPORN	Zelman		1900	68
HERBLUM	Lejbus		1894	68
HERLING	Juma		1908	68
JEGER	Lejbus	BUGAJ		68

KLAJMINC	Zelman		1912	68
KOMOROWSKI	Boruch		1908	68
SZCZESLLIWY	Jankiel		1913	68
SZPIRO	Moszek			68
SZRAJBMAN	Josek		1909	68
SZTAJMAN	Jakub		1910	68
SZTAJMAN	Majer		1911	68
UNGER	Josek		1896	68
UNGER	Moszek		1921	68
ZATERMAN	Izrael			68
ZYLBERBERG	Abram		1893	68
ZYLBERBERG	Chil		1918	68
ERLICHMAN	Juer Chaim			68
BLIMAN	Michel	Werkslhutz	z 1913	68
BLIMAN	Michel		1903	68
FINKIELSZTAJN	Josek		1917	68
GOTLIB	Jankiel		1907	68
GUTWIL	Szymszon		1921	68
AJZENMAN	Boruch		1898	68
BRODBEKIER	Chil		1923	68
BRODBEKIER	Lejbus[2]		1895	68
BRZEGOWSKI	Abram		1925	68
CYMERMAN	Lejbus		1925	68
CUKIERMAN	Hersz		1918	68
DODKIEWICZ	Berek		1920	68
ERLICHSON	Fiszel I		1916	68
FISZMAN	Jankiel		1923	68
FRANKEL	Aleksander		1926	68
FRUCHTMAN	Herszek		1908	68
FRUCHTMAN	Majer		1917	68
GARNCARSKI	Jozef		1921	68
GOLDMAN	Izrael		1924	68
GOLDSZTAJN	Hersz		1913	68

GROJECKI	Lejbus		1923	68
GROJECKI	Srul		1919	68
GROSMAN	Mendel		1910	68
HONIGSBERG	Moszek		1925	68
JOSKOWICZ	Szmul		1910	68
KALMOWICZ	Szymon		1925	68
KENIGSZTAJN	Mordka		1906	68
KIERBEL	Lejbus			68
KUPERBERG	Pinkus		1921	68
LANIENTER	Boruch		1923	68
LIBMAN	Moszek		1910	69
LUBKA	Chanina	M.G.1	1925	69
MORDKOWICZ	Judka		1905	69
MORGENSZTERN	Szmul		1909	69
MOSZKOWICZ	Szlama		1909	69
NAJNUDEL	Fajwel		1902	69
ORZECH	Josek		1921	69
PRUSAK	Szaja		1917	69
PIASKOGORSKI	Beniamin		1913	69
PRZEPIORKA	Izrael			69
PRZEPIORKA	Towia			69
RAJCHCAJG	Chemia		1899	69
ROZENBERG	Herszek		1925	69
ROZENCWAJG	Beniamin		1899	69
ROZENCWAJG	Pinkwas		1926	69
RYCZKE	Mendel			69
SAMET	Chaim		1910	69
SZUCHT	Szmul		1909	69
SZACHTER	Froim		1924	69
SZERMAN	Jankiel		1920	69
SZTERN	Jankiel		1908	69
SZTROSBERG	Mendel		1920	69
SZYKIER	Ezra		1921	69

UNGER	Majer	1922	69
WAJSBLUM	Josek	1912	69
WALSZTAJN	Chaim	1923	69
WARSZAUER	Izrael	1899	69
WIKINSKI	Josek	1925	69
ZACHCINSKI	Abram	1908	69
ZAMBERG	Eliasz	1923	69
ZYNGER	Noe	1910	69
ZAWIERUCHA	Zanwel	1919	69
FIRSTENBERG	Halina	1920	69
KLAJMINC	Perla	1920	69
ZYNGER	Karolina	1912	69
ALTMAN	Lejb	1920	69
BROMBERG	Dawid	1920	69
CHOINA	Majer	1923	69
CIESLA	Cemach	1918	69
CZARNY	Wolf	1919	69
ERLICHMAN	Judka	1896	69
ERLICHMAN	Rachmil	1918	69
FEFERMAN	Rafal	1926	69
FELNER	Ojzer		69
FLANCBAUM	Chaim		69
FUKS	Mordka		69
FRYMEL	Jankiel	1903	69
GARNEK	Moszek	1915	69
GROSMAN	Aron	1913	69
GUTHOLC	Rachmil	1915	69
KESTENBERG	Lewek	1925	69
KLAJMAN	Dawid		69
KOGUT	Ajzyk	1920	69
LUSTMAN	Mendel	1913	69
LUSTMAN	Nusyn	1899	69
MINKOWSKI	Moszek	1926	69

MIODECKI	Chaim		1919	69
MORGENSZTERN	Herszek	E.W.	1915	69
NADULEK	Majer		1893	69
OBERMAN	Eliasz		1918	69
POLIBORSKI	Mojzesz			69
ROCHMAN	Josek		1914	69
RUBMAN	Abram		1914	69
SZACHTER	Noech		1916	69
SZAFIR	Manes		1923	69
SZARFER	Chil		1924	69
SZERMAN	Berek		1915	69
SZTROSBERG	Ajzyk		1924	69
TAREK	Uszer		1922	69
TREFLER	Icek		1921	69
WAJNBAUM	Josek			69
WAINTRAUB	Nusyn			69
ZALKA	Mojzesz		1900	69
ZELINGER	Froim		1913	69
ZYNGER	Dawid		1911	69
ZYLBERBERG	Fiszel I	III	1920	69
AJZENBERG	Symcha		1920	69
BAS	Izrael		1914	69
BERGER	Herszek		1905	69
BERGSON	Gerszon		1911	69
BIRENBAUM	Michal		1913	69
BLATMAN	Herszek		1898	69
BRAND	Zachariasz		1911	69
BRENER	Natan		1917	70
BRODBEKIER	Josef	M.W.A.	1911	70
BRYTT	Szlama		1918	70
CYGIEL	Abram		1923	70
CYMERMAN	Abram		1895	70
ELBERG	Josek		1895	70

ERLICH	Abram	1907	70
ERLICHMAN	Chanina	1910	70
FAJGELMAN	Nuchym	1912	70
FAJGENBAUM	Symcha	1907	70
FISZKOWICZ	Hilel	1914	70
FRYDMAN	Aron	1915	70
GANC	Herszek	1918	70
GARFINKIEL	Hercka	1913	70
GERMAN	Icek Lejb	1917	70
GOLDBACH	Szmul	1912	70
GOLDBERG	Icek	1906	70
GOLDBLUM	Jakub	1903	70
GOLDGRUB	Lejzor	1917	70
GOLDSZTAJN	Abram	1923	70
GROSMAN	Nuta	1925	70
GUTERMAN	Mordka		70
HAJBLUM	Gerszon		70
KLAJMAN	Szulim	1923	70
KORENBLUM	Mordka	1926	70
KUPERIAD	Mordka	1911	70
LICHTENSZTAJN	Bernard	1920	70
LICHTENSZTAJN	Szmul		70
LIBMAN	Izrael	1908	70
LIPSZYC	Szulim	1909	70
MALC	Moszek	1922	71
MASLOWICZ	Berek	1915	71
MASLOWICZ	Szlama	1904	71
MERZEL	Aron	1922	71
MERZEL	Lejbus	1915	71
MINCBERG	Mendel	1923	71
MORDFELD	Josek	1899	71
MORGENSZTERN	Froim	1918	71
NISENBAUM	Josek	1917	71

OLLMER	Izak	1902	71
PUTERMAN	Abram	1904	71
RAJS	Szmul	1920	71
RAFALOWICZ	Wolf	1908	71
ROZENTAL	Icek	1910	71
ROZENTAL	Tadeusz	1900	71
RUBINSZTAJN	Chuna	1906	71
SZECHTER	Tewel	1910	71
SZACHTER	Jankiel	1919	71
SZACHTER	Lejbus	1916	71
SZAFIR	Lejzor	1911	71
SZAJNER	Moszek	1900	71
SZCZERBAKOW	Majer	1918	71
SZERMAN	Josek	1923	71
SZERMAN	Wolf	1902	71
SZPILFOGIEL	Jankiel	1915	71
SZTARKMAN	Majer	1924	71
SZTRAJTMAN	Perec	1919	71
SZWARCBERG	Hersz	1911	71
TAUBMAN	Hersz	1911	71
TENENBAUM	Lejb	1908	71
WARSZAUER	Zysia	1911	71
WAJGENSZPERG	Izak	1898	71
WAJNBERG	Mojzesz	1907	71
WAJNSZTOK	Lejb	1916	71
WAJNSZTOK	Moszek	1918	71
WAJSBLUM	Szlama	1918	71
WASERMAN	Hersz	1915	71
WINOGRAD	Gerszon	1904	71
ZYLBERBERG	Jankiel	1915	71
ZYLBERBERG	Rywan	1917	71
ZYSMAN	Kalaman	1918	71
ZYSMAN	Kalman	1918	71

BERGSON	Fajga	1917	71
BERSON	Fajga	1913	71
ALBIRT	Majer	1923	71
ANIELEWICZ	Jankiel I		71
ANIELEWICZ	Jankiel II		71
ARBEITER	Aron	1925	71
ARBEITER	Izrael	1924	71
ARBEITER	Motel	1922	71
AJZENMAN	Hersz	1906	71
AJZENBERG	Kielman	1925	71
BIDERMAN	Szlama	1925	71
BIDERMAN	Moszek	1923	71
BINSZTOK	Chaim		71
CYMERMAN	Abram	1907	71
CYMERMAN	Moszek	1901	71
FELDMAN	Ela	1916	71
FELDPICER	Zachariasz		71
FELDPICER	Judka	1897	71
FINKLER	Icel	1907	71
FINKIELSZTAJN	Beniamin	1907	71
FINKIELSZTAJN	Herszek	1918	71
FISZ	Judka	1926	71
FRIDENSON	Josef	1922	71
GLIKSMAN	Alter	1912	71
GOLDBERG	Nuchym	1888	71
GOLDFARB	Majer		71
GOLDMAN	Szyja	1916	71
GROCHER	Herszek	1911	71
GROSMAN	Szmul	1923	71
GUTERMAN	Jankiel		71
GUTMAN	Froim	1903	71
GRYNBAUM	Chuna	1926	71
GRYNBERG	Dawid		71

GRYNER	Gamliel	1911	71
GRYNSZTAJN	Aron	1915	71
HERBLUM	Jankiel	1892	71
HERLING	Icek	1916	71
HERLING	Moszek	1909	71
HONIGMAN	Abram	1903	71
KAHAN	Dawid	1924	71
KAMPEL	Fiszel I	1925	71
KANER	Lejzor	1922	71
KIERSZENBAUM	Jakub	1918	72
KLAJMAN	Moszek	1900	72
KORENWASER	Majer	1910	72
KORENWASER	Noech	1918	72
KOSZYKARZ	Chaim		72
KRYS	Mendel	1907	72
KRYS	Pinkus	1900	72
LANGER	Hersz	1915	72
LIBERMAN	Josek	1921	72
LISIEWICZ	Josek	1894	72
LUBLINER	Wolf		72
MAKIEROWICZ	Nachman	1893	72
MANDEL	Chaim	1921	72
MANDEL	Izrael	1919	72
MANDEL	Pinkus	1900	72
MANGARTEN	Dawid	1926	72
MORDFELD	Herszek	1917	72
MYDLARZ	Majer	1918	72
RABINOWICZ	Jakub	1911	72
RABINOWICZ	Jozef	1903	72
RAJZMAN	Moszek	1900	72
ROZENBERG	Lewa	1905	72
ROZENBERG	Lejbus	1923	72
SZACHTER	Moszek	1924	72

SZACHTER	Moszek II	1908	72
SZAFIR	Chaim	1916	72
SZAPSZEWICZ	Jakub	1914	72
SZLEZYNGER	Chaim	1914	72
SZTAJNBAUM	Majer	1898	72
SZTARKMAN	Moszek	1915	72
SZTARKMAN	Szlama	1923	72
TENENBAUM	Szmul	1896	72
WAJSBLAT	Moszek	1908	72
WAJNTRAUB	Mordka	1921	72
WAKSMAN	Pinkus	1911	72
WASERSZTAJN	Pinkus	1912	72
WEKSELMAN	Moszek	1902	72
ZYFERMAN	Lejb	1901	72
ZYLBERBERG	Abram II		72
ZYLBERBERG	Chaskiel		72
ZYLBERBERG	Mendel	1904	72
ZABNER	Dawid	1924	72
APELSZTAJN	Estera	1917	72
CUKIERMAN	Malta	1916	72
CYMERMAN	Malka	1917	72
FRIDENSON	Gitla	1922	72
GUTMAN	Hinda	1923	72
GOLDFARB	Sura	1918	72
GRYNBAUM	Ita	1923	72
GUTMAN	Fajga	1917	72
HERBLUM	Maria	1919	72
HIMELGRYN	Chaja	1912	72
LEWKOWICZ	Romana	1921	72
LEWKOWICZ	Malwina	1924	72
LUSTMAN	Fajga	1925	72
RABINOWICZ	Fajga	1920	72
SZACHTER	Ira	1924	72

SZTARKMAN	Chawa	1919	72
SZTARKMAN	Szajndla	1916	72
WAJCHENDLER	Malta	1922	72
WAJCHENDLER	Sura	1909	72
ZACHCINSKA	Jochweta	1912	72
ZABNER	Estera	1900	72
TENENBAUM	Chaim	1922	72
KOPF	Toba	1921	72
FROJMAN	Rywka	1921	72
BROMBERGER	Czeslawa	1923	72
SZTAJMAN	Toba	1917	72
MANELA	Rachela	1915	72
MANGARTEN	Chawa		72
LUSTMAN	Estera	1919	72
KUMEC	Pesa	1920	72
KLAJMINC	Hinda	1919	72
GEDALOWICZ	Ruchla	1915	72
GROJECKA	Rachela	1922	72
GRABSKA	Szyfra	1922	72
BINSZTOK	Mindla	1908	72
AJZENMAN	Ruchla		72
ABRAMOWICZ	Chana	1921	72
DZIADEK	Tauba	1917	72
ERLICH	Chana	1921	72
LEWENSON	Bela	1919	72
LUSTMAN	Rywka		72
ZELCER	Matla	1917	72
KLAJMAN	Perla	1900	73
MANELA	Laja	1925	73
ERLICHSON	Gucia	1926	73
ERLICHSON	Szajndla	1920	73
KESTENBERG	Mirla		73
KESTENBERG	Syma		73

LIPSTER	Golda	1919	73
LIPSTER	Joachima		73
KURTA	Lea	1918	73
KURTA	Lejzor	1909	73
KRAMARZ	Jakub	1906	73
KAC	Jankiel	1911	73
LEWENSON	Fiszel	1912	73
FRENKIEL	Majer	1896	73
RABINOWICZ	Lejbus	1910	73
HERBLUM	Herszek	1911	73
BLUM	Laja	1909	73
WAJNBERG	Tonia	1898	73
LEWENTON	Pola	1910	73
FINKIELSZTAJN	Dora	1920	73
RUBINSZTAJN	Malka	1924	73
GOTLIB	Lejbus	1910	73
KORENBLIT	Froim		73
KAMINER	Moszek	1919	73
HONIGMAN	Fiszek		73
GRYNBAUM	Ksyl	1919	73
CYTRYN	Dawid	1924	73
DAB	Dawid	1911	73
RUBINSZTAJN	Chuna	1918	73
RUBINSZTAJN	Herszek	1925	73
RUBINSZTAJN	Josef	1895	73
BINSZTOK	Majlech	1897	73
HERBLUM	Alter		73
GARBER	Mendel	1928	73
LUBKA	Pinkus	1913	73
ZYLBERSZTAJN	Icek		73
NUDELMAN	Szmul-Nuta	1913	73
KALIWASER	Abram	1902	73
SZTARKMAN	Ojzer	1907	73

WILCZEK	Hersz	1927	73
SZORFARC	Izrael	1894	73
MINCBERG	Nechemiasz	1925	73
LACHTYNGIER	Abram	1908	73
KOGUT	Moszek	1900	73
HERBLUM	Moszek	1916	73
HERBLUM	Jankiel	1890	73
GOLDBERG	Berek	1893	73
BINSZTOK	Josek	1908	73
HIMELGRYN	Chaim	1912	73
ZELCER	Sura	1907	73
WILCZEK	Ita	1922	73
TENCER	Gitla	1914	73
RABINOWICZ	Rywka	1922	73
MANGARTEN	Malka-Hinda	1892	73
KORENWASER	Hinda	1926	73
KAHAN	Malka	1921	73
AJZENMAN	Pola	1913	73
FRANKFURT	Roma	1920	73
SZNAJDERMAN	Fryda	1920	73
CUKIER	Szyfra	1913	73
BARANEK	Dobra	1902	73
GUTERMAN	Estera	1903	73
KENIGSZTAJN	Bela	1910	73
KOMOROWSKA	Chana	1898	73
LIPSZTAJN	Gucia	1925	73
RUBINSZTAJN	Ita	1923	73
ROZENBLAT	Regina	1918	73
SZTULMAN	Mindla	1916	73
WINOGRAD	Sura	1899	73
WAJNTRAUB	Rywka	1922	73
WARSZAWSKA	Hinda	1915	73
WARSZAWSKA	Hinda	1913	73

ZELCER	Ruchla	1923	73
BIRENCWAJG	Basia	1908	73
TAUBER	Josef	1922	73
ZABNER	Josef	1900	73
HERBLUM	Majer	1914	73
FINKLER	Berek	1923	73
ADLER	Maria	1912	73
ADLER	Esfira	1915	73
ADLER	Estera	1915	73
ADLER	Mojzesz	1917	73
BALTER	Chana	1922	73
BIRENCWAJG	Laja	1908	73
BIRENCWAJG	Sura	1914	74
FAJNTUCH	Chaja	1920	74
HERBLUM	Szajndla	1920	74
LAKS	Anna	1922	74
LAKS	Rozalia	1924	74
MINCBERG	Machcia	1895	74
MINCBERG	Rywka	1924	74
NOSER	Chana	1909	74
OLLMER	Luba	1908	74
RUBINSZTAJN	Ita	1924	74
RUBINSZTAJN	Fajga	1925	74
RUBINSZTAJN	Rachela	1905	74
SZAFIR	Alta	1924	74
SZARFARC	Bela	1910	74
SZPIRO	Ruta	1927	74
TENCER	Rojza	1898	74
TENCER	Chana	1928	74
TENCER	Tauba	1926	74
WOLFOWICZ	Blima	1896	74
WOLFOWICZ	Sura	1910	74
WILCZEK	Ruchla	1904	74

ZYNGER	Perla	1909	74
EJNESMAN	Chaim	1922	74
EJNESMAN	Izrael	1916	74
GOLDBERG	Moszek	1910	74
LAKS	Izak	1895	74
ROZENBERG	Chaim	1926	74
RUBINSZTAJN	Jankiel	1905	74
WILENCZYK	Pinkus	1926	74
WOLFOWICZ	Rachmil	1911	74
ZYLBERBERG	Mania	1926	74
SZCZESLIWA	Rajzla		74
RUBINSZTAJN	Ruchla	1907	74
LANGER	Ruchla	1916	74
ROTSZTAJN	Zelda	1923	74
LEWENSON	Miriam	1921	74
WAJZER	Rywka	1894	74
SZACHTER	Rywka	1907	74
SZACHTER	Ruchla	1925	74
KIERSZENBLUM	Lola	1928	74
MANDELZYS	Estera	1921	74
LOMSKA	Halina	1927	74
NANMAN	Zelda	1894	74
EJNESMAN	Rywka	1917	74
EJNESMAN	Ruchla	1904	74
LAKS	Regina	1926	74
KAC	Brucha	1915	74
BROMBERGER	Teresa	1912	74
BERGSON	Chawa	1920	74
SZTAJNHART	Sura	1921	74
SZTRAJTMAN	Majlech	1894	74
WAJNSZTOK	Josek	1897	74
NAGIEL	Lejbus	1901	74
HERBLUM	Moszek	1915	74

WILCZEK	Jeremiasz	1900	74
WILCZEK	Abram	1922	74
NOWER	Henryk	1903	74
TENCER	Mojzesz	1902	74
KOGUT	Chaim	1919	74
LINDZEN	Azryl	1910	74
LANGLEBEN	Szaja	1900	74
SZCZESLIWY	Szmul	1920	74
RAUF	Icchok	1909	74
ROZENDORN	Szaja	1903	74
SZARFARC	Szaja	1908	74
RUBINSON	Bajrech	1894	74
LERMAN	Chil	1895	74
ZABNER	Josek	1897	74
LEWENSON	Jeremiasz	1893	74
MELCER	Rafal	1915	74
SZUCHT	Josek	1908	74
FELDBERG	Symcha	1917	74
TENENBAUM	Majer		74
SZPIRO	Lejb		74
HERBLUM	Dawid		74
CYMERMAN	Hersz-Abram		74
GOTLIB	Chaim		74
BIRENBAUM	Chaim		74
LEJBMAN	Kielman	1890	74
GOLDGRUB	Chaim	1914	74
DYNER	Abram	1901	74
TOJTER	Chaim	1906	74
WAJCHENDLER	Chaim	1927	74
SZACHTER	Nusyn	1895	74
MEKLER	Lejzor		75
KLAJMAN	Dawid		75
LIPA	Froim		75

KARP	Chaskiel	1924	75
WATMAN	Hersz		75
KESTENBERG	Hanka	1924	75
MANELA	Symcha-Majer		75
HERLING	Towia		75
CISLOWSKI	Dawid		75
WIGDOROWICZ	Hejnoch		75
GROSMAN	Szmul-Nuta		75
ERLICHMAN	Icek		75
BINSZTOK	Majer		75
FISZ	Szlama		75
WAJSBERG	Dawid		75
RABINOWICZ	Abram		75
EJNESMAN	Laja		75
WOLFOWICZ	Rywka		75
BLUM	Marceli		75
FAJGELBAUM	Heniek		75
WATMAN	Abram-Herz		75
WALMAN	Abram-Herz		75
TENENBAUM	Majer		75
SZWARCHAR	Aron		75
ZYLBERBERG	Icek		75

[Page 76 - German]

Anordnung!

In letzter Zeit wurde wiederholt festgestellt, dass Juden am Tage und auch nachts mit und ohne Begleitung von Werkschutzleuten die Julaga verlassen und sich nach Starachowice oder Wierbznik begeben haben.

Zwischen den Polizeidienststellen und der Abwehrstelle wurde folgende Vereinbarung getroffen:

1.) Jeder Jude, der das Lager verlässt und nach Starachowice bzw. Wierbznik will, muss im Besitz einer Bescheinigung sein, die von der Abwehrstelle erstellt und von den Polizeidienststellen abgezeichnet sein muss.

2.) Jeder Jude, der ausserhalb des Lagers oder in der Stadt angetroffen wird, ohne im Besitz dieser Bescheinigung zu sein, wird erschossen.

Der Abwehrbeauftragte!

Starachowice, den 14.4.1943
Bg./Wö.

Verteiler:
1x Julag I
5x " II
1x Akte

Zarządzenie!

Stwierdzono w ostatnim czasie kilkakrotnie, iż żydzi opuszczają w dzień oraz w nocy w otoczeniu wzgl. bez nadzoru wartowników ochrony fabrycznej bozy żydowskie, w celu udania się do Starachowic oraz do Wierzbnik

Pomiędzy posterunkami policji oraz ochroną fabryczną zawarte zostało następujące porozumienie:

1) Każdy żyd, opuszczający obóz i udający się do Wierzbnika wzgl. Starachowic, posiadać musi poświadczenie Ochrony Fabrycznej upełnomocnione przez władze policyjne.

2) Każdy żyd, napotkany poza obozem wzgl. w mieście bez wyżej wymienionego zaświadczenia, będzie zastrzelony.

Starachowice, dnia 14.4.1943

Kierownik Ochrony Fabrycznej

[Page 77 - German]

List of names of Jews who came from Krakow on February 18th, 1943

Please note that the page numbers below refer to the page numbers of the original Yizkor book, not the page numbers in this translation.

Go to the end of the book for the Name Index of this translation pagination.

Family name	First name(s)	Remarks	Year of birth	Page
MLYNARSKI	Marian		1909	77
MYLNARSKIA	Dawid		1918	77
KOPHOLZ	Lothar		1924	77
OGOREK	Samuel		1906	77
SZAFIRMAN	Lejb		1901	77
FLAMM	Romana		1909	77
HEUBLUM	Josef		1910	77
RAJCH	Jakub		1922	77
BORGER	Majer		1925	77
BORGER	Lipek		1924	77
FUKS	Abram		1925	77
HERSZKOWICZ	Moniek		1922	77
HOLENDER	Jakub		1928	77
HOLENDER	Benoa		1922	77
BLUTNER	Izak		1923	77
INFELD	Mozes		1924	77
SZPILMAN	Markus		1915	77
WOLFAJLER	Bernard		1898	77
WIEZA	Icek		1926	77
WINTERFELD	Dawid		1908	77
KELER	Fryderyk		1911	77
JUKIER	Jakub		1921	77
BLANDER	Szymon		1920	77
KURZ	Henryk		1926	77

JUKIER	Chaskiel	1900	77
GOLDWASSER	Hersz	1920	77
PINTER	Mendel	1910	77
GRYNSZPAN	Jakub	1925	77
SZLIWOWIC	Dawid	1906	77
ABSFELD	Josef	1913	77
BANGER	Symcha	1899	77
KLAJN	Henryk	1899	77
RAJEWICZ	Lipa	1926	77
HALBERSZTADT	Osjasz	1923	77
LIPICKI	Szapsza	1898	77
FISZBAJN	Fajwel	1900	77
SZTAJN	Szlama	1922	77
FISZBAJN	Moniek	1923	77
MAJBRUCH	Majer	1908	77
FAJRAJZEN	Josek	1905	77
LIBERMAN	Icek	1925	77
MLYNARSKI	Mendel	1909	77
MYLNARSKI	Rafal I	1905	77
MYLANRSKI	Rafal II	1917	77
BOCHENEK	Abraham	1908	77
LEMPEL	Wilhelm	1897	77
BOCHENEK	Leon	1899	77
ABRAHAM	Ernst	1922	77
FLANCGRABEN	Lazar	1921	77
ROZMARYN	Henryk	1924	77
RAUSCH	Szymon	1926	77
GRYNBERG	Julian	1915	77
GRYNBERG	Alfred	1915	77
TRACHMAN	Abram	1919	77
CUKIERMAN	Mojzesz	1927	77
KLUGER	Jakub	1912	77
KLUGER	Szymon	1910	77

MLYNARSKI	Icek	1925	77
WAJTZENBLUM	Mozes	1899	77
SZNAJDER	Hermann	1897	77
SZNAJDER	Moszel	1926	77
WORCMAN	Josef	1923	77
FRYDRYCH	Majlech	1913	77
FRYDRYCH	Josef	1916	77
WULFF	Pinkus	1907	77
HEFTER	Boruch	1925	77
WAJCMAN	Eliasz	1923	77
BLAT	Majlech	1921	77
LEMPEL	Ferdynand	1926	77
ZYLBERLUST	Arnold	1920	77
BECK	Ossjasz	1923	77
FRYDLANT	Isser	1924	77
CUKIERMAN	Henoch	1912	77
CUKIERMAN	Icek	1916	77
GRYNER	Pinkus	1890	78
ARONOWIC	Dawid	1908	78
WERTAL	Hirsz	1907	78
LAZARUS	Kurt	1912	78
KURZ	Leon	1895	78
GOLDSTOFF	Kiwa	1899	78
ENGLENDER	Aleksander	1923	78
SZPIRO	Szymon	1921	78

List of male workers who came from Radom on October 10th, 1943

Family name	First name(s)	Remarks	Year of birth	Page
KOSZER	Szmul		1922	78

KOSZER	Abram	1920	78
KOSZER	Majer	1905	78
DRESNER	Calel	1920	78
ROSNER	Gerszon	1910	78
WAJCHER	Samuel	1925	78
PELCYK	Jakob	1926	78
WOLF	Dawid	1898	78
WOLF	Lejb	1923	78
BACHNER	Ferdynand	1898	78
ELMAN	Abraham	1923	78
ELMAN	Izak	1905	78
TAUB	Dawid	1924	78

List of male workers
who came from Radom on October 10th, 1943

Please note that the page numbers below refer to the page numbers of the original Yizkor book, not the page numbers in this translation.

Go to the end of the book for the Name Index of this translation pagination.

Family name	First name(s)	Remarks	Year of birth	Page
APFELBAUM	Wolf		1919	78
BLAJWAJS	Hersz		1898	78
BEJGEL	Josek		1916	78
BERKOWICZ	Icek		1903	78
BLAT	Benek		1904	78
BRYT	Pinkus		1903	78
BIALSKI	Chil		1903	78
DANCYGER	Lejb		1919	78
DZIEWIECKI	Moszek		1912	78
EKSELMAN	Jakob		1921	78
FEDERMAN	Herszek		1919	78
FRYDMAN	Lejbus		1921	78
FRYDMAN	Natan		1915	78
GLIKSZTAJN	Rywan		1874	78
GELIEBTER	Chaim		1926	78
GLINKTEWICZ	Moszek		1917	78
GUTMAN	Majer		1909	78
HOLEMAN	Wolf		1913	78
JAMER	Herszek		1894	78
JOSKOWICZ	Abram		1925	78
KOPER	Aron		1913	78
KORMAN	Mojzesz		1918	78
KUPERSZMIDT	Szmul		1900	78
KARAFIOL	Pinkus		1901	78

KIERSZENBLAT	Szlama	1906	78
KIEPS	Judka	1909	78
KLEINBAUM	Pinkus	1924	78
KLEINMAN	Moszek	1894	78
KLEINMAN	Szyja	1926	78
KIERSZENBAUM	Naftali Perec	1913	78
MANDELZYS	Pinkus	1910	78
MANDELBAUM	Symcha	1927	78
NAJMAN	Nachemia	1928	78
NAJFELD	Nuchym	1889	78
NISSENBAUM	Aria	1908	78
OSOB	Mordka	1924	78
PAJAK	Hersz	1884	79
PUTERMAN	Pejsach	1911	79
RAFELD	Gabriel	1924	79
RAJCHMAN	Lewi	1883	79
RAPAPORT	Josek	1923	79
ROZWADOWSKI	Chaim	1902	79
SZAFIR	Froim	1885	79
SZAJNBAUM	Fajwel	1901	79
SZWA REBERG	Motek	1890	79
TAJTELBAUM	Szaja	1919	79
WAJCMAN	Herszek	1897	79
WYSZYNSKI	Jakob	1904	79
WOLKOWICZ	Ignacy	1919	79
WODKA	Mojzesz	1897	79
WROBLEWSKI	Lejb	1900	79
WAJNBERG	Moszek	1909	79
WAJCH	Josek	1921	79
ZYSKIND	Pinkus	1888	79
ZYLBER	Juda	1907	79
SZMUKLER	Moszek		79
WEISFOGEL			79

BRESLAUER	Beniamin			79
APFELBAUM	Felicja		1921	79
BERGEISEN	Mindla		1923	79
CWAJGENBERG	Rajzla		1911	79
DANCYGER	Salomea		1925	79
DEN	Idesa		1899	79
FINKIELSZTAJN	Sura Rywka		1893	79
GOLDSZLEGER	Eta		1894	79
HOCH	Sura		1893	79
HOROWICZ	Stefa		1920	79
HELLER	Regina		1920	79
KESTENBERG	Hindla		1921	79
KUPERSZMIDT	Rachela		1925	79
KUPERSZMIDT	Fajga		1923	79
KLEINMAN	Hanka		1922	79
KARAFIOL	Frania		1927	79
KARAFIOL	Fajga		1899	79
PERCOWICZ	Mania		1925	79
PISKORZ	Mindla		1920	79
POMERANIEC	Mina		1907	79
ROZENKRANC	Chana		1899	79
SZTAJMAN	Syma		1907	79
TUREK	Alta Cypora		1904	79
WOLKOWICZ	Pelagia		1920	79
WROBLEWSKA	Ajdla		1907	79
WERBER	Laja		1918	79
WEISGOGEL	Luba		1923	79
PUTERMAN	Icek	Child	1935	79
WAKSBERG	Jacheta	Child		79
TAJTELBAUM	Bajla	Child		79
KARAFIOL	Bronia	Child		79
KOPER	Ita	Child		79

[Page 80 - German]

List of Jews who arrived on September 16th, 1943 from Mokoszyn

Please note that the page numbers below refer to the page numbers of the original Yizkor book, not the page numbers in this translation.

Go to the end of the book for the Name Index of this translation pagination.

Family name	First name(s)	Remarks	Year of birth	Page
ANIELEWICZ	Salomon		1915	80
BRYKS	Icek		1920	80
BAUM	Hersz		1893	80
BLOCH	Jakub		1911	80
CUKIER	Moszek		1907	80
ERMAN	Majer		1923	80
ERMAN	Bencjan		1910	80
FORTGANG	Gabriel		1907	80
FLIGIELMAN	Symcha		1926	80
FLAMELBAUM	Josek		1914	80
FRANDENRAJCH	Aria		1915	80
GLASMAN	Rafal		1888	80
GLESER	Jakub		1902	80
GOLDSZTAJN	Mojzesa		1913	80
GLAT	Pinkus		1923	80
GLAT	Jakub		1916	80
GOLDMAN	Lejb		1893	80
GOLDSZTAJN	Zelman		1925	80
GOLDMAN	Mojzesz		1913	80
KRAJNDELS	Pinkus		1923	80
KRAJNDELS	Abram		1920	80
KAZIMIERSKI	Jonatan		1918	80
KAPLANSKI	Gerszon		1924	80
KARMESER	Moszek		1914	80

KARMESER	Szlama	1919	80
LUSTMAN	Majer	1924	80
LANGER	Chaskiel	1913	80
ORLEAN	Chaim	1919	80
ORENSZTAJN	Liber	1911	80
PECZYNA	Chil	1908	80
ROTENBERG	Judka	1917	80
SZYMKIEWICZ	Ajzyk	1928	80
SZRAJBMAN	Liber	1925	80
SYNAJ	Szmul	1920	80
SZWARC	Gedel	1922	80
SZAJNWALD	Alter	1924	80
WAJNBERG	Sucher	1912	80
WATMAN	Hersz	1917	80
WATMAN	Mojzesz	1922	80
WAJNBERG	Moszek	1927	80
ZYNGER	Froim	1922	80
ZYLBERMAN	Daniel	1921	80
ZYLBERSZTAJN	Jankiel	1923	80
SZULMAN	Salek	1936	80
BORENSZTAJN	Szajndla	1913	80
BRYKS	Kajla	1923	80
CUKIER	Czesia	1915	80
GRYNBERG	Tauba	1925	80
GRYNBERG	Zysla	1910	80
GROSMAN	Toba	1913	80
GOLDWASER	Halina	1924	80
HERCBERG	Laja	1881	80
KAC	Syma	1926	80
MANDELBAUM	Jadzia	1918	80
MALICKA	Bajla	1912	80
MUNK	Bela	1923	80
ROZENBERG	Matla	1910	80

SZAFRAN	Hela	1915	80
SYNAJ	Sara	1925	80
SYNAJ	Minia	1924	80
SAMBORSKA	Cesia	1920	80
SYNAJ	Estera	1906	80
SZULDMAN	Bajla	1907	80
SZTERENLICHT	Guta	1919	80
WAJNBERG	Estera	1909	80
WAJSROZEN	Malka	1924	80
ZALCMAN	Chana	1918	80
ZAUBERMAN	Matla	1901	80

[Page 81 - German]

List of Jews who came to the camp on September 5th (from Tomaszów)

Please note that the page numbers below refer to the page numbers of the original Yizkor book, not the page numbers in this translation.

Go to the end of the book for the Name Index of this translation pagination.

Family name	First name(s)	Remarks	Year of birth	Page
AJZELSZTAJN	Grojnym		1904	81
ASSJA	Wolf		1912	81
ANTMAN	Martin		1920	81
AJZENBERG	Majer		1917	81
AJZENBERG	Lejzor		1904	81
BULWA	Jakob		1925	81
BLUMENSZTAJN	Josek		1920	81
BOGDANSKI	Abram		1910	81
CYGIELMAN	Majer		1922	81
CURLING	Chaskiel		1922	81
CZOSNIAK	Szansze		1913	81
CYMBERKNOPFT	Hersz		1901	81
FLAMELBAUM	Chaim		1920	81
GROSSMAN	Mendel		1910	81
GRYNSZPAN	Abram		1907	81
GRYNFARB	Icek		1910	81
GOLDKRANC	Jehuda		1912	81
GOMOLINSKI	Szaja		1907	81
GINCBERG	Leon		1893	81
GOLDBERG	Mendel		1906	81
GERSZTAJN	Lejbus		1897	81
HOCH	Moszek		1920	81
HEJNOCHOWICZ	Abram		1903	81
IGIELMAN	Pinkus		1920	81

KLINGERMAN	Moszek	1910	81
KURC	Chaim	1894	81
KOHN	Chaim	1883	81
JAKUBOWICZ	Abram	1926	81
KOZUSZEK	Szmul	1905	81
LEGA	Eliasz	1909	81
LASKASKI	Szmul	1927	81
MUSZKAT	Witold	1896	81
MELDUNG	Szmul	1902	81
NEUSTEMPEL	Szmul	1925	81
OLSZAK	Wolf	1900	81
ROZEN	Majlech	1919	81
RUBINSZTAJN	Abram	1902	81
ROZENBLUM	Tobiasz	1906	81
RABINOWICZ	Lejbus	1922	81
SZMUCIG	Abram	1893	81
SZWARC	Szmul	1920	81
SZTELER	Matys	1903	81
SALEM	Dawid	1916	81
SZTAJNHORN	Symcha	1914	81
TEITELBAUM	Jakob	1914	81
TEITELBAUM	Josef	1907	81
USZEROWICZ	Hejnoch	1914	81
WEINRYCH	Mordka	1924	81
ZONABEND	Moszek	1907	81
ASSJA	Chana	1912	81
GERSZTAJN	Kosia	1924	81
GRYNSZPAN	Rywka	1914	81
GRYNFARB	Estera	1915	81
GROSSMAN	Rajzla	1908	81
MELDUNG	Ruchla	1906	81
ROZENBLUM	Rozia	1914	81
SZETTER	Fajga	1910	81

SZMUCIG	Debora		1918	81
SZEMPEK	Pola		1909	81
ASSJA	Fania	Child	1931	81
GROSSMAN	Tola	Child	1938	81
GRYNSZPAN	Ruta	Child	1936	81
GRYNFARB	Jakob	Child	1943	81
SZETTER	Sara	Child	1933	81
SZETTER	Izaak	Child	1940	81
SZCZUPAK	Madzia	Child	1938	81

[Page 82 - German]

List of male workers who came from Wolanów on July 12th, 1943

Please note that the page numbers below refer to the page numbers of the original Yizkor book, not the page numbers in this translation.

Go to the end of the book for the Name Index of this translation pagination.

Family name	First name(s)	Remarks	Year of birth	Page
ADLER	Jakub Szmul		1920	82
AJZENBERG	Wolf		1915	82
AJZENMESSER	Abram		1914	82
AJZENMESSER	Dawid		1922	82
AKIERMAN	Pejsach		1909	82
BAMEL	Szmul		1913	82
BERKOWICZ	Beniamin		1908	82
BERKOWICZ	Dawid		1910	82
BERKOWICZ	Szymon		1894	82
BERNHOLC	Josek		1913	82
BISTER	Mendel		1924	82
BLACARZ	Izrael		1916	82
BLATMAN	Chil		1915	82
BLATMAN	Hersz		1898	82
BLUMENFARB	Berek		1896	82
BLUMENFARB	Lejzor		1914	82
BOJMAN	Abram		1904	82
BOJMAN	Majer		1915	82
BOJMAN	Szyja		1893	82
BOJMAN	Moszek		1910	82
CEDER	Dawid		1925	82
DABAK	Hejnoch		1900	82
DYMENT	Abram		1919	82
FELDSZTAJN	Motel		1927	82
FISZBAUM	Dawid		1919	82
FLAJSZER	Chaim		1911	82

FRUKENBERG	Motek	1913	82
FRYDMAN	Abram	1900	82
FRYDMAN	Chaim	1922	82
GELBERG	Szaja	1900	82
GISSER	Moszek	1915	82
GLIKSMAN	Dawid	1922	82
GOLDBERG	Naftali	1915	82
GOLDBERG	Izrael	1925	82
GOLDBERG	Mordka	1898	82
GOLCZEWSKI	Chaim	1926	82
GOLCZEWSKI	Lejzor	1926	82
GOLCZEWSKI	Szmul	1921	82
GRYCMAN	Samson	1916	82
GRYNBERG	Rachmil	1913	82
GUT	Jankiel	1903	82
GUTMAN	Abram	1917	82
HABERBERG	Izak	1908	82
HABERBERG	Icek	1924	82
HERSZENFUS	Abram	1924	82
HERSZT	Szyja	1915	82
HOCH	Jozel	1897	82
HOCHENBAUM	Icek	1925	82
HONIGSZTOK	Izrael	1902	82
JERUCHIM	Moszek	1927	82
KAUFMAN	Berek	1915	82
KESTENBERG	Izrael	1924	82
KIERZENBAUM	Chaim	1898	82
KLTUN	Beniamin	1921	82
KOPERWAS	Szyja	1908	82
KOPERWAS	Mordka	1909	82
KORMAN	Majer Ela	1922	82
KORMAN	Izrael	1904	82
KRYGER	Jakub	1926	82

KUNOWSKI	Abram	1918	82
KUNOWSKI	Moszek	1910	82
KUNOWSKI	Szmul	1919	82
KUNOWSKI	Jankiel	1918	82
KURLENDER	Ela	1924	82
LAJZEROWICZ	Mordka	1907	82
LEDERMAN	Lejbus	1903	82
LEWENTAL	Abram	1924	82
LEWENTAL	Izrael	1919	82
LEWENTAL	Jankiel	1926	82
LEWENTAL	Moszek	1922	82
LICHTENSZTAJN	Izrael	1922	82
LICHTENSZTAJN	Josef	1905	82
LIBERMAN	Chaim	1920	82
LINDERBAUM	Josek	1896	82
LINDERBAUM	Szulim	1926	82
LEGA	Moszek	1912	82
LEGA	Majlech	1914	83
LEGA	Chil	1919	83
MALACH	Motek	1908	83
MARGULIS	Icek	1895	83
MARGULIS	Jakub	1926	83
MERKER	Josef	1906	83
NAJDYK	Mordka	1902	83
NISENBAUM	Szlama	1925	83
PASTERNAK	Nachman	1921	83
PATRON	Majer	1914	83
PERCOWICZ	Chaim	1911	83
PIKIER	Rachmil	1925	83
RAPAPORT	Moszek	1927	83
RODBARD	Berek	1924	83
ROZENCWAJG	Lejbus	1911	83
ROZENCWAJG	Abram	1879	83

ROZENSZTAJN	Icek	1882	83
STAROWIESZCZYK	Izrael	1925	83
SZAJNFELD	Moszek	1895	83
SZER	Natan	1908	83
SZLIKIER	Moszek	1909	83
SZPAJZMAN	Gedala	1914	83
SZPIGIEL	Mojzesz	1926	83
SZPIRO	Jankiel	1917	83
SZWICER	Abram	1907	83
TENENBAUM	Jonas	1923	83
TENENBAUM	Mordka	1918	83
TENENBAUM	Pejsach	1920	83
TUCHMAN	Abram	1890	83
TYSZMAN	Nachman	1925	83
TYSZLEN	Izrael	1912	83
TYTELMAN	Chaim	1907	83
WARCKI	Pinkus	1904	83
WAJMAN	Moszek	1923	83
WAJNBERG	Szmul	1903	83
WAJNTRAUB	Josek	1911	83
WAKSBERG	Szmul	1918	83
WAKSBERG	Aron	1895	83
WAKSBERG	Majer	1923	83
WAKSMAN	Chaim	1922	83
WARMAN	Chaim	1912	83
WOLFOWICZ	Mendel	1920	83
ZALCBERG	Wolf	1914	83
ZALCBERG	Chaim	1914	83
KIERSZENBAUM	Mordka	1914	83
KIERSZENBLAT	Chaim	1906	83
WOLANOW			83
WAKSBERG	Fajwek	1937	83
WAJNTRAUB	Cilek	1939	83

PATRON	Herszek	1941	83
TUCHMAN	Rafal	1929	83
KIERSZENBLAT	Abram	1927	83
WAJNBERG	Mendel	1927	83
EN SHRDL CMFWY VBG		1927	83
KOPERWAS	Nuta	1929	83
WAKSMAN	Icek	1930	83
LICHTENSZTAJN	Gedala	1926	83
WAKSBERG	Jukiel	1927	83
RUBINSZTAJN	Dawid	1929	83
KORMAN	Herszek	1928	83
PILICER	Blima	1928	83
CUKIER	Jakub	1928	83
KORMAN	Pinia	1930	83
LICHTENSZTAJN	Icek	1936	83
BERKOWICZ	Moszek	1927	83
WAKSBERG	Uryn	1929	83
MALACH	Abram	1933	83
MALACH	Chaim	1930	83
MALACH	Jenta	1938	83
CERLEWICZ	Chaja	1933	83
CERELEWICZ	Szajndla	1933	83
CERELEWICZ	Rywka	1940	83
BUMENFARB	Chana	1941	83
KOPERWAS	Jankiel	1937	83
KOPERWAS	Cela	1933	83
WAJNTRAUB	Hilek	1939	83
WARSZAWSKA	Ewa	1937	83
SZACHTER			83
WAKSMAN	Lusia		83
BOJMAN	Dwojra		83

Photograph Captions

Please Note: Some of the photos were not included in this English translation of the book. The page numbers in the list below refer to the original Hebrew and Yiddish book.

The original book can be found at:

https://digitalcollections.nypl.org/search/index?utf8=%E2%9C%93&keywords=wierzbnik

Or:

https://www.yiddishbookcenter.org/search?search_api_views_fulltext=wierzbnik&Submit+search=&restrict

When you download the PDF of the original book, you will notice the original page numbers as those below under the word "Page". There are also pages of the PDF, starting with 1. We refer to this numbering as "scan number." Note that after book page number 1, that the scan page number is 32 more than the book page number. This might be helpful when searching for images.

Page	Caption
IX	A general view of the Rynek (town square), in the direction of Kościółna Street
XII	Those active in the book committee in Israel. Standing from right: Malka Weisbloom, Pinchas Hochmitz, Reuven Lis-Shuali, Yeshaya Dekel-Dar Kesler, Chana Tantzer, Rivka Greenberg (Minzberg). Seated from right to left: Menachem Minzberg, Moshe Sali, Simcha Minzberg, Yerachmiel Singer, Menachem Feigenbaum, Tzvi Unger
XIV	Winter in the town
XV	Book committee in Toronto (Canada) Standing from the right: B. Zukerman, G. Rosenwald, A. Zukerman, Leibel Rabinowitz, Hershel Tennenbaum, Max Naiman. Seated from the right: Chana Naiman, Tova Wolfowitz, Esther Zukerman
XVI	The book committee in the United States. Standing right to left: Motel Hilf, Yaakov Katz, Yerachmiel Naiman. Seated from the right: Leibish Herblum, Tzvi Morgenstern
XVII	Editorial Board Right to left: Moshe Sali-Kerberl, Simcha Minzberg, Yerachmiel Zinger, Tzvi Feigenbaum
XX - XXI	Map of the town; Prepared by Sara Postawski Steinhart **Ghetto Streets:** **Kilinskiego, Niska Wysoka, Rynek – the sidewalk – from the end of Wysoka to the end of Niska;** **Krotka, Kolejowa, Radoszewskigo to the cemetary, the alley from Kolejowa to the house of Mermel Dreksler; Ilzecka, Bodzina to the plywood factory.**
1	At the memorial ceremony for the martyrs of our town, held in Tel Aviv. Sitting right to left: Tzvi Feigenbaum, Hershel Weiser, Moshe Sali, Simcha Minzberg, Y. Dreksler-Dekel, Malka Weisbloom, and Avraham Sheiner. {sign at the top: The Yizkor Book Initiative. Remember, and do not forget.} {Sign at the bottom: May the people of Israel remember the martyrs of Starachowice-Wierzbnik who died in sanctification of the Divine Name. Their memory will never be forgotten from our midst.}
2	The Bridge of the Kamienna River

3	At the memorial gathering dedicated to the publication of the book. Right to left: Tzvi Feigenbaum, Moshe Sali (speaking), Rabbi Eidelman, Simcha Minzberg, and Yerachmiel (Rumek) Singer {Note: Same signs as on page 1}
4	Simcha Minzberg Kolejowa Street in Wierzbnik
5	The lumber factory of the Lichtensztajn family
6	Daniel Lichtensztajn Halcia Moshe Pinchas Lichtensztajn
7	Yosef Reuven Lichtensztajn Avraham Lichtensztajn The "Tartak" (sawmill)
8	Piłsudskiego Street in Wierzbnik
15	Wierzbnik residents during the winter, before the disaster struck
16	Inscription on top photo: Wierzbnik, girls of Agudat Israel, 5633 Av (summer 1933) Bottom photo: Bnot Yaakov
17	Yaakov Katz
21	Yerachmiel Zinger
22	The lumber factory of the Lichtensztajn family
24	A typical Jewish house in Wierzbnik. Mordechai Sztarkman (Michlower) next to his house
25	Inscription on photo: Wierzbnik, 1/1 1934. To the Friedman family on the occasion of their *aliya* to the Land of Israel
26	Brit Hachayal (Covenant of the Soldiers) in Wierzbnik in 1938: Godel Kadiszowicz, Shlomo Drajnodel, Noach Fried, Gershon Rozenwald, Mordechai Maslowicz, Leo Zulcer, Avraham Nisker
27	Bnot Agudat Israel (Agudat Israel Girls). Standing right to left: Weizer, Cohen, Sheindel Herblum, Tova Cohen, Dina Rabinowicz, Rivka Przyticka, Komec, Dvora Tenenbaum. Seated from the right: Rabinowicz, Malka Kornwaser, in the center, the teacher Lea Weintraub.
28	Sledding next to the railway station.
30	Elementary school class in Wierzbnik with the teacher.
32	Moshe Sali (Kerbel)
34	Pioneering youth in Wierzbnik in 1938, during the visit of Moshe Sali (Kerbel), who is standing, first on the left.
35	Students of the public school in Wierzbnik (Powszechna)
36	Sawmill (Tartak)
38	Tzvi Feigenbaum
47	The Mizrachi School in 1932. Standing from left to right: The teacher Lipsky, Moshe Szeiner, Yosel Jabner, Kornwasser, Shmuel Weisbloom, Shmuel Tennenbaum, Erlichman, Tennenbaum, Y. Szeiner, M. Neiman, Rotbard, Lipsztejn, Y. Kerbel, Fiszman, Kroizman, Ch. Tennenbaum, Z. Neiman, V. Kelman, Drajnwodel, Sh. Weisbloom
48	The committee for Young Agudat Israel. Right to left: Leibish the son of Reb Shlomo Morgensztern, Leibel Rabinowicz, Tzvi Morgensztern, Abba Komec, Mordechai Zeev Brodbaker
49	Leadership of the Young Agudat Israel movement. Right to left: Moshe Kornwasser, Zisman Cytrynbaum, Tzvi Morgensztern, Shmuel Weizer, Moshe Neiman, Shlomo Sztern
50	The teacher Elimelech and his family
57	A group of youth activists in Wierzbnik: Munik Cukerman, Chanan Rubinsztejn, Akiva Binsztok, Reuven Lis, Moshe Frimerman, and others
58	A group of Wierzbnik youth before the war
59	On an excursion outside of town

	Mendel Szif, Necha Binsztok, and Avraham Cukerman
60	The committee of "Young Hechalutz" Standing from right to left: Hertzka Kleinman, Mottel Reizman, Moshe Kerbel, Mendel Ribak Sitting: Avraham Goldsztejn, Shmuel Meir Ribak, Hershel Herszman, Reuven Lis
61	The chapter of "Young Hechalutz" in Wierzbnik in 1932 The writer of these lines is standing second from the right (in an embroidered shirt)
62	Pioneers of Wierzbnik on *hachshara* [aliya preparation) Meir Rolnicki of blessed memory, Mottel Reizman of blessed memory, Moshe Kerbel, may he live (standing at the right)
63	Wierzbnik youth in nature
65	Jewish soldiers from Wierzbnik, including Avraham Goldsztejn of blessed memory and Reuven Lis (Shuali), may he live
68	"Tarbut" School in Wierzbnik
70	"Young Hechalutz" in Wierzbnik
71	Railway station in Wierzbnik
72	Members of "Young Hechalutz" along with members of the Hama'apil Kibbutz on hachshara in our town Standing from right to left: Leibe Kroizman, Goldsztejn, Herman, Leibel Gruber, Yechiel Mor, Avraham Goldsztejn, Reuven Lis, Meir Rolnicki Sitting in the center: Yaakov Rolnicki with Mottel Reizman at far left Sitting on the floor: rightmost Avraham Manela
75	One of the Beit Yaakov classes with the teacher
76	Grade five of Beit Yaakov
78	The class of the older girls of Beit Yaakov with the teaching staff Right to left: Perl Herzog, Henia Wajntraub, Krolnik, Maslowicz, Pesia Wajnberg, Rivka Proman, Komec, Wajnberg Sitting: Esther Sztern, Reizel Morgensztern, Ita Groszenkorn, (--), center – the teacher
79	In the photo: Malka Leopold (Cohen), Malka Kornwasser, Rivka Cytryn, Bela Weizer, Markowicz, Golda and Esther Cytrynbaum
80	On the right – a teacher from Beit Yaakov. On the left – her sister
81	Maccabee soccer team of Wierzbnik
82 top	A group of youth on bicycle at a sporting competition. The photo was taken before the competition
82 bottom	One of the best Maccabee soccer teams
83 top	Maccabee soccer team
83 bottom	Purim party organized by Maccabee activists in 1933 (March 12, 1933)
86	The Gwiazda soccer team with its activists
90	A group of Beitar activists sailing on the Kamienna River. Among them: Manek Cukerman, Lea Rozenberg, Mendel Szif (--)
92	The Western Wall remains as a memorial to the greatness, glory, and holiness of Jerusalem
95	Reuven Shuali (Lis)
96	Zionist activists From right to left: Reuven Lis-Shuali, Manek Cukerman, Shmuelik Gelbard, Avraham Goldsztein, Akiva Binsztok
101	A group of youths Seated in uniform: Yosef Cytrynbaum; Standing from left to right: Fishel Hirszhorn the son of Reb Shlomo Slopia, Yoel Komec the son of Reb Moshe, Tzvi Herblum the son of Reb Gershon and Tzipora (his story is told in the chapter "Opposition and Rebelliousness" by Tzvi Feigenbaum)
105	The government Public School in Wierzbnik.
107	Matel Kenigsberg the midwife

108	The Drama Club Standing left to right: (--), Gucha Tencer, Miatek Wajgszperg; Seated from left to right: Rivka Lajbenszaft (nee Milman), Chana Tencer, Natsha Cirinska, Mondek Halsztejn, Sala Szarafharc, Yudik Ziskind, and Chaim-Yosef Milman
123 top left	Reb Leibish Tennenbaum, a Hasid of Gur. He immigrated to the United States, where he served as a shochet [ritual slaughterer]. He died in Israel.
123 bottom left	Rabbi Regensberg of blessed memory
123 bottom right	Rabbi Shmuel Isser, a prominent figure in Wierzbnik between the two world wars. He was the head of the community for a time. Perished in the holocaust
124	Reb Yosef Dreksler
128	The Admor of Chemlów accompanied by his Hassidim
130	Reb Leibish Kerbel
133	Shmuel Tennenbaum with his granddaughter Luci
134	Reb Moshe Tennenbaum
137	Uncaptioned drawing. A family at the Sabbath table
146	Photocopy: New decrees against the Jews on a daily basis
147 right	The most difficult decree to this point – the wearing of the yellow patch on the sleeve
147 left	The yellow patch with the word Juif
148 top	The Jews had to leave their residences within three days and move to the concentration area
148 bottom	Placards marking the boundaries of the ghetto (see the map at the beginning of the book, showing the streets of the ghetto) (The placard says: Wohngebiet der Juden Betriten Verboten)
149	Sadistic tortures
150	Standing in line for bread next to the spółdzielnia (cooperative)
151	The entire population was forced to come to the killing place to witness the execution of the prisoners.
153	Everyone, without exception, was ordered by the Germans to leave their homes and gather in one place
157	Dark clouds gathered over the Jewish town
160	Leibush Herblum
161	A gathering near the memorial symbolizing an oven in the death camp
172	Placing a wreath on the common grave of 18,000 victims in the city of Jelenia Góra (Poland)
173	We walked in silent rows with tears in our eyes. Nobody exchanged a word with anyone else. This was a "death march"
175	At the end – destruction and annihilation
176	Menachem Minzberg
177	In the Sieclenice Labor Camp, called the "Konsom"
179	Forced labor workers in Wierzbnik next to the "large oven", the factory for iron products, weapons, and arms
182	On their final journey – to Treblinka
184	The end product of the Satan
185	There were also cases where they forced people to dance "Mah Yafit" (A Sabbath hymn)
186	Persecution and oppression at every step
189	The shipment was not sent to the crematoria, but rather to the women's camp in Birkenau
190	Hanna Tenzer
191	In the Wierzbnik Camp – going out to work
192	We watched our surroundings, and were afraid
193	A natural obstacle around the death camp
194	At the mouth of the abyss
195	The belongings that were collected by "German protocol"
200	Deportations and transfers for various reasons, all leading to annihilation

204	The gloomy future awaited everyone
205 right	Beyond despair
205 left	The friend who saved
207	A mountain of corpses – victims of the Nazi murderers
208	Jewish life was completely worthless
211	Dying at the moment of liberation
213	Fully packed wagons transporting Jews
214	Avraham Zukerman
217	Pinchas Helstein
218	Tzvi (Hersh) Unger
223	Murder and brutality in Nazi nightmare
225	In the hands of the cruel murderers
230	Everywhere there is death and fear
231	A monument for the tragic destruction of European Jewry
233	Pinchas Hochmitz
234	The entrance to the Auschwitz Concentration Camp
235	Roll call in the camp yard
238 top	Malka Weisbloom
238 bottom	Above: The inscription "Arbeit Macht Frei" at the gate of the camp
239	Only death liberates one from Auschwitz
241	Backbreaking work in the Wierzbnik labor camp
242	Next to the crematorium in the Birkenau death camp
245 top	Sara Steinhardt (Postawski)
245 bottom	The torment of the children was sevenfold greater
247	Esther Zukerman-Zilberman
251	Murdered by Hitler's henchmen
252	A Jew at the edge of a pit awaiting death
253	The triumphal march of the Roman soldiers who destroyed the Holy Temple (Translator's note: this is from the Arch of Titus in Rome)
256	The first decree – wearing the Star of David band
257	First aid to hungry refugees
268 Top	Beniek Zukerman
268 Bottom	Soap being produced from Jewish corpses
269	Photocopy: It began with anti-Semitic hate against Jews in words and print
270	Photocopy: A publication of the Nazi "Sturmer" with poisonous anti-Jewish propaganda
272	Starving, worn-out Jewish children – living skeletons
273	Testimony regarding Nazi murderous barbarism
274	Dachau. Germans were forced to look into a pit of corpses
275	Dead bodies of Jewish victims – loaded together on platforms to be carted away
276	Bloody massacres and murders
278	Innocent Jewish victims scattered all over
281	A group of young men from Wierzbnik. On the extreme left is Mendel Brodbeker. He was with the partisans (mentioned in the article)
289	Troubles, persecutions, torment, and wandering
301	David Sali
303	D. Sali in the uniform of a Polish captain
305	David Sali, at the extreme right, among the captains in the ranks of the Polish army
308	Yaakov Shnir (Shiner) in the uniform of a Major in the Soviet Army
311	Yaakov Shnir (Shiner) with his comrades, the captains of his unit
313	From this point on, our progress continued through known obstacles
319	Painting: Like a terrible specter that casts terror and fear on everyone, as was evident during the terrible times of the German occupation. Illustrated by

	this painting.
320	Likely Tzvi Faigenbaum (the author), but possibly Shmuel Dov Faigenbaum (the subject of the chapter)
329	Rivka Greenberg (Mincberg)
330	The search for the victims' remains who were murdered in the Myowka Camp, and gathering them into a communal grave. The native of the city, Gershon Rozenwald, was among those involved in this holy task.
332	Avraham Sheiner in the uniform of a Polish captain
333	A memorial ceremony in Tel Aviv for the town's martyrs who perished in the Holocaust
334	Gershon Rosenwald
346 top	A monument was erected after the liberation. Simcha Minzberg delivering a speech.
346 bottom	At a gathering shortly after the liberation
348	Yerachmiel Zinger (Rumek) and Yitzchak Kerbel next to the monument in memory of those who perished at Bergen Belsen
351	The committee of Wierzbnik natives in Toronto at one of its meetings, dedicated to the publication of the Yizkor Book
353	A group of Jewish soldiers in the Polish Army next to the communal grave (after the war) – Yitzchak Kerbel among them
358	A monument in memory of the murdered Wierzbnik martyrs in the "Beit Olam" cemetery of the Wierzbnik community in Toronto
360	A group of Wierzbnikers in the house of Avraham Zukerman of Toronto
362	At a gathering of the Wierzbnik natives in Toronto at a memorial ceremony in the cemetery, near the monument for the martyrs who were murdered in the Nazi hell.
367	Workers placing flowers at the grave of the fallen heroes of the battle against the Nazi beasts.
369	At a memorial of the Wierzbnik natives in Toronto, Canada
370	Wierzbnik natives in Bergen Belsen, 1945, next to the victory gate erected by the Allies. Standing: Feldpitzer, Y. Kerbel, Zimmerman, and Arbeitsman
377	Reb Hershel Weiser and his wife Rivka
379	Avraham Zukerman, One of the two chairpersons of the United Jewish Fund of the Wierzbniker organization presenting a check to the chairman of the General Jewish United Fund, Gordon Mendele, with the other chairman of the organization of the united fund, Max Nolman, looking on. Present as well was the chairman of the Wierzbnik Organization, Sam Stern, and vice president Willy Kirshenblatt, as well as members of the executive.
384	Y. Kerbel or Shmuel Morgenstern
387	Yisrael Reisler or Avraham Zukerman
388	David Plonski or Shmuel Gelbart
394 right	The head of the family – Reb Shmuel
394 left	The eldest son – Fishel
395	The second son – Yaakov

NAME INDEX

This Name Index refers to the pages of this English Translation.

A

Abraham, 606
Abramowicz, 487, 490
Abramowicz, 573, 579, 597
Absbad, 381
Absbam, 383
Absfeld, 606
Adler, 306
Adler, 573, 578, 600, 619
Aichler, 24
Ajdelkopf, 426
Ajlenberg, 573
Ajsberg, 581
Ajzelsztajn, 616
Ajzenberg, 425
Ajzenberg, 566, 572, 581, 583, 584, 591, 594, 616, 619
Ajzenman, 566, 579, 588, 594, 597, 599
Ajzenmesser, 619
Akierman, 619
Albirt, 594
Alios, 573
Alpert, 584
Altman, 573, 590
Amir-Taubman, 451
Anielewicz, 581, 594, 613
Anisman, 299, 480, 514
Antman, 616
Apelbaum, 566
Apelsztajn, 596
Apfelbaum, 609, 611
Arbeiter, 594

Arbeitsman, 630
Arbeitsman, 564
Aronowic, 607
Assja, 616, 617, 618
Ausdeutscher, 566
Avramovitz, 73

B

Bachner, 608
Bagno, 66, 161, 162, 165
Bajgelman, 566
Balter, 600
Bamel, 619
Banger, 606
Bar, 50
Baran, 566
Baranek, 426, 427, 436, 496, 558
Baranek, 585, 587, 599
Bar-Birenzweig, 429
Barkai – Rosenwald, 249
Bas, 591
Baum, 486
Baum, 573, 579, 581, 585, 613
Baumstein, 52, 426
Baumsztajn, 426
Beck, 607
Bejgel, 609
Beker, 381, 382, 383, 515
Bekermaszin, 428
Bekermaszyn, 501
Bekiermaszyn, 566, 584
Bendet, 564
Benedykt, 566

Ben-Yehuda, 122
Berber-Starkman, 509
Bergeisen, 611
Berger, 591
Bergson, 591, 594, 601
Berkowicz, 609, 619, 623
Bernholc, 619
Bernstein, 24, 30, 50, 53, 55, 56, 94
Berson, 594
Besbaum, 382
Bialski, 609
Biderman, 71, 140, 146, 147, 183, 186, 217, 280, 288, 374, 424, 460, 531
Biderman, 566, 573, 594
Biderman-Rubenstein, 502
Bienstok, 383
Binstock, 46, 53, 106, 109, 180, 254, 391, 416, 428, 541
Binstztok-Shulman, 427
Binsztok, 119, 427, 428, 508, 514, 515, 626, 627
Binsztok, 564, 565, 566, 573, 574, 579, 584, 594, 597, 598, 599, 603
Birenbaum, 566, 574, 591, 602
Birencwajg, 564, 600
Birentzweig, 180, 541
Birenzweig, 27, 50, 52, 54, 56, 64, 139, 150, 188, 430
Birnbaum, 465
Bister, 619
Bittan Weisblum, 235
Blacarz, 619
Blajwajs, 609
Blander, 605
Blass, 347, 553
Blass-Weintraub, 347
Blat, 607, 609
Blatman, 574, 591, 619
Blicher, 566
Bliman, 588

Blisko, 574
Bloch, 613
Blom, 427
Blom-Weintraub, 427
Bluestein, 241
Blum, 159, 361
Blum, 598, 603
Blumenfarb, 619
Blumenfeld, 147, 230
Blumenfeld, 572
Blumensztajn, 616
Blusztajn, 474
Blutner, 605
Bochenek, 606
Bogdanski, 616
Bogdanski-Finkelstein, 469
Boim, 398
Bojman, 619, 623
Bojmelgryn, 566
Bonim, 74
Borensztajn, 566, 574, 614
Borger, 605
Bornstein-Kaufman, 482
Bornsztajn, 427
Borowka, 584
Borstein, 123
Botnik-Finkelstein, 469
Brand, 591
Brandmesser, 425
Brank-Weisblum, 177, 538
Breier, 487
Brener, 591
Breslauer, 611
Brodbaker, 77, 626
Brodbeker, 27, 28, 32, 33, 46, 64, 70, 71, 72, 80, 102, 130, 140, 176, 203, 307, 362, 370, 371, 375, 376, 383, 388, 411, 429, 430, 431, 459, 467, 480, 481, 493, 509, 537, 629
Brodbeker-Rubin, 431

Brodbeker-Unger, 374, 431
Brodbekier, 566, 572, 574, 579, 581, 582, 588, 591
Brodbekker, 173, 535
Broidbeker, 374, 375
Broitbeker, 130
Brojt, 426
Bromberg, 590
Bromberger, 564, 565, 566, 572, 597, 601
Broniewski, 579
Brotbeker, 457
Brykman, 574
Bryks, 613, 614
Bryt, 609
Brytt, 574, 579, 591
Brzegowski, 588
Buchbinder, 71, 410, 411, 474
Buchsbaum, 80
Bulwa, 616
Bumenfarb, 623
Bursztajn, 488
Bzhichiner, 55
Bzizhers-Golombiovski, 298

C

Ceder, 619
Celinski, 482
Cerelewicz, 623
Cerlewicz, 623
Chaitan, 449
Chaitan Kirshelblum, 486
Chajton, 564, 574
Chelminski, 566
Cherinska, 221
Chodorowski, 113
Choina, 590
Cieply, 583
Ciesla, 590

Cipis, 416
Cirinska, 132, 628
Cislowski, 567, 603
Citrinbaum, 72, 84, 138, 405, 408, 411
Cohen, 49, 52, 72, 83, 148, 149, 175, 179, 182, 271, 280, 288, 411, 453, 479, 536, 540, 543, 626
Cohen (Leopold), 201
Cohen-Lichtenstein, 453
Cornwasser, 557
Crystal, 128
Cuker, 477
Cukerman, 119, 492, 626, 627
Cukier, 361, 475, 476
Cukier, 574, 599, 613, 614, 623
Cukierman, 474, 475, 476
Cukierman, 567, 574, 583, 584, 587, 588, 596, 606, 607
Cukierman (Zukerman), 475, 476
Curling, 616
Cwajgenberg, 611
Cygiel, 591
Cygielman, 616
Cymberknopft, 616
Cymerman, 584, 587, 588, 591, 594, 596, 602
Cymrynt, 574, 584
Cypis, 514
Cyprian, 579
Cyrulnik, 579
Cytrym, 574
Cytryn, 104, 473, 627
Cytryn, 574, 579, 582, 598
Cytrynbaum, 78, 104, 126, 474, 626, 627
Czapnik, 579
Czarny, 574, 590
Czepla, 455
Czernikowski, 567
Czernucha, 567
Czosniak, 616

D

Dab, 598
Dabak, 619
Dancyger, 609, 611
Dawidman, 585
Dawidowicz, 436, 496
Dawidowicz, 572
Dekel, 514
Dekel (Dreksler), 437, 438
Dekel-Dar Kesler, 6, 625
Dekel-Dreksler, 514
Delewkowicz, 487, 490
Delewkowicz, 574
Derwic, 581
Diament, 567
Diet, 383
Dinfeld, 436
Disenhaus, 438
Dizenhoiz, 265
Dodkiewicz, 588
Drajnodel, 49, 436, 626
Drajnudek, 583
Drajnudel, 53, 84, 140, 187, 304, 306
Drajnudel, 583, 584
Drajnwodel, 76, 626
Dreier, 564
Dreinodel, 436
Dreinudel, 113
Drejzner, 579
Dreksler, 27, 28, 29, 32, 33, 34, 46, 52, 55, 71, 77, 139, 140, 149, 150, 167, 188, 190, 229, 371, 372, 437, 438, 625, 628
Dreksler, 567, 574, 587
Dreksler-Dekel, 20, 625
Dresner, 608
Drexler, 175, 177, 536, 538, 556
Drobner, 56
Drygant, 574

Dyment, 619
Dyner, 567, 602
Dysenhaus, 567
Dziadek, 597
Dziewiecki, 609

E

Echt, 567
Edison-Erlichsohn, 378
Eetao, 571
Efrati, 211
Eichler, 30
Eidelkopf, 472
Eidelman, 22, 164, 626
Einer, 383
Eisen, 382, 383
Eisenberg, 381, 383, 425
Eisenshtat, 71
Eisenstadt, 176, 537
Eisner, 383
Ejchman, 564
Ejnesman, 564, 574, 601, 603
Ejzenbuch, 567
Ekselman, 609
Elberg, 591
Elbirt, 574
Elman, 608
En Shrdl Cmfwy Vbg, 623
Englender, 607
Enisman, 73, 127, 133, 363, 371, 374, 375, 416, 465
Epstein, 66, 157, 162
Erlich, 585, 592, 597
Erlichman, 76, 626
Erlichman, 574, 584, 585, 588, 590, 592, 603
Erlichsman, 467
Erlichson, 106
Erlichson, 588, 597

Erman, 613

F

Faigenbaum, 14, 20, 22, 126, 131, 146, 183, 190, 301, 317, 344, 398, 410, 630
Faigenbaum (Shraga), 229, 309
Fajgelbaum, 603
Fajgelman, 592
Fajgenbaum, 6, 55, 64, 74, 76, 301, 310, 359, 372, 467
Fajgenbaum, 592
Fajgenbaum (Shraga), 104, 375
Fajntuch, 564, 600
Fajrajzen, 606
Farber, 567
Farbman, 466, 505
Federman, 609
Feferman, 590
Feigenbaum, 69, 176, 179, 351, 468, 537, 540, 560, 625, 626, 627
Feldberg, 602
Feldficer, 476
Feldman, 27, 32, 52, 65, 177, 178, 470, 538, 539
Feldman, 567, 583, 594
Feldpicer, 498, 501
Feldpicer, 564, 567, 574, 584, 594
Feldsher, 235
Feldsztajn, 619
Felner, 579, 590
Ferstenberg, 585
Finkelstein, 356, 472
Finkelsztajn, 469, 485, 500
Finkielsztajn, 564, 572, 574, 585, 588, 594, 598, 611
Finkler, 594, 600
Firstenberg, 590
Fishman, 227
Fisz, 567, 594, 603

Fiszbajn, 606
Fiszbaum, 619
Fiszkowicz, 592
Fiszman, 76, 470, 626
Fiszman, 584, 588
Flajszer, 619
Flamelbaum, 613, 616
Flamm, 605
Flancbaum, 574, 590
Flancgraben, 606
Flantzenbaum, 471
Fligielman, 613
Flikier, 564
Floman, 567
Fortgang, 613
Frajd, 49
Frajdman, 47, 460, 473
Frandenrajch, 613
Frankel, 588
Frankfurt, 599
Freemerman, 331
Frenkel, 473, 478
Frenkiel, 567, 598
Freulich, 574
Fricher, 453
Fridenson, 594, 596
Friedman, 626
Frimerman, 27, 28, 52, 55, 56, 140, 148, 188, 370, 456, 472, 473, 483, 484, 514, 626
Frimmerman, 32, 33, 276
Froiman, 74
Frojman, 597
Froyman, 406
Fruchtman, 471
Fruchtman, 584, 588
Frukenberg, 620
Fruman, 84, 157
Fryc, 574
Fryd, 360

Frydlant, 607
Frydman, 54
Frydman, 567, 585, 592, 609, 620
Frydrych, 607
Frymel, 583, 590
Frymerman, 579, 582, 583
Fryszman, 574, 575
Fuka, 567
Fuks, 590, 605
Funk, 379, 450, 466
Funk-Singer, 466
Furman, 53, 64, 429
Furman, 572

G

Galili-Sternkrantz, 508
Ganc, 575, 592
Garber, 598
Garfinkiel, 592
Garncarski, 588
Garnek, 590
Gatlib, 565
Gdanski, 79
Gdanski, 579
Gedalowicz, 597
Gelbard, 87, 119, 407, 435, 627
Gelbard, 584, 585
Gelbard-Kazimirski, 483
Gelbard-Maslowitz, 435
Gelbart, 237, 630
Gelberg, 620
Gelbtuch, 29, 34, 56
Geliebter, 609
Geller, 206
Gendler, 24, 30
German, 592
Gerszt, 575
Gersztajn, 616, 617

Gertler, 587
Getzko, 50
Gewercer, 572, 579
Gimpel, 501, 502
Gincberg, 50, 53
Gincberg, 616
Gincburg, 434
Gisser, 620
Gitler, 575
Glas, 579
Glaser, 434
Glasman, 613
Glat, 582, 613
Glatt, 434
Gleser, 613
Glick, 465
Gliksman, 467
Gliksman, 579, 594, 620
Gliksztajn, 609
Glinktewicz, 609
Golczewski, 620
Gold, 381, 382, 383, 433
Goldbach, 382, 383
Goldbach, 592
Goldberg, 50, 52, 54, 68, 153, 242, 363, 455, 462
Goldberg, 564, 565, 572, 575, 583, 587, 592, 594,
    599, 601, 616, 620
Goldberg-Enisman, 465
Goldblum, 592
Goldewajg, 564
Goldfarb, 249, 456
Goldfarb, 564, 567, 594, 596
Goldfeld, 567
Goldgrob, 432
Goldgrub, 50, 52, 331
Goldgrub, 592, 602
Goldknopf, 72, 83, 410
Goldkopf, 508
Goldkranc, 616

Goldman, 463
Goldman, 588, 594, 613
Goldstein, 50, 54, 106, 111, 178, 235, 237, 361, 432, 539
Goldstoff, 607
Goldszleger, 611
Goldsztajn, 432, 433
Goldsztajn, 567, 575, 588, 592, 613
Goldsztein, 119, 627
Goldsztejn, 89, 99, 627
Goldwaser, 614
Goldwasser, 606
Golebiowski, 575
Golembiowski, 89, 90
Golombiowski, 476
Goltlib, 575
Gomolinski, 616
Gorfinkel, 458, 506
Gorlib, 567
Gotlib, 74, 512, 516
Gotlib, 564, 565, 575, 588, 598, 602
Gotlieb, 383
Grabska, 597
Grabski, 567
Green, 56
Greenberg, 363
Greenberg (Mincberg), 6, 93, 214, 630
Greenberg (Minzberg), 354, 625
Greenhaut, 124, 125
Greiber (Manela), 461
Grinbaum, 54, 92, 94, 137, 138
Grinszpan, 465
Grober, 79
Grober, 579
Grocher, 582, 594
Groda-Kamec, 476
Grojecka, 597
Grojecki, 589
Grojeski, 568

Grosman, 454
Grosman, 565, 585, 589, 590, 592, 594, 603, 614
Grossman, 52
Grossman, 616, 617, 618
Groszenkorn, 103, 627
Gruber, 99, 435, 627
Grubsztajn, 464
Gruner, 112, 464
Grycman, 620
Gryn, 462
Grynbaum, 502
Grynbaum, 575, 594, 596, 598
Grynberg, 575, 594, 606, 614, 620
Grynberg-Mincberg, 458
Grynblat, 568, 575
Gryncberg, 568
Gryner, 595, 607
Grynfarb, 616, 617, 618
Grynhaut, 436
Grynszpan, 153, 155
Grynszpan, 568, 575, 579, 582, 606, 616, 617, 618
Grynszpan-Goldberg, 153
Grynszporn, 585, 587
Grynsztajn, 568, 585, 595
Guralchik, 55
Gut, 620
Guterman, 27, 46, 52, 53, 54, 71, 72, 79, 83, 88, 140, 147, 175, 176, 272, 424, 433, 480, 536, 537
Guterman, 568, 572, 575, 587, 592, 594, 599
Gutholc, 572, 590
Gutholtz, 185
Gutman, 485, 573
Gutman, 565, 568, 594, 596, 609, 620
Gutsman, 147
Gutterman, 32
Gutvil, 185
Gutwajl, 478

Gutwil, 588
Gynhaut, 436

H

Haberberg, 620
Hajblum, 575, 579, 592
Hakohen, 440, 453
Halbersztadt, 606
Halevi, 158
Halevi, 482
Halsztejn, 132, 628
Halsztuk, 568
Hanna, 584
Hauptman, 575
Hefter, 607
Heilblum, 472
Heinich, 54
Hejnochowicz, 616
Helem, 297
Heler, 181, 542
Heller, 24, 26, 30, 31, 48, 50, 52, 53, 138, 147, 283, 290, 391
Heller, 585, 611
Helstein, 50, 73, 133, 175, 243, 439, 516, 536, 629
Helstoch, 365, 367
Helsztajn, 485, 516
Helsztajn, 565, 566, 579, 585
Hendeles Celinski, 482
Henig, 579
Herblum, 10, 27, 32, 46, 47, 49, 71, 83, 126, 139, 179, 180, 184, 189, 190, 271, 280, 281, 288, 289, 316, 370, 439, 440, 446, 503, 516, 540, 541, 556, 557, 625, 626, 627, 628
Herblum, 565, 575, 584, 587, 595, 596, 598, 599, 600, 601, 602
Herblum-Burman, 439
Hercberg, 614

Hercig, 72, 83, 102, 190, 284
Heriing, 298
Hering, 84
Hering, 568
Herling, 441
Herling, 581, 587, 595, 603
Herman, 99, 627
Hernik, 471
Herschman, 231
Herszenfus, 620
Herszeuhorn, 575
Herszkowicz, 568, 605
Herszman, 89, 515, 627
Herszman, 575
Herszt, 620
Herzberg, 575
Herzog, 103, 276, 627
Heublum, 605
Hilf, 10, 439, 440, 489, 625
Hilf, 568, 583
Himelfarb, 568
Himelgryn, 596, 599
Hirschhorn, 139
Hirszhorn, 126, 434, 627
Hoch, 611, 616, 620
Hochberg-Starkman, 510
Hochblit, 50, 53
Hochenbaum, 620
Hochminc, 581
Hochmitz, 6, 108, 123, 234, 258, 316, 441, 625, 629
Hochnitz, 177, 538
Hoffman, 477
Holcman, 435
Holcman, 585
Holeman, 568, 609
Holender, 605
Hollander, 564
Holtz, 185

Holtzman, 177, 538
Honigman, 595, 598
Honigsberg, 265, 438
Honigsberg, 568, 589
Honigsberg (Ginnosar), 438
Honigsztok, 620
Hopfeld, 443
Horowicz, 575, 584, 611
Horowitz, 95

I

Igielman, 616
Infeld, 605
Isenberg, 45, 46, 53
Isenman, 53, 54
Isser-Herling, 425

J

Jablonski, 565, 568
Jablowski, 426
Jabner, 76, 448, 626
Jacobs, 382, 383
Jakubowicz, 617
Jamer, 609
Janisevitz, 173, 534
Jankielowicz, 585
Jarecki, 575
Jarmula, 568
Jedlinker, 309
Jeger, 587
Jeruchim, 620
Joskowicz, 575, 589, 609
Judkiewicz, 568
Jukier, 605, 606

K

Kac, 471

Kac, 568, 598, 601, 614
Kacman, 428
Kac-Rozenwald, 500
Kadiszewicz, 477, 514
Kadiszowicz, 49, 436, 626
Kadyszewicz, 416
Kae, 568
Kahan, 564, 595, 599
Kaiser-Tenenbaum, 52
Kalechman, 568
Kalichman, 568
Kalikwaser, 575
Kalimowicz, 568
Kaliwaser, 598
Kalman-Singer, 271
Kalmanson, 483, 514
Kalmanzon, 51, 56, 416
Kalmowicz, 580, 589
Kamec, 413, 476
Kamf, 556
Kaminer, 490
Kaminer, 568, 580, 582, 598
Kaminski, 568
Kampel, 595
Kanarek, 575
Kaner, 497
Kaner, 595
Kaninski, 575
Kanner, 380
Kaplan, 575
Kaplanski, 613
Karafiol, 609, 611
Karmeser, 613, 614
Karniszyn, 572
Karp, 568, 603
Kasawaska, 474
Kasztan, 469
Kasztan, 565, 566

Katz, 10, 38, 84, 100, 114, 190, 406, 421, 451, 452, 497, 527, 531, 555, 561, 625, 626
Katzenellenbogen, 67, 72
Katz-Malach, 154
Kaufman, 481, 482, 556
Kaufman, 572, 575, 580, 581, 582, 583, 585, 586, 587, 620
Kaufman-Goldstein, 432
Kazimierski, 24, 30, 51
Kazimierski, 613
Kazimierzski, 237
Kazimirski, 483
Keler, 605
Kelman, 76, 626
Kelmanson, 382, 383
Kenigsberg, 337, 468, 627
Kenigsztajn, 589, 599
Kerbel, 50, 52, 74, 76, 87, 89, 111, 140, 152, 342, 360, 362, 363, 372, 376, 391, 392, 403, 404, 415, 497, 626, 627, 628, 630
Kestenbaum, 576
Kestenberg, 54, 65
Kestenberg, 590, 597, 603, 611, 620
Kieps, 610
Kierbel, 580, 581, 587, 589
Kierszenbaum, 576, 595, 610, 622
Kierszenblat, 610, 622, 623
Kierszenblum, 587, 601
Kierzenbaum, 620
Killman, 331
Kilman, 436, 483, 484, 520, 521
Kilman, 586
Kilman-Singer, 148
Kirschenblatt, 383
Kirshenblatt, 381, 401, 630
Kirszenbaum, 449
Kirszenblat, 474, 484
Kirszenblat, 565
Kirszenblum-Krauzman, 486

Klajman, 568, 572, 576, 583, 590, 592, 595, 597, 602
Klajminc, 580, 588, 590, 597
Klajn, 576, 606
Klajnberg, 565, 566, 581, 584
Klajnmic, 434
Klapper, 586
Klarman, 400, 401
Klausner, 563
Kleiman, 174, 536
Kleinbaum, 610
Kleinbaum (Sne), 54
Kleinbaum-Starkman, 509
Kleinberg, 52, 346, 381, 382, 383, 485, 560
Kleinberg (Baum], 486
Kleiner, 27, 32, 56, 74, 87, 113, 140, 151, 152, 155, 156, 175, 228, 360, 361, 379, 414, 486, 536
Kleinman, 89, 383, 627
Kleinman, 610, 611
Kleparda, 568
Klikwaser, 498
Kliman, 560
Klinger, 569
Klingerman, 617
Klos, 569
Klowenman, 383
Kltun, 620
Kluger, 465, 521
Kluger, 606
Knobel, 569, 576
Kochem, 569
Kochen, 576, 580
Koclowicz, 481
Kogut, 73, 477, 512, 516
Kogut, 569, 572, 576, 590, 599, 602
Kohn, 617
Kojfman, 71, 72, 78, 189
Komarowski, 501, 506

Komec, 49, 77, 103, 126, 496, 626, 627
Komorowska, 599
Komorowski, 565, 588
Konigsberg, 70, 131
Konowicki, 507
Konowiecki, 580
Koper, 586, 609, 611
Koperwas, 620, 623
Kopf, 54, 118, 361, 482, 496
Kopf, 586, 597
Kopholz, 605
Koralnik, 569
Korenblit, 598
Korenblum, 565, 566, 592
Korenwaser, 105, 128
Korenwaser, 565, 569, 572, 583, 586, 595, 599
Korenwasser, 236
Korenwasser-Ajdelkopf, 426
Korman, 609, 620, 623
Kornblum, 489
Kornwaser, 27, 46, 49, 71, 102, 128, 138, 139, 140, 148, 186, 190, 230, 317, 398, 416, 626
Kornwasser, 32, 76, 78, 104, 126, 164, 236, 383, 413, 453, 459, 473, 474, 478, 479, 480, 514, 626, 627
Kornwassser, 480
Korta, 173, 176, 535, 537
Kosovski, 290
Kosowski, 283, 284
Koszer, 607, 608
Koszykarz, 595
Kozuszek, 617
Krajndels, 613
Kramacz, 173, 535
Kramarz, 598
Kramazh, 293
Krausman, 505, 511
Krauzman, 469
Krazman, 556

Kris, 242
Krisztal, 506
Kroizman, 76, 99, 626, 627
Krojzman, 190
Krolnik, 103, 627
Krozman, 64, 71
Kryger, 620
Krys, 595
Krystal, 413
Krysztal, 572, 576, 580, 582, 587
Kumec, 597
Kumetz, 105, 139, 190, 320, 321
Kunowski, 621
Kuper (Reichzeig), 343
Kuperberg, 569, 589
Kuperiad, 592
Kuperman, 425, 471
Kuperman, 569, 578
Kuperminc, 576
Kuperszmidt, 609, 611
Kupfer (Reichzeig), 505
Kurc, 576, 617
Kurlender, 584, 621
Kurta, 598
Kurto, 293
Kurz, 605, 607

L

Lachtyngier, 599
Lajbenszaft, 132, 628
Lajewski, 580
Lajtajzen, 439
Lajtajzen, 569
Lajzerowicz, 621
Laks, 27, 32, 53, 95, 150, 151, 172, 273, 459, 534
Laks, 586, 600, 601
Laks Lerman, 459

Landau, 227, 419, 470
Langelban, 260
Langer, 595, 601, 614
Langleben, 602
Lanienter, 589
Laor (Dreksler), 93, 149, 226
Laps, 178, 539
Las, 580
Laskaski, 617
Laskovski, 26
Lauer (Dreksler), 437, 438
Laufer, 569
Lazarus, 607
Lebman, 186
Leczycki, 584
Lederman, 621
Lega, 576, 617, 621
Leibman, 457
Leigman Kahana, 457
Lejbgot, 569
Lejbman, 576, 580, 583, 602
Lempel, 606, 607
Lencicki (Lang), 476
Lentshitsky, 297
Leopold (Cohen), 104, 627
Leopold-Cohen, 453, 479
Lepek, 383
Lerman, 74, 84, 85, 157, 280, 288, 413, 459
Lerman, 602
Lerner, 580
Lev, 179, 180, 540, 541
Levenstat (Milman], 460
Levin, 381
Levinson, 456, 491
Levinson-Lichtenstein, 453
Levita, 454
Lewa, 576, 587
Lewenson, 578, 597, 598, 601, 602
Lewental, 621

Lewenton, 569, 598
Lewi, 580
Lewin, 576
Lewkowicz, 596
Lewkowicz-Shlesinger, 422
Liberman, 461
Liberman, 583, 595, 606, 621
Liber-Rosenthal, 457
Libeskin, 580
Libman, 569, 589, 592
Lichtenstein, 25, 26, 27, 30, 31, 32, 47, 48, 52,
    54, 71, 80, 113, 131, 140, 148, 173, 177, 180,
    183, 190, 395, 453, 454, 534, 538, 541, 543,
    556
Lichtenstein-Mincberg, 53
Lichtensztajn, 25, 26, 27, 44, 453, 454, 458, 483,
    626
Lichtensztajn, 576, 592, 621, 623
Lichtiger, 72
Liebeskind, 354
Lighteizen, 71
Lilenbaum, 576
Linderbaum, 621
Lindzen, 602
Lipa, 602
Lipicki, 606
Lipman, 252
Lipman, 576, 578
Lipman (Kopf), 482
Lipowicz, 576
Lipski, 87
Lipsky, 76, 626
Lipstein, 27, 33, 52, 109, 174, 175, 187, 188,
    454, 535, 536
Lipster, 598
Lipsztajn, 454
Lipsztajn, 564, 599
Lipsztejn, 76, 626
Lipszyc, 428

Lipszyc, 592
Lis, 55, 56, 89, 92, 99, 119, 139, 140, 455, 626, 627
Lis, 584
Lis (Shuali), 627
Lis Shuali, 91, 105
Lisiewicz, 586, 595
Lisser, 569
Lis-Shuali, 6, 119, 455, 625, 627
Lithuak (Brodbeker), 72
Lithuak Brodbeker, 80
Lomska, 586, 601
Loterman, 490
Lshrdl, 568
Lubianiker, 47
Lubka, 589, 598
Lubliner, 595
Lublinski, 361
Lublin-Taubman, 451
Luksenberg, 576
Lupta, 87, 95, 138, 228
Lusternik, 456
Lustgarten, 365, 391
Lustgarten, 565
Lustig, 53, 54
Lustiger, 54
Lustman, 346, 457
Lustman, 569, 586, 590, 596, 597, 614

M

Machtynger, 569, 581
Magen, 209, 395
Maindel, 569
Maj, 584
Majbruch, 606
Majzels, 569
Makierowicz, 595
Malach, 104, 154, 155
Malach, 621, 623
Malc, 592
Malicka, 614
Malicki, 569
Manche, 130
Mandel, 569, 595
Mandelaum, 456
Mandelbaum, 113
Mandelbaum, 580, 610, 614
Mandelzis, 74, 84, 138, 280, 288, 459
Mandelzys, 580, 601, 610
Manel, 456
Manela, 50, 52, 74, 99, 183, 186, 356, 391, 456, 461, 487, 488, 543, 627
Manela, 576, 597, 603
Mangarten, 573, 595, 597, 599
Mangorten, 569, 582
Manheit, 383
Mann-Neuman, 466
Manowicz, 576
Margulis, 621
Markiewicz, 576
Markovitch (Baranek), 427
Markowicz, 104, 239, 462, 487, 627
Marmorek, 472
Maschliburski, 173, 535
Maskowicz, 500
Maslowicz, 49, 103, 360, 471, 558, 626, 627
Maslowicz, 584, 592
Maslowitz, 530
Mats, 326, 546
Mauer, 576
Mawer, 46
Mekler, 602
Melamed, 179, 180, 190, 540, 541, 556
Melamed (Rendil), 79
Melcer, 602
Melchior, 569
Meldung, 617

Melman, 138, 459
Melman, 569
Mendele, 401
Mendelson, 430
Mentlik, 586, 587
Merker, 621
Merszajn, 576
Merszejn, 569
Merzel, 592
Miernik, 55
Milberg, 584
Milgrom, 576
Miller, 505
Miller, 580, 581
Millman, 298
Milman, 132, 177, 242, 315, 425, 460, 538, 628
Milman-Herling, 177, 538
Milner, 383
Milrad, 78
Milstein, 334
Mincberg, 6, 14, 20, 22, 52, 55, 56, 124, 125, 138, 139, 148, 150, 157, 205, 271, 272, 284, 370, 371, 376, 458
Mincberg, 580, 592, 599, 600
Mincberg-Greenberg, 372
Minkowski, 231, 461
Minkowski, 569, 590
Mintcberg, 6
Minzberg, 23, 30, 276, 378, 563, 625, 626, 628, 630
Miodecki, 591
Miodownik, 576
Miszleborske, 379
Mitelman, 569
Mlynarski, 605, 606, 607
Mlyneker, 47
Mor, 99, 627
Mora, 46, 472
Mordfeld, 592, 595

Mordkowicz, 589
Morgelsztern, 570
Morgenstern, 10, 52, 64, 65, 72, 105, 165, 177, 189, 344, 404, 405, 424, 538, 556, 625, 630
Morgensztajn, 460
Morgensztern, 77, 78, 103, 460, 468, 507, 626, 627
Morgensztern, 570, 576, 583, 587, 589, 591, 592
Morowiec, 570
Moszkowicz, 589
Mune, 565
Munk, 614
Murofska, 558
Muszkat, 617
Mydlarz, 595
Mylanrski, 606
Mylnarski, 606
Mylnarskia, 605
Myncberg, 564
Mysliborski, 45, 88, 131, 140, 245

N

Nachalnik, 136, 137
Nachumawski, 30
Nachumovski, 24
Nadulek, 591
Naftalis, 190
Nagiel, 601
Naiman, 9, 10, 381, 462, 551, 625
Naiman Karstadt, 551
Najdyk, 621
Najfeld, 610
Najman, 27, 55, 64, 74, 109, 149, 395, 429, 462, 474, 477, 509, 510, 552
Najman, 570, 576, 577, 581, 584, 586, 610
Najnudel, 573, 589
Nanman, 601

Neiman, 32, 76, 78, 130, 379, 381, 382, 383, 393, 403, 493, 626
Neiman-Zilberstein, 403
Neinudel, 74, 85
Nemed, 463
Nemed– Kadishevitz, 463
Neufeld, 577
Neuman, 464, 466, 505
Neuman-Silberstein, 448
Neustempel, 617
Nisenbaum, 487
Nisenbaum, 592, 621
Nisker, 49, 297, 429, 500, 626
Niskier, 360
Niskier, 582
Nissenbaum, 610
Nojman, 304
Nolman, 401, 630
Noser, 600
Nower, 602
Nowicki, 504
Nudelman, 110, 112, 187, 331
Nudelman, 565, 573, 577, 582, 598
Nudelman-Rubinstein, 501

O

Oberman, 591
Ofman, 577
Ogorek, 605
Ollmer, 593, 600
Olszak, 617
Olszer, 577
Orbach, 162
Orensztajn, 614
Orlean, 614
Orzech, 570, 584, 589
Osob, 610
Ostrian, 53

Ostrowiecka, 586

P

Pacanowski, 570
Paflower, 176, 537
Pajak, 610
Pajkus, 581
Pancer, 395, 507
Pancer, 580
Papierczyk, 573
Pasternak, 469
Pasternak, 621
Patron, 621, 623
Pavlavor, 559
Paz, 163
Peczyna, 614
Pelcyk, 608
Percowicz, 611, 621
Perelman, 577
Perl, 165
Perl-Toman, 449
Pflichtentrajn, 570, 577
Piaskogorski, 589
Pikier, 621
Pilicer, 623
Pinchevsky, 322, 323, 326, 327, 330, 544, 545, 546, 547, 550
Pinczewski, 469
Pinczewski, 570, 580
Pinkusiewicz, 577
Pinter, 606
Piskorz, 611
Plaitze, 54
Plonski, 630
Plonsky, 407
Pochachevski, 29, 56, 124, 125
Pochachewsky, 175, 536
Poliborski, 591

Pomeranc, 578
Pomeraniec, 611
Postawski – Steinhart, 389
Postawski Steinhart, 625
Postawski-Steinhardt, 83, 156, 196, 198, 271
Potok, 458
Pozner, 580
Praczownyk, 516
Pratzovnik, 50, 52, 111, 123, 188
Prendechiner, 47
Presel, 577
Proman, 103, 627
Proviner, 443
Prusak, 589
Przepiorka, 573, 589
Przyticka, 49, 626
Przytycka, 586
Przytyki, 474
Pszytycki, 71, 138, 149, 416
Puchaczewski, 34
Puterman, 436, 482
Puterman, 593, 610, 611

R

Rabinovitch, 493, 499
Rabinovitch-Rosenberg, 498
Rabinowicz, 49, 54, 66, 68, 72, 73, 77, 140, 184, 194, 252, 279, 287, 387, 411, 423, 499, 522, 626
Rabinowicz, 578, 579, 582, 595, 596, 598, 599, 603, 617
Rabinowitz, 9, 625
Radkowizer, 73, 344
Radkowizer Gotlib, 73
Radolnik, 577
Radzinski, 580
Rafalowicz, 593
Rafeld, 610
Rajch, 605
Rajchcajg, 570, 573, 589
Rajchman, 570, 577, 610
Rajewicz, 606
Rajs, 570, 593
Rajzlik, 577
Rajzman, 577, 580, 595
Rapaport, 610, 621
Rappoport, 165
Rapsztajn, 577
Rauf, 602
Rausch, 606
Razfiner, 47
Rechtman, 570
Redlich, 570
Regensberg, 26, 31, 53, 54, 67, 130, 273, 628
Reichzeig, 343, 505
Reis, 108, 137
Reisler, 407, 504, 630
Reisman, 425
Reizman, 89, 99, 627
Riba, 381, 382, 383
Ribak, 89, 167, 504, 627
Rice, 138
Richtenberg, 475
Riseman, 89, 91
Rochman, 591
Rodbard, 621
Rodowicz, 580
Roichert-Starkman, 509
Roizman-Rubinsztajn, 506
Rolnicki, 73, 84, 89, 91, 99, 441, 499, 627
Rolnicki, 570
Rolnizki, 412
Rosenberg, 50, 52, 175, 179, 235, 247, 280, 288, 328, 356, 362, 412, 455, 498, 503, 536, 540, 548
Rosenbloom, 72, 83
Rosenblum, 431, 511

Rosenkrantz, 161, 165
Rosenkrantz-Toman, 449
Rosenstein, 50, 53
Rosenwald, 9, 52, 73, 113, 236, 276, 299, 348, 356, 359, 370, 400, 401, 456, 493, 500, 530, 625, 630
Rosenwald-Farbman, 275, 466
Rosenzweig (Pasternak), 469
Rosner, 608
Rotbard, 30, 34, 76, 274, 470, 626
Rotbard, 577
Rotbart, 24, 29, 56, 147, 192, 276, 284
Rotenberg, 138
Rotenberg, 614
Rotfeld, 64, 65
Rotfogiel, 586
Rothschild, 71, 72, 102, 410, 508
Rothschild-Szprung, 508
Rotmanovich, 47
Rotsztajn, 601
Rotvand, 44
Rozen, 617
Rozenbaum Brodbeker, 431
Rozenberg, 453, 627
Rozenberg, 570, 577, 582, 589, 595, 601, 614
Rozenblat, 570, 599
Rozenblum, 570, 617
Rozencwajg, 586, 589, 621
Rozendorn, 602
Rozenes, 583
Rozenkranc, 611
Rozensztajn, 622
Rozental, 585, 593
Rozenwald, 49, 355, 500, 626, 630
Rozenwald, 584, 586
Rozenzweig, 429
Rozmaity, 580
Rozmaryn, 606
Rozwadowski, 610

Rubenstein-Lipstein, 454
Rubensztajn, 425, 501
Rubin, 24, 30, 50, 428, 470, 507
Rubinson, 602
Rubinstein, 47, 54, 70, 73, 106, 140, 182, 215, 280, 288, 377, 501, 502, 503, 543
Rubinstein-Erlichsohn, 377
Rubinstein-Hendler, 503
Rubinsztajn, 501, 502, 503, 506
Rubinsztajn, 565, 566, 570, 577, 580, 581, 582, 583, 585, 586, 593, 598, 599, 600, 601, 617, 623
Rubinsztejn, 626
Rubman, 591
Rutenberg, 89
Rutman, 577
Rutmanowicz, 585
Rybak, 167, 188, 356, 362
Rychtenberg, 585
Ryczke, 589

S

Sachs, 383
Saguy, 457
Salem, 617
Sali, 6, 20, 22, 322, 324, 372, 544, 625, 626, 629
Sali (Kerbel), 20, 41, 58, 88, 96, 134, 159, 195, 373, 408, 414, 526, 626
Sali-Kerbel, 15, 141, 151, 372, 415
Sali-Kerberl, 14, 625
Sally-Kerbel, 105
Samborska, 615
Samet, 128, 131, 339, 391, 465, 521
Samet, 570, 586, 589
Sandlar, 73
Sandman-Sternkrantz, 508
Sapirsztajn, 453, 479
Satrajtman, 586

Savidor, 113
Scharfhartz, 32
Scharfharz, 113
Scharfhertz, 177, 538
Schechman, 177, 538
Schechter, 205, 206, 207
Scheinwald-Sternkrantz, 508
Schetland, 492
Schlesinger, 447
Schneider, 105
Schnieder, 560
Schnir, 457
Schoichet, 560
Scislowska, 586
Segilim, 383
Sencer, 132
Senderowicz, 577
Sendorowicz, 570
Sendowski-Kaufman, 481
Shapir, 189
Shapir-Binstok, 513
Shapir-Knobel, 513
Sharfhertz, 177, 538
Shazar, 24, 30
Shefla, 183, 184
Sheiner, 20, 254, 357, 509, 511, 512, 625, 630
Shenner, 141
Sherfer, 512
Shiezinger, 273
Shiner, 50, 73, 106, 109, 312, 325, 340, 341, 353, 357, 364, 372, 629
Shlesinger, 422
Shmiel Isses, 560
Shnir (Sheiner), 454
Shraga, 104, 500
Shraga (Feigenbaum), 475
Shraga Yair, 66
Shraga-Feigenbaum, 468
Shtayrat, 72

Shtramer, 56, 124, 331
Shuali, 522
Shuali (Lis), 118, 352, 627
Shulman-Binstock, 515
Silberberg, 446, 447
Silberberg-Rosenthal, 446
Silberfenig, 483
Silberman, 447
Silbersztajn, 448
Silvemian, 299
Silverberg, 557
Silverman, 443, 447
Singer, 6, 22, 27, 28, 32, 33, 43, 55, 124, 131, 140, 148, 150, 172, 216, 235, 246, 247, 272, 320, 347, 372, 379, 450, 483, 484, 534, 625, 626
Siskind, 177, 538
Skarshiver, 65
Skurnik, 453
Slezinger, 113
Slopia, 126, 627
Smialy, 585
Snir, 111, 346
Snir (Shiner), 331
Spagat, 513
Spiegel, 386
Spitzer, 72
Stajnbaum, 427
Starachovitzer (Shenner), 72
Starkman, 510
Starowieszczyk, 622
Stein, 270, 426, 559
Steinbaum, 175, 177, 317, 536, 538
Steinhardt, 74, 77, 123
Steinhardt (Postawski), 629
Steinhardt Postawski, 74
Steinhart, 252
Steinhart (Pastavsky, 252
Steinhart-Perstovsky, 511

Steinman, 472, 514
Steinman-Frimerman, 472
Stern, 71, 77, 307, 401, 630
Sternkrantz, 322, 508, 544
Sternkranz, 413, 414
Strawczynski, 570
Streitman, 511
Strzyg, 580
Synaj, 614, 615
Szachman, 581
Szachter, 580, 589, 591, 593, 595, 596, 601, 602, 623
Szafir, 591, 593, 596, 600, 610
Szafirman, 605
Szafran, 615
Szajn, 577
Szajnbaum, 610
Szajner, 586, 593
Szajnfeld, 622
Szajnwald, 581, 614
Szapir, 513
Szapiro, 165
Szapszewicz, 596
Szarafharc, 132, 628
Szarfarc, 600, 602
Szarfer, 591
Szarfharc, 27, 52, 74
Szarpharc, 456
Szczerbakow, 593
Szczesliwa, 573, 601
Szczesliwy, 602
Szczeslliwy, 588
Szczupak, 618
Szechter, 593
Szeiner, 76, 512, 626
Szempek, 618
Szer, 622
Szerakowicz, 585
Szerfer, 512

Szerman, 570, 589, 591, 593
Szetter, 617, 618
Szfarcfiter, 571
Szif, 626
Szlezynger, 579, 596
Szlikier, 622
Szliwowic, 606
Szmucig, 617, 618
Szmukler, 610
Szmuklerman, 570
Sznajder, 607
Sznajderman, 599
Szorfarc, 599
Szpagat, 513
Szpagat, 585, 586
Szpajzman, 622
Szpigiel, 622
Szpilman, 605
Szpiro, 588, 600, 602, 607, 622
Szrajbman, 588, 614
Sztabholc, 577
Sztajman, 588, 597, 611
Sztajn, 606
Sztajnbaum, 577, 583, 596
Sztajnhart, 511
Sztajnhart, 570, 601
Sztajnhorn, 617
Sztajnowicz, 581
Sztal, 570
Sztarkman, 74, 475, 509, 510, 626
Sztarkman, 566, 573, 579, 593, 596, 597, 598
Sztarkman (Michlower), 46
Szteler, 617
Szterenlicht, 615
Szterenszus, 573, 577
Sztern, 78, 103, 626, 627
Sztern, 589
Szternkrantz, 53, 54
Sztrajtfeld, 570

Sztrajtman, 593, 601
Sztreitman, 511
Sztrosberg, 570, 577, 589, 591
Sztulman, 583, 599
Szuch, 571, 586
Szucht, 589, 602
Szuldman, 615
Szulman, 614
Szwa Reberg, 610
Szwarc, 614, 617
Szwarcberg, 571, 593
Szwarchar, 603
Szwicer, 622
Szwicman, 581
Szyff, 565
Szyfman, 571
Szykier, 589
Szymanowski, 577
Szymkiewicz, 614

T

Taiblum, 71
Taichman, 78, 340
Taichman Shenner, 78
Tajblum, 577
Tajchman, 577
Tajtelbaum, 511
Tajtelbaum, 610, 611
Tannenbaum, 164
Tantzer, 6, 625
Tarek, 591
Taub, 608
Tauber, 600
Taubman, 53, 451
Taubman, 577, 581, 586, 593
Tauman, 165
Tchatchke, 293
Teichman, 506

Teitelbaum, 480
Teitelbaum, 617
Tencer, 30, 32, 132, 279, 450, 628
Tencer, 599, 600, 602
Tenenbaum, 27, 46, 49, 52, 53, 64, 66, 71, 72, 76, 84, 87, 125, 140, 150, 184, 235, 236, 284, 423, 428, 449, 470, 490, 491, 492, 493, 508, 626
Tenenbaum, 571, 582, 583, 585, 587, 593, 596, 597, 602, 603, 622
Tennenbaum, 9, 32, 76, 114, 160, 161, 162, 163, 164, 165, 166, 276, 404, 625, 626, 628
Tenser, 218
Tentzer, 175, 177, 536, 538
Tenzer, 24, 27, 52, 53, 56, 125, 150, 220, 287, 628
Tobman, 449
Tojter, 602
Toman, 449
Trachman, 606
Trajster, 586
Traper, 33
Trefler, 571, 591
Trofa, 165, 166
Troper, 28, 452, 492
Tropper, 428
Trupa, 180, 541
Tubman, 147
Tuchman, 622, 623
Tuchszeler, 507
Turek, 611
Turkeltaub, 513
Turko, 565, 571
Tyszlen, 622
Tyszman, 622
Tytelman, 622

U

Ulsztat, 578
Ungar, 515
Unger, 6, 27, 33, 50, 52, 53, 123, 132, 150, 172, 173, 174, 235, 244, 245, 291, 348, 349, 359, 424, 456, 534, 535, 625, 629
Unger, 571, 573, 588, 590
Urbach, 72
Uris, 94
Uszerowicz, 566, 617

V

Vaigenshperg, 54
Vakselman, 185
Veffer, 104, 153, 154, 155
Verthime, 333, 334
Vigdorovich, 53, 72, 88, 111, 274, 340
Vilkovski, 65
Volberg, 44

W

Wagman, 508
Waigman, 344
Wajch, 610
Wajchendler, 571, 573, 577, 581, 587, 597, 602
Wajcher, 608
Wajcman, 607, 610
Wajdenbaum, 573
Wajgszparg, 516
Wajgszperg, 132, 628
Wajman, 310
Wajman, 622
Wajnbaum, 571, 573, 591
Wajnberg, 103, 627
Wajnberg, 571, 578, 581, 583, 586, 593, 598, 610, 614, 615, 622, 623
Wajnerman, 581
Wajngort, 571
Wajnman, 428
Wajnper, 573
Wajnryb, 583
Wajnsztajn, 571, 578
Wajnsztok, 578, 581, 593, 601
Wajntraub, 49, 103, 627
Wajntraub, 573, 581, 596, 599, 622, 623
Wajs, 578
Wajsberg, 582, 603
Wajsblat, 581, 596
Wajsblum, 571, 578, 582, 586, 590, 593
Wajsdorf, 582
Wajskopf, 571
Wajsmehl, 583
Wajsrozen, 615
Wajtceken-Kogut, 477
Wajtzenblum, 607
Wajzer, 74, 84, 102, 105, 138, 157, 190, 235, 363, 372, 398, 399, 411
Wajzer, 573, 578, 585, 601
Waksberg, 582, 611, 622, 623
Waksman, 578, 596, 622, 623
Wakszal, 579
Waldman, 426
Waldman, 565
Walgroch, 571
Walman, 603
Warcki, 571, 622
Warda, 581
Wargon, 581
Warman, 622
Warsewski, 487, 488
Warszauer, 582, 590, 593
Warszawska, 599, 623
Waserman, 571, 593
Wasersztajn, 596
Watman, 571, 603, 614
Weichandler, 445

Weichnik, 445
Weinberg, 205, 441
Weinrych, 617
Weintraub, 72, 84, 230, 239, 347, 432, 434, 442, 553, 626
Weintraub-Goldstein, 432
Weisberg, 188, 356, 362, 497
Weisbloom, 6, 20, 35, 54, 76, 109, 123, 234, 235, 258, 260, 264, 316, 352, 356, 625, 626, 629
Weisblum, 326, 442, 443, 547
Weisblum-Dawidowicz, 436
Weisblum-Rosenberg, 503
Weisdorf, 383
Weisenfeld Kleiner, 486
Weiser, 20, 625, 630
Weisfogel, 610
Weisglas, 445
Weisgogel, 611
Weitzendler, 445
Weitzman, 175, 536
Weizer, 49, 78, 104, 479, 531, 626, 627
Wejgman, 578
Wekselman, 581, 596
Weksler, 460
Werber, 279, 287
Werber, 611
Wertal, 607
Wicznik, 445
Wiegensprech, 177, 538
Wiesenfeld, 87, 152, 228, 415
Wietrznik, 571
Wieza, 605
Wieznik, 79
Wigdorowicz, 603
Wikinski, 590
Wilczek, 316, 395, 396
Wilczek, 599, 600, 602
Wilenchik, 331, 444
Wilenczyk, 74, 342, 391, 444

Wilenczyk, 601
Wilfowicz (Kopf), 482
Wilinski, 578
Winograd, 46, 443, 444
Winograd, 565, 566, 571, 573, 593, 599
Winograd (Goldzhak), 46
Winterfeld, 605
Wiser, 398
Wisla, 586
Wisniewski, 571
Wissotzky, 48
Wloszczowski, 578
Wodka, 610
Wolanow, 622
Wolf, 608
Wolfajler, 605
Wolfovich, 252, 493
Wolfovitch, 299
Wolfowicz, 371, 374, 416, 514
Wolfowicz, 600, 601, 603, 622
Wolfowitz, 9, 625
Wolkowicz, 610, 611
Worcman, 607
Wroblewska, 611
Wroblewski, 610
Wulff, 607
Wyszynski, 610

Y

Yaffe, 354
Yankalevski, 67
Yash, 109

Z

Zabner, 587, 596, 597, 600, 602
Zachcinska, 597
Zachcinski, 446

Zachcinski, 571, 590
Zagerman, 383
Zajfman, 45, 52, 73, 139
Zalcberg, 622
Zalcman, 571, 578, 615
Zalka, 591
Zamberg, 590
Zanvil, 25
Zarnowiecki, 572
Zaterman, 588
Zauberman, 578, 586, 615
Zawierucha, 590
Zawner, 413
Zeifman, 511
Zejgman, 572, 578
Zelcer, 571, 572, 573, 597, 599, 600
Zelekowicz, 490
Zelinger, 591
Zemel, 581
Zerubavel, 53
Zheloni, 50
Zielinski, 585
Zilberberg, 32, 34, 447
Zilberman, 250, 426, 461
Zilberstein, 403, 423
Zimerman, 190
Zimmerman, 495, 502, 630
Zinger, 14, 560, 625, 626, 630
Zirenska, 177, 538
Ziskind, 132, 273, 447, 628
Zitelna, 102
Zoberman, 72, 83, 183, 446, 475

Zolna, 578, 582, 585
Zonabend, 578, 617
Zuckerman, 175, 176, 536, 537, 560
Zuker, 448
Zukerman, 9, 84, 106, 140, 241, 283, 284, 290, 292, 293, 294, 380, 381, 382, 383, 384, 401, 407, 410, 422, 474, 493, 494, 551, 625, 629, 630
Zukerman-Schlesinger, 447
Zukerman-Zilberman, 249, 273, 629
Zulcer, 49, 626
Zvuliner, 206
Zweig-Cohen, 453, 479
Zyferman, 596
Zylber, 53
Zylber, 610
Zylberberg, 27, 29, 52, 149, 150, 190, 416, 446, 457, 483, 514
Zylberberg, 572, 578, 581, 582, 583, 587, 588, 591, 593, 596, 601, 603
Zylberberg-Tobman, 449
Zylberfenig, 583
Zylberlust, 607
Zylberman, 53
Zylberman, 614
Zylbershtein, 381
Zylberstein, 67, 68, 74, 220, 552
Zylbersztajn, 572, 587, 598, 614
Zynger, 587, 590, 591, 601, 614
Zyngman, 578
Zyskind, 582, 610
Zysman, 593

www.ingramcontent.com/pod-product-compliance
Lightning Source LLC
Chambersburg PA
CBHW082009150426
42814CB00005BA/268